Designing Object-Oriented User Interfaces

Acquisitions Editor: *Tim Cox*
Executive Editor: *Dan Joraanstad*
Editorial Assistant: *Laura Cheu*
Text Design Assistance: *Lisa Jahred*
Cover Design and Execution: *Yvo Riezebos Design*
Marketing Manager: *Mary Tudor*
Senior Promotions Specialist: *Jim Fisher*
Production Editor: *Ray Kanarr*
Copy Editor: *Chris Grisonich*
Proofreader: *Elizabeth Gehrman*
Technical Assistance: *Craig Johnson*

Camera-ready copy for this book was prepared using FrameMaker.

Instructional Material Disclaimer
The examples presented in this book have been included for their instructional value. They have been tested with care, but are not guaranteed for any particular purpose. Neither the publisher nor the author offer any warranties or representations, nor do they accept any liabilities with respect to the programs or examples.

Library of Congress Cataloging-in-Publication Data

Collins, Dave (David Hunter), 1943–
Designing object-oriented user interfaces / Dave Collins.
p. cm.
Includes bibliographical references and index.
ISBN 0-8053-5350-X
1. object-oriented programming (Computer science) 2. User interfaces (Computer systems) I. Title.
QA76.64.C663 1994
005. 1'2--dc20 94-24586
CIP

ISBN 0-8053-5350-X
1 2 3 4 5 6 7 8 9 10 -MA- 98 97 96 95 94

The Benjamin/Cummings Publishing Company, Inc.
390 Bridge Parkway
Redwood City, CA 94065

Contents

Part III Internal Design 301

Preface

Designing Object-Oriented User Interfaces presents a principled approach to developing user interfaces for modern hardware and software platforms. It defines what an object-oriented user interface is, and provides a methodology for designing the visible interface and its underlying software. The principles and practices presented here are based on development experience and academic research. The book is intended for both working developers and for students and teachers in academic and industrial settings.

Object-orientation reflects the way people—including end users and system developers—perceive, think, and act. The foundation for this book is the idea that the same set of object-oriented principles can be applied to end user interfaces and to the internal system structures that implement them. This results in a user interface design methodology that fits seamlessly into object-oriented design and development processes for entire systems.

Design, if it is meaningful, occurs in the context of development (even for students, exercises must assess how the design will function when it is built). To get the most out of this book, it is important to go beyond it and do real designs. Start with tasks that people do, sketch designs for interfaces, implement the sketches, and show the results to potential users. Designers are often surprised by how hard it is to implement simple ideas, and by the way users respond to them. This surprise factor never goes away; becoming comfortable with it is a sign of maturity as a user interface designer.

The same thing goes for this book. I have tested the principles and practices in my own projects and by analyzing their use in other projects large and small. Nevertheless, I am sure there are still surprises in store, and lessons to be learned. I invite your comments and suggestions about any aspect of the book, particularly its applicability to development projects you are involved in. Comments can be sent by electronic mail to dcollins@acm.org, or by post to P. O. Box 24, Pleasantville, NY 10570, USA.

Background

Though I was not aware of it at the time, the motivation for this book probably came in 1984 when I first saw an Apple Macintosh computer. I was already a user of graphics systems, but the idea of a computer on which *everything* was done by manipulating visible images was novel, and profoundly appealing.

Conscious work started in early 1988, when my colleague, Chamond Liu, was putting together a conference on object-oriented systems (held at the IBM Education Center at Thornwood, New York). I was interested both in object-oriented programming languages and in the usability of human-computer interfaces, and Chamond asked me to chair a session on object-oriented user interfaces. He also asked me to make a presentation dealing with the connection (or lack of connection) between the principles of objects, classes, and inheritance as applied to programming languages, and analogous principles applied to the external behavior of user interfaces.

Chamond's request started me on a long journey. As I digested literature from areas as diverse as computer architecture and cognitive psychology, connections became apparent not only between user interfaces and programming, but between systems and methods used to develop them. These connections were manifest in the construction of many significant object-oriented systems, as described by the people who had designed and built them. Since then, my understanding of the connections has been deepened by experience as both developer and user of systems with object-oriented user interfaces.

Starting with my talk at the conference in November of 1988, discussion and presentation of the ideas went on through many tutorials and short courses on aspects of object-oriented user interfaces. Talking with designers and implementors who attended these helped to confirm the basic ideas, and expanded my understanding in areas where I lacked personal experience.

There is now a large body of ideas and methods for object-oriented user interface design. I think it is fair to say that a consensus exists on at least the broad outline of a methodology. By 1992 I felt that making these ideas and methods available within a coherent development framework would advance the practice of design, and the result is this book.

Production This book was produced in camera-ready form from a manuscript written in Microsoft Word and FrameMaker, running on Microsoft Windows. It is set in fonts from the TrueType Lucida family. Screen images and halftone art were processed with ImagePals, from Ulead Systems. Line art was prepared with CorelDraw, from Corel. Application examples done specifically for the book were coded with Smalltalk/V from Digitalk, ParcPlace Smalltalk, and Borland C++.

The availability of tools allowing an author to produce a book, with all its text and artwork, is a remarkable example of what computers can do, and part of a revolution as profound as what followed the invention of moveable type in the 16th century. I thank the developers of the products that allowed me to accomplish this feat, and encourage them to make it easier in the future.

Acknowledgments

A book as broad as this synthesizes the work of many people. Ideas have come from published papers, presentations, conversations, and user interface implementations in products and research prototypes. Specific ideas that I have used are acknowledged in the text. In addition, many people have contributed to my general understanding of the field and opened my eyes to possibilities for user interface designs. Though I take full responsibility for any deficiencies in this book, its value could not have been achieved without those people.

The first twenty years of my career in the computer industry were spent in daily contact with customers and end users of computers. I owe my first debt to them, for teaching me things about the experience of human-computer interaction that I could not have learned in any other way.

I have given courses and tutorials based on this material to people from many disciplines and with varying amounts of background knowledge. I thank all the students in those courses for their patience and their feedback. Students pointing out problems based on their experiences led to many improvements in the ideas and methods.

Developing a curriculum in software usability for IBM over the period 1988-1992 provided the opportunity to hear ideas from leading people in the field of user interface design. Contact with people like Bill Buxton, Charles Irby, Ted Nelson, Ben Shneiderman, Edward Tufte, and many others was both educational and inspiring. I am grateful for the support of the human factors community within IBM during that same period. People too numerous to mention gave up their time to help me understand how human factors could be applied in development. Walter Baker, John Bennett, John Gould, Dick Granda, Richard Halstead-Nussloch, and Ron Shapiro were particularly generous. The information development and graphic design communities in IBM also helped me to understand the role of those disciplines in user interface design and development.

Managers and colleagues at the IBM Systems Research Education Center and at the User Interface Institute of IBM Research were consistently helpful and supportive. Chamond Liu, as mentioned above, provided the key idea that got me started. Bob Mack encouraged both the book and the research behind many of the ideas about implementation. Many others provided helpful ideas and encouragement.

Thanks to Dan Joraanstad, of Benjamin/Cummings, and Grady Booch, series editor for the Object-Oriented Software Engineering series, for encouraging the book at its inception. Thanks also to Tim Cox, Ari Davidow, Ray Kanarr, Laura Cheu, Melissa Standen, Lisa Jahred, and others at Benjamin/Cummings for keeping it on track as we went along.

The following people provided concrete help while the book was being written, in the form of discussions or reviews of chapter drafts: Walter Baker, Steve Berczuk, Katherine Betz, Grady Booch, Steve Goetze, Reza Jalili, Chamond Liu, Bob Mack, Linn Marks, Brad A. Myers, Steve Otto, Jim Poretta, James Purtilo, Mary Beth Rosson, Kenneth S. Rubin, Drasko Sotirovski, George Vanecek, Mark Wilkes, and Kirk Wolf. Their feedback improved both the content and style of the book.

Thanks most of all to Linn Marks. She has given me a steady stream of visual design ideas for user interfaces and for the book itself. Many ideas here were generated or sharpened in the course of long discussions on the art and science of design. She also provided the constant encouragement I needed to persevere through the period of more than a year, while I struggled to get these ideas down on paper in the form in which you now see them.

1

Introduction

This book is about designing object-oriented user interfaces. It covers the design of the visible interface and the software that implements it. I base both aspects of design on object-oriented principles, which brings coherence to the software development process. Theory is presented where it is needed, but the emphasis is on good development practice and on building high-quality systems.

Design, as presented here, includes much of what usually falls under analysis. The book also contains material on implementation. This is partly because "analysis," "design," and "implementation" are overlapping ideas. More importantly, object-orientation reveals deep structural correspondences between the artifacts of analysis, design, and implementation. These correspondences are particularly important in user interface design, and they can be exploited by coupling the separate development phases more closely than you may be accustomed to.

This book primarily targets applications with graphical, iconic interfaces implemented on platforms such as the Apple Macintosh Desktop, Microsoft Windows, the OS/2 Workplace Shell, NeXTSTEP, and OSF/Motif. Designing these interfaces requires skilled people from disciplines including object-oriented analysis, design, and programming, human factors, and graphic design. Larger multidisciplinary teams will be needed in the future when capabilities such as speech recognition and multimedia output become common.

The structure of this book is based on the development process. It provides a framework for the efforts of the whole team, as well as specific information for each discipline. You can learn what you need to know about the framework quickly, then focus on topics that are important to you. In a project team, you also need to know how your work relates to that of others. The best way to do that is to understand the whole process, so you will benefit by looking at all the topics in the book.

The approach here emphasizes mainstream object-oriented principles as the central theme for object-oriented user interfaces ("mainstream" meaning object-orientation just as it is used in object-oriented programming or object-oriented databases). Other interface design methods center on things like graphic design or human factors principles. Those approaches do not contradict the one here, and they fit as components in an inclusive framework.

This introductory chapter covers:

- A definition of the user interface and an overview of how it is treated in this book.
- The general plan of the book and aids provided for the reader.
- Information about the people who make up the audience for this book.
- How this book relates to other methods and books in the field of user interface design.

1.1 The User Interface

What *is* a user interface? Everyone knows the answer to this question—but the answer is different, depending on who I ask.

Programmers focus on using operating systems, processor hardware, storage, etc., to give functional capabilities to users. They think in terms of programming languages and computer artifacts, and they view the user interface as something designers add to the system[1] to make it "user friendly."

Analysts think about the system in terms of the end user's job; they see the user interface as a replica of the forms, books, control panels, or other objects in the user's world.

Human factors experts may treat the user interface as a behavioral science experiment. Their goal in design is to provide users with the stimulus and response mechanisms that maximize performance in the experimental task.

Graphic designers, often with backgrounds in print media, view the user interface as a succession of screens that are like pages in a magazine—each one designed to be attractive, to flow, and to convey information.

These answers are caricatures, but they summarize points of view that are prevalent among different specialists. Each point of view is valu-

[1] The term *system* refers to a complete, standalone environment, which defines all the basic services available to end users. *Application* refers to a program that provides a subset of end user services which runs on a system in conjunction with other applications. Where the difference is not important, I will often use them interchangeably.

Figure 1-1 Bennett's model of the user interface

able, but each sees only part of the user interface. Figure 1-1 is a holistic view, based on John Bennett's work.[1] It shows:

- A *conceptual model*, representing the user's understanding of his or her task. It includes goals for using the system, and knowledge of how the capabilities of the computer system relate to the objects and processes of the real-world task domain.
- A *presentation language*, the form in which the system presents information to the user. Typically this is visual information on a display, but it may take other forms and includes manuals and training materials on how to use the system.
- An *action language*, the mechanisms the designer provides to allow the user to interact with the system. This includes commands typed on the keyboard, menus, use of a mouse to point at things, etc.
- An *implementation model*, the design of the software and hardware that provide the system's functional capabilities.

The figure shows a static view of the interface. Bennett emphasizes the dynamics of a user's interaction with the computer:

- The user starts with a goal to be accomplished.
- Based on a conceptual model of the task domain and the system, the user formulates a plan of action to reach the goal.
- The user translates actions in the plan into the steps required to

[1] See [Ben77], [Ben83]. The ideas in this model have been around for a long time. The concept of presentation and action languages, for example, was presented in 1966 by W. R. Sutherland in his Ph.D. thesis (see [Fol74]).

accomplish them through the medium of the computer.

- Using the action language, the user executes the steps in the plan.
- The system processes each user input, which may involve computation, accessing data, formatting output, etc.
- After each step, feedback through the presentation language shows the result of the previous actions and provides guidance on what to do next.

Bennett's model is used throughout the book. Chapter 3, *Two User Interface Styles*, introduces a method for analyzing user interfaces based on it. Chapter 7, *Users, Tasks, and Task Analysis,* expands on this analysis method. Chapter 5, *Three Domains of OO Design for the User Interface*, shows how object-orientation fosters a closer coupling of the elements, particularly the conceptual and implementation models. The conceptual model is the focus of Chapter 8, *The User's Conceptual Model.* Chapter 9, *Information Presentation*, and Chapter 10, *Interaction and Control Mechanisms*, cover the design of the presentation and action languages. Chapter 12, *Information Models*, deals with the semantics of the implementation model, and Chapter 13, *Presentation and Interaction Objects*, deals with implementing the presentation and action languages.

Object-Oriented User Interfaces

This book is about designing *object-oriented* user interfaces (usually abbreviated to *OOUIs*). OOUIs can be defined in several different ways. OOUIs are often equated to graphical user interfaces (GUIs), characterized by overlapping windows, pulldown menus, buttons, etc. Some people restrict the term OOUI to GUIs that use icons and other graphical techniques to represent "real objects," such as documents, to the end user.

Programmers who *implement* user interfaces using an object-oriented programming language may define them as object-oriented. This is particularly prevalent among Smalltalk programmers, since much of the "look and feel" of modern user interfaces comes from research done by the developers of Smalltalk at the Xerox Palo Alto Research Center.

These definitions identify parts of OOUIs, or things that make implementing OOUIs easier. Although I do not agree with it, the last definition alludes to an important connection between object-oriented interfaces and object-oriented programming languages—a theme that will recur later in this book.

Deep issues are involved in characterizing OOUIs. These are covered in Chapter 3, *Two User Interface Styles*, and Chapter 4, *Applying Object-Orientation to User Interfaces.* For the time being, here is a working definition:

- Users perceive and act on objects.
- Users can classify objects based on how they behave.

- In the context of what users are trying to do, all the interface objects fit together into a coherent overall representation.

Figure 1-2 shows an example of one type of OOUI, an object-oriented shell or "desktop" holding things the user needs.[1] The overall representation suggests an office. The user operates on things like `Godwin letter`,[2] which is a document in the `Word processing` folder. In the implementation model, the folder may be a directory in the computer's file system, and `Godwin letter` may be a text file associated with a particular application program. The shell conceals this from the user, who deals only with documents, folders, etc. Objects interact by direct manipulation. For example, the user can "pick up" a document icon by pressing a mouse button while the pointer is over the icon. As the user moves the mouse the icon moves, and it "drops" when the button is released. If the document is dropped on a folder, it disappears from its original location and moves to the folder. This can be verified by clicking the mouse button twice while the pointer is

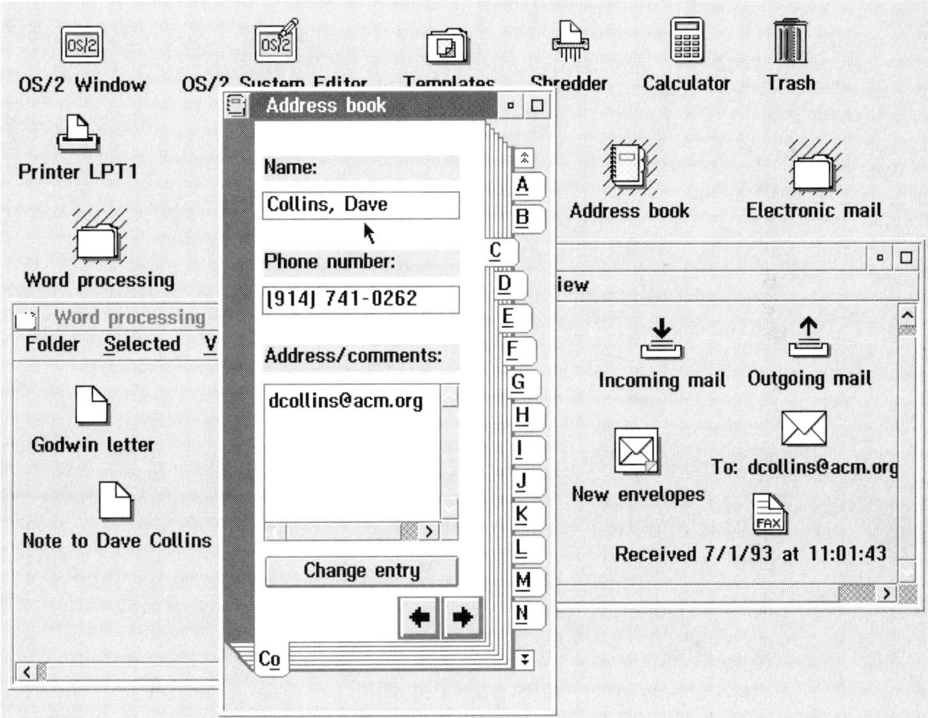

Figure 1-2 An object-oriented user interface

[1] The prototype for this example, and others in the book that are not specifically credited, was developed using Digitalk Smalltalk/V on Microsoft Windows [sDig92a] or OS/2 [sDig92b].

[2] The `monospaced font` is used for computer commands, object names, programming code, etc.

over the folder, which opens a window showing the folder's contents.

Object representations reflect "real world" counterparts. This reinforces the office model and makes things easier for users, by providing clues to how objects will behave. For instance, a user will probably expect that dropping objects on the `Shredder` icon permanently deletes them, whereas dropping objects on the `Trash` icon is reversible. Just as in the real world, the user can open the trash can and retrieve objects that have been discarded.

Classification, in the ordinary sense of the word,[1] is helpful to the user of this interface. He or she will surmise by visual appearance that `Godwin letter` and `Note to Dave Collins` are "the same kind of object." The behavior of the objects will confirm this. The user might also guess that objects like `Godwin letter` and `Received 7/1/93 at 11:01:43 AM` are similar, though not of the same type. They are both kinds of documents, which can be opened and read, printed (by dropping their icons on `Printer LPT1`), etc. (It should go without saying that we, the designers, must choose representations for objects that are unambiguous, and fulfill the expectations they generate.)

To understand representational coherence, consider the "story" that you can read from left to right at the bottom of Figure 1-2:

- The user has written a note to Dave Collins and wants to mail it.
- Dave's address is found in the address book and put on an envelope.
- When the note is placed in the envelope and the envelope is dropped into the outgoing mail, it will be sent to Dave.

This story could occur in the real world or in the simulated world of the computer system. I use this example because it is familiar to most people, but the principle is the same in other domains as well.

1.2 Plan of the Book

This book has three major parts:

1. *Foundations* is a base for the following sections. It covers material on user interfaces and how object-orientation applies to user interfaces.
2. *External Design* presents methods for designing what the end user perceives. This includes the conceptual model and the "look and feel" (presentation and action languages). Part II also describes the people and skills involved in OOUI design, and how they fit into the larger object-oriented development process.
3. *Internal Design* describes general software architectures, methods,

[1] As opposed to the technical sense used in object-oriented analysis and design. Chapter 4 will clarify the connection between the two senses.

and tools for implementing OOUIs, illustrated with examples.

A final chapter, *Summary and Directions*, summarizes important points about OOUI design and speculates about future OOUIs. Two appendices include a case study used for exercises in several chapters and a brief tutorial on object-orientation. There is a glossary of technical terms and an annotated bibliography of journal articles, books, videotapes, and software packages. The bibliography includes all the cited references and additional materials for exploring the literature on OOUIs.

Each part has several chapters, and each chapter contains:

- A short introduction. Reading the chapter introductions provides a quick overview (or later, a review) of the entire book.
- The chapter content, with diagrams and pictures, examples, and case studies to illustrate and reinforce concepts.
- A chapter summary that lists the key "rules of thumb" or design techniques presented in the chapter. Whereas the chapter introduction is an overview of content, the summary focuses on operational guidelines.
- A section called *To Explore Further*, which lists journal articles, books, and software for pursuing topics covered in the chapter.
- Exercises to provide practice in the material covered in the chapter. Some exercises have two formulations: one for the student, and one for the working developer, which can be applied to a current project.

What the Book Is About

This book's overall approach resembles a spiral, making a complete circle around the material several times. Each one uses understanding developed in the prior circle as a base for a deeper understanding of the subject. The spiral approach[1] provides a broad grasp of OOUI design as you learn specific techniques.

Foundations Many of us are victims of what Wurman [Wur89] calls "information anxiety." Conscious that new knowledge is published—and old knowledge becomes obsolete—at a frightening rate, we struggle to make sense of the flood of information from books, journals, and other media. I have often felt this anxiety about the field of object-oriented user interfaces during the last few years.

Experience over a lifetime of learning, however, has convinced me that there is an "80/20" rule in knowledge—20 percent of the information contributes 80 percent of the knowledge. Every discipline has its fundamental principles. These principles form the core of the discipline, organize the remaining knowledge, and do not change very fast. If this seems implausible, look at object-orientation itself as an example—though the

[1]Conceptually, this is similar to the "spiral process" for software development [Boe88].

amount *published* about OO has multiplied astronomically in recent years, the amount of basic knowledge has not. Most of the important principles of OO were known to the developers of Simula-67 in 1967 [Nyg81], to the developers of Smalltalk in 1972 [Kay93], and to researchers in the theory of abstract data types [Lis74] in the 1960s and '70s.

This 80/20 rule motivated Part I of the book (Chapters 2–4) on *Foundations.* I encourage you to read it, despite urgings to get on to the "meat," the chapters covering specific methods for designing and implementing OOUIs. The fundamentals presented in *Foundations* provide a framework for understanding a broad range of current and future user interface technology and design methods.

I have tried throughout the book to emphasize methods, architectures, and techniques that will endure and serve you well in the future. While writing, I am implementing prototype interfaces on several platforms. The amount of information necessary for programming on each one continually amazes me. The secret of not being overwhelmed is to recognize that implementations are like the leaves of a tree, whose branches are a few general principles.[1]

External design A good user interface cannot be designed in isolation. It is part of a system, and must be designed and implemented along with other parts of the system. Part II, *External Design,* begins by describing how interface design fits in with the whole development process. Chapter 5, *Three Domains of OO Design for the User Interface,* shows how object-orientation provides a coherent view of design and helps to integrate different phases of development. Chapter 6, *OOUI Design: Process and Team,* outlines the design process, describes the skills used for aspects of OOUI design, and discusses the role of the user interface design team during each phase of development.

What ultimately motivates the use of a system or application is the function it offers. The system reveals its function, and provides access to it, through the user interface. The remainder of Part II is about designing not only the "look and feel" of the user interface, but also how the functions of the system are organized. Chapter 7, *Users, Tasks, and Task Analysis,* deals with functionality and its organization from an object-oriented perspective. Presenting system concepts clearly is the subject of Chapter 8, *The User's Conceptual Model.* Chapter 9, *Information Presentation,* and Chapter 10, *Interaction and Control Mechanisms,* deal with designing the "look and feel" of OOUIs.

Internal design The last part of the book, *Internal Design,* is about using object-oriented software to implement systems with OOUIs. Chapter 11, *Object-Oriented System Architectures,* is a general view of OO implementa-

[1] If this sounds like classification in object-oriented programming, you are right on the mark. Chapter 14 shows how this principle can be applied to building user interface frameworks that are portable across platforms.

tion for typical systems and applications. It shows how the software components that compose the user interface fit into the larger architecture; the remainder of Part III specifically addresses the user interface components. Chapter 12, *Information Models*, presents the software components corresponding to the user's conceptual model. Chapter 13, *Presentation and Interaction Objects*, covers the "look and feel" components. Chapter 14, *Tools for Prototyping and Implementation*, classifies the tools that are available, gives examples, discusses pros and cons, and provides a checklist for evaluating tools. This part ends with Chapter 15, *Design Examples*, which discusses pragmatic issues of OOUI implementation and examines four applications that illuminate them.

Chapter 16, *Summary and Directions*, reviews key points of the book and discusses the effects of new technology on user interfaces. This includes not only input and output technologies for the interface itself, but technologies that provide new, more complex functional capabilities. These capabilities, in turn, demand new user interfaces to make them more accessible.

What the Book Is Not About

I have said what the book is intended to do, and it is only fair to point out what it is *not* intended to do. My goal is to help you design and build better user interfaces, by enhancing your knowledge of OOUI concepts and technology. This book is not a polemic defense of the OOUI, nor is it an attempt to prove that OOUIs are invariably "better" than other kinds of user interfaces. Object-oriented techniques can help to map the ideas and expectations of end users into designs, but they do not guarantee success.

The third part of the book talks about many different platforms and tools for implementing OOUIs. People attending courses I teach are sometimes disappointed because they do not receive detailed guidance on the particular combination of platforms and tools they are interested in; those people will be disappointed here as well. A single book cannot provide detailed coverage of every tool. Even if it tried, the information would quickly be outdated. So while I could have written *OOUI Implementation on Microsoft Windows with C++ and the Borland Class Library*, or *OOUI Implementation on OS/2 Presentation Manager with Digitalk Smalltalk/V*, I wrote this book instead. It offers general principles, with examples, that will be applicable in many different environments.

Finally, this is a guide for practical design, not a scholarly work. It emphasizes breadth, not depth, to cover the many areas with which a designer needs to be familiar. For further study, references are cited in the text, in the section *To Explore Further* in each chapter, and in the bibliography.

1.3 Audiences for the Book

Designing OOUIs involves many roles and skills. The material here is comprehensible and valuable to people in many disciplines—software design and development, graphic and information design, human factors and usability, technology planning, and market analysis, to name a few. The plan of the book addresses the general skill categories of external design, internal design, and project management.

Prerequisites

To avoid making the book too basic, I assume a few prerequisites. You should have some familiarity with the concepts of object-orientation, perhaps from programming with an object-oriented language. If not, read Appendix 2, *Introduction to Object-Orientation*, before beginning the body of the book. Code examples in the book use Smalltalk and C++, and Appendix 2 briefly summarizes these languages.

I also assume you are familiar with one or more of the GUIs on the market, since these are the platforms on which OOUIs are typically implemented. If not, you should get some experience while you read the book. Much of the material relates to the dynamic behavior of interfaces, and can't be shown with still images. Hands-on experience is the only way to get a "feel" for these ideas.

Audience Categories

This book is primarily directed at an audience of software developers (or students of subjects related to software development). By "software developer" I mean anyone involved in a project whose outcome will be a new software system or application. This broad category includes many skills that play key roles in designing and building OOUIs. A project may not have all these roles; you may fit more than one, or assume different roles over the life of a project. The categories overlap because names and definitions vary from project to project. Figure 1-3 shows the life cycle of a typical software project, and where the various roles come into play.

Developers tend to be most interested in one of three categories of knowledge, and the structure of the book is designed to accommodate a focus on one or another of them:

- Analysts, human factors engineers, graphic and media designers, and information developers are usually most interested in *external design knowledge*. This is applicable to phases in Figure 1-3 from *strategic planning* through *information/media development* and is covered in Parts I and II of the book.
- Programmers and software engineers are usually most interested in *internal design knowledge*. This is applicable to phases from *system and software design* through *implementation* and is covered in Part III.

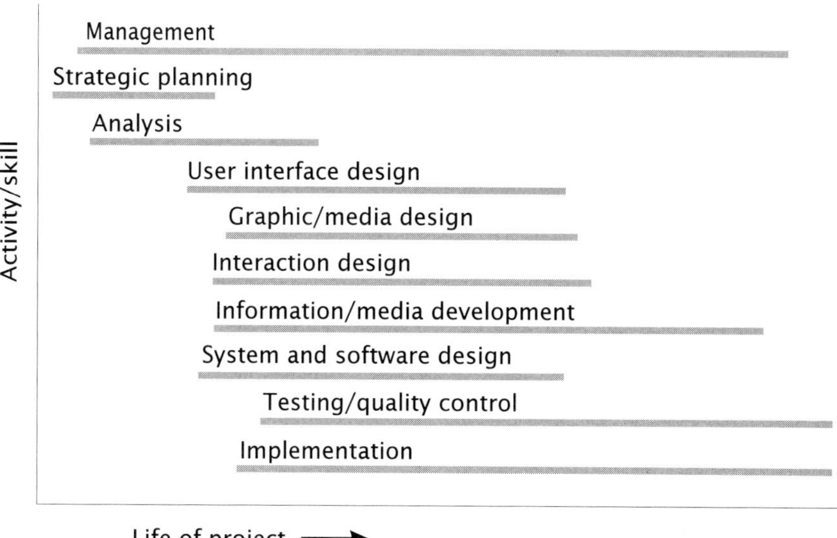

Figure 1-3 Skills in context: a view of the project life cycle

- Managers, project leaders and consultants, and planners typically seek *overview knowledge*. Reading Part I and Chapter 16 and skimming the remainder of the book will provide this overview.

These categories are not hard and fast. There are human factors engineers who do their own programming, and programmers who do external user interface design. Testing engineers may be interested in internals or externals, depending upon the kind of testing. In any case, you will benefit from reading outside your speciality. The affinity between externals and internals in OO systems means that a point in one discipline may be illuminated by an explanation from another.

Students In addition to software developers, this book will interest several categories of students:

- Students in corporate training courses that teach a specific development skill.
- Students learning a tool or programming language for implementing applications with OOUIs. The material in this book covers general principles that complement the learning of a particular tool.
- In a university computer science curriculum, this book may be supplementary reading in a course on object-oriented programming languages, or one that teaches human-computer interaction design as a software engineering discipline.

- In a university curriculum in psychology or human factors, this book may be supplementary reading in a course on human-computer interaction.

1.4 Relation to Other Design Approaches

We are seeing the crests of two technology waves. One is "object technology," a catch-all term for the application of object-oriented principles to computer systems. The other is a loosely-defined set of hardware and software technologies underlying "graphical user interfaces" (GUIs). Examples include the Apple Macintosh, personal computers running Microsoft Windows or OS/2, and a variety of UNIX-based workstations.

Designing Object-Oriented User Interfaces rides both waves. There is a large literature on user interface design, object-oriented design, and GUI design, so I would like to position this book with respect to other methods in the field.

Solid circles in Figure 1-4 represent categories of design methods. The gray circle shows what this book covers. The other methods are valuable—I have studied them, and I use them. This book presents a comprehensive design methodology for object-oriented user interfaces, but it does not supersede all other methods.

Object-oriented software engineering applies object-oriented principles to building software systems and applications. There are several excellent texts covering it, for instance Grady Booch's *Object-Oriented Analysis and Design with Applications* [Boo94] and Ivar Jacobson's *Object-Oriented Software Engineering* [Jac92].

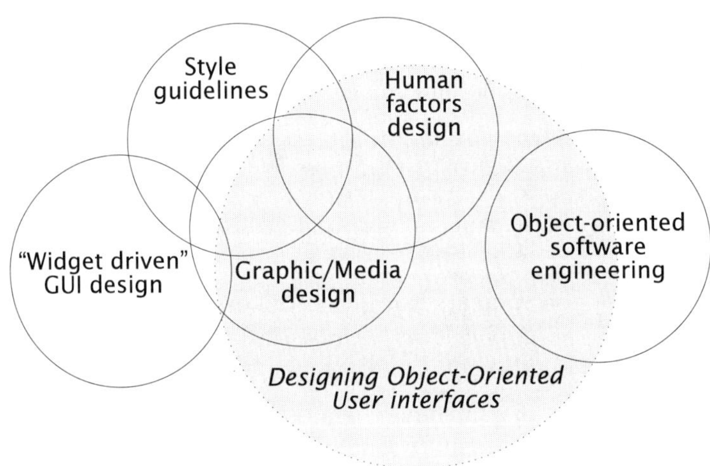

Figure 1-4 Approaches to OOUI design

Quite remarkably, no text I have seen in this field provides significant coverage of user interface design or implementation. Contrast this with the fact that, in modern systems on average, *about half* of both code and development effort goes to implementing user interfaces [Mye92]. This is an average; for systems with GUIs the proportion is higher—in some cases over 90 percent.

On the other side, published methods for user interface design largely ignore the fact that it is part of product development. In spite of this gap in the literature, the same principles and techniques we apply to development as a whole can be successfully applied to user interface development. One of the tasks of this book is to show how to move user interface design and implementation into the mainstream of object-oriented software engineering.

Human factors design is based upon the capabilities and limitations of people. It draws from psychology and physiology, as well as using techniques developed specifically for human-computer interaction. Methods in this approach include empirical design guidelines and iterative improvement through usability testing. Ben Shneiderman's *Designing the User Interface* [Shn92] is one of many texts that teach this approach.

Human factors design is an indispensable component of software development, but it has two limitations that prevent it from being the *primary* approach to design:

- It does not provide principles that integrate it into the mainstream of development.
- Although human factors principles are good at iteratively improving a user interface, the starting point for design comes from a conceptual model of the system. Current human factors methods are weak in this area.

Object modeling (as presented in the literature of OO software engineering) is a strong technique for generating initial ideas for the user interface.[1] I have found that developers are more receptive to human factors issues in object-oriented environments. I attribute this to the fact that OO programming language constructs are closer to objects in the application domain, making it easier for developers to take the user's point of view.

Graphic/media design has traditionally dealt with presenting visual information through media such as television, the printed page, advertising posters, etc. Its applicability to user interface design is obvious, since computer interfaces present visual information on something that is essentially a TV screen. As with human factors, this is an indispensable component of user interface design. Every developer could benefit by

[1] Object modeling *is*, in a sense, a human factors approach to design. Chapter 4 argues that object-orientation is congruent with the way people perceive and think about the world, and this may be the key to its success.

reading Edward Tufte's *Envisioning Information* [Tuf90], a treatise on presenting information efficiently, elegantly, and without clutter. But this approach is also limited:

- It is not integrated into mainstream development.
- In practice, many designers forget that there are significant differences between the computer and other media (many developers forget that there are similarities, but that's another story).
- Graphic/media design does not address interactivity and input devices.

Style guidelines are sets of rules and suggestions for designing interfaces. The most important examples are published by computer vendors for interfaces implemented on their platforms. Examples include *Macintosh Human Interface Guidelines* from Apple Computer [App92]; *Object-Oriented Interface Design: IBM Common User Access Guidelines* [IBM92] from IBM; and *The Windows Interface: An Application Design Guide* [Mic92] from Microsoft. Together with working examples and tools for implementing a style, guidelines simplify the work of design. As with the previous approaches, however, guidelines alone are not sufficient. A user interface needs content, not just style.

Widget-driven design is related to the style guidelines approach. A widget[1] is an interactive object presented on the display, such as a window, button, or scroll bar. Platform vendors supply toolkits with code for implementing standard widgets, and high-level tools provide visual palettes of widgets for building user interfaces. The developer can "tear off" copies of the widgets and "paste" them onto the screen at the desired location. The tool generates code that allows the developer to connect the widgets to application code. These tools are valuable within a more principled design method. Basing the design on the tool, however, creates complex and confusing user interfaces, cluttered with windows and buttons.

My objective here is not to criticize these methods, but to show how they fit into a broader design methodology as components. In fact, most of the proponents of these methods broaden them as well. Shneiderman's book [Shn92] is an example—it incorporates graphic design principles and discusses guidelines and toolkits. The IBM style guide, as its title implies, presents general principles for designing OOUIs. The Apple style guide has a discussion of how user interface design fits into the development process. Aaron Marcus, in a book on graphic design for user interfaces [Mar92], addresses human factors issues and interactive components of interfaces.

User interface experts of all sorts have told me that their influence

[1] The term "widget" originated in the X Window System [Sch86].

on product quality is less than it ought to be—in spite of the effort devoted to developing user interfaces and their acknowledged importance in today's market. To correct this situation, we need to fill the gap between user interface design and "system design" as practiced by software engineers. I believe that object-oriented user interface design, as presented here, does that. I have provided new methods where I think they are required and adopted existing ones where they are adequate.

This book alone cannot provide all the detailed knowledge you need to develop a particular OOUI. It can give you the blueprint you need to integrate diverse design methods and the background to understand why the blueprint works.

I

Foundations

The fundamentals presented in this first part of the book provide a framework for understanding object-oriented user interfaces.

Chapter 2, *Evolution of the OOUI*, explores two contexts for the historical evolution of OOUIs. One is the characteristics of end users and the work they do with computers. The other is the thirty-year history of ideas leading up to modern graphical and object-oriented user interfaces. Understanding this evolution will broaden and deepen the knowledge you bring to current designs.

Chapter 3, *Two User Interface Styles*, analyzes character-based and graphical interfaces for similar applications. Its objectives are to bring out some of the key differences between OOUIs and other interfaces and to introduce an analysis method that will be expanded later in the book.

Chapter 4, *Applying Object-Orientation to User Interfaces*, defines object-orientation and shows how object-oriented principles apply to the external characteristics of user interfaces. The basis for the principles in cognitive psychology is also discussed.

Though most directly related to the externals of user interfaces, this part is valuable for implementors as well. A key aspect of object-orientation is its ability to provide conceptual models for systems that cut across all phases and activities in the development process. Examples and discussion in Part III, *Internal Design*, will show that clear conceptual models of objects and relationships can guide the design of internal architectures as well as external user interfaces.

2

Evolution of the OOUI

In the early 1980s, a new breed of user interface came to town. They were led by the Xerox Star workstation, and made famous by the Apple Macintosh. They featured documents that looked like paper, not computer screens, and objects represented by little pictures called "icons." Users "pointed and clicked" instead of typing commands. By the early 1990s, they dominated the personal computer and workstation market.

Why this change? Are they really better, or was it just a high-tech fashion show? Is one vendor's interface better than another's? Where will they go in the future? This chapter examines these questions by looking at the historical and social context in which these interfaces developed. The context includes people and their environments, as well as computers and computer applications. If you are a strategic planner or market analyst, understanding this context will help you predict future requirements. If you are a developer, it will help you to understand the characteristics that make a successful product.

The first electronic computers appeared about fifty years ago. Since then, more changes have occurred in computing technology than in all of prior history. Improvements in the coming decade may again exceed all prior advances. Technology forecasts predict computers in the 21st century that we can hardly imagine today.

Computers have become cheaper as well as faster. In a time when cost inflation is a serious concern, computer costs have been *declining* at double digit rates, and this trend will continue. Telecommunications technology, needed to satisfy the information appetite of today's computers, shows similar curves of advancing capability and declining cost. It has become a cliché to say that we are in the midst of a revolution fueled by the processing of information.

True historical revolutions cause dramatic changes in the way people live. In the "information revolution," the vehicle for these changes is the interface between computers and people.

Basic human capabilities for perceiving, thinking, and acting on objects in the world have not changed for thousands of years, and these capabilities will not change within the lifetime of anyone reading this book. This creates a tension between rapidly changing technology on one side of the interface and the unchanging capabilities of the human on the other side. There are two ways of resolving it: designers can use technology to create user interfaces that fit the capabilities and limitations of their human users; and—though basic human capabilities are fixed—culture can change, altering attitudes, styles of work and play, and the set of tasks to which we apply computers.

Cultural change takes time. This is true for "corporate culture" and the culture at large. Pervasive use of computers in industry and commerce dates from the 1960s and '70s, and computers dedicated to individuals have been common for less than two decades. Machines powerful enough to support OOUIs have only become widely available within the last ten years. In historical terms, this is a very short period, and a period in which the rapidity of change exceeded the rate at which culture could change in response.

Though radical changes, such as telecommuting and paperless offices, have indeed occurred, they exist in small pockets. Much of the basic work that people do with computers (keeping accounts, writing letters, etc.) has been done for centuries. On the whole, we do things faster with computers, but we do not do different things. Many experts believe that until we start to restructure our work based on computer capabilities, we will not fulfill the promise of the information revolution.

The material in this chapter is somewhat diffuse and far-reaching, but it has definite objectives:

- To provide a framework for thinking about design "in the large"—in the context of life within corporations, families, etc. In the long run, it is design in the large that determines the success of technology applications.
- To identify, in the history of user interfaces, ideas about human-computer interaction that have endured and proven their value.

2.1 People, Work, and Technological Change

Anyone who has been in the computer business for a few years has been through the following cycle, perhaps many times:

- A new technology becomes available, or becomes cheap enough to be widely used. Examples are mainframe database systems in the 1970s, single-user workstations in the 1980s, and multimedia systems in the 1990s.

- A project is started to automate existing work[1] using the new technology.
- A new system or application results, which is then offered (or forced upon) the affected workers.

What happens next? Users may greet the system with anything from wild enthusiasm to staunch resistance. There are many published case studies dealing with the process. For instance, [Per82] describes the rapid acceptance of the technology of video games; [Bor91] discusses the dramatic difference in the acceptance of facsimile transmission (Fax) versus electronic mail; [Kra89] shows how the introduction of a large system can have both positive and negative effects. Why these differences? Do they merely reflect superficial attitudes toward new technology?

Studies done over the last few years suggest that user attitudes may be symptomatic of deeper and more important issues. Gary Loveman, then at the MIT Sloan School, proposed in the late 1980s that investments in computers and other information technologies were not correlated with improvements in productivity. Since then Loveman [Lov91] and others [Gle93] have concluded that although the technology can have significant effects, it is not a panacea. Real productivity improvement comes when companies reengineer the way they do work to capitalize on the potential in the new technologies. My intuition is that Loveman and the other experts are right, though there is by no means complete agreement, and certain basic notions such as "productivity" are hard to define and measure [Bry93].

A Reengineering Example

I was involved with a communications utility that planned to apply computer technology to the process of providing leased line communications facilities to customers. The work flow at the time involved these steps:

1. A designer received the customer's order for service and prepared a circuit design based on the class of service requested, location of the endpoints, location of intermediate nodes, etc.
2. The design was passed to an assignment clerk, who worked from printed books holding the inventory of equipment at each node location, and links, by type, between nodes. The clerk attempted to provide a circuit conforming to the design, using the components that were available.
3. If available equipment would not support the design, the clerk sent it back to the designer. The designer attempted a redesign, and step 2

[1] Similar scenarios can be found in contexts other than work, but the process and outcomes are similar. For example, the system might be a multimedia tool for education, or a new computer game. You might suppose that work is different because workers have no choice. The 19th-century Luddites are a well-known counterexample, and more subtle resistance to technology is common.

was repeated. (If the redesign could not be done, another process was invoked to order additional facilities or equipment.)

4. When the assignment of equipment and links to the design was successful, the inventory books were updated, and the design and assignment information were sent to an order clerk. This clerk prepared work orders for the implementation of the design and sent them to the affected node locations.
5. After technicians at each node did the work, they notified the order clerk. After all the work was completed, the clerk sent a notification to technicians at the endpoints, and these technicians tested the circuit. If it worked correctly, the customer was notified. The clerk also posted information to the billing department so that billing of the customer could begin.
6. When a customer discontinued use of facilities, a process was invoked to disconnect the physical circuits and to post the changes to the inventory books so that equipment and links could be reused.

The most serious bottleneck in this process was the set of inventory books. If one clerk was using the book for a particular location, no other clerk could work on a design involving that location. Because of the manual updating of the books, errors in the inventory were common (typically either lost items because the discontinuance processing was not done, or double assignment of items due to clerical errors). The process was time-consuming, and it resulted in customer dissatisfaction.

The initial proposal was to automate the inventory books using a database system. This would reduce clerical errors, enable clerks to access the information without leaving their desks, and prevent a clerk from locking out an entire location while searching the inventory. This would have enhanced the process, but after further study, the whole process was reengineered. The system designers added capabilities to the automated system to support these new process steps:

1. The customer's order for service was electronically transferred to a designer, who prepared a circuit design interactively. The design was based upon the class of service requested, the location of the endpoints, location of intermediate nodes, *and* information on the availability of equipment and links, which the system dynamically extracted from the database. When the designer approved the design, the system automatically reserved the items in the database, and work orders were generated and transmitted electronically to affected locations. (If the items needed to support the design were not available, the designer could immediately transfer information to the process that ordered additional facilities or equipment.)
2. After technicians at each node did the work, they posted a completion in the system. After all the work was completed, the system sent a notification to the endpoints where technicians tested the circuit. If

it worked correctly, the system generated a notification for the customer and posted information to the billing department.

3. When a customer discontinued the use of facilities, a process was invoked to disconnect the physical circuits and to post the changes to the database so that equipment and links could be reused. The discontinuance order could not be purged from the system until the inventory updates had been posted.

Without reengineering, this might have gone down as an expenditure that failed to produce a commensurate gain in productivity. As it was, the effort was a success. Notice that though the new system reduced the number of process steps from six to three and changed the process flow, the *objects* involved did not change. Customers, service orders, nodes, equipment, links, etc., were invariant across the reengineering. This suggests that reengineering benefits from an object-oriented perspective.

Streamlining the process was small comfort to the assignment and order clerks whose jobs were eliminated. Management handled this situation by promoting some clerks to designers and reassigning others. These human aspects of new technology affect its payback, and the effects are not always handled so well. A subtle effect of the new system is that the designers have more control over their product since they control more of the process steps related to its production. Again, this reflects the value of a focus on objects. (It is only fair to point out that increasing control may decrease social contact with others involved in the process, a potential negative effect [Kra89].)

Characterizing People, Tasks, and Environments

These examples suggest that predicting the success of new systems requires a broader focus than just the technology. My experience confirms that of experts in human factors and industrial psychology. These experts say we need to look at three factors besides the technology:[1]

- The characteristics of the end users.
- The characteristics of the tasks they do.
- The characteristics of the environments in which they work.

Figure 2-1 shows some characteristics of end users, all of which affect the acceptance of technology.[2] Being sensitive to the importance of these factors will help to avoid unpleasant surprises:

- *Physiological*: Physical size and strength; physiological reaction to stimuli and range of motion for muscular action; comfort levels for

[1] See, e.g., Baker in [Dic84], [Bak89]. I am indebted to Dr. Baker for helping to educate me on this topic over a period of several years when we worked together.

[2] The "onionskin" diagram follows [Bak89]. It suggests that what we see of users is always filtered through all the layers.

ambient light, temperature, etc.; sensitivity to environmental stresses, fatigue, etc.

- *Sensory/motor*: Capabilities and limitations of the senses of sight, hearing, touch, etc.; strength, range, and speed of motor (muscular) action. People have little or no conscious control over this pre-attentive level of mental processing. It plays a major role in the presentation and action languages in the user interface model of Figure 1-1.
- *Cognitive*: The ways in which users process information; use of memory and processing resources in perception, thought, and action. This level of processing is conscious, but the individual may have little control over it. Training can move some of the processing to lower levels. For instance, when learning to ride a bicycle, we are conscious of all the actions being performed. Once learned, most of the processing is done automatically at the sensory/motor level. The cognitive layer corresponds to the conceptual model in Figure 1-1.
- *Cultural*: The influence of the entire body of knowledge and beliefs to which users have been exposed through other people, documents, films, etc. An important component of culture for most people is the "corporate culture" in their work environment, which may be quite different from, say, the culture of the community where they live. Designers of products for an international market or a multinational company must consider the cultural differences that arise from such factors as nationality and ethnicity.

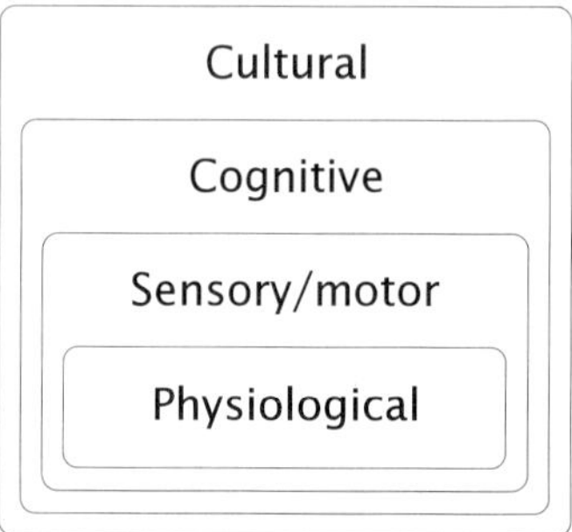

Figure 2-1 Characteristics of end users

The basic capabilities of the first three levels, the physiological, sensory/motor, and cognitive, are very difficult to change. The user's background and education affect the cognitive level, but in practice these capabilities are beyond the control of technology implementors. Improvement of sensory/motor and cognitive capabilities through training may delude designers into thinking that users can learn *anything*, but this is not true. The average user can be taught (with difficulty) to touch-type; the same person cannot be taught to remember a new ten-digit numeric password every week. It is simply outside the range of normal human accomplishment. The cultural level has a significant influence on individuals, but this occurs over time and is difficult to predict. Other things being equal, technology succeeds when it recognizes the basic capabilities and limitations of individuals.

When a system is first tried by its intended users, their reactions are often surprising to the developers. "Great features" of the system are ignored, things that appear obvious to the developers are confusing to the users, things the developers like, the users dislike (and vice versa). A common human reaction is to reject any implied criticism of deeply held beliefs, and developers may manifest this. Often in my career I have heard developers (even when face to face with users!) imply that problems reflected deficiencies in the users' intelligence or education, not in the system.

The similarity in basic human characteristics may make us forget that significant differences exist in cognitive models and culture. This is particularly true for computers, where developers usually have mental models and corporate cultures that differ greatly from those of users.[1] As you design a system, taking the time to reflect on your *own* characteristics, as well as those of users, can change this situation dramatically. Instead of a confrontation, meeting with users can become an enjoyable and creative partnership.

As an example of analyzing user characteristics, consider a simple user interface device—the computer keyboard. Here are examples of issues at the four levels:

- *Physiological* stress resulting from computer keyboard use is a significant problem, and has, quite literally, crippled some users [Fur93]. This is a multifactorial problem [Bak89], and it involves the task and environment, not just the keyboard. The ultimate cause, though, is a violation of physiological and biomechanical limits of the human organism.
- Typing involves s*ensory/motor* skills. There is a great difference between touch typists and those who "hunt and peck" on the keyboard; this is an example of performance improvement by training. The touch typist is using his or her sensory/motor systems in a different and more efficient way. Touch typists are often initially frustrated when they try to use a mouse, since a new sensory/motor skill must be learned. (Though unlike touch typing, users typically learn mouse skills quickly without formal training.)
- To illustrate *cognitive* aspects of keyboard use, I will relate a true anecdote. I was teaching someone how to use an electronic office system. The first step was to log in, and I asked the user to type `logon` followed by his user ID. He appeared confused and unable to do this, and I could not figure out why. It turned out he had never used a

[1] The same problem may arise with respect to physical differences. I have seen a videotape of a five-foot-tall operator attempting to clean a tape drive that had been designed by a six-foot-two-inch engineer. The task was nearly impossible.

typewriter or computer keyboard in his life. Even users who do not touch-type usually have a mental model of where things are on the keyboard, and how to operate the keys. Having no such model, this individual had no sense of how to find the right keys, or what action would enter the letters into the computer.

- Another true story illustrates the effect of *cultural* influences. In the mid-1980s, a forward-thinking company decided to give every middle manager and executive a personal computer for their use at home. They could use it for whatever they wanted—the point was simply to give them an incentive to understand the new technology. Later the company found that, almost without exception, the managers had given the PCs to their children and never used them. After probing, it turned out that rejection of the PCs stemmed from the need to use the keyboard to operate them. In this company, keyboard use stereotyped the user as a clerk, typist, or secretary, and was not something a manager was willing to do, even in private.

As this example illustrates, a developer needs to understand what is going on at all these levels to reliably predict whether a design will succeed.

Tasks The next major area is that of tasks. Figure 2-2 shows a layered view of tasks, analogous to Figure 2-1. A task[1] is a sequence of actions a person performs to reach some goal. An example would be the sequence of actions required to type a letter.

The layers are:

- *Physical objects and events*: tools used to accomplish the task, material objects that form the starting point for the task, and physical events that occur as the user does the task. In typing, we have the typewriter or computer keyboard and a blank sheet of paper (or a blank screen), and the events associated with hitting the keys, etc.

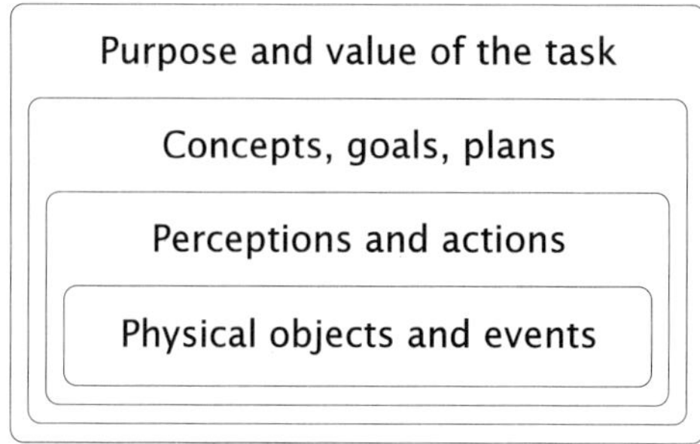

Figure 2-2 Characteristics of tasks

[1] This use of "task" is somewhat more exact than the dictionary definition and corresponds to the use of the word in the literature of psychology and human factors. This is covered in Chapter 7, *Users, Tasks, and Task Analysis.*

- *Perceptions and actions*: things a user is aware of during the task, and the actions the user performs. For skilled users, this occurs at the sensory/motor level. In typing a letter, the user sees characters appearing on the page, strikes the keys and receives tactile feedback, etc.
- *Concepts, goals, plans*: the user's understanding of the objects and the task, the goal to be attained, and a plan or mental image of the steps to be taken. In typing, the typist decomposes the letter into strings of characters separated by white space; the action language of the keyboard then requires striking the keys to produce the characters, spaces, and blank lines on the page. Visual feedback is used to check the state of the typed page against the goal (the typist's idea of the letter to be produced).
- *Purpose and value of the task*: why is this task being done? What is its value? This is usually referred to the larger cultural context, including the corporate culture in which work is done. In the example cited above, *typing* was a valuable subtask for clerical employees, whereas managers were accustomed to performing the subtask of writing (by hand) or dictating a draft. These two subtasks together produced the final typed output. There the social and cultural dimensions of the task were quite explicit, since it was done by a team of people, not a single individual.

Environments Figure 2-3 shows the corresponding layers for the environment in which someone does a task.

The layers are:

- *The physical world*: all the physical objects and events in the environment of the user.
- *Stimuli/affordances*: stimuli are events generated in the environment that cause perceptions in the user. Affordances are perceived properties of objects that "afford" action. Examples of affordances are handles on doors, or the keys on a typewriter.[1]
- *Language and concepts*: the user's background knowledge about objects in the environment, and the language available for thinking and talking about them. Language and concepts are intimately connected. Some people (e.g., the linguist Benjamin Whorf [Who56]) assert that language effectively dictates the set of thinkable concepts..
- *Society* is the carrier of culture. It is embodied in the set of people the user encounters, at work or in society at large. Society has a strong influence on the individual's perception of the purpose and value of

[1] The term "affordance" was coined by Gibson [Gib79]. Norman explores affordances at length in [Nor88].

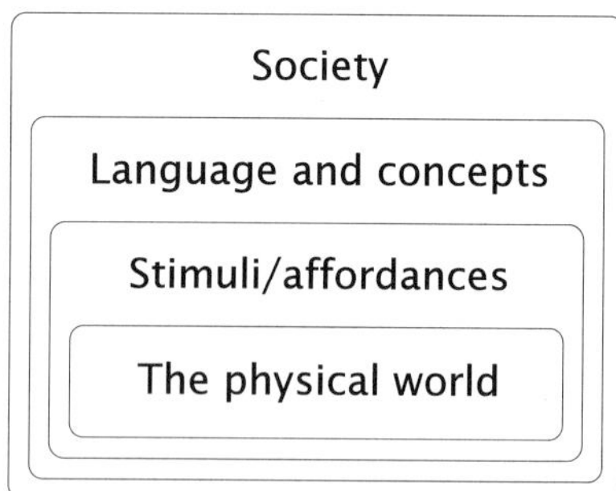

Figure 2-3 Characteristics of task environments

a task.[1] In the case of the non-typing managers, once a few courageous individuals started using PCs, it became much easier for others to follow. The transition was also eased by the emergence of new tasks, such as entering data into a computer spreadsheet, which were "managerial" and therefore placed a new cultural value on typing skills. In most cases, the social environment is either part of the task (if it is done by more than one person) or is involved with the task inputs and outputs.

As another example of the use, and the need, for analysis, consider providing speech recognition technology for typists. There are many obvious issues to think about, and some not-so-obvious ones. Because speech can be overheard, users may fear that people will think they are talking to themselves; or they may fear that the privacy of letters or other documents is being compromised. Ambient noise, such as air conditioners or other people talking, may degrade the recognition rate. Speech recognition may not be consistent with the overall management and structuring of tasks. For instance, secretaries often type while answering routine phone calls; this would not be possible if speech replaced the keyboard as the input mechanism.

Too often, this sort of analysis is done only after a product has failed in the market. Failure can be avoided by understanding factors that make technology acceptable or unacceptable for users and tasks, and how individuals, groups, cultures, and technology interact.

Production Workers and Knowledge Workers

An important interaction between technology and culture that influenced the evolution of OOUIs is the trend toward fewer *production workers* and more *knowledge workers*. Production workers make physical goods, and they have dominated the economies of developed nations for most of the last couple of centuries. Knowledge workers primarily create, process, or transmit information.

[1] See [Ber67] for a strong view on the "social construction" of reality.

Though economists and social scientists do not have precise definitions of "production" and "knowledge" work, there is general agreement on a trend that has been going on since the late 19th century. The number of workers in industries whose main content is information (such as banking, publishing, postal and telephone communications, etc.) has been increasing at the expense of workers in the production and agriculture sectors [Bel80]. The same trend has occurred *within* companies, favoring departments such as planning, marketing, and information systems. This trend has accelerated since the end of World War II, in part due to dramatic improvements in information technologies. The US Bureau of Labor Statistics predicts that jobs in the production, unskilled labor, and agriculture sectors will continue to grow more slowly than population, or decline. Jobs with a large knowledge content, ranging from computer programming to nursing, will increase faster than population [Woo93].

My assessment of the trend is that the important issue is not simply "goods versus information," but the amount of value that information adds to the end product. Even for manufactured goods like automobiles, information (on sales, market trends, automated design and production processes, etc.) is now a significant component in the value of the end product. The trend in manufacturing is to have more options, smaller raw materials inventories, faster delivery to customers, and shorter product development times. These factors demand manufacturing processes that change quickly in response to new information.

Processes in many traditional "production" industries are shifting, over time, away from production and toward knowledge work. In contrast, there are bureaucratic processes in businesses and public agencies where employees do little more than "push paper," without responding to changes in the information content of the forms they process. These processes are routine, repetitive, and non-adaptive—more like production than knowledge work, although economists might put these jobs into the knowledge sector. The key issue is repetition versus variety; rigid structure versus flexibility.

For the better part of this century, an approach known as "Taylorism" (after Frederick W. Taylor, who pioneered "scientific management" in the early 1900s) has been applied to structured work. Taylor himself focused mainly on production work, applying techniques like "time and motion" studies to increase efficiency. He analyzed each worker's part of an overall process, and modified each part to produce the maximum output with the least effort. Since then, his approach has been applied to all kinds of repetitive, process-oriented work. Examples include processing of routine forms, such as insurance claims, handling of directory assistance calls by telephone operators, and many others. The Taylor approach, however, fails to account for several things:[1]

[1] This is not a criticism of Taylor himself, who improved conditions both for workers and management, but rather of blanket application of his methods in inappropriate contexts.

- The success of this method is based on intensive analysis of processes that are repeated without significant variation. Knowledge-intensive processes are often highly variable.
- It looks primarily at the process, not the product. Each process has inputs and outputs that the worker focuses on exclusively. The analysis ignores issues that require a global view of the end product.
- It assumes that work in process flows linearly from worker to worker. Analyzing processes involving the simultaneous collaboration of groups of workers is much more difficult.
- Skilled, knowledgeable people like to feel that they have mastery over the task, and can control how they do it. This attitude works against "scientific management." The Taylor approach does not consider either individual or cultural factors not directly related to the production process.

Some thinkers, such as Drucker [Dru89] and Toffler [Tof85], have concluded that information and information technology radically and pervasively change the nature of work, and that managers must learn to cope with the lack of structure that prevails in the "information-based organization." If this view is correct, it implies that user interfaces must adapt to new work structures. The right approach seems to me to be provided by Bennett's research [Ben83] on decision support systems. These systems help decision makers to simulate, visualize, and evaluate alternatives, based on data and assumptions.

Information technology has tended to "automate away" the highly structured, repetitive aspects of jobs, leaving the unstructured components (which require decision-making) to the worker. Branch banking is an example. Most of what a teller does is repetitive, such as handling deposits and withdrawals. Automated teller machines (ATMs) can handle this component of banking. Other functions, such as auditing, evaluating credit ratings, etc., are less structured and have a high decision-making component. The number of people employed in these latter jobs is increasing, while the number of tellers is declining [Woo93].

More and more of the job content of knowledge workers is decision-making, and the systems they use are taking on more characteristics of decision support systems. This is true for professional office work [Mac87], and also for industrial process automation systems [Zub88].

Decision support tasks are unstructured, but involve some or all of the following activities:

1. Obtaining, formulating, or analyzing general assumptions and constraints on the range of possible decisions.
2. Obtaining and inspecting data pertinent to the decision being made.
3. Transforming, summarizing, and reviewing the data.
4. Evaluating the consequences of trial decisions by simulation,

inspection of data, etc.

5. Iterating some combination of steps 1–4 based on the consequences of the trial decision.

6. Putting decisions into a form in which they can be communicated to others, or directly implemented.

Bennett concluded that in decision support systems, the user interface cannot provide the structure that is lacking in the task itself. The interface can, however, provide a context for interaction to guide the user through a space of possible actions and results. The context is a rich, graphical representation of the data or other objects of interest, and a means of showing users what actions are possible at each point in the process. Mack and Nielsen [Mac87] arrived at similar conclusions after studying integration issues in software for office professionals. They explicitly mentioned an "object-oriented" approach to representing the things that concerned office users; this seems to be an appropriate term for Bennett's ideas as well.

Publishing exemplifies these issues. Though classified as part of the knowledge sector, until recently much of the process was routine and highly structured. Publishing a book involved many steps, each done by someone with a different skill: writing, layout, graphics production, typesetting, copy editing, etc. No one involved was responsible for the entire product. Many decisions made within process steps were routinized, or, if non-routine, were referred to a manager or other higher authority. Global "creative control" was separated from process details. New computer technology, however, has changed all this.

As the author of a technical book, I have become very aware of how closely the publishing process is now coupled to the knowledge that is driving the product—that is, the process has become more information-intensive. Desktop publishing systems have begun to look like Bennett's decision support systems. An author can now do almost all the tasks associated with publishing a book, except for the actual printing. The author has at his or her disposal a word processor, automatic spelling checker and thesaurus, grammar checker, graphics and image processing programs, a page layout program to put everything together, and a laser printer to produce "camera ready" final copy for the printer.[1]

This changes the publishing process significantly. The decision content of each step increases because the author has an integrated view of the final product and the freedom to explore alternatives while in the midst of the process. The means for doing this is an object-oriented interface, where the objects are words, paragraphs, pages, pictures, etc. Showing the objects as they will appear in print, with tool icons and menus expressing the possibilities for action, provides a context to guide the author's work.

[1] In many cases, even literature searches and other research can be done online.

I have suggested that the increase in knowledge work is motivating OOUIs. However, many jobs are still repetitive and highly structured. Even knowledge workers typically do some tasks that have more the character of production work. For such tasks, the freedom and flexibility associated with typical OOUIs may not be necessary or desirable. Chapter 7, *Users, Tasks, and Task Analysis*, discusses designing interfaces for highly structured tasks within the object paradigm.

2.2 History of the OOUI

The previous section talked about production and knowledge work from a broad social perspective. We now take up the thread of how the human-computer interface was evolving to support emerging demand for "knowledge systems." This thread begins thirty years before "GUI" became a household word in the computer industry. The evolution was driven by visionaries such as Ivan Sutherland, Doug Engelbart, and Alan Kay—people who, to paraphrase Engelbart [Eng68], proposed augmenting human intellect rather than automating production tasks.[1] These pioneers, unlike many designers today, did not have a mass of powerful technology for which they were trying to find a use. They had powerful *ideas*, and struggled to implement them on relatively crude machines.

This section traces some of the main currents of ideas that led to the modern OOUI, as represented on major commercial platforms. The next section, *User Interface Technology Evolution*, takes a broader and more speculative look at the relationship between users, computers, and technology.

Early History

Figure 2-4 is a representation of the history of the OOUI. This chart is not "the compleat history of the OOUI"—not every system and user interface that played a role is shown. I apologize if I have left out any reader's favorite interface; if the figure contained them all, it would be impossibly detailed. An arrow from one system to another indicates an influence. The nature of the influence varies, and in some cases it is obscure or controversial (the relationship between the Apple Macintosh and Microsoft Windows, for instance, is still being debated in the courts as I write).

In the early days of modern computing, there was an optimism about what computers could accomplish which is hard to find today, amid books with titles like *DOS for Dummies* and *Windows for the Complete Idiot*.[2] JOSS, an example of the youthful excitement, was developed at the RAND Corporation on a 1953 computer that was pathetically underpowered, "to demonstrate, on a small scale, the value . . . of easy access to computing

[1] Which is not to say that automating production is unimportant. If properly done, automation frees up humans for better things.

[2] If you do not believe these titles, browse in any well-stocked computer bookstore.

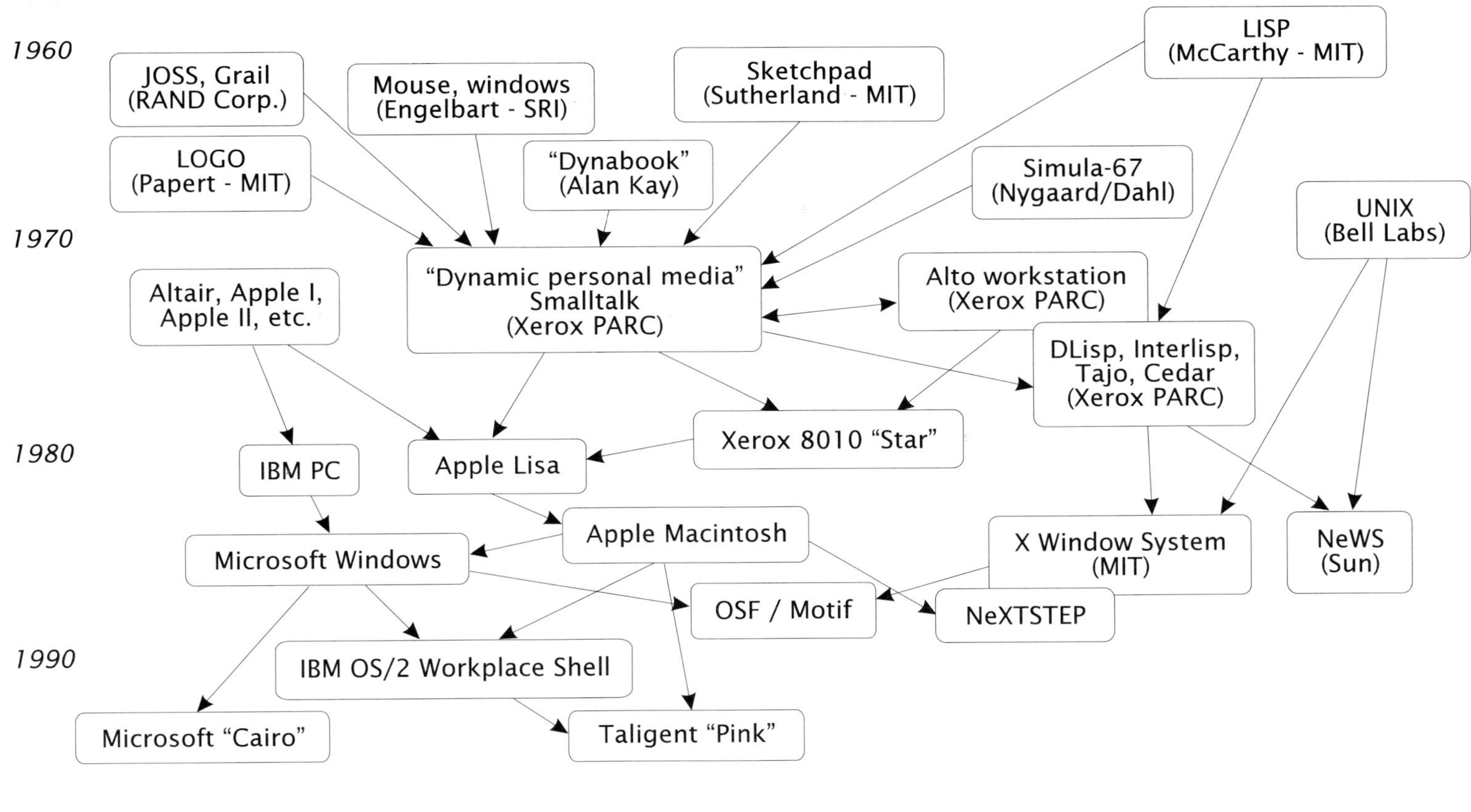

Figure 2-4 Some linkages in the history of the OOUI

power for the non-programmer" [Mark82]. In spite of its deficiencies, JOSS became addicting to many users. It was neither graphical nor object-oriented, but it pioneered an approach to user interfaces (described in the principles below) that was used successfully on more powerful systems at RAND and elsewhere. The JOSS command language, developed by Cliff Shaw, could be summarized for users on a single page. It was built around several key principles:

- *Readability*: The language was tailored to the users (mainly mathematicians). Not only the syntax, but the semantics or "conceptual model" reflected the user's domain, not the computer's. I would expand this and call it *comprehensibility*.
- *High degree of interaction*: A user entered a program in small steps that were immediately interpreted by the computer. Error messages again used the language of the user and allowed the user to correct the error and continue.
- *Power of expression*: Ease of use alone is not sufficient to make a computer system popular. The system must *do something* that is important for its users, and do it efficiently. JOSS allowed users to do powerful computations with just a few statements.
- *Timesharing*: To paraphrase Alan Kay [Kay93], timesharing was an innovation on the road to personal computing. Instead of breaking down a large computer into data stores and programs, timesharing divided it into *smaller computers*, one for each user.

These principles, or similar ones, motivated a great deal of early work. Viewed from the user's seat, systems of astonishing power often resulted. In the early 1960s, Tom Ellis at RAND invented the RAND Tablet, which allowed the use of a pen-like stylus as a pointing or writing device. RAND programmers built a system called GRAIL around the tablet, with which the user could interactively sketch flowcharts. The system recognized flowchart symbols, hand printed characters, and gestures based on proofreaders' marks. The graceful interactivity of GRAIL was a match for any of today's pen-based systems (though it took a dedicated System 360/44 mainframe to handle a single user).[1]

One of the most important systems of this early period was Ivan Sutherland's Sketchpad system [Sut63b].[2] This was tremendously influential in the field of object-orientation, as well as in the field of computer graphics. Every computer-aided design system, every "paint" program, owes a debt to Sketchpad. It introduced several ideas that have become key principles of modern graphical interfaces:

- The interface was highly interactive (using a graphic display and light

[1] A film clip of GRAIL in operation can be seen on [vKay87]. See also [Kay93], p. 73.
[2] The citation for [Sut63b] in the bibliography refers to two videotapes of Sketchpad.

pen), and the user interacted directly with the geometric objects of interest.

- Users could create "master" or template objects, from which many identical copies or instances could be created. If the master was changed, all instances would be changed as well.
- Users could apply constraints to composite objects, for instance that two lines should meet at a right angle. Sketchpad would then redraw the object to satisfy the constraint.
- The display was a "window" onto a large drawing. The window could be resized by zooming in and out of the drawing.

Though based upon principles similar to those underlying JOSS, Sketchpad (like GRAIL) had the advantage of being able to display and operate directly on objects with a natural graphic representation, without the need for an intermediate command language. Where commands were used, they could be simplified, since the user indicated the object to be operated on by pointing at it.

Notice the similarity between Sketchpad and Bennett's characterization of a decision support system. This connection is strengthened by understanding Sutherland's objective, which was *not* simply to build a drafting system. He envisioned that the objects in the drawing would be active entities modeling the properties of the real objects they represented. In a circuit diagram, each component would understand its electrical characteristics; in an architectural drawing, building components would be aware of their own strength, stresses, etc.

The most stunning fact about Sketchpad is that Sutherland implemented it—on hardware we would consider almost incredibly crude—and essentially invented object-oriented programming in the process. The credit for being the first OOP language goes to Simula-67, but only because Sutherland did not generalize his work. This quotation captures (for me) the quintessence of object-orientation. It precedes a technical description of the type system for geometric objects in Sketchpad, which we would now call a class hierarchy:

> The organization of the elements of the drawing into types has facilitated the generalization of the programs which comprise the Sketchpad system. . . . Those subroutines which had to do with a single kind of drawing part were collected together and specifically labeled, both in the coding sheets and block diagrams, but most importantly in the mind, as belonging to that particular kind of entity.[1]

While Sutherland was building Sketchpad at MIT, a group led by Doug Engelbart at the Stanford Research Institute (SRI) was also helping to invent the future of user interfaces. He and his colleagues at the Augmented Human Intellect Research Center invented the mouse and did

[1] [Sut63a], p. 49.

much of the fundamental research underlying its use as a pointing device for text and graphics editing. Other contributions included the first practical implementation of hypertext, multiple tiled windows,[1] separation of the semantic content of information from how it is viewed, collaborative editing of documents, and video conferencing [Eng68].

They recognized early on that productivity went beyond supporting individuals with technology. They addressed issues involving multiple users in a corporate and cultural context, and saw that real productivity gains required that work be restructured as well as "automated." Engelbart and his colleagues were ahead of their time. This, and the fact that their systems emphasized expert use and made few concessions to novices, limited their immediate impact. Their goal to "augment" groups and even entire enterprises was particularly difficult in the sociocultural dimension. But later researchers used technical innovations such as the mouse, and the implementation of ideas that few others had even thought of helped push the field generally. Engelbart's group at SRI also seeded people into many other organizations, notably the Xerox Palo Alto Research Center (PARC).

The systems described so far, though they were grounded in an understanding of human factors, were built by computer scientists. Other developments were occurring which were more explicit attempts to use computers for understanding human cognition. John McCarthy at MIT developed the LISP language in the late 1950s [McC60]. He designed LISP to process symbols represented as character strings, besides "crunching numbers." Then as now, LISP was used as a tool for artificial intelligence (AI) research. As a programming language, LISP had an influence on later languages such as Smalltalk. More importantly, perhaps, the AI community at MIT and Stanford created an environment in which many researchers were studying the question of how to use computers to simulate and augment human intelligence.

Seymour Papert, at MIT, developed a language called LOGO for helping children to learn [Pap80]. LOGO systems feature an object called a "turtle," which moves around the computer screen and draws lines in response to commands.[2] In early LOGO systems, the turtle was a physical device that rolled around on the floor, drawing on a large sheet of paper. Children worked with the turtle by "teaching" it to compose primitive commands into programs to draw complex geometric objects. (A modern OO programmer would call these programs methods.) This very physical, object-oriented interface allowed even small children to work successfully with the computer—a fact that was not lost on later researchers. Children are just as "smart" as adults at using computers (try playing a Nintendo game with the average 12-year-old if you do not believe it), but they have less patience. This makes them good subjects for experiments exploring

[1] Tiled windows are like rectangular tiles that cover the display without overlapping.

[2] If you are a Smalltalk programmer, the global object `Turtle`, an instance of class `Pen`, is the direct descendant of the LOGO turtle.

how to make computers easier to use.

Xerox PARC For reasons that may be serendipitous historical accidents, all the ideas and technology I have described came together in the Learning Research Group (LRG) at the Xerox Palo Alto Research Center (PARC) in the early 1970s. Alan Kay started the group to implement his vision of a *Dynabook*, a lightweight, powerful computer about the size of a book [Kay77a]. Knowing that the technology to build an actual Dynabook would not be available for many years, they set out to build a simulation, or "interim Dynabook," on the Xerox Alto workstation. Harking back to the JOSS principles, they wanted a user interface for the Dynabook that anyone could use, while allowing expert users full access to the power of the computer. The result was a series of Smalltalk systems.[1]

As a language, Smalltalk had its roots in LISP, LOGO, and Simula-67. Its development environment was influenced by LISP, LOGO, and JOSS, and its user interface incorporated specific ideas and general philosophy from Sketchpad, GRAIL, LOGO, and Engelbart's NLS system. It used a bitmapped graphical display, a mouse for pointing, and multiple moveable windows with popup menus (enhancements to Engelbart's tiled windows). The windows on the screen were intended to suggest loosely arranged sheets of paper on a desk or table. Each window had properties far beyond paper, permitting the user to mix text, graphics, and animation in powerful ways.

The Smalltalk language was co-designed with its user interface. Larry Tesler, one of the researchers, pointed out the strong connection between the properties of objects in object-oriented languages and the properties of corresponding objects on the screen.[2] Dan Ingalls, one of the principal designers and implementors of Smalltalk, proposed the *reactive principle* as the basic idea behind the Smalltalk interface: "Every component accessible to the user should be able to present itself in a meaningful way for observation and manipulation" [Ing81].

Something that will surprise anyone who has never seen the "classic" Smalltalk interface[3] is that, by today's standards, it is not very graphical. A user can put graphics on the screen, and text is displayed in a variety of fonts and sizes, but most object representations are variables, class names, etc., presented in text. Other work going on at PARC during the 1970s resulted in interfaces that looked more like what we see today. The object-oriented conceptual model and architecture of Smalltalk facilitated these later developments. Ingalls' reactive principle gave coherence to graphical user interfaces, and the *Model-View-Controller* (MVC) architecture of Smalltalk provided the technical foundation for implementing them.[4]

---

[1] Early Smalltalks were complete operating systems and development environments, as well as programming languages. See [Gol83], [Kay93].

[2] Tesler did this in a paper in which he coined the term "object-oriented user interface" [Tes83].

[3] Commercially available in [sDig86] and early versions of [sPar89].

[4] MVC is covered in detail in Chapters 11–13.

Two other projects at PARC are worth mentioning. David Canfield Smith, in his Pygmalion system [Smi75], invented the idea of "iconic programming," where the user manipulated icons on the screen to accomplish a task. Smith implemented Pygmalion using the Smalltalk-72 system.[1] Though Pygmalion represented icons as rectangles enclosing text, they had the semantics of the icons in today's graphical OOUIs. DLisp and Interlisp were windowed development environments written in LISP. They were influenced by Smalltalk, and in turn they influenced a series of programming development environments done at PARC and by the Xerox Systems Development Division. The first of these environments, Tajo, incorporated pictorial icons, including icons representing minimized or "collapsed" windows, thus becoming the first system to manifest the general look and feel of modern GUIs [Tei86].

A characteristic of the "youthful enthusiasm" stage of user interface research was that the people with the ideas were also the people doing the implementation. The time came when user interface design and user interface development became separated. A beneficial consequence of this was the notion of "window systems," layered software architectures that concealed messy implementation details from programmers who only wanted to write applications. All the major commercial platforms today use this form of architecture; many of the basic technical ideas were developed at Xerox PARC, along with the external appearance of the GUI. Several ideas are particularly important:

- The display screen as a resource that is shared among many programs, just like any other system resource. This requires serializing access to the display, assigning input events to their proper program recipients, and notifying programs when their screen windows have been overlaid and must be restored.
- Event-driven systems. Earlier systems (and many later ones) assumed a flow of conversation where the user entered something, then waited until the system had responded. The PARC window systems, particularly Tajo, were *event-driven.* The user could enter any number of inputs such as keystrokes and mouse button pushes; programs that responded to these events had to be ready to receive them at any time.
- Separation of application functions from the look and feel of the user interface. Smalltalk pioneered this [Ing78], and later systems evolved more sophisticated architectures. DLisp was the first window system in which applications communicated over a network with a display server on a different machine—an idea that was later used in the design of the X Window System [Sch86].

[1] Suffixes for PARC Smalltalk systems were 72, 76, and 80, designating the year they were released. [sPar89] and other commercial products are based on Smalltalk-80.

The Xerox Star and Apple Lisa

Two developments in the late 1970s resulted in commercialization of the ideas developed at Xerox PARC. First, the Xerox Systems Development Division decided to develop a workstation for office professionals, based upon user interface ideas and document editing and printing technology developed at PARC. The result was the Xerox 8010 "Star" office workstation.[1] Second, Steve Jobs, cofounder of Apple, visited PARC, liked what he saw, and eventually hired several researchers, including Larry Tesler. Jobs' interest led first to the Apple Lisa, and later to the Macintosh.

Xerox shipped the Star to customers in 1981, priced at about $15,000; Apple shipped the Lisa in 1983, at just under $10,000. Neither was a commercial success—partly due to price, partly because they were underpowered and slow, and they provided a limited number of applications. The Macintosh, with nearly as much function as the Lisa (networking support was a notable exception) and a similar user interface, cost less than $3000—low enough to become popular and to compete credibly against the IBM PC family, which had started shipping in 1981. Technical innovations in the Macintosh were largely "under the covers," and enabled the low price—but the Mac finally brought the GUI to a mass audience, and changed the industry permanently.

Figure 2-5 shows the interface for the Star, arguably the most famous user interface ever implemented. Already, in 1981, it exhibited all the common characteristics of the modern GUI:

- Icons represent data objects (documents), containers (file drawers, folders), and tools (printers, in and out mailboxes). Users express object interactions and commands by moving icons and dropping them on other icons.
- Icons can be asked to show their properties, or their contents, in windows. Views show the state of the objects as accurately as possible, as in the document displayed in the open window in Figure 2-5.
- Window contents are scrollable, and have menus and control icons along the top border.
- Commands are expressed almost entirely by pointing and clicking with the mouse.[2] The keyboard is used mostly for entering text or filling in forms.
- The environment is represented graphically, using images of familiar objects. The idea of an office desktop is used as an overarching metaphor to suggest the kinds of operations that are possible in the system.

---

[1] 8010 is the official name. "Star" was a development code name, which stuck after it was used in papers written about the 8010.

[2] The Star actually had a small number of special keys for common commands [Smi82]. The Apple Lisa, and almost all subsequent systems, used mouse and menu operations instead.

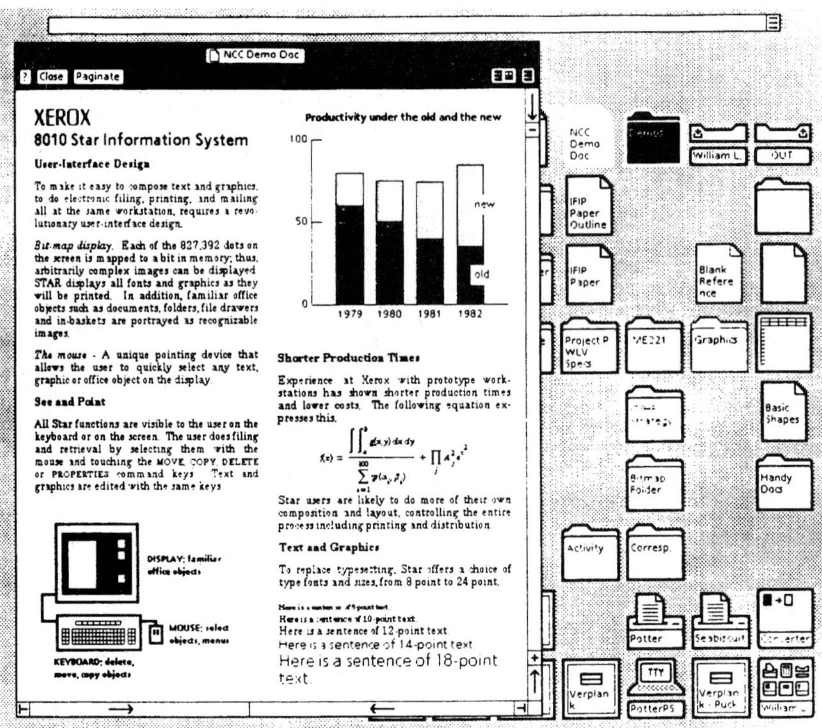

Figure 2-5 User interface for the Xerox Star

Xerox invested 30 person-years[1] in the external design of the interface. It was done by a large and talented team led by Charles Irby, and including David Canfield Smith, of icon fame, as well as graphic designers and human factors experts [Smi82]. The methodology used for the basic design had previously been codified by a team led by Irby, and including Larry Tesler [Irb77]. (Tesler then left for Apple and led the design of the Lisa.) Star is generally credited with launching the GUI era because it was shipped before the Lisa, and because the Lisa designers had seen the Star while they were still at work. But the Lisa was a parallel derivative of the same body of technology [Mor83]. The Lisa interface is not shown here because it was substantially the same as that of the Macintosh, which in turn determined the basic "look and feel" of most of the systems that followed.

The Star interface still exists almost unchanged in the Xerox GlobalView user interface, which runs on more powerful descendants of the 8010. Charles Irby later left Xerox, after he and some of his colleagues failed to convince management that the Star concept ought to be applied

[1] To illustrate the thoroughness of the approach, the design of the Star involved, in addition to numerous informal tests, 400 subject-hours of formal human factors testing done in a laboratory setting [Bew83].

to a more general workstation for professional decision support. They founded Metaphor Computer Systems (subsequently acquired by IBM) and designed a user interface for their *Data Interpretation System* which still looks much like the Star [IBM89].

Later Developments

Both the Xerox 8010 and the Apple Lisa (and the IBM PC) were directed at commercial end user environments where the primary applications were word processing, data analysis, and presentation graphics. Parallel developments were occurring directed at the growing market of professional computer system analysts, designers, programmers, and other high-end users such as VLSI circuit designers.

Though its developers emphasized its usability by "everyone," Smalltalk was a programming language and program development environment. DLisp, Interlisp, Tajo, and Cedar were also development environments first and foremost. The Bell Labs UNIX system [Lib89] was an environment designed by programmers for programmers, and it found a natural synergy with the PARC graphical development environments. The computer science connection made UNIX the system of choice for many universities, so it was a natural base for non-computer science applications at these universities.

One prominent result of this was the X Window System, developed as part of Project Athena, an ambitious campus-wide networking project at MIT. Two key technical ideas emerged from the X Windows project:

- The application does not need to be on the same machine that provides window management services.
- Providing low-level graphics and event-handling services without dictating the look and feel of the user interface is valuable.

X Windows has become an industry standard, and it provides the substrate for many UNIX GUIs. The proliferation of GUIs has had an impact on one of the main objectives of UNIX—portability across hardware platforms. The typical GUI has an application programming interface (API) with hundreds of function calls, and no two APIs are alike. As a result, porting an application from one platform to another can be a major effort for the programmer.[1] In addition, users may need to relearn the same application on a different platform, simply because details of the user interfaces differ.

Suitable development tools can address both user-level consistency and API compatibility. The Open Systems Foundation, a consortium of UNIX vendors, has supplied a base for such tools with OSF/Motif [Berl91]. Motif provides a standard API and a standard look and feel across multiple platforms. The fact that Motif was based on a submission by Microsoft and Hewlett-Packard, derived from Microsoft Windows, is an indication

[1] Technical issues in portability are discussed in Chapter 14.

that we are at the end of an era. Twenty years of widely divergent experiments funneled into Xerox PARC. After a decade of research and a decade of commercialization, we are left with a plethora of GUIs, but they all look much the same. This is the crux of the portability issue—if moving to a different GUI platform provides little new function, why should a large programming cost be required to do the port?

Systems like the Xerox 8010 and the Apple Lisa did not make much of a distinction between the platform or "shell," and the applications. Platform function was rich, and the relatively few applications were developed by the system vendor. Today each major platform has thousands of applications from many providers. The focus of innovation has shifted from platforms or shells to applications, but innovation is restricted by the need to harmonize with the host GUI.

Figure 2-6 is an example; the tool bar, a row of icons representing commonly used functions, has become standard in applications from Microsoft and other vendors. The diversity of such innovations is such that no historical pattern has emerged, yet the range of diversity is constrained by the prevailing styles. The tool bar fits well because it is conceptually similar to the action bar menu above it, and reflects the graphical style of the GUI platform. The next section discusses some of the issues raised by this state of affairs; others are deferred until later in the book.

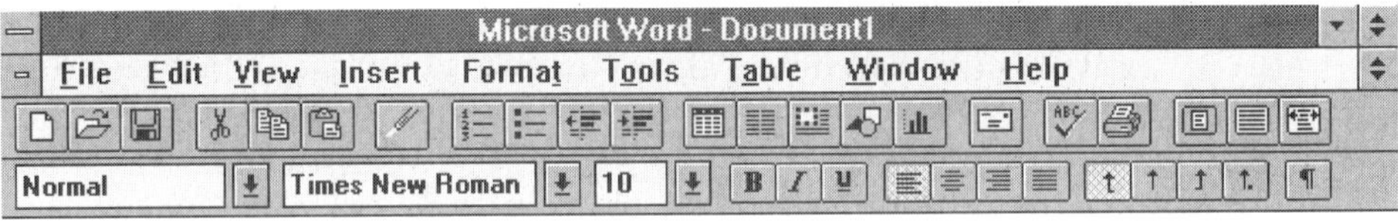

Figure 2-6 Tool bar in Microsoft Word

2.3 User Interface Technology Evolution

In 1946, a seminal report [Bur46] articulated what we now call the *von Neumann architecture*, the standard blueprint for most of the computers built since then. In the report, the authors[1] state: "Inasmuch as the completed device will be a general-purpose computing machine it should contain certain main organs relating to arithmetic, memory storage, control and connection with the human operator." Since the beginning of the computer age, then, the user interface, the "connection with the human operator," has been considered a fundamental component of the system. David Parnas, well known for his contributions to software engineering, was also an advocate of giving the user interface first-class status in the design of

[1] One of whom was the mathematician John von Neumann, whose name is attached to the architecture.

computer systems. In 1969 he wrote, "Several papers [including two by Parnas] . . . have argued that the proper procedure for computer system design involves going 'top-down' or 'outside-inwards'—in other words, designing the user interface *first*" [Par69].[1]

Throughout the history of computing, a strong ongoing thread is devoted to the human side. Fortran (FORmula TRANslation), the first popular high-level computer language, was motivated by the desire to provide an input language that is more compatible with the language of the users of the computer (who were mainly mathematicians at that time). John Backus, who led the design of FORTRAN, saw in the early 1950s that the cost of the human operators and programmers of computers would come to dominate the cost of computer hardware [Bas86]. COBOL (COmmon Business Oriented Language) was also motivated by the "human factors" aspect of programming languages. The verbose lexicon and syntax of COBOL were intended to make it easier for managers and other non-programmers to understand the logic of a program [Weg76].

The previous section described research specifically aimed at improving user interfaces. The consequences of usability (or lack of it) were also understood in the commercial arena. In a remarkable short article written in 1958 [Gol58], Robert Goldman says: "Too many people think that a computer is a complex, diabolical device . . . Their attitude is quite satisfying to those of us who work with computers . . . The trouble is, the people who hold the complex, diabolical view are often right; one way to convince them would be to actually make the computer easier to use." The average computer user of today would resonate with this statement, though not with the solution he described—an interpretive machine language interface, said to be easier than programming with wires on a plugboard!

Goldman makes two key points, which are still issues today:

- System designers faced the tradeoff of using expensive circuits to increase the computational speed of the machine, or to enhance the user interface.
- Unless the user interface was enhanced, the market for computers would be restricted by the small number of people capable of using them.

From the days of plugboards and wires, the industry has gone through several generations of user interface style and technology. Figure 2-7 summarizes these generations. The hardware technology generations are the conventional ones, and the next two columns show the predominant user interface devices and interaction languages. Each generation has limitations which are constraints imposed by the relationship between technology and its human users (maximum typing speed, for example). My description of the fifth generation is speculative—it is not clear yet what

[1] The Xerox Star is an example of taking this advice seriously.

"post GUI" user interfaces will look (and feel) like.[1]

An anthropologist might observe that interaction languages become part of the culture, both for users and developers. Many people resist the transition to a new language, like any other cultural change. Doherty has observed [Doh91] that the bandwidth of many of today's networks and user interfaces evolved around human typing speed. This is just one example of design based on technology constraints that no longer exist, but continue to influence designers through cultural inertia.

Generation	Hardware technology	User interface devices	User interface languages
First	Vacuum tubes (valves)	Plugboards, switch panels, indicator lights, paper tape, punched cards	Machine languages
Second	Discrete transistors	Typewriter terminals, paper tape, punched cards	Programming languages, command languages
Third	Integrated circuits	Typewriter terminals, character-based CRTs, vector graphics displays	Command languages, menus, text entry, form fill-in
Fourth	Very large scale integration (VLSI)	Graphical user interface and associated devices, "event-driven" interfaces	Icon manipulation, menus, commands, text entry, form fill-in
Fifth	Ultralarge scale integration	Current GUI, multimedia, speech/gesture recognition, artificial intelligence, "virtual reality," etc.	Enhanced OOUI, high bandwidth direct manipulation, agents, etc.

Figure 2-7 User interface and technology generations

Technology has changed since Goldman wrote about usability in 1958, but his main points are still valid. It is just as true today that acceptance of computers is limited by the size of the population that is comfortable using them. They are not yet the ubiquitous "information appliances" that some have envisioned.

His first point, the difficulty of the technology trade-off, has changed in character. There are still hardware constraints—no matter how good the design, it will not be successful if performance is inadequate, or if excessive cost deters customers from buying it. However, personal computers

[1] The characteristics of post-GUI interfaces are discussed further in Chapter 16.

are available today[1] that offer more computational power than the mainframe supercomputers of five years ago. For most users, the bottleneck is the user interface—controlling the computation, and understanding the flood of information the computer can produce. This is a constraint primarily imposed by our current ability to develop software, which is something I hope can be improved by the methods described in this book.

One thing that has not changed very much is the people who use computers. People interact with computers in a way that is, in general, no different from the way in which they interact with other artifacts in the world. We must use the same hands, the same eyes and ears, the same brains that we have used for millennia. Thus, if new interface styles are not *solely* that, simply *styles*, they must exploit our existing capabilities in new ways.

2.4 Summary

This chapter presents some of the long-range factors driving the market for systems and applications with object-oriented user interfaces. These include social, cultural, and demographic factors as well as the availability of enabling technologies. These factors interact through feedback loops that affect the rate at which the mainstream population of computer users can assimilate new technology. The most important demographic factor affecting the market for OOUIs is the shift from production work to knowledge work that has been occurring in the developed world for most of this century. This shift demands computer technology oriented toward flexibility, individual empowerment, and peer collaboration, rather than functional "assembly line" processes and hierarchical organizations.

Figure 2-8 sketches the interaction of these factors. Changing technology itself fosters related technology change. New processor chips spur the production of new memory chips; new processor and memory chips make the production of larger, faster displays feasible; this in turn influences user interface design. When applied to human activities such as work, technology enables individuals and groups to work faster, to do different work, and to work in different ways.

"Fourth generation" technology has facilitated knowledge work, individual self-reliance, creativity, and empowerment. As the technology and new work roles become more pervasive, they begin to affect the structure and style of corporations, shifting power from hierarchies of managers to networks of workers. We can see similar changes in areas as diverse as shopping and military tactics. These cultural shifts generate needs that in turn influence the future direction of technology.

Some rules of thumb for planners, analysts, and designers that can be drawn from this chapter are:

[1] Based on the Sun SPARC, the Intel Pentium, or the Apple/IBM/Motorola PowerPC RISC processor.

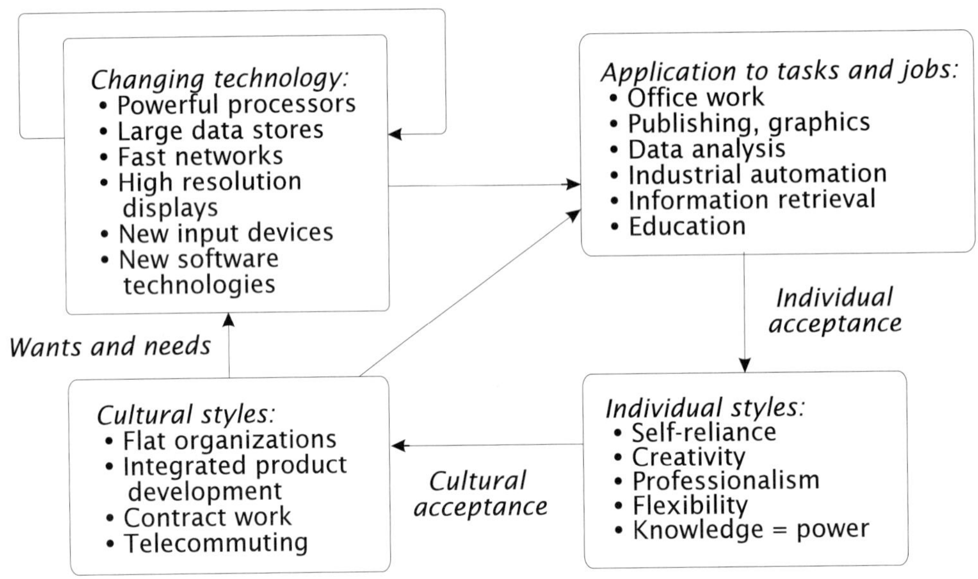

Figure 2-8 The cycle of change for object-oriented user interfaces

- Individuals, corporate cultures, and the culture at large may resist the introduction of new tools. *Do* take this into account. *Do not* use it as an excuse by blaming the flaws in a design on "user resistance."
- The strategic planning that drives design may need to account for long-term demographic and cultural trends, of which current technology users are probably unaware.
- Products are used in a context—they must fit the user, the task, and the environment (including other products being used).
- The technology for the next generation of commercial applications probably already exists in research laboratories.

2.5 To Explore Further

The ideas in Section 2.1, *People, Work, and Technological Change*, come from many sources. I have filtered them through my own experience and presented what I thought most important. To go further, I would encourage you to study a little sociology and anthropology, as well as psychology and human factors.

[Nor88] is an unorthodox, but highly entertaining, introduction to some of the key ideas of human factors. [Bak89] emphasizes the multifactorial nature of usability. [Tho89] presents an "ecological" perspective on user interface design, which is very much in the spirit of this chapter.

[Shn92] is a good general book on human factors and interface design, and the first chapter talks about some of the larger goals we should be seeking so that our designs add value to people's lives.

Production Workers and Knowledge Workers in section 2.1 expresses ideas that have almost become clichés in certain circles. Magazines such as *Business Week* and *Fortune* will keep you abreast of major developments that affect business information systems. Articles in journals such as the *Harvard Business Review* provide more depth on selected aspects. Of the literature cited in the text, [Bel80] is particularly useful for understanding the long-term trends. Public libraries can supply more detailed and up-to-date information (for instance, census data), but the raw data is complicated and hard to digest. [Tof85] and [Dru89] are good places to start for a look at future trends in the information-based corporation. [Zub88] is filled with accounts of how workers react to information technology. It is somewhat hard going, but the perspective Zuboff provides on the problems is a useful counterbalance to the optimistic (and sometimes shallow) view of other authors. [Ben83] offers insights into the kinds of systems knowledge workers need.

[Per85] is an account of the history of PARC, and discusses many of the user interface-related developments that occurred there. [Gol83] describes the Smalltalk language. [Per89] is a short and well-written summary of all the technical developments leading to the modern GUI. The best single account of all the material in this section through the PARC years is [Kay93]. [vKay87] covers roughly the same material and includes film clips of many of the interfaces described. [Tei86] covers the non-Smalltalk windowing systems developed at PARC. [Joh89] is an assessment of the Star project. [Smi82] presents the design principles behind the Star. [Mor83] discusses the development of Apple's Lisa. Besides these and other cited references, [Gol88], the record of an ACM conference on the history of personal workstations, contains papers covering many early developments.

The modern implications of much of the history here will be covered in subsequent chapters. Emerging technologies that will play a role in tomorrow's user interfaces will be discussed in Chapter 16, *Summary and Directions.*

2.6 Exercises

1. List a few tasks you do that involve the use of computers.

   - Are the tasks structured to maximize the benefit of the computer?
   - If not, how could they be reengineered to be more effective?

   (*For developers*: Try this exercise on your development process activities.)

2. Pick a GUI (e.g., the Macintosh Desktop, OSF/Motif, etc.). Describe yourself briefly in terms of physiological, sensory/motor, cognitive, and cultural characteristics. (Cognitive may be a little difficult. Think about verbal versus visual thinking, memory capacity, ability to tolerate uncertainty, etc.)

    a. Find some specific characteristics of the GUI that suit you either well or badly on these four dimensions.

    b. Describe a hypothetical person who differs significantly from you on these dimensions. (It will help to think of people you know who are different from you.) Take the *same characteristics* of the GUI you used in part (a). How well or badly do they suit your hypothetical person?

    (*For developers*: This is a valuable exercise to do for the product you are working on.)

3. Pick some jobs that you are familiar with (perhaps including your own, or your spouse's). Trace out the process flow that leads to the delivery of the good or service the job produces. Classify the "inputs" to the process. How much of the input is knowledge or information, versus materials or energy? What is the cost of information inputs, versus others (or, what is the value added to the final product by information inputs)? Has the relative amount or value of the information changed over the last 1, 5, or 10 years? How effective do think the computer support for this job is? (This is a hard exercise to do in detail, so you might want to experiment and find jobs where the answers are more obvious.)

4. [vSIGGRAPH] 56, 1 (1990) is a detailed exposition of the Xerox Star user interface, presented by Charles Irby and David Canfield Smith. Look at this tape and critique the Star user interface. What do you like? What don't you like?

5. Find currently existing examples of first, second, third, and fourth generation user interfaces. (For first generation, you may have to look at devices other than computers.) Look only at the interface devices and languages—not at the implementation technology. Is the use of each generation appropriate, given the function performed and the technology available to the designers?

3

Two User Interface Styles

This chapter introduces a technique for analyzing a user interface from the user's point of view and applies it to two styles for user interfaces. Chapter 4 will define one of these as "object-oriented." The analysis here is "naive" because it does not rely directly on object-oriented principles. It is not trivial, however, because it brings out basic issues in the user's perception of the quality of an application or system, as revealed through its interface.

For most users, the interface *is* the computer, the system, or the application. Technology, as such, is invisible. What the user sees, hears, feels, etc., are the artifacts of the user interface. The user's perception of whether a task can be done, and whether it is hard or easy, rests on those artifacts. Though the exact measure of ease or difficulty is hard to define, users generally have a good idea of how hard a task ought to be when done on a computer. Why? Because they understand the task, though they may not know much about computers. This is the basis for our analysis and for exploring the benefits and hazards of an object-oriented approach.

Since the analysis in this chapter is brief and high-level, it will raise issues and questions that are explored in detail only later in the book. Meanwhile, I encourage you to speculate, examine alternatives, and to apply this analysis technique to other interfaces you encounter—as developer, or as end user.

3.1 Analyzing User Interfaces

To judge whether a user interface is efficient, easy to use, etc., we need to understand what users want to accomplish with it. This is the premise underlying the method used in this chapter.[1] Methods such as this, called *user-centered*, can be used to develop new interface designs from user requirements. Here, we will analyze *existing* user interfaces.

The method is presented here in an "object neutral" way—that is, without using any specifically object-oriented techniques of modeling or analysis. This points out that the focus of user interface design has to be first and foremost on *users*. Chapter 7 will expand on this method, and show how it is synergistic with several well-known approaches to object-oriented analysis and design.

The Method

This analysis method is based on the model for user interfaces in Chapter 1 (Section 1.1), and Figure 1-1 is useful as a reference point. The objective is to assess the ease of using an interface by examining the steps required to perform representative tasks. For the purposes of this chapter, the method can be summarized in the following steps:

- Develop a task scenario—a description of one or more tasks someone would do using the system being analyzed. The description should be, as much as possible, independent of the computer implementation. For example, "produce a typewritten letter," not "use the word processor to type a letter"; "take the customer's order," not "invoke the order processing transaction," and so forth.
- Using the scenario, list the steps a user would execute to accomplish the task(s) with the system's user interface.
- Answer the following questions:
  1. What does the user need to know before beginning the task? How much of this knowledge is about objects and actions that are fundamental to the task, and how much is only about the computer system?
  2. What action does the user take to accomplish each step on the computer (type a command, select from a menu, etc.)? Is it easy to do? What information does the system provide about the next step? What happens if the user gets lost?
  3. What feedback does the system give after each action? Does the feedback contain too much information, or not enough? Is it easy to perceive and understand? Does the user need to remember

[1] The method described here is a synthesis of the work of many authors, filtered through my own experience. I have been influenced by [Ben83], [Ben84b], [Gou88], and [Whi88]. I am particularly indebted to Bennett.

large amounts of information in going from one step to the next?

4. Looking at a *series* of actions done by the user, is it efficient? Are all the steps necessary? Are any transitions awkward (for example, going from keyboard to mouse)? Are the steps related to steps in the task, or are they related more to managing the user interface?

To adhere to the spirit of the method, keep in mind that the user's task should always be easier *with* a computer than *without* one.[1]

Do not expect black and white answers to these questions. User interface design always involves tradeoffs. Since no two users or tasks are exactly the same, rarely can one find a single "ideal user interface" for an application or system. That does not mean that one interface cannot be better than another in some particular context, set by the market for the product. How well *those* users do their tasks with your interface ultimately decides its success or failure.

Chapter 7, *Users, Tasks, and Task Analysis*, presents the basis for this sort of analysis and shows how it can be used to generate designs. Right now we will apply it to understand some of the differences between user interface styles.

3.2 The Interfaces

In this section the method is applied to the user interfaces for two applications. One is an application for calculating. The other is an environment or "shell" for other applications. The objectives of the analysis are to illustrate the method and to pull out some characteristics differentiating the "two styles" of the chapter title.

A Four-Function Calculator

The first application is simple—performing basic calculations. It essentially emulates a typical four-function desk calculator. In spite of its limited function, this is a fairly popular application for occasional use by people who already have personal computers or workstations for other reasons. I call the first of the two interfaces for this application "traditional" because it is typical of command line interfaces that have been in use for decades on mainframes and minicomputers. The second I will call "object-based," because it tries to represent objects as they appear in the world.[2]

The first interface (shown in Figure 3-1) is typical of applications designed to run on terminals and personal computers capable only of

[1] This paraphrases something said by Ted Nelson [Nel87]. The point may seem obvious to the point of absurdity, yet I have run across systems that fail to satisfy this basic criterion.

[2] There are, of course, other styles besides these two, such as menus and form fill-in.

displaying characters. The session that is shown should be self-explanatory. The user's entries are lower case, following a prompt message; the computer's responses are capitalized.

```
C:\>calc
  NOW IN CALCULATOR MODE
  ENTER EXPRESSION:
    991.54 + 78.87 =
  RESULT IS    1070.41
  ENTER EXPRESSION:
  m+
  RESULT ADDED TO MEMORY. MEMORY IS   1070.41
  ENTER EXPRESSION:
    23 + 54.a =
  BAD ARITHMETIC CONVERSION.
  YOU HAD A SYNTAX ERROR.
  CHECK YOUR EXPRESSION AND TRY AGAIN:
    23 + 54.2 =
  RESULT IS    77.2
  ENTER EXPRESSION:
  quit
  LEAVING CALCULATOR MODE. HAVE A NICE DAY.
  C:\>
```

Figure 3-1 Command line interface to a calculator application

This interface works in a straightforward way, but it has some problems. Using addition of numbers as a representative task, the analysis questions lead to the following observations:

- The overall structure of the application is not visible to users. Though they already understand the task, users need to learn the details of the interface (through training or reading a manual) to discover that it is basically a four-function calculator.
- Actions are simple once the command syntax is learned, unless the user is unfamiliar with the keyboard. Errors in typing or memory lapses cause syntax errors that must be corrected by re-entering the entire command. Although users will normally know what to do next, the mechanism for exiting the application (`quit` command) is not obvious. If the screen is cleared, it is not obvious that the system is in "calculator mode." For a user who has *not* learned the command syntax, the next step at any point can be paradoxically both obvious and non-obvious. The user knows *what* to do, but not *how* to do it. (This is analogous to Ali Baba's brother Cassim, in the tale of "Ali Baba and

the Forty Thieves," from *The Arabian Nights*: Cassim could not remember the password "open sesame!" to exit from the cave of the thieves, and he was killed when they returned.)

- Feedback seems simple and obvious. For errors in command entry, additional information on the exact cause of the error might be desirable.
- The main possibility for awkwardness is that users are constantly conscious of using a computer, which may reduce the amount of attention they can pay to the task.

The command line interface style of Figure 3-1 dates from a time when character-based terminals, connected by telephone lines, provided the only affordable access to computers for most users. The technology of the terminals constrained interfaces not only to be character-based, but to use commands and responses that minimized the number of characters typed and transmitted over the line.

Raw technology for building workstations has become cheaper, and additional capabilities are now common. Information can be displayed in more sophisticated ways on graphic displays. Pointing devices, such as mice and touch screens, reduce the need for typing. Users are directly connected to desktop computers, so line transmission is not a constraint. Computational power can be devoted to making interfaces more interactive.

One approach to making interfaces easier to use, facilitated by this technology, is to present things in a way that is closer to the "real world" of users. Interfaces that are "object-based" in this sense—presenting a model intended to represent "real world objects"—are often billed by their designers as a solution to the problem of usability. (Looking at product advertisements in the computer trade press will provide a wealth of examples.)

The graphical calculator in Figure 3-2 is an example of this approach.[1] The "real world objects" are the whole calculator and its component parts (buttons and display). Users can "press" the calculator "buttons" by moving the mouse pointer over a button on the display and then pressing the left mouse button. On a touch screen display, the calculator buttons can be directly "pushed."

Alternatively, a user can type the expressions, using corresponding keys on the computer keyboard (which facilitates "expert use," a topic we will return to later). The speed of desk calculators can be matched or exceeded by use of the numeric keypad provided on many personal computer keyboards (shown in Figure 3-3). Exploiting this capability is an important, and easily overlooked, feature of a good interface to the calculator application.

This interface to the calculator has several potential advantages,

[1] Based on a Smalltalk implementation given to me by Derek Dickson.

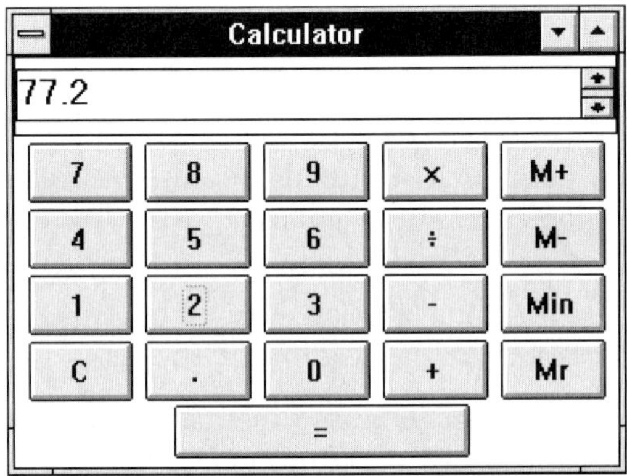

Figure 3-2 Graphical, object-based interface to a calculator application

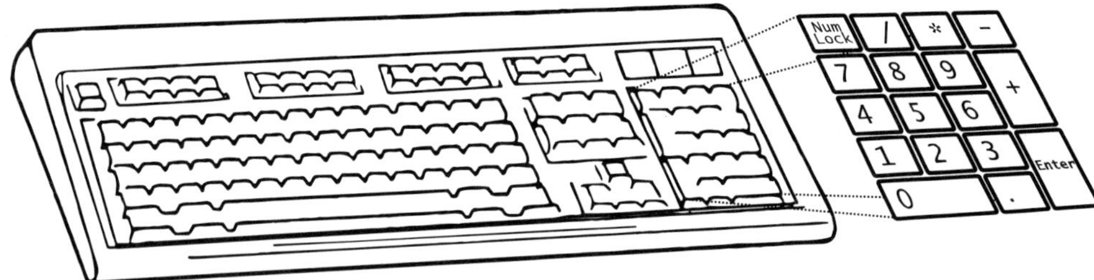

Figure 3-3 Computer keyboard and numeric keypad layout

though realization of these advantages (as I have discovered from using many calculator applications) depends on good design and attention to details in the implementation. Applying the task-based analysis method (again for the task of adding numbers) we find:

- If the user is familiar with typical calculators, the overall structure of the application is immediately visible. No training is required. It is not true to say that the user needs to know nothing about the interface (the keys, their meaning, and the display); the interface simply takes advantage of the fact that most users have *already* learned it from using real calculators (psychologists call this "transfer of learning").
- No command syntax is required. Most syntax errors thus simply cannot occur.[1] For "calculator literate" users, the gulf between knowing what to do and knowing how to do it is smaller than for the command line interface. "Computer literacy" has some positive effect on

[1]Most calculator applications, like most "real" calculators, ignore erroneous entries, such as function keys pressed when a numeric entry is expected. In addition, the set of actions available on the simulated calculator keyboard is highly constrained.

users of the command line interface, but not as much. This is because the graphical calculator visually shows the user the set of valid keys, and because calculator interfaces are fairly standard. The visual display of the calculator constantly reminds the user of being in "calculator mode."

- Most feedback is obvious, since it mimics a real calculator. This user interface also mimics certain problems of real calculators.[1] Typical calculators display numeric key entries, but do not display functions as they are entered. Users need to remember what function they entered, and cannot verify that it was done correctly. (This problem shows the hazards of being bound too closely to a real-world model. It could easily be fixed by displaying the function as it is typed the way the command line does.) Also, an entry sequence such as `3 x + + 4` (with an extra function key pressed) simply uses the last function entered, without providing any feedback. Some implementations provide a scrollable display that saves a "tape" recording users' actions; otherwise they must remember the previous results and actions.
- Because they are familiar with calculators, users may feel closer to the task, and devote less attention to irrelevant details of computer usage. The "feel" of the interface is quite natural and efficient, particularly if the application supports keyboard or touch screen use. In principle, the "look" of the interface has one inefficiency relative to the command line—it takes up space on the screen to display the keys, which might be important for a user with many windows open. In practice, command line interfaces do not exploit this potential advantage; they typically use the full screen, or open an unnecessarily large window.

The benefits of the graphical calculator interface depend on providing the user with the sense of working with familiar objects rather than "asking the computer to do something." This sense is both visual and tactile. The casual user can approximate the "feel" of a real calculator with a touch screen or mouse, and the expert can get it with the numeric keypad.

Before going on to the next interface comparison, consider the "grain of analysis" for the calculator application. This was chosen because it is revealing in spite of its simplicity, and the task of doing simple calculations is well understood and easy to analyze. In a real design situation, we always need to ask ourselves (and our users) whether the analysis is being done at the right level.

To test this, look at the context for the task being analyzed. Suppose, for example, that a user is preparing a report that includes a table of numbers, and wants to show the sum of the numbers. If the report application provides no calculation capability, the user must open a separate application (such as the one in Figure 3-2) to do the computation. The calculator

[1] [Joh85] explores this problem in more depth.

may be efficient in the context of calculation, but it is inefficient in the larger task context, because extra steps are needed to open it and transfer numbers. There is a theme here which will recur throughout this book—*analyze in context.*

Personal Computing Environments

Computer users often work with large collections of objects representing information being processed to do some task. In writing this book, for instance, I worked with documents containing chapters and appendices, and graphic files containing figures. Other examples from various application areas include letters, bills, insurance claims, engineering drawings, etc. Users also work with "tools" (such as the calculator above), where the emphasis is on the function performed, and data is transitory.

Even where the information is paramount, it is associated with a set of functions. I create and edit my chapters with a word processing program; the insurance clerk uses a claims processing application. Multiple packages of functions may exist for a single type of information. One engineer may use a graphics application to modify an engineering drawing; another may use a package that extracts part counts from the same drawing, to compute pricing information.

In environments containing many information and tool objects, storing, accessing, and managing these objects becomes a task in itself. We will use the following scenario as a concrete example to look at two different approaches to this task: An author has a set of chapters for a book. Each chapter contains text and figures. Figures may be bitmaps, line drawings, etc.; the figures are separate objects, but they are linked into the chapter text. The author wants to do the following:

- Read the text of a particular chapter.
- Make some modifications to it.
- Produce a new printed version of the chapter to give to a proofreader.
- While doing this work, the author wants to keep track of work in progress—to know where things are, which chapters have been completed, what figures exist, etc.

Most of the action in this scenario occurs in the word processor (and ancillary applications, such as graphic editors) used by the author. The focus here, however, is on facilities provided by the computing environment (often called the "shell"). These facilities help the author to organize, store, and find information, and invoke functions to process it.

Figure 3-4 shows a command line interface for displaying and manipulating computer files. This is from the MS-DOS operating system; it is similar to other command line interfaces found on interactive mainframe

```
C:\>dir \dooui\word

 Volume in drive C is AVANTI486_A
 Volume Serial Number is 3B4D-09FA
 Directory of C:\DOOUI\WORD

.             <DIR>      02-21-93  10:25a
..            <DIR>      02-21-93  10:25a
DOOUI001 DOC      42697 03-04-93   2:06a
DOOUI002 DOC      66469 03-05-93  11:30p
DOOUI003 DOC      69182 02-23-93   1:21a
FIG3-5   BMP       8126 02-23-93   1:25a
        6 file(s)      186474 bytes
                     53598208 bytes free
C:\>word \dooui\word\dooui003.doc
```

Figure 3-4 Command line interface to a personal computing environment

systems, personal computers, and workstations.[1]

In the figure, the visible information objects are files representing components of this book. DOOUI003.DOC, for instance, is the text file containing this chapter; FIG3-5.BMP is the bitmap for Figure 3-5 below. To access or manipulate information, the user types commands that specify an application or function that will operate on the information, then the name of the file containing the information. In the example, I typed `word \dooui\word\dooui003.doc` to indicate that Microsoft Word is the application, and I wish to edit the file containing Chapter 3.

The sequence of steps to do the task in the scenario is:

- Type the command to invoke the word processor, giving it the file name for the text to be edited. Alternatively, the word processor can be invoked without a file, then the file can be selected from a list of eligible files accessed after the application opens.
- After the word processor starts, edit the text and save the file, which updates it to incorporate the changes.
- Depending on the word processor, invoke a command to print the text from within the application, or type a separate command (for example, `print \dooui\word\dooui003.doc`) after exiting from the application.

[1] The MS-DOS interface is partly based on the command language of the UNIX operating system. It is worth noting that one of the criteria in the development of the UNIX command language was that it should be useful in the construction of *programs*, or "shell scripts" (see [Lib89]).

The analysis questions from page 50 lead to the following observations:

- Besides the task, the most important things the user needs to know are the structure of the computer file system, and the mapping of "user" information objects, such as chapters, to computer files. The file specification `\dooui\word\dooui003.doc` says that in the file system "root directory" there is a directory `dooui`, which contains a directory `word`, which contains the file named `dooui003.doc`. The user must map this structure to the fact that "in the materials for my book I have chapters, and I am interested in Chapter 3." There is no visible clue to where the file is; its location must be remembered, or deduced from a series of `dir` (directory list) commands. The user must also remember the name and argument format of the command that invokes the application.
- If the user remembers file names and command formats, actions are simple (typing). The system provides no indication of the range of possible actions, so "navigation" is entirely the responsibility of the user. Most command line interfaces provide help commands—though the user must remember their format in order to be helped.
- The primary feedback is the opening of the application, or printing of the document. Feedback from errors may be difficult to interpret. For instance, issuing a command without a required argument causes the message `required parameter missing`, with no clue about what kind of parameters are needed.

  Sometimes the system provides too much feedback. For example, if the user is just trying to locate a file, most of the information in Figure 3-4 is superfluous.
- The sequence of actions is efficient, if correctly performed. Inefficiency arises if the user needs help on command syntax, or cannot locate the file. Depending on the application, transitions might or might not be smooth. The environment provides an interaction technique, typing commands, which may be inconsistent with interactions in the application at many levels. The application may use menu selection rather than command typing; the application may use the command `delete` to remove things, while the shell uses `erase`. (This can be particularly confusing, or dangerous, if the same command name means different things in different contexts.)

Figure 3-5 shows a very different computing environment, Hewlett-Packard's NewWave [sHew92]. There are many other examples of this style, such as the Apple Macintosh and the IBM OS/2 Workplace Shell. Here we not only have a visually different representation, and a different interaction style, but also a different *conceptual model*. It is called the "desktop metaphor"[1] because the interface is supposed to resemble the user's real desktop. Instead of being based upon computer artifacts such as directories and files, it shows icons representing documents[2] and other objects stored in folders and file cabinets. The desktop also displays tools, such as the calculator in the upper right. Double-clicking on its icon brings up the calculator as seen in Figure 3-2.

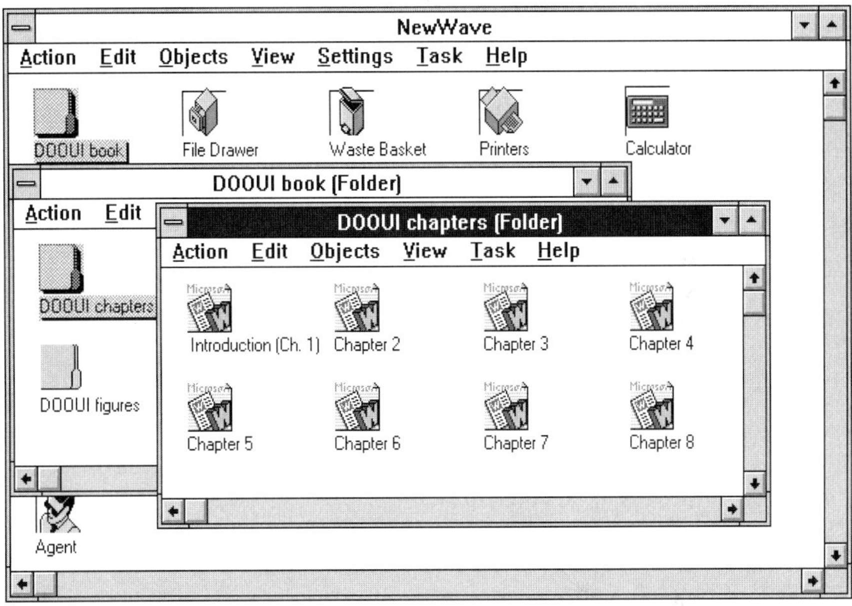

Figure 3-5 Iconic interface to a personal computing environment (HP NewWave)

The sequence of steps to perform the task in this object-based environment is:

- Locate the icon representing the chapter to be edited (labeled `Chapter 3` in Figure 3-5), and double-click on it (or click on the icon to select it, then select `Open` from the `Objects` menu at the top of the window).
- After the word processor starts, edit the text and save the file, which updates it to incorporate the changes. Notice that this step is unchanged from the command line environment.
- Drag the `Chapter 3` icon to the `Printers` icon and drop it.

[1] "Office metaphor" would be more appropriate, since objects such as wastebaskets are not normally found on top of a desk. The term comes from the Xerox Star designers.
[2] The form of the document icons identifies the application that created them (Microsoft Word in this case).

Analysis of this environment leads to these observations:

- Users do not need to know the structure of the computer file system. The interface represents text files as documents stored in folders. Just as in the real world, however, users are responsible for remembering which folder contains the document of interest. Here there is a `DOOUI book` folder, which contains a `DOOUI chapters` folder, which contains a Microsoft Word document called `Chapter 3`. Users do not need to remember any command syntax to edit or print the document.
- Once they are learned, the actions here are simpler than in the command line interface; the user typically points at visible objects and clicks a mouse button, or drags visible objects around the screen. Selecting actions from menus is more complex, and may require searching for the correct action. For example, one might expect to find the `Open` action on the `Action` menu, rather than on the `Objects` menu, which is actually where it is in NewWave.
- The primary feedback here is the opening of the application, or the printing of the document. Feedback from errors may be hard to interpret in this environment. For instance, dropping a document on the calculator results in the message `This object or tool cannot contain other objects`, without any further indication of why the drop was inappropriate.

  Here, also, the system may provide too much feedback. With more elements on the screen, it is possible to create a useful visual context, *or* visual clutter.
- The sequence of actions seems efficient; incorrect actions are less likely, because of visual cues and the direct manipulation of objects. In principle, inconsistent interaction techniques could be a problem here as in the command line interface. In practice, the convergence in graphical user interfaces has resulted in fairly consistent techniques between shell environments and applications (though some inconsistencies do occur). One new source of awkward transitions here stems from reliance on mouse interactions. Text editing relies heavily on the keyboard, so mouse interactions may require users to move their hands back and forth between keyboard and mouse. Poor performance will also impair efficiency, and is more of an issue here; presenting objects in a graphical format and moving them rapidly around the screen requires more computer resources.

Looking at these shell environments in the larger task context brings up other issues. Chapter 2 discusses differences between knowledge workers and production workers. The graphical desktop environment allows multiple overlapping windows, each representing a different piece of work. For example, since I am now editing Chapter 3, but referring to Chapter 2, I might have windows opened to view both of them. Knowledge workers often multiplex in this way, and get additional benefits from the object-based shell. Knowledge workers also tend to work with different kinds of objects and applications. As a result, they benefit from the generally higher level of consistency found in object-based shells and the reduced need to learn verbal command syntax.

Production workers, on the other hand, perform a small number of tasks repetitively. For example, a professional typist might use the same word processor constantly, typing, proofreading, and printing one document after another. Such workers do not usually multiplex, are not as exposed to consistency problems, and have no trouble remembering a constantly used command syntax.[1] Many production tasks done on computers are keyboard-intensive. The lack of mouse support may not be a detriment, and interactive keying performance is often better in an exclusively character-based environment.

Because of these factors, some designers believe that object-based shells are superior for knowledge workers, but that production workers should stick to command line and other character-based interfaces. The performance issue is going away, however, as machines get faster. Vendors of graphical "production" applications, particularly word processors, have paid more attention to production tasks in order to increase their market share. As a result, the trend is toward object-based interfaces for all workers, and command line interfaces are a vanishing breed in most environments.

Systems like JOSS show that many characteristics of a good interface transcend whether it is graphical or character-based. These lessons should not be forgotten, and supporting production tasks with object-based interfaces will be revisited in Chapter 7. We will now examine some "gray areas" between the two styles, then discuss them from a general perspective.

3.3 Discussion

Life for user interface designers would be easier if I could say "here are two interface styles," and let it go at that. But there is a spectrum of styles between the two extremes of "character-based, command line" and "graphical, object-based." This is unfortunate because it complicates the designer's work, but it is fortunate because it affords wide latitude for creativity. Even saying "a spectrum" underestimates the situation, because it implies that user interfaces fall along a one-dimensional continuum. There are *many* dimensions along which interfaces can vary. "Character based—graphical" and "functional (command line)—object based" are only two of these many dimensions, but these already imply more than a linear continuum of styles.

[1] Though learning it may be a problem, especially in industries with high employee turnover.

Hybrid User Interface Styles

This section looks at user interfaces that have elements of both styles. They vary along three design dimensions:

- The *kinds* of things that users deal with.
- How things are *represented* in the user interface.
- How the user *conceptualizes* them.

The possibilities we have seen so far for the kinds of things are:

- Commands, functions, or applications as the fundamental entities.
- Information objects (documents, etc.) as the fundamental entities.

The possibilities we have seen for representation are:

- Character strings identifying entities.
- Visual (graphical) objects identifying entities.

Finally, we have seen two alternatives for conceptualization:

- Entities presented by the user interface are understood as artifacts of the computer system (applications or data files).
- Entities presented by the user interface are understood as "real world" objects (documents, tools, etc.).[1]

Looking again at the two examples presented to illustrate "two user interface styles," we can place them more carefully, based on the criteria above. The first one, the "command line" or "traditional" style, has the following characteristics:

- Commands or applications (functions) are the fundamental entities.
- Entities are represented by character strings that name them.
- The conceptual model is based on computer artifacts.

The characteristics of the second, the "object based" style, are:

- Information objects (data) are fundamental.
- Entities are represented by graphical pictures.
- The conceptual model is based on objects from the real world.

Many user interfaces show mixtures of these characteristics and do not precisely fit either style. Figure 3-6 shows the File Manager application from Microsoft Windows. Though the details vary, similar graphical presentations of file structures are found on many platforms. Objects here are presented graphically, but the conceptual model is based upon com-

[1] This is a simplified view, presenting black and white alternatives. Users may see shades of gray, and we need to observe and question to find this out.

puter artifacts. The names of objects are their computer file names; in spite of the suggestive "document" and "folder" mini-icons, most users are thinking of them as files, not "chapters in a book," "engineering drawings," etc.

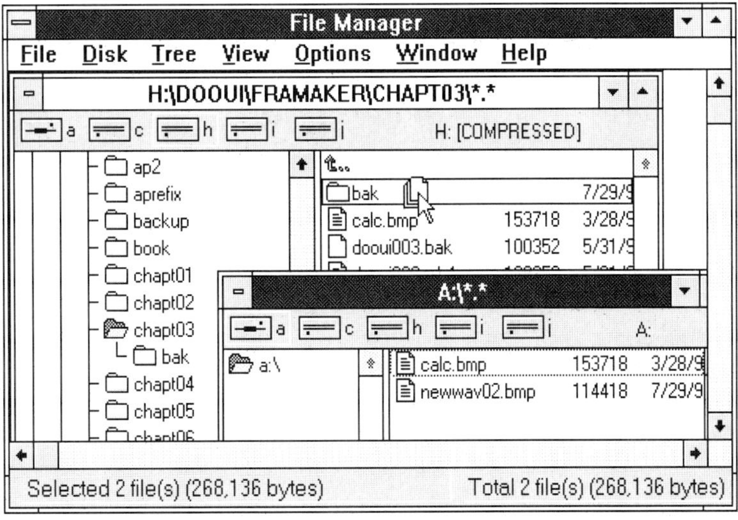

Figure 3-6 Graphical view of a file system (Microsoft Windows File Manager)

Regardless of the conceptual model, this is a useful application. Users can copy or move files and directories by dragging their icons within the visual representation; other commands (such as renaming) can be executed by selecting the file icon, then selecting the command from a pull-down menu. Studies show that for representative samples of file management tasks, users work faster and make fewer errors with the graphical file manager, versus typing commands.[1]

Figure 3-7 shows another user interface, the Microsoft Windows Program Manager, which is graphical but not object-based.[2] The entities represented by the user interface are applications (such as `Microsoft Word` and `File Manager`) or groups of applications (such as `Visual C++` and `Accessories`). The application groups may be shown as icons, or opened to windows (such as `Main`) that show their contents. When an application icon is opened (by selecting it and choosing `Open` from the `File` menu, or by double-clicking on it), the application is invoked, as if the appropriate command had been typed on a command line. (A command line window can also be brought up by opening the `DOS Prompt` icon.)

[1] See, e.g., [Kar87], [Sen91]. There are some cases, e.g., commands involving pattern matching on file names, where command typing is superior.

[2] MS Windows 3.1 allows users to associate a data file with the program represented by an icon, and also to customize the icon. This allows at least a partially object-based interface, but most users do not seem to be aware of this capability. Windows 4.0, code-named "Chicago," will be fully object-based.

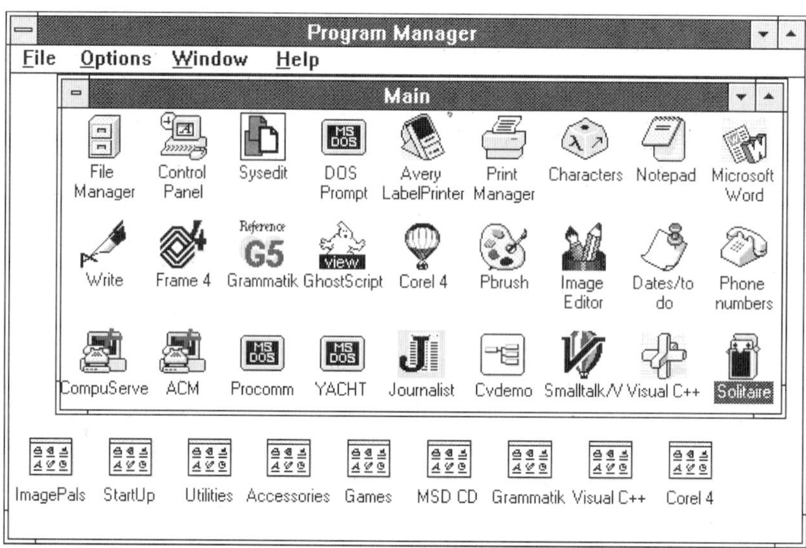

Figure 3-7 Iconic command invocation (Microsoft Windows Program Manager)

Studies on the use of icons do not show a clear advantage for this sort of interface. Well-designed icons allow faster location of visible objects, but icons the size of the ones in Figure 3-7 restrict the number of objects that can be shown (versus the small "mini-icons" in Figure 3-6, or a list of text titles). Many interfaces allow users to customize the representation, choosing either icons or text. Though Microsoft Windows allows only icons, NewWave provides the option of icons or text, and the Apple Macintosh allows large icons, mini-icons, or text. Most users prefer icons, but it is not clear whether this is motivated by aesthetics or productivity.

Chapter 4 analyzes these design dimensions from the point of view of object-orientation, which provides more tools for making decisions. Hybrid user interfaces may have their place, but should be used consciously, with an understanding of their intended effect.

Benefits of the Object-Based Style

You may have guessed that I am biased toward object-based user interfaces. You could legitimately ask (or complain), "well, how do we *know* that one style is really *better* than the other?" I could answer, "well, it's intuitively obvious." But that answer is convincing only to those who share my intuition, and even then it may be wrong.

For a specific application like the calculator we can do standard usability tests on the two styles—do users learn faster, make fewer errors, complete tasks faster with one than the other? We may have to test several implementations to be convinced it is the *style* rather than the specific design that is superior. In an environment containing many applications (or objects), the task is more difficult. Testing requires a suite of benchmark tasks, say for standard sorts of office work, and an extensive series of comparisons across the two styles. Here again, the issue of style versus particular implementation crops up, and it is difficult to extrapolate beyond the benchmark environment.

Many features of the calculator, the desktop, and similar applications can be characterized as *direct manipulation.* This term was coined by Ben Shneiderman to describe interfaces that give the user a sense of "directness," through visual representation of objects and immediate feedback. Shneiderman cited anecdotal evidence and some studies suggesting that direct manipulation interfaces are easier to use, and more popular among users, than the traditional command line or menu selection styles. Following his original work on the subject [Shn83], additional studies[1] and interface examples (including many done at Shneiderman's laboratory at the University of Maryland) have validated the technique. Other aspects of the object-based style, such as the value of good visual representations, have also been validated in specific contexts.

Nevertheless, readers looking for the general and definitive study comparing the "goodness" of object-based (or object-oriented) user interfaces to other styles will be disappointed. No truly comprehensive studies have been done, and the published reports are sketchy and ambiguous.[2] So, though many user interfaces are claimed to be superior because of their "object-orientation," at present we must rely primarily on the intuition of the designer to choose this style, and case-by-case testing to verify the intuition. Do not be too disappointed by this state of affairs. After all, that is the special sort of intuition that distinguishes good designers—the ability to fit form to function in a way that delights the user of the end product.

Since refining your intuition for what makes interfaces work well is one of the goals of this book, we will now look at some of the factors involved in differentiating the object-based approach to the user interfaces we have just examined:

- They provide a rich context to guide the user's activities. The context in the examples shown here is primarily visual, but also includes tactile elements. Sound can be useful too. Providing this sort of context is easier when a real-world model is available to guide the design. This is consistent with Bennett's findings in studying decision support systems, presented in Chapter 2.
- It cannot be shown with still images, but the success of these interfaces depends upon their interactivity. In dealing with objects in the real world, people are accustomed to immediate responses. For example, when dealing with real calculators, pressing a numeric key

[1] In addition to the file management studies mentioned earlier, see, for example, [Hut85], [Mor91], and Chapter 5 of [Shn92].

[2] See, for instance, [TBS90]. Among other things, this study uses the general category "graphical user interface," which is too broad to cover just object-based interfaces.

causes an *immediate* change in the display.[1] Computer applications must provide similar performance to give users the sense of dealing with real objects. One of the most frequent defects I observe in object-based interfaces is poor interactive performance.

- Object-based interfaces have their most obvious appeal to novice users, who are not familiar with the applications. A successful interface will not lose its appeal as the user becomes expert, and will take advantage of any expertise the user brings to the application from prior experience. The use of the numeric keypad in the calculator application is a good example of a user interface that "scales up" to expert use. Similar capabilities may not be so obvious in more complex applications, but they are just as important.

3.4 Summary

The choice of an object-based style provides significant opportunities to benefit the user, although this may have to be shown on a case-by-case basis. Often the choice is not an issue, since an object-based style (or at least, the visible accouterments of the style) is dictated by the platform. For consistency, it would not make sense to implement anything else on most of the leading commercial workstation and personal computer systems.

The choice of a style does not absolve the designer of responsibility. In any style, both good and bad designs are possible. I would not be writing this book if I did not believe that in many cases, object-oriented user interfaces are the best choice the designer can make. Attaining the potential benefits requires that you be well grounded in the fundamental concepts and issues and in techniques of design and implementation. The remainder of the book provides that grounding.

The key "rules of thumb" for designers that can be drawn from the analysis in this chapter are:

- Base designs on an understanding of users and their tasks, and evaluate them in terms of the ease of performing tasks.
- Analyze tasks in context; the grain of analysis should be large enough to capture the *whole* task, but small enough to see the important details.
- Where possible, help users by presenting analogs to familiar objects; keep in mind that these objects must facilitate task performance. Designers should not let real world-models preclude them from exploiting the power of the computer.

[1] Immediacy is something that can be measured, as the longest interval which is perceived as "no delay." This is typically 50–100 milliseconds (See [Car83], pp. 49–50). This is discussed further in Chapter 10.

- Interactive performance is critical to providing the sense of "working with real objects."
- Do not bias interfaces in favor of either novices or experts; try to accommodate both.
- Do not apply object technology dogmatically. Be skeptical—but be skeptical on behalf of the user, not just to prove you are smart.

3.5 To Explore Further

The material in this chapter is covered in more detail elsewhere in the book. The primary focus here is on taking a serious, analytic approach to understanding how people will perform tasks using the interface to a system. It follows that doing the exercises below will be more valuable than any additional reading.

For more information on calculator interfaces, see [Bay84], [Joh85], and [You81]. To learn more about the full range of user interface styles, see [Shn92].

Almost everyone these days has a personal computing environment, and exploring it with a critical attitude is the best way to learn more. [Joh87] is an example of this attitude.

3.6 Exercises

1. Write down scenarios for the following tasks (you don't need a lot of detail, but make sure you list all the separate steps required for the task).

   a. Making a withdrawal from a savings account at your bank, using the services of a teller.

   b. Making a withdrawal from a savings account at your bank, using an ATM.

   c. Moving a file from one place to another, using a command line interface (UNIX, MS-DOS, your favorite mainframe, etc.).

   d. Moving a file from one place to another, using a graphical interface (Macintosh, NeXTSTEP, OS/2, etc.).

   Compare (a) to (b), and (c) to (d). For each comparison,

   - Which of the two scenarios required fewer steps?
   - Which was faster? Was it the one with fewer steps?
   - In which of the two scenarios was the user more likely to make a serious error (being unable to complete the task, accidentally deleting a file, etc.).

(*For developers*: For an application domain you are involved in, develop and analyze scenarios comparing:

- A current method to a method in the system you are developing.
- Two alternative approaches to a task to be performed by users of the system you are developing.)

2. If you have access to these systems, compare an Apply Macintosh to any system with a "graphical file manager" (e.g., many graphical interfaces for UNIX systems, Microsoft Windows, OS/2 presentation manager, etc.). What is good (or bad) about the Macintosh for tasks such as locating documents, copying documents (to other folders on the hard drive, or to diskettes), and opening documents?
3. Take a real hand calculator. (If you use one, a wristwatch with a calculator, such as those made by Casio, will do.) Analyze the things you do with the calculator, paying particular attention to errors you make and capabilities you wish your calculator had. Sketch a graphical interface for a computer calculator that you would enjoy and use productively. Do not add any new functions, unless they relate directly to things you think about while using the calculator.

4

Applying Object-Orientation to User Interfaces

Representing what end users need to know about applications and systems is a critical success factor in development. The representation must be consistent with how users "naturally" perceive, think about, and act on objects in the domain of the application.

This representation of knowledge is not "artificial intelligence," though it relates to techniques used in AI. It does not require object-orientation, but object-orientation makes it easier. The basis of the representation is understanding how users think about their world. Many aspects are domain-dependent, but much of thinking and perceiving involves cognitive, or information-processing, capabilities that are common to all human activities.

Some people say that OO designs, OO programs, OO databases, and OO user interfaces do not have much in common. I think this opinion is wrong—the object paradigm's unified view across systems is uniquely valuable. This chapter presents a basis for objects in human cognition and shows how that basis applies to user interfaces. Chapter 5, *Three Domains of OO Design for the User Interface*, relates OOUI design to other applications of object-orientation in system development. In subsequent chapters, the effect of this paradigm on all aspects of the development process will unfold.

Chapter 3 introduces one dimension of user interface analysis, based on users' tasks. This chapter adds another, based on objects. The application of object-oriented principles to user interfaces is not trivial or shallow, and it goes far beyond icons and implementation techniques. The philosophy of ideals. For those who are not philosophically inclined, I mention this only to stress the fact that these ideas have been around for a very long time.

More practically, (1) states that everything is an object, and that objects are encapsulated; and (2), if we substitute "instance" for "manifestation" and "class" for "idea," is the notion of classes in object-oriented programming. Kay's ideas, which can be interpreted in the domain of human cognition or of computer science, are the "first principles" for the model developed in this section.

Kay gives another formulation of (1): "each Smalltalk object is a recursion of the entire possibilities of the computer. Thus its semantics are a bit like having thousands and thousands of computers all hooked together by a very fast network."[1] What he says here about Smalltalk is true of any "pure" OO language where objects are completely encapsulated and communicate only by message passing. Recursive composition thought of in this way is a powerful principle. It can describe client-server networks, as well as individual systems and programs. This metaphor of "object as little computer" suggests three corollaries:

- Objects can be created, and they persist until they are destroyed. The notion of an object implies persistence over some finite time and the potential of indefinite persistence.
- Because it encapsulates state and process (methods), an object is potentially the locus of a thread of control; that is, it is potentially active concurrently with other objects.
- Objects are autonomous. The object receiving a message is responsible for invoking the correct process or rejecting the message. This implies dynamic typing. From the sender's point of view, the type of object receiving its message may be unknown or only partially known, and it may dynamically change. This does not mean that an object can change its type; it only means that objects of different types can be substituted for one another, if they all respond appropriately to messages that are sent to them.[2]

These are not merely tautologies. Indefinite persistence, for instance, implies that objects may persist across events such as starting and stopping application programs. This could involve destroying objects "under the covers," but saving their state in another form from which they can be recreated on demand. In any *implementation* of objects, persistence, concurrency, and dynamic typing raise serious issues. An abstract model of object-orientation, however, should permit the free expression of the inherent potentialities of objects. If a particular use of the model demands that the potentialities become actualities, at that point—when a real sys-

[1] [Kay93], p. 70.

[2] Even strongly typed languages such as C++ support some level of dynamic typing, usually "inheritance polymorphism" (described below).

tem is being designed—implementation issues should be raised.

This view of concurrency and dynamic typing is supported by Hoare's work on "communicating sequential processes" [Hoa78], in which he says "input, output, and concurrency should be regarded as primitives of programming, which underlie many familiar and less familiar programming concepts." ("Input" and "output" here mean essentially the same thing as message passing.) The notion of "actors" [Agh87] is even more suggestive than "objects" of this inherent potentiality for persistence, concurrency, and autonomy.

Kay's second principle, objects as manifestations of ideas, implies *classes* that embody the ideas manifested in sets of objects. Classes imply classification, the abstraction of a set of ideas into a more general idea. Classification of objects and ideas is an essential feature of human thought. It affords a cognitive economy—in a bank, for instance, we do not need to know everything about money market accounts because we already understand bank accounts in general. We can reuse knowledge about the superclass to understand the subclass.

Classification, or *inheritance*, is a defining characteristic of object-orientation. At the level of OO programming, inheritance is the subject of technical debates, but in the general model inheritance is used to classify and represent relevant knowledge from the domain being modeled. A major dichotomy in object-oriented programming languages (OOPLs) is whether a class can inherit from more than one superclass (multiple inheritance). Both in OOPLs and in general knowledge structures there are tradeoffs between the richness of multiple inheritance, and the appealing simplicity of single inheritance.

The next section will discuss psychological views of objects and classes. The evidence from psychology is that people usually think in terms of concrete "prototypes" that represent all the members of a class, not in terms of the abstract class itself. Some OO languages are "classless," and use the equivalent of these prototypes to implement shared behavior [Ste89]. The model here uses this idea as an alternative formulation of the class concept because of its importance in human cognition.

Kay's first principle emphasizes not only objects, but the composition of objects. Composition, as a programming language principle, is not unique to object-oriented languages, and it is not usually given as part of the definition of OOP. The model here includes it because composition is an essential characteristic of any object-oriented simulation model.

Booch also considers composition part of the object model. *Hierarchy* is one of his model's essential elements, and he discriminates two senses of hierarchy: the class hierarchy (corresponding to the principle of inheritance), and the "object structure" hierarchy (corresponding to the principle of composition). Another of Booch's essential elements, *modularity*, also involves composition. A module is composed of objects, and a system is composed of modules.

There are varieties of composition. Containment is a loose coupling between independent objects, for instance, a pile of documents in a folder.

Construction is a tight coupling, in which the composite is built from its parts, which relinquish some independence to contribute to the behavior of the whole. A window on a computer screen, constructed from components such as scroll bars, menus, frame, border, graphic or text display area, is an example, as is the composite document described below.

Polymorphism (from Greek roots meaning "many forms") is the ability of objects to respond to the same message in a variety of ways, depending on the object type.[1] As an example, a composite document containing text, bitmapped images, and vector graphics objects might react to the message `display` by sending `display` to each of its components. Each object would respond differently, but appropriately, to render itself on the display screen. This seems sensible, and in some way each object's `display` method is a specialization of the general idea of displaying. We might infer that each object's class inherits from a class `DisplayableObject`. This is an example of what Wegner calls "inheritance polymorphism" [Weg87b]. He also talks about *ad hoc* polymorphism, where objects of unrelated classes implement (or "overload") the display operation. In either case, this is closely related to the idea of autonomy (or dynamic typing), since the exact behavior invoked by `display` is determined by the receiver.

Polymorphism is an important feature of object-oriented models. I include it under inheritance, because it is often an essential feature of classes that share a common ancestor. For example, all subclasses of bank accounts must support a `deposit` operation, but the processing is not likely to be identical in all of them. Even *ad hoc* polymorphism, if it is used sensibly, will tend to make an observer infer a common ancestor as the source of the generic operation. This is relevant in the context of interfaces, since the user's inferences are all-important.

An Object Model for Designing OOUIs

Here is a statement of the model of object-orientation (the object metamodel) to which this section has been leading. It will be restated in Section 4.2 from a cognitive point of view and in Section 4.3 from a user interface design point of view.

1. An *object* is a building block for simulation models. Objects respond to messages by returning themselves or another object. From the history of an object's responses, we can infer that it has a hidden *state*. The state changes only as a result of messages sent to the object, and the state is revealed only through the object's responses to messages. We can also infer the existence of *processes* (methods or member functions) within an object, one for each message the object accepts.

   a. Unless changed as a result of a message, an object's state *persists*

[1] I use *type* synonymously with *class*. The two concepts are sometimes distinguished in the literature of programming languages; see, e.g., [Weg87b].

for the lifetime of the object. The nature of the simulation model determines the appropriate lifetime for its objects.

   b. The executing process within an object may be *concurrent* with executing processes in other objects.

   c. Objects are autonomous; the receiver of a message is responsible for invoking the associated process, or rejecting the message. From the sender's point of view, this is *dynamic typing.*

2. Objects may be *composite.* The externally visible behavior of composite objects is internally synthesized from the behavior of their component sub-objects. The sub-objects are values[1] of state variables in the composite object, which may return the sub-objects as message responses and make them visible to other objects. Composition comes in two varieties: containment and construction.[2] These are two ends of a spectrum:

   a. *Containment* is a loose coupling. The behavior of the composition is the sum of the behavior of the container and its contained objects.

   b. *Construction* is a tight coupling in which the composite is "built from" its parts and exhibits "emergent" behavior—behavior that is more than the sum of the behavior of the parts. Construction puts more constraints on the independence of sub-objects than does containment.

3. Part of the state of every object is its *class,* which determines its behavior in the sense that two objects of the same class will respond differently to messages only if their states differ. Another way of looking at this is to say that every object has a sub-object, its class, which is a repository for the processes invoked by messages it receives. An object is called an *instance* of its class, and classes act as "factory objects" [Cox91] or "cookie cutters" for the construction of new instances.

*3. As an alternative to (3), an object can have a sub-object called its *prototype,* to which it *delegates* some or all of its behavior, by referring messages to the prototype. The prototype can function as a template, which is copied to construct new objects.[3]

4. A class may have subclasses (or derived classes); the class is called a superclass (or base class) relative to its subclasses, which *inherit*

[1] I mean "value" in the general sense. The distinction between value and reference, made in some programming languages, is not important here.

[2] This area has no standard terminology. Many authors (e.g., [Boo94]) use "aggregation" for what I mean by composition. Codd [Cod79] used the terms "cover aggregation" and "Cartesian aggregation" to express what I call containment and construction.

[3] This is a simplified view of "classless" approaches to OO. For the full story, see [Ste89]. Templates that are copied to create new objects are not quite the same as cookie cutters or factories that "manufacture" new objects.

from it. If a subclass does not define a process to handle a particular message, instances of the subclass invoke the process defined in the superclass for that message. A class may have more than one direct superclass (this is called *multiple inheritance*). Inheritance is transitive—a class may inherit from a superclass of its superclass.

a. If all subclasses of a class have processes (either unique or inherited) to handle a given message, the message is called a *polymorphic* operation, and instances of the subclasses are called polymorphic objects (with respect to the given message). More generally, if related or unrelated classes all have processes to handle the same message, their instances can be called polymorphic objects relative to the given message.[1]

Comparison of four object models Figure 4-1 compares this model with three others. (In the Booch column, entries marked * are "minor elements.") All the concepts are present in each. The differences lie in which concepts are emphasized, and this depends on the purpose of the model. Alan Kay proposes the simplest set of principles that will encompass his conception of objects. Wegner's model is intended to classify programming languages. The Booch model expresses not only objects, but object-oriented software engineering.

Kay [Kay93]	**Wegner [Weg87a]**	**Booch [Boo94]**	**DOOUI**
Objects	Objects	Encapsulation Concurrency* Persistence*	Objects · Concurrency · Persistence · Autonomy
		Modularity Hierarchy (2)	Composition · Containment · Construction
Ideas	Classes	Abstraction Typing*	Classes
	Inheritance	Hierarchy (1)	Inheritance · Polymorphism

Figure 4-1 Four models of object-orientation

The model used in this book provides a set of general concepts that can be applied across the entire development process, besides covering

[1] Polymorphism, in general, may require the dynamic typing of (1c).

the user interface. It does not supplant other models, but it is more useful for understanding the key issues in user interface design, both external and internal.

4.2 Cognitive Models of Objects

What is an object? We spent the last section discussing this question, but . . . what is an object? All the formalism obscures the fact that every human being, every moment of his or her life, faces this difficult question—what is an object? We are normally unaware of the difficulty, because our sensory mechanisms operate below the threshold of consciousness to constantly answer the question in real time. An object is something we perceive as distinguished from the rest of the world. We understand it when we can identify it as a member of a class. This section discusses how these cognitive issues relate to the object model of Section 4.1

Objects and Classification

Figure 4-2 is an example, well known in the literature of psychology, that makes us deal with the issue of object perception consciously. Can you see

Figure 4-2 Can you find the object?

the object in the picture? Some people see the object immediately; some see it after they are told what it is; and some can see it only after it is outlined on the picture. The object is a dog, a Dalmatian. It is facing down and left; its nose is pressed to the ground in the center of the picture, and its tail is in the air on the right.

The picture, of course, is intended to confuse. Finding the object is a difficult exercise, which brings out points that are important to analysts and user interface designers as well as psychologists. Computer systems and their interfaces are part of the world, and users struggle to "find the objects," just as you did with Figure 4-2.

People integrate data from multiple senses to parse the world into objects. Touch is a particularly important sense, which cooperates with vision and is used to explore the surfaces of objects.[1] Touch can also be used actively (as can the human voice) to elicit behavior from objects.

Piaget [Pia74] and other psychologists have discovered that all of us, as children, do a great deal of experimentation to discover objects and their properties. (Put a child down in front of the Dalmatian and see if she relies only on vision!) The fortunate consequence of this experimentation is that we grow up to be adults who "understand the world." The unfortunate consequence is that we forget that our world view is based on experiment, observation, and what other people tell us.[2]

As adults, if we cannot see the Dalmatian, we may claim that it simply is not there. The old saying goes "seeing is believing." Among psychologists, the saying goes a little differently—"believing is seeing." If this can be true for concrete objects, it is more likely to be true for abstractions. This has important consequences when people from different cultures, such as system developers and end users, come together to try to reach a common understanding of some domain.

Now look at Figure 4-3. For most people, this is the opposite of Figure 4-2. In Figure 4-2, it is hard to find the object; here it is hard *not* to find it. In the left-hand part of the figure, most people see clues from which they infer the existence of the cube in the right-hand part of the figure, though it is not really there.[3]

A great deal of what people do in making sense of the world is to identify objects as members of a class. This is because we economize on our cognitive structures by understanding the characteristics of a class, then characterizing individual objects in terms of the class. Eleanor Rosch [Rosch78], her colleagues, and other researchers[4] have discovered many interesting things about classes. (Psychologists and linguists often prefer the term "categories" to "classes," since "categories" has no associations

---

[1] This is called *haptic* touch; haptic perception in general uses active exploration to discover object properties.This topic is revisited in Chapters 9 and 10.

[2] But see [Carr84] and [Carr85] for a perspective on "active learning" in computer users.

[3] Some people, instead of a cube, see a flat six-sided polygon in the left-hand figure. The same point is made—the object is illusory.

[4] See [Lak87] for a summary of the work of psychologists, linguists, and others in this area.

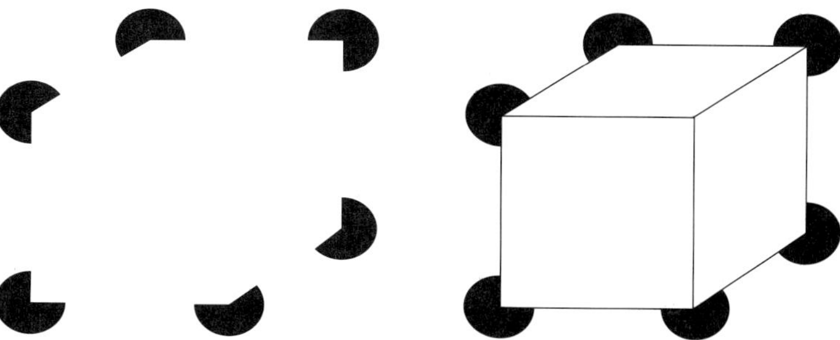

Figure 4-3 An illusory object

to mathematics or formal logic. I will use the two terms interchangeably.) Two results, due to Rosch, are particularly important:

- The "classical" notion of a class as a set of members that share well-defined common characteristics is almost assuredly wrong as a model of how people typically think about the world. People actually deal with concrete images of "prototypical class members," rather than abstract sets of characteristics. To understand this, think for a moment about your notion of the class *bird*. What did you think of? Most people think of images and characteristics associated with "typical birds." Typicality is something that psychologists can test, and it turns out that robins, for example, are very typical birds, whereas chickens are not.
- There are certain levels in the class hierarchy, or taxonomy, in any domain that have special significance. Rosch called these "basic level categories." Anyone who has experience of the objects in the domain will probably recognize the basic categories. There tends to be less knowledge, and less agreement, on categories in the class hierarchy either above or below the basic level. Speaking and thinking involves basic level categories more than any others, and people associate them more strongly with "prototypical member" images. *Bird* is a basic level category that is universal. The level above it (the "superordinate" or superclass) is usually something like *animal*, and the level below it (the "subordinate" or subclass) is a specific kind of bird. Anywhere in the world, robin-like birds are better prototypes than chicken-like birds, and people associate birds with behavior such as "flies," "twitters or sings," "pecks," "hops around when on the ground," etc., besides visual characteristics such as body shape, wings, tails, clawed feet, etc.

The significance of this to analysis and design should be clear. First, do not expect people to be able to formulate naturally the categories in any domain in terms of abstract characteristics. Do expect them to be comfortable with prototypical representations. In the words of an apocryphal end user, "I can't tell you what I want, but I'll know it when I see it."

Second, in any domain, the basic level categories are anchor points for "finding the objects." Here are some examples of basic level categories in domains in which computers are important. Each category is bracketed with its superordinate category and a sample subordinate category:

- Account–bank account–checking account
- Document–letter–order confirmation letter
- Container–folder–pending orders folder
- Graphical object–drawing–architectural blueprint
- Computer–laptop computer–Toshiba T4500C

Basic level categories have several characteristics that help to identify them:

- People name things more readily at the basic level, and languages have simpler words for things at that level.
- People tend to perceive things at the basic level holistically, and to think about them using images of prototypes (this has significance for choosing icons and other visual representations of objects). Superordinate categories are more difficult to think about and represent. People tend to define subordinate categories in terms of differences from basic level categories.
- It is easier to remember things at the basic level, and people learn things at the basic level earlier in life.
- "Folk taxonomies" are classification schemes that people develop informally. If a scientific or formal category structure exists for a domain, it tends to agree with the folk taxonomy at the basic level, but not at higher or lower levels. (This says that although the basic level is the anchor point for object-oriented analysis, the definition of higher and lower levels requires close cooperation between analysts and users.)

Figure 4-4 illustrates these points, using an example domain (biological classification, with birds as the basic level category) that psychologists have studied extensively. What are the objects? Can you predict their behavior? Will the object on the lower right behave differently from the object on the lower left? The answers are obvious, of course. If you think about it, it is quite an achievement to be able to predict the behavior of objects we have never seen before. Classification enables us to store information with the class that is applicable to all its instances.

There is a danger here, though—if we misclassify an object, our predictions will be wrong. This is important in user interface design—if a user correctly classifies the objects displayed, their behavior is predictable and

Figure 4-4 Prototypical instances of subclasses of Bird

the interface is easy to use. Misclassification causes confusion and difficulty, but can be largely avoided by good design.

Figures 4-2, 4-3, and 4-4 illustrate two techniques people use constantly to make sense of the world. The first is matching perceptual patterns to prototypical objects. Once we know that Figure 4-2 shows a dog, it becomes easier to make sense of it. The task of analysis is reduced to recognizing a known pattern. Given a prototype bird, we can classify the objects in Figure 4-4 based on how they differ from the prototype.

People also make sense of things by composing objects from their parts. In Figure 4-2, the dog's head, front legs, and hind legs are the most salient parts (probably in that order). Recognizing those parts, we can fit them together into the dog. In Figure 4-3, the black filled arcs delineate the visible edges and corners of the cube, from which the whole can be constructed. In Figure 4-4, we can recognize features such as wings, beaks, etc. These two techniques are related. Studies by Tversky [Tve84] indicate that people classify objects in basic level categories based on their composition from parts.

Besides using "pure perception" for classification, people classify or categorize based on two other schemes. The actions that can be taken on an object help to fit it into a category. Brown [Bro58], among others, observed that people tend to form basic level categories around sets of actions that are common to members of the category. This is consistent with Tversky's findings. Her subjects identified parts, such as frets and strings on a guitar, which are associated with actions taken on, or with, the object.

The conceptual,[1] or cognitive, model [Lak87] of the context in which the object occurs also helps to classify it. For instance, "drafting tools" is a category determined by the context of the job of drafting or drawing. "Baseball bat" is another example of a category determined by its context. Presenting context, or overall representation, can help users classify and understand interface objects.

Another Look at the OOUI Object Model

Now, let us relate these findings to the terminology of the object model presented in Section 4.1.

1. *Objects* are building blocks for simulation models of the world, or parts of it, that we carry in our heads. Objects respond to "messages" by reflecting light, reacting to touch and other actions, etc. We infer that objects have internal states and processes, based on their visual appearance and other behavior. Our inferences about objects are influenced by how we classify them, and how they fit into a larger conceptual model.

   a. Objects persist, and do not vanish arbitrarily.

   b. Objects are active simultaneous with the activity of other objects.

   c. Objects autonomously determine their own behavior.

2. Objects may be *composite*. The externally visible behavior of composite objects is synthesized from the behavior of their component subobjects. Composition may be

   a. Containment, for example a set of objects in a box, where composite behavior is the sum of the behavior of the container and its contained objects.

   b. Construction, for example a clock or an engine, where composite behavior "emerges" from the behavior of the components. Subobjects in a construction appear less autonomous than those in a container.

3. We may describe an object as a member of a *class*, which influences our prediction of its behavior. We recognize an object as a member of a class by its resemblance to a *prototype* member of the class. Lacking other evidence, we predict the behavior of an instance based on how the prototype would behave.

4. A class may have subclasses (or subordinate classes); the class is called a superclass (or superordinate class) relative to its subclasses, which *inherit* from it. Knowledge of behavior that is common to instances of all subclasses of a class is based on (or delegated to) the

[1] The term "conceptual model" is used here for what Lakoff calls a cognitive model, because it is more common in the field of HCI.

superclass, or its prototype. An object may be thought of as belonging to more than one class, in which case we have *multiple inheritance.*

a. Objects are *polymorphic.* We may take the same action on objects of different classes, and expect each to respond according to its own nature.

Taken to extremes, the notion of object autonomy is animism. One form of animism is anthropomorphism, the idea that things behave as if they were people. This is important because thinking of objects as "little people" has been widely observed in object-oriented designers and programmers [Ross90]. Some authors recommend it as a technique to designers.[1] Seymour Papert, the designer of the programming language LOGO, may have been the first to comment on the value of the "little man metaphor of computing" [Pap70], which he used in teaching computers to children.

Objects and Symbols

The discussion so far has left out an important dimension of human thought. We think about objects, and represent them externally to ourselves, as symbols. User interfaces are examples of symbolic representations of objects, actions, and conceptual models. Understanding how people think about, and with, symbols is therefore important for understanding user interfaces.

We can talk about symbols at two levels. Symbols shown on a user interface, such as icons and text strings, *are* objects in and of themselves, which the end user must recognize and understand. The symbols also *represent* objects. The user must be able to identify what is being represented.

One way of understanding the relation between people, objects, and symbols for objects is to study how children develop capabilities for dealing with objects and symbols. The psychologist Jean Piaget pioneered this approach [Pia74] and found that capabilities we take for granted are not inborn, but develop in stages as the child matures. The major periods of development Piaget delineated[2] are:

- *Sensorimotor*[3] (age 0–2): in this stage the child is primarily oriented to direct perception and simple actions (such as grasping) in the "here and now." Objects are identified with the direct actions they afford, and object persistence is not well established (the child may assume that objects vanish when they are outside the field of vision or touch).

---

[1] See, e.g., [Wir90].

[2] This simplifies a large body of research, and only covers what is directly important to the treatment of user interfaces in this book. Though some of the details of Piaget's stages are controversial, staged development is generally accepted ([Kag84], [Bow93]).

[3] This is a variant spelling of "sensory/motor." Note that the age ranges given here are typical, and they may vary considerably.

- *Concrete operations* (age 2–11): in this stage the child understands that objects are persistent. Notions of physical space, time, and causality develop. The child thinks about objects, or operations on objects, mainly with concrete visual or tactile images, or words associated with concrete images. Object states are more important than transformations between states. The child develops the ability to classify objects.
- *Formal operations* (age 11–15): In this stage the child develops the ability to reason by operating on symbolic representations of operations, detached from symbols or images of the objects themselves. The child can think of operations and transformations between states as objects, permitting the development of logical and mathematical thought.

This advancement in the use of symbols raises a question about user interfaces: if the use of direct actions and images is more "primitive" than the use of more abstract symbols representing operations, is issuing commands a more "advanced" (and perhaps "better") technique than using direct action on iconic images? To make this concrete, Figure 4-5 shows how the object `January report` can be deleted by moving its icon to the "trash can." In a command interface, the user might type `erase January report`. The situation is not as simple as it might seem, however.

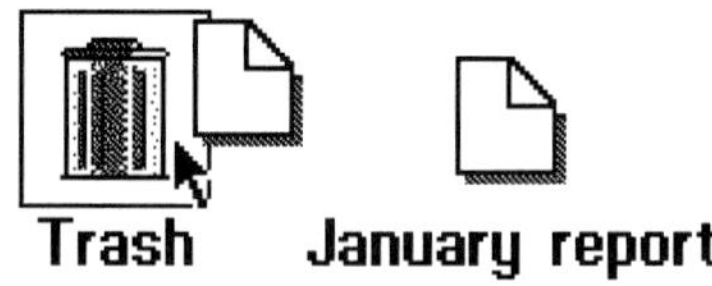

Figure 4-5 File deletion by direct manipulation of icons

Piaget did not simply say that the reasoning methods of one stage are superseded by those that develop in the next. Each stage integrates the accomplishments of the prior stage into its more sophisticated structure.[1] So a child's reasoning from images may be more primitive that an adult's reasoning from abstract symbols. That does not imply that an adult's use of imagery and direct manipulation are necessarily more primitive than the same adult's use of linguistic symbols. In a well-known study of creativity [Had54], the French mathematician Hadamard found that almost all his colleagues (including such thinkers as Einstein) relied on visual and kinesthetic (touch and movement) imagery in doing their work. Piaget's work shows that adults possess a larger and more sophisticated "cognitive toolkit" than children. The issue in choosing a tool from this kit is not which is more "advanced," but which is more *efficient* for the task at hand.

Figure 4-6, which shows the major systems in the cognitive toolkit,

[1] [Pia74], p. 51.

will help explain what efficiency means in this context. At higher levels in the figure, there is more abstraction and more reasoning power. But mapping to higher levels, and then back down to the level of objects and actions, takes time and effort.

Borrowing an example from Ben Shneiderman [Shn92], do a thought experiment. Imagine being in your automobile, and coming to a corner. Would you prefer to turn the car using the steering wheel, or would you like to issue a command (using speech recognition, perhaps) such as "turn right 90"? If you think about it, it is unlikely you will conclude that the command interface is superior. Driving is not a matter of performing an action, thinking about it, then performing another action. Driving requires constant feedback and coordination between visual, tactile, and kinesthetic sensations and motor actions. The mapping to the level of symbolic operations and back down to actions cannot be performed fast enough. So we continue to rely primarily on the sensorimotor and image levels to drive. (If you had a chauffeur, of course, it would be different, because you would be delegating the moment-to-moment coordination tasks.)

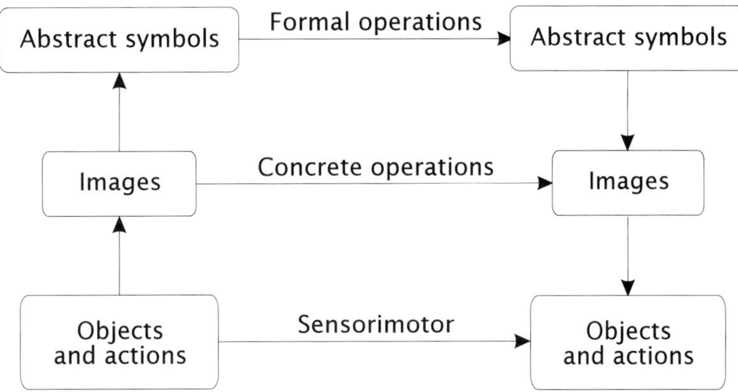

Figure 4-6 Cognitive systems

Jerome Bruner, another psychologist, emphasized the persistence of the three systems: "human beings . . . have developed three parallel systems for processing information and for representing it—one through manipulation and action, one through perceptual organization and imagery, and one through symbolic apparatus."[1] Through their writings, both Piaget and Bruner influenced the Learning Research Group at Xerox PARC, which developed Smalltalk.

I would like to end this section by stressing the important relationship between classification, composition, and conceptual models. Examine Figure 4-7 *before* you turn the book upside down. What are the two objects? How are they constructed from their parts?

[1] [Bru66], p. 28.

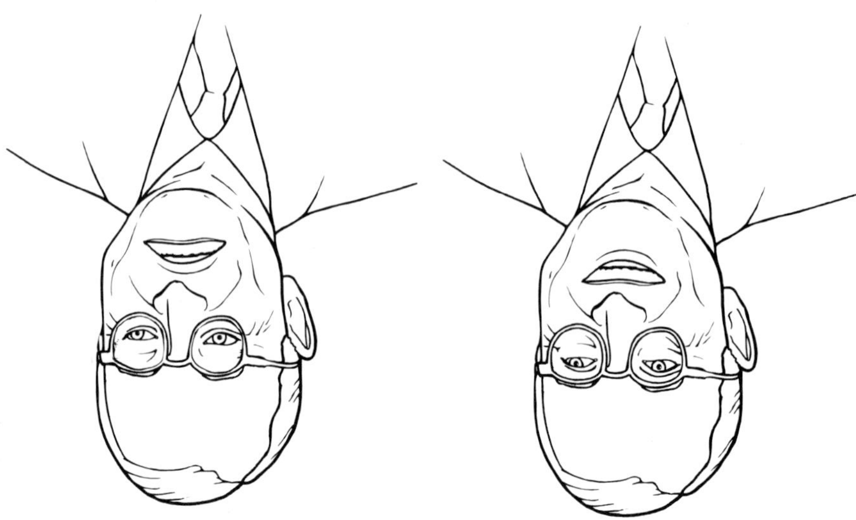

Figure 4-7 What's wrong with this picture?

Now turn the book over to see the two faces "right side up." Were you surprised? Why do the faces look different upside down? The answer seems to be that in the upside-down view, the individual parts of the face (eyes, nose, mouth, etc.) look correct. The fact that the face is not in its normal aspect prevents us from seeing the parts in context. When we turn the book upside down and see the faces in the normal position, we realize that one of them is terribly wrong, because it is not composed properly from its parts.[1]

The fact that the problem is so subtle from one point of view, and so blatant from another, is something to think about. I use this as an example in my classes because it illustrates a problem I see in user interfaces. Developers, lacking a holistic appreciation of the user's world, put together an interface in which all the parts are present, though perhaps not "quite right." The user, seeing everything in context, reacts as you did when you turned the book over.

4.3 Object-Orientation in User Interfaces

Section 4.1 presented a model of object-orientation, and Section 4.2 discussed its cognitive foundations. The choice of topics and examples emphasized aspects of the model that are important to user interface design. This section shows how the model applies to user interfaces, and how it

[1] I first saw an example of this phenomenon in [vKay87]. [Roc74] discusses the general problem of perceiving upside down faces.

relates to several definitions of OOUIs.

Larry Tesler coined the term "object-oriented user interface" in a short paper published in 1983 [Tes83]. His idea of an OOUI included the characteristics listed here, which I have elaborated based on the ideas in this chapter.

- *Users see objects and choices displayed graphically*, and choose them by pointing with the mouse cursor. As in Bennett's decision support systems (described in Chapter 2), displaying choices provides affordances for user actions. When the number of choices is large, it is easier for users to recognize the right one when it is displayed, than to recall it from memory.
- *The syntax of commands is "object-action"*; the user selects an object (by pointing and clicking) and then specifies an action on it. Since viewing or transforming some object is the focus of the user's task, this helps because only actions relevant to the selected object are displayed.
- *Users get immediate feedback from actions.* This is part of providing the feeling of *direct manipulation* [Shn83], discussed in this chapter and in Chapter 3.
- *The interface is modeless.* Modes are global states of the interface that affect the meaning of user actions. An example, still prevalent today, is "insert mode" in text editors, which determines whether typed characters will be inserted, or will overlay existing text. Modes can be useful, but if they are not visible, they can be disturbing because they interfere with the user's ability to predict the results of actions. An example of a mode in the real world is the *loaded* state of a firearm, as in "I didn't know the gun was loaded."

  The situation is more complicated than Tesler envisioned. As Jacob points out [Jaco86], OOUIs are indeed moded, but the selected object determines the mode. If the object is visible, actions will be predictable. I prefer to see modelessness as a consequence of other OOUI design features, rather than as an end in itself. However, this is a good checklist item. Raise a red flag when you hear a user say, "I didn't expect *that* to happen!"
- *The interface displays objects in WYSIWYG form* ("What You See Is What You Get"). An example is document formatting, where the document is shown on the display screen just as it will print. More generally, this could be rephrased as "what you see is what you've got," meaning that objects accurately display their current state. This goes along with giving users visible feedback when their actions have changed the state of an object.

  The type of WYSIWYG representation should be appropriate for the task. The formatted document is a "high fidelity" representation, and this is useful in controlling the appearance of the printed text. If the task is to file the document away in a folder, the user only needs to identify the right document. An icon suffices for this task; a large window showing the text would waste time and resources. The icon has conceptual, rather than physical, fidelity.[1]

- *Objects and actions are consistent* both within an application, and across different applications. This is an application of polymorphism, and it often reflects a development focus on reusable objects. An action such as `print`, for example, should produce consistent results for different object types. (The exact meaning of "consistent," here and elsewhere, is context dependent.) Consistency and WYSIWYG go a long way toward reducing modes and their associated problems.

Bill Verplank, one of the designers of the Xerox Star, provided a definition that supplements Tesler's. "What can be called 'object-oriented' direct manipulation interfaces . . . defines a class of interfaces which rely on concrete and visible objects, simplified sets of user actions and rapid feedback where the key activity is visibly moving screen images by pointing at them."[2] This adds to Tesler's list the idea that actions can be expressed by object interaction. Even an action on a single object, such as `print` on a document, can be expressed as an interaction between the document and a printer object.

Verplank talks about "the *illusion* of manipulable objects," recognizing that the things on the interface are really symbols, not the objects themselves. To sustain the illusion, the symbols need to be "direct" representations of the objects portrayed. Hutchins, Hollan, and Norman [Hut85], talk about two forms of directness.[3] The presentation language is *semantically direct* when users understand the displayed objects with a minimum of cognitive effort ("what you see is what you've got"). The interface has *articulatory directness* when users' intentions map easily to the action language ("what you want is what you get").

These ideas are illustrated by a scenario where the user is thinking something like "OK, I need to move that paragraph to the bottom of the page . . . hmmm . . . is that really the start of the paragraph there? . . . now . . . what are the commands I use to do that?" Directness relates to putting things at the right cognitive level in Figure 4-6, as well as to the specific representation. The less abstract, the more direct. The best guideline for defining "directness" is to understand the domain you are designing for, and how users think about it.

[1] Thanks to Janet Fath for pointing this out. There are also cases where document recognition is helped by showing an iconically sized, but physically detailed, representation. Wang's Freestyle system [vWang89] is an example; the vicon browser in Chapter 15 of this book is another.

[2] [Ver88], p. 365.

[3] This topic will be discussed further in Chapter 10.

A Definition of OOUI

Here is a more detailed version of the definition of an OOUI that was summarized in Chapter 1. It describes features of interfaces (such as the Xerox Star) that are generally considered object-oriented, and is consistent with other definitions (such as Tesler's).

It prescribes a set of characteristics for interfaces that meet the criterion of "representing what an end user needs to know." The prescription is not a cure-all, and needs to be applied by experts—but that is what the rest of this book is about.

1. *Users perceive and act on objects.* This is simple in principle and hard in practice. User interface objects must provide appearance and behavior needed for users' tasks, while concealing implementation details. The encapsulation of objects does not preclude object interactions, such as dragging a document icon to the trash icon to delete it. These interactions are part of the external behavior of the objects. Behavior also includes visual appearance, changes in appearance to reflect state changes, and responses to user actions such as mouse clicks.
2. *Users can classify objects based on how they behave.* This does not imply that a user could write down a class hierarchy, but simply that users will make predictions based on how they classify what they see and interact with. You can verify this informally by asking users to predict the behavior of various objects in the interface. Their performance improves if they can classify objects as similar to other objects whose behavior they already know ("this is the same kind of object as that one," "this object is similar to that one," etc.). In spite of the benefits, designing an interface to use classes and inheritance is more difficult than simply using objects. Some of the issues are discussed below.
3. *In the context of what users are trying to accomplish, all the interface objects fit together into a coherent overall representation (user's conceptual model).* This means that the composition of interface objects provides users with a representation that is meaningful in context. No object is an island. The interface directly represents the collective behavior and interaction of objects, not just the individual objects. The composite representation fosters a conceptual model of the domain modeled by the user interface. There are two sorts of composition:

    - Objects contain other objects. For example, a filing cabinet contains drawers, which contain folders, which contain documents.
    - Objects are constructed from other objects. For example, a window on the display is built from a title bar, a border, scroll bars, etc.

In both cases, the user sees the total behavior of the composed object as arising from its parts, although the coupling of parts is looser in containment than in construction.

This definition is based entirely on the external appearance and behavior of the user interface. It says nothing about how the interface is implemented.[1] Observing users is the ultimate test of conformance to it. It should also be clear that simply using the visible paraphernalia of GUIs (overlapping windows, icons, etc.) does not necessarily make an interface object-oriented.

Applying the OOUI Object Model

Now I return to the model presented in Section 4.1, to make some points about the relation between the abstract model, its cognitive basis, how it is manifested in OOUIs, and the definition of an OOUI.

1. A user interface *object* is a building block for simulation models of the domain the end user is interested in. This corresponds to point (1) of the definition. Objects respond to messages sent to them by the user and by other objects. Users infer the internal states and processes of objects based on their visual appearance and other behavior. Classification of objects, and how they fit into a larger conceptual model, influence the user's inferences.

   a. The nature of the simulation model determines the appropriate lifetime for any user interface object. For example, a user may expect that a window on the screen, after being closed and reopened, will reappear at the same location, and with the same size. This requires some persistence mechanism in the implementation.

   b. The executing process within an object may be *concurrent* with executing processes in other objects. Users expect concurrency in interface controls, though they do not often get it.[2] Imagine driving a car, however. Downshifting while turning a corner involves concurrent use of controls for speed (accelerator and brake pedals), shifting (clutch and gearshift), and turning (steering wheel).

   c. User interface objects are autonomous. Users expect anything they identify as an object to have its own behavior. They also expect dynamic typing in appropriate contexts. For example, users may expect to be able to put any type of object in a folder.

2. User interface objects may be *composite*. The visible behavior of composite objects (in response to message passing) is internally synthe-

[1] I will claim that it is extremely difficult to implement an OOUI without using techniques, if not languages, that are object-oriented. But that claim is not part of the definition.

[2] Chapter 10 will talk about concurrency in user interface controls.

sized from the behavior of their component sub-objects. This relates to point (3) in the definition, since the entire content of the display is a composite object that must make sense to the user. Composition is manifested on a spectrum from containment to construction.

   a. Containers may be "typed" to hold only certain kinds of objects (for instance, an outgoing mail container may hold only things in envelopes), but the type must be made clear to the user.

   b. Construction constrains object autonomy; a user would not normally expect to disconnect a scroll bar from its window and put it somewhere else, for example.

   When designing, thinking of "composition" in the way it is used by artists and musicians is not a bad idea. As Figure 4-7 shows, poor composition can have a disastrous effect on a user's perception of quality.

3. Part of the state of a user interface object is its *class*, which determines its general behavior. An object is called an *instance* of its class, and classes act as templates for the construction of new instances. Developers may implement classes that users do not recognize as classes, or *vice versa*. This is particularly problematic if we expect users to properly recognize an entire hierarchy of classes, as is discussed below. Representation of the template aspect of classes is also an issue. Since "class" is quite abstract, the use of concrete *prototypical objects*, which are copied to make new objects, is common in OOUIs.

4. A class of user interface objects may have subclasses; the class is called a superclass relative to its subclasses, which inherit from it. This and the previous point relate to point (2) in the definition. The key issue is whether users recognize the inheritance structure that the designer intended; this is discussed below.

   a. *Polymorphism* can be used very effectively in OOUIs to reduce the number of commands or operations the user needs to learn and remember.

Classes and Inheritance

The application of classes and inheritance to user interfaces is not straightforward. The more abstract a thing is, the more difficult it is to symbolize it in a concrete way. Classes are quite abstract, indicated by the fact that people appear to use prototypical members, not classes, in their thinking.

Everyone classifies, and there is substantial agreement on classes corresponding to basic level categories. But taxonomies (class hierarchies) may vary significantly between individuals, and people may classify the same object differently depending upon the context. This makes it hard to design a class hierarchy that will satisfy all the users all the time. Multiple inheritance also complicates the situation. A single multiple inheritance lattice may appear as a multitude of simple inheritance trees, depending on the point of view.

One solution to the problem of representing classes is to portray them as concrete templates used to create instances. The Apple Lisa designers pioneered the "stationery pad" metaphor. Any document could be saved as "stationery" and would be represented visually as a pad of paper, from which new instances of the document could be "torn off."

This metaphor can be applied generally, as it has in the IBM Common User Access style [IBM92b]. Figure 4-8 (left to right, in sequence) shows a user creating an envelope from a New envelopes template by dragging the mouse pointer over it. The turned up corner in the lower right of the template icon is intended to suggest a "pad" of envelopes.

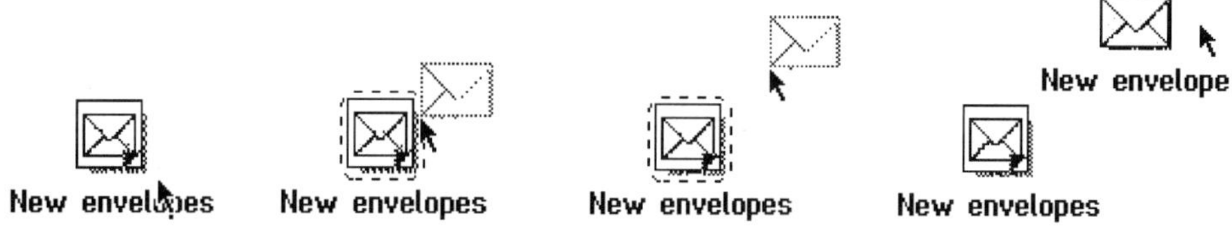

Figure 4-8 Creating an instance from a template

In this example the stationery pad metaphor is stretched, but still works. It is probably not universally applicable, and you may need to create new template metaphors for other domains. A similar solution, more generally applicable, is to allow the use of existing instances as templates, by copying them. This too has its problems, such as what to do when no instance exists for copying and whether to copy the state of the prototype instance. In general, the right solution depends on the domain.

Inheritance hierarchies for classifying objects in a user interface have been explicitly mentioned by designers. Figure 4-9 is the hierarchy of icon types for the Xerox Star, as presented in [Smi82]. I would surmise that the basic level categories are the leaf nodes in the tree (`Document`, etc.). It seems clear that understanding the various classes of concrete objects helps the user, but it is less clear whether higher level categories such as `Data icon` and `Function icon` are beneficial. Charles Irby, who led the Star design effort, said later that inheritance had not been important in the design [Irb89]. He emphasized, however, that they had taken pains to define a simple, consistent set of actions applicable to all objects. [Smi82] also makes it clear that common commands were primarily important to the designers and classification was secondary.

Irby's "simple, consistent set of actions applicable to all objects" are what I call polymorphic operations. A common example is the action of double-clicking the mouse on an object (or of selecting the object, then selecting the `Open` command from a menu). This will cause different results depending on the kind of object. A text document will display itself as ed-

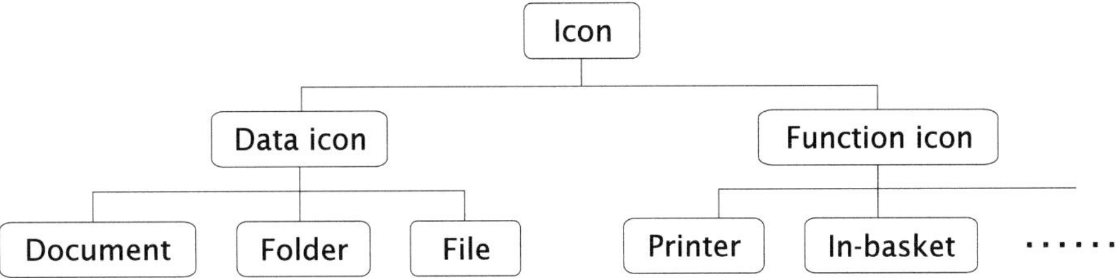

Figure 4-9 Xerox Star user interface class hierarchy

itable text in a window, a chart will display itself graphically, a calculator will open to a full-sized desk calculator, etc. Polymorphism can be detrimental to usability if the results of user actions appear arbitrary, capricious, or unpredictable. Thus the emphasis in the Star design on consistent command operation (though again, consistency is context dependent and sometimes hard to define [Kel87]).

Actions as objects Star's "function icons" illustrate a tradeoff between objects and actions. Having many actions (commands) for each class of object can be confusing to users and hard to implement consistently. Given `anObject` and a command `doSomething`, we can substitute a `somethingDoer` object for the command. Users can then drop `anObject`'s icon on the `somethingDoer` icon to execute the command.[1] Examples of this technique in the Star (and in most other object-oriented shells) include printing by moving a document icon to the printer icon, and mailing by moving an item to the out-basket icon.

Function objects may seem not to be very object-oriented, but examples are common in the real world—mailboxes, calculators, copiers, shredders, etc. Objects like these, with concrete representations, are good candidates for user interface metaphors. In using this technique, designers must walk a line between too many actions, leading to menu clutter, and too many objects, leading to desktop clutter.

Figure 4-10 shows a more recent user interface class hierarchy, defined for IBM's Common User Access (CUA) style. Both the CUA hierarchy and the Star's appear intuitively reasonable—certainly a user should benefit from understanding the general behavior of containers or devices as represented in the user interface, for example. (Device is equivalent to `Function icon` in the Star.)

I use and recommend class hierarchies as a design tool, but this is based on intuition and informal observation of users, not hard data. The Star, the OS/2 Workplace, and similar shell environments have relatively few object types. With a rich set of applications, the number of object types increases, and classification is more useful. General classes, such as

[1] Chapter 10 discusses uses, issues, and tradeoffs of this technique; Chapter 13 discusses implementation.

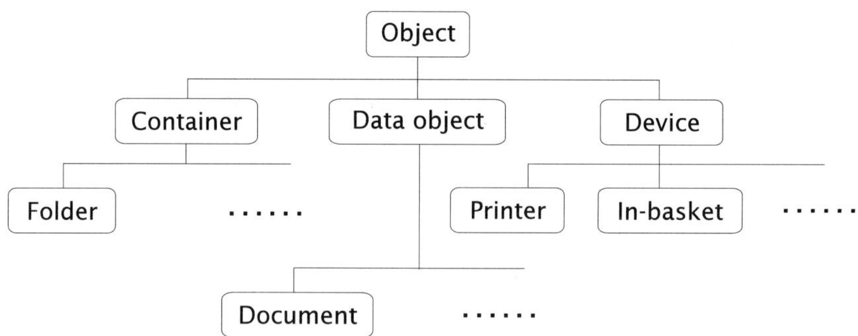

Figure 4-10 IBM CUA user interface class hierarchy [IBM92]

`Container` and `Document`, can foster consistency if they are used as abstract superclasses of application-specific classes such as `PendingInvoiceFolder` and Invoice.

Real users are the final judges of classification schemes. People classify objects based on what they see, touch, and think, regardless of the designer's intention. Finding out how the users of a system classify objects in the application domain is useful across *all* facets of design.[1]

4.4 Summary

Employing user interface objects to represent an application domain to users, including the possibilities for action on objects in the domain, is a critical success factor for application development on GUI platforms. Design of these objects should use a general object-oriented model, and exploit what psychologists have learned about how people perceive, think about, and interact with objects and symbols. The result is an object-oriented user interface (OOUI).

The key "rules of thumb" for designers that can be drawn from this chapter are:

- The principles of object-orientation can be formulated in a way that facilitates application to a variety of disciplines in the software development process.
- Understanding the psychological basis for OO principles helps in applying them to user interface design. Understanding the theory, however, will not substitute for knowledge of how *your* users understand the application domain and the system. This usually comes from observing them doing their work.

[1] Chapters 5 and 11-13 discuss the relationship between externally visible classes and implementation class hierarchies.

- Composition—how well you "compose" your representation of complex objects, including the overall conceptual model of the application, can make or break a user interface.
- Representing objects is the most straightforward aspect of designing an OOUI, but requires a lot of attention to details. Accurately representing classes and class hierarchies is more difficult, and must be done carefully to ensure that object behaviors will be predictable to users.
- Designing a small set of generic or polymorphic operations applicable to all user interface objects can make things simpler for users.

4.5 To Explore Further

John Sowa started me thinking about user interface design as a problem of knowledge representation. His book [Sow84] is a treasure trove of information on how people and machines acquire and represent knowledge.

The model in Section 4.1 includes what most experts consider the essential attributes of object-orientation. Since there is no universally accepted formulation, it draws on a variety of sources. These include a characterization of object-orientation in programming languages [Weg87a], a set of definitions being used by ANSI and the Object Management Group [Sny93], the object model presented in [Boo94], and [Ste89], a discussion of alternatives to classes for sharing behavior in object-oriented systems.

For understanding objects, my favorite blend of computer science, psychology, and vision comes from Alan Kay [vKay87, Kay93]. Beyond the works already cited, the best place to find current thinking about object-orientation is in the proceedings of the annual OOPSLA conference, published as special issues of *SIGPLAN Notices*.

Of the literature cited in Section 4.2, I particularly recommend [Lak87]. Lakoff summarizes all the major findings in the field, and his book is readable as well as scholarly. Finding and understanding objects in computer interfaces is studied by Carroll and Mack in two papers on "active learning" ([Carr84] and [Carr85]). [Nor88] is an innovative approach to applying findings from cognitive psychology to understanding user interfaces and other objects in the world. [Lewi91] presents a theory of interface design based on allocation of cognitive resources, which complements the material on Piaget and Bruner in this chapter.

[Shn92] is a good introduction to looking at user interfaces. Shneiderman's concept of direct manipulation is particularly relevant to OOUIs. [Smi82] and other literature on the Xerox Star is still a good source of coherent design guidance for OOUIs. The most important thing is to *look at user interfaces*, preferably by using them. The next best thing is videotape; various issues of [vSIGGRAPH] are a good source.

4.6 Exercises

1. List examples of objects in the following application domains that exhibit concurrency and persistence. Think first of "conceptual" concurrency and persistence; do not worry about whether you would need true concurrency in the implementation.

   - Vehicle scheduling for a taxi service
   - Branch banking (including the use of ATMs)
   - Communications network management

   (*For developers*: Try this exercise on an application domain you are involved in.)

2. List tasks you do frequently on a computer system.

   a. Which of them would benefit from true (implementation) concurrency? (I.e., from a true multitasking system such as UNIX, OS/2, or Windows/NT.)

   b. Design a visual interface that will allow you to control these tasks (start, suspend/resume, cancel, check status, etc.). Try a *control panel* metaphor, with labeled buttons, indicators, etc., if you can't find a better visual representation.

3. Make copies of Figure 4-2, the left half only of Figure 4-3, and Figure 4-7. Show them and discuss them with several people.

   a. For Figure 4-2, how far did you need to go in pointing out the Dalmatian before people recognized it?

   b. For Figure 4-3, what objects did people see?

   c. For Figure 4-7, was everyone surprised? If not, did they have an explanation?

4. Show some computer users a copy of Figure 1-2 (or a screen print from your favorite GUI), explaining the icons if necessary. Explain the concept of a class hierarchy or taxonomy, and ask your "test subjects" to diagram their classification of the icons.

   a. Were the taxonomies similar?

   b. Did you get any clues from your subjects about how you could make the representations more obvious?

   (*For developers*: Try this exercise on a user interface you are involved in developing. You might want to try sketches or prototypes of various alternatives.)

II

External Design

Part I of this book was about ideas that underlie OOUI design methods. This part presents methodology and techniques for designing the tangible objects that users see, hear, touch, and think about. Part III will connect external design to the software structures that implement it.

Chapter 5, *Three Domains of OO Design for the User Interface*, works through a sample application to show how object-orientation provides a design language that integrates diverse activities in development. Chapter 5 also shows the breadth and depth of OO user interfaces, which include more than "what's on the glass."

Chapter 6, *OOUI Design: Process and Team*, presents an overall methodology for OOUI design, describes the people and skills involved, and discusses how OOUI design fits into the development of a whole system or application.

Chapter 7, *Users, Tasks, and Task Analysis*, begins the detailed exposition of design activities. It provides an object-oriented perspective on analyzing the tasks for which an OOUI is designed. Chapter 8, *The User's Conceptual Model*, shows how to use this analysis in designing a conceptual model that structures the visible aspects of the interface.

The user's conceptual model drives the design of the look and feel of the interface—the presentation and action languages. These are covered in Chapter 9, *Information Presentation*, and Chapter 10, *Interaction and Control Mechanisms.*

5

Three Domains of OO Design for the User Interface

Some user interfaces look like poorly related collections of features. They create confusion as users move from one function to another, and integrating the work of several functions is difficult. In contrast, other interfaces appear seamless—functions are consistent, and they flow naturally from one to another.

Crafting seamless interfaces requires a broad view of design and of what makes up a user interface. A good interface is much more than what's "on the glass"—the deep structure of the system works with the surface to represent what users need to know. As a result, user interface issues are pervasive in the design of systems and applications. Overall architecture, organization of functions, database design, and many other factors influence the quality of the user interface. Bringing them all together requires a high level of teamwork and coordination across the development process.

Coordination in large projects is often difficult because of the many languages used to express facets of system design. Teamwork suffers when communication is difficult. Object-orientation eases this problem by providing a common language with a vocabulary focused initially on the problem domain. The vocabulary can be extended gracefully to computer artifacts as the process moves toward implementation, without losing sight of the problem.

The "three domains" of the chapter title are the conceptual model of the system, the representation of objects provided by the user interface, and the deep structures of the system that implement the functional capabilities of objects. All these domains[1] are important to user interface designers, and the common language of objects provides cohesion between them.

This chapter does the following:

- Describes the "three domain" perspective.
- Discusses its relevance to the issue of providing a common language to developers.
- Illustrates it with a worked-out example.

The example occupies most of the chapter, and takes a small problem from concept through analysis, design, and implementation. A simulation model of the problem domain is used to validate the analysis and prototype a simple user interface.

5.1 Designing for Understandability

Many problems in the development and use of systems boil down to lack of understanding. A function is missing because an analyst misunderstood the application requirements. Interactive performance is poor because the designers didn't know the target platform. A feature has bugs because the programmers didn't understand the specification. Users were not trained, so the interface appears complex and confusing. The list could go on and on.

Misunderstandings may stem from the complexity of the conceptual constructs we deal with, or the complexity of the languages we use to communicate them. Object-orientation helps to alleviate the latter problem, by providing a common language for diverse activities.

Understandability and Complexity

The problem domains we work in, the processes of design and development, and the systems we design, are all complex. An understanding of user requirements must traverse a long chain of people and events before it finally appears in a running implementation. This process resembles *Telephone*, a children's game I used to play. The first child whispered a message to the second, who whispered it to the third, and so on. The object of the game was to deliver the message unaltered to the last child, but we seldom succeeded—it was usually garbled beyond recognition. Something similar has happened when users see an implementation that does not meet the requirements they thought they had conveyed to developers.

Figure 5-1 shows the process that often introduces misunderstanding and unnecessary complexity into the process of developing a system

[1] "Domain," like "model," is a heavily-used word in our business. Besides the "three domains," there is the "problem domain" or "application domain," the world outside the computer in which users do their work.

or application. This is a simplified picture, but even here there are four processes (analysis, system design, user interface design, and implementation), probably done by different people, and producing four deliverables: a statement of requirements, specifications for both the system internals and the user interface, and the implemented source code. Each is written in its own technical language. Forward translation (from requirements to code) is difficult, and reverse translation (extracting requirements from source code, for instance, when the system needs maintenance) is often impossible.

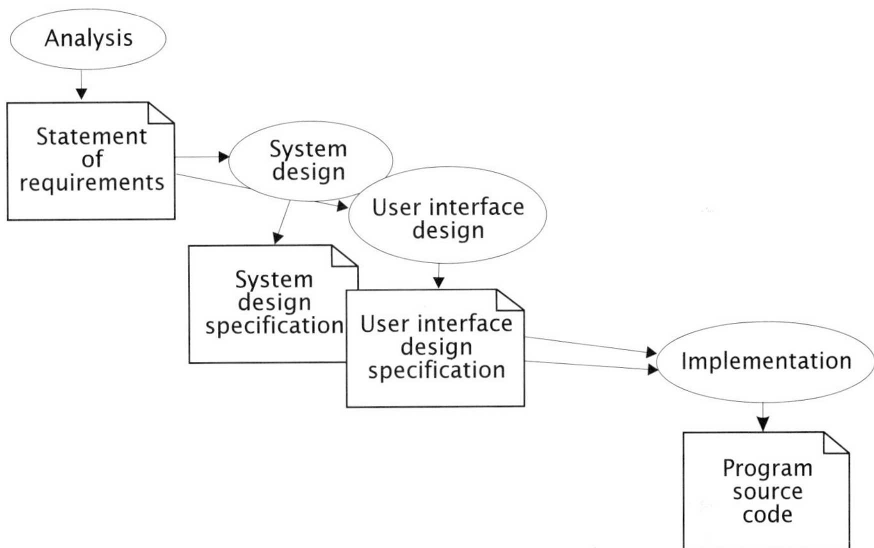

Figure 5-1 Processes and deliverables in software development

Our focus here is on user interface design, which is frequently removed from the mainstream of system design. The deliverable specification may be a prototype, or a set of sketches with text describing interface features. If the specification is a prototype, it may be written in a programming language different from the implementation language for the system. Here is a rich source of problems—can the prototype be translated into the system implementation language? How do user interface objects connect to functional modules? If the interface needs to be changed late in the cycle, where is the code we need to change, and will changing it break other parts of the system? This sounds pessimistic, but I think it is fair to say that these problems afflict most projects. Fixing them with management attention, walkthroughs, controls, and constant testing is expensive; we would rather make them less likely.

Essential and Accidental Complexity

Fred Brooks [Broo87] distinguishes two kinds of complexity. The first is *essential* complexity, which we need in software to model the inherent complexity of problem domains. The second is *accidental* complexity, which is introduced as an artifact of the development process.

There is a criterion (attributed to Einstein) for the adequacy of a model: "as simple as possible, but no simpler." In physics, this means that a model or theory should be as simple as possible, but rich enough to explain the observable facts. In the realm of software systems, a design should be as simple as possible, but rich enough to model the essential elements of the application domain—those that are important to the system's users. To manage complexity, we need to minimize accidental complexity, and handle essential complexity efficiently.

In [Boo94], Booch offers five characteristics[1] of "complex systems":

1. Complex systems can be hierarchically decomposed.
2. The choice of what to select as the components of a system may depend on the observer.
3. Linkages or communications *within* components are stronger or more dense than linkages or communications *between* components.
4. Certain patterns, or subsystem types, recur in different systems, and in different places within the same system.
5. Complex systems do not appear all at once; they evolve from simpler systems.

He also calls these "the five attributes of *well-formed* complex systems" (my italics). Fundamentally, these are characteristics of complex systems that people can understand. Most of the application domains software designers deal with are well formed, because they have been organized over time by the people who work in them. A few examples are office work, accounting, banking, and publishing.

These five attributes characterize well-formed systems *as we see them*. Another way of saying this is that they are *ways of seeing* systems to make them comprehensible. Many design methods emphasize *representing* what we see, but *how we see* it is also important. *Representing* can mean anything from writing lines of code, to implementing the visible "look and feel" artifacts of a user interface. *How we see things* relates to the clarity of the ideas that drive the representation.

Brooks points out that "the essence of a software entity is a construct of interlocking concepts . . . this essence is abstract in that such a conceptual construct is the same under many different representations. It is nonetheless highly precise and richly detailed" [Broo87]. He goes on to say that he believes the hard part is developing the conceptual construct,

[1] Drawn from [Cur85]. The list here is paraphrased from [Boo94], Chapter 1.

not representing it (for instance, as code in a programming language). The same thing is true in many intellectual activities—the hard part is not writing (either prose or code), it is knowing what to write.

To illustrate the generality of the "essence," or conceptual model, these attributes (parallel to the ones listed above) characterize "well formed" complex user interfaces:

1. Like object-oriented systems in general, user interfaces can be decomposed along the dimensions of objects ("part-of" hierarchies) and classes of objects ("kind-of" or class hierarchies).
2. The choice of what to select as the visible components of an interface may depend on the observer. Here there is a privileged observer, the end user. Fortunately, in a given problem domain (banking, office work, insurance, etc.) users tend to think alike. Designers need to understand and exploit the "natural" component selection and classification schemes provided by users—not only in the user interface, but in the system design as well.
3. Linkages or communications *within* components are stronger or more dense than those *between* components. The well-formed interface will show clearly where linkages are strong or weak. This task is easier if linkages in the user interface match corresponding linkages in the underlying functional structures of the system.
4. Certain patterns, or subsystem types, recur in different interfaces, and in different places within the same user interface. Well-formed interfaces exploit consistency among their parts, and with other interfaces used by the same end users. This is manifested as common objects, similar object types, and common (polymorphic) interaction techniques.
5. The evolution of complex systems from simpler ones is manifested in "progressive disclosure"[1]—a set of essential core objects and functions that are easy to find and use, with more complex variants that extend the basic entities. This can mirror the process of incremental development—core objects and functions are developed first, then extended to provide the full capabilities of the system.

Complex problem domains lead to complex systems, which have complex user interfaces. If the only problem were the problem domain, things would be difficult, but more straightforward than they are now.

There is also a second "problem domain"—the computer and its associated hardware and software. Because of this, developers must walk a tightrope. On the one hand, the computer should remain a "problem domain" only for the developers, not the users. On the other hand, developers must be constantly aware of the user's problem, and not concentrate exclusively on artifacts of the computer domain. Adopting the perspective

[1] One of the principles used by designers of the Xerox Star; see [Joh89].

described in the next section makes this balancing act easier.

5.2 The Three Domains

Understanding something can be equated with possessing a knowledge structure to represent it. The structure can be "in the head"—a mental or conceptual model. The conceptual model may also exist as a written description, using words and diagrams. This is the first domain of user interface design, and it corresponds roughly to the analysis phase of software development.[1]

The second domain is what is "on the glass," what the user sees as the visible user interface. The third domain of user interface design encompasses things "under the hood"—the program modules, databases, etc., that make up the underlying structures of the system. I will call these three domains the *conceptual model*, the *user interface model*, and the *implementation model*.[2]

The third domain, the implementation model, breaks down into the structures that directly implement features of the visible user interface (windows, controls, icons, graphic displays, etc.) and the "functional" structures of the system. Functional structures make up the *information model*;[3] they implement the content or semantics of the user interface, as opposed to the style. The information model is stressed in this chapter, for a couple of reasons. First, most user interface designers are already convinced that style issues are important. Second, it is relatively easy to iteratively improve the style of an interface if the content is solid. Changing the information model is usually more difficult, so it should be validated early in development.

This is not to say that designing the entire system is part of user interface design. However, the user interface is a window into objects and functions provided by the underlying information model, which always ends up being visible to the user, though perhaps only indirectly. Trygve Reenskaug, who worked on the development of user interface concepts for Smalltalk, said "More than twenty years of experience has shown that a bad system design can never be hidden from the user, even by a masterfully designed user interface" [Ree81]. What he calls a "bad design" is a system structure that does not map to the conceptual structure of the application domain, which is why the third domain is critical.

Designing in the Three Domains

The process of designing an OOUI comes full circle. We extract, through analysis, a formalization of the conceptual model held by experts in the

[1] This domain is discussed in detail in Chapter 8, *The User's Conceptual Model.*

[2] This terminology matches Figure 1-1 (Chapter 1) if the user interface model is decomposed into its parts, the presentation and action languages (look and feel).

[3] The term "information model" in this context is due to Adele Goldberg [Gol90].

application area; design an internal representation of the objects, behaviors, and relationships found in the conceptual model; the internal representation supports an external representation (the user interface) that presents knowledge of the application in a form that is understandable and usable. Finally, this external representation fosters the development of an "expert" conceptual model in the mind of a new user.

In a system developed using object-oriented methods, finding the right model in any domain involves the same basic steps:

- What are the objects?
- How do objects interact with one another?
- How are objects similar to one another (how can they be classified)?
- How do objects fit together into structures, collections, etc.?

There is one additional question to be asked in designing an object-oriented user interface:

- How should objects be presented to the user, in terms of appearance and interaction behavior?[1]

This last question can be generalized: What needs to be added when implementing the "core objects" discovered in analysis? For user interfaces, the question translates to presentation and interaction behavior, and may involve adding additional objects such as icons, buttons, scroll bars, etc., that are not in the analysis model. Analogous questions are asked in the domain of object-oriented programs and object-oriented databases: Given some set of objects, how do we represent them in a program? How do we store the objects, so multiple users can access them concurrently, update them, etc.? In these cases too, additional objects (not found in the analysis model) may be added to the implementation domain.

Figure 5-2 illustrates the expansion of a set of classes that model an application domain. The "blobs" are classes;[2] classes shown in gray have been added in moving from analysis to design or implementation. The analysis classes model the first domain, and the visible user interface classes model the second. View/controller classes, system implementation classes, and database object types model the third domain. The structure of the analysis classes is mirrored in each domain.

Database object types are shown separately to emphasize the isomorphism[3] (structural similarity) of the analysis or "conceptual model" classes to the core classes in all the major components of the system. Each domain and subdomain in Figure 5-2 contains a simulation model of the

[1] Recall Dan Ingalls' *reactive principle* from Chapter 2: "Every component accessible to the user should be able to present itself in a meaningful way for observation and manipulation" [Ing81].

[2] This is Booch notation, from [Boo94]; the concepts are independent of any particular notation.

[3] Isomorphism is a mathematical term. I am using it here rather loosely, but the notion of "approximate isomorphism" can be well defined; see [Apo61].

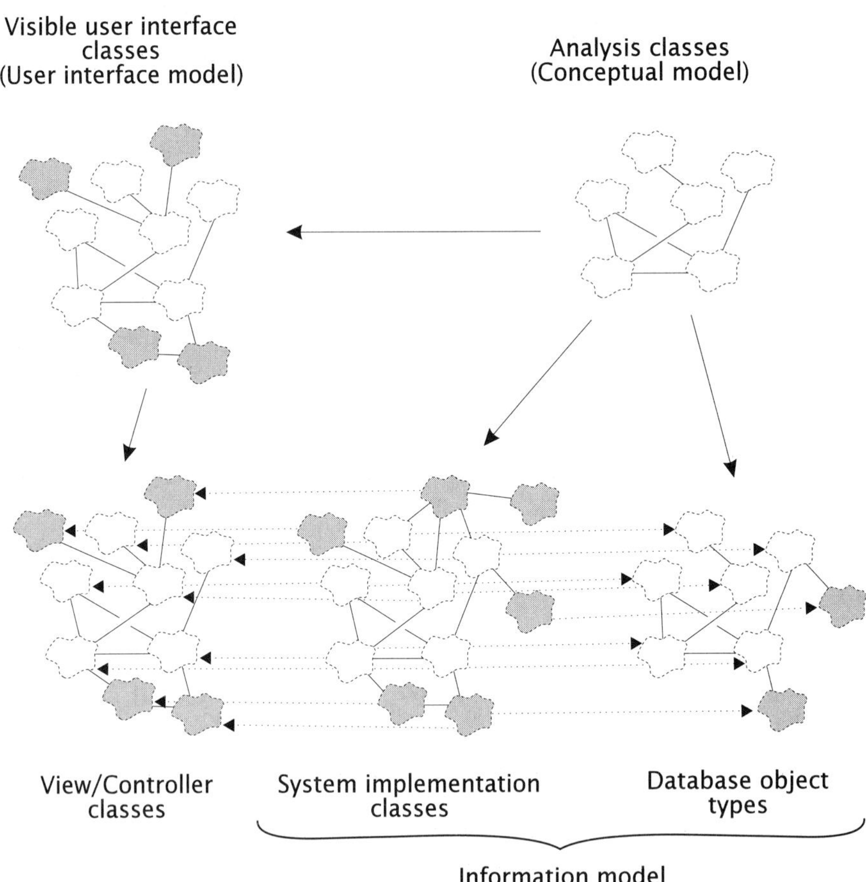

Figure 5-2 Mapping from analysis or "conceptual model" classes

application domain, represented by the core classes. The dotted lines in the figure reinforce this, by showing that objects in the database are the persistent forms of system objects, and objects in the user interface are the visible forms of system objects.

Part III, *Internal Design*, will describe an architecture for implementing user interfaces called "Model-View-Controller," or MVC. The view and controller of MVC are software objects that implement the objects in the visible user interface. They correspond to the presentation language and action language in Bennett's user interface model, and they are shown in Figure 5-2 as the view/controller classes. The "model" of MVC is the underlying functional code for the system. (I prefer the term *information model* for this concept, to differentiate it from other uses of "model").

Isomorphism

Isomorphism between the conceptual model of the system and a set of core classes in the user interface and the implementation is the key to attacking the problems of misunderstanding discussed in Section 5.1. The system conceptual model is the core of a common language across the development team and the development process. It keeps the people and the process focused on the problem they are solving, even as they extend it with objects related to the implementation domain.

Figure 5-3 is another perspective on the same idea. It shows that ideally, the user interface is a window that reveals an underlying information model. The user has a conceptual model of the application domain that matches the structure of the information model, as presented by the visible user interface model. Objects in the user's conceptual model that need to be persistent are always there, because the database component of the information model mirrors the conceptual model. This is an ideal view; the reality is more complex, and may involve compromises. All these domains affect aspects of the interface that are important to users, so compromises should be made only when clearly necessary.[1]

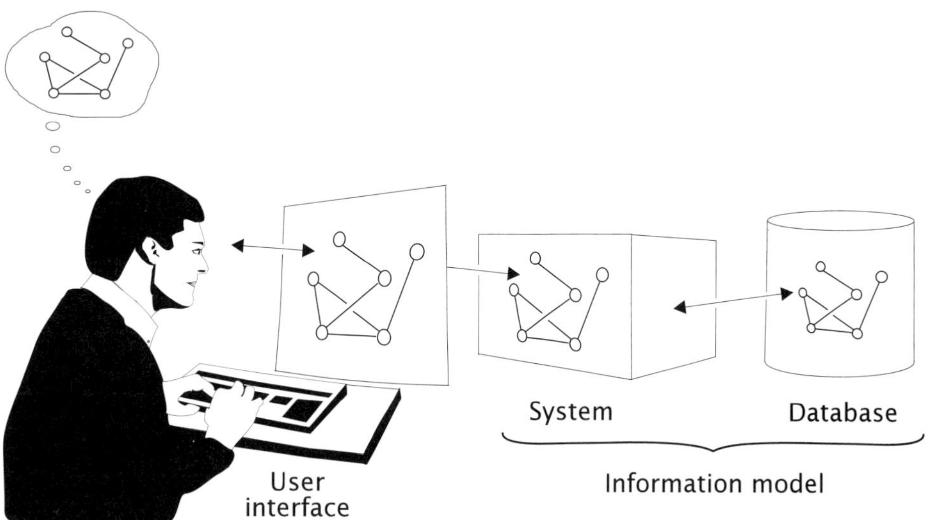

Figure 5-3 An idealized view of the user interface

Software development is complex and difficult, and anything that simplifies it is valuable. "Semantic gaps" between differently structured system components are a source of complexity. A key advantage of OO design is that the basic method can be uniformly applied across many sys-

[1] Another way of saying this is that the accidental complexities of implementation should not make us lose sight of the essential elements of the problem.

tem areas, thus helping to bridge the gaps. Striving for the ideal of isomorphism makes the system easier to understand, for programmers as well as users.

To summarize, there are three domains in which an OOUI designer operates. The first, the *conceptual model*, may be in the user's head, in the designer's head, or written down as an application domain analysis. The second, the *user interface model*, is what is visible to the user, the look and feel of the interface. The third domain includes the underlying functional objects of the system (the *information model*), and the software structures that implement the visible user interface. Making the mapping between these domains as simple as possible will simplify life for developers and end users.

5.3 An Example: "Klondike" Solitaire

This section works through an example application, to illustrate how a designer operates in the three domains. It emphasizes the information model and its mapping to the visible user interface. The application is a card game, Klondike (a type of solitaire), and the user interface will allow the user to interactively play the game.

Why a card game? This is a good example for several reasons. It is a popular application. Klondike solitaire was bundled with Microsoft Windows version 3.0, and for many users of Windows it offered a simple entré into the new style of graphical presentation and mouse interaction. IBM's OS/2 Workplace Shell also includes a Klondike game. NeXT bundles a poker game, which has similar characteristics.

The basic "requirements" for card games are well understood, and codified in rule books.[1] The analysis of the application domain is small and easily understood; yet it is non-trivial, and illustrates important principles. There is an obvious and natural set of presentation and interaction techniques for card games, but applying them involves subtle details. Finally, there are other example card games available, and comparing them is a useful exercise after working through this one.

Methodology To develop this example, I started with CRC cards [Bec89]. This method uses ordinary 3 by 5 inch index cards on which the designer writes the name of a class, its responsibilities, and the classes with which it collaborates. The important thing about CRC cards is that they can be rearranged, rewritten, or thrown away. Early stages of analysis and design require flexibility. Arriving at a good solution usually depends on throwing away lots of bad ones, and CRC cards encourage this. More formal methods, particularly if they are supported by computer tools that produce elaborate outputs, discourage rearranging and throwing away ideas.

[1]For this example, I used *Official Rules of Card Games*, edited by Albert H. Morehead (New York: Fawcett Crest, 1968).

What CRC cards do not provide is a formal check on whether the design will really work. The next steps are to document the design more carefully, and begin running simulation models to verify it. There are many tools and notations for documentation; I picked Booch diagrams here because they are easy to understand, and people who are knowledgeable in the application domain can inspect them and provide feedback. The simulation model is an abstract version of the design (usually implemented with a high-level programming language) and a set of test cases that can be run against it. The test cases are based on usage scenarios for the application, and help to verify that the analysis has captured everything correctly.[1]

Smalltalk is a good tool for building simulation models. Even if I intend to switch to C++, I find it faster to rapidly iterate in Smalltalk, then port the work to C++. I do not feel dogmatic about this, though, and skilled C++ programmers may disagree. The important thing to recognize is that in the early stages of analysis and design, the environment should permit rapid iteration and experimentation. The criterion for a tool is that it allows rapid exploration and testing of design ideas, whatever the programming language.[2]

The Application

Now, for the application itself. Figure 5-4 shows the layout for a game of Klondike. Klondike is a solitaire game for one player.[3] Here is a brief summary of the rules.

From a standard 52-*card* deck called the *stock*, deal seven *tableau piles*. This is done by dealing a card to the first *pile* face up, then cards to the other six piles face down. This process is repeated, starting with the second, then third, etc., piles. The resulting layout for the *tableau* is shown in the figure. The remainder of the stock (24 cards) is kept as a *face-down pile*, and play goes as follows. Cards are turned over one at a time from the stock to a *face-up pile* called the *talon*. When an ace appears as the face-up card in any pile (talon or tableau) it can be moved to a *foundation pile*. In the same way, cards can be moved to partially completed foundation piles—two of spades can be placed on top of ace of spades, etc. If the bottom card on a tableau face-up pile is one rank lower, and a different color, than the top card on another tableau pile, the entire face-up pile can be moved. (For example, the ten of spades can be placed on a jack of hearts or diamonds.) The top face-down card is then turned over. Cards from the

[1] If it sounds like I am mixing up analysis and design, you're right. The analysis classes always show up as a subset of the design classes, so I don't worry about it. I am not alone in believing that the traditional separation between analysis and design tends to break down in object-oriented development. See, e.g., [Thom89].

[2] This may depend as much on the development environment and the available class library as on the choice of language.

[3] Though it seems like a contradiction in terms, there are also solitaire games for two players.

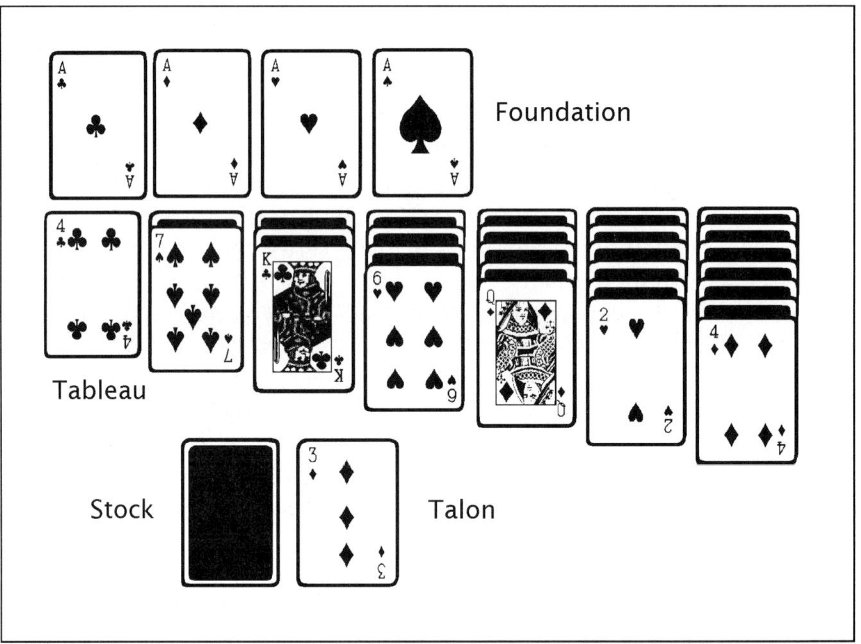

Figure 5-4 Layout for the game of Klondike solitaire

talon can also be moved in this way to the tableau. When the stock is exhausted and no further plays are possible, the player wins if all of the cards are on the *foundation.* Otherwise, he or she loses.

There is a variation, which differs only in how cards are dealt from the stock to the talon. In this version, three cards at a time are dealt from the stock and turned over. When the stock is exhausted the player turns over the talon to form a new stock, and continues playing. The game ends only when no further plays are possible.

Klondike involves both skill and luck; some people take the game seriously and get quite good at it. Others play mostly to pass the time. Over time, players develop a quick visual sense for what moves are permissible. They also develop the motor skills involved in moving cards around, and may play quite rapidly. Visual, motor, and cognitive skills developed in other card games are transferable; a skilled player of other card games will tend to learn Klondike faster. Although cards are standard, there is some variation, mostly for aesthetic reasons.

Rule books for card games provide more details, but this is the sort of description a "domain expert" would provide. In the first paragraph describing the game, I italicized some of the nouns, with their modifiers, that seem to identify objects that are important in Klondike. These objects can be classified according to their behavior. There is also a composition, or part-subpart, structure in the game. CRC cards representing the objects can be rearranged to show the classification or the composition of the objects, and from this I developed two diagrams showing the analysis. (I find this less confusing than showing the class hierarchy and the part-subpart hierarchy on the same diagram.)[1]

Analysis and Design

Figure 5-5 shows the composition structure. Some classes in the diagram are duplicated for clarity. The numbers on the "has" links are rules for quantities of cards and piles in the composition. This diagram reflects some decisions I made about identifying classes. For example, `Foundation` could have been a class, but is modeled as a collection of `FoundationPiles` managed by the `KlondikeGame`. I arrived at that decision after developing the simulation model, and discovering that all of the interesting behavior of the foundation was part of `FoundationPile`, or was coordinated by the `KlondikeGame`. I made a similar decision about the tableau. The implementation of the "has" links in the simulation uses the Smalltalk `OrderedCollection` class, which is not shown in the diagram. Libraries in almost all development environments provide standard collection classes, so this can readily be translated to another language.

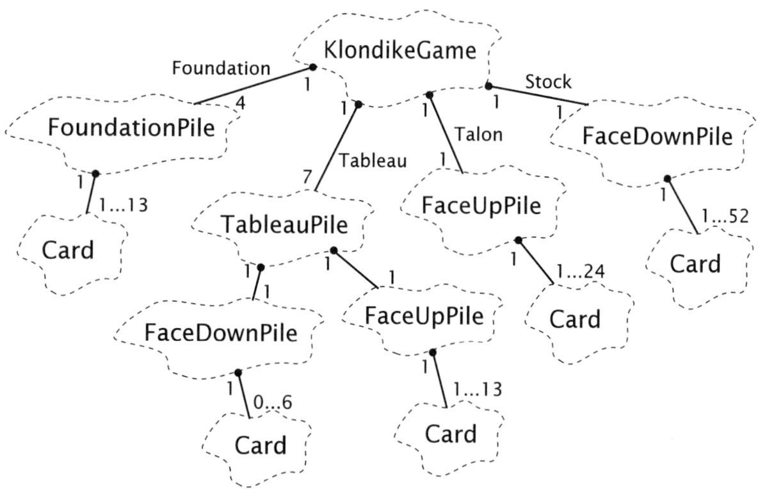

Figure 5-5 Composition diagram for the Klondike classes

Figure 5-6 shows the inheritance structure of the classes. Two of the classes, `Object` and `Model`, are grayed, which is my convention for a design class that is not part of the analysis. The simulation model uses Smalltalk-

[1] Looking for nouns is a simplistic way of "finding objects"; it works here because of familiarity with the task scenarios in which the objects are used.

80, where `Object` is the root of all classes, and `Model` is the root for classes used as information models in the model-view-controller framework. Using these classes is not a problem, even if the implementation uses C++; for the purposes of this design, the necessary protocols from Object and Model can be duplicated easily in the C++ classes. Some of these protocols are important for implementing the user interface, though, so the classes are in the diagram as a reminder. The remaining classes in Figure 5-6 are the same as those in Figure 5-5.

Behavior for the classes in Figure 5-6 comes from exploring a game scenario. Instances of `Card` can provide their value, suit, and color. Instances of `Pile` subclasses provide behaviors for dealing, turning over cards, testing whether a card or pile can be dropped on them, adding a card or pile, and so on. In analyzing the behavior of the various card piles, I concluded that foundation piles and tableau piles need to incorporate rules that are quite specific to this game. Stock and talon piles, on the other hand, are similar to piles in other card games. As a result, instead of classes called `Stock` and `Talon`, I designed the more generic `FaceDownPile` and `FaceUpPile`. Later, this could make these classes reusable in the development of other card games. At this point, the important thing is that generic classes reuse the user's knowledge of other card games.

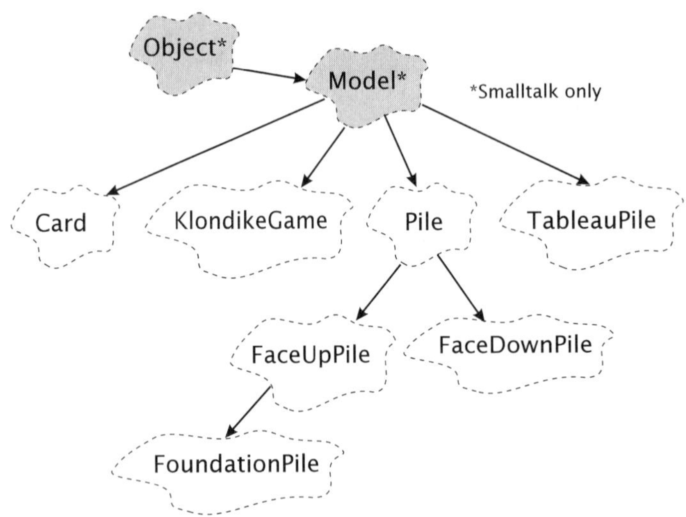

Figure 5-6 Classification diagram for the Klondike game classes

By using scenarios, the behavior of objects is defined based on what end users want to do with them. Though the analysis so far does not address the visible user interface, it has built a structure of classes that models an expert user's concept of the game. (This must be validated, of course, by testing the model with users.)

Implementing the Information Model

To provide a feel for building the simulation model, here is a listing of the public protocols for the class `KlondikeGame`, in Smalltalk-80.[1] The complete code listing is not shown, just the class definition, method definitions, and comments. The comments relate the code to the diagrams and other documentation, and serve as a notepad for documenting the analysis. These protocols, along with public protocols in the other classes, describe the semantics for playing the game of Klondike.

```
Model subclass: #KlondikeGame
      instanceVariableNames: 'stock talon talonRule tableau
             foundation'
      category: 'Solitaire'
      comment: 'KlondikeGame models the game of Klondike
      solitaire. Its protocols handle interaction behavior
      between the various parts of the game. Instance variables
      stock, talon, tableau, and foundation hold the component
      piles. Piles are responsible for their own behavior,
      including adding and removing cards if valid, and
      rejecting invalid adds and removes, according to the
      rules of the game.'
KlondikeGame methodsFor: 'Public accessing'
newGame
      "Deal a new game by dealing out the tableau piles from a
      new 52-card stock."
setTalonRule: anInteger
      "Set the rule for dealing from the stock to the talon. If
      anInteger is 1, one card at a time is dealt, and the
      game is over when the stock is exhausted. If anInteger is
      3, three cards are dealt, and when the stock is
      exhausted, the talon is turned over to form a new stock."
dealTalon
      "Deal from the stock to the talon. Answer the card(s)
      dealt, or nil if no cards were dealt because the stock
      was exhausted."
tableau: fromInteger toFoundation: toInteger
      "Move the top card from tableau pile fromInteger to
      foundation pile toInteger. Answer true if the move was
      done, false if the move is illegal and could not be done."
tableau: fromInteger toTableau: toInteger
      "Move the face up pile from tableau pile fromInteger to
```

[1] Smalltalk examples in this chapter were done with ParcPlace Smalltalk [sPar92]. C++ examples were done with Borland Turbo C++ [sBor92].

```
        tableau pile toInteger. Answer true if the move was done,
        false if the move is illegal and could not be done."
talonToFoundation: anInteger
        "Move the top card of the talon to foundation pile
        anInteger. Answer true if the move was done, false if the
        move is illegal and could not be done."
talonToTableau: anInteger
        "Move the top card of the talon to tableau pile
        anInteger. Answer true if the move was done, false if the
        move is illegal and could not be done."
turnTableauTopCard: anInteger
        "Turn over the top card of tableau pile anInteger."
tableau
        "Answer the tableau collection. For use by views
        displaying the receiver."
foundation
        "Answer the foundation collection. For use by views
        displaying the receiver."
talon
        "Answer the talon FaceUpPile. For use by views displaying
        the receiver."
stock
        "Answer the stock FaceDownPile. For use by views
        displaying the receiver."
```

To show that this can readily be translated to another language, here is the same information from a C++ header file:

```
// KlondikeGame models the game of Klondike solitaire. Its
// member functions handle interaction behavior between the
// parts of the game. Member variables stock talon, tableau,
// and foundation hold the component piles. talonRule
// specifies which dealing rule is used (1 or 3).

class KlondikeGame {
 public:
   void newGame(); // Deal a new game.
   // Set the number of cards dealt from the talon.
   void setTalonRule(int);
   // Deal from the stock to the talon.
   FaceUpPile* dealTalon();
   // Move top card from a tableau pile to a foundation pile.
   BOOLEAN tableauToFoundation(int, int);
   // Move the face up pile from a tableau pile to another
```

```
        // tableau pile.
    BOOLEAN tableauToTableau(int, int);
    // Move the top card from the talon to a foundation pile.
    BOOLEAN talonToFoundation(int);
    // Move top card from the talon to a tableau pile.
    BOOLEAN talonToTableau(int);
    // Turn over the top card of a tableau pile.
    void turnTableauTopCard(int);
    // Answer the tableau collection. For use by views.
    TableauPile** tableau();
    // Answer the foundation collection. For use by views.
    FoundationPile** foundation();
    // Answer the talon. For use by views.
    FaceUpPile* talon();
    // Answer the stock. For use by views.
    FaceDownPile* stock();
     private:
   FoundationPile **foundation;
   TableauPile **tableau;
   FaceUpPile *talon;
   FaceDownPile *stock;
   int talonRule;
};
```

The point here is not to start writing code for the sake of writing code. The purpose of the simulation model is to verify that the right information has been captured from the problem domain. As it turns out, the structure of the simulation model is often a good base for the "real" architecture of the system. This is not surprising—the qualities of completeness, economy, and elegance that make a good architecture are precisely the qualities of a good conceptual model.

Testing the Model

For running initial tests on the model, I use a very crude form of "user interface." In Smalltalk, objects can implement a `printOn:` method, which presents the object as a string. These `printOn:` methods, used recursively, show the state of complex objects; here is an example, showing how a `FaceUpPile` displays itself and its cards:

```
FaceUpPile>>printOn: aStream
   aStream nextPutAll: 'aFaceUpPile: '.
   self cards do: [
      : eachCard |
      eachCard printOn: aStream].
```

```
Card>>printOn: aStream
    aStream cr; nextPutAll:
        '   ', self value asString, ' of ',
        self suit asString.
```

A sample output from this is

```
aFaceUpPile:
   Ten of hearts
   Ace of spades
   Six of clubs
```

This simple user interface, together with the object inspectors that are part of the Smalltalk environment, allows early testing of the model. Testing involves constructing some objects, sending them messages, and inspecting their state. The same technique can be used in C++. The equivalent of a `printOn:` method is overloading the output stream << operator. Here is an example, for the same classes:

```
// FaceUpPile non-member function--overload of << operator
ostream& operator<<(ostream& os, FaceUpPile& pile)  {
   os << "aFaceUpPile: ";
   for (int i = 0; i < pile.size(); i++)  // Print each card
     os << pile.at(i);
   return os;
}
// Card non-member function--overload of << operator
ostream& operator<<(ostream& os, Card& card)  {
   os << '\n' << "   " << card.value()
              << " of " << card.suit();
   return os;
}
```

In a C++ environment without interactive inspection tools, simple programs such as the following can be developed as test scenarios. (These can also be saved to form the core of a regression testing library.)

```
#include "card.h"
#include "faceup.h"
int main() {
   FaceUpPile pile;
   pile.add(new Card('Ten', 'hearts'));
   pile.add(new Card('Ace', 'spades'));
   pile.add(new Card('Six', 'clubs'));
   cout << pile;
}
```

There is one downside to the method in this example. Coding an executable model is valuable, because it gives both end users and developers a concrete sense of the analysis model, particularly its dynamic aspects. The danger is that the simulation model is coded with a particular tool, and it is hard to avoid biasing the model toward what is easy to do with the tool. To avoid this, dialogue with end users is needed while testing the model. At the very least, an analyst who is not involved in building it should act as an advocate of the end user's position. I have emphasized the concrete things I can present here, such as program code. In real life, user feedback plays just as important a role.

User testing After basic testing of the simulation model is complete, the next step is to go back to the users or domain experts who provided the basis for the model.

Referring back to Figure 5-3 on page 107, an interface designer wants to know two things—whether the user interface provides a clear window into the functionality of the system, and whether the functionality itself is clear. Developers often ask users to look at diagrams such as Figures 5-5 and 5-6, or the output from test programs such as the one described above. Even if we are only interested in the semantics of the information model, this is not enough. To evaluate the clarity of the model, users need to dynamically interact with it, and we are asking too much if we expect them to infer the interaction from a set of diagrams. They need an actual user interface.

Ideally, we would design and prototype something that looks and feels like the interface to the intended system. Here we might like to provide something like Figure 5-7, which is the interface to the Klondike game bundled with Microsoft Windows. An interface such as this, however, may involve thousands of lines of low-level code (even in a high-level language like Smalltalk), not to mention extensive graphic design work. We would like to quickly develop an interface that effectively reveals the structure of the conceptual model, while skimping on elegant (but expensive) features such as high-quality graphics and direct manipulation.[1]

A comprehensible user interface reflects an appropriate model of the application domain. Object-orientation provides a mechanism for accomplishing this, the isomorphism discussed in Section 5-2; Figure 5-8 is an example. The solitaire game composition is presented to users by making the composition structure of the information model (shown in Figure 5-5) directly visible in the interface. Similarly, the behavioral relationships in the class hierarchy of the model (shown in Figure 5-6) can be made visible in the user interface.

The user interface shown in Figure 5-9 took two days to build. It is crude and not intended to mimic the "look and feel" of the ultimate application. It represents the cards with text strings, and the piles as lists.

[1] In some cases, rapid prototyping tools may allow more professional-looking interfaces to be built quickly. Currently, this is not possible for the kind of direct manipulation used in the interface shown in Figure 5-7.

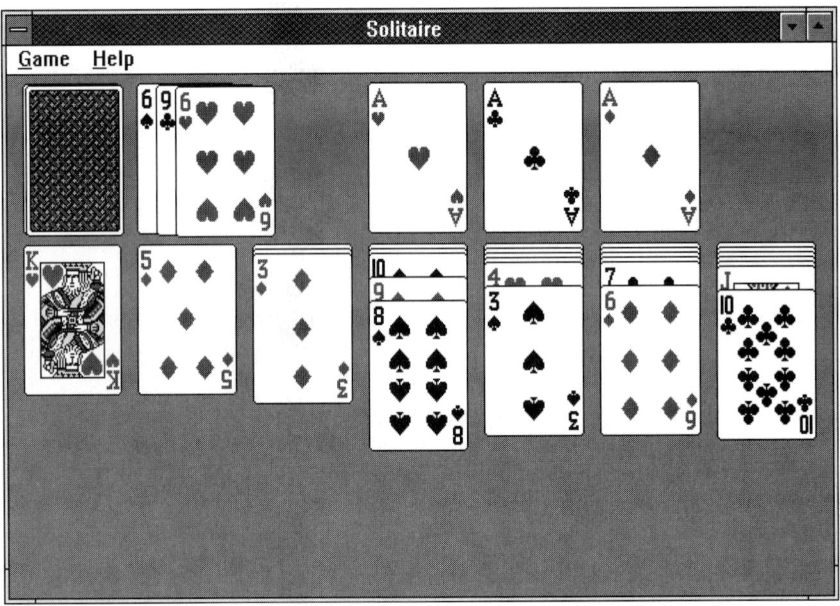

Figure 5-7 Klondike solitaire from Microsoft

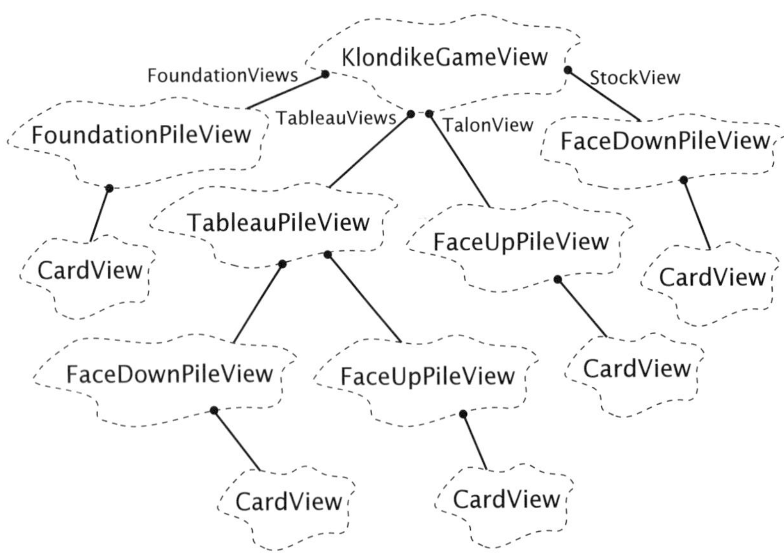

Figure 5-8 Composition of user interface objects for the Klondike game

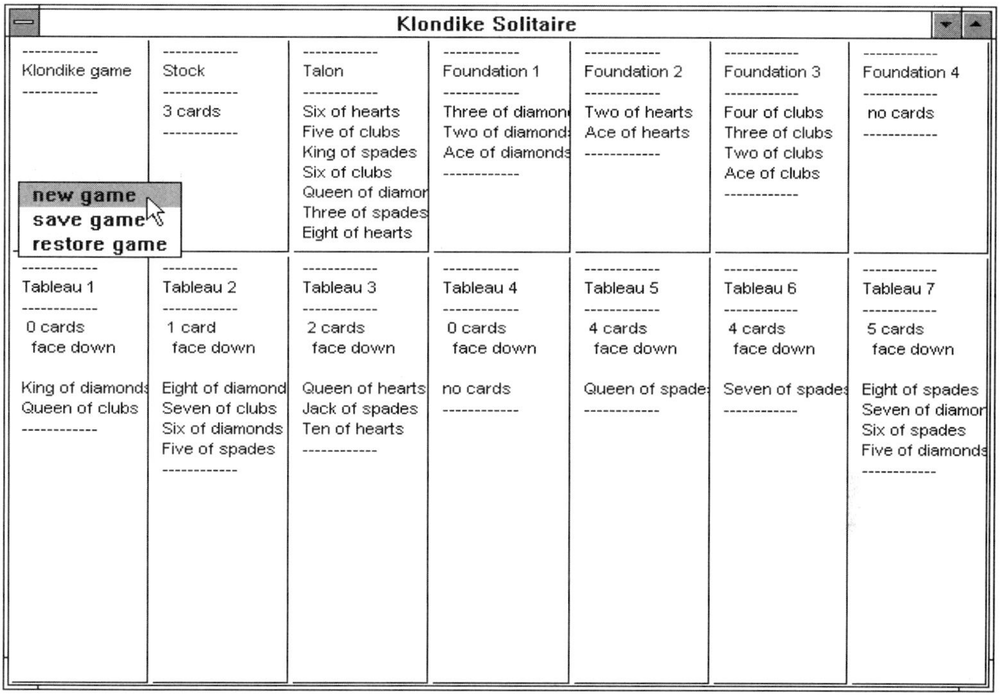

Klondike Solitaire

Klondike game	Stock	Talon	Foundation 1	Foundation 2	Foundation 3	Foundation 4
new game save game restore game	3 cards	Six of hearts Five of clubs King of spades Six of clubs Queen of diamor Three of spades Eight of hearts	Three of diamon Two of diamond Ace of diamonds	Two of hearts Ace of hearts	Four of clubs Three of clubs Two of clubs Ace of clubs	no cards

Tableau 1	Tableau 2	Tableau 3	Tableau 4	Tableau 5	Tableau 6	Tableau 7
0 cards face down	1 card face down	2 cards face down	0 cards face down	4 cards face down	4 cards face down	5 cards face down
King of diamond Queen of clubs	Eight of diamond Seven of clubs Six of diamonds Five of spades	Queen of hearts Jack of spades Ten of hearts	no cards	Queen of spade	Seven of spade	Eight of spades Seven of diamor Six of spades Five of diamonds

Figure 5-9 A simple user interface for testing the simulation model

Some functions are invoked with popup menus, such as the one in the upper left, which presents options for the entire game. In the real game, most actions consist of moving cards from one place to another. Here, users do this by moving the mouse to the pile with the card to be moved, clicking the left button, moving to the target pile, and clicking again. This is nearly as efficient as the interaction technique in Microsoft Klondike, where the mouse is used to drag cards from one pile to another. The main problem with this interface is that the lack of a familiar visual representation makes things more difficult for the player.

In spite of faults, it is adequate for testing the information model. A user can play solitaire with it, and verify that the model of the game is correct (or point out areas where it is incorrect).

The classes in Figure 5-8 reflect the implementation architecture for the interface in Figure 5-9, though not all of them are coded as they would be in the ultimate interface of Figure 5-7. `CardView`, for instance, is simply a text display, and most of the other view classes are implemented using the Smalltalk `ListView` class. The architecture will not change, though, as the implementation is scaled up to be more like Figure 5-7.

At a high level this design would be the same on different platforms, or implemented in different languages. At a lower level, there is considerable variation among different platforms and tools. For example, Figure

5-8 does not show the `Controller` class associated with each `View` class. Controllers handle interaction behavior; though they are associated with Smalltalk, this is not really a language issue. It is one of many variations found in object-oriented class libraries for building user interfaces. A full discussion of the issues raised here is deferred here to Part III, *Internal Design.*

User experience While testing the simulation model for the Klondike game, I was pleasantly surprised by the fact that after a few minutes, I became absorbed in the game and forgot the interface. Another user, an avid solitaire player, also tested it. She quickly learned how to play rapid solitaire (after one game), and seemed to enjoy the games she played.

I take this as a validation of the conceptual model, and of the value of a sound conceptual model in general. The converse of what Reenskaug said (that a bad design cannot be hidden from the user, even by a good user interface) is that a good design shows through, even if the user interface has a few warts. This implies that a definition of the user interface including only the surface artifacts of presentation and interaction is too narrow. Most of the interface action goes on inside the user's head, and that is why the conceptual model (and its reflection in software) is so important.

The cost of modeling this application was low. I spent about an hour with CRC cards, four hours designing and making diagrams, and four days coding (some of which was really iterative design). I needed about four hours to write enough C++ code to convince myself that the design was portable. The "final test," with myself and one other user, took two hours. The value of this work is a good conceptual model, a basic software structure for the information model, and a skeleton for the user interface implementation.

This is a small application, in a well-defined problem domain. Larger problems take more work, but the work can often be done in stages. Typically, information models with many classes can be broken down into loosely connected submodels that can be developed separately. Some classes in a large model play subsidiary roles, and can be left out of a "first cut" prototype. Though prototyping a large model takes more time and effort, the effort returns more value. The conceptual structure of the system has been developed, and will be a guiding vision for subsequent development of a user interface design and a detailed system design.

An interesting sidelight to this little project is a validation of the conclusion of [Mye92] that about 50 percent of code, on average, is devoted to the user interface. The application totals 1124 lines of Smalltalk code, of which 481 (43 percent) are in the user interface portion. These figures are exact because the user interface code is carefully separated from the information model—the public protocols in the Smalltalk and C++ listings above make up the *only* interface between the two components. The information model, at this point, is more complete than the user interface, which I would expect to be about 75 percent of the final application code.

As a result of the separation, development of the user interface and the information model could proceed in parallel from this point, with periodic checkpoints to make sure they are synchronized.

5.4 Summary

Covering up an ill-conceived system structure with a user interface that matches the user's expectations is difficult at best. A user interface must make the connection between the user's goals and actions, and the facilities provided "under the covers" to accomplish the goals. Using OO principles to provide structural similarity, or isomorphism, across system components helps everyone involved; but this structural similarity must be designed in from the beginning.

Some rules of thumb for designers that can be drawn from this chapter are:

- Understandability—of your design, the system, and the user interface—benefits both end users and developers.
- The "core classes" that model the application domain are the basis for designing both the user interface and the underlying system.
- The information model, which embodies the conceptual model of the system, can be rapidly prototyped and validated using object-oriented tools.

5.5 To Explore Further

Information models and view/controller objects are covered in Part III of the book, *Internal Design.*

Using software architectures to separate "content" from "style" in the user interface is a holy grail in the field of HCI research ([Pfa85], [Edm92]). The ITS system [Wie90] is interesting because it implements "style" at two levels. Designers specify styles generically (e.g., by calling for a "one and only one of many" choice to be presented to the user). The generic specification invokes code from a style library that implements a particular platform style. This essentially separates "style semantics" from lower level aspects of look and feel. The classic object-oriented approach to content/style separation is the Smalltalk model-view-controller architecture ([Kras88], [Gol90]).

5.6 Exercises

1. Pick an application you are familiar with, as a user. Word processing and spreadsheets are good examples.

   a. Work out some of the objects in the conceptual model.

   b. Can you find these objects in the user interface? If not, how does it affect your ability to work with the system?

   c. Are there aspects of the underlying implementation that are not part of the conceptual model, but show through to the user interface? If so, how does this affect your ability to work with the system?

   (*For developers*: Do the exercise for an application or system you are working on.)

2. Compare two different computer card games. The Klondike solitaire games on Microsoft Windows and OS/2 are good examples; others depend on the platforms you use. Video game arcades may also be sources of card games. Are there differences in how clearly the "conceptual model" of the game comes across? If you are using different games, pick a common part, such as a deck from which cards can be dealt, and look at its conceptual model.

3. Examine the display in Figure 5-9.

   a. The display of the talon violates the normal convention. How? (If in doubt, consult a rule book or other solitaire players.)

   b. From looking at Figure 5-8, what would you conclude about the source of the problem? (Hint: note that the display of face-up piles in the tableau *is* correct.)

   c. Discuss the pros and cons of fixing the problem by changing only the view classes (Figure 5-8) versus changing the talon in the information model (Figure 5-5).

6

OOUI Design: Process and Team

This chapter is about the people and processes involved in designing object-oriented user interfaces. The processes are imbedded in the larger context of system development, and are affected by how development is done in an organization. As far as possible, this chapter is independent of any particular organizational or process model—it describes activities, skills needed to do them, and how they fit into a variety of software development processes.

Software development is like politics or religion—a subject for strong opinions and vigorous debate, not always based on empirical data. I have tried to base what I say here on observation and analysis of real projects, both successful and unsuccessful. Though success is not guaranteed in this world, certain things seem to be consistently done in successful projects (many of them applicable to "conventional" as well as OO development).

After stating a few modest assumptions about the development process, and defining some terms, this chapter covers three things:

- The activities that occur while designing an OOUI
- The people and skills required for those activities
- Managing them within the constraints of particular process models.

The overall objective is not to assert that a particular kind of development process is required to build OOUIs, but to show how OOUI design works in a broad range of situations.

6.1 Development Process Models

A process model abstracts and organizes the objectives, activities, and products of a generic development project. Such models are important to OOUI designers because they provide context and constraints on the design process. This section informally defines the most important models, and spells out assumptions this book makes about software development processes.

Most process models assume that the process is *phased*. We plan to do something, analyze the requirements, synthesize a design, and then build it; each of these activities is a phase. There may be *iteration*, meaning we anticipate that some things may be done more than once. For example, in a process that permits iteration between design and implementation, one purpose of the early part of the implementation phase may be to find problems in the design. It is anticipated that the design phase will be revisited to correct them. (Another approach to this is a mini-implementation phase, called *prototyping*, that occurs at the end of design.)

There may be *concurrency* between phases, where the timelines for successive phases overlap. Concurrency can be a consequence of iteration; anticipating that each phase may be iterated based on discoveries in the next phase, it makes sense not to declare a phase "finished" until we are well into the next one. Concurrency can also be a consequence of a staged release or evolutionary strategy, where a basic product is developed rapidly and released, in parallel with the development of "add-on" features to be released later.

This book assumes that object-oriented methods are used in development. That does not mean the system will necessarily be implemented using an object-oriented programming language such as C++ or Smalltalk. It does assume that object-oriented analysis, design, and programming techniques will be used, whatever the implementation language.[1]

The Waterfall Model

Figure 6-1 is a view of software development called the "waterfall model" because it assumes that everything goes in one direction. The number of phases, their names, and their exact content may vary depending upon organization and project size. That does not change the characteristics of the model. The general layout of phases in the waterfall model is common to other process models as well.

The lack of overlap and iteration between phases in a waterfall process implies that if the deliverables of each phase (the plan, the analysis, the design, etc.) meet their "exit criteria," they are guaranteed for the life of the project. The model also assumes that knowledge existing at the

[1] Though difficult, it is possible to implement OO designs with non-OO programming languages. See [Dav93] and [Yan88] for examples. Implementing an OOUI in an environment where no other OO techniques are used is almost a contradiction in terms, and is unlikely to succeed.

beginning of the project (about user requirements, technology, etc.) will not change significantly over the life of the project.

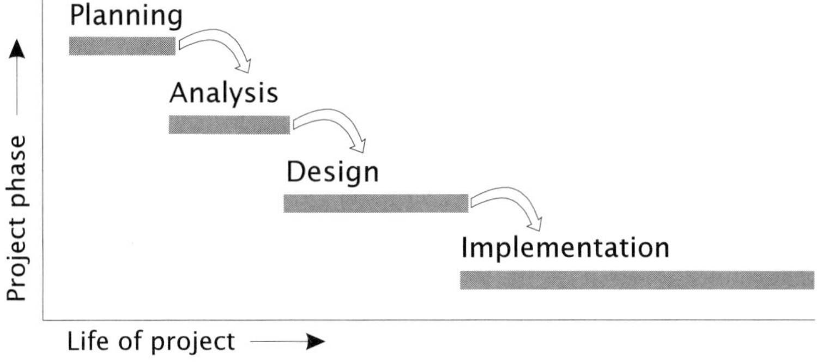

Figure 6-1 Waterfall model of software development

Many people believe that the assumptions of the waterfall model are risky. In most environments, ascertaining that all the relevant data has been collected during planning and analysis is difficult, and the data may change over the life of the project. In fact, the data may change *because of* the project, as users change their goals and tasks in response to new possibilities revealed by the computer system. Another risky assumption is that no significant flaws in the design are found during implementation. Any problems are considered defects, and rework or "bug fixing" is done to correct them. (The danger here is underscored by the fact that in real projects, most of the problems, and the most expensive to fix, are introduced during analysis and design.[1]) Some waterfall processes specify a prototyping phase at the end of design, in an attempt to reduce the risk.

The OOUI design activities described in Section 6.2 can fit within a waterfall process, and may even reduce the risks. Performing user and task analysis within the planning and analysis phases won't protect the project against changes in requirements, but it will enhance the quality of the analysis. Involving end users during the design phase reduces the risk of design errors based on misunderstanding of requirements and other causes. Iteration in a waterfall process must be done within phases and not across phases. (In reality, iteration across phases is often done, but is hidden under "defect removal.")

Spiral, Iterative, and Concurrent Models

Barry Boehm proposed a "spiral process" to manage the risks associated with the waterfall model [Boe88]. Figure 6-2 shows this model. The spiral essentially goes through an entire waterfall development cycle several

[1] This was documented by Boehm in the '70s [Boe76], and subsequent studies (e.g., [Curt88]) confirm the conclusion.

times. Each iteration of the cycle produces a prototype of the system, which helps to assess the risks involved in committing to build the final product. Based on risk assessment, additional iterations may be scheduled. Iterations may address specific risk factors, such as uncertain requirements, performance concerns, etc. The final cycle is a conventional waterfall that delivers the end product.

Spiral development is synergistic with OOUI design activities. If risk factors are associated with the user interface (complex and varied tasks, lack of understanding of users, etc.), one or more iterations can focus on the interface. In any case, the user interface design can be refined in each iteration, in parallel with other activities.

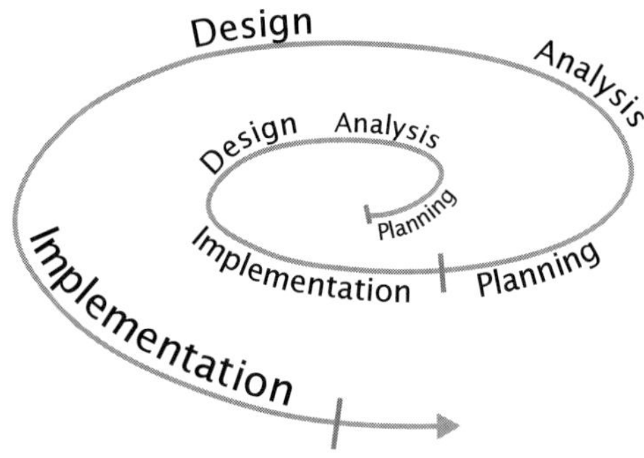

Figure 6-2 A spiral development process

Another approach to managing the risks associated with waterfall development is shown in Figure 6-3. It assumes overlap or concurrency[1] of phases, so that the deliverable from phase n can be validated in phase $n+1$ before phase n ends. It also assumes that iteration can occur; this could result in a spiral, though there is no assumption that all phases will be redone in sequence.

Iteration and concurrency are typical in OOUI design. No one can imagine a user interface, and understand its users, so clearly that there won't be any surprises when the users see it for the first time. Doing activities concurrently avoids getting all the surprises at the end of the design process. Iterating design, implementation, and testing helps to avoid delivering the product with surprises still intact.

Most experts on software development espouse some form of iteration and concurrency,[2] so these assumptions seem safe. A common problem is that though the assumptions are granted at the outset, they later fall by the wayside. Concurrent activities are more difficult to control, and

[1] Concurrency can also be taken to mean running many small processes in parallel, and combining their outputs; see [Aoy93].

[2] See, e.g., [Broo87], [Boe88], [Gil88], [Gou91], [Boo94], [Coc93].

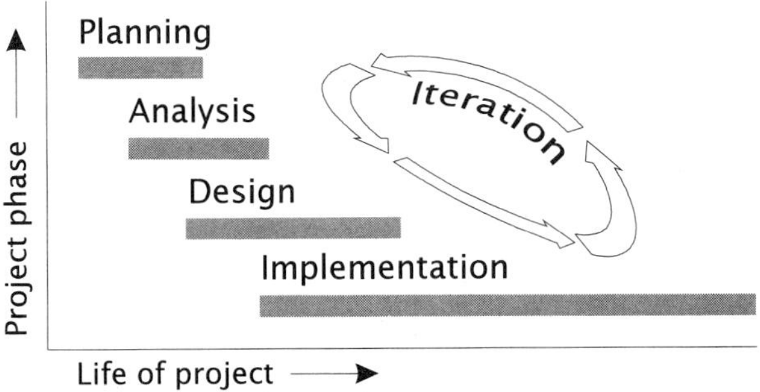

Figure 6-3 A concurrent, iterative development process

iteration implies that some of your time will be spent going "backwards." This combination of apparent lack of control and lack of progress may induce panic in managers who are up against deadlines. Following the design process given in this chapter will help, enabling you to show progress by exhibiting functional prototypes that have been inspected and verified by the system's end users (the solitaire game of Chapter 5 is an example).

Evolutionary development The concurrent and spiral models may include delivering partial products to end users over time, as opposed to delivering a complete, fully functional product all at once. This sometimes happens *ad hoc*, when developers discover that partial delivery is the only way to meet a deadline. An unplanned evolutionary or incremental development process can result in user interfaces where objects and features appear "tacked on" instead of being part of a coherent whole. Once done, this is difficult to undo; end users may resist changes to the interface after they have invested effort in learning it. This underscores the need for a coherent conceptual model of the system, to structure the introduction of new elements.

Models of a single phase Each phase mirrors the activities of an entire project on a smaller scale. The activities of the phase are planned, deliverables from the prior phase are analyzed, and the products of this phase are designed, implemented, and delivered to the next phase. As Booch points out [Boo94], similar structures within and across phases are particularly evident in object-oriented development, because of the common language of objects and classes. Each phase can have its own assumptions and practices regarding iteration and concurrency, which may be different from the assumptions of the process as a whole. Activities within a phase need to be managed, just as does the whole project.

6.2 The OOUI Design Process

Words, sentences, and paragraphs appear on paper in a linear order, one after another. This is not necessarily the form of the things being described. The process of designing OOUIs, like design in general, is a creative process, and solutions emerge from an initially chaotic interplay of thinking and doing, problems and trial solutions. It is difficult to manage groups of people who are engaged in this sort of activity, which may explain why managers often want to linearize it. Anyhow, think of the process as it is done, not as it is written.

Activities in OOUI design fall into three clusters—finding the right conceptual model, making its objects tangible, and evaluating the result. The conceptual model (often loosely called the "metaphor"[1]) is a set of concepts in terms of which users can easily understand the application and its interface. Sometimes this is straightforward, as in the solitaire application of Chapter 5. Sometimes it is less simple, as in the "desktop metaphor." Sometimes it is very difficult, where there are no established conceptual models to draw on. The "metaphor," once found, is a perfectly definite thing: a collection of objects, actions on objects, and relations between objects.

The second cluster of activities makes the objects in the conceptual model tangible. This includes designing the presentation language—how objects are presented, visually or otherwise—and the action language—how the user interacts with them. The third major cluster is testing and evaluating the results of the first two. Evaluation can go on concurrently, based on rough sketches, verbal descriptions, or simple prototypes. More formal testing and evaluation are done when the design is complete.

Design Process Activities

Figure 6-4 shows the flow of the activities that make up these clusters, and how they are interrelated.[2] The arrows in the background indicate that they may be iterated several times during the design process. Each activity in OOUI design is covered in detail in subsequent chapters, and summarized here.

Analysis of users and tasks is done to understand the users of the interface and the work they do. In the development of a commercial product, the early part of this activity may tie in with market research done to decide who could benefit from the proposed product. In systems for use within the company doing the development, user and task analysis help to establish the scope of the project.

[1] "The essence of metaphor is understanding and experiencing one kind of thing in terms of another" ([Lak80], p. 5). Usage of the terms "metaphor" and "conceptual model" will be clarified in Chapter 8.

[2] "Object-oriented analysis" in the figure is part of the analysis phase for the entire project, and not directly part of OOUI design. It is included in the figure because of its close ties to user and task analysis.

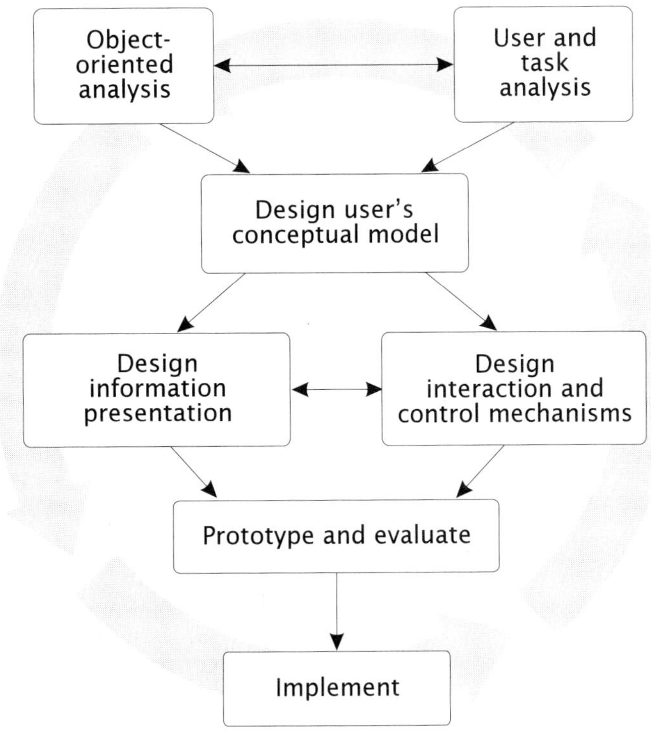

Figure 6-4 Activities in the OOUI design process

Users need to be understood along the dimensions described in Chapter 2—physiological, sensory/motor, cognitive and cultural; factors as varied as the physical size and educational background of users will influence the design of the user interface. Tasks, in an object-oriented context, are analyzed to understand how the objects of the problem domain are used. This is helpful in the design of the whole system, as well as the user interface.

Task analysis may look like extra work for overburdened analysts and designers. However, most object-oriented methodologies already use similar methods. Jacobson's object-oriented software engineering (OOSE) method [Jac92] includes *use cases*, sequences of actions that define the specific ways in which users use the system. Booch [Boo94] also recommends use case analysis. The object modeling technique (OMT) [Rum91] uses *scenarios*, which are similar to use cases, to drive the modeling of system dynamics. Wirfs-Brock and colleagues [Wir90] advocate scenarios as a tool for discovering object responsibilities. Object behavior analysis (OBA) [Rub92] uses *scripts*, which are formal descriptions of "use scenarios." All these methods collect and use information on user tasks. The results of task analysis are thus shared resources for the entire development process.[1]

This is also the place to develop measurable usability objectives. These are specific, quantified targets for things like time to learn the system, time to perform each task, acceptable error rates, interactive response time, etc. Depending on the type of development being done, these objectives will be based on some combination of user requirements, how good the competition is, and what the designers think is possible. The basis for objectives should be well-documented, so that other members of the development team understand their importance. Where possible, objectives should be related to specific usage scenarios.

User analysis, task analysis, and usage scenarios are covered in Chapter 7, *Users, Tasks, and Task Analysis.*

Designing the user's conceptual model is the key activity in object-oriented user interface design. The first activity feeds this one, and the conceptual model will strongly guide subsequent activities. I recommend not starting this activity until user and task analysis are well underway. Conceptual models are powerful tools, and adopting one prematurely can bias the activity of collecting information about users and what they do.

Many OO development teams see this activity as something that goes beyond the user interface. The conceptual model ties the results of analysis together, and its software embodiment is the core of the system implementation. Chapter 8, *The User's Conceptual Model*, presents the details of this activity, and clarifies terms such as "metaphor." Chapter 8 will also explain why I say "designing" rather than "discovering" the conceptual model.

The next two activities, designing the presentation and action languages, may occur partly in parallel with this. Doing a trial design of presentation and interaction is a way of evaluating the conceptual model, and may suggest changes to it. Working out how to present the objects and actions in the application domain may even suggest an entirely new metaphor.

Designing the information presentation This is the design of the object representations, or views, that make up the presentation language. Views are designed along with mechanisms that allow the user to interact with the displayed information, and Figure 6-4 shows this activity proceeding in parallel with the design of interaction and control mechanisms.

If these two activities are normally done in parallel, and by the same people, why not merge them? The separation reflects the separability of the "feel" of the user interface from its "look." It may be valuable to design several different looks and feels, and choose the best combination. This may even be a requirement, when disparate groups of users require different presentation and interaction mechanisms for the same information

[1] Some CASE tools support use cases or scenarios, e.g., Objectory [Jac92] and HOMSuite [sHat94].

objects. For example, people with vision problems may need special information presentations; people with different motor skills (including children and the elderly) may need different ways of interacting.

Some applications have large amounts of media "content" which is designed and produced separately from the information display "form." Examples are information retrieval systems and multimedia applications with significant video and sound content. Sometimes, as in generalized retrieval systems, the user interface is independent of the content. In many multimedia applications the user interface may be content-specific, and it is important that the design of presentation and control mechanisms be integrated with the development of the content.[1]

A similar situation occurs in the development of online user help, manuals, and training materials for any application or system. The design of these ancillary products must be integrated with the design of the system itself. (Some people argue that manuals and online help are part of the user interface to a system, which suggests even more strongly that their design must be integrated with user interface design.)

Chapter 9, *Information Presentation*, covers the activity of designing information displays.

Interaction and control mechanisms This is the design of the action language. It is quite possible to design a variety of interaction techniques for the same information presentation—typing commands, function keys, pointing at objects and menus with a mouse, voice commands, etc. The development of user interface "feels" is currently not nearly as rich as the "looks" of modern GUIs, so this activity offers the development team an opportunity to differentiate their product. Though many features of the presentation and action languages are independent, there are many dependencies as well, which is why their design normally occurs in parallel. This activity is covered in Chapter 10, *Interaction and Control Mechanisms*.

Some developers think of "user interface design" as simply the design of information presentation and interaction. This is prevalent in older design methods based on functional decomposition, where there is no clear externalized conceptual model; it also appears in "widget driven" design methods for GUIs. The solitaire game, the desktop metaphor, and many other examples show that a good conceptual model guides the design of look and feel and provides coherence to the user interface that is hard to obtain otherwise. As a result, design of the look and feel of the interface should not start until the conceptual model has been at least sketched out.

Prototyping, evaluation, and iteration Some design processes end with documents specifying the system. Users inspecting these documents must try to do two things—first, to generate an image of what the system will look like, and second, to evaluate the image against what they want. The

[1] For multimedia applications, this issue is addressed in [Marks95].

second step, for users who understand the tasks to be done with the system, is easy. The first step, almost by definition, is difficult—if it were easy, why would highly paid professionals be employed to design systems? In practice, users cannot do this very well, and the result is the familiar syndrome of "well, yes, I signed off on the design, but I didn't know it would look like *that!*" Prototyping allows them to focus on step two, and to provide the designers with valuable feedback *before* extensive resources have been committed to implementation.

Chapter 5 illustrates using a prototype to test the information model. Testing the basic software architecture of the system is a strong argument in favor of doing the prototype, even when time is short. This depends, of course, on building the prototype using either the target implementation language, or a language that can support the same class and object structures. In the worst case, if the prototype becomes the product, it is likely to be more extensible and maintainable.

Chapters 9 and 10 discuss issues in using prototypes as documentation of the design. Prototyping tools are discussed in Chapter 14, *Tools for Prototyping and Implementation.*

Evaluation and iteration occur at many levels in the design process. At first, it is an individual designer looking at part of the design to see whether it can be improved. Later, other designers may be called upon for opinions. Eventually, the users of the proposed system should evaluate the design.

Early in the design process, evaluation should be informal and non-judgemental, since generating ideas is the priority. Later, as the design gets closer to completion, evaluation can become more methodical and critical. Likewise at the beginning of the process, the artifacts to be evaluated should be informal—rough sketches or partially implemented prototypes that can be easily discarded or changed. Later, more faithful prototypes can be implemented.

Figure 6-5 shows two areas where a lot of iteration typically occurs. After analyzing users and tasks and beginning to work on the conceptual model, iterating between the two activities results in a better model and a better understanding of tasks. After developing an adequate conceptual model, the focus shifts to making the objects tangible—designing the look and feel of the interface. Iteration then takes place between design and prototyping. Several competing approaches may be tried, to see which is best. Results of the design-prototype iteration may reveal problems with the conceptual model, in which case the first pair of activities is reiterated. The figure emphasizes that users of the system are at the center of these activities.

Besides ongoing evaluations, a formal evaluation should be done at the end of the design process, with the usability objectives (developed in user and task analysis) as criteria. If the objectives are not met, either they must be revised, or the design process needs to be reiterated. If the information model prototype has been validated by the developers who will be

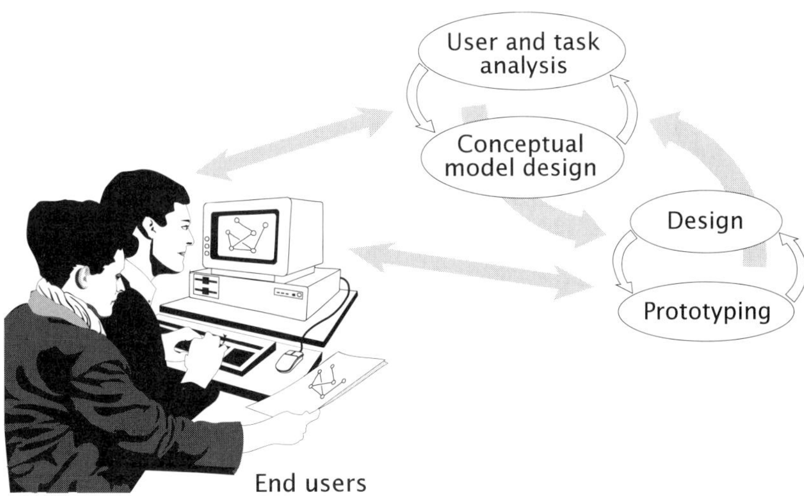

Figure 6-5 Iterative, user-centered design

implementing it, you now have a good sense of the feasibility of the implementation.

These activities may seem familiar if you have been involved in user interface design before; they could be components of any interface design process. The specifics are different, of course, for OOUI designs. Task analysis emphasizes the objects that are acted on instead of the procedures in which the objects appear. Designers of object-oriented user interfaces pay more attention to the conceptual model; prototyping the information model as a way of validating the conceptual model is also novel. The differences mainly extend existing user interface design philosophies, and should be welcome additions to a designer's tool kit.

Role of the OOUI Design Team in Development

The value of weaving user interface design into the fabric of the larger development process, instead of considering it a separate activity, is better quality at lower cost. Better quality comes not only from a better user interface, but from the contribution that user interface specialists can make to the process of gathering and analyzing requirements. Lower cost comes from sharing data between user interface design and the design of other aspects of the system. Enhancing the possibility of sharing is an argument in favor of object-oriented design, since objects provide a common language for diverse activities.

Figure 6-6 shows how the activities of OOUI design fit into the development life cycle. This is a rough sketch, which will vary based on development process model, the size of the project, and preferences of individual organizations. In a strict waterfall model, for instance, "User and task analysis" may have to be arbitrarily split into a part in the

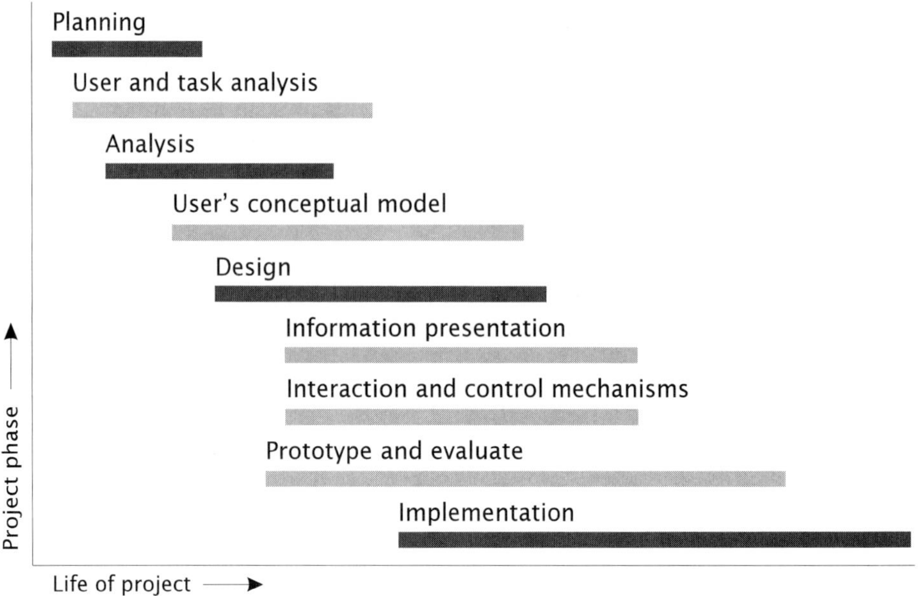

Figure 6-6 OOUI design activities in context

planning phase, a part that occurs during analysis, and a part that occurs during design.

Planning usually precedes development proper, to establish the scope of the project and identify the users. Planners begin the job of analyzing users and tasks to decide what the proposed system should do.

A complaint I frequently hear from end users, and one that is well documented [Cha82], is that computer systems are not task-oriented. That is, they appear to have been designed as collections of features and functions by developers who did not understand the tasks for which they would be used. Part of the problem is that system features are specified based on planning processes that do not have enough data. High-level market analyses, requirements aggregated from many customers, and conversations with managers who are not close to the work are often the basis for deciding the scope of systems.

The data available to planners can be improved by involving human factors engineers from the user interface design team. Well-designed surveys, on-site interviews, focus groups, etc., will repay their cost with higher product quality. The activity of user and task analysis should begin in this phase, to avoid making decisions that later make it more difficult to do a good design. The user interface team should also focus on communication and education during the planning phase. Establishing rapport with other developers, and making them familiar with the activities involved in designing the user interface, will pay dividends later.

Analysis The work of the user interface team in the analysis phase has two aspects. The first is continuing the work of analyzing users and tasks that was begun in the planning phase. This work will provide input to later user interface design activities. The second aspect is joint work with developers who are building the analysis model that will drive system design. The analysis model is a structure of classes, along with diagrams and text explaining their dynamic interactions. It should support all the scenarios implied by the system requirements.

Usage scenarios based on task analysis are helpful in building and validating the analysis model, and for constructing meaningful test cases for the system. Developing scenarios through collaboration between the user interface team and the analysis team has many benefits. The analysts get a better product for less of their own work. Interface designers avoid duplicating the efforts of analysts and insure that their design is driven by the same model that drives system design. As mentioned on page 129, task-driven usage scenarios are synergistic with many popular OO analysis and design methodologies.

The analysis model itself should be structurally similar to the user's conceptual model of the system. If not, it is much easier to iron out differences at this point than later, when users discover the mismatch. The process of resolving differences will result in a better analysis model and a better design model for the user interface.

Design At the point of entering the design phase, a task model based on usage scenarios should already be in place, and the analysis model for system design should reflect a concern for users' tasks and conceptual models. Development of the user's conceptual model may be well underway at this point, in which case designing presentation and interaction mechanisms can begin.

As in analysis, collaboration with system designers is important. The realization of the analysis model and the realization of the user's conceptual model need to be coordinated. To validate the design, a common prototyping effort for the information model will benefit both teams. If prototyping is done by programmers or designers who will be involved in the implementation, it provides continuity between phases, and between the user interface and other parts of the system. The prototype can become a "living specification" for verifying conformance to functional requirements and usability objectives as the project evolves.

User interface designers are sometimes brought on board only after the design phase begins, and they are expected to hand off a complete design when it ends. Norm Cox, a graphic designer who worked on the Xerox Star, calls this "putting lipstick on the bulldog"—it reflects the belief that a good interface can hide all the system's warts. Unfortunately for the users of these systems, it cannot. In one sense this simplifies things; all user interface activities occur in sequence within a single phase, and little coordination is required. But no designer with integrity enjoys being in this situation.

Application Domain Expertise

Knowledge of the domain for which a system or application is being developed is an obvious and important skill, to be applied at many points through the design of the user interface. It is needed while analyzing users and the nature of their tasks, and on an ongoing basis as the design evolves and is evaluated.

The best way of accessing task-oriented knowledge of the application domain is to find potential users of the system who are willing to be part of the design process. In an accounting domain, for example, an accountant can define problems to be solved, answer questions, and evaluate proposed designs. Involving end users does not mean that they design the interface. Computer interface design requires specialized skills, and we would not be employed if users could do it themselves.[1]

Consultants who know the domain can also help, particularly in educating members of the development team on what the application is. At least one member of the team, typically an analyst, should become an expert in the domain (unless you find a user willing to sign on for the duration of the project). This person will act as the user's ombudsman throughout development of the interface. For help in understanding the relevant characteristics of the user population and the environment, trained human factors people are invaluable. They will notice things that other developers won't.

There are well-known cases in the computer industry where a lone developer, or a small group, seems to have come up with a brilliant and successful idea without involving users. On closer inspection, we find that they did the things suggested here, though perhaps in an informal way. A case in point is perhaps the most innovative and successful user interface idea in the history of computing, the spreadsheet. Dan Bricklin, who conceived the idea that led to VisiCalc, had a rare combination of talents.[2] An accomplished programmer, he was also a graduate student at the Harvard Business School, and thus an expert in the problem domain. Besides using his own knowledge, he discussed issues with other students and professors who did financial analysis. Though the success of VisiCalc depended on clever design and programming by Bricklin and Bob Frankston, the brilliance of the basic idea came from Bricklin's experience in the problem domain.

Object-Oriented Design and Programming

It is often desirable to prototype aspects of the interface look and feel without worrying about the ultimate implementation. On the other hand, it may be helpful to develop a prototype of the information model, and to give the system implementors a sense of how the user interface software

[1] Users often do make significant contributions; my point here is that, as professional designers, we should be able to do better than what users can envision.

[2] The history of the spreadsheet and VisiCalc are described in [Lam86], pp. 131–150, and [Lic89].

should be developed. Doing these things requires someone who is a talented object-oriented designer.

Someone who can do this is usually an object-oriented programmer with additional skills in user interface design and implementation. Such a person is invaluable in the rapid generation of prototypes. Typically the individual will be a professional programmer or software engineer. I have seen many cases, however, where nonprogrammers in the field of user interface design have developed the skills to do the job themselves. In one case, a human factors engineer with a background in psychology went back to school and obtained a Master's degree in computer science for this purpose.

There is an important side benefit of having a programmer on the user interface design team. Convincing other developers of the value of user interface features is much easier if the design team can give them a sense of how the features are to be implemented. Having someone on the team who speaks the language of programming makes this possible. It also helps the user interface design team to assess both the costs and benefits of implementing a feature before proposing it.

Human Factors

Human factors engineers are experts in the scientific and engineering aspects of the human side of interfaces between people and machines. They apply knowledge from psychology, physiology, etc., to improve the efficiency and comfort of user interfaces. I also include knowledge of sociology, social psychology, and anthropology under the umbrella of human factors. This kind of knowledge is useful for studying users and tasks, especially where tasks require collaboration between groups of users. No matter how motivated the average developer, it is hard to substitute for specialized training in human factors and related social science disciplines.

The discipline of human factors contributes to all phases of OOUI design. Findings from cognitive psychology (discussed in Chapters 4 and 8) are useful in developing and validating conceptual models. The design of interaction (the action language) has been researched for many years, and there is a large body of useful (and underutilized) results. Knowledge of the human factors of perception is also important, as an adjunct to the design of graphics and other visual media used in the interface.

Graphic and Media Design

A medium (plural media) is an entity that transmits something (in this context, information), often transforming it in the process. Media design is the process of choosing media (graphics, text, video, etc.) to convey information, and laying out the information for efficient presentation. All these media can be part of a user interface, so appropriate skills are needed to design their content. Today that most often means graphic design skills (for the layout of text and graphic elements on the flat surface of a computer display). Other media, such as video, may be important as well.

Professional graphic and other media designers have talents developed through years of training and experience. These are artistic talents, and not something we should expect to find in a typical group of software designers or programmers. Particularly for commercially marketed products, these skills are critical to the success of a user interface. As interfaces become more graphical, the lack of graphic design becomes more obvious. As the number of products multiplies, making a good first impression on potential users becomes more important. The talents of graphic designers and other media experts go beyond "first impressions," however. Well-designed media presentations express things in a way that is clear and simple, not just aesthetically pleasing.

Even the most graphical user interfaces often have lots of text, in messages, help panels, and tutorials. When presenting a rich information model, clarity is essential; it follows that professional writers should be employed for the writing task, not designers or programmers. This does not absolve designers of the task of integrating writing (and other media presentations) into the design of the total system.

What if you don't have all the required skills? You may not have people with all these skills on the development team, though I assume your organization at least recognizes the need for them.

Except for highly innovative research projects, application domain expertise always exists somewhere. Users or potential users of your system are often happy to supply their knowledge, especially for internal projects (where users and developers work for the same company). Some persuasion may be necessary to convince their managers that their time is being well spent. This is usually not hard; it is often more difficult to convince the project manager that developers should be "distracted" from designing and programming to talk to users. A solid plan for designing the user interface is a good vehicle for persuading managers that investing resources in design will save rework later, and produce a quality product faster.[1]

In any project using OO development methods, object-oriented design and programming skills are available. The problem is typically to convince the project manager that the skills should be applied to user interface design and prototyping. One tactic for doing this is the quality argument—that several iterations of good prototypes will result in a significantly better design, and fewer problems requiring rework later. The other argument is that prototyping the information model and the user interface implementation will benefit other parts of the project. This argument is particularly strong if prototyping can be done in the system implementation language.

Many large companies have human factors engineers within research

[1] [Gou88] has a number of practical suggestions for getting user feedback on design ideas without a large investment.

or development organizations. They are often in short supply, and function more as consultants than as full members of the team. If your company does not have human factors people on the staff, outside consultants can be employed. It is generally not feasible to employ these consultants full time, so they need to be integrated into the team. Points in the process where human factors knowledge is particularly valuable were discussed above. Consultants can be involved at those points, with a full-time team member coordinating their work.

A similar situation exists with respect to graphic and media designers. Large organizations may have full-time graphic designers; smaller organizations may need to hire design consultants. Again, a team member should be given the responsibility for coordinating the graphic design aspects of the project and effectively using graphic design consultants. Similar considerations apply to integrating other media design activities, for instance, video design and production for a multimedia application.

6.4 Managing the OOUI Design Process

Figure 6-7 is another view of the concurrent development process of Figure 6-3. Overlapping parts of phases are in lighter gray. These areas are just that—"gray areas." Compare the waterfall process of Figure 6-1, where only one thing is happening at a time. Object-oriented design in general fosters processes with gray areas. Though more likely to be successful, according to their proponents, they are more challenging to manage.

Part of the difficulty is illusory; in a project staffed by competent people, managers usually need less control than they think they do. Part of the difficulty is real, and is a factor that drives managers toward the apparent simplicity of the waterfall process. Demonstrating that you can control the progress of the iterative and concurrent set of OOUI design activities will help in selling them to project managers.

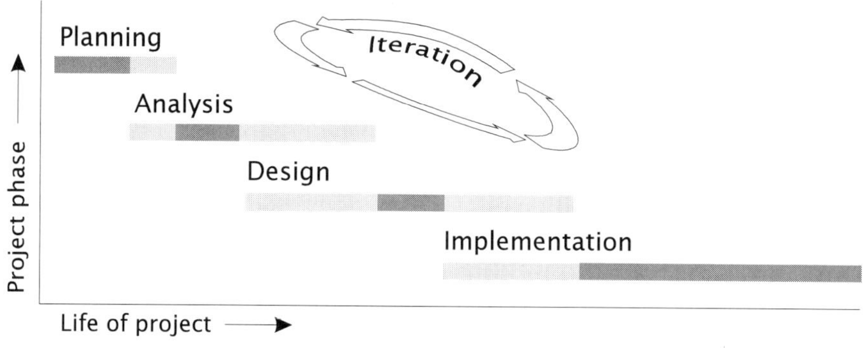

Figure 6-7 Areas of uncertainty in a concurrent, iterative process

Style Guides

Style guides, typically provided by platform vendors, contain guidelines, instructions, and examples for creating the "look and feel" appropriate to the platform. Style guides are described in more detail in Chapter 10, but they are also relevant here because of their potential as tools for management.

In principle, style guides can help manage the quality of applications. They promise standard, consistent presentation and interaction styles based on following rules. This should reduce the need for prototyping, iteration, and testing. In practice, the promise is only partially fulfilled. Style guides can reduce the need for design decisions about the surface elements of look and feel, but designers need education and experience to interpret the rules correctly.

It is important that all developers understand the ground rules for using style guides. Issues need to be resolved as early as possible in the life of the project. Making the user interface design team into a "style police force" is guaranteed to arouse hostility among other developers. Programmers are especially liable to resent the imposition of rules without guidance on how to implement them.

One task of a programmer on the user interface design team is to help develop tools to support the style guide. An alternative is to convince the project manager to designate a development programmer as the "style guru." This should not be a hard sale, if the manager is already convinced of the need for the style guide. Object-oriented programming techniques allow style rules to be abstracted and encapsulated as reusable classes. This helps implementors and simplifies prototyping.

Prototyping

Prototyping, though it is recommended by many authors and assumed in most development process models, still generates controversy. Even where deadline panic is not a factor, there is disagreement on the value of prototyping to explore and evaluate design alternatives.

A variety of things are called prototypes, from rough sketches of displays, to running simulations involving tens or hundreds of thousands of lines of code. Taking as the defining characteristic the existence of at least some running code, the arguments go as follows.[1]

Prototyping is *good*, because

- Prototypes allow users to evaluate something that looks enough like the real thing to provide meaningful feedback.
- Prototyping exposes errors in requirements analysis and design early in the development cycle.

[1] The section on prototyping in [Agr86] confirms this summary of what I have observed over a twenty-year period.

- Prototypes document the design more faithfully than a paper specification.
- Prototypes provide a visible focal point for discussions about requirements and design, for developers and project managers as well as users.

Prototyping is *bad*, because

- Realistic prototypes of complex user interfaces require large amounts of coding, which takes resources away from building the product.
- Prototyping is an excuse for not doing a careful job of requirements analysis and design.
- Prototypes do not differentiate between essential features of the design, and accidental features introduced by the prototyping tool.
- Prototypes are misleading. Managers and end users, because they do not understand what is involved in development, will see a prototype and believe that the project is much closer to completion than it really is.

There is some truth to both sets of statements. Certainly, users can give better feedback after seeing a prototype.[1] Anyone who has been through a couple of projects from start to finish knows that errors in interpreting requirements are more glaring when the user sees an implementation. Prototypes do document some design features better than specifications, and they do provide a focal point for meaningful discussion. I have seen designers argue for weeks over features that could have been prototyped and evaluated directly in a couple of days. On the other hand, I have seen all the problems that people cite to show that prototyping is harmful.

Prototyping must be managed to be successful. A prototype is an experiment. A designer should have an idea of what questions it will answer before beginning, and be able to explain the purpose of the experiment to management or customers. The right amount of prototyping, and the right tools, vary from project to project. Following a few guidelines will help to optimize the process, and keep managers and customers happy.

Have a plan (however informal) for what the prototype will accomplish, and use the cheapest method available. In the early stages of design, when ideas are fluid, rough sketches may be better than high-fidelity prototypes. Usability objectives will help to select areas that need more thorough testing. Write down factors that support prototyping; frequently changing requirements, for example, may suggest that a prototype would help users to explore the problem domain.

[1] Chapter 36 of [Tog92] works through a case study in which prototyping was essential to get the level of feedback needed to make an informed design decision.

Make a conscious decision, as early as possible, about whether the final product will be delivered in increments. If incremental or evolutionary development is planned, each step in the evolution can start as a prototype.

Do not use prototypes as the sole documentation for a design. Too many things are left out (such as performance requirements) and too many things creep in accidentally (such as artifacts of the prototyping tool that are not part of the design).

Other things being equal, a prototype has more value if its implementation is close to that of the real system. Complex interaction techniques, for example, require complex coding on typical GUI platforms. Reusing code, or at least design, in the implementation phase reduces the cost of user interface features. Do not assume that using the system implementation language will always be more difficult. I have found that many interaction techniques are *easier* to prototype in Smalltalk or C++ than in higher level tools, because high-level tools often trade off power for ease of programming.

Other things are not always equal, particularly cost. Gould ([Gou85], [Gou88]) points out many inexpensive ways of getting feedback on designs. Putting up design sketches or simple prototypes in public areas, with a log book for comments, will elicit valuable ideas. Technical writers on the project can use the instruction manual as a "prototype"—manuals are often unclear because the system design is hard to understand. Brainstorming within the development team can produce ideas for low-cost prototypes, besides making developers feel more involved in the process.

Managing Iteration

Iteration is important in user interface design. When it is done privately, say by a group of developers iterating design sketches on a whiteboard, it doesn't raise any eyebrows. When it becomes a public part of the development process, questions are raised by project and product managers—"Why can't you do it right the first time?" "How many times will it take to get it right?"

For iteration to be successful and cost effective, two conditions are necessary. The trial design must be close enough to the target design when iteration starts, and the iteration must converge toward a better design at a reasonable rate of speed and cost. "Reasonable" depends on the context. More time and money would be spent on iteration in a groundbreaking research project than in the development of a system for a well-understood domain such as accounting or word processing.

The converse of these conditions leads to uncontrolled iteration. Skimping on "up front" design work is often excused by saying "don't worry, we're going to iterate until we get it right." This may be an inefficient way of getting to the right design, or may prevent the process from getting there at all. Cycling through iterations without making any overall improvement is also possible. These problems waste time and money, and make development managers reluctant to commit resources to further iteration.

Figure 6-8 is a portrait of the ideal iterative process. There is an optimum solution somewhere in the space of possible designs, and a succession of prototypes spirals in on it. Good management of iteration insures that an approximation to the ideal really exists by monitoring the process to keep it on track, moving through each iteration cycle in the least practical time and cost, and avoiding unproductive iteration.

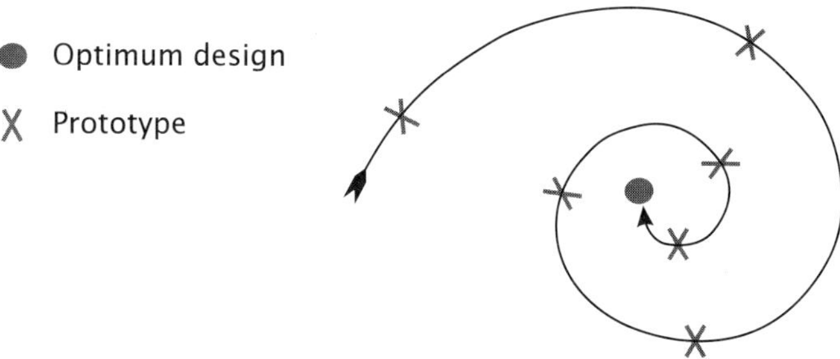

Figure 6-8 Idealized view of iterative design

Figure 6-8 implies that there is a single optimum design for the user interface. In reality, there may be many "locally optimal" designs. For some combination of system features, a given user interface design may be optimal; for another combination, a different user interface may be best. If functions or objects are added, removed, or reorganized, the optimum may change. Figure 6-9 illustrates the problem this can cause. Iteration may converge to a design that is not "best" overall, or may wander unproductively and not converge at all.

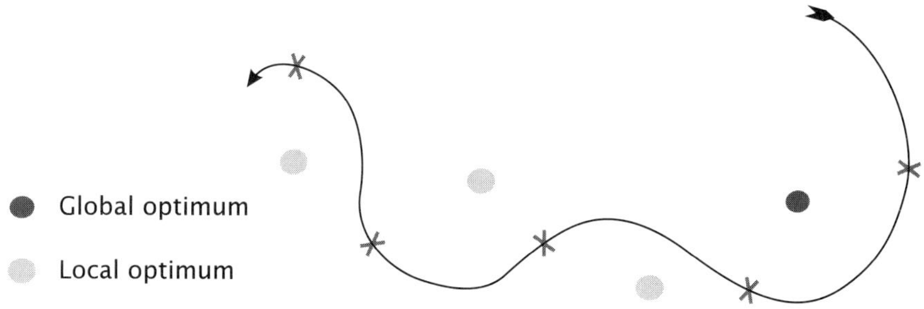

Figure 6-9 Iteration around multiple optimal designs

A prime cause of wandering iteration is not having a good conceptual model of the system. This forces users and developers to evaluate designs in a haphazard way, by looking at the goodness of individual "look and feel" features and trying to synthesize a comprehensive figure of merit. A design that presents a clear conceptual model will stand out, because it organizes all the features into a coherent whole.

It is quite possible, though, that situations will arise where more than one interface needs to be provided, or where users should be given facilities for tailoring the interface. If the system has several different types of users, for example, there may a different "best interface design" for each type. Doing a good job of analyzing users and tasks will provide the information needed to detect this situation.

Figure 6-10 shows another potential problem with iteration. Designs circle the optimum without clear improvement. Nothing is more frustrating to a manager than spending time and money on iteration, only to discover that no one can agree on whether the new solution is better or worse than the old one! A common cause for this is the lack of a definition of "goodness." Without objectives for evaluating the interface, judgements may rely on subjective opinions rather than facts. You may even be as close to the optimum as necessary with *all* the prototype designs and not know it. Developing measurable objectives is the best way to avoid this problem.

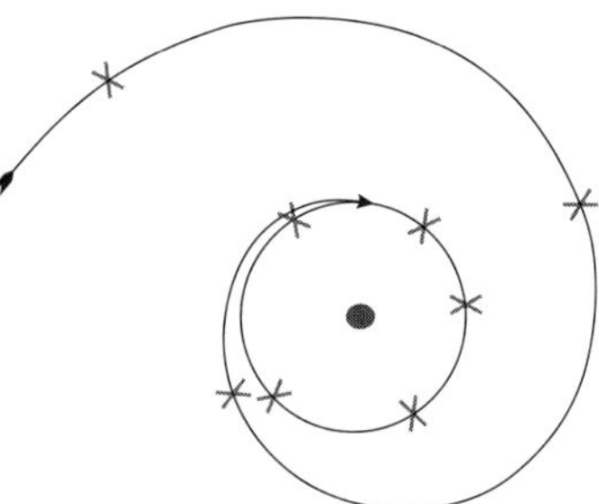

Figure 6-10 Iteration fails to converge

Managers with a technical understanding of OOUIs can do a better job of managing iteration. Designers may disagree about how much iteration is enough, or what defines success. Lacking managers with technical understanding, the loudest voice often wins the argument. Managing OOUI development successfully involves "managing down" to get the interface design done, and "managing up," to show that the process is under control and will converge to a successful outcome.

6.5 Summary

The activities in the OOUI design process are

1. Finding the right conceptual model:
    - Analysis of users and tasks
    - Designing the user's conceptual model
2. Making the objects tangible:
    - Designing the information display
    - Designing control mechanisms
3. Testing and iteration:
    - Prototyping
    - Evaluation and iteration

The details of these activities vary depending on the application, the size of the project, and the way in which the activities are imbedded in the larger process of system development.

OOUI design is a team process, because it requires many different skills. Well-functioning teams need an appropriate culture, leadership, and motivated individual members. Necessary skills include:

- Application domain knowledge
- OO design and programming
- Human factors
- Graphic and media design.

Some key rules of thumb for managing OOUI design processes are:

- OOUI design fits most development process models. Commitment to quality and rapport between all the members of the development team are critical success factors.
- Get involved as early as possible in the process, and be prepared to educate other developers on the value you can add to the product.
- Prototyping and iteration are important for good user interfaces, but they must be managed—to secure credibility with upper management, and to optimize the process.

Acknowledgments

The design process described in this chapter is based on a methodology developed in 1976 by staff members from the Xerox Palo Alto Research Center and the Xerox Systems Development Division, led by Charles Irby ([Irb77], [Smi82], [Irb89]). Many ideas they used, such as task analysis, were already well established in the practice of human factors engineering. Others, such as conceptual models based on objects and actions, emerged from other work going in at Xerox PARC ([Smi75], [Car88], [Kay93]). The document that resulted from their work, however, was the first codified set of procedures for systematically designing an object-oriented user interface. It was subsequently used for designing the Star user interface. Though other work has extended some points of the methodology, their framework has stood the test of time, and I have used it without much alteration.

The model-view-controller architecture [Gol90] developed for Smalltalk-80 was a second major influence on my thinking. The three elements of MVC correspond to the conceptual model, information presentation, and control mechanisms in the Xerox user interface design methodology, and to the conceptual model, presentation language, and action language in Bennett's model of the user interface [Ben83]. Chamond Liu started me thinking about this in 1989, by pointing out the similarity between the MVC triad and the elements of Bennett's model.

6.6 To Explore Further

The technical content of the activities described in this chapter is covered in more detail in later chapters. The general characteristics of the methodology described here were first articulated by Charles Irby and colleagues, as described above; [Smi82] is the most accessible source of further information.

This book does not cover many topics under the rubric of *usability engineering* that are important to software product and process quality. These include usability objectives, user testing, and other activities generic to any user interface development process. Many good sources of information on usability engineering exist.

[Ben84b] and [Nie92b] present frameworks for incorporating usability engineering principles into the development process. Usability objectives are covered in [Whi88], which is specifically about usability, and [Gil88], which covers objectives for system attributes in general. [Gou88] and [Rubin84] are particularly good sources if you are motivated to improve the usability of your software, but don't have human factors experts who can help.

[Shn92] provides general information and techniques for usability, examples, and pointers to other literature. It includes a "lifecycle for interactive-systems development" which is a useful checklist to use against your process. [Hel88] is a massive compendium of modern thinking on all aspects of user interface design and the human factors of HCI. [Tog92] supplies practical advice, entertainingly presented, for user interface designers. Chapters 11-14 and 34-36 address process issues. [Nie94] has a wealth of ideas on evaluating usability and effectively using the results of evaluations within software development organizations.

There is a large body of literature on the software development process; [Agr86] is a good place to start. *IEEE Software* 10, 5 (September 1993) is a special issue on "lessons learned" from software engineering practice. It contains assessments of many aspects of modern development. Much of the software engineering literature implicitly assumes that tools and techniques either have solved, or will solve, problems such as low productivity and excessive error rates. [Curt88], based on extensive interviews with project teams, argues that human behavior is the dominant factor in the success or failure of software projects. [Boe81] is a major effort to derive development models from empirical data collected in many projects.

There is also literature from the software engineering community specifically dealing with iteration, concurrency, prototyping, and evolutionary delivery. [Gil88] and [Boe88] are good starting points. [Ala84] is an empirical assessment of prototyping, and worthwhile despite having been done more than ten years ago; it is one of several papers on prototyping reprinted in [Agr86]. [Gou88] discusses these same issues from the perspective of designing for good usability.

Many books on object-oriented software technology, such as [Jac92] and [Boo94], discuss the development process specifically for OO systems. [Love93] is mainly devoted to OO development process issues.

A major frustration for user interface designers is the general lack of understanding of "common sense" principles for developing systems with usable interfaces. Gould and Lewis [Gou85] confirm this, but also offer some useful advice that may help you to improve the level of understanding within your development organization.

Lack of teamwork is a problem that confronts many development organizations. It often stems from misunderstandings and conflicts between people in the different disciplines involved in user interface design (programming, graphic design, human factors, etc.). Scott Kim [Kim90] provides an excellent description of the problem, along with advice on how to solve it.

6.7 Exercises

1. If you are familiar with the details of at least one successful, and at least one unsuccessful, project with a large graphical user interface component, compare them using the following criteria:
   - Skills used to design the user interface.
   - Relationship of user interface design to the development process as a whole.
   - Amount of iteration and concurrency in the user interface design process.
   - How prototyping was done.

- Interpersonal dynamics within the development team.

If you are not familiar with any projects, read [Smi82] for an account of one that is generally judged a success. Failures are seldom written up as case studies, though they can be just as valuable for learning.

2. Pick an application you frequently use, such as a word processor, program development environment, etc. Develop three or four usability objectives for it. (Example objectives might be "a new user should be able to learn to write and print a letter within an hour," "a programmer should be able to change a source statement in an existing program and recompile the program within three minutes," etc.) Could you convince a development manager that satisfaction of these objectives is important to the success of the product?

3. Ask someone from a different discipline how he or she would solve a typical problem, and then explain to him or her how you would solve that particular problem (for example, if you are a programmer ask a graphic designer, or *vice versa*). Do you find that you and your colleague have different ways of thinking about problems? Would differences in strategies be complementary if you were working on different aspects of the same problem? ([Kim90] has other exercises of this sort.)

4. (This is based on a technique presented in [Lim92].) Pick a development process model that you are familiar with, and a set of activities associated with user interface design (for instance, the activities described in this chapter). (*For developers*: Try this on the process you use in your work.)

   a. Draw a table, with columns labeled by development process phases and rows labeled by interface design activities. Place an "x" at intersections where a design activity takes place in a given phase.

   b. Revise the results of (a) by replacing "x" with a difficulty level, indicating how easy or hard it is to do the activity within the phase. Base this on your experience, if possible. (In a classroom situation, students can compare and discuss their results.) You can use a scale of "easy-moderate-difficult," or a numeric scale such as "1 (very easy)–10 (very hard)."

   c. For at least one activity you rated "hard" in (b), assess whether you think it is difficult because of the nature of the activity, or because of the process phase in which it occurs. What could you change to make it easier?

7

Users, Tasks, and Task Analysis

So far we have covered foundations and context for OOUI design. Chapters 1–4 presented ideas and definitions that underlie OOUI design methods. The example application in Chapter 5 showed the breadth and depth of OOUI design. Chapter 6 summarized skills and activities in OOUI design and showed how they fit into the software development process. This chapter begins the detailed exposition of activities in the design process.

Analysis of users and tasks is the first step in designing the externally visible aspects of the user interface. Chapter 8 explains how the results of task analysis become part of the user's conceptual model of the system, the first of the "three domains" of Chapter 5. Chapters 9 and 10 cover the design of the "look and feel" of the interface, the second of the three domains. Part III of the book covers the third domain, internal design and implementation.

Customers have many reasons for purchasing software or contracting its development. Price, availability, feature lists, and superficial appearance are all factors. The fundamental driver of system requirements, though, is work that needs to be done. In the long run, the success of a system or application is decided by how well it helps users with their tasks.

A task is a meaningful unit of work, a unit within a person's activities. Whereas the aim of the analysis phase of development is to define *what* services the system must provide, the objective of task analysis is to *organize and sequence* these services to support end user tasks. Analysis and task analysis use much of the same data; task analysis is particularly synergistic with several well-known methodologies for object-oriented analysis and design.

This chapter fills out the method used in Chapter 3 with more details on the following:

- Understanding users, tasks, and work environments.
- Analyzing and documenting tasks.
- An object-oriented perspective on tasks, including the idea of tasks themselves as objects.
- The use of task analysis data in OOUI design.

The last topic, using analysis data in design, begins here and continues in Chapter 8. Here and in Chapter 8 the grain of analysis is at the level of what users would call tasks and subtasks. Chapter 10 covers tasks at a finer grain, the level of individual actions such as keystrokes and mouse clicks.

An important attribute of "seamlessness" in applications is that when an object or function is needed for the task in progress, it is "right there." Successful software developers recognize this. An advertisement for Microsoft *Office*[1] reads: "It understands how you work . . . It performs your routine tasks for you so you can focus on your data . . . And our IntelliSense™ technology recognizes what you want to do and helps you do it." The key to achieving a seamless flow, and making good on promises like these, is to understand your end users' tasks.

7.1 Why Task Analysis?

No explicit task analysis was presented in the solitaire game example of Chapter 5. Not much analysis was needed, because the "obvious" user interface design simply mimics the real-world game, and presents all the objects and services of the application in a single window. Anything the user needs to access is readily at hand. In larger applications, failing to explicitly consider and understand user tasks can cause problems.

Take, for example, the user interface for a bank's automated teller machine (ATM). The tasks done by a typical customer, such as depositing and withdrawing money, are simple. Overall, the structure may be simpler than the solitaire game. Because an ATM interface has a limited ability to present information, however, more care is needed to insure that it presents what the user needs.

Suppose monitoring an ATM shows that nearly every customer who makes a withdrawal also makes a balance inquiry immediately afterwards. This could happen because the transaction record for the withdrawal does not print out the new balance. This annoys customers, particularly if (as with many ATMs) they have to initiate a new transaction and rekey their personal identification numbers (PINs) to obtain the account balance. The

[1] *Time*, November 1, 1993, pp. 38–39.

problem is that the customer's definition of the task "make a withdrawal" includes the step "verify the new account balance"; the system's definition of the task does not. A task or unit of work is relative to the customer or user, so this is a failure in task analysis.

Desktop publishing applications usually support defining "style templates" separate from the text and graphics in documents. Templates specify things like paragraph styles, type sizes for headings, and the location and numbering of footnotes. The application I am using to write this book supports the task of creating a formatted document with the following steps:

- Create a template document with layout and style information.
- Open an existing text document.
- Apply the template layout to the text document.

I create a single template representing the chapter format, and apply it to every chapter's text file. I would like to open the text file, then point to an existing template document to be applied.[1] But I must first open the template, though I am not creating or modifying it. This is a minor problem; in complex applications such as this, however, it is often the sum of minor problems that causes overall dissatisfaction.

One more example shows how, in some situations, object-orientation facilitates task orientation. In many electronic mail systems, users compose notes on personal computers, then upload them to the e-mail system. For a user, "upload the note file" is a step in the task "send a note." The system views these as disjoint tasks, and requires the user to invoke the file transfer program, upload the file, exit the file transfer program, and invoke the mail program to send the note.

This kind of problem is common, and hard to avoid, on systems where tasks are accomplished by invoking a series of programs. Frequent tasks can sometimes be automated using macros or command scripts, but this adds the burden of remembering additional command names and parameters. An object-oriented system could provide a single view of a logical file system incorporating both host and PC files. The user could then identify the note file and transfer it (by command entry or direct manipulation) to an "out mail box" representing the e-mail function.

The converse of this problem can also occur, and will be discussed later in the chapter. A task that can be readily automated using a command script in a "functional" system may require execution of many steps in a system with an OOUI. This is not a defect in the OO approach; it is a failure in task analysis.

When task analysis is done well, the result is often delightful. Testing programs in C++ is complicated, since a program is composed of many

[1] As often happens, supporting the task in a different way also suggests ideas for the user interface; in this case, dragging a template icon and dropping it on the icon representing the text document.

files, and the programmer must construct a "make" file describing all the interrelationships between them. This is a tedious and error-prone job. When I first started using a graphical "workbench" environment for C++, I found that I could simply select a file and apply the action "run" to it. The environment would analyze the dependencies between files, recompile and relink whatever was necessary, and run the program. The job was much easier, because the system understood the task in my terms.

Failure to efficiently support users' tasks is a common problem. Typical symptoms are users hunting around in menus and rummaging through help text, saying "I know I ought to be able to do that at this point, but I can't figure out how"; writing down information on scraps of paper, or retyping information from one part of the system into another; constantly moving between windows, or rearranging windows to get through a task. You can probably find many examples—from your own experience, by talking to users of complex applications, and by reading product reviews in the computer trade press.

Solving these problems is not simple. Significant applications have many users, with different backgrounds and expectations. Besides obvious differences, such as language, education, and physical capabilities, users may have different styles of working, leading to different definitions of what appear to be the same tasks. Accommodating this heterogeneity starts with understanding it, which is the subject of the next section.

7.2 Users and Their Tasks

In talking about what makes technology successful, Chapter 2 proposed that it is necessary to understand the characteristics of the end users, the tasks they will use the technology for, and the environments where they work. The first step is to know who the users of your system will be. This may be easy or difficult, depending on the system. You may be developing a very specific application for a single client, or a general-purpose package for a broad market. In either case, the more you know about your users, the better.

Understanding Users

Developers often underestimate both the similarities and the differences among users. When asked why users were not involved in designing a user interface, a designer responded "what's the point—ask ten different users, you'll get ten different answers." But when asked how he knew an interface was easy to use, the same designer said "well, it's easy for me," implicitly assuming that it was therefore easy for everyone.

Users *do* differ, in all the dimensions described in Chapter 2—physical and physiological, sensory/motor, cognitive, and cultural. They have different levels of expertise in the problem domain, and in their knowledge of system functions. They may use the system every day, or once a month. Their use of the system may be optional, or it may be a critical part of their job.

Individual differences can be large. Even on simple text editing tasks, the performance of individual users (for various reasons) may differ by nearly an order of magnitude [Ega88]. The good news is that interface designers who are aware of these differences can minimize their effects. More robust interfaces, interfaces that are adaptable or customizable by users, online help for common problems, and well-designed tutorials can compensate for many differences. For example, an experiment was performed using a database query system [Ega88]. The original interface used SQL,[1] and user performance varied by a 2:1 ratio; the difference was correlated with logical aptitude. By changing the interface so that the query logic could be specified by selecting examples from tables, the formerly poor performers did nearly as well as the "expert" users.

Details vary, but the first step is to understand the differences among potential users. This process can start early in development, though some differences may not show up until testing is done with a user interface prototype. The second step is to try to understand *why* the differences exist, and the third step is to develop design alternatives to handle them. Even if you decide not to address the differences, knowledge of their impact will allow you to gauge the effect of this decision. The bottom line on differences is that a user who cannot perform tasks successfully using a system is a user who will not buy it, or a user who will remain unsatisfied.

International users Production of computer software for use outside the country in which it is developed is steadily increasing. Many large US software companies earn the majority of their revenues outside the US—for Microsoft, for instance, the figure is 60 percent and increasing [Russ93]. Countries such as India ([Nid93], [Pres93]) are emerging as providers of software written for use in Europe and America. As the world becomes more open, the success of more products will depend on acceptability in several countries. Even within a single country, you may have to consider use by people of different cultures. In New York City, for example, there are significant minority populations for whom English is a second language. Many bank ATMs offer users a choice of English and other languages, such as Spanish and Chinese.

Experts recommend a two-step process to develop software for international users [Russ93]. The first step, *internationalization*, separates elements, such as messages in a particular language, that are unique to one environment. This step requires a knowledge of user characteristics in all the target countries, since it may involve diverse cultural issues as well as languages. The second step, developing *localized* versions, requires a knowledge of the users for whom the particular version is being devel-

[1] Structured Query Language, a commonly used language for expressing the logic of a query.

oped. Again, language is the most obvious but not the only issue. As a couple of examples, cultural norms may determine icon symbolism, and local laws may affect functional aspects of applications.

Users with disabilities The heading is somewhat misleading, since it implies that there is a sharp distinction between the "able bodied" and the "disabled." We all have abilities and disabilities. One of the promises of computer technology is that it can compensate for disabilities, and allow everyone to use their abilities. As I write this, I am wearing glasses; without them I could not read the text on my screen. If I lost the glasses, however, I could adjust the size of the displayed text to make it large enough to read without them. This is typical of the sort of accommodation a modern interface can make.

Disabilities are generally classified as visual, auditory, mobility, and cognitive. Many people are considered disabled (about 43 million in the US [Fil93]), so there is a high probability that someone with a disability may need to use any system you develop.[1] Employers may encounter laws or regulations requiring them to provide accommodations for disabilities (for instance, the "Americans with Disabilities Act" in the US). Currently, "adaptive technology" is an add-on to existing applications, so providing designed-in accommodations can be valuable to customers for your products. Most accommodations are made in the presentation and interaction components of the user interface.

Technology can erase individual differences. Before the industrial revolution, a worker's output varied tremendously based on physical strength and stamina. Today, for most jobs, this is no longer an issue. Machines amplify or replace human muscle power.

Computers can amplify the power of the human mind and senses as well. Disabled users are one example; they can usually function at the same level of productivity as "normal" users, when provided with suitable technology.[2] There are other examples of applications, in areas as diverse as mathematics and publishing, that allow novices to perform at levels formerly accessible only by experts, and experts to perform at levels that were never possible before. Using computers in ways that augment the powers of humans[3] is the key to productivity for everyone.

Contextual Analysis

Besides understanding users and tasks, we need to understand the environment in which tasks are done. These factors are not neatly separable. Imagine doing a task, say cooking a dish for a meal. In some sense the task can be separated out, as a recipe in a cookbook. But what you probably

[1] Nearly 10 percent of all males have some form of color blindness, for example. Children and senior citizens, though not classified as "disabled," may need similar accommodations.

[2] See [Brow92], [Fil93].

[3] Recall Doug Engelbart's concept of human augmentation [Eng73], discussed in Chapter 2.

imagine is a gestalt composed of the cookbook procedure, your own skills and feelings about the task, and the kitchen in which you work. The cookbook recipe leaves out all kinds of critical factors such as interruptions by small children, how easy it is to locate ingredients, and the idiosyncratic behavior of your stove.

Factors like these are just as important in the tasks people do with computers. As an example, LeMaster and Herz [Lem90] provide a case study of task analysis for an expert system that helps loaders generate plans for stacking cargo into trucks. By observing and talking to workers, they found that expert loaders take pride and pleasure in the challenge of designing loading plans. They were able to design a user interface that took this factor into account; it helped novice loaders perform more like experts, but did not take away the experts' feeling of being in control of the task.[1] The satisfaction derived from expertise, and the help that newer workers get from experts, are important contextual factors in most work environments, but they will not be found in official job descriptions.

Designing a system's user interface based on large amounts of context-free task data is risky. I hear (and have observed) many stories of systems that work well in some environments, but not in others. Analysis after the fact usually turns up factors that could have been discovered in advance. So I recommend analyzing in context, at least to validate, if not collect, data about users, tasks, and environments.

Contextual analysis has been used extensively for product development at the Digital Equipment Corporation, as reported by Wixon and colleagues [Wix90]. They recommend the following steps[2] for understanding user requirements and tasks:

1. Interview and observe users in the work environment. Choose users strategically to represent the diversity of the user population.
2. Be concrete; talk about what the users are doing. Let the users lead the conversation, but ask questions, probe their assumptions, and feed back your understanding of what they have said.
3. Summarize your understanding of users, tasks, and environment; let the users critique it.
4. Based on your understanding, design and build prototypes. Have the users test these, preferably in the work environment. Iterate if necessary.

There are cases, such as international products, where contextual analysis is difficult. At the very least, consultants from each target area can validate task analysis and user interface design. It often happens that contextual analysis is difficult because users are remote from developers, which usually means that developers do not know much about them.

[1] [Zub88] reports many cases where this sort of contextual analysis was not done, leading to loss of job satisfaction after computers were introduced.

[2] I have summarized and paraphrased these from [Wix90].

These are exactly the situations where contextual analysis provides the greatest benefit.

7.3 Task Analysis and Task Synthesis

Tasks can be defined in two ways. From a conceptual or "top-down" point of view, a task is a meaningful unit of work, intended to satisfy some goal. From a procedural or "bottom-up" point of view, it is a sequence of actions on objects. Both perspectives are important in designing user interfaces.

Designers work with two sets of tasks. One makes up the users' current work, and is the subject matter for *task analysis.* The second set, produced by designers through *task synthesis,* will create a new work environment after the system or application under development is completed.

Task Analysis

Task analysis describes current tasks, and extracts information that will help in reengineering them for the new system environment. The analysis output is used for task synthesis—developing task descriptions for the new system. Analysis of current tasks should focus on goals, because the task steps may be based on existing technology that will be replaced.

The top-down and bottom-up perspectives are not either-or. While analyzing tasks top-down, awareness of task steps helps in understanding goals and identifying objects involved in the task. While analyzing task performance bottom-up with the new system, keep the user's goals and the overall flow of tasks in mind. The analysis of the calculator interface in Chapter 3 illustrated the point that an efficient interface at one level may not be efficient in serving higher level goals. These goals might be served best by reorganizing or eliminating lower level tasks.

As an example of these ideas, consider the development of a computer system to replace the manual card catalog in a library.[1] Bottom-up analysis of existing tasks is misleading. They involve objects, such as cards in the catalog, that are artifacts of the existing technology. We can put these objects in perspective by thinking in terms of the users' goals, for example, "locate all the books about user interface design." On the other hand, we do not want to ignore the current system. We may need objects in the new system that capture the semantics of catalog cards. So, although tasks should be described in terms of goals and the essential abstractions of the problem domain, the description should also correlate these items to the objects and actions of the task as it is currently done.

We could go even further, and say that library books themselves are artifacts of technology (the printing press). The task goal might then be "find all available information about user interface design," which would

[1]This example was inspired by one in [John85].

open up possibilities such as an "all digital" library. The test for this sort of exercise is its appeal to the end users and the project sponsors. In most cases today, physical books are fundamental objects in the domain of library systems. I suggest raising the level of abstraction until it becomes clear that you are no longer in the domain of the original problem, then backing off one level. This leads to an open-ended design, and may suggest new capabilities for the system (for example, providing access to online information as well as books in the library).

Synergy with OO analysis methods Most object-oriented methodologies incorporate methods similar to task analysis for collecting analysis data. Exploiting the synergy between task analysis and OO analysis methods can reduce the total cost and effort. Because of this, the method of documenting tasks presented here should be taken as a sample. Develop a single method for documenting tasks by merging it with your chosen method for documenting object-oriented use cases or scenarios.[1]

Task Synthesis

Task analysis and other analysis activities provide several outputs:

- Requirements for the system or application being developed.
- An analysis model of objects, classes, and services that are necessary to meet the system requirements.
- Descriptions of tasks done in the current environment, their goals and interrelationships, and the objects and actions involved. Objects and actions are described in terms of the current environment, and in terms of how they map to the objects and services of the system analysis model.

The first two outputs are standard parts of any object-oriented analysis phase. The third output is described in more detail in the next section, *Documenting Task Analysis*. All three help to build a model of how users will employ the new system to do their work.

In general, the way the work breaks down into tasks will be different in the new environment. Some tasks now done by users will disappear, new tasks will be added, and tasks that remain will be done differently. Thus part of building a model of the new system is *task synthesis*—describing tasks, their goals and interrelationships, and what objects and actions they involve in the new environment.

Building a model of how users will operate in the new environment is the subject of Chapter 8, *The User's Conceptual Model*. The model has two components. The first is the *system model*, which is based on the system analysis model along with metaphors that help users to understand it. The

[1] This was discussed in Chapter 6 under *Design Process Activities* (in Section 6.2). If you are not currently using use cases or an equivalent method, look at [Jac92], Chapter 7, and [Rub92] to understand the rationale for use case or scenario-driven analysis.

second component is the *task model*, which is the result of task synthesis. These models will guide the design of the presentation and interaction components of the user interface, which translate the abstract objects and actions of the conceptual model into the concrete details of how users see and interact with objects.

The design is validated by comparing the results of task synthesis to the descriptions of tasks in the current environment. Every goal in the original task set should either be satisfied by some new task, or clearly be no longer needed. The new tasks are then analyzed procedurally (as in Chapter 3) to verify that the steps involved are efficient, and accomplish the desired result. Subsequently, they become test cases for verifying that the system satisfies functional requirements and usability objectives. Finally, since the task descriptions reflect the way end users work, they are the basis for instruction manuals and tutorials.

Collaborative Tasks

Most approaches to task analysis implicitly assume that tasks are done by a single user, or at least that a single user is the primary agent in accomplishing a task. In the real world, people do most of their work in collaboration with other people, and we may need to account for this in modeling tasks.

There are two categories that cover most situations. In *sequential collaboration*, a task is done by multiple users working one at a time on an object or components of an object. Production on an assembly line is an example, as well as insurance claim processing, order processing, and many other "paper processing" tasks. In *parallel collaboration*, a task is done by multiple users working simultaneously on an object. Many creative tasks fit this model; imagine several designers working in a room with a whiteboard, all sketching parts of a system diagram on the board simultaneously.

Sequential collaboration tasks are well understood in most businesses, and they are described using workflow networks. Managing these tasks requires knowing what conditions must exist for a task to start, what new tasks can start when a task has finished, and how to detect violation of rules or constraints, for instance that a task must be finished by a certain date. The next section deals with documenting these tasks. Section 7.5, *Tasks as Objects*, discusses situations where it is convenient or necessary to model tasks and associated rules and events as objects in the system.

Cooperative parallel tasks are more difficult to manage, and more difficult to support with computers. Many current examples are research prototypes, such as document editors permitting concurrent editing in real time by multiple users [Ell91]. Designers often rework these tasks to be "pseudo-parallel." This can be done by breaking task objects into subobjects that can be worked on separately and then combined, or by locking and unlocking task objects to serialize access.

Viable commercial products for cooperative parallel tasks are starting to emerge for applications such as desktop conferencing [sFuj93] and sharing of "virtual notebooks" [sFor93]. Since collaboration is a feature of tasks in the real world, it is important not to "analyze it away" simply because technology is not currently available to implement it. Collaboration requirements should be recorded in task analysis, even if you decide not to support them in the design.

Unstructured and Content-Driven Work

Many systems and applications are "task driven." The user has definite goals that motivate the use of the system, and the satisfaction of the goals entails a step-by-step process of use. Many computer games also fall into this category.

The applications that Bennett classified as "decision support" do not directly lend themselves to this approach. As discussed in Chapter 2, they are driven by objects and the services or operations the objects provide. So in a sense, the task *steps* are given in advance, though the order in which they are performed is not. The user has some goal in mind, perhaps very general, and when the goal is achieved, we can retrospectively describe the task steps that led to it.

Unstructured tasks should not be overanalyzed. The ability to explore and try different things is usually important to users. The focus of analysis should be on what capabilities are required, and on minimizing constraints on the ordering of task steps. Where task steps will change object states, users may benefit from the capability of undoing the changes, or of making a temporary "working" copy of the object to operate on, if undo is not possible.

There is another class of application in which *content* is the essential driver, and it is difficult to see any "task" that can be broken down into steps. Works of literature and films are examples of this—what is the task of the reader of a Hemingway novel, or the viewer of a Fellini film? The same issue arises in education. In cases where a student is learning a specific practical discipline, such as a computer programming language, task analysis is helpful in structuring the training. In a course on art history or abstract mathematics, it may not be.

Many current multimedia applications, particularly in education and entertainment, fall into the content-driven category. Certain aspects of these, such as the design of presentation and interaction components, have much in common with OOUIs. The overall structure of the application and its content, however, draws more from art, literature, or film directing than from the techniques described in this book. For these applications, "integrative design" [Marks95], based on content, must be used in addition to, or instead of, task analysis.

7.4 Documenting Task Analysis

Figure 7-1 shows a useful format for documenting the relationship between users and tasks. The application in this example is a word processor; rows identify tasks done by users, and columns identify different types of users for the product. In theory, there could be a third dimension to this table, to classify the environments in which the tasks are done. It is often simpler, where the same type of user may operate in different environments, to create new user categories—for example, "Office typist" and "Plant floor typist."

	Typist	Secretary	Author or technical writer	Business professional
Create letter	often	often	sometimes	sometimes
Create multichapter document	never	never	often	never
Create report	never	sometimes	often	often
Create style template	never	sometimes	sometimes	never
Insert graphics in text	never	sometimes	often	often
Insert table in text	sometimes	sometimes	sometimes	often
Format type font/size	sometimes	sometimes	often	sometimes
Print document	often	often	often	often
Revise document text	often	often	often	often
Revise document format	sometimes	sometimes	often	sometimes

Figure 7-1 Task/user table, with frequency of tasks

The table cells in the figure show how often each type of user performs a given task. The cells could also contain task goals for this type of user, usability objectives (elapsed time for the task, anticipated frequency of errors, etc.), or other information.

Versions of the table can be made both for the current environment and the new system. A spreadsheet application is a good tool for maintaining them. Most spreadsheets have additional functions that may be useful, such as the ability to summarize, print reports, maintain multiple dimensions of information for each cell, etc. You will undoubtedly want more information than the sample shows, but it will vary depending on the size and complexity of the system, and the number of different types of users.

Documentation on users is always a good idea. The information needed is variable, but might include:

- Job description for each user type, including other tasks that are related to the functions provided by the new system.
- Characteristics of the job environment that affect task performance. For example, the fact that secretaries are frequently interrupted and interleave several tasks may be significant.
- Other systems used by users that may condition their expectations.
- Characteristics such as education, physical skills and disabilities, etc., that affect the user's ability to use the interface.

For custom development, the client's personnel department often provides information on users. For general products, there may be market analysis data developed during the planning phase. While this data is valuable, it is often insufficient. Contextual analysis, described earlier, is the best way to supplement or validate the existing data.

You will certainly want a full description of the tasks listed in the table. A task description should contain the following information:

- *Preconditions* for the task, expressed as constraints on the state of the objects involved. For example, for the task "revise document text," the document must already exist.
- *Goals* of the task. These can be described in terms of object states, such as "produce a letter containing the text dictated to the secretary." Relate goals to higher-level goals and processes, particularly in the description of current tasks; for instance, "the company tries to respond to customer complaints in writing within 24 hours."
- *Breakdowns*, situations where the flow of the current task is awkward, or some goal cannot be satisfied due to current limitations. Breakdowns are opportunities for improvement in the new system.
- *Postconditions* of the task. These include object states resulting from the task that are not directly relevant to the goal. For instance, assigning document ownership to the creator may be a postcondition of "create letter," though not an explicit part of the goal.
- *Agents*,[1] the people directly involved in the task. An agent designates a user in a particular role, such as "typist." Agents are distinguished from users because the same user may be more than one kind of agent. For example, a bank teller might also be a customer of the bank.
- *Objects* involved in the task. In the analysis of current tasks, describe

[1] Other terms may be used for agent, such as "actor" [Jac92] or "participant" [Rub92].

existing task artifacts, such as "subject card from the card catalog." Artifacts should also be described abstractly: "carries subject classification of the book it describes." This separates the object's semantics from its implementation in the current system.[1]

- *Steps* in doing the task. These should be specified in terms of actions on the task objects. Some steps may be subtasks common to several tasks. For example, "select a block of text in the document" is common to many word processing tasks. Common subtasks can be described separately and referred to when needed.
- *Critical features* of the task.[2] These are aspects of the task that are fundamentally important. For example, in the library system the task "update card catalog" may not exist in the new system, because the equivalent function is done automatically by the system. But the underlying idea, that indexing information must be updated when the library's holdings change, needs to be preserved. Critical features may include breakdowns, key objects, required actions, and procedures that reflect business rules or legal requirements.

To be as clear as possible, use a vocabulary of names for objects, actions, and other items in task descriptions that is consistent among all the descriptions, and consistent with other project documentation. A glossary or data dictionary is needed for any sizeable project.[3] Task descriptions are not "once and for all" documents; expect to revise the descriptions as your understanding of the application domain improves.

This format also works for unstructured tasks, such as exploratory data analysis in decision support applications. Some task steps may need to be described as independent subtasks with no particular ordering. For example, suppose an analyst is looking at a set of data points. The initial step might be to look at the points as a scatter plot. The next step might be to look at a histogram, linear fit to the points, exponential fit to the points, etc., depending on the analyst's intuition from looking at the scatter plot. A task description should make this clear, to avoid introducing unnecessary constraints. Critical features might include the need to undo state changes, if the user needs to back out a task step and try a different approach.

Some of the tasks in Figure 7-1 may be too large to be useful. "Print document" can be considered a unit, and simply needs a detailed description. "Create multichapter document" is probably a composite of smaller tasks, which may extend over weeks or months. Where the smaller tasks are common to several tasks, they should be documented separately. Where they are part of one larger task, they can be shown as an indented list below the major task.

[1] These object descriptions should cross-reference object descriptions in the analysis model.

[2] I am indebted to Linn Marks for suggesting this aspect of task description.

[3] Glossaries are explicitly part of the OBA methodology [Rub92].

The converse of tasks that are too large is tasks that are too small. Most tasks are not done in isolation; they are part of larger units of work. In systems of any size, it is difficult to grasp the logic of how larger tasks are composed from smaller ones just from reading task descriptions. One approach to this problem is to have a hierarchy of task descriptions. Higher level tasks can be described in a "pseudocode" notation[1] showing their composition, for example:

```
task deliver report {
   subtask create report;
   while (graphics to insert)
      subtask insert graphics;
   while (tables to insert)
      subtask insert tables;
   while (report is not error free) {
      subtask print report;
      subtask proofread report;
      subtask revise text;
   }
} // end task "deliver report"
```

A flow diagram can also show task logic and flow. Figure 7-2 shows an example for the same "deliver report" task.

Task analysis should occur in parallel with other analysis activities, since looking at the objects used in the performance of tasks helps in "finding the objects" for the analysis model of the system. As objects are discovered, additional tables, relating object types and tasks, can be created. Figures 7-3 and 7-4 show examples.

Tables like Figure 7-3 are useful where there is one main object per task. Each entry shows two numbers; the first shows the relative frequency[2] of the task, and the second shows the proportion of total time spent on that task. This data may be necessary if measured user productivity is a key objective; it can be gathered by observing users or by written surveys. Tasks such as "insert table in text," where the proportion of time spent is large compared to the frequency, should be examined to find out why. Analysis of this sort often reveals areas where improvement is possible.

Where tasks involve more than one object, a table such as Figure 7-4 summarizes the relation between objects and tasks. It shows tasks a customer might perform at a bank ATM. ✓ indicates the object is involved in the task along with other checked objects. ☑ indicates that only one of the checked objects is involved in any instance of the task. As analysis progresses, information can be added to the cells to summarize which ser-

[1] Use any notation that makes sense, but be consistent within a project.

[2] That is, the ratio of the number of times the particular task is done to the total number of all task executions.

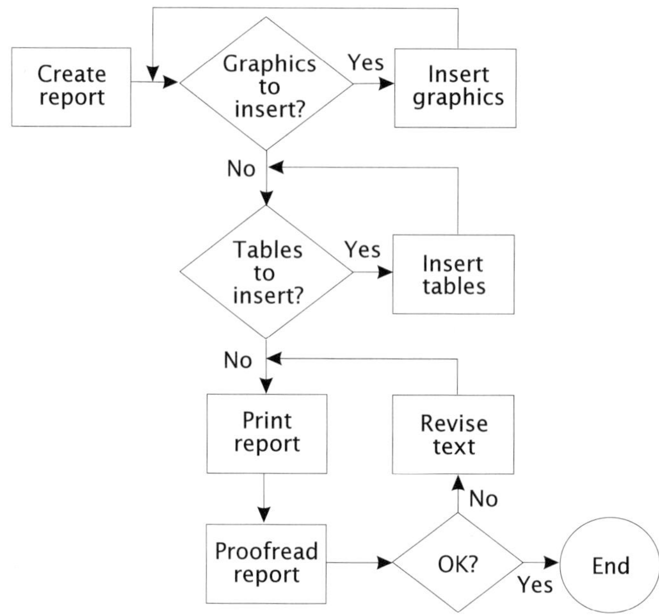

Figure 7-2 Flow diagram for the "deliver report" task

	Letter	Multipage report	Multichapter report
Create	.60 / .50	.30 / .20	.05 / .20
Insert graphics in text	0 / 0	.05 / .05	.05 / .05
Insert table in text	.05 / .20	.10 / .10	.05 / .10
Format type font/size	0 / 0	.05 / .05	.05 / .10
Print	.05 / .05	.10 / .05	.02 / .02
Revise text	.25 / .10	.30 / .35	.75 / .45
Revise format	.05 / .15	.10 / .20	.03 / .08

Figure 7-3 Task/object table with relative frequency / fraction of elapsed time of tasks

vices or responsibilities of the object are involved in the given task.

Figure 7-5 shows a more detailed view of a single task from Figure 7-4. This is called an interaction diagram [Jac92]. The vertical dimension is time (increasing from top to bottom), and it shows the flow of events between the agent and objects of the task.

	Savings account	Checking account
Deposit	☑	☑
Withdraw	☑	☑
Transfer	✓	✓
Balance inquiry	☑	☑

Figure 7-4 Task/object table showing objects involved in task

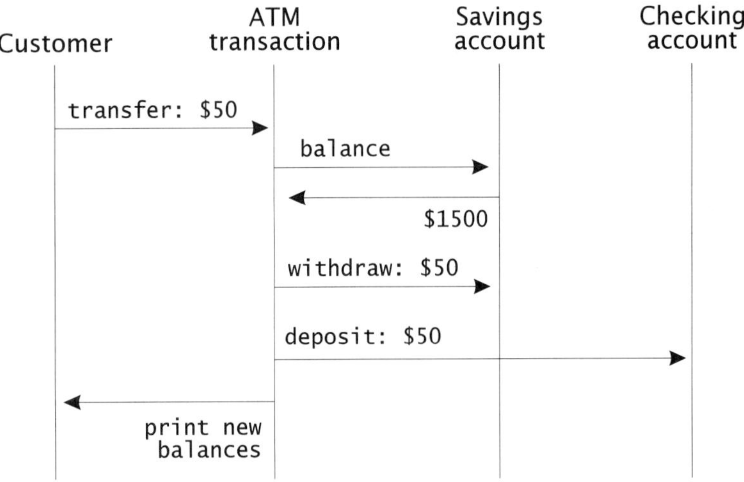

Figure 7-5 Interaction diagram for the "transfer" task

Collaborative tasks Documentation for sequential collaborative tasks extends the formats used for single-user tasks. Task descriptions can be supplemented with information on inputs, outputs, and constraints related to collaboration. Task flow pseudocode and flow diagrams such as Figure 7-2 can also document sequential collaborative tasks. As an example, suppose the task "deliver report" is done by several people working on the same document: a writer, and artist, and an editor. The pseudocode is augmented to show the agent for each task:

```
task deliver report {
 Writer: subtask create report;
   while (graphics to insert)
      Artist: subtask insert graphics;
   while (tables to insert)
      Artist: subtask insert tables;
   while (report is not error free) {
      Writer: subtask print report;
      Editor: subtask proofread report;
      Writer: subtask revise text;
   }
} // end task "deliver report"
```

Similar changes would be made to the flow diagram. Where timing and precedence constraints on subtasks are important, work management diagramming techniques such as PERT/CPM [Hur93] are useful. Parallel collaboration tasks can be documented by extending the notation to indicate the involvement of several agents and what each one does. Design for parallel tasks may bring up difficult issues in concurrent programming and data access, but these issues do not necessarily have to be exposed in the analysis.

Levels of Detail

Task analysis can be done in great detail, producing reams of documentation, or it can be done at a summary level. A highly detailed task analysis may make sense when the cost of failure in task performance is high. The control system for a nuclear power plant, or an on-board navigation system for a spacecraft, are examples. In many such cases, the client for the system will mandate task analysis standards.[1]

The opposite end of the spectrum is a system intended for tasks that do not yet exist in their envisioned form. Many research projects fall into this category, as well as some commercial projects. For these projects, an initial detailed task analysis may be harmful, because it discourages exploration. A task *focus* is still important, and a very general scenario, or several alternative scenarios, can provide it. The approach is top-down, using needs, desires, and goals to generate ideas about tasks and technologies that might satisfy them.

An example of a project of this kind is the "Global Desktop," done at IBM Research.[2] Technology was being developed to link "desktop" user interfaces and server machines in a heterogeneous network, and the following is an extract from one of several scenarios developed to help un-

[1] Many examples of detailed task analyses can be found in the human factors literature, e.g., [Phil88] and [Car83].

[2] I worked on this with Wendy A. Kellogg, John Vlissides, and John T. Richards. A prototype of the Desktop, built by Daniel Yellin and colleagues, was shown at OOPSLA'93.

derstand how the technology might be used:

> Dr. Janet Quinn is a physician and occasional computer user. . . The scenario begins on a Sunday morning in Janet's home. She's in the market for a car . . . and has decided to use the Desktop to find a good one. . . Janet begins with **AutoAdvisor**. She decides to look up information on the Saturn . . . Janet decides to open the **Financier** and see how expensive the Saturn is to insure. . . But when she looks back at the **Financier** worksheet, she realizes she won't be able to tell unless she re-enters all the information. . . [Janet gets tired of reentering the same information into both applications, so she calls up customer service for advice. The consultant explains *collaborations*, objects which allow separate applications to function cooperatively.] . . . Knowing she will also want to look at ads, Janet decides to try a collaboration between **AutoAdvisor** and the **Classifieds**. . . [Janet ends up with a collaboration including these objects and **Geographer**, which shows the location of car dealers with the model she's looking for.]. . . Janet selects an ad and sure enough, a dot on the map highlights . . .[1]

This scenario started as a "back of the envelope" sketch, and was expanded, refined, and revised based on feedback from potential users; when it contained sufficient detail, it became the basis for a prototype that was used to explore the scenario further. Notice the emphasis on a familiar task, buying a car, though the detailed methods and technology are novel. Scenarios like this can be valuable even for projects where current tasks are well defined. Asking "what if" questions may reveal goals and tasks that are important to users, but not feasible in the current environment. This can lead to unexpected benefits from the new system.

Whatever the level of analysis, to be useful it must be used. Tables like the ones in the figures look good at project status presentations, but that is not enough to justify the cost of generating them. As a check on the level of detail, ask yourself the following questions:

- Will prospective users of the system read the analysis and provide feedback on its correctness and completeness?
- Will you and other developers use the analysis as you design the user interface?
- Will all, or a representative sample, of the tasks be used to test the correctness and usability of the user interface?

If the answer to any of these questions is *no*, you are probably collecting too much data, or not presenting your analysis in a useful form. In many environments, using any task analysis data at all is an improvement over current practices. Even a high-level analysis is valuable if developers and customers use it, and it may precipitate discussion and questions that lead to a more detailed analysis.

[1] Bracketed sentences are my summaries. The scenario is copyright 1993, IBM Corporation, and the extract is reprinted with permission.

7.5 Tasks as Objects

This chapter contains expressions like "a task is a single meaningful unit of work," or "tasks that will be performed," where *task* occurs as a noun. This is an "objectification" of something normally seen as a process. Modeling tasks explicitly as objects is sometimes quite useful.

The general rule is that when a task has behavior or properties that are interesting outside the context of performing it, it is a candidate for modeling as a separate object. An example of interesting behavior for tasks is the ability to run themselves on command, or when some designated set of events has occurred. Examples of interesting properties are when the task was last done, other tasks that must finish before it can start, and objects that are modified by the task.

Task objects can be components of larger objects. *Projects* may include both task and non-task objects related to specific projects. *Business processes* are objects composed of linked tasks.

This section has two general examples. One is the problem, mentioned earlier, where tasks that can be automated using a procedural command script require execution of many steps in a system with an OOUI. The second is the problem of managing complex sequential collaboration tasks. Both can be solved with task objects, and the solutions illustrate how these objects play a role in analyzing tasks.

Structured and Unstructured Tasks

"Production" applications such as sales order entry and insurance claims processing often involve well-structured tasks that can be functionally decomposed into subtasks. Viewed bottom-up, this suggests execution of a sequence of commands, each representing one subtask. Many systems provide the capability of using something like a procedural programming language to compose "shell scripts" or "command scripts." These are lists of subtask commands, with imbedded procedural logic, that can be invoked with a single command.

Viewed top-down, functional decomposition suggests a user interface based on a hierarchy of menus. This works well if the menu hierarchy conforms to the structure of the tasks, but is confusing and difficult otherwise. Command scripts and menus are usually optimal for some tasks, and difficult for others.[1]

Users doing "knowledge work" seldom have tasks amenable to functional decomposition. Office work, as done by a manager or professional, is an example. The goal of the task is difficult to state in simple terms. It consists of numerous items of completed work, spread out over time—memos, papers, designs, plans, etc. The user's viewpoint is object-centered, rather than process-centered. This suggests a user interface that provides a set of operations or "microtasks" clustered with each object.

[1] See [Shn92], Chapter 3, for a discussion of menus, and Chapter 4 for a discussion of command languages.

Eventually these microtasks sum up to an overall goal, but it is not clear that the path to the goal is representable in a user interface.[1]

Many OOUIs are optimized for "knowledge based" applications, and can be inefficient for tasks that are well structured and performed repetitively. However, any well-structured task can be defined as a procedural "program" of operations on some set of objects. These programs can be modeled as `execute` methods for object classes representing task types. In this way, a level of efficiency equivalent to command scripts can be provided without compromising the structure of an OOUI.

The equivalent of a hierarchical menu structure can also be provided in an OOUI, as a hierarchy of containers holding task objects. Task objects can implement rules and constraints on tasks, such as checking preconditions or verifying the identity of the user executing the task, and they can execute based on events, such as clock time or the completion of other tasks.[2]

Task objects can simply be hard-coded parts of the system implementation, or users can be given the ability to create task objects. An example of user programming is the capsule facility from the IBM Data Interpretation System [IBM89], developed by Metaphor Computer Systems. Suppose a sales analyst performs the following task steps each week for her manager:

1. Query the sales database for the products her group is responsible for.
2. Upload the query results to a spreadsheet for analysis.
3. Plot a graph of sales by week for the largest-selling product.
4. Mail the plot and the spreadsheet to her manager.

Though the analyst is a knowledge worker, this is a repetitive, well-structured task. It can be automated by creating a capsule, copying the icons representing the objects used in the task, and connecting the icons to represent data flow between them. Figure 7-6 shows the result. The plot has been opened for inspection. The `Query`, `Spreadsheet`, `Plot`, `Envelope`, and `Mail Tray` icons have been "wired together" to accomplish the desired task, which executes when the user clicks on the `Run` button.

Hewlett-Packard's NewWave environment [sHew92] has a similar idea. The user can create "agent tasks" in a manner similar to macro recording. A new task is created, and user actions are recorded and stored while the user does the task. The task can then be executed by dropping its icon on the `Agent` icon.[3] A command language script, which the user

[1] A large part of the problem of representing knowledge work procedurally is that workers are driven by events in real time. Event-driven systems in general are compatible with OO methods; this topic is discussed in Chapter 11.

[2] In systems where tasks are modeled as objects, explicitly modeling *rules* and *events* as objects may also be worthwhile.

[3] Note that this use of "agent" is different from its use in task descriptions.

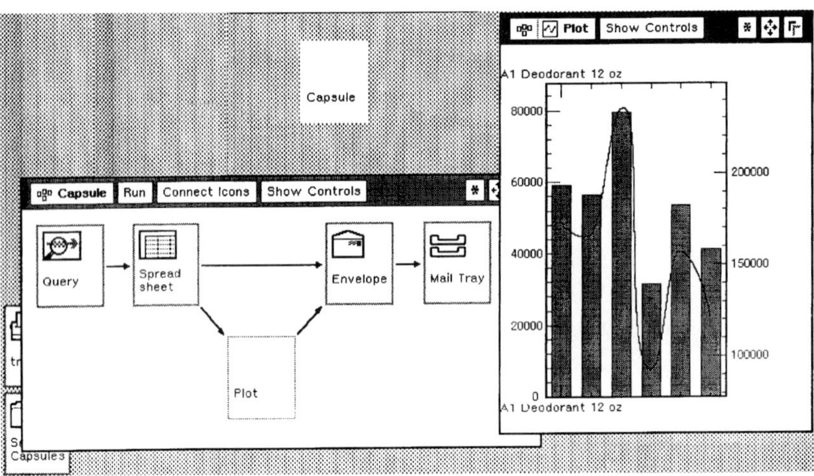

Figure 7-6 A capsule in the Metaphor system

can edit, is stored in the task object. Since the language can specify procedural logic (using `if-then-else` and `do`), it is more powerful than the capsule facility. NewWave also contains a calendar called the `Agent schedule`. Dropping a task's icon on a day in the calendar causes it to be scheduled on that date. The user specifies the time of execution in a dialogue box, and whether the task is to be executed regularly (for example, on the 25th of every month).

Several products from Microsoft, for instance Visual Basic [sMic93d], use the concept of *wizards.* A wizard is an icon or button that executes all the steps in some common task. Wizards shipped with products reflect their designers' analysis of multistep tasks that users often need to do.

Collaborative Tasks and Workflow Management

Task objects can model collaboration between users involved in the same task. Modeling collaboration requires objects representing users as well, with attributes such as tasks the user is involved in, agent roles the user can play, and what objects the user has locked or "checked out." Collaborative tasks may also require modeling of rules, such as constraints based on business requirements, and events, such as notification of task completion.

Social and cultural issues often dominate cooperative tasks, and are difficult to capture or model explicitly. Contextual analysis and iterative design are important for supporting these tasks.

Modeling many types of parallel collaboration tasks, such as remote conferences, primarily involves user objects and simple task objects. Tasks that involve collaborative creation or updating of documents or other objects may require extensions to the behavior of those objects, to indicate, for example, who is involved or who has control. Similar technical issues arise in distributed object-oriented databases.

Typical businesses have many sequential tasks that involve moving work (in the form of materials, documents, or computer files) through a complex network of people. Managing these tasks involves knowing what conditions must exist for a task to start, what new tasks can start when a task has finished, and how to detect violation of business rules. Computer applications to manage the workflow in these tasks have existed for many years, mostly as special purpose packages for specific areas.

Recently, general-purpose workflow management applications with OOUIs, such as Xerox's *InConcert* [sXer93], have been developed. Using graphical manipulations similar to those in the Metaphor capsule environment, the user can link task objects in a workflow and specify their properties. Packages such as InConcert can be used to model and document task flows, besides implementing them from component objects.

7.6 Summary

Understanding users and their work is critical in giving your system or application a "seamless" feel. I recommend the following task analysis steps as part of the analysis phase of development:

1. *Categorize users* of the proposed system. Depending on the situation, categories may be based on physical differences, education, language and culture, job category, or other factors.
2. *Establish the major tasks* users will do with the system. Build a table of tasks versus users, and a set of task descriptions, to organize your knowledge.
3. As objects are identified, *define tasks as sequences of actions on objects.* In unstructured tasks, do not introduce unnecessary constraints on the ordering of actions.
4. *If necessary, define "task objects"* that encapsulate the actions for structured, repetitive tasks.
5. *Use the task analysis data for task synthesis,* which produces a model of tasks in the new system. Reengineer to maximize the added value of the new system.
6. *Analyze in context*; visit users in their work environments.

7.7 To Explore Further

[Ega88] is an eye-opener on the magnitude of differences among individual users, even within demographically similar groups. [Russ93] is a good short summary of differences between users of different nationalities. [Pres93] discusses both the technical and marketing issues of international software products. *Communications of the ACM* 35, 5 (May 1992) is a special issue on computers and people with disabilities.

[Gou87] describes the design of a messaging system for Olympic athletes that needed to support 12 languages. It is an example of contextual design, as well as supporting international users. [Wix90] describes contextual design, a perspective that enhances conventional task analysis approaches. [Hol93] is a more recent and complete treatment of contextual design, and presents some worthwhile techniques for diagramming tasks and workflows. [Kir93] is a business-oriented view of contextual issues.

Most books on human factors and user interface design cover task analysis, e.g., [Shn92] and [Rubin84]. In my opinion, much of the literature presents methods that are too detailed to be useful in practical development situations (e.g., [Car83], [Phil88], [Pot89]). Nevertheless, reading the literature is worthwhile to provide raw material for methods that are appropriate for your particular situation.

A large literature on "groupware," or computer supported cooperative work is available. [Ell91] presents an overview of issues. Proceedings of the biennial ACM conference on CSCW (computer supported cooperative work) are a source of more information. Designing and implementing support for parallel tasks is still a research issue, though some support for concurrent OO design is provided in [Rum91] and [Boo94].

7.8 Exercises

1. List categories of people who might play the Klondike solitaire game in Chapter 5.
   a. Will any of these need (or want) a different user interface?
   b. For international users, what is the problem in the prototype user interface of Figure 5-9 that does *not* exist in the interface of Figure 5-7?
2. List the set of tasks performed by the player of the Klondike solitaire game in Chapter 5. For at least one task, say "move face up cards from one tableau pile to another," describe the task in detail (preconditions, goal, etc.).
3. Ask one or more people to write a description of some task they do. Without looking at theirs, write down your own description based on observing them doing the task. (Ask them to explain if you see behavior you do not understand.) Include in your description any environmental factors that seem to influence the task. Do the two descriptions agree?

4. Read through *Fax Case Study* (Appendix 1). Correlate what you read with your own experience with facsimile transmission. Using this information, do the following:

   a. Choose an environment for the application to be designed. This could be a general business environment, or the particular environment in your company or university. Categorize and describe the users of a fax application in your environment.

   b. Using the format shown in Figure 7-1, list the tasks these users perform.

   c. Describe each task, along the lines suggested in Section 7-4.

   d. Make a "first pass" at identifying objects used in the tasks, and relate them to tasks using the format in Figure 7-4.

   e. For at least one task involving more than one object, draw an interaction diagram like the one in Figure 7-5.

   The results of this exercise will be used for additional exercises in Chapters 8, 9, and 10.

8

The User's Conceptual Model

The classes and relationships discovered in analysis were described in Chapter 5 as a "conceptual model" of the system. That description glossed over some key points, and this chapter presents a method for developing a more comprehensive conceptual model. It is based on the analysis model, information about tasks (described in Chapter 7), and *metaphors* that help to structure the user's experience of the system or application. The user's conceptual model drives the design of the concrete presentation and interaction components of the user interface, covered in Chapters 9 and 10.

The user's conceptual model is a roadmap of the system. It provides an overview of objects and capabilities, gives "driving instructions" for specific trips through the functions of the system, and helps users to reason about navigation through unfamiliar areas. Since we are designing the roadmap (the conceptual model) *as* we design the system, we can test the map as we go along and use the results to simplify the design of the system itself.

The last paragraph starts with a metaphor—it explains an unfamiliar concept (the user's conceptual model) in terms of a familiar one (a roadmap). Metaphors expressed in user interfaces, such as the "desktop metaphor," have similar purposes. They help provide overall structure for two interlocking parts of the user's conceptual model: the *system model*, which incorporates knowledge of objects, and the *task model*, which incorporates procedural knowledge about tasks.

The material in this chapter is difficult to teach, and difficult to successfully apply—perhaps more difficult than anything else in the book. I am convinced that it is critical for designing good user interfaces, and statements from successful software developers reinforce my conviction. Here's what Bill Gates, CEO of Microsoft, had to say about it:

> You can see that the metaphor question is entirely separate from concepts such as graphic icons or windows. It is also a much more difficult issue to deal with. The effort, however, will definitely be worth our while: it is in this area, more than any other, that we can make the breakthroughs that will allow the ordinary user to view the computer as simple.[1]

Microsoft illustrates both the importance and the difficulty of designing good conceptual models. Products that turned out to be highly successful nevertheless went through many iterations before finding market acceptance. Differences among users form one of the obstacles in the path of developing conceptual models that are widely helpful for learning and using a system. Another is the conflict between designers' models, often based on technology, and users' models based on the application domain.

There is no formula for cranking out great conceptual models. There are methods, however, for systematically generating and exploring ideas for models that will help users. Effort put into this process will be rewarded by effort saved in designing the presentation and action languages, and better quality in the end product.

After explaining some terminology, this chapter covers:

- Several examples that reinforce the idea of a user's conceptual model, and how it helps users.
- A method for designing and evaluating components of a user's conceptual model.
- A catalog of user interface metaphors that you can use to generate design ideas.

8.1 Models and Metaphors

Model is a heavily used term in the fields of design and engineering. This book discusses object models, conceptual models, information models, user's conceptual models, designers' models, task models, etc. A model is a structure in one domain that explains, simulates, predicts, or controls behavior in another domain. Think of a model airplane. In the hands of a small boy, a model plane teaches simple things about aircraft design and aerodynamics. More sophisticated versions in a wind tunnel can teach things to a scientist. Nowadays, both the plane and the wind tunnel are likely to be modeled inside a computer.

Models range from drawings on cave walls and diagrams in the sand, to sophisticated physical mockups or computer programs. Throughout recorded history, models have been used to explain, simulate, and predict. Only in modern times, and particularly in the computer age, do we have

[1] [Gat83], p. 403.

the means to control reality by manipulating models.[1] Examples range from electronic stock markets to direct manipulation interfaces for industrial process control. The ability to understand *and* control by means of a single visible model is fundamental to OOUIs.

This section explains three kinds of models. *Mental models* are structures in our minds that we use to explain, simulate, predict, or control objects in the world. *Conceptual models* are externalized representations of mental models, in words or pictures, that can be shared. *Metaphors* are models that help us understand one thing in terms of another; metaphors can be components in mental and conceptual models.

Metaphors

Metaphor, in rhetoric, is a figure of speech that substitutes one kind of thing for another, as when Shakespeare says "all the world's a stage."[2] Its purpose is to make the reader or listener understand things in a different way, by pointing out an analogy between the things being compared. Though the world is *not* literally a stage, thinking of it that way can lead to seeing people's behavior in a new light. ("See in a new light" is also a metaphor; we use metaphors constantly and are hardly aware of them.) Several metaphors can form a coherent whole. When Shakespeare says, in the same passage, "one man in his time plays many parts," the metaphor *man as actor* is coherent, or congruent, with the metaphor *the world as a stage.*

Metaphors in user interfaces have similar purposes: *the computer display as desktop, the computer display as spreadsheet, windows, buttons,* etc. Though the term "metaphor" has become popular in the context of GUIs, even command line interfaces use metaphors. When we `copy` or `erase` a file, we invoke a metaphoric understanding of the operations based on written documents (or tape recorders, which were initially understood in the same metaphoric way). When a computer screen presents entry fields to be filled in, we understand it in terms of paper forms. These metaphors help people both to learn and use systems.

Metaphors can lead to misunderstanding as well as understanding. *Word processor as typewriter* is helpful in understanding word processors. But the space bar and the `BkSp` key on most typewriters simply move the carriage, whereas they erase the text in most word processors. (The space bar may insert spaces and reflow the text, which is also unlike the action of a typewriter.) One study attributed 60 percent of the errors made by people learning a text editor to "mismatches" with the typewriter metaphor [Carr88b].

Simile is a figure of speech that explicitly compares two unlike things, as opposed to the implicit comparison in metaphor. "The world is *like* a stage" is a simile. User interfaces almost always express metaphors, not similes. It is good practice, however, to use similes, not metaphors, in

[1] Though this has always been a dream, evidenced by "voodoo dolls" and other artifacts of sympathetic magic.

[2] *As You Like It* II, 7.

help text, manuals, and training material. Saying "think of a word processor as a typewriter" can lead to the problems described above. It is better to say "a word processor is like a typewriter, but there are some differences . . ."[1]

The word "metaphor" comes from a Greek word meaning "transfer." Metaphors transfer understanding from things we already know, to new things. There is a cognitive economy in this, which is the basis for its value—in ordinary language, and in the presentation and action languages of the user interface.

Mental Models and Conceptual Models

Usage of the terms "mental model" and "conceptual model" varies widely in psychology and cognitive science, and in the literature on human-computer interaction. Most psychologists[2] distinguish between internal states in an individual's mind, which they call *mental models*, and external abstractions or descriptions of those internal states. I will use *conceptual model* to refer to an external abstraction, such as a written description or diagram that expresses some part of a person's knowledge.

These terms can be tricky. I might ask an experienced user to write down how she thinks about some system—thus asking her to create a conceptual model based on her mental model. I could then give her conceptual model to another user, telling him it will help him learn the system. As he learns to use the system, he will assimilate some or all of the first user's conceptual model into his mental model. Eventually, his mental model may come to resemble hers, based on transfer of knowledge through the conceptual model.

To see how mental models work, look at Figure 8-1. Which of the four upright objects looks tallest? Most people see the heights increasing as they go from left to right in the picture. As you can verify with a ruler, however, the four objects are identical in all their dimensions. Most explanations for this kind of illusion posit a mental model that causes the incorrect judgement. The most plausible theory is that our mental model of visual perspective says that converging lines mean increasing distance, and the apparent size of objects decreases with distance. Thus a distant object (the rightmost) with the same *apparent* size as a close object (the leftmost) is "seen" to be larger.[3]

This mental model is hard to get at, since it is outside our consciousness. Even "conscious" models are hard to describe; thinking always involves processes that go on outside awareness. In fact, when people are asked to describe a mental model, what they produce is a conceptual model—a theory about how they think. Getting at the "real" mental model

[1] This example is based on one in [Carr88b].
[2] See, e.g., [Nor83a], [Carr88a].
[3] See [Greg79], Chapter 9.

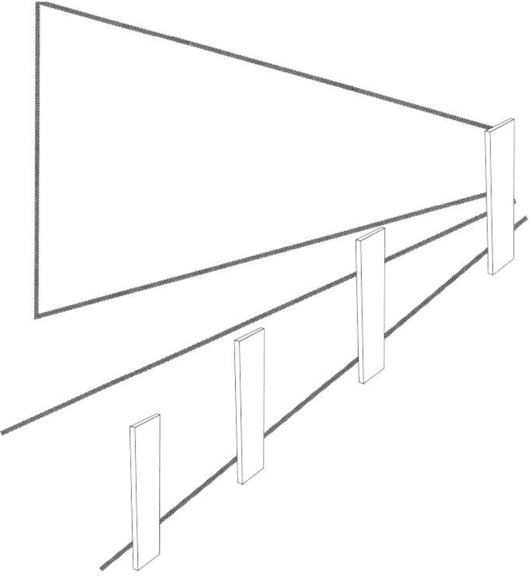

Figure 8-1 A visual illusion

may be surprisingly difficult.[1]

Mental models are important to designers because they determine how, and what, users think about computer systems, applications, and user interfaces. Conceptual models are important because they are tools the designer can use to help users think correctly about a system. They can be embodied in the user interface and in manuals and training materials, and become part of users' mental models.

The *user's conceptual model* is not—in spite of the name—the way a particular user conceives of the system.[2] It is a shared abstraction. It incorporates the way experts think about the problem domain, but may also have facets that help novices to learn the system. In the design process, it is a model for thinking about a computer system that has not yet been completely designed. We get around the apparent circularity—a conceptual model of a system that the conceptual model will help us design—through an iterative process.

I will close this section by reiterating that usage of the terms "conceptual model," "mental model," and "metaphor" varies widely. Writers in the computer trade press use them loosely to mean just about anything. Metaphor, in particular, refers to everything from the user's conceptual model, to the visual appearance of the user interface. In psychology and human-computer interaction, "mental model" is often used to refer to what I have called a conceptual model.[3] For instance, [IBM92b] says "A

[1] [Pay91] is an instructive case study of investigating the mental models used by people to understand the operation of bank teller machines.

[2] It might be better to coin a new term, but "user's conceptual model" is widely used in the literature of HCI.

[3] Or sometimes, e.g. in [Carr88a], to refer only to the *system model* component of the conceptual model (described in the next section).

user's conceptual model is a mental model consisting of the set of relationships that a person perceives to exist among the elements of any situation."

It is important to maintain the distinction between internal mental states and external abstractions of these states, so I separate the terms. In this book "mental model" refers to a private construct in someone's mind. A "conceptual model" can be written down and shared.

8.2 Users' Models of Systems

This section illustrates, mostly by example, what a user's conceptual model is; Section 8.3 presents a method for designing it. For OOUI design, it is convenient to identify three parts of the conceptual model:

- The *system model*, a static model of the objects in the system and their relationships.
- The *task model*, a dynamic model of how the user can interact with objects in the system to accomplish tasks.[1]
- Metaphors, which help users apply knowledge about the structure of things they already understand to the structure of the system and task models.

Figure 8-2 graphically illustrates concepts associated with conceptual and mental models. The cartoon is about communicating a mental model, and most of us have had both of the experiences shown here.

The tourist has asked the police officer for directions to a point of interest. The officer has a mental model of the city; notice that the cartoonist shares it with us by portraying it as a roadmap, which is a common conceptual model. The officer is probably giving directions in a procedural, or task-oriented, form: "go past the next traffic light, turn right at the circle, then left at the next corner," etc. The tourist tries to synthesize a map-like representation based on what the officer is saying, but fails. We know that he will be lost again at the next corner.

This little drama, repeated thousands of times a day, is Shakespearean in its universality, and captures the essence of many avoidable failures in human communication. We have a mental model and assume it is a conceptual model that our listeners share; they do not, so what we say makes little sense. As Don Norman points out [Nor88], this is the tragedy of many user interfaces—the designer has a clear model of how the system works, but the "system image" (which includes the user interface, manuals, training, etc.) does not convey it, and the user gets lost.

The cartoon clearly shows the first two elements of a user's conceptual model. The system model is a model of streets, traffic lights, build-

[1]Psychologists refer to knowledge of the system model as *declarative knowledge*, and knowledge of the task model as *procedural knowledge*. See, e.g., [Moran81].

Figure 8-2 Communicating a mental model
(Drawing by Stevenson; © 1976 The New Yorker Magazine, Inc.)

ings, etc., and their relationships. The task model contains procedural or "rote" knowledge of a set of routes. It also contains knowledge of how to construct *new* routes, based on the system model and knowledge of "microtasks" such as turning at corners, traveling in the correct direction on one-way streets, etc. The third element, metaphor, is also present. How does the cartoonist convince us that the police officer has a clear mental model of the city? By using the roadmap as a metaphor—being able to draw a map implies a knowledge of the geography the map describes.

The relation between the system and task models is important. We all develop procedural knowledge of common tasks such as driving to work. Developing this knowledge in the first place is easier if we have a map to provide a spatial analogue of the route, so memorizing a set of directions is not necessary. If the procedure fails, for instance if a road is closed and we need to detour, we are lost without the map.

Metaphor is important too. Flying over the earth and seeing a bird's-eye view of it is the metaphor that allows us to understand the use of maps. Most of us have forgotten this, since we do not remember what it was like not to be able to use a map. The experience of using a new and unfamiliar user interface can revive the feeling of "not knowing how to use a map."

So Simple a Child Could Understand

Here is another example, which leads into a discussion of conceptual models for computer systems.[1] Responding to concerns about the safety of riders entering subway (underground) stations at night, the New York City Transit Authority initiated a system of color-coded lights outside the stations in 1981. The coding was intended to advise passengers as to whether it was safe to enter the station.

A green light means that the station has a token booth that is open 24 hours (riders must purchase tokens in order to proceed to the train). A yellow light indicates that there is no token booth, but a rider who already has a token can enter through a turnstile gate. A red light means either that the token booth and entrance are open only during the day, or that what appears to be an entrance is really an exit.

In 1990, a *Times* reporter decided to find out (by asking people) whether subway riders understood this simple "user interface." He found that most did not. Some people had explanations that were far off the mark. When he saw station entrances with red and green lights, one man surmised that the lights were decorations for the upcoming Christmas holiday. One young girl, however, knew what they meant. Her mother had given her a metaphor for understanding them—a traffic light. Green meant it was safe to go in, yellow meant caution, and red meant "don't go!"

This may seem trivial, but remember that the Transit Authority had spent large sums on signs and posters to educate people, and it had failed. The little girl's mother succeeded, with a simple metaphor that allowed her daughter to understand the lights in terms of what she already knew. Whoever designed the lighting scheme probably had this metaphor in mind, but it was not communicated to the public. Perhaps it seemed too simple.

Users' Models for Computer Systems

A traffic light is a special case of using one or more indicator lights to show red, yellow, and green, meaning danger, caution, and no danger, respectively. These lights are used in control panels for all kinds of electrical or electrically monitored equipment, which makes the metaphor a prime candidate for helping users understand control systems implemented on computers.

An example is the Omegamon II product, from Candle Corporation.[2] Omegamon monitors the performance of workloads running on IBM's MVS (Multiple Virtual Systems), an operating system for large mainframes. MVS systems may run hundreds of batch jobs and interactive transactions concurrently, and a single human operator may need to monitor several sys-

[1] This is based on "Subway Lights: Dim Message or Holiday Cheer?" *The New York Times*, November 11, 1990, p. 36.

[2] I am indebted to Jim Poretta, of Candle, for supplying me with additional information on Omegamon II; [Por92] summarizes his experience.

tems. Workload performance is determined by complex interactions between the jobs that are running and the system resources available for processing. The operator must detect and solve performance problems. Solving them may entail canceling a job that is using too many resources, shifting resources among jobs, or finding a problem that needs to be diagnosed by a technician.

Omegamon II uses an implicit *control panel* metaphor in representing system information, along with a *status light* metaphor to help the operator find problems quickly. Screen displays show key information about aspects of the system. A computer display, unlike a physical control panel, is "soft"—many different panels can be successively (or concurrently) shown on a single display. Omegamon II manages a hierarchical structure of panels. At the lowest level, the panels display information on components of a single job or system resource. At higher levels, they display aggregated information on classes of jobs and resources.

Each job, resource, or aggregation displays in a color that is its "status light." Green means service levels (preset performance levels) are being met; yellow indicates a warning level or potential problem; and red means a critical problem, such as complete resource failure. Most displays have more than one component, and each component has its own status indication. Operators monitor high-level aggregates until a problem occurs. Then, pointing at the problem component causes a panel to appear for that component, with its subcomponents. Subcomponents will again show their status with red, yellow, or green. In most cases, operators can quickly pinpoint the source of problems.

This design may sound like a simple insight, but many computerized monitoring and control systems simply spew out a sequential stream of status messages whenever a state change occurs. The operator must constantly monitor these messages to see when performance thresholds are exceeded, and synthesize a structural understanding of how system components are interacting. Omegamon II improves the operator's performance, because its design incorporates three simple, but powerful, ideas:

- It maintains and displays a model of the domain being monitored (jobs and resources).
- Its user interface is based on an understanding of the capabilities and limits of operators, and the tasks they perform.
- It uses metaphors (control panels and status lights) to make the interface easier to understand.

These elements correspond to the components of a user's conceptual model.

Coherence in Conceptual Models

Coherence means that the elements of a model fit together in a way that makes sense to the user. *Congruence* of elements is another term that describes this situation. Coherence (or incoherence) can arise in several ways.

Coherence in the system model is fundamental. One possible source of incoherence is the application domain itself—work may be disorganized, or different users may have inconsistent views of the objects in the domain. Another source of incoherence is the modeling process. These are issues primarily of system analysis, not user interface design. I will not discuss them further, except to point out that the sort of prototyping advocated in Chapter 5 can expose these problems early in the development cycle.

Parts of the task model can be incoherent, for instance if a task step negates the operation of a prior step, or violates a rule of the business. Going back to Figure 8-2, "driving in circles" might be the result of the tourist's acquiring an incoherent task model from the police officer. The task model can also be incongruent with the system model, if it implies a relationship between objects that does not exist in the system model. In the driving context, a task that requires a left turn where only a right turn is possible illustrates this kind of incoherence. Avoiding these problems is part of task synthesis, described in the next section. If the problems persist, it suggests a need for reiteration of system analysis and task analysis.

Coherence among metaphors is also important. Note that designers cannot completely control the metaphors that people use. If a "red-yellow-green" visual indicator appears, some users will apply the *traffic light* and *status indicator* metaphors, whatever the designer's intent. Metaphors may be congruent or incongruent with each other, or with the system and task models. In Omegamon II, the two metaphors are congruent with each other, and with the system and the tasks. Status indicators are reasonable objects to find on control panels. Control panels are reasonable models of the system, and they support the operators' tasks.

In another example, a communications network management application used a red-yellow-green scheme. A "roadmap" of the network provided the overall structure. Individual nodes in the network, such as switches and multiplexors, were colored to show their status. This example is interesting because the *roadmap* metaphor is congruent with both the *traffic light* and *status indicator* metaphors. In the traffic light metaphor, a red light suggests that "traffic is stopped" at a point in the flow. In the status indicator metaphor, it indicates that a node's "control panel" has an error indication.

Metaphorical coherence is particularly important to interface designers, because metaphors are significant leverage points for design. The system and task models are largely determined by the nature of the problem domain. Metaphor selection is more creative and can significantly improve the interface. Good interface metaphors often appear childishly simple, but that is a mark of their sophistication. Many studies[1] show the value of

[1] See, e.g., [Carr82], [Carr88a], [Fei93], [Kel87], [Pay91].

metaphors and metaphorical coherence. These studies also show that the designer cannot choose whether or not users have metaphors—if all else fails, they simply invent their own.

Real systems are complex, and users typically understand them in terms of models that incorporate many metaphors—some provided by the system image, some by the users themselves. Metaphors can mislead as well as lead, and it is difficult to insure that metaphors are congruent with the system and with each other. As an example, consider some metaphors[1] we might employ to help people learn and use a word processing system: "It is like a typewriter." "The display is like a television." "The display is like a sheet of paper." "The places where you put your files are like file cabinets and folders." "You can change fonts, as with a typesetter." "It can make copies of your documents, like an office copier." The following table shows some of the ways in which these metaphors interact with the user's experience of the system.

Metaphor	Computer keyboard	"Saving" files	Printing documents
Typewriter	Space and backspace are incongruent	Incongruent	Incongruent
Television	Depends on user	No connection	Congruent
Sheet of paper	Paper is "magic"	Incongruent	Incongruent
File cabinets/folders	No connection	Congruent	Incongruent
Typesetter	Congruent	Incongruent	Congruent
Office copier	No connection	Congruent	Congruent

Figure 8-3 Metaphor mappings for word processing

I will explain a few of the table entries; the rest I leave to the reader as an exercise.[2] The issue with the space bar and BkSp key was discussed on page 179. "Printing" as a separate step is incongruent with the idea of a typewriter, which prints the document as it is typed. How the keyboard relates to television is not clear; users with computer experience may find it congruent, others may not. The ability to erase and retype is what makes

[1] Expressed here as similes.

[2] In fact, you might argue with some of my entries. Only by testing these against real users could we be sure about who was right.

the paper "magic." This is incongruent with real paper, but for most users it is a comprehensible and desirable extension to the real-world metaphor.

This complexity is typical of the systems you will be designing. Though it seems that there are many problems here, they are manageable. Areas where metaphors are incongruent with the system will be harder for users to learn [Carr88a], but they can be identified and pointed out in manuals and training: "it is like this, except that . . ." Users are generally willing to accept "training wheels" as they assimilate the model of a new system. In domains that have been studied, evidence shows that users' models tend to converge to a common "expert model" as they learn [Carr88a].

If users have experience with other computer systems, they can become metaphors for the new system. This is particularly evident with word processing applications. It has good or bad effects, depending upon the congruency of the old and new systems. As part of user and task analysis, it may be important to understand what models users possess from prior computer experience.

8.3 Designing the User's Conceptual Model

Simple examples of OOUIs, such as calculators and solitaire games, can suggest the naive idea that the user's conceptual model is just a transcription of the way every user thinks about the application domain. In these examples, it is almost true. In more complex situations, most users are expert only in certain facets of the domain, and their knowledge is structured by the "metaphor" of the technology they currently use. For calculators and card games, that's fine—we are happy to use the existing technology as a user interface metaphor. In most situations, we plan to change the technology and the tasks in the interest of efficiency—so we must *design* a new conceptual model to help users.

This section sequentially presents the activities of designing the system and task models, and finding metaphors. However, they are part of a gestalt, not separate activities. The *Journalist* application [sPed93] is an example of this. CompuServe[1] provides access to sources of news articles, photographs, and maps, which users can download and display on their computers. Existing CompuServe facilities implicitly define the system and task models in terms of files, applications, and download procedures. Journalist uses a *newspaper* metaphor—users can lay out pages, with space for specific kinds of stories and pictures. The story and picture objects on the page automatically download the proper data to fill themselves. The use of this metaphor adds new objects to the system model, and dramatically changes the task model.

[1] A popular online information service in the US. Journalist is discussed in more detail in Chapter 15, *Design Examples.*

Designing the System Model

The system model is based on the analysis model of the system. Object-oriented analysis provides a classification of objects in the problem domain, and various submodels of static and dynamic relationships between objects.

Journalist shows why designing the user's conceptual model should start during the analysis phase—a creative idea for the conceptual model may lead to a different object decomposition in analysis. In Journalist, some of the original analysis objects (such as files) migrate to the design model as implementation objects. They are replaced in the analysis model by objects more attuned to what users are really trying to do—access news.

Once the analysis model is developed, the main job of user interface designers is to decide what needs to be presented when, and to whom.

In some systems, everything is visible to everyone, so the system model is essentially just the analysis model. The solitaire game is an example of this situation. There is one other simple case, where there are many loosely coupled objects. "Desktop" systems, such as the Apple Macintosh Finder and the IBM OS/2 Workplace Shell, are examples. Most objects on the desktop can be understood individually, so there is a set of system models, and users learn those they need. There is also an overall system model for the desktop itself, which describes common interactions such as placing objects into folders; this overall model does not depend on the details of the individual objects.

Class hierarchies for "desktop" systems were discussed in Chapter 4, Section 4.3. Figure 4-10 showed a typical hierarchy, with abstract classes `Container`, `Data object`, and `Device`. Users can understand the overall system model in terms of these abstract classes, which specify common interaction protocols. The common protocols do not interact much with object behavior that is specific to an application domain such as word processing.

There are cases where users are interested in specific facets of a complex system model. Suppose an aircraft manufacturer has a system that deals with all aspects of building a new plane. Having a single model that captures information about the plane may be advantageous, but not every user needs to see all of it. An engineer may be interested only in the geometry of a part, whereas an accountant may be interested only in its cost. Or a user may only be interested in the plane as a whole, not the parts it is composed of. Figure 8-4 shows a way of accommodating this sort of situation. Each user's system model has a proxy object (shown in gray) which may collapse the properties of several objects, or represent a facet of a single object.[1]

In another common case, each user is interested in a subset of the

[1] Implementation issues of proxy or "schema" objects and partitioned models are discussed in Chapter 12, *Information Models.*

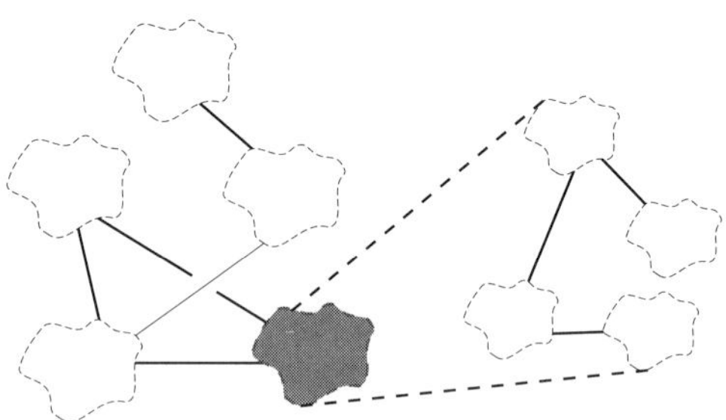

Figure 8-4 A proxy object in a user's system model

objects in the analysis model. For example, an application for an automobile dealership may have objects of interest to everyone in the dealership, such as cars and customers, objects of interest only to the sales staff, such as car loans, and objects of interest only to the service department, such as parts in the inventory. This can be handled by partitioning the analysis model into system models for different types of users, as shown in Figure 8-5.

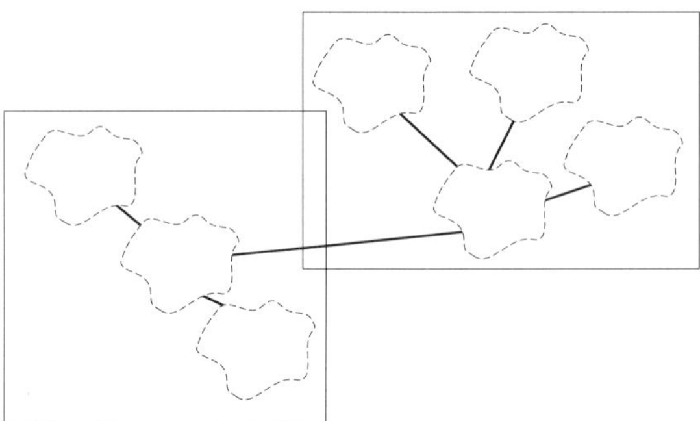

Figure 8-5 Partitioning a system model

Documentation of system models (including faceted or partitioned models) consists of pictures like Figures 8-4 and 8-5 and text describing how objects apply to different types of users. As much as possible, analysis documentation should be reused for documenting system models.

Designing the Task Model

Many designs simply replicate the flow of current tasks in the system under development. (The solitaire game and the calculator are examples.) Whether or not this is a good idea, it simplifies task synthesis. We just reformulate the current task descriptions (created in the task analysis activity) in terms of objects and behaviors in the system model.

At the other extreme, the new tasks may be very unlike the current ones. Designing the new tasks is usually a large effort, whose scope goes beyond the software development team. Task synthesis in these cases should be driven by business process reengineering[1] based on a creative dialogue between business experts, system analysts, and user interface designers. Task analysis data can help identify opportunities for restructuring, and creative metaphors can ease the transition for users.

There is always a tension between current ways of doing things, which are comfortable to users, and new ways, which may be more efficient. Some companies have made the transition in several steps. From the point of view of user interface design, managing the transition involves not just managing the change in software and systems, but also managing the change in the way users see the systems. As the following example illustrates, it is possible to gracefully migrate through several conceptual models, each one providing "handles" to help users understand the new tasks.

Cigna Insurance,[2] like most insurance companies, relies heavily on processing of forms—applications, claims, bills, accident reports, and so forth. For people who use a form constantly, it becomes an important object in its own right, often eclipsing the objects it refers to (customers, material goods, etc.). Many tasks in business are structured by the rules for filling out and moving forms around the company; thus forms become metaphors for tasks, processes, and systems.

Computer systems can eliminate forms by allowing users to operate directly on representations of the underlying objects. Making this change involves reengineering the business—the flow of tasks changes, and some current tasks (and jobs) are eliminated. Users, without the familiar metaphor of forms, may find new systems difficult to learn and use. Many companies, Cigna among them, have elected to make the change in stages.

The first step for Cigna was to enhance the process of filling out forms by presenting an image of each form on a computer display. This eliminated the need to stock blank forms; it also reduced errors, since the form and its fields could provide immediate feedback to the user. After filling out the form online, the user printed it out to be mailed and processed as before.

The second step, after users were comfortable with forms on the computer, was to mail them electronically instead of on paper. The benefits of this are obvious. The third step was to act directly on the objects the form referred to, instead of on the form itself. The originator, though, still has a form-like user interface.

This is not a new idea. Character-based user interfaces have exploited the *form metaphor* for years, and many database packages offer

[1] See [Gle93], [Stewa93]. Process reengineering (discussed in Chapter 2) can be applied to areas as varied as science and games, not just commercial businesses.

[2] The information on Cigna and their systems is from [Smit93]. The case also involves networking and other issues that are not discussed here.

rapid development tools for building form-based interfaces to databases. The key idea that Cigna exploited was the use of a metaphor, the form, as a common thread through significant changes in tasks and task flows. This case illustrates the close connection between the parts of the user's conceptual model. The form metaphor represents the system model (because fields in forms correspond to object classes), and provides a visual picture of the tasks to be done.

The output of task synthesis is always a set of task descriptions for the new system, in terms of actions on objects in the system model.[1] Relevant metaphors can be used in the descriptions. Task descriptions, besides documenting the task model, can be the basis for manuals and training materials.

Finding Good Metaphors

The Journalist example (page 188) shows that metaphors are not a superficial aspect of design, but may restructure the system in a deep way. Developing the "right" metaphor is difficult, but it can be a key factor in the success of a software product.

The spreadsheet is one of the best examples of this. Spreadsheets have been used for hundreds of years in business and commerce. In the 19th century the spreadsheet was already a source of metaphor, as this quotation from Charles Dickens shows: "Mr Lorry sat at great books ruled for figures, with perpendicular iron bars to his window as if that were ruled for figures too, and everything under the clouds were a sum."[2] The notion of a paper spreadsheet is comfortable and familiar to most users; the computer version preserves this, but adds speed and functional power.

Computer spreadsheet applications are an example of what Randall Smith [Smith87] calls "the tension between literalism and magic." A *literal* interpretation of the metaphor would demand that the user open a computer calculator to do sums, then type the results back into the spreadsheet. But the spreadsheet is *magical*—the cells in a row or column can sum themselves, and automatically update the cell containing the sum. Literalism maximizes understanding, but does not add any power; magic maximizes power, but may interfere with understanding.

The brilliance of the computer spreadsheet, designed by Dan Bricklin for VisiCalc [Lic89], is that it adds magic in ways that mostly delight, rather than baffle, the user. In doing so, it overcomes the limitations of the metaphor, while preserving its value as a tool for understanding.

An example of magic that goes too far is the use of the *trash can* metaphor, as implemented on the Apple Macintosh,[3] for ejecting diskettes. If confined to its role as a container for deleted objects, the trash

[1] These tasks can be documented using the format for current tasks described in Chapter 7.

[2] *A Tale of Two Cities*, Chapter 12.

[3] This metaphor is illustrated in Chapter 4, Figure 4-5.

can is an excellent metaphor. Though quite literal in this context, it provides a powerful capability that most computer systems lack—the ability to undo accidental deletion. It is also used to eject diskettes from the drive, as the Macintosh has no ejection button. Dropping a diskette's icon on the trash can icon causes it to eject, which turns out to be either baffling ("why should I do *that* to eject the disk?") or frightening ("won't it destroy my data if I throw it in the trash?"). This bit of magic is too strange for most users.[1]

Figure 8-6 shows an example of an interface metaphor that is near the literal end of the spectrum. This was built with LabVIEW [sNat89], a product from National Instruments for creating interfaces to laboratory data acquisition hardware.

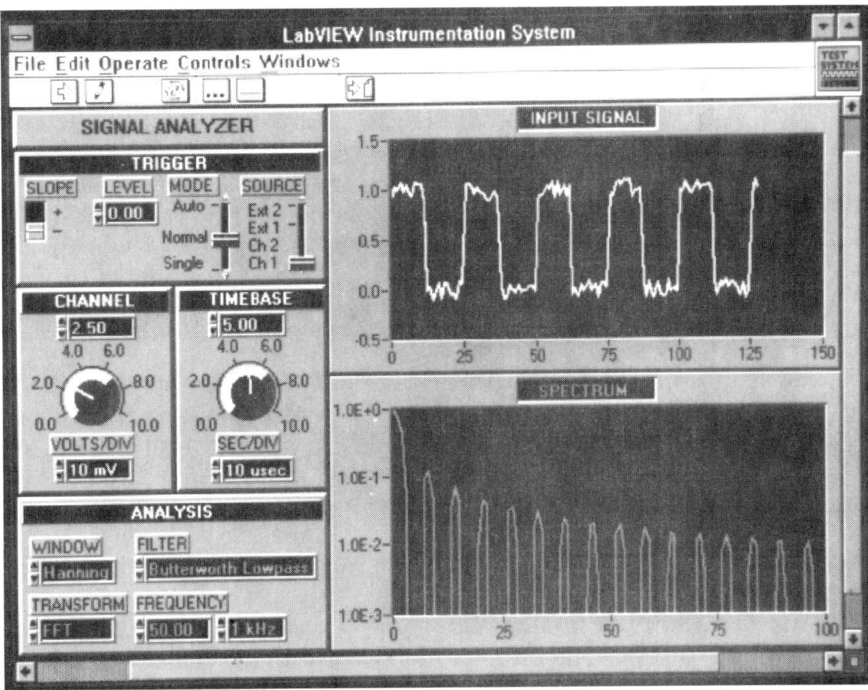

Figure 8-6 A virtual control panel user interface

One of LabVIEW's strengths is its ability to provide technicians with realistic simulations of control panels (here, a typical laboratory oscilloscope). Literalism in the interface is key to this. A good designer, of course, will discover many ways in which this interface could transcend its metaphor.[2] Figure 8-7, a single part from another LabVIEW interface, is

[1] Another questionable use of the trash can metaphor, in *Lotus Organizer*, will be shown in Chapter 9.

[2] See Exercise 2.

one example. Notice the detailing of the screws in the lower corners of the meter. This enhances the user's sense of the meter as a familiar object. Notice also the digital display reading `.8000` below the dial. This is "magic"—analog meters in the real world do not have this feature.

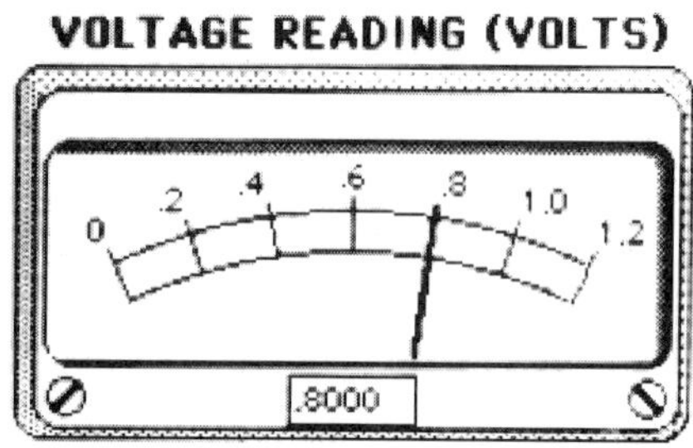

Figure 8-7 A user interface metaphor with both literal and magical features

Comparing interfaces recently built with LabVIEW[1] with those done in the early days of the product (about six years ago) tells an interesting story. Over time, there are fewer literal features such as the screws, and more use of standard GUI controls. This reflects the fact that over the same period the end users have become more comfortable with computers and are willing to trade literalism for more power. Like the forms used by Cigna (page 191), the control panel metaphor here allows users to make a smooth transition.

The literalism-magic dimension is valuable in finding, evaluating, and extending metaphors. Exploring breakdowns (situations where things do not work as users would like them to) can lead to magic that seems very natural. The "magic paper" of word processing is an example. Breakdowns in typing include mistakes that have to be erased, insertions that require a whole document to be retyped, etc. Users are delighted when these aspects of the real-world object go away.

Steps in finding metaphors The activity of "finding metaphors" is highly creative and difficult to structure, but there are some steps that will help.

The first step is to use brainstorming, or some similar technique, to generate ideas for metaphors.[2] Do this with users, or with people who understand the application domain. A designer unfamiliar with the domain is unlikely to come up with the best idea; whereas users almost always have existing metaphors that are valuable, at least as starting points. No criticism is allowed during this process—the purpose of brainstorming is to generate as many ideas as possible.

[1] LabVIEW has an object-oriented visual interface builder, which incidentally validates the isomorphism principle explained in Chapter 5. Each visible object—in the visual builder, and in the resulting user interface—corresponds to a software object in the system. (Thanks to Roxanne Green, of National Instruments, for a helpful discussion of this and the user migration issue.)

[2] [Ada86] has lots of good techniques for generating ideas.

Besides ideas from users and designers, here are other starting points:

- Objects in the problem domain such as forms, tools, containers, etc.
- Metaphors used in existing applications for the domain, and for similar domains.
- Metaphors based on generalizations of the domain. For example, *forms processing* is a generalization of *insurance claims processing.*
- Metaphors based on domains that contain the target domain. For example, *word processing* is contained in *office work.*
- Metaphors from Section 8.4, *A Catalog of Metaphors.*

Metaphors generated in the first step are then sorted into clusters. If two metaphors are simply restatements of each other, they can be combined. If metaphors are congruent, they can be put in the same cluster. (Tables like Figure 8-3 on page 187 can be used to evaluate congruence.) Metaphors may end up in more than one cluster. For instance, the *form* metaphor is congruent with the *spreadsheet* metaphor, the *desktop* metaphor, and the *magic paper* metaphor.

The next step is to test metaphors for *fit* and *extensibility.* Fit is the extent to which the metaphor really helps users understand the system and task models. It corresponds to literalism in the literalism-magic polarity. Extensibility is the extent to which the metaphor supports the "magic" that will enhance its power without detracting from understandability.

Tables such as those shown in Figures 8-3 and 8-8 are useful in evaluating metaphors. In Figure 8-8, several metaphors for an application are examined by looking at the objects involved in them, and how those objects might appear to a user. You can elaborate on the columns labeled "Objects" and "Tangible presentation and interactions" with descriptive text and sketches to provide a feel for both extensibility and fit.

A final criterion for metaphors is one that was mentioned in Chapter 5: "as simple as possible, but no simpler." Other things being equal, the best metaphor will be as simple as possible, but also cover the problem domain completely (either directly, or through extensions).

8.4 A Catalog of Metaphors

Lakoff and Johnson [Lak80] propose that understanding is always metaphoric—we build comprehension in layers, structuring knowledge of new things in terms of what we already know. These layers are built up from basic physical experiences:

- Our existence in space, with orientations such as up-down, left-right, and front-back, and the ability to move in space.
- Our ability to directly manipulate objects.

Application	Metaphor	Objects	Tangible presentation and interactions
Reading news stories online	Ticker tape	words, paragraphs	passive reading of text
	Encyclopedia	words, paragraphs, pictures, subjects, cross-references	passive reading, picture viewing, search, indexing, cross-referencing
	Newspaper	words, paragraphs, headlines, stories, pictures, topic and layout preferences	passive reading, visual scan, choosing topics, designing layout

Figure 8-8 Evaluating metaphors

- The interactional or behavioral properties of objects, relative to us and to other objects.
- Causal connections, and our ability to organize our activities around desirable states or goals.

This view is similar to that of Piaget and Bruner (discussed in chapter 4), but more radical, since it implies that even abstract symbolic understanding is based on metaphors.

Command Language Metaphors

To see how pervasive basic metaphors are, I examined several command languages[1] for operating systems and utility programs (such as editors) incorporated in the systems. I found 109 commands that can be interpreted as examples of basic metaphor categories similar to those listed above. Based on my own usage, I would guess that these commands account for a large proportion of the total usage of these systems.

Here are the categories and commands. Each command is in the category that seems primary, though in many cases commands fit more than one metaphor.

1. *Position, size, orientation, or motion of objects in space:* `back`, `backup`, `continue`, `down`, `escape`, `exit`, `first`, `fork`, `forward`, `goto`, `last`, `more`, `next`, `on`, `path`, `pause`, `run`, `stream`, `up`, `threads`. Lakoff and Johnson

[1]From UNIX, Microsoft MS-DOS, Digital Vax/VMS, and IBM VM/CMS. Many commands are common across several of these systems.

point out that our own sense of position in space is the basis for understanding the spatial properties of other objects. This is illustrated by terms such as "front" and "back."

2. *Direct manipulation of objects:* `append`, `attach`, `bell`, `break`, `close`, `compress`, `connect`, `deposit`, `disconnect`, `dump`, `expand`, `extract`, `hash`, `link`, `load`, `merge`, `move`, `open`, `pipe`, `push`, `recover`, `remove`, `replace`, `restore`, `retain`, `select`, `set`, `shift`, `sort`, `stack`, `switch`, `take`, `unlock`. This category is closely related to category (1), since we manipulate objects in space. It also is related to *human activities* in category (4), but focuses on the object manipulation itself rather than the purpose of the manipulation.

3. *Body parts, biological objects and functions, physical actions on humans and animals:* `abort`, `debug`, `disable`, `dismount`, `head`, `kill`, `mount`, `purge`, `shell`, `sleep`, `tail`, `spawn`, `tree`. These metaphors are very direct, but they are emotionally charged in most cultures;[1] I suggest not using them in interfaces. Many are particularly offensive if depicted graphically. References to lower animals (`debug`, `shell`) or common abstractions (`head`, `tail`) may be less offensive, and some plant metaphors, such as `tree`, are innocuous. This category, and (5), are more specific subcategories of (2).

4. *Human capabilities, activities, and interactions:* `answer`, `call`, `command`, `create`, `do`, `echo`, `examine`, `find`, `help`, `inquire`, `job`, `make`, `prompt`, `quit`, `recall`, `reply`, `search`, `send`, `server`, `share`, `show`, `view`. Notice that these are abstract, or refer to sensory, intellectual, or speech activities that do not require physical contact with other humans; thus they do not fall into category (3).

5. *Writing and printing, including the production, transmission, and storage of printed media:* `archive`, `copy`, `delete`, `directory`, `edit`, `erase`, `file`, `font`, `format`, `label`, `library`, `list`, `log`, `mail`, `mark`, `menu`, `print`, `read`, `type`, `volume`, `write`. Writing and printing are preferred metaphors for command languages, since they are character-based. Graphical interfaces can also use metaphors based on drawings and other visual media. In general, each "old" technology becomes a metaphor for the new technology that replaces it.

Finding metaphors in command languages is instructive, because it argues that metaphor is a tool for understanding even where the interface has limited representational capabilities. In GUIs the field of metaphorical representation is larger, but the metaphors still have the same basis in human experience.

[1] You can verify this from an anthropology textbook, or by trying them out on friends who are not computer programmers. These metaphors are common in command languages for historical reasons—most such languages were developed by young male programmers, for use by other young male programmers.

Metaphors Based on Human Activities

Most of the metaphors described below are based on objects—books, game tables, forms, desktops, etc. However, ideas for metaphors may originally occur to you as actions or activities: shopping, driving, touring a museum, eating in a restaurant, etc.

My preference is to reformulate action-based metaphors as object-based. Shopping, for example, would lead to a *supermarket* metaphor, perhaps, or a *used car lot* metaphor. Making abstract metaphors concrete, or providing concrete examples, helps in deciding how to represent them. If you keep the associated objects in mind, activity or action-based metaphors can suggest useful contextual representations.

Agents Everyone understands the notion of an *agent* who does a task or activity on someone else's behalf. This is a powerful metaphor that should be used carefully. Raising expectations that cannot be met will only confuse the user, so the interface must make the limitations of the agent very clear [Lau92]. The *agent task* in Hewlett-Packard's NewWave environment[1] [sHew92] is a simple example.

There are cases, even in the best graphical interfaces, where textual commands are useful. For example, if I want to find all the objects that are chapters in this book, the pattern matching command `find dooui*chapt*` may be faster than a visual search. Agents (in this case an "object finder") are useful metaphors for the objects that receive such commands.

Stage and theater A theater can be a spatial metaphor, but the interaction between people (the actors and the audience) is more salient. *Programming by Rehearsal* [Fin84] was an example in which a programmer could get "actors" from "central casting" and "rehearse" them for tasks in a program. Brenda Laurel argues that *theater* is a fundamental metaphor for user interfaces, and has related it to the *agent* metaphor [Lau90a].

Sensory Metaphors

One dimension for classifying metaphors is by what senses they involve. Since the conventional GUI is the dominant platform for OOUIs, visual metaphors predominate. We can enrich our understanding, however, by thinking about metaphors in terms of other senses. What does a book mean to a blind person? This question leads to things like talking books, which are useful for sighted as well as blind people.

Tactile/kinesthetic metaphors play a role in user interfaces involving controls and control panels, perhaps coupled with visual and auditory feedback. There are arcade games based on automobile controls, some of which provide force feedback through the steering wheel. High-end flight simulators have real tactile and force feedback; tactile feedback plays a metaphorical role even on personal computer flight simulator games.

Auditory metaphors such as talking books are worth exploring. Audi-

[1] Described in Chapter 7 (Section 7.5).

tory metaphors can be conveyed visually, by using cartoon "speech balloons." The Macintosh has used sounds for years to signal various events. Now that sound cards have become widely available, users can easily connect "earcons" (icons for the ear [Bla89]) to objects and events. All the sounds of the real world are available, including digitized speech.

I include olfactory metaphors for completeness, though I have never "smelled" one used on a computer. Perfume is sometimes used to enhance magazine ads, and presumably exploits the metaphor "things that smell sweet are good."

Containers

Containers are spatial metaphors that can have any number of dimensions. A line is a 1-D container for its points; a text string is a 1-D array of characters. Most of the 2-D, 2½-D, and 3-D metaphors described below are, in some sense, containers for objects.

Objects in containers can be ordered or unordered. Containers suggest activities such as searching, finding, linking objects, and generally organizing the things they hold. Besides the containers mentioned below, a ten-minute tour of your house will reveal hundreds more—trash cans, closets, backpacks and luggage, pockets in clothing, chests and bureaus, file cabinets, spice racks, dish drainers, bookcases, etc. Outside the house there are thousands more, from supermarket shelves to automobile trunks.

2-D Spatial Metaphors

These are metaphors based on spatial layout of subobjects on a two dimensional (flat) surface. They obviously lend themselves well to presentation on computer displays.

Pieces of paper Paper generalizes many other metaphors, such as letters, pages, posters, forms, spreadsheets, etc. Paper is also a component of other metaphors such as books, drafting tables, etc. Paper can have all sorts of "magical" properties.

Forms are seen constantly in the real world and imitated on computers. Many database programs, dialog boxes, and complete applications are based on forms. A form often incorporates a representation (such as a routing checkoff) of the business process that it is a part of. This makes forms candidates for representing task objects.

Forms can be "magical" without impairing understanding. Subobjects (fields) in a form can provide help to users who are filling them out—popup lists of valid values, immediate notification and explanation when an error is made, etc. Form fields can also interact directly with the objects they describe. A customer icon, for example, can be dropped on a form to fill the customer name and address fields. Forms can also provide spreadsheet-like abilities to automatically calculate sums of fields, etc.

Spreadsheets In a way, spreadsheets are highly specialized forms. They are also structured containers for their cells, which leads to new ideas about what might be in a cell—a picture, a set of objects, a communications link to an information source, etc. Spreadsheet cells can cooperate among themselves to produce all kinds of calculations, summaries, etc.

Many spreadsheets now are 2½ dimensional—that is, they represent stacks of 2-D sheets for different periods, locations, etc.

Pages are 2-D surfaces that hold various information objects—text, paragraphs, pictures, etc. Pages in a computer application can be magical—they can hold objects, such as full-motion video displays, which could not exist on a real physical page. Pages can be composed into objects such as books, notebooks, newspapers, etc.

The *Journalist* application is an example of a *newspaper page*. The key idea of a newspaper is that it is organized to quickly provide an overview, but can also provide details. Computer newspapers can be magical, for example by showing video as well as pictures.

Page layout is a general visual and tactile metaphor for the construction of pages. I say "tactile" because the metaphor includes the notion of "cut and paste," and picking up objects such as graphics to "drag" onto the page.

Drafting tables The idea of a drafting table is that it presents drawing tools arrayed around a large work surface containing the drawing being produced. Sketchpad was the first of many examples, ranging from simple "paint" programs to high end commercial art and computer aided design (CAD) applications. The drafting table metaphor is congruent with *paper, page, page layout*, and many other metaphors.

Light tables are flat, translucent surfaces, lit from below, for viewing slides or film. They allow photographers to get a quick overview of many pictures. As more computers are capable of displaying high-resolution images, this is becoming a popular metaphor. The "magic" is that you can click on a picture, and see it full size (perhaps in full motion, if it represents a video or film clip).

A computer light table, unlike a real one, can allow a user to edit pictures as well as look at them. This leads to a merger of the *light table* with the *drafting table*. [Garb92] describes a prototype for such a system.

Game tables Pong (1972) was the original example of a game table [Per82]. You'll find hundreds of other examples (including the solitaire game discussed in Chapter 5).

Instrument and control panels Figure 8-6 showed an example of a control panel metaphor. When portrayed literally, control panels lend themselves to computer display. They are discussed below, under *Machine Metaphors.*

Menus start from the real objects found in restaurants throughout the world. They add magic in a way that relates to the *control panel* metaphor—each entry on the menu is a "button" that invokes the object or function described. Menus may be shown as arrays of buttons, rather than as text lists.

Maps have been around for millennia, and are among the earliest and most important ways of representing information on a flat surface [All92]. Maps represent information analogically—even a paper map is a metaphor for the territory it represents.

Geographic information systems (GIS) use the map metaphor quite literally. Even there, there is plenty of room for magic. Different categories of information, such as roads, population density, rainfall, etc., can appear as transparent layers, which can be added or removed by the user. Points on the map may have behavior—a city might provide statistics on itself, for example. The basic "bird's-eye" metaphor of maps can be implemented with a vengeance, by allowing users to rapidly pan over the map and zoom in and out. Users may become part of the map, as in applications that use inertial navigation devices to pinpoint the location of a moving car on a roadmap.

More abstract topological maps can be metaphors for workflows, communications networks, semantic networks, etc.

Picture frames and windows The essence of a picture frame is that it establishes the border of a space and tells us that what is inside it is a representation, not the real thing. A window has similar properties; it says that what is seen through it is real, but in a different space from that of the observer. A window also cuts out a specific piece of a larger space for viewing. "Windows" on computer displays are obvious examples of these metaphors.

Blackboards and whiteboards Blackboards are good metaphors for collaborative work, since people use them that way in the real world. Hiroshi Ishii [Ish92] describes a wonderful example of adding magic to this metaphor. A "clearboard" is shared by remote collaborators, who see themselves (by means of video cameras) on opposite sides of a clear surface on which everyone can write or draw.

2½-D Spatial Metaphors

These are metaphors that are more than two dimensional, but only in the sense of incorporating several layers of stacked 2-D surfaces. Each surface in the stack has a 2-D metaphor that should be congruent with the metaphor of the stack. Examples include pages in a book, or stacks of documents in a file folder.

Desktops and briefcases The *desktop* metaphor has already been explained. I call this a 2½-D metaphor because almost all desktop systems support the "messy desk" model—open windows representing documents can be stacked on top of one another. This is a literal feature of desktops, and it causes problems in the real world as it does on computer screens.

One "magical" solution to messy desks is a set of tools for finding objects, through lists or queries. Another idea is the ability to have *many* messy desks, which can be hidden and retrieved at will. Briefcases are one of several metaphors that can represent desktops that are not currently in use.

Desktops often contain other containers to help organize the clutter. File cabinets, folders, drawers, books, etc., are congruent with the desktop metaphor.

Books with pages are obvious choices for many applications. Subcategories include notebooks with index tabs, scrapbooks, photo albums, cookbooks, etc. Newspapers are similar.

Books of all sorts can support the magic of hypertext, which links parts of the book and allows users to travel directly along the links, instead of moving in a linear way through the book. Hypertext links are somewhat like *doors.*

Notebooks add index tabs to the basic book metaphor, and also have an informal "I'm here to be used" feel. *Lotus Organizer* [sLot93] is a good example, which also uses hypertext to move between pages of the notebook and presents desktop accessories arrayed around the notebook pages.

The *Virtual Notebook System* [sFor93] uses a notebook as a metaphor for collaborative work. Users can create, modify, or comment on individual pages, which contain text, images, and commentary. Pages can be viewed simultaneously by many users.

Index card files Card files with index tabs are widely used in the real world. Implementations on computers range from the simple *Cardfile* application that comes with Microsoft Windows, to Apple's *HyperCard,* which uses magic extensively to link cards via buttons and add text, graphics, and full motion video to them.

Early Smalltalk-80 systems have window labels that do not extend completely across the top of the windows, but look like index tabs. This allows windows to be arranged like a card file on the desktop.[1]

Doors and rooms Rooms are containers for organizing things; for example, you could have a room for each project you are working on, each with its own desktop. Doors are ways of getting from room to room. In the real world, doors open only to adjacent rooms. In computer systems, magical doors can take you anywhere.

I call this a 2½-D metaphor because most current implementations, such as *Rooms for Windows* [sXer92] from Xerox, present 2-D doors as access points into 2-D rooms. When better technology is available, we will no doubt see true rooms with depth, in which a user can move around. (The *Ark Workspace* shown below is an example.)

[1] An example appears in Chapter 11 (Figure 11-11).

3-D Spatial Metaphors

3-D space is a powerful metaphor. Most people can remember, in great detail, houses they lived in many years ago. Learning a new space, though, can be difficult. "Magical" navigation capabilities can ease this process for new users.

Doorways Doors were just described as a 2½-D metaphor, but have 3-D implications as well. A door is a metaphor for something that opens to another space. Randall Smith's Alternate Reality Kit [Smith87] had a space warp or "wormhole" to connect widely separated places on a very large simulated workspace or desktop. An extension would be a *transporter* metaphor (as in *Star Trek*) to create doorways at will between arbitrary points in 3-D space.

Buildings Figure 8-9 shows the *Ark Workspace* [sArk92].[1] The drawers on the right side of the room hold sets of objects for projects, which the user can move to the desk. The bookshelves on the left hold general tools, such as a calculator and calendar. Other objects, such as the calendar hanging on the wall, are also functional and have behavior. Large areas on the display are "inert," and are there only to support the 3-D illusion. Efficient use of the 3-D metaphor requires the ability to "move around" in space. Forthcoming products from Ark and other vendors will support user-controlled motion through 3-D spaces.

Other special cases of buildings in 3-D space may prove useful in certain applications—Post Offices, libraries, museums, homes, castles, dungeons, etc.

Earth's surface and atmosphere, outer space Many computer games, ranging from auto races through undersea adventures to flight simulators, exploit these metaphors. Flight simulators show that you can give the user a "true" 3-D space, even with a 2-D display. They do this by allowing users to move in the space.

There are research systems that allow a user to "fly" through data.[2] The ultimate extension of this is the *cyberspace* described in William Gibson's visionary novels [Gib84]. It is not clear yet how very large data spaces can be best organized. The earth, solar system, etc., are good organizers for data about themselves, of course; they may be good metaphors for other domains as well.

Spacewar, the earliest graphical computer game [Bra74], used space as a metaphor, and was quite difficult, even though the space was not truly 3-D. Users of data-intensive applications, however, may be willing to become "rocket jockeys" on high-performance user interfaces.

[1] US Patent 07/786,291. © 1992-1994 Ark Interface, Inc. All rights reserved.
[2] One called *Info Navigator*, from Silicon Graphics, appears in the film *Jurassic Park*.

Figure 8-9 Ark Workspace "room" metaphor

Space and Time

People deal with space better than time, as philosophers from St. Augustine to Einstein have known. This has been validated for modern computer users as well [Carr82]. Transforming from the temporal to the spatial domain is a rich source of metaphors, in ordinary language and user interfaces: "Time marches on." "At what point in time were you there?" "Looking forward to the future."

Time is a one-dimensional medium, which permits motion in only one direction ("forward," toward the future). Space is a three-dimensional medium, but motion in space can be restricted to one dimension and direction by one-way roads, railroad tracks, etc. In these contexts, motion in space equals motion in time.

Many applications in science deal with the measurement and understanding of events in time, and commercial applications often require the management of complex activities occurring over time. Abstract spatial representations of temporal events have been in use for centuries, and are an obvious source of ideas for computer representation. Gantt charts,[1]

[1]Named after H. L. Gantt, an associate of Frederick Taylor. The "timeline" charts of development in Chapter 6 are Gantt charts. PERT charts show networks of tasks in a workflow involving parallel activities.

showing parallel timelines, and PERT charts, which show intersecting timelines, are examples. ("Intersecting timelines" is a complex idea, but can be explained with a metaphor of intersecting roads or railroad tracks.)

Clocks and calendars Gantt and PERT charts show time as a line punctuated by significant events or "milestones" (another spatial metaphor). People also structure time with standard units—hours, days, weeks, etc. Clocks show time as one dimensional, but circular, emphasizing the recurrence of minutes, hours, and days. Clock time can also be laid out in a straight line, as it is in a daily appointment schedule.

Standard wall calendars are a 2-D representation of time, based on the recurrent unit of the week. The passage of weeks is shown on the vertical axis, and the passage of days on the horizontal. For timelines extending over weeks or months, the calendar may enable users to grasp durations more easily than the timeline in a Gantt chart. The 2-D organization also facilitates accessing individual days quickly, which is why "month at a glance" schedules use this format.

Computer implementations can add magic to these metaphors by changing representations on demand, and by "zooming in and out" in time. The calendar in Lotus Organizer is an example—clicking on a date in the monthly calendar brings up the appointment schedule for that day.

There is another, quite different, use of the ability to transform between time and space. Computer screens have limited ability to display information, compared to books or maps. By changing the display rapidly under user control, allowing users to home in on the information they need, the limitation can often be overcome. This technique substitutes successive display in time for simultaneous display in space.

Machine Metaphors

This is a category for old technology that acts as a metaphor for new technology. Most machine metaphors, such as the typewriter, focus on objects that are tools. The tools, in turn, help the user to manipulate the ultimate objects of interest (in the case of the typewriter, characters and words on paper). Success with a machine metaphor depends on understanding which aspects of the old technology can help users navigate in the new environment, and which ones need to be thrown away or transcended with "magic."

Instrument and control panels are basically 2-D, so they readily lend themselves to computer displays. LabVIEW, shown in Figure 8-6, is an example. Control panels are congruent with other metaphors, and are used in all sorts of applications such as flight simulators. VCR controls, which are congruent with the *television* metaphor, are widely used to control multimedia applications.[1]

Radio buttons, used in all GUIs, are based on a control panel (the

[1] An example is shown in Chapter 15 (Figure 15-7).

Just as the stage magician uses simple mechanisms, and showmanship, to give the audience the illusion of supernatural powers, the designer uses computer technology, and good design, to give the user the illusion of an environment based on the problem domain. Audiences (at magic shows or user interfaces) are willing, even desirous, of believing the illusion, as long as it is seamless. Tog points out a few things designers can learn from magicians about making seamless illusions.

8.5 Summary

The "user's conceptual model" is something we design to help people learn and use a system or application. Its design is based on discovering what expert users know about the problem domain, and designing a representation of objects and services appropriate to the computer domain. It includes procedures as well as objects and relationships. The user's conceptual model includes a *system model*, incorporating knowledge of objects and relationships, and a *task model*, incorporating procedural knowledge about doing tasks. *Metaphors* help give overall structure to the model. You can think of the user's conceptual model as a roadmap and driver's guidebook to the system.

In reality, different users have their own private mental models of the system. Even in the best case, these will differ based on needs and experience. The most successful applications, such as spreadsheets and word processors, show that a good model can be useful to many different users.

Design of the user's conceptual model starts with the data from system and task analysis. Brainstorming and other creative techniques will yield metaphors that provide structure. Effort spent in this activity will lead to a more usable system, and will simplify the process of designing the "look and feel" of the user interface.

8.6 To Explore Further

My exploration of models and metaphors started with the work of Jack Carroll and his colleagues. [Carr82] is an early, but clear, presentation of issues and guidelines for using metaphors in computer interfaces. [Carr88b] provides additional insight, examples, and guidance on picking the right metaphor. [Carr88a] is a guide to research in mental models, and how they may help or hinder computer users.

Though in some ways the use of metaphors in user interfaces is "obvious," it is a technique that is difficult to apply. Developers often have trouble generalizing from simple examples to the more complex situations they encounter in real projects. I recommend the work of George Lakoff and Mark Johnson for further study, even though their book, *Metaphors*

We Live By [Lak80], is not about computers or interfaces. Metaphors, they argue, are fundamental to our understanding of things in the world. So, just as fish probably do not pay much attention to water, we swim through this "cognitive sea" of metaphors without noticing it. Paying attention to metaphors in everyday life will sharpen your appreciation of how they can help people to understand computer systems.

Lewis [Lew91] discusses direct metaphoric understanding versus symbol manipulation. He argues that the task of the user interface designer is to allocate users' cognitive processing resources to the tasks they do best.

Vernor Vinge's *True Names* [Ving87] is the best example I know showing the use of magic in user interfaces. Science fiction novels such as this and William Gibson's *Neuromancer* [Gib84] are good tools for jump-starting the process of finding metaphors.

8.7 Exercises

1. Write a short description of some computer application or system, as though you were explaining the system to someone who was unfamiliar with it. Analyze what you have written, looking for metaphors and similes. See how many alternate metaphors you can invent for the same concepts. By changing metaphors, can you make your explanation more coherent?
2. Ask yourself the question "if an instrument control panel had magical properties, what could it do?"
   a. Based on your answer, how could you enhance the control panel metaphor shown in Figure 8-6?
   b. Besides adding "magic" to the metaphor, is there any benefit to having both analog and digital displays in Figure 8-7? (Think of tasks the user of this interface might be doing.)
3. Pick one or more metaphors from Section 8.4, *A Catalog of Metaphors*. Find as many examples as you can of computer applications or systems that use the metaphors you chose.
4. Take one or more of the application concepts in the table below. List as many metaphors as you can for the concept. Decide whether each metaphor is congruent or incongruent with the objects required by the problem domain. What tangible representation does each metaphor suggest for the important objects and actions?

Application	Metaphor	Objects	Tangible presentation and interactions
Database/file server			
Communications network			
Repair shop scheduling			
Image database query			

5. Use Appendix 1, *Fax Case Study*, and the results from Chapter 7, Exercise 4, to design a user's conceptual model.
   a. Develop a system model and diagram it using Booch [Boo94], OMT [Rum91], or your favorite notation. You will need to do a little analysis "on the fly," based on your task analysis data.
   b. Design a task model based on the system model and task analysis. Describe the tasks using the same format you used for existing task descriptions.
   c. Describe metaphors you think will help users understand the objects and tasks.

9

Information Presentation

Chapter 8 covered the user's conceptual model, which structures the way that users perceive and interact with objects. This chapter is about representing objects through the physical medium of the computer and its output devices. Chapter 10 addresses techniques for interacting with the objects.

As Alan Kay said [Kay77b], computers, as media, can simulate all other media. A window on a computer display can be a book, a painting, or a television. Computers can play music, speak, and produce tactile sensations. This makes the topic of "representing objects through the medium of the computer" almost limitless.

However, current technology limits the actual computer medium. In terms of size, resolution and color, paper is still better than a computer display. Presenting digital sound and pictures requires more storage than many computers provide. Devices that present data to sense organs other than the eyes and ears are crude or nonexistent.

The style in art called *trompe-l'œil* (French for "fool the eye") refers to paintings that make the viewer think they are real objects. *Trompe-l'œil* is a metaphor for the design of object-oriented user interfaces within the limits of technology. We need to "fool" the senses, and more importantly, the mind, to provide the feeling of working with real objects.

"Real objects" is a broad concept. To a mathematician, for example, the expression $\Sigma f(x)\Delta x$ represents a perfectly good object. The goal of the OOUI designer is not to deny the abstract nature of objects such as these, but to provide useful, concrete ways of seeing and interacting with them. This reduces the burden on users—of translating objects and actions between their language and the computer's language.

Computer users are exposed every day to high-quality media design in magazines, newspapers, television, radio, and commercial audio disks. In this area, perhaps more than any other, professional designers can enhance the look of an interface. This is not simply a matter of aesthetics or "polish"—graphic and other media designers can help present information *efficiently* within the confined surface of a computer display.

This chapter presents the elements used in composing designs on computer displays, and a step-by-step method for designing the appearance of OOUIs. Covering every aspect of information design in one chapter is not possible, so I will concentrate on three areas:

- Relations between computer output and human sensory input.
- Using principles of object-orientation in presenting information.
- Basing the overall structure of information presentation on the user's conceptual model.

Knowledge of these topics will foster a fruitful collaboration between OO software designers and media design specialists.

9.1 Human Senses, Information, and Technology

Most human-computer interfaces are "sensist" in favoring vision above other senses. Sound is available as an output medium on many platforms, and haptic (touch and force) information will eventually be part of user interfaces as well. Because technology is rapidly changing, it behooves designers to have a broad perspective on presenting information.

Consider this item of information: "a force of five pounds." I have expressed it in language, as visual text. I could express the text as sound—as spoken words, or in a non-verbal form with the convention that increased loudness means more force. This suggests a visual portrayal such as lines or bars whose size corresponds to the amount of force. With an appropriate device, we could present the force in the most direct possible way, to the sense of touch (the user would feel the force directly on a body part such as the hand). All these presentations are valid, and useful in the right context. The key variables in the context are the capabilities (or preferences) of the user, and the nature of the task. Visual presentation will not work if the user is blind; audio presentation will not work if the user is deaf. In solving a physics problem a graph may be appropriate; in giving feedback to the operator of a remote robot, tactile force may be required to do the task.

The Senses

The five conventional senses are sight, hearing, smell, taste, and touch. Sight is the sense most exploited in user interfaces, with hearing next, and touch a very distant third.

Sight Vision is the dominant sense for most people, which partly explains the predominance of visual presentation in user interfaces. People with normal vision get more information through this sense than others, and in the presence of conflicting sensory information, most people give precedence to vision [How87]. Listening to amplified sound is an example—when listening to someone singing into a microphone, we locate the sound at the singer, not the loudspeaker, if the loudspeaker is not too far away from the singer.[1]

Another reason for the predominance of visual effects in user interfaces is that visual displays have been in use longer than any other computer output devices.[2] The quality of sound output devices for computers is now as good as that of visual displays, but except for people with visual deficiencies, they supplement rather than replace vision.

Visual media are two-dimensional, so vision has a dimensional advantage over hearing. Spoken words are linear, and synthesizing the "big picture" relies on the memory of the listener. Older computer interfaces, which display output one line at a time, suffer a similar disadvantage.

Hearing Sound is a rich information medium, underused in computer interfaces. Capabilities such as identifying a familiar voice in the babble of a noisy room, or picking out the clarinet in a symphony orchestra, are remarkable [Moo87].

Blind people rely extensively on sound and are skilled at using it to synthesize a sense of objects in space. Sighted people are also good at localizing sound sources in three dimensions, but they rely more on vision for their global sense of space.

Sound, from bells, sirens, and other alarms, is widely used for alerting people to things they must pay immediate attention to. Sound is superior for this function because it is omnidirectional; people will miss visual cues if they are not looking in the right direction. Sound as an alarm must be used carefully. I have seen monitoring applications in which alarms are presented constantly, in which case the operators simply ignore them (or turn off the sound).

People can multiprocess among the different senses, and this is particularly evident with hearing and sight.[3] Most people can listen to a radio while driving a car, without being distracted; many people listen to "talking books" while driving. This capability can increase the information bandwidth of a user interface. For example, presenting help or tutorial information with recorded speech allows a user to pay attention visually to the problem area, while still attending to the help information. (This also avoids the common problem of having the help text cover up the display the user needed help understanding.)

Smell and taste Dog owners know that "olfactory space" is an important

[1] "Too far away" is typically an angular distance of about 30°.

[2] I include typewriters as visual displays.

[3] This is not quite so simple as I make it out to be; see [San85], Chapter 4.

part of canine life. Though less important for humans, there are situations where smell is a prominent component of experience. Walking down Mulberry Street, in lower Manhattan, I pass through the district known as Little Italy. Regions of space are permeated with the smells of garlic, oregano, and other spices from restaurants, or wine, cheese, and espresso from outdoor cafés. Crossing Canal Street, I enter Chinatown and the character of olfactory space changes—now there is the smell of Chinese cooking, sidewalk fish markets, and incense from gift shops.

Remarkably, smell was used in a completely mechanical prototype "virtual reality" device called *Sensorama*, developed in Hollywood in the 1950s.[1] Sensorama provided the sights, sounds, feel, and smell of a motorcycle ride through Brooklyn, New York. Small fans wafted smells across the user's nose at the appropriate moments. I am not aware of any computer interface that exploits the olfactory sense (or the related sense of taste).

Touch and haptic senses The general category "touch" covers many different sensory capabilities, including the ability to feel pressure, vibration, heat, and pain. We also have kinaesthetic sensors, which register forces on muscles and joints, and help us figure out our position and motion in space. There is a *haptic* sense of touch, which involves coordination between sensory and motor capabilities as we touch, grasp, or handle objects. It is this haptic sense we use, for example, in identifying objects by texture (think of running your fingers over velvet, or sandpaper).

Small children use haptic touch constantly to "find the objects" and make sense out of the world [Pia67]. Most adults rely more on vision, at least for familiar objects. Haptic touch influences the "feel" of a user interface. This is obvious in the use of physical devices such as the keyboard and mouse, and there is also a *virtual* haptic sense. If a user "picks up" and "drags" an icon across the display, visual feedback when the mouse moves should be instantaneous. If it is not—if there is a perceptible delay—users will sometimes report that the mouse "feels sticky," though there is no physical difference.

Touch as a presentation medium is not generally available outside research laboratories. This is because of the difficulty of implementing it, not because it would not be useful. Its value to blind users is clear—imagine being able to move your hand across a computer "desktop" and identify objects by touch, or read text by touch on a Braille display [Web93]. Touchable objects would also benefit sighted users, particularly in a 3-D interface (the proof of this is that we rely on it in the real world). Touch can convey large amounts of information, illustrated by the ability to discriminate textures such as different grades of sandpaper.

Simple devices such as a mouse with force feedback [Pen93] will probably be available within a few years. Virtual touch, as in the "sticky mouse" example above, is important to designers today.

[1]Discussed in [Rhei91], Chapter 2. [Cot93], p. 30, shows a picture of Sensorama.

Sensory coordination Senses do not operate in isolation. First, they are substitutable. Blind people acquire much the same knowledge of the world as those with sight, though they use different senses ([Sac93], [Gre87a]). Second, we synthesize many properties of objects from several senses. Texture, for example, has visual and tactile components. Third, sensory perceptions may evoke other, different perceptions. Smelling a familiar food (pizza, say, for those in the US and Europe) can evoke a visual impression; reading a description in a novel can evoke the sights and sounds of the scene.

Many virtual reality applications provide striking examples of sensory coordination [Rhei91]. I used a system [Wen93] intended to demonstrate the creation of a virtual "acoustic space." The sound sources were high-fidelity, and localized in 3-D space. It also used a very low-resolution head-mounted display to allow users to "see" the objects. When the sound was turned on, there was a sudden and remarkable increase in the "reality" of the seen objects. A similar phenomenon has been reported in multimedia applications. When accompanied by high-fidelity stereo sound, the apparent quality of the displayed video improves.[1]

People not only coordinate their senses, they coordinate sensory and motor activity, as in haptic touch. In virtual reality applications such as the one just described, the sense of reality increases if the user can move around the objects,[2] particularly if they can be touched or grasped. This is true in the real world as well—we understand objects as a gestalt of their interactional properties, not just based on a single sense.

Coordination of senses and motor activity has implications for user interface design. By following a couple of principles, designers can help users get "the sense of objects" and a better understanding of what they see. First, provide redundant information through different senses or different aspects of the same sense. Graphical information, for example, can be shown through outline, shading, and color, and supplemented with textual description and sound. Second, allow users to see objects from different points of view. Graphical information can be shown in different scales, rotated and resized, or reformatted. Objects with the ability to make sounds can alter their volume or timbre to indicate a change in position relative to the user.

Sensory Information Capacity[3]

The raw materials designers work with include physical devices for displaying information. These devices have output capacities that we can measure in bits per second, and it seems reasonable to ask about the input

[1] I have experienced this; I have also heard studies mentioned by Nicholas Negroponte and Brenda Laurel, though I have not seen them in the literature.

[2] You can experience this phenomenon with flight simulators such as Microsoft's [sMic93a].

[3] I am indebted to Bernice Rogowitz for a discussion on this topic with respect to vision.

capacity of the sensory channels they are aimed at. How much information do we need to throw at users, and how much can they catch?

Take vision as an example. Computer displays cannot fill the entire visual field with a "realistic" view; this suggests that the output bandwidth of displays is less than the input bandwidth of human vision. The question is not so simple, however. People are constantly presented with large sensory fields, but pay attention only to small parts of them. Furthermore, attention is divided between a central or focal part of the field, and a peripheral part. The central part gets most of the attention, but changes in the periphery can cause attention to shift rapidly.[1]

I have heard figures as high as three gigabits per second proposed as the capacity of the human visual system, but I have seen no evidence to support such rates. I can imagine following a fast-paced hockey game on TV, which pushes the limits of my visual ability. Transmitting this requires about 100 megabits per second.[2] The TV screen only fills about 1% of my visual field,[3] but it includes the central region, where acuity is greatest. I am attending mostly to the hockey puck and the players near it, not the entire field; this would certainly put the upper limit in the megabit, not gigabit range.

Based on physiological and neurological factors, psychologists estimate the input bandwidth of the visual system to be about 600 kilobits per second [Dit87]. A quick calculation gives a figure of about 2.5 megabits to show static data on an SVGA display,[4] typical for personal computers. This means that the eye cannot instantaneously process all the data on the display, but over a brief period it can scan and assimilate what is on the display and in the surrounding visual field.

Similar considerations apply to the other senses. Bandwidth for human sound processing is estimated at about 10 kilobits per second [Dit87]. Audio CDs record sound at 640 kilobits per second,[5] and are still unlikely to fool people into hearing live sound. This is primarily because the CD sound, though stereophonic, presents a single audio "point of view," and does not change its characteristics to match the listener's movements. (Current implementations of "immersive" sound require hundreds of MIPS of processing power per sound source [Wen93].) People can move around a crowded and noisy room, rapidly shifting attention from one conversation to another while blocking out what they are not attending to. So, as with vision, assimilating large amounts of information from the environment occurs over time, not instantaneously.

Total bandwidth for tactile information has the same order of magni-

[1] The human eye can move across the visual field at 800° per second.

[2] This is for the "raw" signal; data compression reduces it to less than 10 mb/s [Mil94].

[3] The entire visual field is about 100° both horizontally and vertically. At typical viewing distance, a TV occupies less than 10° in both dimensions. The central part of the retina, the fovea, covers about 2°.

[4] 640 by 480 pixels, at 8 bits per pixel. SVGA is a display standard for IBM-compatible PCs.

[5] 40,000 16-bit samples per second.

tude as that for sound [Shi93]. The environment presents a large quantity of information that we ignore, such as the feel of the clothes we are wearing. We can focus rapidly on novel sensations, such as the feel of a crawling insect.

The key message here for designers is that the information that is most important to the user should be presented "centrally" in the sensory field. (The meaning of "central" is obvious in vision, and can be found by experiment for other senses.) Move less important information to the periphery and mute it, so it does not distract. If an item of peripheral information becomes important, use strong sensory cues such as sounds or color changes to draw attention to it. Do not waste space in the center of the field on information that does not change—users will become habituated and ignore it. The user's bandwidth is large, but it should not be wasted on information that is not relevant to the task.

Technological and sensory limits How close is technology to matching human perceptual capabilities? Computers can overwhelm users with pure quantity of information, and the designer's task is to filter and organize it. People are very good at zooming in on details, so the rendering of those details helps determine the quality of the interface. Vision illustrates this.

Under ideal conditions, the human eye can discriminate objects covering about one minute of arc in the visual field. At a typical viewing distance for a computer display, say 24 inches (61 centimeters), this corresponds to a "picture element" (pixel) about .007 inches (.018 cm) across. The pixel density is about 143 per inch, or 56 per centimeter. This is as good as the best commercial CRT displays (typical displays are under 100 pixels per inch). A laboratory prototype LCD from Xerox [Wer93] can display 284 pixels per inch (112/cm). This is still not up to paper—high quality typesetters print at 1200 or 2400 dots per inch (472 or 945/cm). For most visual tasks, however, it is equivalent.

Putting this sort of data together with data on the bandwidth of sensory input, the technology we have today (at least for sight and sound) can match human capabilities, but only from a single point of view. It is the ability of people to rapidly shift their attention and point of view that stresses the available output devices. I suspect this is the origin of the "three gigabit" figure—though the eye cannot absorb all this at one instant, the display needs the higher bandwidth to create the whole visual field. The whole field is needed because we cannot predict where the user will want to look.

This problem is a point of leverage for designers. By anticipating users' information needs (through task analysis) we can present what is most important in the foreground, and provide ways of changing to other points of view. By understanding how people think about the information (through conceptual modeling) we can present it in the most efficient form. The task is to apply knowledge of human senses and cognition to maximize the power of available display technology.

9.2 Views, Presentation Metaphors, and Patterns

Figure 9-1 shows elements from typical GUIs. There is a large area (the display screen) which contains smaller areas (windows).[1] Windows contain objects, including smaller sub-windows. Windows may be tiled (non-overlapping), as in the window on the upper right, where the rectangular sub-windows fit together like tiles. Except for tiled areas, the space of the screen appears 2½-dimensional—windows overlap one another like flat sheets of paper. Objects such as the button that says `Push Me` can be shaded to suggest that they are 3-dimensional. There are also non-rectangular "windows," such as the cartoon character saying "Need help?"

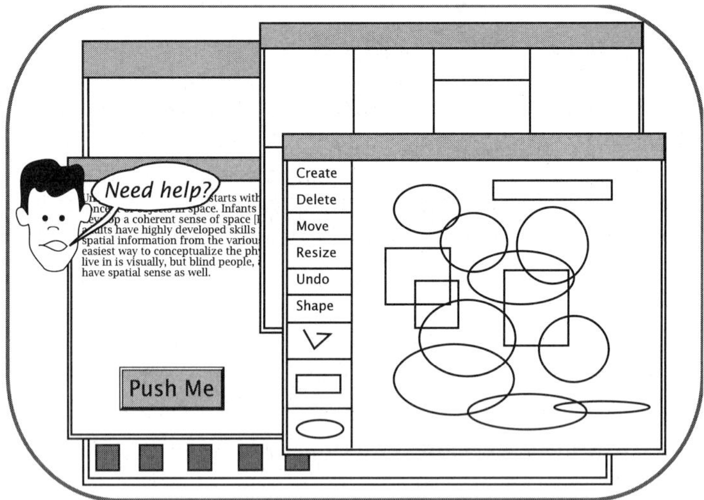

Figure 9-1 Visual elements in a graphical user interface

The general metaphor in Figure 9-1 is *objects in space* that the user can manipulate. The space is visual, but the metaphor is more general; if the objects had the right behavior, the space could just as well be apprehended through touch or hearing. Almost all of the metaphors in Section 8.4, *A Catalog of Metaphors*, invoke the *objects in space* metaphor.

Objects in space-time might be more accurate, since the behavior of objects occurs in time as the user interacts with them. Time is critical in computer presentation, since the display space is limited. Information that cannot be presented all at once must be revealed over time. Individual objects present themselves using subsidiary metaphors such as *human conversation* (the cartoon character) or a *drafting table* (the drawing window).

These ideas are the starting point for designing a presentation space

[1] Technically, windows are areas on the physical display managed by a window or presentation manager; they usually contain object views plus associated framing and control mechanisms. Where no danger of confusion exists, I use "window" and "view" synonymously.

for the OOUI: views of objects, placed in space (or in a hierarchy of containing spaces), whose behavior unfolds over time.

Views

Each object on the screen that displays the behavior of some object in the implementation model is a *view*. Views may be composed from smaller views, as in the window on the lower right in Figure 9-1, containing rectangles and ellipses. The notion of an object in the implementation is unambiguous, at least if the system is built using an object-oriented programming language. "An object on the screen" bears further discussion, since it can only be reasonably defined based on what users perceive.

Take Figure 9-2 as an example. What are the objects in the interface? There are seven icons in the lower left of the display, and a window in the upper right, which has sub-objects—the title bar, a sizing border, the menu at the left, the small window titled `Tools`, and the shapes drawn within the main area of the window. The menu and the `Tools` window also have sub-objects, such as the area that says `Create` and the icons under `Tools`.

Users see these as objects partly by visually parsing what is on the display. This is not the whole story, since haptic or behavioral properties play a role. In interface styles such as CUA or OSF/Motif, window borders can be "grabbed" with the mouse and directly manipulated to resize the window. If they did *not* have that capability, the borders might appear to be decorations, not separate objects.

Objects presented as views on the screen fall into two categories:

- Objects in the system model component of the user's conceptual model.

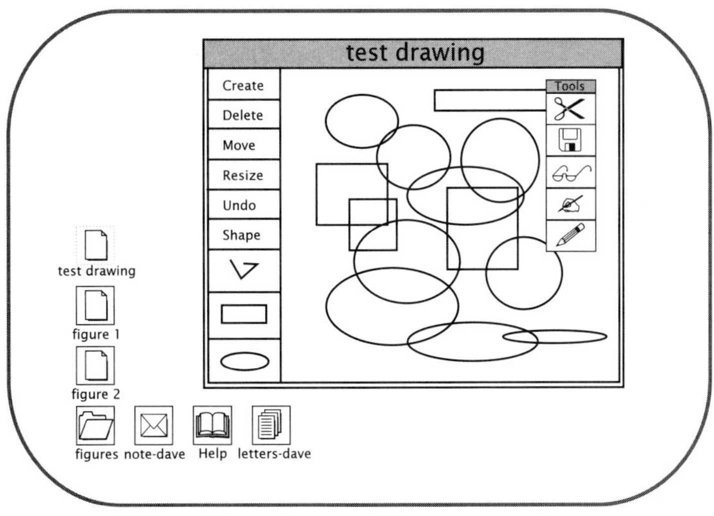

Figure 9-2 Views in a graphical user interface

- Representations of mechanisms that allow the user to manage and interact with views in the first category.

The user's perception decides whether we have succeeded in representing these objects of interest.

Figure 9-3 shows what we are trying to do in designing the display. Objects in the conceptual model are *information objects*—these are the problem domain objects users are interested in. They appear in the interface as *information object views*, which allow users to view and interact with them. Information object views have associated objects called *frames*, which include things like the title bar and window border. Views that allow the user to interact with information, to edit text or graphics for example, have control mechanisms. Many of these, such as menus, scroll bars, and message boxes, have *control mechanism views* that make them visible to the user.

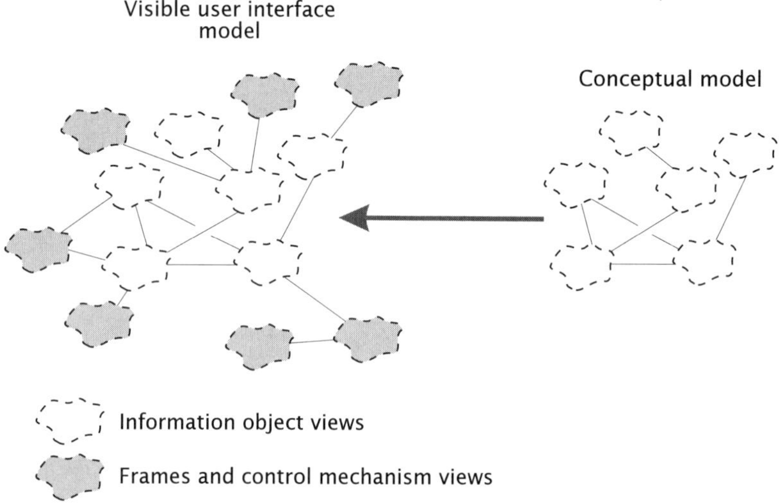

Figure 9-3 Mapping from the conceptual model

An information object may have any number of views. Two major categories are *icons* and *content views*. Icons economize on display space; they identify the object, and afford interactions such as opening a content view or dropping on other icons. They can also display simple state changes. For example, the dashed border around the icon for the object `test drawing` in Figure 9-2 shows that a content view is open on the object.

Figure 9-4 shows three different content views of the same information object, a collection of customers of `First National Bank`. Icon views, such as (a), are useful where rapid visual identification of object types is important. Here, where there is only one object type, it is not very efficient. Unless it is important to visually emphasize the "objectness" of the customers, a list view, as in (b), is easier to scan and makes better use of screen space. Items in the list can be dragged with the mouse, just as in the icon view. Mini-icons (small icons) can be placed to the left of each text item to use space efficiently, but still provide the icon as a visual "handle" for the object.

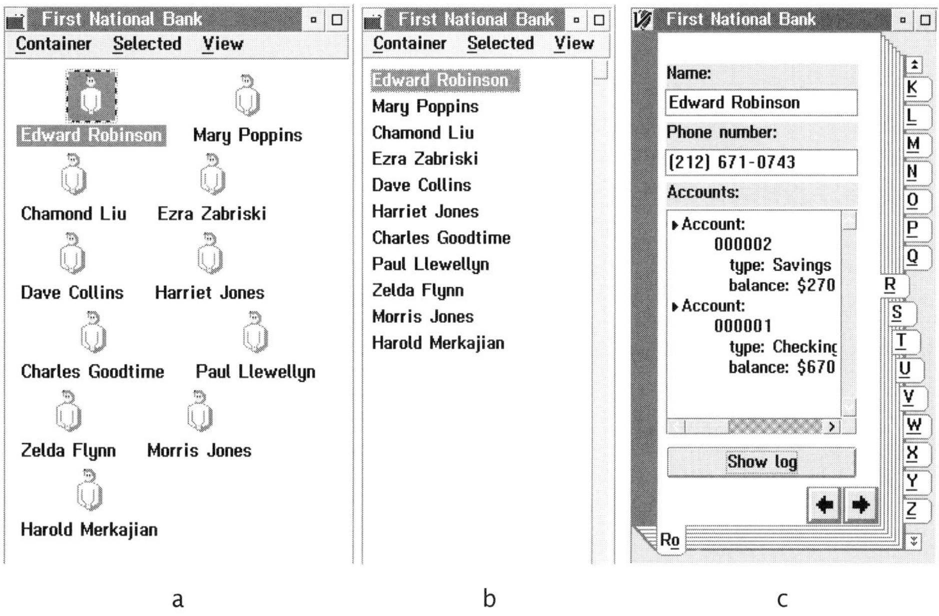

Figure 9-4 Three views of a collection of objects

In views (a) and (b), seeing details for an individual customer requires some additional action, such as double-clicking to open a content view. View (c), which uses the notebook metaphor, supports tasks in which the user needs to see summary information for the customer. Pages in the notebook (one per customer) show the content of the collection; each page individually is a summarized content view of a customer.

Viewing objects in containers or collections is a generic task for which there are many standard design solutions. Designing views is not always simple, and is usually specific to the problem domain for the objects of interest. Applications in some domains, such as graphics and word processing, have existed for long enough that there are standard representations. These may serve, with modifications, for other domains as well.

Presentation Metaphors

Metaphors help structure the user's conceptual model by portraying the unfamiliar (the metaphor target) in terms of the familiar (the metaphor source). The source is usually more concrete, and has visual or other sensory content. Presentation metaphors are simply concrete realizations of the concepts expressed by metaphors—as Figure 9-4 (c) concretizes the *notebook metaphor*, for example. Presenting the sensory content of metaphors in the user interface helps users to recognize or learn the conceptual model.[1]

Most presentation metaphors are visual, though they often represent more general spatial ideas that could be conveyed through other senses. In principle, metaphors should be presented through at least their most strongly associated senses—vision for written text or pictures, and hearing for speech. In practice, this is about as far as current interfaces go in terms of supporting the senses.

Objects in space and time Understanding the world starts with developing an idea of objects in space that persist and evolve over time. An important property of real objects, often violated in user interfaces, is continuity—real objects do not appear, disappear, or change state in arbitrary ways. Causal connections should be clear, and metaphors can reinforce them. An example is the appearance of a content view when the user "opens" an icon. In some interfaces[2] the opening of the content window is animated to show it exploding outward from the icon. This provides visual continuity and reinforces the causal link.

Causality unfolds in time. This is important for information presentation because our experience with objects in the world conditions how we expect them to behave on the screen. Imagine seeing a child throwing a ball. The ball passes behind a tree, which generates an expectation that it will momentarily reappear on the other side. If it does not, you sense an interruption in the normal flow of events. Now imagine coming back to the same spot a week later and finding that the tree is gone. What happened? Again, the expected flow is interrupted, and you expend mental energy trying to figure things out.

Users should focus their energies on the problem domain, not the interface. Failure to support expectations about object constancy and continuity interferes with this.

Three-dimensional space Objects in most user interfaces are at most 2½-dimensional; though they can overlap one another, they have no true depth. The Ark workspace shown in Figure 8-9 (Chapter 8) is an example of portraying objects in 3-D space. The advantage of 3-D space is that the higher dimensionality provides a structure that helps the user locate more objects by position.

Fully exploiting the 3-D metaphor requires that users be able to shift their point of view. Otherwise, as in the Ark system, much of the screen space contains details that support the 3-D illusion, but have no real information content. To preserve the sense of object constancy, motion in space must seem smooth and continuous in response to user control [Macki91]. This is possible on a standard flat display, but requires more

[1] Broad categories are discussed here; almost all the metaphors in Section 8.4, *A Catalog of Metaphors*, have obvious concrete representations.

[2] The Macintosh Desktop and the OS/2 Workplace Shell, for example.

graphics power than is available in many desktop machines today.

Frames The idea of a frame is that something goes on inside it that is different from what goes on outside. Picture frames, window frames, and fences are all examples, as are the tabs, rings, and binder that frame a notebook. Frames may exclude (as the fence does) or they may invite (as does the frame of an open door). Interesting frames for user interfaces invite at least visual inspection of their content. Frames are important metaphors in OOUIs, since they justify the constrained space in which object views exist.

Frames that are visually too strong can distract the user's attention from what is being framed. The visual system is optimized for edge detection, so it does not take much to create a frame or border. Look at this page, for example. The white space around the text forms a strong border all by itself.[1]

Media metaphors As Marshall McLuhan pointed out [McLu65], old media serve as metaphors for new ones. Since computer displays can simulate books, newspapers, television, etc., replicating them is an obvious source of presentation metaphors. Media metaphors have various levels of generality—for example, *paper documents*, *forms*, and *insurance claim forms*.

Users of media are sensitive to fine nuances in presentation, which designers should understand when presenting the information on a new medium. Text, for example, is not just text, it is a visual pattern of position, color, typography, and even the color of paper (think of reading a newspaper that is yellowed with age). Nygren and colleagues showed that experts in a domain understood a great deal from the visual pattern of data on a paper form, and from "accidental" characteristics such as whether fields were written in pen or pencil [Nygr92]. Doctors, for example, could correctly "read" a patient's condition from visual patterns in a textual report where all the characters had been replaced by "X." They could not grasp the information as quickly when it was presented on a computer display.

Adding magic to media metaphors is often as simple as making one medium part of the content of another, in a way that would not be possible in the real world. For example, *The Seventh Guest*, a popular CD-ROM "interactive fiction" product, presents a book on the computer screen; the pages of the book have "pictures" that are like TV screens, in that they can show video as well as still images.

Human conversation Hutchins, Hollan and Norman [Hut85] characterized user interfaces in terms of two metaphors: *conversation* and *model worlds*. The latter is the dominant metaphor in OOUIs; it corresponds to the idea of objects in space that the user can manipulate. The conversational metaphor dominates in command language interfaces, where the user talks

[1] Figure 4-3 (Chapter 4) is an example of a type of "border effect" that is undesirable unless it is intentional. [Tuf90] has other examples. These are easy to inadvertently produce, and quite distracting.

while the system listens, then the system talks while the user listens, and so forth.

Model worlds can include the conversational metaphor in a literal way, as when the cartoon-like "agent" in Figure 9-1 says "Need help?" It is also applicable in a more abstract form. In talking with other people, we have expectations about the flow of the conversation—when to expect feedback from the other party, for example. Each object in a model world should respect the protocols of ordinary conversation. This is mainly a topic for Chapter 10, since it is part of interaction. But the presentation language is the vehicle for conversational responses from objects, and insuring that the user recognizes them is part of presentation design.

Design Patterns

The architect Christopher Alexander developed the idea of *pattern languages*, which describe how large entities such as buildings and towns are created from smaller architectural patterns such as courtyards, terraces, and streets [Alex79]. The idea of standard patterns from which large structures can be designed is very general, and has been applied to object-oriented design [Gam94]. It is also applicable to designing interactive user interfaces.[1]

Alexander emphasized the interplay of patterns of *events*, and patterns of *space*. In a user interface, these correspond to the user's tasks and actions, and the spatial layout of windows and other objects on the display. Patterns use spatial structures to resolve tensions created by events. For example, in designing a workshop, there is a need to have tools close at hand, but also a conflicting need to have an uncluttered space for working. The architect balances these needs by providing something like wall racks, that keep the tools close to the worker without cluttering the work area.

Workshops illustrate a connection between design patterns and metaphors—"real world" patterns often serve as metaphors for user interface patterns. The workshop pattern, with tools arrayed around the periphery of the work area, is common in computer applications such as graphics and word processing.

Here are a few more examples of "pattern thinking":

- *Windows* resolve the tension between wanting to be in one place, but see what is going on somewhere else. To be successful, a design should minimize the effort to move to the window. In user interfaces, windows can be *workspaces*, or *doors*, reflecting patterns of movement between different workspaces.
- *Tool bars* are an obvious implementation of the *workshop* pattern; *Popup menus* are a bit of magic to enhance it. Suppose you could snap your fingers and make all the tools for a particular piece of

[1] I am indebted to Ward Cunningham for pointing this out to me.

work appear—that's what popup menus do, by presenting appropriate options for the selected object with minimum hand motion.

- *Notebooks* resolve the tension between wanting a tabbed indexing system, and needing more immediate access than a file cabinet would provide.
- *Hypertext* resolves the tension that results when users need a collection of information for multiple tasks, each of which requires a different ordering of the information.

Patterns provide an additional handle for thinking about metaphors. They emphasize the interplay of dynamic activity with static structure and reinforce the need to observe users at work. They unify the primarily spatial approach of this chapter, and the action-based design of Chapter 10.

9.3 Step-by-Step Presentation Design

Here, as in other places in this book, take "step-by-step" in the right spirit. Adherents of the waterfall development model may think of troops marching in formation, but design resembles more the progress of a football team down the field. Team members are working together, but doing different things simultaneously; there is motion both forward and backward as they progress toward the goal.

Figure 9-5 shows an overview of information presentation design, expanded in the context of the whole design process (from Chapter 6, Figure

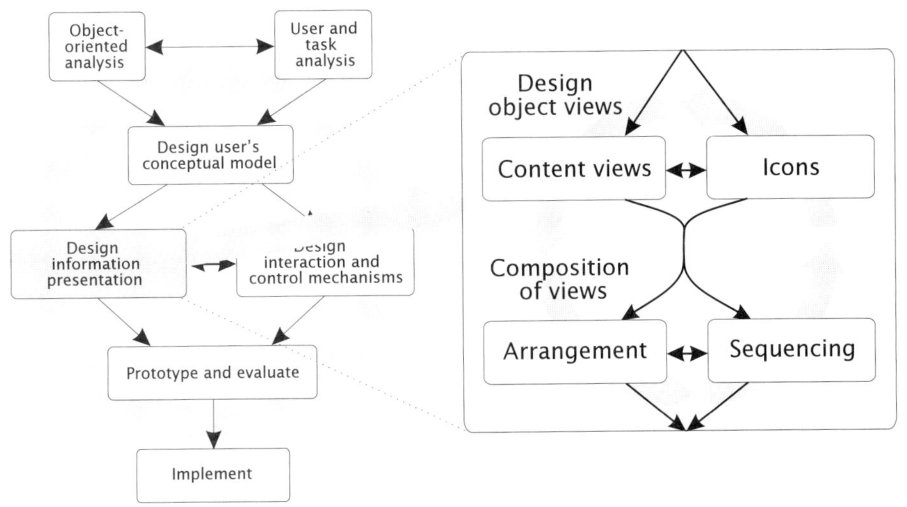

Figure 9-5 Flow of information presentation design

6-4). Starting from the user's conceptual model, views are designed for each visible object, followed by the composition of the entire interface. These steps are iterative, and closely tied to the design of interaction.

Preliminaries

Presentation design, viewed as an innovative artistic endeavor, can appear overwhelming. Whereas previous activities have a high analytical content, here you are up against a blank screen that you must fill by sheer creative effort.

Art historian George Kubler said, "Everything made now is either a replica or a variant of something made a little time ago."[1] In utilitarian design particularly, radical ideas are not necessary, and are not even desirable unless they offer radical improvements in function. Even innovations such as the Xerox Star or Apple's HyperCard relied on earlier work. This is not to say that creativity is not part of the design process—only that it is typically applied to the details of a problem, and to discovering the right framework for a particular application. Inventing entirely new frameworks is seldom required.

Getting started Where is the starting point for design? First, remember that we begin from a user's conceptual model that describes the application domain and provides concrete metaphors for visualizing it.[2] It is one of several sources of concrete ideas for presentation design:

- Metaphors from the user's conceptual model. This is not only a good starting point, it is a requirement—users will probably not use the intended metaphors if they are not embodied in the presentation language.
- Design patterns derived from studying the work activities of users.
- Current representations of the application content in other media. Though they are not binding, existing forms, charts, etc., are reasonable places to start.
- Existing applications in this or similar domains. This goes beyond copying—analyzing user interfaces will show how to use their strengths and improve their weak points.
- Style guides and *de facto* style standards for the implementation platform.

These starting points can be found more quickly, and better utilized, by people trained in the presentation media. Taking graphics as an example, visual designers are invaluable at this point. They can also be involved in developing the user's conceptual model, since most metaphors have

[1] [Kub62], p. 2.

[2] If conceptual modeling is skipped, the design of look and feel truly is a formidable task. Iterating on style without an understanding of content is unlikely to produce a good interface.

visual content. Visual *artists* (who may be the same people as the designers) are needed to execute the designs.[1]

Style guides are manuals for interface design based on a platform, such as the Apple Macintosh, or on a class of platforms, such as OSF/Motif for UNIX systems. They provide general advice on style, and specific instructions for standard elements such as windows and dialogue boxes. They may include working examples and implementation tools.

Typical OOUIs display tens to hundreds of objects at the level of windows, and hundreds to thousands of objects at the level of icons, buttons, menus, bitmaps, text fields, etc.—all on a display surface smaller than an ordinary piece of letter paper. Doing work with such an interface is like living in a ship's cabin. Efficient task performance depends on a consistent scheme for organizing and identifying objects, and a style guide can help provide that. Style guides are also catalogs of ideas for visual display and interaction techniques, and save much of the work of detailed design on buttons, dialogue boxes, and the like.

Since style guides cover both the presentation and action languages, Chapter 10 discusses them in more detail.

User differences Most interfaces are used by people with varying expertise, both in the problem domain and the interface itself. This is one of many ways in which users of an interface differ; others include age, education and aptitudes, and physical abilities. The capability of providing multiple content views of the same information helps adapt the interface to these differences.

In most media, helping the user who lacks knowledge adds clutter and makes the result less useful to the expert. In a book, this means extra explanations, sidebars, footnotes, cross-references, etc. Computer interfaces, however, can hide added tutorial information and produce it only when necessary. They can also provide choices of colors, text sizes, etc. to adapt to different levels of perceptual ability.

Experience shows that adaptations like these are difficult to retrofit to existing interfaces, but relatively easy to design in from the beginning. The idea is that objects can have multiple externally visible behavior sets, each appropriate in some context. Part of the preliminary work in presentation (and interaction) design is to decide what adaptations are needed, based on user profiles developed in task analysis.

Internationalization needs to be addressed early in design. Developing software for international markets involves "internationalizing" the software to partition elements that are unique to one environment, then developing local versions for target cultures and languages. Though the work of separating translatable resources occurs during implementation, identification of such resources is part of presentation design.

[1] I use the term visual designer/artist, since there seems to be a general visualization talent. There are also specific talents involved in designing and producing graphics, photographic images, video, etc.

Text is the most obvious concern. Text that is part of the application, such as help and dialogue text, should be designed in two steps: first outline the semantic content, then write the text in the primary language. Translating text requires knowledge of the task and the computer system, since the necessary technical words may not be part of the ordinary vocabulary. Maintaining text as a separate resource makes iterative design and testing easier, and simplifies the process of localizing the interface for a particular market.

Representing character sets on the display is an issue for some languages. Graphics that express general symbolic meaning (not specific to the problem domain) may also require translation. Things like color symbolism, though less important, should be evaluated for each local version of the system. Languages that read right-to-left (Arabic and Hebrew) may require some redesign, to reverse the typical default left-to-right layout of display elements.

Portability Target platforms for the design should be reviewed here. OOUI applications portable across major platforms such as Apple, IBM, and UNIX are quite feasible using object-oriented implementation tools, but require planning.

An application on a graphical platform will have presentation objects that are generic to the platform (such as window frames and scroll bars), and objects that are unique to the application. Many generic objects are nearly identical, except for visual details, across platforms; these generic objects are also supported by platform tools and are therefore easy to implement. Some objects may not be available everywhere, however. The notebook of Figure 9-4 (c) is an example; it is a standard part of the IBM OS/2 Workplace Shell, but is not available on many other platforms.

Because some things are standard and others are not, a compromise must be made. The extreme alternatives are:

- Use only visual elements that are available on all the platforms to which the application will be ported.
- Use the optimal set of elements from one platform, and reimplement those that do not exist on platforms to which the application is ported later.

This is not just an issue of implementation ease. There may be a trade-off between function and ease of learning, if controls are introduced that are not consistent with a given platform style.

Object Views

Having accomplished the necessary preliminaries, the next step is to design views for each object in the user's conceptual model. This step is based on the system model and metaphors. Objects for which views are designed include:

- Simple information objects displayed as pictures and blocks of text.

- Composite objects, which contain primitive objects as components. There are various types of visual composition. Compound documents contain non-overlapping areas of text, graphics, and other media as sub-objects. Books contain pages in various formats. Graphic documents such as maps and blueprints often contain layers, where each layer presents a different type of information.
- Containers, which are loosely coupled compositions; they imply only that the contained objects are stored in the same place (and perhaps ordering constraints such as alphabetical sorting). The system model may explicitly specify the content of containers, or users may decide what goes in them.
- "Maps" or other visual devices that give the user an overview that organizes objects conceptually and provides access paths to them. Hierarchical representations of file systems are common examples. The form of a map may be suggested by a metaphor in the user's conceptual model.

Objects may have content views, covered below in Section 9.4, and icons, covered in Section 9.5.

Though object views precede composition of the interface in my exposition, it is not a linear process. There is an analogy here to visual art—a painter must work out and execute the details of individual figures in the painting, and also work out the composition. One or the other may be the starting point, but they evolve in parallel. Here you do a little object view design, then a little composition, then go around again.

Object views and composition are mutually supportive. The behavior of individual objects supports the overall concept; the composition presents the concept and helps the user understand the behavior of individual objects. An example is the *drafting table* as a concept that composes its individual objects—the drawing, its graphical content, and various tools.

Composition of the Interface

Regarding composition, the painter Henri Matisse said: "All that is not useful in a picture is detrimental."[1] In user interfaces, screen space is precious, and so is space in the user's mind. Studies show that GUI users spend a significant amount of time moving, resizing and rearranging windows [Bil88]; anything done to make information visible when and where the user needs it will help.

There are two aspects to composition. At any point in time, objects are arranged in space on the display. There is also a time sequence of events, which results in successive spatial arrangements of objects. As in a film, ballet, or any other form that unfolds in time, these two aspects must be gracefully related in terms the user can understand.

[1] Quoted in [Can58].

Studies of work ([Bil88], [Mand92]) have concluded that people tend to organize work on their desks in two ways:

- In piles related to particular tasks.
- In sequence within a pile based on the anticipated order of use.[1]

This task-based desktop organization coexists with more permanent organizations in folders, file cabinets, and shelves of binders. It can also happen that a folder in the permanent filing system becomes part of a pile on the desk for immediate attention (for instance, the pending orders file for a customer who has complained about late shipments).

This leads to two principles of composition—one based on how objects collaborate in tasks, and one based on how they are organized for storage and retrieval.[2] The application of these principles is complicated (just as it is in the real world) by the fact that no single organization is optimal for every purpose. It is also complicated by the fact that users control the organization of their computer desktops, so the designer can at best provide a reasonable default, with facilities for organizing and finding things.

Corresponding to piles and other forms of organization in the real world, we have presentation metaphors such as folders, notebooks, toolboxes, briefcases, and of course the ubiquitous window.[3] Organization may be loose, as in folders, or more structured as in notebooks.

Figure 9-6 shows several methods of organizing screen space. In (a), windows are tiled; the user can control only the proportion of the tiled space that each window takes. In (b), windows can overlap and are resizable, but they are clipped by the border of a containing, or parent, window.[4] In (c), there are no restrictions on the size or positions of the windows, except the borders of the physical display; the user has complete freedom. On Apple's Macintosh II computers, the display border itself does not even restrict windows. Multiple physical displays may be attached to form a single connected surface; when a window is moved beyond the edge of one display, it appears on the adjacent one. Windows are not restricted to being rectangular, though most window systems do not facilitate non-rectangular windows.

Preserving the user's organization of objects is a capability that designers often fail to provide. If, in a display such as (b) in Figure 9-6, the user arranges and sizes the child windows and then closes the parent window, the arrangement should reappear when it is opened. Failing to do so not only makes the user do extra work to restore order, but violates a

[1] You can probably confirm these studies by observing the way you arrange papers and other work on your own desk.

[2] By considering "storage and retrieval" to be general tasks applicable to all objects, these could be reduced to a single principle of task-based organization.

[3] And even (literally) piles—see [Mand92].

[4] In Microsoft Windows and the OS/2 Presentation Manager, this is called an MDI (multiple document interface).

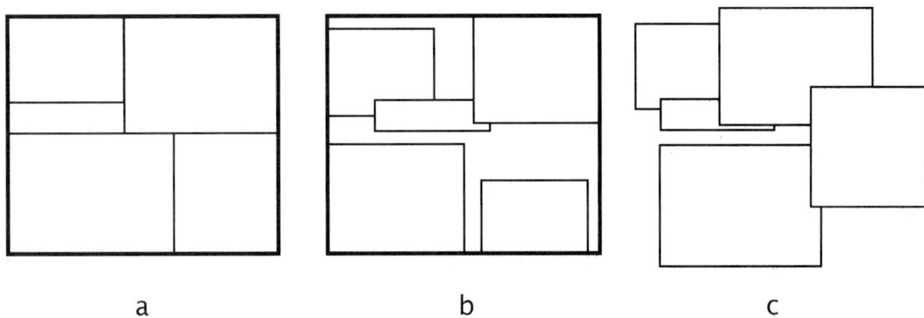

Figure 9-6 Organizing collections of windows on the display

fundamental property of objects—they do not move or disappear without cause. This is similar to the frustration you might feel if someone tidied up your desk for you, and left things in unaccustomed places so you could not find them.

In designing compositions of objects, we can add organizers such as visual overviews, links between distant objects, etc. These may be suggested by a metaphor, as in the notebook in Figure 9-7. They may also be magical, as in hypertext links, or the capability in some systems to keep multiple "shadow copies" of objects in different places.

Designers must often compromise between providing helpful visible organizers and conserving space for displaying information. In Figure 9-7, the apparatus of the notebook, as opposed to the displayed information, takes nearly 50% of the space. The tabs show indexing information, but almost 40% of the display space is taken by borders, rings, and other things that simply say, "This is a notebook."

Pattern thinking (page 224) helps in designing compositions. In architecture, a room, a house, or a street must accommodate many patterns

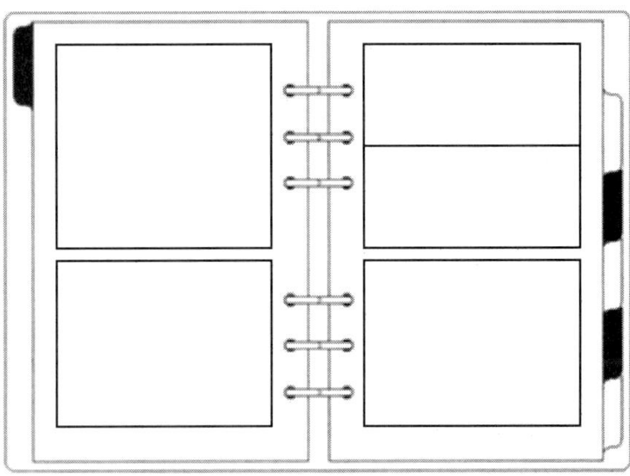

Figure 9-7 A notebook as organizer

of activity, and similarly for any artifact in a user interface. A good design solution is one that encourages and facilitates patterns that satisfy user needs, and discourages undesirable activities. This requires many cycles like the following:

- Take a set of activities associated with a task, and sketch the arrangement of display elements that is optimal for it.
- Test your sketch against another task. Are there tensions? Try to develop a structural pattern that minimizes conflicts between the tasks.
- Continue with other tasks, and iterate until you are satisfied.

Since these steps involve interaction as well as presentation, they overlap the material presented in the next chapter.

Documenting and Testing the Design

Documentation of the external aspects of a user interface helps to exchange ideas among the user interface design team, to communicate them to users for evaluation, and to pass specifications from designers to implementors. Techniques useful for all these purposes are presented here and in Chapter 10.

Documentation may be transient, generated to try an idea and then discarded; it may be worthwhile to save transient documents in a design notebook, as a history of what alternatives were evaluated. More formal documents (including prototypes) will be a permanent part of the project record.

Rough sketches In the early stages of design, it is important to generate lots of ideas. Rough sketches are *rough*—they can be produced quickly, and they express an idea without investing too much in it, so criticism is acceptable.

Once a rough sketch looks promising, it can be drawn more legibly using a graphics package to allow careful examination of the idea and its visible expression. Figures 9-1 and 9-2, done with CorelDraw [sCor92], are examples. An advantage of graphics on paper is that several ideas can be evaluated side-by-side more easily than if they are shown on a computer display. Sketches can also be produced for audio components of interfaces, using a tape recorder and sound sources that approximate the desired result.

Videotape Stopping to document design ideas sometimes disrupts the flow; a video camera can capture ideas, including whiteboard sketches, on the fly. Video can show the sequencing of events on a display, by "animating" a series of sketches placed successively in front of the camera.

When a finished prototype is available, video can supplement it. Showing the prototype in operation, with running commentary on its operation and the rationale for specific features, is valuable for users, designers and implementors.

Prototypes Any visualization, including rough sketches, can be considered a prototype of sorts. The term is usually applied to a "mock-up" that shows some or all of an interface exactly as it will appear to users.

For evaluating information presentation, high-fidelity prototypes can be "display only," with a minimum of interactive function. Window contents can be static bitmaps generated by graphics and word-processing applications. Both printed "screen dumps" and actual displays are useful for evaluating alternatives side-by-side.

In showing display-only prototypes, keep in mind that the whole of the user interface is more than the sum of its parts. Display prototypes leave things out, such as the "feel" of moving windows around to reveal portions of their contents, artifacts that occur from moving objects on the screen, and error displays produced by application functionality.

Information presentation is only part of the gestalt of the user interface. A working "look and feel" prototype integrates documentation of the presentation and action languages. This topic will be discussed further in Chapter 10.

Testing Subject to the caveats just mentioned, everything from rough sketches to running prototypes helps to test and evaluate the design as you go along. Those who are lucky enough to have users involved directly in the design process will save time by discussing ideas with them in the rough sketch stage, before going further.

Formal testing of user performance cannot be done effectively based only on presentation design, and should be deferred to a point where interaction and simulation of function are available in a prototype. Various partial and informal tests can be done, though, and will provide empirical data to help improve the design. Examples of testable elements include:

- Whether the composition (arrangement and sequence) of presentation elements supports the flow of tasks.
- Readability and understandability of text, icons, and other presentation elements.
- For international products, the adequacy of translation.

Lacking real users, people such as secretaries, managers, and developers not involved in the design can be test subjects for some elements, such as text readability.

9.4 Content View Design

The interfaces you design will probably be predominantly visual, and this section is primarily about visual design; Section 9.6 covers views with nonvisual information. Whole books are devoted to visual design,[1] and I will

[1] E.g., [Mar92], [Ran85], and [Tuf90].

require n bits per pixel to store 2^n colors or shades of gray, so detailed images can be expensive to store. Compression techniques reduce the size of stored images, but increase the time it takes to display them.

It is difficult to scale images up without producing an unacceptable appearance. It is also difficult to scale them down, since the right choice of which pixels to discard is a visual problem that algorithms cannot completely capture. The latter problem is important in applications that allow users to browse image libraries by viewing collections of images scaled down to icon size.

"Graphics" versus "image" is a technical distinction that is not always apparent to users. A line drawing presented with image data is a single object, whereas the same drawing presented with graphics has sub-objects such as lines and polygons. If the drawing has different behavior in the two cases, users may need to know which they are seeing.

Video, essentially a succession of halftone images, is becoming more common in multimedia computer interfaces. It is useful or essential for presenting certain types of information. Designing the content of video presentation requires close cooperation between interface designers, domain experts, and people skilled in the video medium. On current desktop machines, video presentation must also be carefully designed to minimize storage requirements. Even with the best compression techniques, it requires 10-15 megabytes per minute.

The ability to display graphics and images is a fundamental advantage of GUIs, and is key to making object properties and behaviors visible. Performance is a problem on current machines, and will probably continue to be a problem—as machines get faster and storage devices get larger, there is always a conflict between improving display performance and improving image quality.

When using graphics and images, always ask what information the user needs from the picture. Line drawings are often used in technical manuals instead of photographs, because they capture essential details that are obscured by the inessential "realism" of the halftone image. Task analysis, content analysis, and user testing can all help in making the right compromise between the quantity and quality of images, and interactive performance.

Color appears in user interfaces in several contexts. The most important kinds of color are:

- *Intrinsic* color, which is part of images or video displayed on the interface. In this case, color is not a separable design issue.
- *Supplementary* color, used to enhance text and graphic presentations. Color is a separable issue in this context, though it certainly interacts with other graphical elements.

The best advice on the supplementary use of color comes from Edward Tufte: "*Above all, do no harm.*"[1] His advice is prompted by the obser-

[1] [Tuf90], p. 81. Italics are his.

vation that inappropriate use of color distracts the user and obscures the information. I use one general rule for supplementary color: Design first in black and white, then add color to emphasize important elements or to code quantitative values.

This rule forces me to think about why I am using color, which motivates improvements in the design. It also allows for monochrome displays,[1] and for people with color vision deficiencies. Color can enhance other means of conveying the information, such as shape, size, spatial separation, etc.

Here are other guidelines, summarized from various sources:[2]

- Do not use more colors than you need. Marcus recommends five plus or minus two for coding discrete values. More may be appropriate for coding a continuous value, such as temperature, but they should be spectrally related (points along a color spectrum, or along an intensity gradient for a single color).
- Minimize the use of bright, highly saturated (pure) colors. In large doses they are distracting and fatigue the eyes; use them in small areas for labeling or emphasis. The lens of the human eye suffers from chromatic aberration, and does not focus properly on pure (saturated) blue; it should be avoided for text and lines. For large areas of color, such as screen and window backgrounds, use grays or muted pastel colors.
- Understand physiological limits on color perception. For example, nearly 10% of the population have some form of red-green "color blindness." The blue aberration just mentioned is another important fact.[3]
- Use conventional coding if possible, such as red-yellow-green for stop-caution-all clear. If there is no standard convention, adopt one and use it consistently. Be aware of cultural differences in color conventions [Dre72].
- Well-drawn maps show that color, used correctly to enhance information presentation, is aesthetically pleasing as well. Resist the urge to use color *purely* for decoration. If users complain that an interface is boring, this is a symptom of lack of content, not lack of color.

In spite of these guidelines, letting users choose their own colors, based on needs (such as visual deficiencies) or preferences, is appropriate. Designers should provide reasonable default colors. Since interfaces usually have many coordinated colors, it is common to provide default "color schemes" to users, which simultaneously change all the interface colors.

---

[1] NeXT machines originally supported displays with black, white, and two shades of gray. In spite of this, many NeXT applications are superb examples of clear information display.

[2] Particularly [Tuf90], [Shn92], and Marcus's "ten commandments of color" [Mar92].

[3] Good sources of information include [Mar92], [Greg79], and [Snyd88].

Tufte points out that nature is a good source of color schemes. OS/2 has palettes based on the seasons, and Microsoft Windows uses palettes based on place, such as *Arizona* and *Ocean*.[1]

Color, like all interface elements, should be tested. Even a standard design from another medium, such as paper, may look very different on a computer display [Snyd88].

Composition is simply the way all the other elements are put together, though, of course, it is not simple at all. There are general principles for the composition of content views, some of which are listed under typography, color, etc. Others can be found in the literature of graphic design and art. There are also principles that will be specific to the domain of the information being presented.

An apparent paradox in the HCI literature is that many studies conclude that the less information a display contains, the better users do on tasks [Tul88] (subject to the constraint that the information is sufficient for the task). On the other hand, graphic designers often recommend dense displays. Tufte says, "less is a bore" [Tuf90], and shows convincing examples of displays that are clear, yet dense with information.

Most of the studies cited by Tullis [Tul88] were done on alphanumeric displays, with little capability for organizing information. These studies also used simple, structured tasks. He cites other studies showing the power of organizing information into "chunks." The key to resolving the conflict is to recognize the organizing powers available on the display. Properly composed displays can show large amounts of information, but the user "sees" only that which is relevant at a point in time.

Graphic designers are skilled at exploiting the organizational capabilities of visual media, but must exercise their general skills in the context of the specific domain, and the properties of computer displays. Most domains have conventional ways of representing information that users are trained to understand. These, and task structures, need to be integrated with general graphic design principles. Providing more than one content representation is sometimes the best way to resolve conflicts raised by the need to support different tasks and different users. Examples such as the spreadsheet, though, show that good representations can serve many different purposes.

Screen real estate Conventional representations of information often conflict with the fact that computer screens cannot display as much information as pages in a book, magazine, or newspaper. Whereas paper media usually have more "spatial real estate," computers have more "temporal real estate"—that is, they can change the information display more rapidly. This difference requires a compromise between time and space.

Users often need to make visual comparisons between tables, graphs, etc.; this is difficult if the items are presented sequentially instead

[1] Not to mention *Black Leather Jacket* and *Hotdog Stand*, which I do not recommend.

of side-by-side. The problem cannot always be solved in a satisfactory way. One approach is to provide the option of seeing the compared items together at a reduced size, or sequentially at full size.

Because of the real estate problem, the design may need to explicitly account for physical screen size. Typical personal computers display 640 by 480 pixels, while 1024 by 768 is a common size in high-end workstations. The larger display has more than 2.5 times the area of the smaller;[1] this is significant, given that the typical personal computer display screen is about the size of an unfolded holiday greeting card. You may either have to specify a requirement for the larger size, design different views for the different displays, or use a "least common denominator" design that will work on both.

9.5 Icon Design

Icons, more than anything else, represent the popular notion of an OOUI. Though there is more to it than that, icons *are* important—not only to provide object representations, but to give the impression of an interface that has been designed with care. All the design elements mentioned above must be applied under stringent conditions. Icon sizes vary from platform to platform, but are usually in the range of 32-64 pixels square.

Icons are not always the most efficient representation of objects, as the example in Figure 9-4 illustrated (page 221). In the right context, icons can portray complex objects and functions in a small space, and allow users to identify things more quickly than by reading text. Icon design is both art and science. I have read scores of papers, examined thousands of icons in interfaces, and spent hundreds of hours designing and drawing icons.[2] There is no formula for producing good icons, but there are some rules of thumb.

Are icons intuitive? The most commonly asserted (and rejected) claim about icons is that users with no prior exposure can understand their meanings. This is certainly not always true, and we should not rely on it in user interfaces. Even for very common icons such as those used in international airports, understanding is mostly based on prior familiarity or an accompanying text sign. For most interfaces, this is fine—it is a pleasant surprise when users deduce an icon meaning on their own, but the important issue is whether they find the icon "intuitive" and easy to use after learning what it means.

[1] Since the area is measured in pixels, it maps directly to the amount of information that can be legibly displayed.

[2] I do not consider myself a graphic designer; though I have learned a lot about icons, I would always get a professional designer, or use a professionally designed icon library, if at all possible.

What Makes a Good Icon?

Good icons are distinguished by both visual and conceptual properties:

- They are congruent with metaphors from the user's conceptual model. They do not evoke negative or emotionally charged metaphors.
- They are visually simple, so they can be quickly apprehended without being distracting.
- They are readily distinguishable, but use a consistent graphical style.
- They are easy to learn and remember.

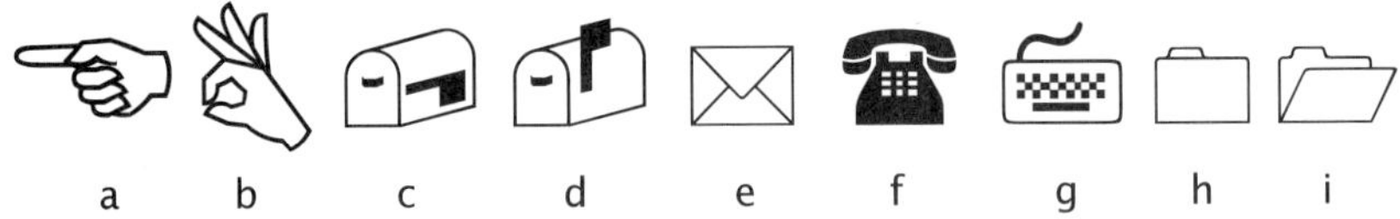

Figure 9-9 Examples of icons

Concrete metaphors Most good icons are representations of concrete objects. All the icons in Figure 9-9 are examples of concrete representation, though that does not automatically make them good icons.

Icons (a) and (b) are examples of the *body part* metaphors I warned against in Chapter 8. The gestures portrayed here have specific, and innocuous, meanings in most parts of the US. Their meaning varies around the world, however; in some places they are obscene or threatening.[1] This sort of metaphor should be avoided, and it underscores the need to understand the audience for a system or application.

Icons (c) and (d) portray a style of mailbox found in many parts of the United States. This does not suffer from any emotional associations, as do (a) and (b), but exemplifies the issue of "intuitiveness." These icons will be intuitive to many Americans, but non-intuitive to others. That does not necessarily make them bad icons. There is no universally recognized visual sign for "mail," so your choice is to use different icons for different countries, or to assume that users can learn one standard icon.[2]

Icon metaphors, being parts of the representation of the user's conceptual model, must be evaluated for both visual and conceptual congruence and consistency. In Figure 9-10, icons (f) and (g) are congruent—paper goes with envelopes. (g) is also congruent with both (a) and (b)—paper goes with printers. Visually, (g) is more consistent with (a) than with (b), whose representation of paper is different from that in (g).

[1] Small, stylized hands are sometimes used as pointer icons for turning pages, etc. This may be acceptable; I have not seen any data.

[2] ISO [ISO92] has proposed a standard icon for mail, based on the office mail tray:
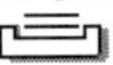

Figure 9-10 More examples of icons

Icons can represent functions or actions as well as objects. Concrete metaphors for actions include tools associated with the action (for instance a pencil, ✐, for line drawing, or a printer for printing), and representations of the object state that will result from the action (for instance an open folder, 🗁, for the action of opening a directory in the file system). Tools can be used as pointer icons, which track the mouse. This can indicate a mode (such as draw versus erase) or show what actions are possible in a given area (as when the pointer changes to the "I-beam" text editing cursor when it is over editable text).

Images of concrete objects are easier to learn and remember than abstractions, so it is worth some effort to find good metaphors. This applies to both information object and tool icons.

Visual properties of icons Complex visual forms take more time and effort to parse and understand. Since the point of icons is to allow rapid visual recognition, the simpler they are, the better—as long as they adequately portray the desired concept. Icons representing different classes of object should be readily distinguishable; similar objects, or objects with similar components, should have visual similarity. Conveying fine differences visually may be counterproductive if it takes users longer to identify the differences than it would to read text labels on the icons [Byrn93].

In certain situations it is appropriate to convey lots of detail in an icon, namely when the icon represents an object that is a visual image. Icons representing individual items in a library of video clips or still images are examples. The Freestyle system [vWang89], from Wang Laboratories, uses icons that are scanned images of the documents they represent. The theory behind this is that users will visually recognize the general "shape" of a document in cases where they will not remember its name.

Text labels on icons help users identify them. Labels are required where many instances of the same icon must be differentiated, as with the customer icons in Figure 9-4. In other cases it is a trade-off between ease of understanding and screen space. Tool bars and tool palettes typically do not include text labels, thus saving space; experienced users don't miss them. An information area on the screen that displays the names of icons as the mouse moves over them will help novice users.

Text labels and graphic images for icons should be maintained as separate resources. This allows users to rename icons, and makes translation easier. Icons containing textual elements in the image, or culture-specific images, may have to be translated into different graphics for local versions of a system. Keeping resources separate from the programs that use them makes this easier.

Though icons should be distinguishable, they should also have a general visual consistency. The principle here is essentially typographic. It is more difficult to read words **like** *this*, because the font changes cause visual confusion; similarly, icons that are not consistent in style are harder to "read." In Figure 9-10, (h) is stylistically different from all the other icons in obvious ways. There are more subtle differences between (a) and (d), which are head-on with drop shadows, and (b) and (c), which are seen at a different angle and have a more 3-dimensional look.

Icons can reflect state changes in the object they represent, and this contributes to the sense that the icon "is" the object. Figure 9-2 illustrated this with a dashed outline for an icon whose object had an open content view. Folders and other containers can be shown as "open" or "closed" by icon state changes (versus). In Figure 9-9 (d), the raised flag indicates there is mail in the mailbox.

Animation, though not easy to implement, can indicate state changes or help users understand the meaning of icons [Bae91]. It can also hinder understanding. There is a wonderful bit of animation in Lotus Organizer [sLot93]. Organizer has a wastebasket, , into which the user can drag items to delete them. When something is dropped into the basket, it goes up in flames. This is impressive, but it is the wrong metaphor. The flames say that the deleted item is gone forever, but in fact the deletion is undoable. The moral of the story is that if you think the user will get bored, ship a video game with your product. Graphic effects within an application should support the right conceptual model.[1]

Icon libraries Designing and producing even a single icon that is concrete, expresses a concept clearly, and is visually distinguishable and attractive (without being distracting) is a non-trivial task. Most applications that use icons will need tens or hundreds of them. Furthermore, icons for one application usually need to be visually and conceptually consistent with icons used by other applications, and with icons in the platform shell or desktop.

Professional looking icons are designed by professionals; a graphic designer should be employed if original icons are needed. Even when professionally done, icon production is time consuming; do not reinvent the wheel if you don't have to. An application may need hundreds of icons, but most of these should represent variations on a smaller number of basic types, which may already be available on the platform you are using. Reusing existing icon designs not only saves work, it often makes the system easier to use, because users have fewer icon types to learn.

Platforms may make icons available as editable bitmaps. Graphic design firms have icon libraries, and there are printed sources of designs

[1] I use Organizer, and in other respects I find it an excellent product.

([Dre72], [Mod76]). Using these sources will save time and testing as you build your own icon library. One note of caution—icon designs may be copyrighted, so be sure you have the right to use a design, particularly in a commercially marketed product. Some sources, for example IBM [IBM91], explicitly permit duplication of icons.

Documentation and Testing

Icon designs should be documented to relate them to the system concepts they represent. The following example can serve as a guide.[1] It documents a folder icon, but the elements used are generic.

- *Icon Name:* Folder
- *Metaphor:* Office environment, desktop
- *Abstract object type:* Container for holding objects
- *Specific object type:* File folder for holding documents
- *Visual appearance:* Manila office folder
- *Visual components:* Front cover, back cover, index tab protruding above back cover
- *Function:* Folders contain objects, such as documents and other folders. Folders open to views of the icons for objects they contain. If an icon is dropped on an open or closed (iconic) folder, the icon is moved or copied to the folder.
- *System model object(s) represented:* (In documentation for a specific system, a pointer to documentation of the object for which the icon is a view.)
- *Technical information:* (A description of the implementation of the icon, perhaps by identifying bitmap files.)

Testing icons You cannot be sure that an icon works until it is tested. I have seen some remarkable results; for instance, that 25% of users saw an icon representing a mail tray with an envelope in it as a coffee cup.[2]

In testing icons, it is important to know what questions are to be answered. For example, should users understand icon meanings on first sight, or is it sufficient that they be usable after a training session? Important issues, such as how fast icons can be visually discriminated, are sometimes subtle and difficult to test. Many problems with icons will emerge quickly from simple tests, though, such as the fact that users frequently mistake two icons for one another, or that an icon image offends some people.

[1] This is based on the ISO recommendation for standardizing icons [ISO92].
[2] [Bew83] and [Ver88] give other examples of this sort.

9.6 Non-Visual Information

Several forms of non-visual presentation either are common today, or will become common within a few years. The two main categories are sounds and simple forms of tactile feedback. Sound can be further classified as speech and non-speech audio.

Two different motivations have driven the use of non-visual information. One is the need to make computers accessible to people with visual deficiencies. The second is the limited bandwidth of computer interfaces that use only the visual channel. Adding additional sensory modalities enhances performance in many applications. The two motivations are not incompatible—techniques developed for visually impaired users benefit those with normal sight, and vice versa.

Audio

Many years ago, as a technician in the US Marine Corps, I used a radar set that tracked objects on the ground. When the signal was reflected from a moving object, its frequency shifted (this is the Doppler effect, which is also the basis for speed detection radar used by police). The shift for interesting objects was in the audio range, and it was used to present an "audio display" to the operator. Most objects have different parts that move at different speeds (for instance, the body, arms, and legs of a walking man), and all the Doppler-shifted signals combine to form a complex sound. Skilled operators readily made very fine distinctions, such as differentiating types of vehicles, or telling whether a man was walking or running.

Sonar operators develop similar skills. The human capability exploited by this type of interface is the ability to distinguish *timbres*, which are determined by the sound waveform. Though keeping track of the spatial position of objects is easier with a visual display, the audio display allows finer discrimination of individual objects. This is an example of an audio capability that is useful to both normally sighted and blind people. Audio supplements the visual channel to achieve a higher total bandwidth through the interface.

My experience while using the radar was that after a while I did not hear the sound, I heard *the object* making the sound. This is the key to understanding non-visual presentation in object-oriented terms: sound is simply another behavior an object can present to the user.

Audio "GUIs" Graphical user interfaces, while beneficial to users with normal vision, are a problem for blind people who need to use computers. Screen readers allow blind people to use character interfaces by "reading" (with a speech synthesizer) the contents of the display, which is available as coded text in a buffer. The GUI screen is an uncoded bitmap, so this technique will not work. GUIs also display non-text elements, and require input from a pointing device besides the text keyboard.

The problem of GUI use by the blind has been only partially solved.[1] The problem is not intrinsic, since most properties of GUIs are spatial, not strictly visual. It lies more in the fact that GUIs are designed for visual use, and lack the implementation "hooks" for non-visual behavior.

Soundtrack [Edw89], a "graphical" word processor, is designed specifically for blind users. Intended as a test bed, it helps to illuminate the nature of an OOUI: "The interface is constructed from *auditory objects.* An auditory object is defined by its spatial location, a name, an action, and a tone."[1] The tone of an object (a musical tone) signals that the mouse pointer has passed over it. Tones vary in pitch to indicate position on the display. When the mouse is clicked on an object, a speech synthesizer reads its name. Soundtrack also has auditory mechanisms specific to objects that are menu items, scrolling controls, and content windows (which display text).

SonicFinder In contrast to Soundtrack, SonicFinder [Gav89] is an enhancement to an existing interface (the Apple Macintosh *Finder*, or desktop manager), and is used primarily by users with normal vision.

In SonicFinder, Gaver took an approach to auditory icons that I find compelling, though no empirical testing has been done. In contrast to Soundtrack, where arbitrary tones or speech represent icons,[2] "Objects in the computer world should be represented by the objects involved in sound-producing events; actions by the interactions that cause sound; and attributes of the system environment (e.g., processing load or available memory) by attributes of the sonic environment (e.g., reverberation time)."[3]

As an example, take the operation of dragging a file to the trash. Object types in SonicFinder are represented by material types—wood, in the case of files. Object selection is represented by the sound of the material being tapped; the size of the object affects the timbre of the sound. So when the file is selected, the user hears the "thunk" of wood being tapped; as it is dragged across the desktop, a scraping sound is heard; the trash can emits a "clink" when the file contacts it; and finally a crash is heard when the user drops the file.

Gaver reported one definite performance improvement. The "clink" provided confirmation that the file was actually over the trash, avoiding the common error of dropping the file icon without quite hitting the trash.[4] It seems plausible that well-designed sounds can help in other ways, and an interface like this would surely benefit people with visual impairments.

"Sonic design" for user interfaces is in its infancy compared to visual design, and there are no standard guidelines for using sound in a general-purpose interface. For users with normal vision, it should be used moder-

[1] [vIBM92] shows one example of a partial solution.

[1] [Edw89], page 54.

[2] Arbitrary tones were also used as "earcons" by Blattner and her colleagues [Bla89].

[3] [Gav89], page 76.

[4] This is a general problem with many iconic drag and drop systems—the visual feedback indicating a target "hit" is not quite obvious enough.

ately, to supplement visual presentation. Since sound is omnidirectional, its effects on people in the environment, as well as on the individual user, must be considered.

Haptic Information

Haptic refers to a variety of "touch" or "feel" senses, ranging from true tactile information, perceived through receptors in the skin, to force feedback, perceived through proprioceptive receptors in the joints. A variety of applications exist, ranging from force feedback in the steering wheels of cars in arcade games [Min89] to a system that helps chemists "visualize" the forces between molecules [Broo90].

Haptic displays are usually used together with visual displays. It seems plausible that they could also be used with audio displays. For example, the *Feelmouse* [Pen93] is a mouse that provides a synthesized tactile feedback indicating the quality of the surface its pointer is passing over on a visual display. Used with an audio interface like SonicFinder, this could be very valuable to blind users.

GROPE A series of systems developed at the University of North Carolina provide examples of the capabilities of haptic display [Broo90]. One of the most recent, GROPE-IIIB, supports a chemistry application, molecular docking. The efficacy of drugs is often governed by how well their molecules fit or "dock" with other molecules. Docking depends on a complex force field determined by atoms of both molecules near the point of contact. Chemists use 3-D models to analyze the docking of molecules, but it is a difficult problem.

In the GROPE system, the chemist places his or her hands in grips that provide force feedback with six degrees of freedom.[1] The chemist sees a 3-D display of the molecules, and can "grab" and try to force them together in various positions. The system provides feedback through the grips by calculating the atomic forces in real time. Force feedback improved the chemists' performance in the docking task by more than a factor of two.

GROPE is one of the few systems that has been extensively tested, but there is no reason to doubt that haptic devices will be useful in many applications. From the OO perspective, exerting force is just another behavior it is reasonable for certain objects to have.

9.7 Summary

Human senses have a broad range of capabilities, which we must exploit using relatively limited computer display devices. This provides leverage for designers, to anticipate users' information needs and present what is most important in the foreground.

[1] Three dimensions of position and rotation around the three spatial axes.

Though limited in some ways, computers have the flexibility to simulate almost any medium—books, pictures, and television, for example. And unlike these media, computers are interactive; users can shift points of view and rapidly explore large information spaces.

The presentation medium for most OOUIs is a flat surface that shows a view of a large space. Within this space are views of objects. Objects may be containers (desktops, folders, etc.), resulting in a hierarchy of spaces. The overall metaphor is *objects in space* that evolve in time and can be manipulated by the user. This is usually presented visually, but it is comprehensible in terms of touch and sound as well as vision.

Views include:

- *Information object views*, which allow the user to view and interact with representations of domain objects. These may be:
    - *Icons*, which identify the object, show major state changes, and permit interaction with the object as a whole.
    - *Content views*, which "open" the object for inspection or editing, and allow users to interact with components of the object.
- *Frames*, which are display mechanisms associated with information object views, such as window title bars and borders.
- *Control mechanism views*, which make interaction mechanisms visible to the user. Examples include menus, scroll bars, and buttons.

The typical visual display for graphical OOUIs shows areas of text, graphics, still images, and full-motion video. The raw materials for creating the display are typography, graphic elements, images and video, color, and the layout of these elements on the screen. "Design"—coherency between elements—can make or break the appearance of a user interface. Designers of traditional media such as print and video currently have the best skills to provide this coherency.

Visual metaphors for information presentation using words and pictures exist in all domains, and can be used by OOUI designers. Providing behavior above and beyond visual appearance contributes to the sense of "working with real objects." Audio output can supplement or replace visual presentation, and tactile output devices may be available in the future. The ability of computer displays to simulate multiple media, and to rapidly move through information spaces under user control, can overcome the limitations of display size and resolution.

Designing good interfaces involves understanding both the similarities and the differences between computers and other media. Lessons from media design are important for designing computer presentations, but other media are passive. The computer is the only medium that provides significant interactivity. Even in a fast-paced medium like TV, there are just pictures and sound, albeit moving. In a computer we can conceive of pictures and sound as ways in which objects interact with users, which adds another dimension to design.

That additional dimension, the "feel" of the interface, is the subject of the next chapter.

9.8 To Explore Further

The relationship between psychology and principles of object-orientation, and the application of OO principles to user interfaces, are covered in more detail in Chapter 4.

I am indebted to Edward Tufte for helping me, through his books and lectures, to work out my own understanding of visual design. [Tuf83], though mainly about statistical graphics, is a rich source of design principles and visual metaphors for presenting information. [Tuf90] is more general; the examples are mainly drawn from print media, but they are transferable to design for computer displays.

Other print media designers are also good sources of ideas and inspiration. Richard Saul Wurman offers general principles in [Wur89], and examples in [Wur84] and his other Access guidebooks. [Mar92] covers design principles applicable both to print media and computer interfaces.

[IBM92b], Chapter 6, has a worked-out example of application design. The application supports various functions for an automobile dealership, and is taken through requirements, conceptual modeling, and the design of presentation and interaction. Among other things, it is a good illustration of how a style guide determines many aspects of user interface design (the style in this case is IBM's Common User Access, or CUA).

[Dre72] and [Mod76] are sourcebooks for icon symbols; both books cover international symbols. [Bie94] is a dictionary of meanings for traditional symbols, many of them visual. It is a source of metaphors and their visual representations. These books are sources of ideas, not substitutes for user testing of icons. [App92] and [IBM91] are sources of icons that have been tested on their specific platforms; they also supply general advice on developing and testing icons.

9.9 Exercises

1. Suppose you are given the requirement of developing customized roadmaps for trips between widely separated cities (for example, Rome and Paris). Users are interested only in information about things along the route.

   a. Design a presentation of the desired information, in a compact form, on a paper map. (A good solution to this problem was published by John Ogilby in 1675 [All92], and is still used by the Automobile Club of America. Tufte discusses this problem in [Tuf90], pp. 112-113.)

b. Design a solution for a personal computer that can be carried in an auto. List differences between a good paper solution and a good computer solution. (See [Lan93] for examples of commercial mapping products.)

2. Internationalization, described on page 227, involves separating interface elements that are specific to one country, then translating them for each target market. Generalize this two-step process, and show how it supports development of product versions for any heterogeneous user population (based on education, physical abilities, etc.).

3. A familiar maxim in OO design methods is: "Find real-world objects." Finding real-world metaphors for abstract objects is an extension of this. Suppose the object of interest is a database containing customer information.

   a. For the user of a customer-related application, does the database correspond to a real-world object? To a real-world metaphor?

   b. How would you present the database visually to the end user?

   c. Now suppose you are designing an application for database administration functions. Does the database correspond to a real-world object? How would you present it visually to an administrator?

4. Using the results of Chapter 7, Exercise 4, and Chapter 8, Exercise 5, design icons and content views for the fax application. You can use a platform style of your choice, or the style described in Appendix 1, Section A1.3, *The "Office" Style Guide*.

   a. Document content views with sketches. Copies of the screen dumps in Appendix 1, *Fax Case Study*, can be used to sketch the integration of the fax application with the "Office" shell (assuming you are using the same style).

   b. Make sketches of icons you are adding, and document them using the format given in Section 9.5. Do not forget to relate icon documentation back to the conceptual model documentation developed in Exercise 8-5.

10

Interaction and Control Mechanisms

Interactivity is a key difference between computers and all other media. This chapter deals with the design of that interactivity.

In the narrow sense, interaction covers the *action language* of the user interface, as opposed to the *presentation language*. More broadly, interaction is a cycle that includes information presentation as a response to user action. This chapter focuses on the details of the action language, but also ties presentation and action together into a holistic view of interaction ("look and feel" design).

Shoshana Zuboff, in her study of the impact of information technology on work, reports that " 'Work' becomes the manipulation of symbols, and when this occurs, the nature of skill is redefined."[1] "Computerized" workers manipulate information, not physical things, and feel disconnected from their own skills as well as the work. Even for knowledge workers accustomed to symbolic work, the information being manipulated loses some of its reality as it moves from the concrete world of pen and paper to the virtual world of the computer.

Well-designed interaction can restore the sense of directness to work and minimize the distancing effect of the computer. It reinvolves the sensory and motor systems in a coordinated process. Effective interaction design involves all of Bruner's levels—physical manipulation, perceptual imagery, and abstract symbols—resulting in better task performance and greater satisfaction.[2]

[1] [Zub88], p, 23.

[2] Bruner's concept of coexisting levels or cognitive systems was described in Chapter 4.

Video games, though trivial in some respects, are good lessons in interaction design. Unlike many systems designed for work, games do not distance users, or make them feel they have no control over outcomes. Games that do not engage users fail and disappear; the successful ones are well designed, at least at the levels of manipulation and imagery.

This chapter covers:

- The nature of interactivity.
- Interaction devices, viewed as physical mechanisms and as logical capabilities.
- A step-by-step approach to designing the feel of the OOUI.

It also covers two topics that tie together material on interaction and information presentation:

- The use of style guides in designing OOUIs.
- Documenting user interface "look and feel" design.

There are no set formulas for discovering interaction techniques that will make your interface "come alive." This chapter focuses on principles, guidelines, and issues, illustrated by examples. It provides a general framework for thinking about interaction, and will help refine your intuition for finding the right techniques for your specific tasks, users, and environments.

10.1 Interactivity

Interaction is mutual or reciprocal action. Interactivity is an ongoing process of interaction. People normally have a high rate of interaction with other people and objects in their environment, and it is natural to want such interaction with computer systems. Many studies show that for almost all applications, users prefer high interaction rates.[1] These rates come from good system performance, and from a user interface with the right "feel."

"The right feel" implies a natural sequence of motor actions, which comes from familiarity, efficiency, and ease. Familiarity comes from common actions such as grasping or pointing, actions used in physical situations the application is modeling, or actions learned from other computer systems. Efficiency and ease come from minimizing the effort, movement distance, or time to accomplish a result. Motor actions are not one-way, usually requiring sensory feedback to be done easily. They may be haptic, directed at getting information (for instance, exploring a surface by feel).

[1] See [Shn92], Chapter 7.

Case Study: Video Games

Many video games are excellent examples of interactivity. Take *Pong*, the first successful arcade game. Developed in 1972, one of its design goals was to run on very cheap hardware [Per82]. The result was the almost absurdly simple game shown in Figure 10-1.

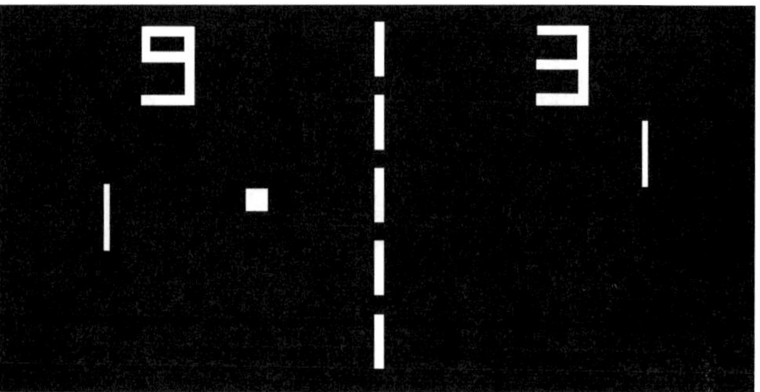

Figure 10-1 Display for the video game Pong

It is a version of ping-pong for two players. The display shows the players' scores at the top, the "net" in the middle, a paddle for each player, and a "ball" that is hit back and forth with the paddles. The graphic display was so crude that it showed the ball as a square. The paddles had a single degree of freedom—they could only move up and down. In spite of its simplicity, it was a huge commercial success.

Pong's interface mirrors the simplicity of the game itself—the only objects of interest are the ball, the paddles, and the scores, and that's about all that is displayed (the net is irrelevant). Actions are direct, and the game provides immediate feedback.

Given the hardware constraints, the simple graphics were a good design decision. Devoting all the limited power of the chip set to moving the ball and paddles provided a sense of "real objects" that was key to making the game absorbing. Aside from its immediacy, visual feedback on the motion of the paddles and ball is clear and simple; there is no clutter on the display.

A system built by Pausch and colleagues [Pau92] makes an important point about Pong, video games, and interactivity. It used a novel input device (a Polhemus tracker attached to the wrist) to allow children with cerebral palsy to play Pong on a computer. On average, the children did nearly as well as "able bodied" players. Interaction here (and in general) involves integrated use of vision, cognition, and motor actions. Separating these for analysis allowed the researchers to see that motor action was the problem area, and develop a new action language that compensated for it.

Arcade games often have controls customized for the game. Developing games for home computers is more challenging, since the largest market is obtained if they use devices available on all machines. Pinball

Figure 10-4 The cycle of interaction

the selected object.) The user's action initiates a process in the implementation model. Its completion is indicated by an output coded in the presentation language, which acknowledges that the action was done, shows how it changed the states of objects, and indicates the range of actions that can be taken next. The user modifies the state of his mental model based on the new information, and the cycle repeats.

This picture clarifies the notion of "distance." Hutchins, Hollan, and Norman [Hut85] talk about the "gulf of execution," the effort a user expends in translating conceptual intentions into the action language, and the "gulf of evaluation," effort in translating the presentation language into the terms of the conceptual model. As an example, imagine that instead of having a joystick to move the paddle in the Pong game, the user had to type commands, such as `moveTo: 5`. The conceptual intent is visual, and needs to be translated into text symbols; this is the gulf of execution. If the game displayed the ball location textually (say as numeric coordinates) this would be a gulf of evaluation—the user would need to translate from text to a visual image.

Textual commands for Pong illustrate *articulatory distance*—the action of moving a joystick is physically close to the conceptual action of moving a paddle, and typing a command is physically far away. The file concept in most computer system interfaces is an example of *semantic distance*. The user's concept is typically something like a document, and there is a semantic gap between this and a file.

The cycle of interaction has the same structure of thought-action-computation-feedback at all levels. (The *thought* is not necessarily conscious at the lower levels; in fact, for many interactions, the sense of directness relies on the fact that processing is pre-conscious.) Take the task of deleting a document by dragging its icon to the trash can icon. This is part of some larger task such as organizing the file system, which has this cycle:[1]

- Understand which documents need to be moved, deleted, etc.
- Perform the required actions.
- Verify the state of the file system.

The cycle for deleting a single document is:

- Decide to delete the document.
- Select the document icon, drag it to the trash can icon, and drop it.
- Observe a state change in the trash icon,[2] and/or the disappearance of the document.

This task has subtasks, each of which has its own cycle. For instance, to select the document:

- Decide to select the document.
- Move the mouse until the pointer is over the document and press the button.
- See that the document icon highlights.

This has an even lower level, the subtask of moving the mouse pointer. The user picks out the target for the mouse movement, moves the mouse, and observes that the pointer moves on the display to the desired location. Even this can be decomposed further, into cycles of pick a nearby location–move the mouse–observe pointer movement.[3]

Stuart Card and colleagues suggest that there is a natural division of interaction tasks into three levels, with three time scales ([Car83], [Car91], [Macki91]):

- *Perceptual* tasks, taking 100 milliseconds or less. A typical perceptual task is tracking the motion of an object, as in moving the mouse pointer from one place to another. We handle these tasks without conscious processing.
- *Immediate* tasks, taking about one second. This is the time scale of the smallest discrete actions we are conscious of starting and ending. Selecting an object is an example. It is also the time we will wait after

[1] These descriptions leave out the computation step, since only its results are visible to the user.

[2] In Macintosh System/7, for example, the trash can icon bulges when something drops into it.

[3] See [Wal93] for a detailed analysis at this level.

asking a question before worrying that the other party did not hear us.[1]

- *Unit* tasks, taking about ten seconds. This ten-second time is based on the capacity of short-term memory—it is the average time that a person can hold action planning, action, and feedback in consciousness as a unit.

Understanding and supporting users' interaction cycles is critical to providing a good feel to the interface. At the lowest level, if visual feedback lags behind movement of the user's hand, it significantly increases error rates and task difficulty [MacK93b]. At any level, the user can have difficulty formulating an action plan because of a bad conceptual model; the action language may require too many steps, or steps that are too hard; computational delay can introduce lag; feedback may be missing or confusing.

Interaction cycles are like human conversations. Bill Buxton [Bux90b] talks about the "phrasing" of interaction, invoking the idea of both conversational and musical phrases. He considers tension to be what binds smaller actions into phrases or gestures. In deleting the file there is first a relaxed state, then tension increases as the mouse is moved with the button pressed down, and the tension is released by letting up on the button when the icon reaches its target. The tension is both physical and mental, and there is an optimal level—just enough to bind together the components of the action, not enough to cause fatigue or a sense of effort. Both Buxton and Shneiderman [Shn92] emphasize the need for *closure*, the sense that the action is finished. In this example, closure is provided by the release of muscular tension and the visible state change as the icon drops on the trash can.

In the conversation metaphor, objects are anthropomorphized—and, like people, they can behave badly. Inconsistent behavior and lack of feedback make the conversation difficult.

The language model of interaction We can use language in a more formal way for understanding interaction. Linguists use a model with three levels [Cho72]. The *lexical* level describes the form of tokens in the language. For example, *l'œil* and *the eye* are different lexical tokens referring to the same object. The *syntactic* level describes meaningful sequences of tokens. For instance, "cabbages see furiously" is a syntactically correct sentence. The *semantic* level describes how the language relates to real objects and relationships. It is at this level that "cabbages see furiously" fails to be meaningful.

In describing interaction, the levels are as follows:

[1] [Guy88] relates response time to anxiety; for the reported response times that were more than 1.25 seconds, anxiety increased over the task; for shorter response times, anxiety slightly decreased.

- The *lexical* level describes the mapping of physical devices and actions to the action language. For example, the first token in an object-oriented "sentence" is the object to be operated on. Typing the object's name and selecting an icon with a mouse are two different lexical forms for specifying it. In both cases there is a visible indication of the user's action; this is *lexical feedback*.
- The *syntactic* level describes the form of meaningful sequences of tokens in an interaction. Selecting a menu action without selecting the object to which it applies, for instance, is syntactically incorrect.[1] Syntax can be specified independently of implementation; "select an object" might map to "click the left mouse button while over the object's icon" at the lexical level.
- The *semantic* level describes how tokens and sequences relate to objects, actions, and relationships in the implementation model. For example, selecting an object and choosing the `delete` action causes the object to be deleted.

The language model is a tool for analyzing interaction, with a view toward efficiency, providing appropriate feedback, blocking errors if possible, and helping the user recover from them if not. Many interaction sequences can be described using regular expression grammars [Aho86]; this means they can be analyzed and documented with state transition diagrams, described below in Section 10.3.

Fitting the control to the task Studies of interaction by human factors researchers are useful to interface designers. *Stimulus-response (s-r) compatibility* [Fit53] is the idea that controls and displays should be designed to minimize the effort needed to translate between displayed information and actions, or between the operation of a control and the displayed feedback.[2] An example is moving the display pointer in the same direction as the physical movement of the mouse. Perceptions of response compatibility can be based on convention, such as "red = danger," or on expectations about the behavior of physical objects.

"Fitting the control to the task" includes stimulus-response compatibility and other ways of using knowledge of users and tasks. These ideas have been applied in many areas, for example the design of aircraft controls. Fitts and Jones [Fit47] studied aircraft accidents attributed to "pilot error" during World War II. From interviews with survivors and analysis of controls and displays in aircraft, they showed that most "pilot errors" were caused or facilitated by poor design or inconsistent design. For instance, to lower the flaps a pilot needed to push a control on one plane, and pull it on another.

General guidelines on designing controls and interaction come from

[1] This is a common error made by novice users; it is reasonable to correct it by saving the action and asking the user for an object specification.

[2] This is similar to the "gulfs" of [Hut85].

this research, which are just as applicable to computers as to aircraft:

- Make the control and display compatible:
    - Use analogic display where possible, as with the mouse pointer.
    - Respect conventions, such as up equals on or higher intensity.[1]
    - If all else fails, establish a standard and use it consistently.
- Do not require complex motor action if it is not necessary; if it is necessary, recognize the training requirement. This is the principle of "as simple as possible, but no simpler."
- Provide appropriate feedback to show the results of an action.
- Analyze user performance, especially user errors, to improve controls and interaction.

In aircraft design, these issues are life and death matters. In video games, they spell the difference between commercial success and failure. In all interfaces, they affect user productivity and satisfaction.

Interactive Performance

Performance has its own heading to emphasize its importance. I have seen more than one nice-looking graphical application that replaced an "old" character based application, but performed worse than its predecessor, even for text display. There are cases, such as WYSIWYG editors for desktop publishing, where lower performance may be a reasonable price to pay for the superior display. In general, it is not reasonable—nor is it necessary, if designers and implementors pay enough attention to interactive performance.

Observing and playing computer games on all sorts of processors suggests that people are willing to put up with low-quality graphics, if the "feel" is very direct. If performance is poor, and actions do not produce immediate responses, a game loses its appeal.

There are numerous studies reporting the effects of poor performance,[2] in two categories. "Response time" is the time it takes the system to respond to a significant unit of user entry, such as a data query. Fine grained response, such as how fast the display tracks the keyboard or mouse, is called "lag." In both categories, linear degradation in computer performance causes non-linear degradation in user performance and satisfaction.

Non-linear degradation is explained by the time constants proposed by Card and colleagues (described on page 257). If feedback from a task such as moving the mouse exceeds 100 milliseconds, the task can no

[1] But verify the convention; I am told that in some countries, the convention for light switches is up = off.

[2] Many are summarized in [Shn92], Chapter 7; see also [Doh86], [Guy88], [MacK93b], [Rush86], [Tha81].

longer be handled by the perceptual and motor systems without conscious attention. Try thinking consciously about what you are doing while, say, riding a bicycle, and you will see how this degrades task performance. If feedback from an immediate task exceeds about one second, the user may become anxious and make mistakes. When response time in a unit task exceeds about 10 seconds, short-term memory capacity is exceeded; the user makes mistakes, or adopts a strategy of keeping information in long-term memory, which takes longer to access, or of writing it on paper.

It is not easy to measure, but poor performance also degrades the user's perception of working with objects. Lag violates perceptual assumptions about object constancy and continuity. Lag and poor or inconsistent response time violate cognitive assumptions about causality.

For many applications today, good interactive performance *and* high-quality graphics (and video) are requirements. This demands powerful processors—whereas an Intel 386 processor looks blindingly fast running a character-based word processor, a 486 (or even a Pentium) is barely adequate for high-end publishing packages, which must accurately show graphics and typography. Situations like this should not cause designers to throw up their hands, or say "wait until the machines get faster." The machines will never be fast enough.[1]

Users are willing to accept compromises if they retain control. "Draft mode" for graphics is a capability that allows good performance with adequate graphics rendering; if the user needs the best rendering, draft mode can be turned off. The best solution is to anticipate user needs. Microsoft Word has a creative solution. If a user is paging through a document rapidly, graphics are not shown. When the user pauses, graphics for the displayed page are rendered.

10.2 Interaction Devices

Many types of input devices are available for computers, though only a few are widely used. Just as display devices can be classified based on the senses they use, input devices can be classified based on effector muscles. Almost any muscle can drive an input device. Users with motor disabilities may employ the tongue, the diaphragm (via a breath-actuated switch), or the muscles that rotate the eye (via gaze-tracking cameras) to provide input to computers.

In typical OOUIs, many control mechanisms are *virtual devices*—buttons, dials, sliding switches, etc. painted on the screen and actuated using a physical device such as a mouse. A large part of interaction design is deciding which physical devices and actions are most natural and efficient

[1] I say this because "interesting" problems tend to be solved by algorithms whose performance is non-linear in the size of the problem, whereas the human expectation is that if the machine is twice as fast, the problems that can be solved ought to be twice as large. Resolving this tension will always be a creative challenge to designers.

for operating these virtual controls. Users may also operate directly on domain objects displayed as icons.

Human Effectors

Motor bandwidth, the amount of information that can be transferred through an effector, is much lower than that of the senses. Whereas sensory bandwidths range from a few thousand to hundreds of thousands of bits per second, motor bandwidths range from about 5 bits per second for head and neck movements to about 35 bits per second for finger movements ([Car90], [Greg86a]). Besides bandwidth, coding and stimulus-response compatibility must be considered. For example, the bandwidth for arm and wrist muscles is between 10 and 20 bits/second, so in principle, touch typing is faster than "mousing." In practice, it depends on the task. While this is true for text entry, the mouse is better for pointing and selection tasks.[1]

The hand The motor cortex in the human brain devotes more of its "hardware" to controlling the hands than to any other area except the speech muscles [Pri71]. Figure 10-5 suggests only a few of the myriad activities and gestures of the hand. Most input devices exploit a small subset of its capabilities—tasks with mice, trackballs, and styluses mostly involve pointing and pressing buttons.

The most complex use of the hand (for input to computer systems) is in keyboarding. Though its use as a data entry device is recent, the keyboard has been used in musical instruments for centuries. Using keyboards can be considered a "natural" activity, though one requiring much practice.

For many people, the use of handwriting and gestures is more natural than keyboarding, and more expressive than pointing at things. This makes handwriting and gesture recognition a promising input technology, though (as with speech recognition) the accuracy of existing technology is barely adequate to support a reasonable rate of interaction.

Figure 10-5 The hand: grasping, pointing, using a stylus

Speech A large part of the motor cortex is devoted to the speech muscles, and speech is a relatively high-bandwidth communication channel. It requires a complex transducer, which is why it is only beginning to appear in

[1] [Car78] is one of many studies demonstrating this.

computer interfaces. Speech often combines with hand gestures, as when someone says "could you [touching someone] move over there [pointing out a place]." Combinations of speech and gesture have been found effective in computer interaction ([Bol80], [Hau89]). Since people can multiprocess effector outputs, just as they do with inputs from different receptors, this increases the total bandwidth.

Other effectors Position-sensing devices can be attached to almost any part of the body that moves.[1] The head is not as efficient as the hands, but its status as a carrier of sense organs (the eyes and ears) makes it important for virtual reality applications. Head trackers, in conjunction with head-mounted displays, make the virtual eye position and orientation follow the head.

Individual differences For users with disabilities, devices are often used simply to take advantage of functioning muscles. Even "normal" users show significant differences in motor abilities. It is important to permit different devices for the same function, and to allow user adjustment.

The use of logical devices (described below) is a design technique that allows different devices for the same task. An example of user adjustment is the sizing border on windows in Microsoft Windows, OS/2, and OSF/Motif. The default width of the border is three pixels, which was considered a reasonable compromise between making it easy to "grab," and minimizing the amount of screen space taken up. For many people this is too small, but it can be changed. Mouse tracking gain is also adjustable, so that a given movement of the hand will produce more or less movement of the display pointer.

Physical Devices

Figure 10-6 illustrates some common devices for pointing and selecting with button pushes. The keyboard, not shown in the figure, is also an important device used as input to most computer systems.

Touch-sensitive screens allow direct use of the hand, though many commercial touch screens have poor resolution and cause arm fatigue. Researchers at the University of Maryland [Sea92] have produced touch

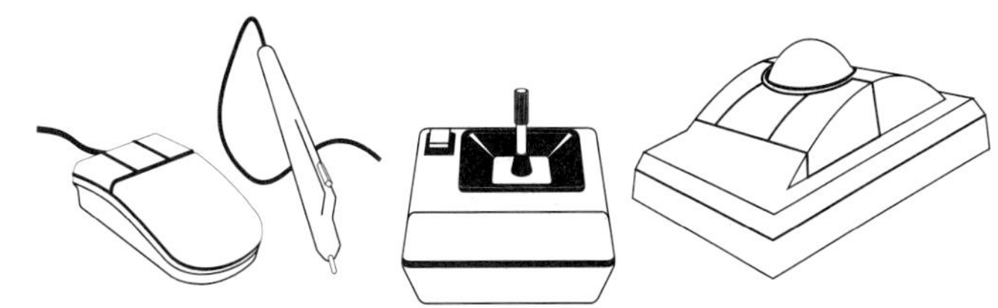

Figure 10-6 Extensions of the hand: mouse, stylus, joystick, trackball

[1] The Polhemus electromagnetic tracker is an example of such a device.

screens with elegant interaction techniques and single-pixel pointing precision (precision is achieved by using time-averaged position when the hand is moving slowly). Placing the screen at the proper angle reduces fatigue. For public-access applications, touch screens are a good choice, because they are rugged and (if the display is well designed) intuitive.

The stylus in Figure 10-6 is used with a position-sensing tablet. The tablet senses position in absolute coordinates, unlike a mouse, which senses relative movement. Like the mouse, the movement of the stylus is indirectly coordinated with visual feedback. Touch screens are more direct—the thing pointed to is the thing seen. Fingers as pointers leave something to be desired, since they are large enough to obscure what they are pointing at. A good compromise is to use a stylus, or *pen*, to "write" directly on a touch-sensitive display (see Figure 10-7).[1] Though the mouse and stylus/tablet combination do as well in most tasks, they require some learning; pens do too, but almost everyone gets that in their first few years of school.

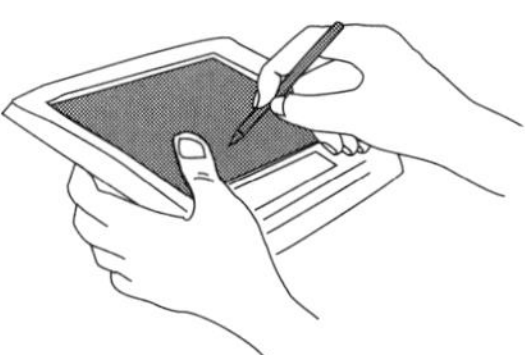

Figure 10-7 The pen as an input device

The "paper" on which the pen writes is important too. Real paper and pens have coevolved, and the paper has just the right friction to stabilize the pen without dragging. Writing surfaces on pen-based computers often feel unnatural because they are too slippery.

It is important to analyze physical devices in a task context. As an example, the trackball performs well for pointing tasks (though the mouse is superior); it does poorly on dragging and selection tasks, since it is awkward to push the buttons while positioning with the ball [MacK91].[2] It is also important to look at the larger environmental context. Though the trackball is a poor choice compared with the mouse based on task analysis, it has a very small "footprint" compared to a mouse. I normally use my laptop computer with a mouse and pad, which takes up about 100 square inches on my desk (625 cm^2). On an airplane I use a trackball, which occupies about 4 square inches (25 cm^2).

Another example of contextual analysis is the issue of homing time to move from one device to another when both are used in the same task. The classic example is text editing, using the keyboard for data entry and the mouse for positioning the cursor in the text. Studies show that for the

[1] I am talking here about modern pen-based systems [Mez93], not the older lightpen, which has all the disadvantages of the finger, and is heavy enough to quickly fatigue the user.

[2] It is worthwhile to develop benchmark tasks for evaluating input devices. See Exercise 1 for an example.

positioning subtask, the mouse is faster than any other method [Car78]. Nevertheless, for editing that requires significant text entry, it may be faster overall to use the arrow keys on the keyboard for positioning, to avoid the homing time when the user's hand moves between the mouse and keyboard.

A better solution for text editing is to put a pointing device (essentially a small joystick) in the keyboard. Though this is not quite as good as a mouse for a pure positioning task, it is better overall for text editing [vIBM90]. Figure 10-8 shows one implementation of this device. The device also has the advantage of a much smaller footprint than the mouse.

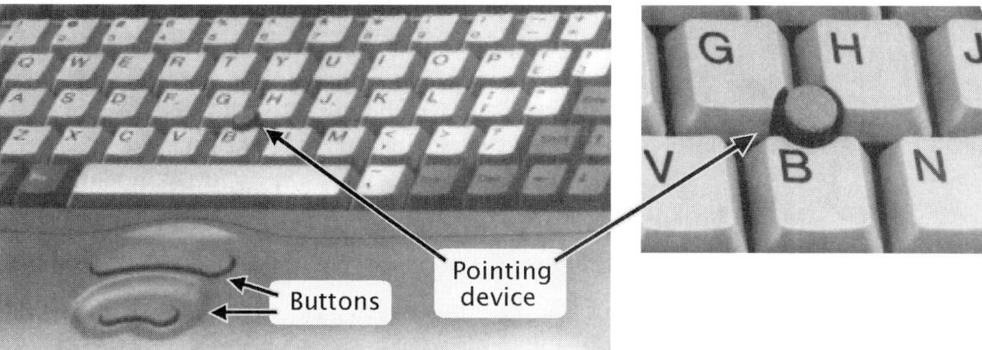

Figure 10-8 Pointing device in keyboard (Toshiba T3400CT)

Sensing body position Devices like the mouse and trackball are mechanical transducers that convert the force or position of body parts such as hands into signals the computer can interpret. Position and orientation can also be sensed in ways that are more direct and less obtrusive.

Myron Krueger has developed several systems that detect body and hand position in real time by processing video images [Kru91]. In his Videodesk system an overhead camera tracks the user's hands, which can function as positioning devices for objects on a computer display. Since there are no "buttons," alternative methods are needed to detect that the hand wants to grasp or move an object. One technique is to assume that when the hand has rested on an object for a certain length of time, it is to be picked up. Similarly, when the hand has moved an object and then stops, the object is dropped.

Figure 10-9 shows two techniques from Videodesk. They would work with any device able to sense hand position and the orientation of the fingers, for instance the VPL Dataglove.[1] The left side of the figure shows the user moving documents on a "desktop"; the right side shows a graphics application in which the fingers serve as control points for a spline curve.

[1] A glove containing sensors which register all the finger joint positions; see [Rhei91], Chapter 7. [vSIGGRAPH] 27, 2 (1987) shows the Dataglove in operation.

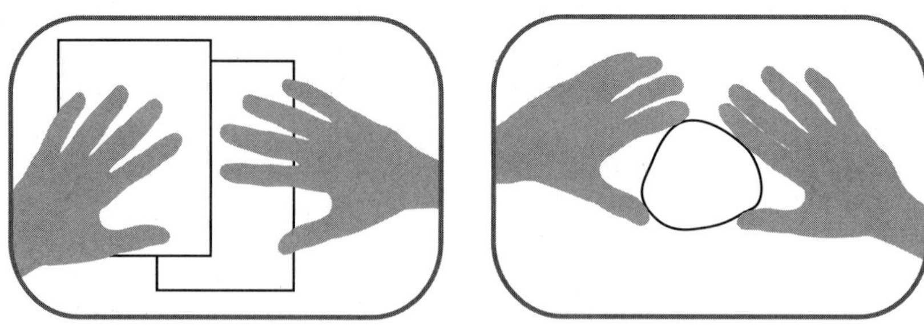

Figure 10-9 Hands as interaction devices in Krueger's Videodesk system

A common way of indicating an object of interest is to look at it. People are good at detecting the direction in which other people are looking, and it turns out that machines can do this too. Devices are available that reflect a spot of infrared light off a user's eye and use a video camera to detect the gaze direction [Sta90]. Again, some additional technique such as gaze fixation over time is needed to select an object.

Techniques such as these can help disabled users even today [Pau92], though they are not in the commercial mainstream. The price of the technology is falling fast enough to make it widely available within the next decade.

Concurrent input People can simultaneously perform more than one motor task; for instance, turning a corner while changing gears in a car. Three tasks are going on simultaneously here (turning, controlling speed, and changing gears) using five controls (steering wheel, accelerator, brake, clutch, and gearshift). Unrelated tasks can be done concurrently—I saw a mother in a restaurant rocking her baby's carriage with one foot while eating her meal and carrying on a conversation.

Studies have shown that users can easily and effectively use two-handed input for existing computer applications [Bux86], and that user interface software can support concurrency [Hil86]. Studies also show the effectiveness of concurrent speech and gesture input ([Bol80], [Hau89]). Users often use the keyboard and mouse almost simultaneously in text editing tasks, and would probably use true concurrency if it were available. Given the evidence, it is surprising that platforms (even those with multitasking operating systems) do not support concurrent input.

Modeling human performance OOUIs involve a high intensity of interaction, so small differences in performance can affect efficiency, cause fatigue, and result in repetitive strain injuries [Fur93]. Predicting user performance at this level has been the subject of research into "keystroke models" for many years [Car83].

One of the most successful models is Fitts's law [Fit54], which predicts user performance in movement and pointing tasks. Though Fitts was not studying computer interfaces, his result is very general; it fits a variety of pointing, selection, and dragging tasks in OOUIs [MacK91]. The "law" is based on information theory and experimental results, and has been extensively validated. It says that the minimum time taken to accurately point (say with a finger) to a target, by moving the pointer, is given by

$$MT = a + b \log_2((A / W) + 1).$$

MT is the movement time, A is the "amplitude" or distance to the target, W is the target width in the direction of motion, and a and b are empirically determined constants.[1]

Fitts proposed, and experiments have confirmed, that the lower limit on MT (for targets within arm's reach) is attained using the finger or a simple device such as a pencil. This is because the capacities of nerves and muscles determine lower limits for a and b. Device design can worsen performance compared with unaided muscles, but cannot improve it.

Fitts's law has many practical consequences, such as the fact that a keyboard is faster than any other use of the hands for text entry. Many experiments (see, for example [Jel90], [MacK91]) have shown that in terms of speed, the mouse is the best device available for pointing and dragging. Given the number of "new and improved" devices on the market, Fitts's law is a valuable tool for separating fact from hype.

The validity of performance models depends on correct analysis of the whole problem. Pointing at text, as an isolated task, is faster with a mouse than with keyboard cursor positioning. But in word processing, use of the mouse may raise the number of Fitts's law tasks to three: 1) move the hand from the keyboard to the mouse; 2) point with the mouse; 3) move the hand back to the keyboard. As another example, [Jel90] reports no performance improvement from varying the "gain" of a mouse (gain is the ratio of pointer movement distance to hand movement distance). However, increasing the gain reduces the amount of space needed for mouse movement, which may improve performance by avoiding the problem of "tripping over" items on the desk while moving the mouse.

The table in Figure 10-10 summarizes some common and not-so-common input devices. Many of these devices can emulate mice, and can be freely interchanged if device drivers are available for the implementation platform. (In fact, the designer may have no control over which device the user chooses). Others, like the pen, may require special features such as handwriting recognition software.

The sources listed in *To Explore Further* provide more information on these and other devices. As the in-keyboard pointing device illustrates, innovation is constant; 3-D devices, in particular, are likely to improve greatly over the next few years.

Direct Manipulation

Ben Shneiderman coined the term "direct manipulation" [Shn83] to describe a class of user interfaces he had observed. Users were enthusiastic

[1] This is one of a number of variants; see [MacK91].

about them, and reported higher productivity. These interfaces appeared in applications ranging from text editors to video games, but they all shared certain characteristics:

- Objects from the problem domain were continuously represented on the display.
- Operations were effected through direct actions on object representations.
- The effects of actions on objects were immediately visible.

He also noted that direct actions were often reversible in an obvious way; having moved some text, the user could simply move it back to undo the action. In addition, the syntax of direct manipulation was simple,

	Pointing	Dragging	Text	Comments
Keyboard	poor	poor	excellent	
Mouse	excellent	excellent	*note 3*	senses relative motion
Stylus/tablet	excellent	excellent	*note 2*	senses absolute position
Pen	excellent	*note 1*	*note 2*	very natural
Lightpen	good	good	*note 3*	fatiguing
Touchscreen	good	*note 1*	*note 3*	very natural
Gaze tracker	good	*note 1*	n/a	
Trackball	good	fair	n/a	small footprint
In-keyboard pointer	good	good	n/a	very small footprint
Joystick	good	fair	n/a	small footprint; rugged
Dataglove	good	good	n/a	uncomfortable
3-D stylus	good	good	n/a	fatiguing
3-D mouse	good	good	n/a	fatiguing
3-D tracker	*note 4*	*note 1*	n/a	fatiguing; poor tracking and lag with some devices
Speech recognition	poor	poor	poor to good	Good with limited vocabulary

Note 1: A mechanism is needed to signal drag start/stop.
Note 2: Handwriting recognition is required.
Note 3: Text entry is possible on "soft" keyboards.
Note 4: Pointing performance depends on body part tracked (e.g., the hand is

Figure 10-10 Summary of some important input devices

because direct actions replaced command entry or menu selection.

Direct manipulation does not solve all problems—though Shneiderman and others have shown that it has a large range. Direct manipulation works effectively with other modalities, such as speech. Bolt [Bol80] describes a system in which the user points at objects on a display, simultaneously giving voice commands such as "put *that* [pointing to an object] *there* [pointing to the target location]."

Constrained natural language combined with direct manipulation may solve one problem direct manipulation alone does not always handle well—the selection of sets of objects by description. Whereas a small set of objects can be shown and visibly selected by the user, this does not work well for large sets such as objects in a database.[1]

Experience and studies show that nothing fosters the sense of "working with objects" more than direct manipulation. Compromises may be necessary, since the most direct technique is not always the most efficient. Users place a high value on the sense of being in control and "being there" with objects in the problem domain—so when in doubt, bias compromises toward direct manipulation.

Levels of directness Shneiderman, in [Shn83], considered character-based full screen editors "direct manipulation" as compared to line editors. For example, to move a block of text lines in a full screen editor, the user might do the following:

- Type `mm` to the left of the starting and ending lines in the block to be moved.
- Type `p` (for `previous`) to the left of the line after the insertion point for the text.

This contrasts with line editor command sequences such as `m 10 5 27` (meaning "move 5 lines, starting at line 10, to a position before line 27"). The full screen editor provided a direct visual model of what was going on, resulting in faster task time and reduced errors. The action language was still somewhat cumbersome, requiring command mnemonics and positioning using the keyboard.

Cut-copy-paste, first seen commercially in the Apple Lisa and Macintosh, is conceptually similar but physically and visually more direct:

- Select the text to be moved using the mouse.
- Pull down or pop up a menu, and select the action `cut`. This deletes the selected text and moves it to a non-visible object, the *clipboard*.
- Using the mouse, place the insertion point at the desired location in the text. Alternatively, a block of text can be selected to be overlaid by the moved text. (In the first case, the insertion point can be

[1] Shneiderman and colleagues have developed an elegant approach based on direct manipulation of query parameter values [Ahl92], which handles many cases of database query.

considered a "nil selection" that the moved text replaces.)

- Select the menu action `paste`, which moves the text from the clipboard to the desired location.

This is much faster to execute than to describe, but notice the indirection of the extra object, the clipboard. It would be more direct to select the text to be moved, select the insertion point, and then pick `move` from a menu. This would preserve the arguably simpler conceptual model from the line editor,[1] along with the physical directness of the GUI action language.

The Xerox Star and the Metaphor Data Interpretation System use a method that avoids the need for a clipboard:

- Select the object to be moved.
- Press a `Move` button on the keyboard (which could just as well be a menu pick). The mouse pointer changes to indicate "move mode."
- Move the pointer to the insertion or drop point, and press the left mouse button to complete the move.

This is essentially drag and drop, which is implemented in some word processors, such as Microsoft Word, in a more conventional way. Instead of using a mode, the user presses a mouse button to drag the text to the insertion point, then drops it by releasing the button. In Word, as in the Star or Metaphor, there is a loss of visual continuity. The mouse pointer becomes a small rectangle; the actual text appears at the drop point when the mouse button is released. Moving the image of the text itself would be the most direct possible way. Figure 10-11 shows this; the user is dragging the text "JCN announces the Pentawidget . . ." from the left window to the right one.[2]

There is a subtle problem in the drag and drop technique—either the source and target points must both be visible during the drag, or the user must be able to perform an auxiliary action while dragging, to expose the target. In systems that exploit drag and drop extensively, this is a problem for users when there are many open windows obscuring one another [Mac93]. In such cases, the clipboard becomes a useful object again, as a place to hold objects while the insertion point is located.

The examples in Figure 10-12 illustrate degrees of directness and show that "directness" may be relative to the task. The application is a counter that can be incremented and decremented. `Menu Counter` is the least direct,[3] requiring selection of the action from a menu. `Slider`

[1] One could also argue that the cut-copy-paste model is simpler because it does not require multiple selection, does not require memory for operand ordering, and exploits the metaphor of cut-copy-paste with real paper.

[2] This is a prototype. I am not aware of any product that implements it.

[3] But `Menu Counter` is more direct than typing commands. What about *speaking* commands—would it be more direct? Would it change the user's perception of the type of the object receiving the command? I leave this as an exercise for the reader.

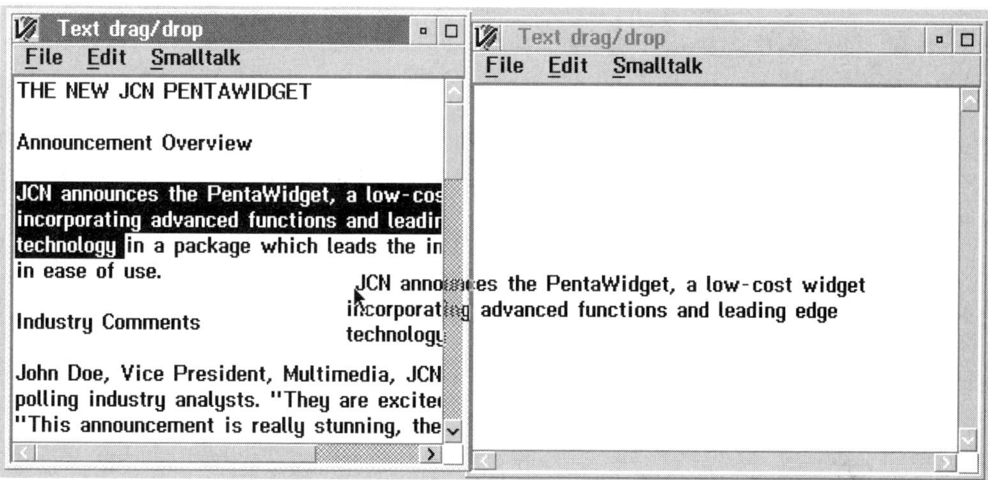

Figure 10-11 Direct manipulation in a text editor

`Counter` and `Dial/Button Counter` are more direct, but support different tasks. The slider,[1] a continuous control, makes it easy to change the value by large amounts quickly, but the push buttons make it easier to enter discrete increments accurately. `DM Counter`, on the right, is controlled by "grabbing" the dial pointer with the mouse and moving it.

`DM Counter` brings out several issues in direct manipulation. The direct manipulation control and the display are tied closely together, and this control mechanism would not work with the digital display. Though the mechanism is direct, it is not visible. Whether users discover it may depend on their expectations about the manipulability of objects in the interface. Although `DM Counter` is *physically* more direct, `Dial/Button Counter` is conceptually more direct for discrete increments and decrements, and the digital display probably provides better stimulus-response compatibility in this task.

"Directness" is not a simple property, and must be evaluated at the

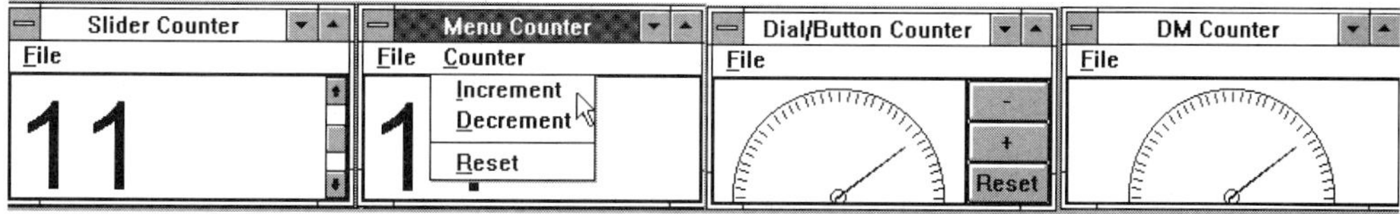

Figure 10-12 Direct and indirect manipulation

[1] My use of a scrolling control for a slider is questionable, since the conceptual model of a scrollbar implies position within a document; see [App92], [IBM92b].

semantic, syntactic, and lexical levels. Since it makes sense to map the most direct interaction techniques to the most frequent actions, careful analysis and testing are required to ensure that they are efficient.

Logical Devices

There are disadvantages to dealing with physical devices. Designers initially care about what a device needs to do, not its physical details. Interface tuning, new technology, or user needs and preferences may motivate a change from one device to another. Changes are easier if the design specifies what the device does, without dictating how it is done.

Designers of computer graphics systems developed the idea of *logical devices,*[1] corresponding to the syntactic level in the language model. Take the logical device called a *pick* in graphics terminology, which selects objects. A mouse implements a pick, as do many other devices—trackballs, light pens, styluses, etc. A keyboard can also be a pick—the user can type in the coordinates of the object to be picked, or use the arrow keys to locate the object and the `Enter` key to signal the pick.

The devices below are a combination of the sets from [Fol92] and [ANS84], with some changes in terminology.[2]

- A *locator* provides a position and/or orientation. Position may have any number of dimensions, so there are corresponding classes of locators. A mouse is a two-dimensional locator. Virtual reality applications often use devices with six dimensions (x, y, z, roll, pitch, and yaw[3]), specifying position and orientation in 3-D space.
- A *button* provides its identity and state (pressed or not). Buttons and locators are basic primitives from which other logical devices can be constructed. A selector, for example, is a locator plus a button to signal that the object at the current location should be selected. Physical buttons were common on first and second generation computers, and virtual buttons are just as common on GUIs.
- A *selector* returns the identity of an object that the user has picked. This is called a *pick* in the graphics literature, but *selector* describes its function better in OOUIs. Unlike choices (described below), selectors operate on information objects and are asynchronous.
- A *drag* device provides a sequence of positions between a start and end location. It is called a *stroke* in graphics, referring to its use in drawing lines. It also supports "rubberbanding" to vary the size of a line, rectangle, etc.
- A *valuator* provides a real number, which makes it a one-dimensional locator. It is treated separately because obtaining a single value is

[1] These are sometimes called *virtual devices,* but I prefer to reserve this term for "soft" visual controls on the display, such as menus, buttons, etc.
[2] The *composite* device is my addition.
[3] Roll, pitch, and yaw are the amounts of rotation around the x, y, and z axes.

such a common interaction task. Though physical devices exist, such as dials, GUIs usually use virtual controls (actuated by a device such as a mouse) as valuators. Figure 8-6 (Chapter 8) shows a control panel interface with several virtual valuators.

- A *choice* device returns values chosen from a finite set. Examples of choices are radio buttons (for choosing one and only one item from a set), menus (for choosing zero or one items from a set), and list boxes (for choosing zero, one, or many items from a set). Choices are similar to selectors, but choice sets are presented synchronously in response to user actions. Selectors operate asynchronously on information objects in content views.
- A *keyboard* inputs text strings. Besides physical keyboards there are virtual or "soft" keyboards, shown on the display and "typed on" with the mouse; these are useful for special symbols, foreign alphabets, etc., and for simple devices such as calculators. Speech and handwriting recognizers can also be logical keyboards.
- A *composite* device is any logical device constructed from the basic devices. For example, a standard scroll bar logically consists of a valuator and four buttons (line up/down and page up/down).

The devices in this list cover all common forms of interaction. Composites can construct novel input devices; for example, [Ble88] describes an input device that simulates an artist's charcoal, allowing the position, line width, and color density to be dynamically varied.

Basic interaction tasks A complementary way to look at the logic of interaction is in terms of low-level tasks the user does with devices. [Fol92] proposes the following set of *basic interaction tasks*:[1]

- *Position* specification, corresponding to the *locator* device.
- *Dragging*. This specifies a continuous series of positions, and corresponds to the *drag* device.
- *Selection* from a variable set, corresponding to the *selector* device.
- *Selection* from a fixed set, corresponding to the *choice* device.
- *Text* entry.
- *Quantification*, corresponding to the *valuator* device.
- *Rotation* of an object in space.

These basic tasks can be used to synthesize more global interactions, such as moving objects from one container to another.

[1] I have added dragging to the list, because of its importance in OOUIs.

10.3 Step-by-Step Interaction Design

As in Chapter 9, "step-by-step" means the presentation is linear, not that design will be done without backtracking and iteration. There are many dependencies between the action and presentation languages, so their design occurs in parallel and is usually done by the same people. It is possible to design different "feels" for the same "look," so activities here and in Chapter 9 will have varying degrees of integration.

Figure 10-12 shows the flow of designing interaction and control mechanisms, expanded in the context of the overall design process. Basic object interactions are identified for icons and content views, and mechanisms for implementing them are designed, or chosen from a style guide. Then the larger, task-related, cycles of interaction are designed.

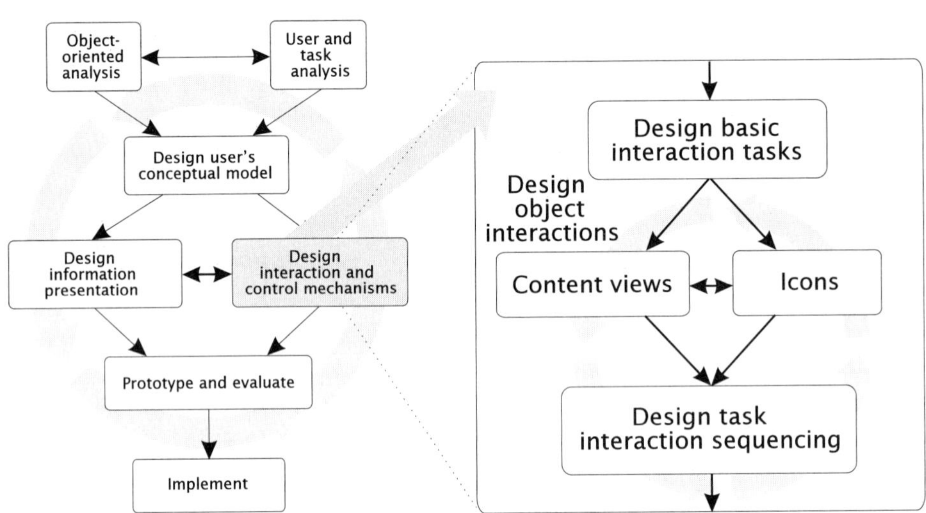

Figure 10-13 Flow of interaction and control mechanism design

This chapter looks at many low-level issues in interaction, so it is worth reviewing the general idea of an OOUI and how interaction design plays a part in it. Users see and act on *objects*, which can be classified based on behavior. All the interface objects fit together into a coherent representation based on the task domain.

To produce the sense of "acting on objects," the objects must "act back" in reasonable ways. This ranges from good performance that fosters a sense of object continuity, to consistency with the user's conceptual model. Object classification depends on interactions that are consistent across a class, and consistent in an abstract way across subclasses of a common base class. Coherence requires interactions that are congruent with the conceptual model, and support the actions needed for tasks.

Preliminaries

Interaction design, like presentation design, does not start from scratch. Interaction techniques for computer interfaces are less advanced than information displays, so even quite innovative interfaces can be constructed from well-known techniques.

Here are some starting points; since they parallel the starting points for presentation design, it may make sense to do them concurrently:

- Metaphors from the user's conceptual model, such as *control panels*, are sometimes direct sources of ideas. In other cases, brainstorming about how users might want to interact with objects or navigate in the metaphoric space will generate ideas.
- Studying the work activities of users in existing tasks will suggest ways of interacting.
- Existing applications often create *de facto* standards for interaction, which should be followed unless you can provide something significantly better. This is particularly true if users have formed motor habits based on standard techniques.
- Platform style guides often provide specific and detailed guidance on interaction techniques based on mouse, keyboard, and the visual controls provided by the platform vendor.

As an example of idea generation, consider the following problem. A company needs to forecast the effects of economic trends, and wants an application for building financial models. After building a model, financial analysts want to dynamically vary parameters such as interest rates or revenue growth, and see the results immediately. Suppose we have chosen the *spreadsheet* as a metaphor for building the model, with various data graphs for viewing outputs.

There are many excellent spreadsheets on the market, all with graphic output capabilities. Users of the application we are designing have probably used at least one of them, so it makes sense to use these existing applications as sources of interaction techniques for building and inspecting the models.

Standard spreadsheets do not provide the capability of rapidly and dynamically varying the models, because they require retyping of the data for every change. Exploring this requirement with the users yields statements like "I want to tweak that parameter up and down a little, and watch what happens," or "I'd really like to just grab that growth trend and pull it down, to see what it does to the bottom line."

These statements suggest additional interaction techniques to enhance the spreadsheet. Virtual dials or sliders can be linked to values in the spreadsheet, allowing users to change parameter values rapidly and continuously. Output graphics can function as input controls, using direct manipulation of the displayed lines, bars, etc. to control the underlying data. These techniques extend and complement standard spreadsheet interactions.[1]

Graphic design and human factors Control mechanisms such as menus, buttons, and scroll bars have visual aspects. These may make up a significant part of the visual appearance of an application, so they should be professionally designed and executed. Often these controls are part of platform toolkits, but for application-specific controls, graphic designers are just as important here as in presentation design.

Designing controls that work well requires human factors expertise, just as designing ones that look good requires graphic designers. This is true even where interface elements come from toolkits. Controls are not used in isolation, and human factors knowledge applies to their composition. It is common to use human factors experts to test a design after the product has been built. At that point it is too late and too expensive to do much about the inevitable problems that are found. The leverage point for specialized expertise is in the design phase.

Basic Interaction Tasks

Improving user performance in interaction has both top-down and bottom-up aspects. High-level issues include things like matching visible controls to metaphors in the user's conceptual model. Low-level issues relate to the performance of basic interaction tasks such as pointing or entering text. Larger interactions are usually synthesized from a small set of basic tasks, so it is worth some careful effort to optimize them.

Basic interaction tasks can be described using logical devices. In the financial analysis example above, *valuators* vary parameters of the financial models. Direct manipulation of graphics is one novel way of implementing valuators; a physical device such as a joystick is another possibility. Formulating the problem in terms of a logical device allows exploration of the design space of physical interaction devices to be independent of the functional requirements of the application.

Logical and physical devices can be modeled as finite state machines, so basic interaction tasks can be documented using state transition diagrams. Figure 10-14 is an example, showing a transition diagram for dragging an icon with the mouse. If button 2 on the mouse is pressed when it is over an icon, it signals the *start drag* event and goes to a dragging state. The dragging state is left when the user hits the Esc key (*cancel drag*), or releases the mouse button (*drop*). In either state, *mouse move* is signaled when the user moves the mouse.[2]

Besides maintaining device independence, logical devices and basic interaction tasks are tools for designing interaction and improving its efficiency. The task model in the user's conceptual model can be decomposed

[1] The idea of attaching controls to spreadsheet cells was suggested by Bill Buxton in a tutorial presentation [Bux91]. It also appears in a in a product called *Sliders & Dials* [sGol92].

[2] Exercise 2 illustrates the use of state transition diagrams to solve a design problem.

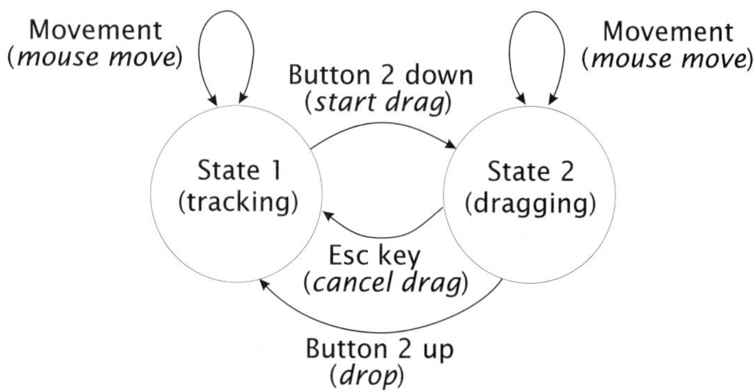

'e 10-14 State transition diagram for drag and drop

into a set of basic interaction tasks, a specification of the generic objects used in these tasks, and the logical devices required. Higher level tasks are synthesized from these. Logical devices can then be mapped to physical and virtual devices that optimize the performance of the tasks, subject to other constraints such as cost or size. This typically requires several round trips between top-down analysis and bottom-up synthesis and optimization.

Users of OOUIs may perform hundreds of low-level interactions per hour, so even a small saving per task can result in substantial improvement. Style guides may dictate standard ways of accomplishing interactions such as object selection, but this does not preclude providing alternative "shortcut" methods.

Once users are habituated to a motor action sequence, it is fixed in memory and difficult to change [Pri79]. As an example, WordStar, an early, successful word processing program for PCs, used abbreviated keystroke combinations for commands. An attempt by WordStar developers to introduce a more rational command language failed, because users could not unlearn the old commands [Tel90]. So it pays to analyze, test, and iterate in design—you may not get a second chance.

Object Interactions

Objects in the user interface must provide behaviors that support the task model component of the user's conceptual model. Use cases, interaction diagrams, and the sort of decomposition just described are tools for designing object interactions. They produce results at two levels.

Dealing with "keystroke level" or lexical issues such as hand movement, visual feedback, and the use of optimal devices produces low-level efficiency. Higher level issues must be considered at the same time. Interactions should be consistent across objects of the same class; where possible, operations should be polymorphic—applicable to different object types. This reduces the number of interaction behaviors and simplifies the interface. Visual controls should be congruent with one another and with the user's conceptual model.

Interaction in content views Objects are represented by content views and icons. Content views will have a much richer set of interactions than icons, so encouraging the sense that the icon and the content view are the same object is an issue in interaction design.

The standard approach to this is to create a menu on the content view menu bar with actions applicable to the object as a whole, such as `Print`, and to implement these same actions for the icon. Most GUI platforms have a standard for this that is not very object-oriented. The action bar menu is labeled `File`, and it often contains actions that foster an "application and file" view of the interface. The menu should be labeled by the object type, such as `Folder` or `Document`. Object/action tables (shown in Figure 10-15 on page 282) will help in assessing individual menu items.

Sub-objects in a content view should support the standard interactions for their class. For example, if a text document has an embedded graphic, the graphic object should provide editing behavior that is consistent with its behavior in any other context. The containing object can do things like move and scale the sub-object as a whole, but should respect its encapsulation by not imposing behavior on it.

A common example of a view with sub-objects is the form (represented by a dialogue box) which contains text entry fields, lists, buttons, etc. Behavior for these sub-objects can exploit inheritance. For instance, a text entry field has generic behavior such as accepting keystrokes, supporting simple editing, etc. This behavior should be consistent in all instances of the type. (Many GUIs violate this by not supporting cut/copy/paste consistently in text entry fields.) Now suppose we have a text entry field for entering address information, which supports *autocompletion*. This means that in the state field, for example, if the user types `New Y`, it is automatically completed to `New York`, since no other state name will match. An autocompletion text entry field should appear as a subclass of the generic text entry field; implementing its interaction behavior as a clean extension of the generic behavior is the key to presenting this appearance.

For form-based applications or others that use views composed from smaller objects, it is worthwhile to "brainstorm" and find useful behaviors for the sub-objects. Doing this in advance and designing a class hierarchy will help insure behavior that is consistent and useful.

Sub-objects in views can function as icons, and interact with other views. The direct manipulation text editor shown in Figure 10-11 is an example. Figure 9-4 (Chapter 9) is another potential example—dropping a customer icon on a `Customer name` text entry field might cause the field to fill itself by sending a message to the customer to retrieve the name.

Style guides and toolkits provided by platform vendors dictate solutions to many design problems in object interaction. Vendors are becoming more conscious of object-orientation, and we can expect to see more support (both style guides and tools such as OO class libraries) for providing consistent interaction techniques for object classes.

Controlling displayed information No presentation design is perfect for all purposes. For reasons ranging from physical to conceptual, user requirements for presentation vary even for people performing the same tasks. An important use of interaction is to allow users to change the presentation in content views. They may want to change type sizes or colors, the size of visual controls such as the mouse pointer, the national language, etc.

Controls that compensate for individual differences have other benefits as well. For example, when laying out small graphical elements in text, I may want to see it at twice its actual size. When evaluating the layout of an entire page, I want to see it at half size. The ability to change point of view is a prominent aspect of our interaction with objects in the real world—providing this capability in the interface enhances the sense of objects and improves task performance.

Icon interactions Several methods are commonly used for interacting with iconic object representations:

- Direct action on the icon to initiate an operation. For example, most GUIs support opening the default content view of an object when the mouse is double-clicked over its icon.
- Direct action on the icon to pop up a menu of actions for the object. The menu is context sensitive and only enables actions valid for the object in its current state. Many platforms use a special mouse button for this purpose.
- Selection of an icon, followed by selection of an action from a global menu provided by a content view or the "desktop" (which is really a content view of all objects currently on the desk).
- Dragging an icon and dropping it on another icon.

Several of these may be available for the same action, to allow choices based on preference or efficiency. For example, in OS/2 a user can open a default content view by double-clicking over the icon, selecting it and pressing `Enter` on the keyboard, selecting it and then selecting `Open` from a global menu, or pressing mouse button 2 over the icon and selecting `Open` from its context menu. Providing redundant mechanisms is helpful if they are used consistently. If double-clicking, for example, produces different results depending on the object, users will probably be confused.

Menus should enable only the operations that are valid for currently selected objects but should always show the same set of actions, graying or otherwise indicating those that are not enabled. This allows users to form motor habits for clicking on menu items (since they are always in the same place), while showing which ones are currently valid. One of many uses for a status information area on the display is to provide a brief, one-line explanation of menu actions as the pointer passes over them. For disabled actions, the explanation can say why the action is not valid.

Context menus that pop up at the mouse pointer location are mechanically efficient, since they require less hand motion. Some interfaces also allow menu bar menus to be "torn off" and moved near the object the user is working on. Floating tool palettes also minimize hand motion. Keystroke commands are useful for experienced users performing repetitive operations—one hand points to the object, the other actuates the command keys. Two-handed concurrent pointing would be useful in the same situation, though most platforms do not support it—one hand points at the object, the other at the menu.

Drag and drop is a powerful technique, and more than anything else provides the illusion that the icons are objects. Careful design is needed, because there is no visible indication of what will happen when a user drops one icon on another. In its basic form, drag-drop provides a single polymorphic operation:

```
droppedOnObject doSomethingWith: droppedObject.
```

In order for this technique to be successful, it must be clear to users what `doSomethingWith:` means.[1] If not, particularly if drag-drop implements destructive operations such as deleting objects, it will have the opposite of the desired effect—instead of feeling empowered, users will become anxious and slow down their work.

Several techniques can help in the design of drag and drop interactions. The most valuable (and the most difficult) is a conceptual model so clear that nothing else is needed. Objects representing functions, such as printers and trash cans, help to make the model clear and visible. Function objects that are containers, like the trash, are particularly useful because they facilitate *reversible operations*. If an operation is done by dropping an object into a container, it can be undone by opening the container and taking the object back out. Having an `Undo` action on the global menu is a less imaginative alternative, but one that is consistently applicable to all operations.

Finally, there is a technique that is useful for any pointing or dragging operation, including menu selection. The Xerox Star designers first said it explicitly [Smi82]: *feedback on button down, action on button up.* This means that as the mouse pointer is moved with the button pressed, the system gives some indication of what action will result when it is released (no action is taken until then).[2] For menus, this can be a one-line explanation in a status area. For drag-drop, a frequently used form of feedback is displaying the "not allowed" cursor, ⃠, if the pointer is over an icon that will not accept the drop. More informative feedback would be

[1] The Smalltalk-like syntax here is for analytic purposes—not to suggest that users consciously think of it this way.

[2] "Action on button up" also provides a satisfying sense of closure or "phrasing"—see page 258.

useful; a wider range of iconic cursor feedback is possible, and the status area can be used to dynamically display whether a drop is possible, and what will happen if the drop occurs.

Designers often forget that the user may decide not to drop after starting a drag. This can cause panic if there is no "safe" place to drop the object. The easy solution is to provide an escape mechanism, such as pressing the `Esc` key, that cancels the operation.

Drag-drop can implement more operations by using command modifiers. It is conventional in GUIs to use the keyboard for this purpose; using mouse buttons is possible but relies on having a mouse with the requisite number of buttons. The *de facto* standard is to perform a `move` operation on a normal drag, and a `copy` if the `Ctrl` key is pressed. This creates two situations, for move:

```
droppedOnObject doSomethingWith: droppedObject
```

and copy:

```
droppedOnObject doSomethingWith: droppedObject copy.
```

The meaning of these will depend on the objects involved. It is also possible to select multiple objects and drop them all at once, for instance when deleting several objects. This equates to

```
droppedOnObject doSomethingWith: droppedCollection.
```

As more operations are loaded onto drag and drop, it becomes more difficult to present a clear conceptual model, especially if the command modifier is not visible. I have seen interfaces with different meanings for dragging depending on which of the `Ctrl`, `Alt`, or `Shift` keys was pressed. Users need "crib sheets" to remember the modifier meanings, which defeats the purpose of using direct manipulation.

Where dragging accomplishes more than one operation, the cursor shape can change to indicate the mode. Graphics programs use dragging for drawing lines, adjusting spline points, rotating objects, resizing objects, etc. To change modes, the user clicks on a menu item or tool icon, and the cursor changes to reflect the mode (┼ , ▶ , ↻ , and ✖ for the operations listed). For dragging icons, the mode indicator should be placed in a consistent position relative to the image of the dragged icon—normally at the "hot spot" for the pointer.[1]

Documenting object interactions Figures 10-15 and 10-16 illustrate useful tabular formats for documenting object interactions. Figure 10-15 shows actions and results for object types. Where objects are part of a class hierarchy, typographical conventions (italics and indentation) show the class/subclass relationships. The *Document* class is an example, with subclasses **Note** and **Chart**. Notice that some actions are "inherited." The

[1] The mouse is a locator device, and the pointer hot spot is the visual point that is returned as the locator value. Letting the user know where the pointer is really pointing is an important part of direct manipulation.

	Open	**Print**	**Delete**
Document	Open editor view	Print document	Delete document
Note	Open text editor	Print note	Same as superclass
Chart	Open graphic editor	Print chart	Same as superclass
Container	Open view showing contained objects	Print list of contained items	Delete container and contents after user confirms
Folder	Same as superclass	Print list of items in folder	Same as superclass
Trash can	Same as superclass	Print list of deleted items	⃠
Device	Specified by subclasses	Specified by subclasses	Remove device from system after user confirms
Printer	Display printer queue	⃠	Same as superclass

Figure 10-15 Object/action table

action column heading can show multiple ways of invoking the action, for example, "Open/double click/`Ctrl` + O" instead of "Open." The results in the cells may include visible state changes or other feedback from the action.

Each cell in Figure 10-16 shows the action that occurs when the row object is dropped on the column object. If command modifiers exist, each cell will contain multiple entries, one per modifier. ⃠ in a cell shows that a drop is not permitted.[1] Subclassing relationships can be shown and used here as well.

Part of the value of these tables is to be able to see the large scope of interaction at a glance, and compare one table against another. For instance, Figures 10-15 and 10-16 can be compared to verify that menu actions are consistent with drag-drop actions. The tables can be maintained using spreadsheet programs.

Besides checking for completeness and consistency of actions, there are some "rule of thumb" analysis techniques to apply:

- If the number of object types is large (more than ten or so), a class hierarchy may help to reduce complexity.

[1] Asymmetries in Figure 10-16, such as permitting documents to be dropped on folders but not vice versa, are typical of actual platforms.

	Document	Folder	Printer	Trash can
Document	⃠	Put document in folder	Print document	Delete document
Folder	⃠	Put folder in folder	Print list of items in folder	Delete folder after user confirms
Printer	⃠	⃠	⃠	Remove printer from system after user confirms
Trash can	⃠	⃠	Print list of deleted items	Not possible—trash can is unique

Figure 10-16 Object/object interaction table

- If the number of actions is much larger than the number of object types (more than twice as large), it may be possible to reduce the number by developing more general polymorphic actions. For example, `Print`, `Plot`, and `Generate PostScript` can all be subsumed under a polymorphic `Print`.
- If the number of actions is much larger than the number of object types, consider adding tool or function objects to provide visible "handles" for actions that can be represented concretely.
- If an action has many variants based on parameters, consider adding a tool object whose instances represent commonly used parameter values. For example, mail tray objects can represent distribution lists for document mailing.

These guidelines are based on the premise that reducing the user's memory load makes the interface easier to learn and use. Memory load is reduced by having a small, orthogonal command set, classified by object type.

Task Interaction Sequencing

Task interaction sequencing deals with global issues in supporting user tasks. It is related to composition in information presentation, particularly the sequencing aspect of composition. Composition is concerned with where things appear and what they look like, and secondarily with when they appear. Interaction sequencing deals with when they appear and how the user causes them to appear.

Task analysis and the task model portion of the user's conceptual model are the main guidelines here. This activity may compete with information presentation for scarce display space. The more visual controls, the easier it is to navigate around the system—but the less space is available to display the information users want to see.

"Computer administrative debris" [Tuf90] is Edward Tufte's derisive term for interface controls that are not part of the end user's information. Even well-designed interfaces can contain amazing numbers of controls and widgets. Figure 10-17 shows a display from FrameMaker [sFra92], the package I used to prepare copy for this book. The window frame, menus, tool bars, rulers, etc., take up 35% of the display space.

This machinery is useful, even necessary, but it creates a conflict between tools and space to display the object being worked on. To put this in perspective, I inventoried a few work areas outside the computer domain: a carpentry workshop, a kitchen, and a dentist's operating room. In these cases, places to lay out and store tools took up about 50% of the space, so 35% is not bad. The problem stems from limited space on current computer displays, and making them big enough would largely solve it. (Or at least provide the raw materials to solve it.)[1]

Until we do get desk-sized displays, the space conflict will be an issue in design. Partial solutions include:

- Allow users to hide and show controls. In the FrameMaker example,

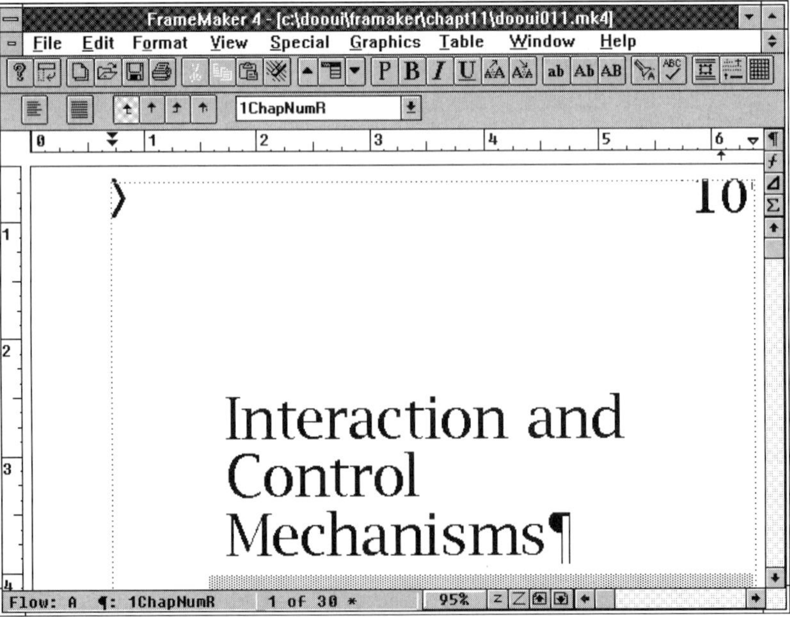

Figure 10-17 Visual controls and screen real estate

[1] As an example, visual control mechanisms become no larger when moving from a 640 x 480 display to 1024 x 786; in fact they usually can be made a little smaller due to increased legibility. So all the extra space goes to the user's information.

rulers and tool bars can be hidden to reclaim about two thirds of the space devoted to controls.

- Provide alternative interaction techniques that do not require visible controls. (`DM Counter` in Figure 10-12 is an example of this.)
- Use mechanisms such as pulldowns, popups, and rollups to allow users to quickly reveal hidden functions. (Inspecting current GUIs will provide a wealth of examples.)
- Allow users to customize tool bars and menus to provide access to the most frequently used functions.

These techniques, particularly the last, do not excuse poor design. Task analysis will help to provide an organization of tools and controls that works for most users. Ideally, users will customize by hiding or showing controls in large groups, or by setting global parameters governing visibility.

Organizing work Work is usually organized based on general categories of objects; users need tools for each category. Objects of interest may reside in a more or less permanently organized filing system, to be retrieved only when needed. When the user needs to access these objects, mechanisms such as lists, queries, etc. must be available to find and retrieve them.

Current work is kept in piles or other temporary organizations. Typical OOUIs represent piles by folders or other containers holding icons representing work items. The distinction between items still in the pile and items the user is looking at corresponds to the distinction between icons and windows showing content views. Users need two capabilities:

- The ability to manage and track work in the piles or temporary folders. Interaction mechanisms associated with the permanent filing system, such as querying, can also be applied to the temporary one.
- The ability to manage collections of open views. This is more difficult because of the limited space on the display compared to a real desktop, but more power can be brought to bear on it. Grouping windows into projects or workspaces, providing window lists that allow rapid switching between different windows, and saving layout information when windows are closed are all useful.

These capabilities can significantly improve user productivity—finding things (including submerged windows) and adjusting window layouts are major time wasters in complex application environments.

Users also deal with objects outside the boundaries of their workstations, accessed through electronic mail or network file servers. What they need here is seamless integration of external objects into their work. In terms of interaction design, this means interacting with external objects directly and in the same way as "local" objects. This is mainly an implementation issue (sometimes a difficult one), but recognizing the need is part of external user interface design.[1]

The complexity of work done on computers varies. Some users work primarily in a single application, processing documents sequentially. Others may multitask between dozens of different documents and applications. I have never seen a system with too much organization for users, though I have seen systems with organizing functions that were too complicated to use. Task analysis will help to provide organization in ways that support the real work of the users.

Task organization metaphors A few metaphors are very frequently used for organizing and sequencing work, both in the real world and on computer screens.

Agents perform tasks for the user. "Intelligent" agents are on the frontiers of research, but even unintelligent ones can be quite useful. The design challenge is to provide an agent capability that is easy to use. Looking at task analysis data, or watching people work, is the best way to find tasks that are easily automated.

Calendars, *clocks*, and *flow diagrams* are all "containers" for time-ordered events. If users know they need to work on certain objects at definite times, these metaphors will help.

Workshops and *workbenches* organize tools relative to objects being worked on. Figure 10-17 is a typical example of an application that uses this metaphor. The menu bar appearing at the top or side of a window is an abstract version of the workbench metaphor. Agents, calendars, clocks, and control panels can be integrated as tools in workbenches.

Microsoft Office [sMic93b] uses the workbench metaphor in an innovative way to integrate multiple applications. Microsoft Word is a compound document editor, which allows various types of graphic objects to be imbedded in text. In the Office environment, if a user is editing a document and clicks on a graphic object, the Word tool bar is replaced by the tool bar for the application that created the graphic (Microsoft Excel, for example). The user can edit the graphic in context, without the usual time-consuming and visually distracting process of opening a new window. When the user clicks in the text again, the Word tool bar is restored.

Control panels provide central control of devices, and can function metaphorically in computer interfaces for controlling tasks. Panels are work organizers when they group controls for performing tasks, switching contexts, finding things, etc. Figure 8-6 (page 193) is a literal example of this metaphor. Figures 13-2 (page 376) and 14-7 (page 441) are examples of control panels for finding files.

Control panels have a "functional" feel; workbenches tend to be more object-oriented, and are preferable in OOUIs. Video editing is an example of a task that uses a complex panel to control the sequencing of video frames, special effects, etc. Computer implementations of video editors use control panels, but also workbenches where video clips and frames

[1] Several examples are covered in Chapter 15, *Design Examples.*

can be laid out, rearranged, and spliced together [MacN92].

Design patterns Many tensions become apparent during design: conflicts over use of display space, between novices and experts, among incompatible tasks, etc. As described in Chapter 9, Alexander encountered similar problems in building design, and developed the idea of design patterns as a solution. His patterns evolved over time to minimize tensions in the pattern of activities in a place.

Chapter 9 applied pattern thinking by iteratively resolving conflicts over information presentation for different tasks and activities. The same iterative cycle can resolve conflicts over control mechanisms. The example of Pinball Construction Set (page 254) illustrates how display and controls can be handled separately. Where controls are visible objects on the display, the cycles can be combined.

Here is the analogue, for interaction design, of the list on page 232 in Chapter 9:

- Take a set of activities for a task, and design an arrangement of controls that is optimal for it. Show the sequencing of events on the display as users do the task.
- If there are tensions in the design, for instance between control and display space, or between different types of users, try to find or develop patterns that resolve the tension.
- Test the design against another task. Are there tensions? Try to develop a structural pattern that minimizes conflicts between the tasks.
- Continue with other tasks. Include large units of work that encompass several tasks; these may reveal new tensions related to finding things and navigating from task to task. Iterate until you are satisfied.

Patterns have much in common with metaphors, including the fact that small units can be congruent or incongruent with one another, or with larger units of which they are a part. The style guides described below document patterns for small tasks, such as choosing a file to open. Larger patterns can be documented in project notebooks or as extensions to existing style guides.

10.4 Style Guides

The design space for graphical user interfaces includes designs for character and keyboard based interfaces as a subspace, and adds the dimensions of typography, graphics, video, sound, and the interaction devices described in this chapter. Enlarging the space increases the number of possible *bad* designs as well as the number of good ones. To constrain the space, standards and guidelines have been developed. Their purpose is to exclude bad designs, and sometimes to exclude even good ones that are inconsistent with a standard "style."

Consistent style in presentation and interaction can help users, because they can transfer knowledge of the style to multiple applications. On many platforms, use of a vendor's style guide is almost mandatory. The common look and feel of Apple Macintosh applications, for example, is so well known that a new product is unlikely to succeed if it is inconsistent with existing applications.

I prefer the term "style guide" to "standards" or "guidelines." Standards imply legislation by an organization such as ISO, whereas "look and feel standards" are less formal. "Guidelines" in user interface design usually refer to general advice such as "maintain consistency," or "minimize user memory load."[1] Style guides may include standards, guidelines, advice, and examples for maintaining a consistent look and feel across multiple products. User interface style guides are analogous to style guides for writing and graphic design, used by publishers to achieve a consistent "look" and level of quality.

Style guides cannot substitute for basic skills needed in designing OOUIs, such as graphic design and human factors engineering. What they can do is help people learn and apply the surface details of a particular style. They can also save time in development, because many standard interface elements come directly from the style guide.

Content of Style Guides

Style guides are available for many platforms, such as Apple Macintosh [App92], IBM CUA [IBM92b], Sun Open Look [Sun90], Microsoft Windows [Mic92], and OSF/Motif [OSF90]. Most of them have three levels of content:

- High level guidelines such as "maintain consistency," "use concrete representations of objects," etc.
- General advice or directions on presentation and interaction techniques, such as "when the user must make one and only one choice from a set, use radio buttons."
- Specific details of presentation and interaction techniques, such as "use mouse button 1 for selecting objects" or "follow the example in Figure 1 when presenting a button in its pressed and unpressed states."

The level of detail varies; there are style guides of less than 100 pages, and others with nearly 500 pages. Some rely entirely on printed text and pictures; others include running programs as examples, and even program source code for implementing styles.

[1] Such guidelines are valuable tools. See [Rubin84] and [Shn92], Chapter 2, for useful sets of guidelines.

De facto **style guides** The production of a style guide is a lengthy process, and interface designers do not sit around waiting for the next edition. If an application incorporating novel interface elements becomes commercially successful and is imitated, the new elements may become *de facto* standards. Some of the Microsoft applications, such as Word and the Excel spreadsheet, are examples. Innovative devices such as tool bars, developed for these applications, have become a standard for all applications on Microsoft Windows.

Tool bars have spread beyond the Windows platform, and are seen on OS/2 and UNIX applications. Tool bars and other controls are part of a sort of *de facto* "metastandard" for GUIs. Every platform style guide has elements like scroll bars, radio buttons, pulldown menus, and sizeable windows. Viewed as composite logical devices, they have almost identical interaction behavior on any platform—only their visual appearances differ. Thus logical devices can be considered abstract classes, with concrete subclasses for each platform.

Use and Misuse of Style Guides

My experience, confirmed by reports in the literature [Thov91], is that many designers like style guides, because they think that arguments over details of the interface are unproductive. They would rather have the choice dictated by a style guide, so they can get on with things they consider more important. On the other hand, some people do not want choices dictated, because they feel that it limits creativity. Many designers overestimate the extent to which style guides "dictate" what the interface should be like; it is harder than they think to implement standard styles, and easier to be creative within standard styles.[1]

Looking at a set of successful applications within the same style is a good way of exploring the use of style guidelines. (Applications on the Apple Macintosh, Microsoft Windows, NeXT, and other platforms can furnish examples.) Developers have relied primarily on the platform vendor to develop the style guide, rather than creating their own. They have used the style guide for consistency, so users can transfer their skills from one application to another. Successful developers have not hesitated to break the rules, particularly by introducing new widgets, such as tool bars. But they break rules for good reason, not just to be "creative."

Studies have been done on the use of style guides ([Tetzl91], [Thov91], [Nie92a]), and most of their conclusions are similar. Style guides in books are useful, but designers also need working examples that dynamically illustrate presentation and interaction techniques. Programmers want sample code that shows how to implement them. Developers also benefit from a library of commonly asked questions, with answers. [Tog92] is an example; it answers many questions about the Apple Macin-

[1]For music lovers, I like to cite the case of J. S. Bach, who worked within an extremely rigid set of style rules (which he broke when necessary). This obviously did not impair his creativity.

tosh style that are not answered in the style guide itself.

Designers have the greatest difficulty with higher level rules in the style guide. Take a style rule such as "Use mouse button 1 for selecting icons. Indicate selection by highlighting the icon in reverse video." This is unambiguous. On the other hand, consider "When designing objects for an object-oriented user interface, a designer should consider the tasks a user will want to accomplish and then ensure that the characteristics of the objects support the user's tasks." This is from the IBM CUA style guide ([IBM92b], page 31); similar statements occur in others. They are subject to interpretation, and do not make much sense at all to designers without experience in object-orientation.

That is why the background chapters in this book are so extensive. I do not believe that anyone can provide a simple set of rules for designing interfaces that conform to broad, abstract principles such as "object-oriented." Nielsen [Nie92a] found that "lack of object-orientation" caused the most usability problems, and the most serious problems, in interfaces designed by people with no prior experience in GUI design.

A similar problem arises in understanding "consistency," one of the main arguments for style guides. Consistency is straightforward when applied to low level issues such as colors, mouse button usage, function key assignments, etc. Suppose, however, we have two applications that operate on "documents"—what does it mean for the "document concept" to be consistent between the two applications? I have stressed the importance of conceptual models, and indeed it turns out that lack of "conceptual consistency" is a problem for users [Kel87]. But conceptual consistency cannot be defined by simple rules.

Practical Advice

The consensus is that the sort of consistency provided by style guides is valuable to users. Based on experience, discussions with colleagues,[1] and reports in the literature, I offer the following advice on using style guides effectively in OOUI development:

- Do not expect style guides to help much with high level issues such as object-orientation. Applying abstract principles requires education and experience.
- Building a customized style guide is a long, expensive process. If possible, rely on vendor style guides. Your energy is best spent on developing tools, examples, and checklists that highlight the aspects of the style that are most important in your environment.
- Successful commercial platforms and applications often become *de facto* style guides by providing examples of new techniques. Do not hesitate to incorporate them into your own style, but decide in advance on which elements to use.

[1] Particularly Mark Wilkes, who has extensive experience with the CUA style.

- Inspecting designs for conformance to the style is worthwhile, but not as simple as it sounds. Avoid setting up a "style police force." Conformance checkers should clearly understand that the goal is usability and quality, not points on a checklist.
- Encourage the development of "style gurus" who can help other designers and developers.
- Object-oriented libraries and frameworks can capture style rules as reusable code. Enhancing and expanding libraries should be a project goal.[1]

It is important that all developers understand the purpose of the style guide. Disputes about its adequacy need to be resolved early in the life of a project. Putting the user interface design team in the position of being a "police force" for enforcing style rules is guaranteed to arouse hostility among other developers. Programmers are especially likely to resent the imposition of rules without any guidance on how to implement them. (The best solution to this problem is to buy or develop style libraries, or tools that generate code from a style specification.)

One reason for having a programmer on the user interface design team is to help develop and promulgate tools to support the style guide. An alternative is to convince the project manager to designate a development programmer as the "style guru." This should not be a hard sell, if the manager already believes the style guide is necessary.

10.5 Documenting Look and Feel

Chapter 9, under *Documenting and Testing the Design* (page 232), discussed techniques such as sketches and videotape for documenting the presentation component of the interface design. These are also useful for documenting interaction. The design activities converge on "prototype and evaluate." At that point, all the documentation is merged into a single "user interface design specification."

The complete design specification can be evaluated by users, and specifies what needs to be implemented. It typically includes:

- A working prototype with the intended look and feel, and enough simulated application function for testing.
- Supporting documentation that describes essential characteristics of the prototype more formally.
- Documentation explaining the rationale for user interface elements and relating them to the requirements statement and other project documents.

[1]Implementation aspects of this are discussed in Chapter 14.

- Measurable objectives for usability, performance, etc.
- Descriptions of tasks as they are performed using the interface, which are also the basis for online help, manuals, and training material.

Prototypes as Design Documents

Prototypes allow users to evaluate something that looks and feels enough like the real thing to provide meaningful feedback. This is true during design, and in the formal testing that may occur as an exit criterion for the design phase. Both for users and implementors, prototypes document the gestalt of the design more faithfully than a paper specification.

Typical OOUI prototypes inadvertently document much more than the intended design. They are built on some platform using a particular tool, and contain many features that are accidental. A window opens—is its size and location part of the design, or a platform default? A choice dialogue shows radio buttons—is that essential, or are radio buttons the default for the prototyping tool? Supplementary documentation answers these questions.

Prototypes, together with supplementary materials, are efficient forms of documentation. For example, Figure 10-15 shows an object/action table, which is an abstract list of actions. A prototype shows an explicit organization of those actions into a menu hierarchy, tool bars, etc. Referring to the prototype in the object/action table formalizes its menu organization as part of the design specification. Using prototypes in this way requires version control, since they are then "officially" part of the specification.

Bitmapped images of the prototype can be captured from the screen and annotated, either by hand after they are printed, or by importing them into a graphics application. This is an easy and accurate method for showing whether visual details are essential.

Interaction details that are critical can be documented using tables like those shown in Figures 10-15 and 10-16, state transition diagrams as shown in Figure 10-14, or other methods, including free form text description. Descriptions can refer to the prototype. Videotape can couple a verbal description directly to the prototype.

In practice, a working prototype may not be complete in all details. It might provide only a critical subset of look and feel, with the remainder documented on paper. In these cases, project documentation should summarize what has been tested with the prototype and what has been inspected only on paper. There is also an assumption about application function. To adequately test look and feel, a prototype must simulate the underlying information model. The accuracy of the simulation should be monitored to insure the validity of testing results.

Other Documentation

The elements that must be documented for the interface "look" are

- Object views, both content and iconic.
- The overall composition of views, including spatial arrangement and temporal sequencing.
- The appearance of controls, including visible feedback.

For the "feel," the following must be documented:

- Interaction techniques for individual object views.
- More global interactions that control the sequencing and organization of tasks.
- Details on individual controls.

These need not be documented in detail if they are standard elements from a style guide. There is an obvious correspondence between the two lists, reflecting the fact that in a well-designed interface, users have a unified perception of presentation and action. Sometimes—for example, when supporting users with disabilities—multiple looks and feels are required. In these cases presentation and interaction documentation may need to be separated.

Many techniques besides prototypes are useful for documentation. It is worthwhile to save even rough documentation in a project history that goes along with other documentation. This helps in tracing design rationale, and can be used in "after the fact" analysis, with the aim of improving the design process.

Rough sketches are useful for rapidly documenting interaction, for the same reasons given for presentation. Sketches should be "storyboards" showing sequences of events and specifying the user actions that cause them. Figure 10-18 shows a sketch of the design for this task scenario:

- Look in the `Electronic Mail` folder.
- Open the `In Basket`.
- Open the item `Note from Joe`.
- Move text, by selecting and dragging it, from the note into the opened `Jan. Spreadsheet`.

Videotape can capture dynamics and verbal description simultaneously, and is a good medium for documenting design ideas. Sophisticated video equipment can show the computer screen, with insets showing hand motions on the mouse and keyboard. Videotape is widely used in usability testing, to capture user interactions for later analysis.

Videotapes and rough sketches can be combined. Rough sketches presented in succession can be taped, with a designer pointing at elements

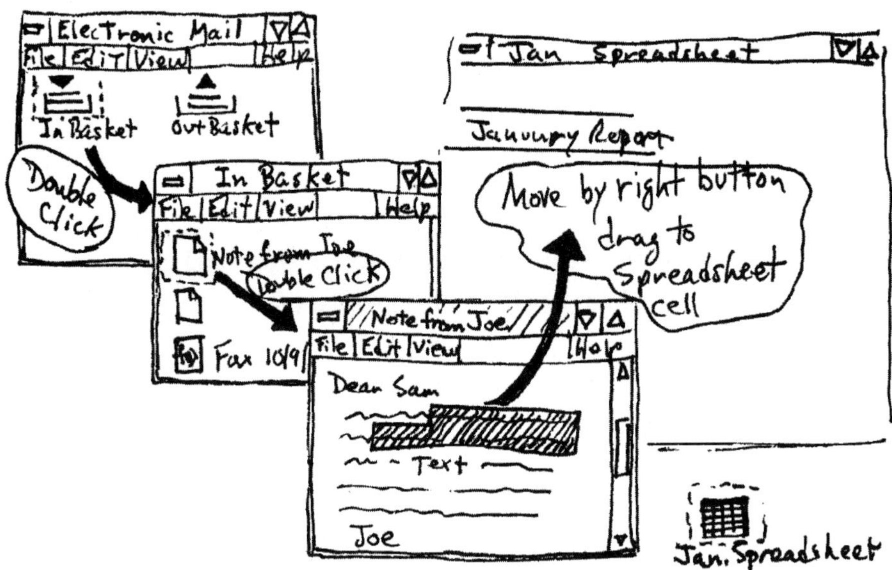

Figure 10-18 Storyboard sketch for a user interface design

and explaining the interaction sequences. Tapes can be passed around to other designers and users to get early feedback.

Formal methods There are many formal methods for user interface documentation. Most of these address interaction and time sequencing of events. Besides state transition diagrams, the interaction diagrams and task flow notations in Chapter 7 are useful for documenting low-level interaction tasks as well as higher level task flows. Although improving on a picture for documenting a static presentation is difficult, numerical specification of proportions, sizes, resolutions, and colors is sometimes necessary to supplement the picture.

I am not in favor of unnecessary formality, but there are areas in presentation and interaction design that require precision. Programmers will not implement complex interaction techniques correctly based on "handwaving" descriptions, so precise diagraming can save much discussion and rework time.

Objectives Two kinds of objectives can be documented as part of the design—objectives for machine performance, and objectives for human performance. A good working prototype allows testing of the human performance, but normally not the machine performance (since that depends on the real implementation).

Machine performance objectives are critical. Section 10.1 talks about different time scales for interaction cycles. These are based on fundamental constants in the human nervous system, so certain techniques simply will not work if things do not happen fast enough. Sometimes "fast enough" can be determined from the literature of human factors; in other cases it may have to be discovered through experimentation with a prototype.

Charles Irby was once asked what he would do differently on the Xerox Star project if he could do it over [Irb89]. His reply was to the effect that he would have had a closer integration between design and implementation. Because of performance problems, techniques that worked well in the prototypes did not work well in the implementation. This was a factor in the poor acceptance of the Star in the market.

Unlike machine performance targets, objectives for human performance should exist prior to design, since they are part of the system requirements. They include required task completion times, error rates, and other similar factors. During design they can be refined if necessary, and the relationship between human and machine performance objectives can be established and documented.

Traceability and design rationale Besides documenting what has been designed, we need to relate the design to other documents in the development process.

Traceability is the ability to relate a design feature to the user requirement it satisfies, or vice versa. This requires supplementary documentation (usually text) relating objects to the analysis model, actions to object behavior, sequencing to the task model, and so forth.

Design rationale is an explanation of why particular design features were chosen over alternatives. Collecting rationale encourages designers to think about alternatives, which is a benefit in itself. If developers find it difficult to implement features of the user interface design, the rationale explains why the feature is important, and why it cannot be done in another way. And it avoids the question, asked by users or designers of future product releases, "Why did you do it that way?" Often, even the original designers have forgotten why they did it the way it was done, leading to a process of reinvention to discover the rationale.[1]

Rationale usually takes the form of text documentation accompanying the design. Hypertext systems can provide easier access to rationale when needed, without cluttering the design documentation [MacL89]. A videotape narrative by a designer going through a prototype can document rationale; this is easy to do if video is part of the design documentation anyway.

Rationale relates to traceability, since the rationale for a feature is often that it satisfies a user requirement in a non-obvious way. This is particularly true of design features needed to satisfy usability and performance objectives.

[1] Published documents on the Xerox Star (cited in Chapter 2) contain many discussions of rationale that benefited not only developers at Xerox, but others in the industry as well who were working in the same domain.

10.6 Summary

Interaction is mutual or reciprocal action. It unifies the look and feel of a user interface with the underlying system implementation in a cycle of thought-action-computation-feedback. This cycle recurs at many levels, from jobs and tasks to low-level interactions such as pointing at objects. For almost all applications, users prefer, and are more productive with, high interaction rates. A high rate comes from good system performance and a user interface with the right "feel."

"Feel" can be analyzed at the levels of lexical action (physical devices and actions), syntax (allowable sequences of actions), and semantics (the meaning of action sequences in the context of an application).

Interaction is implemented with physical devices such as mouse and keyboard, virtual devices such as "buttons" displayed on the screen, and techniques for interacting with them. Direct manipulation is particularly important for OOUIs. Devices can be analyzed as *logical devices*, which are independent of their implementation. Physical devices act as transducers, converting users' physical actions into logical values.

The design of interaction and control mechanisms can be analytically separated from presentation design, but they are closely connected. Controls in OOUIs are typically visible on the display, so each control has both "look" and "feel."

Interaction design includes designing interactions with individual objects, and basic interaction tasks such as pointing, selection, and text entry. It also includes the composition of global interactions that organize work and task flows. In interfaces with a good feel, both low-level and high-level tasks seem easy and efficient.

Style guides contain advice and guidance on look and feel design, and details of specific standard elements for presentation and interaction. They are usually provided by platform vendors, and can be supplemented with application-specific information. They can save time in design, and are particularly valuable when used with object-oriented class libraries that implement style "widgets."

Documentation that specifies the design of the entire user interface is developed during presentation and interaction design. It typically consists of:

- A working prototype.
- More formal supporting documentation.
- Design rationale and relationships between interface elements and user requirements.
- Objectives for usability and performance.
- Descriptions of tasks as they are performed using the interface.

Some key points of advice for designers from this chapter are:

- Low-level performance is important to user productivity and satisfaction. It depends on good machine performance, and careful design based on analysis of low-level basic interaction tasks.
- Studying style guides and commercially successful applications will help you build a repertoire of solutions to typical OOUI design problems. For low-level interactivity, video games are often better examples than "business" applications.
- There are many tensions between conflicting requirements, such as screen space for information display versus visible control mechanisms. Expect to have to iterate to resolve these tensions.
- Designing good controls for OOUIs requires both graphic design and human factors expertise.

10.7 To Explore Further

[Per82] is a comprehensive treatment of early video games. [Tetz93] is a recent update. [Lam86] has interviews with Toru Iwatani, designer of Pac-Man, and Jaron Lanier, formerly a game programmer for Atari and later founder of VPL, the virtual reality company.

[Fol92] and other textbooks on graphics provide more detail on input devices. [Fol92] is also a good source on physical and logical interaction, the language model of interaction (which Foley was instrumental in developing), and formal methods based on it.

A program for evaluating input devices using Fitts's law is available from the University of Guelph (Canada). It runs on the Apple Macintosh, and is an excellent educational tool. It is available to researchers by anonymous FTP from `snowhite.cis.uoguelph.ca`, in directory `pub/fitts-law`. [MacK93a] describes the tool.

I have found Bill Buxton's papers and forthcoming book [Bux91] to be a source of both inspiration and knowledge. More than anyone else in the field of HCI, he has pushed to get "equal time" for interaction techniques.

[Shn92], Chapter 5, covers direct manipulation and provides many examples. Shneiderman and colleagues have proven the direct manipulation technique by way of many elegant examples; for instance, the dynamic query system described in [Ahl92].

[Roo93] summarizes pragmatic issues of developing and using style guides, based on surveying developers and designers at the CHI'92 conference. [Tetzl91], [Thov91], and [Nie92a] provide assessments of the effectiveness of style guides in helping designers. The case for style guides is presented in [Mar92], which also describes a company-specific style guide done by Kodak.

Human Factors in Computer Systems, the proceedings of the annual conference of ACM SIGCHI conference, is a good source of both new and proven ideas for interaction techniques.

Vendors of interactive devices Literature provided by vendors of interactive input devices is a source of information on capabilities. [Des93] lists vendors of keyboards, mice, and trackballs; many of these manufacture other devices as well. Advertisements in the trade press are a source of vendor contacts. Journals devoted to computer graphics and virtual reality are the best source of advertising and articles on new devices. Here are a few vendors of devices other than mice and keyboards:

- Elographics, Inc. (touch screens and tablets)
  105 Randolph Road
  Oak Ridge, TN 37830, USA
- Koala Technologies (touch tablets)
  3100 Patrick Henry Drive
  Santa Clara, CA 95050, USA
- Kurta (digitizing tablets)
  3007 East Chambers
  Phoenix, AZ 85040, USA
- LC Technologies, Inc. (eye gaze tracking systems)
  4415 Glenn Rose Street
  Fairfax, VA 22032, USA
- Polhemus (6-D electromagnetic tracking devices)
  P.O. Box 560
  Colchester, VT 05446, USA
- VPL Research Inc. (DataGlove)
  656 Bair Island Road, Suite 304
  Redwood City, CA 94063, USA

10.8 Exercises

1. Try the following on any GUI with a mouse or other pointing device:

   - Select the lowercase “i” in a word processing application, using a proportional font.
   - Select the `File/Open` menu entry, starting from the lower right corner of the screen.
   - In a drawing editor or paint program, sign your name.

   What was easy in these tasks? What was difficult? If possible, compare two different pointing devices on these tasks.[1]

[1] This was inspired by [Bux91] where he advocates defining benchmark tasks for testing interaction devices.

2. Consider a requirement for providing an on/off control by means of a touch screen. Three possibilities for visual presentation of the control (pushbutton, lever, and slider) are shown below. State diagrams for two ways of interacting with the touch screen are also shown. In (a), there are two states and a *press* can be registered either when state 1 is entered or when it is left (both alternatives can be found in interfaces). In (b), a *press* alone is registered only if the user's finger is lifted without being moved on the screen. If the finger is moved, the *dragging* state is entered, and is left when the finger is lifted off.[1] Recalling the notion of s-r (stimulus-response) compatibility from page 259, Propose a method of interacting with the three switches using the two states in (a). How would you rank the three switches in terms of s-r compatibility using this method?

   Now answer the same question, but design your interaction based on the three-state model of the screen in (b).

   See [Pla92] for a description of a real application of touch screen on/off switches. [Green88], p. 498, describes an experiment by Valk to test touch screen operation of visual buttons and toggle switches.

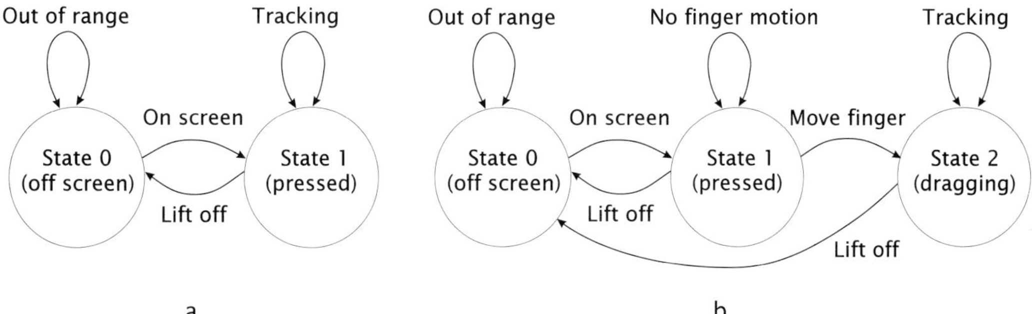

3. Draw a state transition diagram for the technique of moving an object described on page 265, in conjunction with Myron Krueger's Videodesk system.

[1]The state numbering is from Buxton's "three state" model for pointing and dragging devices [Bux90a].

4. Design interaction mechanisms for the roadmap application in Chapter 9, Exercise (1b).

   a. For navigating within the map itself.

   b. For providing additional information to users, such as the location and quality of restaurants and inns along the route.

5. Using a style guide for a user interface you have access to, try to assess whether the interface conforms to the style.

   a. Is it easy to do this? How could it be made easier?

   b. Do you think the interface will be more consistent with other applications on this platform if it conforms?

   c. Will conformance make the interface easier to use?

   (*For developers*: if you use either a company or vendor style guide in your work, use it for this exercise.)

6. Using the results of Chapter 7, Exercise 4, Chapter 8, Exercise 5, and Chapter 9, Exercise 4, finish your paper design for the fax application.

   a. Update your content view sketches from Exercise 8-5 to include menus, tool bars, buttons, etc. that you have added. Sketch any dialogue boxes you have added for controlling the application.

   b. Use tables like those in Figures 10-15 and 10-16 to document actions and interactions for your fax objects; include interactions between fax objects and existing “Office” objects.

   c. Document task interaction sequencing with sketches along the lines of Figure 10-18. Copies of the screen dumps in Appendix 1, *Fax Case Study*, can be used to sketch the integration of the fax application with the “Office” shell.

Internal Design

Part I of this book explained the application of object-orientation to user interfaces and presented ideas that underlie OOUI design methods. Part II provided specific techniques for understanding users and their tasks, developing a conceptual model of the system, and designing the look and feel of the interface. This part covers aspects of designing the implementation model that are important to user interface designers.

An ideal development process exploits the synergy between OO representations in all parts of the system. The implementation should reflect the structure of the problem domain, which requires that interface designers understand implementation issues and work with programmers on an ongoing basis. In the other direction, programmers can benefit from a deeper understanding of how implementation decisions affect external properties of the user interface.

Chapter 11, *Object-Oriented System Architectures*, overviews key architectures used in OOUI implementations and ways of structuring user interface code relative to other parts of systems. Chapter 12, *Information Models*, covers the software that implements the user's conceptual model. Software objects implementing the presentation and action languages are the subject of Chapter 13, *Presentation and Interaction Objects.*

Tool support, ranging from OO class libraries to visual interface builders, can significantly ease OOUI implementation. The available tools are too numerous to cover in detail, but Chapter 14, *Tools for Prototyping and Implementation*, describes categories and criteria to help in choosing the right ones.

Chapter 15, *Design Examples*, presents four example systems with OOUIs. They illustrate all the points in this book in the context of significant projects.

These chapters use code examples in Smalltalk and C++ to illustrate points about design. Even non-programmers can get some benefit from these by skimming the comments and descriptions. For programmers unfamiliar with the languages, Section A2.3 of Appendix 2, *Introduction to Object-Orientation*, has brief tutorials on Smalltalk and C++.

11

Object-Oriented System Architectures

Graphical OOUIs have a reputation for being easy on users, but tough on developers. Programmers developing character-based interfaces have been accustomed to a simple input-process-output flow of control. Input and output consist of character strings read and written to a terminal stream. Simple programs such as "hello, world" [Ker78] can be dashed off by novice programmers in just a few lines of code.

Thrown into a GUI environment, developers face a huge increase in complexity. Coming from *read* and *print*, they are confronted by window system programming interfaces with hundreds of function calls. Input-process-output is replaced by multithreaded, asynchronous event processing. "Hello, world" has gone from five lines to one hundred. Added to this is the trend toward client-server and other distributed application architectures. "Process" may now involve pulling together data and functions from multiple computers, and "input-output" may be controlled by a computer that is remote from the application.

There is some good news amid the complexity. Research and practice in several fields, including user interfaces and heterogeneous networks, has converged on an object-oriented approach to hiding implementation complexity from both users and programmers. It is based on communication by events or messages, and object layers that separate major functions such as application logic, user interface, and communications infrastructure.

This chapter presents the architecture behind the object layers. Its principles are part of a common language for developers and should be understood by both designers and implementors. The chapter has three objectives:

- To contrast OO applications and systems with their "conventional" equivalents, in terms of concept, architecture, and implementation.
- To overview the concepts of window managers and other components that form the implementation infrastructure for OOUIs.
- To present general ways of structuring user interface code relative to other parts of systems.

"Other parts of the system" include an *information model*, which implements functional content, and a *technical infrastructure* of communications, databases, etc. These are covered in Chapter 12. Chapter 13 describes software structures that implement the visible user interface.

11.1 An OO View of Systems and Applications

This section presents a general structure for object-oriented systems. It emphasizes the software components that implement the user interface, and contrasts OO with "conventional" views of implementation. It also introduces the model-view-controller (MVC) architecture, which provides a useful vocabulary for discussing system implementations.

Model-View-Controller

Starting in Chapter 1 with Figure 1-1, we have seen several perspectives on a three-way factoring of the components of a user's interaction with a computer system:

- The user's conceptual model of the system captures the semantics of objects, relationships, and behavior.
- The presentation language, or "look," of the interface represents objects concretely.
- The action language, or "feel," provides mechanisms for acting on objects.

Model-view-controller [Gol90], a framework for building interactive applications, is based on this three-way factoring. MVC was developed as part of Smalltalk-80 [Gol83], but has influenced many other OO application architectures.

The three components of MVC correspond to the three external components of the user interface. Figure 11-1 is an expansion of Figure 1-1 showing the internal software components of the user interface. It uses a convention called "doughnut diagrams" to represent objects: . The idea is that an outer ring of methods (or member functions) encapsulates the object's state. This explicit representation emphasizes that the interface components are *objects*—not functions or programs.

Figure 11-1 also evokes the idea of isomorphism, or structural similarity (illustrated in Figure 5-3, Chapter 5). This is an idealized view of the heterogeneous world of real systems. Assuming a completely object-oriented environment, the *model* (or *information model*) mirrors the structure of the user's conceptual model; the *view* shares the same structure, and presents the model in tangible form; the *controller* allows the user to interact with the model.

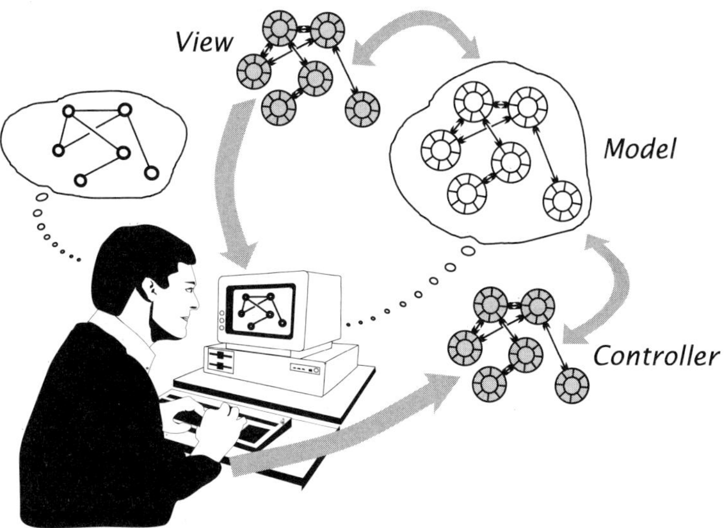

Figure 11-1 Model-view-controller

Model, view, and controller in the figure are composite objects whose components collaborate to produce the desired behavior. In Smalltalk-80, both the components and the composite objects are instances of subclasses of three abstract classes—`Model`, `View`, and `Controller`. Other systems and class libraries use different names, but provide similar behaviors.

`Model` represents the semantics of entities in the application domain. Subclasses of `Model` synthesize semantic behaviors from lower-level capabilities such as database and network access, computational methods, etc. A model may have component objects, or be a component object of a larger model. A model is not aware of views and controllers, except through messages they send to obtain or change its state.

Instances of `View` present the state of a model, for example on a graphic display.[1] A view and its model are connected by a dependency mechanism. The view registers itself as a dependent of the model; the model broadcasts a notification of any change in its state, so views that

[1] Where the meaning is obvious in context, I will say things like "instances of `View`" as a shorthand for "instances of subclasses of `View`."

depend on it can update their displays. Views can contain subviews, which display different parts or facets of the model.

Instances of `Controller` handle interaction between end users and the model or its views (to modify the display, to edit or change the underlying model, etc.). Controllers implement the action language by translating keystrokes, mouse clicks, etc., into actions on the model objects. Each view that permits interaction has an associated controller; in a composite view, there is a hierarchy of controllers associated with the hierarchy of subviews.

Most systems do not implement controller behavior in a separate class; rather, they mix the behaviors of view and controller into a single kind of object. Where view and control behavior are combined, I refer to the combination as a *view* or *view layer*. It is also possible to combine everything into a single object type, and this is often done. It is bad software engineering to do so,[1] and the assumption here is that models and views are separate.

Systems as Communicating Objects

The typical view of "conventional" systems is that they are modular structures based on top-down functional decomposition. As Bertrand Meyer points out,[2] however, most systems of any size (operating systems or transaction-driven applications, for instance) do not have any "top" from which you could decompose them. A UNIX system, for example, is best thought of as a collection of asynchronous processes, operating on each other and on objects in a hierarchically composed file system. In distributed systems, these process and file objects may reside in nodes on a local or wide-area network.

Combining process instances and files into objects makes the top level of systems object-based; applying this uniformly is the core of the OO view. Classes and inheritance are easy steps from the paradigm shift that occurs in passing from functions to objects. In the object-based view, a system is a network of objects that communicate by message passing. The objects may be distributed across multiple platforms. Some objects are subsystems or applications, which are composed of smaller networks of communicating objects.

Layers in OO systems Figure 11-2 shows an OO system. Its objects are distributed between a client, which provides the user interface, and a server, which provides functions that supplement the resources of the client. There are three main layers in the system:

- The *view* layer includes the action and presentation components of the user interface—all the software that implements the visible interface.

---

[1] This statement is justified in Section 11.4 and in Chapter 12.

[2] [Mey88], p. 47.

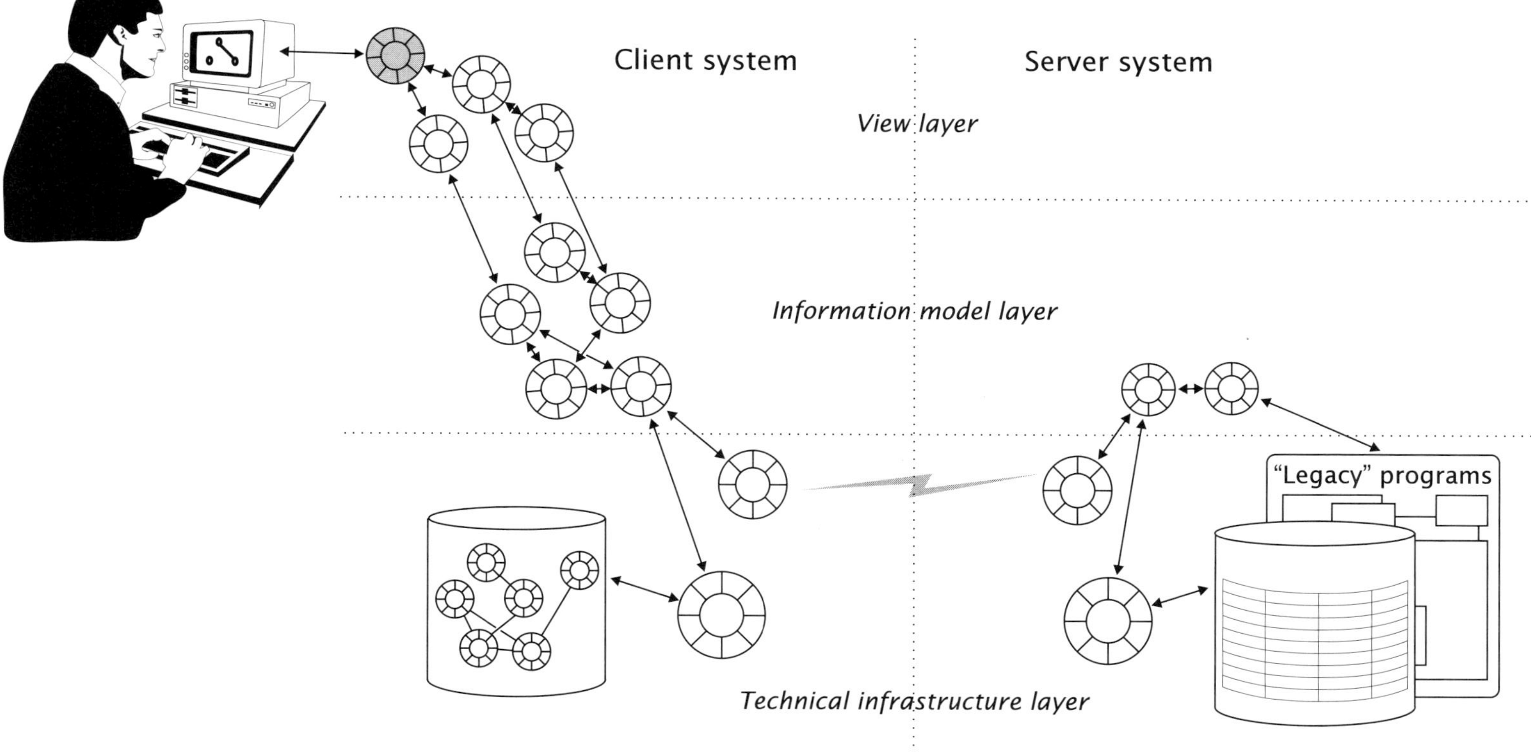

Figure 11-2 An object-oriented distributed system

- The *information model* layer includes all the software implementing the application functionality (or model in the MVC sense).
- The *technical infrastructure* layer includes services such as networking and database that are not parts of the model, but are required to implement it.

The view layer consists of views and controllers, or functionally equivalent objects. The gray object in the upper left of the figure represents an infrastructure sublayer of the view layer. This sublayer, the *display manager*, handles the mapping to physical devices such as the mouse, keyboard, and display. It translates window management and operating system interfaces into messages to and from views and controllers.

The information model layer in a distributed environment has three major interfaces. As in a standalone application, it has an upward interface to the view layer and a downward interface to the infrastructure layer. This layer also has a horizontal interface (through networking services in the infrastructure) to model layers in server systems. Parts of the information model may be mirrored on client and server. In Figure 11-2, the bottom two objects in the model layer on the client side may be "surrogates" for information that actually resides on the server system. Thus the information model accessed by a user consists of client information objects, plus the two objects in the model layer on the server system.

The technical infrastructure layer includes objects that provide general services to models, such as database and communications access. In most systems this layer includes non-OO components that the designer of the OO system needs to take into consideration. These include non-OO databases that store object state information, and non-OO programs that supply portions of the behavior of objects.

Databases, whether OO or not, make objects persistent and shareable. The "lightning bolt" connecting client and server represents a communications link. It can make remote objects appear to be local, or allow local objects to "shadow" remote objects in a way that is transparent to users of the local objects.

The link can also allow the behavior of a single object type to be transparently distributed. This is valuable when some facet of behavior is complex and already exists as a "legacy program" written in a non-OO language. As an example, suppose client machines have an object type representing high-resolution scanned images. We want to display images and allow users to interact with them on client workstations, but we also want to take advantage of image transformation subroutines (such as a fast Fourier transform) that run on a vector computer elsewhere in the network. Properly encapsulated communications can make these routines appear to be member functions of the image class on the client.

The X Window System [Sch86] is the base for GUIs on most UNIX platforms. It uses a definition of "client" and "server" that often confuses people, so it merits a brief explanation. X also shows why user interface designers may need to understand issues deep in the implementation domain.

The common notion of "client" assumes that the client application runs on the end user's workstation. Figure 11-2 illustrates this view. Its "client system" can be decomposed into the following components:

- A *display server* (the object shown in gray on the upper left) that provides an interface to the physical display and input devices.
- A *window manager* that manages the allocation of the display and input devices to more than one application.
- A *client application*, consisting of the view and information model objects running on the client system. View objects in the client application communicate with the window manager and display server.

X Windows assumes that these three components may run on separate nodes on a network, as shown in Figure 11-3. The source of confusion is that the end user's workstation, normally thought of as the client, is now called a server; a remote machine is the client. The confusion is only apparent. The X Windows terminology works in all cases; it reduces to the "ordinary" terminology in the case where the client application, window manager, and display server are all on the same node, which is then called simply "the client."

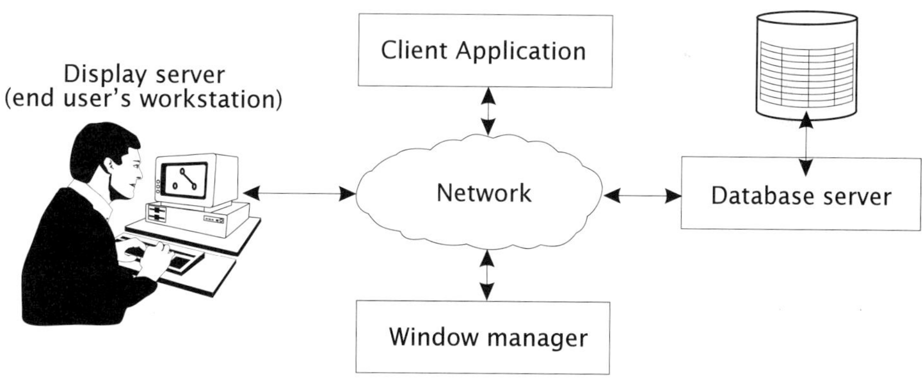

Figure 11-3 Architecture of the X Window System

X was developed in the early '80s for Project Athena at MIT and assumed that the typical end user station had little power to run applications. This assumption influenced the choice of architecture. The architecture has also turned out to be useful for areas, such as scientific visualization and virtual reality, that need powerful special-purpose display servers.

Today, many X applications run on the same machine as the window manager and display server. Where the display server is remote from the application, achieving good performance for highly interactive user interfaces may be difficult. Except for performance implications, the finer grain of distribution in X is concealed from both user and programmer. In other commercial systems, such as Microsoft Windows, window management and display services always run on the same platform as the client application.

OO applications If systems are collections of communicating objects, what are "applications"? Most Smalltalk applications are built entirely from models, views, and controllers. Large applications are constructed by composing finer-grained models and views; the larger composite objects contain task-based sequencing and other logic that is not part of the smaller objects.

One could argue, however, that "application" is a packaging concept and should be modeled using a different kind of object. Many OO class libraries take this approach and provide an `Application` class in addition to models and views.

Smalltalk makes it possible to have "nothing but objects." C++ needs a "main" program that is a function, not an object. As this skeletal example shows, in a "pure" OO program, `main` does no more than create one or more objects, start them off, and end when they are finished:

```
int main() {
    // Create the application object
    MyApplicationClass appObject;
    appObject.run(); // Tell it to run
    // Exit when the application is finished
    return appObject.returnCode();
}
```

Notice that `main` is not "the application"—that role is assumed by the instance of `MyApplicationClass`.

However structured, an OO application is a way of packaging a collaborating set of objects for the purpose of providing a service to users. This is appropriate since, like operating systems, most large applications do not have a functional "top." This packaging is similar to Booch's notion of a *module* [Boo94].[1] There are also *subsystem* objects, which package services such as database management.

11.2 User Interface Implementation Models

An implementation model has two aspects. It is an architecture that constrains the way software can be written and structured to build systems, and it is also a conceptual model of the implementation domain. This sec-

[1] A large application or subsystem may be built from many modules.

tion presents two influential models from a conceptual point of view. Section 11.4 discusses several implementations based on one of them, the *event model.*

User interface designers need to know about implementation models because the internal design ultimately dictates external behavior. Developing an appropriate internal model in parallel with the external design avoids unpleasant surprises, such as being unable to support desirable features in the implementation.

The Language Model

Figure 11-4 is based on the *Seeheim model* for user interfaces, so-called because it was developed at a conference held in Seeheim [Pfa85]. The figure shows in parentheses elements of the closely related language model [Fol92]. This model proposes that software implementing the user interface be divided between three modules:

- A presentation module that maps between logical tokens in the presentation and action languages and their physical or lexical form. The lexical form is a particular representation or interaction technique using the display or input devices.
- A dialogue control module that maps output from the application to the presentation language, and maps the action language to a sequence of inputs to the application.
- An application interface that maps tokens in the action and presentation languages to objects and actions in the application.

So far, this sounds similar to the MVC scheme. The difference is the assumption of a single channel connecting adjacent modules, as opposed to many objects sending messages to each other across layer boundaries. A single channel is attractive because it means that the dialogue control module can contain a logical specification of the behavior of the entire interface. This specification is independent of the application semantics and independent of the interface implementation.

The Seeheim model implies that the dialogue specification can be

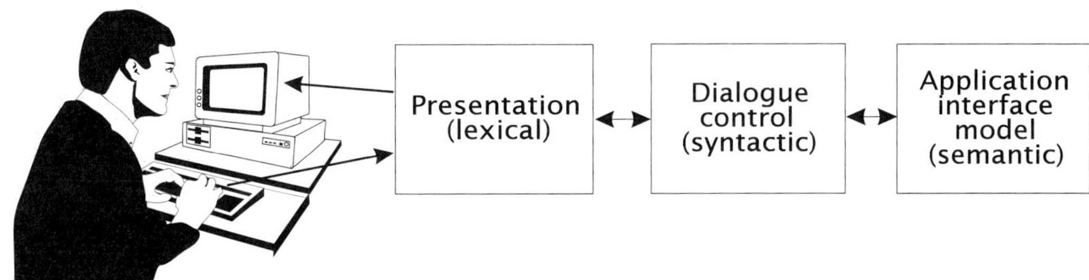

Figure 11-4 Seeheim model of the user interface, with linguistic attributes

written and "compiled" into a user interface implementation, analogously to compilation of programs. Systems have been built along these lines, though for relatively simple interfaces. They are amenable to top-down functional decomposition, with "process user input" as the top function.

As an example, here is a specification, using BNF notation,[1] of part of a command language grammar:

```
<Command> :: <CopyCommand> | . . .
<CopyCommand> :: Copy <FromFileSpec> <ToFileSpec>
<FromFileSpec> :: [ <DiskSpec> ] : [ <DirectorySpec> ]
                    <Filename> | <FilenamePatternSpec>.
              <FileExtension> | <FileExtensionPatternSpec>
<ToFileSpec> :: [ <DiskSpec>: ] : [ <DirectorySpec> ]
                    [ <Filename> . <FileExtension> ]

. . . . . .
```

This grammar can be compiled into programs that will accept commands such as

```
copy c:\docs\myfile.doc d:\docs
```

and invoke appropriate action routines to perform them.

Grammars like this are adequate for user interfaces based on command languages or simple menus. The single channel of communication, in fact, mirrors the environments in which these interface styles developed. Figure 11-4 is a good picture of a character-based terminal attached to a processor through a communications link. There the cycle of interaction has a large grain—the user formulates a complete command, enters it, and waits for the system to process it and respond.

Many command languages are simple enough to be expressed as regular expression grammars, which can be graphically represented by state transition diagrams. More complex context-free grammars can be represented by augmented transition networks with subnetworks that can be recursively invoked. Some simple transition networks were shown in Chapter 10; these networks rapidly escalate in complexity as larger portions of the interface are represented.[2]

The language model and OOUIs As a specification of the entire structure of an OOUI, the language model has two problems. First, grammars and transition networks are reasonable representations only if the number of states is small. In an OOUI, the global interface state is the Cartesian product of the states of all the individual objects, which makes linguistic specifications impractical. They are too difficult to understand, implement, and maintain.

[1] Backus-Nauer form, widely used for specifying programming languages [Aho86].

[2] Harel statecharts [Har88] improve this somewhat, but they are still very complex for large systems.

Second, the language model assumes that all the tokens in a "sentence" can be parsed before any semantic response is needed. This is a good assumption for a command language interface, but it is not valid for OOUIs. As an example, to delete a file using a command language, a user might type

```
delete myfile.doc
```

The lexical component in Figure 11-4 would accept the input tokens (typed characters), parse them into syntactic tokens (words), and provide lexical feedback by displaying the characters as they were typed. If the syntactic component detected an error, it would provide syntactic feedback to the user with a message such as

```
Invalid command syntax. Reenter.
```

After the entire command had been syntactically parsed, it would be passed to the application, which would perform the desired action. Finally, the user would get semantic feedback:

```
File myfile.doc has been deleted.
```

To delete a file in an OOUI, the user might drag the file's icon to the `Trash` icon and drop it. Lexical feedback in this case is the visual movement of the icon. Semantic feedback at the end of the operation might be given by the disappearance of the file icon, accompanied by a change in the appearance of the `Trash` icon.

What if the user drags the file icon over another icon, for example a folder, on the way to the trash? At the time this occurs, the user's intent is not known, so it is appropriate to provide feedback on what would happen if the icon were dropped. (This is the principle of *feedback on button down, action on button up,* discussed in Chapter 10.) This feedback depends upon the semantics of the two objects represented by the icons, so it cannot be provided by the lexical component.

Mark Green points out one problem of using a grammar to represent this kind of interaction: whether appropriate feedback is even possible will depend upon the parsing algorithm being used [Gree86]. Performance is another problem. To provide continuous semantic feedback, every input token passes through all the modules in Figure 11-4. Since these modules are monolithic, large case statements must be executed for each token to determine how to process it.

Although the language model is problematic as a global implementation strategy, it works to describe individual objects. Chapter 10 shows examples where this model is useful in specifying and analyzing individual interactions. This conclusion mirrors the situation in programming languages. In principle, it is possible to view any software system, however large, as a single program. In practice, doing so is disastrous. Objects decompose the complexity of large user interfaces just as they do for large programs in general.

The Event Model

Command or menu-based user interfaces operate on fully formed commands as input, with fully formed responses as output. The file-dragging example shows that thinking of OOUIs in this way is not adequate. In an OOUI, the input is a stream of primitive *events*, characterized by the event type, the device that generated it, and the destination of the event. Event destinations, or *event handlers* (views or visible controls), are usually determined by the visual pointer location. The output is also a stream of events, many of them direct responses to the input events.

Primitive input events include such things as movements of the mouse, button presses, and keystrokes. Sequences of primitive events can be combined to create new events. An example is combining *button down/ mouse move/button up,* while the pointer is on a scrollbar, into a *scroll* event. Output events include displaying text and graphics, and creating sounds.

Though the event model is pragmatically motivated, it can be formalized. Green [Gree86] has shown that a formal event model has at least as much expressive power as any commonly used language model. This means that any interface that can be specified by a context-free grammar or transition network can be specified in terms of events and event handlers. In practice, as dragging and other examples illustrate [Hil86], many interface styles can only be expressed using events or some equivalent model.

The essence of the event model is that it removes the burden of global specification and control of the interface by distributing it across multiple autonomous event handlers. In Green's formulation, the model includes:

- *Events*, generated by devices or event handlers. In OO terms, these correspond to messages sent to objects.
- *Event queues* that distribute events to event handlers. The destination handler for an event may be determined by a state variable such as the mouse pointer location, or by a handler's having registered itself as the recipient of certain events.
- *Event handlers* that receive and process events. Event handlers correspond to objects, and the processing routines for particular events correspond to methods or member functions. Event handlers may generate events and create new event handlers dynamically.
- *Templates* describing the behavior of event handlers. These correspond to classes.

Specification of event handlers Robert Jacob developed a specification language for direct manipulation interfaces [Jaco86] that illustrates both the language and event models. Jacob points out that while grammars and transition networks are not adequate to express the entire interface, they can specify the behavior of individual interaction objects. His specification notation uses both text and graphical transition diagrams, as shown by this example. It is a visual button that can be "pressed" using the left mouse button.[1]

```
INTERACTION_OBJECT SimpleButton is
IVARS:
position := { x1, y1, x2, y2 } --screen rectangle
METHODS:
Draw() { DrawTextButton(position, "Display"); }
TOKENS:
iLeftButtonClick     { --Left mouse button clicked-- }
iEnter               { --Pointer enters button rectangle-- }
iExit                { --Pointer leaves button rectangle-- }
oHighlight           { --Invert color of button-- }
oDehighlight         { --Invert color of button-- }
SYNTAX:
```

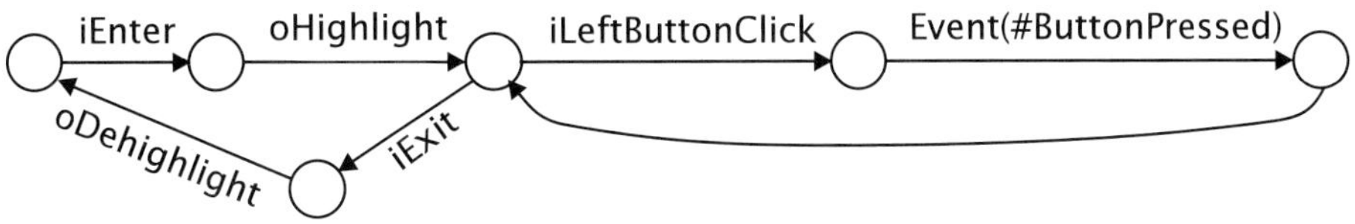

Figure 11-5 Syntax diagram for SimpleButton

Figure 11-5 shows the button syntax. Transitions between states may be caused by input events, such as `iEnter`, or output events generated by the interaction object, such as `oHighlight`. Transitions may invoke semantic actions, such as `Event(#ButtonPressed)`, which signals another object.

The specification, including the syntax diagram, can be compiled and executed. Jacob's system also includes inheritance and composite objects. It was proposed as a "high level" specification language for user interfaces. Like many such languages, it is essentially an object-oriented programming language.

Sibert and colleagues [Sib86] arrived at a conclusion similar to Jacob's. They characterized the situation in terms reminiscent of the *conversation* and *model world* metaphors [Hut85] discussed in Chapters 9 and 10. They distinguished *linguistic* and *spatial* models—the latter corresponding to event models. Linguistic models fail as global specifications because they are linear. GUIs present spaces that are at least two-dimensional, and in which several threads of activity can be simultaneously active. On the other hand, each thread is linear in time, and a linguistic model can be used to represent it.

[1]Based on an example in [Jaco86]. I have modified the notation somewhat.

Space and events are connected in most implementations, where events are associated with the object the user is pointing to. This is quite explicit in some systems, for instance Apple's HyperCard [Goo87]. Programming in HyperCard is accomplished by defining areas on the display as "buttons" and attaching scripts to them. The scripts define how the buttons handle events such as mouse clicks or typing characters.

11.3 Event-Driven Window Managers

GUI platforms use the event model as the basis for display and window management, and are synergistic with OO languages. Even GUI applications written in non-OO languages such as C have an OO "flavor." The details of how platforms such as the Macintosh, Microsoft Windows, OS/2, and X Windows implement the event model vary considerably. This section describes a conceptual model that covers all of them and helps in mastering the details of specific platforms.

Besides event dispatching, which deals mainly with input, window managers provide *imaging models* for output. These are conceptual models for the content of individual windows, embodied in programming interfaces for displaying graphics and text. Most platforms support imaging models based on standard 2-D graphics primitive [Fol92] and *BitBlt* (bitmapped) primitives originally developed for Smalltalk [Gol83]. The Sun NeWS [Ster87] and NeXT [Garf93] systems use imaging models based on the PostScript page description language [Ado86].

A treatment of imaging models is beyond the scope of this book. Textbooks on graphics ([Fol92], for example), cover the basic ideas, which are well established. Standards are emerging for other media types such as audio and video, but are not currently supported in a standard way by window managers.

OO class libraries are good vehicles for providing standard imaging models and programming interfaces. An example is the *Smalltalk Portable Imaging Model* in ParcPlace Smalltalk release 4 [Lei92]. It provides code portability across many of the major platforms. The ideal would be an industry standard portable imaging model; in spite of efforts like NeXT's use of PostScript, however, there seems to be no move toward a single standard.

Events and Event Dispatching

"I/O" in event-driven systems is user-driven. In command line interfaces, input from the user is permitted only when the program is ready to receive it, and output is provided when the program is ready to send it. The situation in GUIs is reversed. The user is in control of the dialogue and can initiate events whether or not the program is ready for them. These events may be mouse button presses and keyboard characters or input from virtual devices such as buttons and scroll bars.

Higher-level input events may be synthesized from lower-level events. An example is shown in Figure 11-6. `Window 1` has two sub-windows, buttons labeled `OK` and `Cancel`. Suppose that clicking the left mouse button signals to a button that it has been "pushed." So when the `OK` button, for instance, receives the events *leftButtonDown* and *leftButtonUp*, it generates a new event, *ButtonPressed*, which is sent to `Window 1`. (This is similar to the `SimpleButton` example on page 315.)

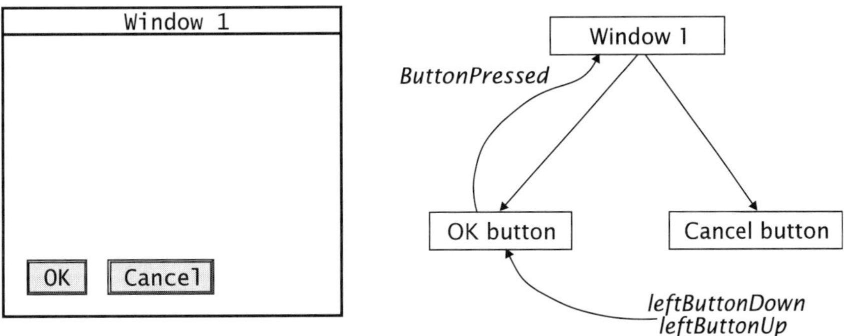

Figure 11-6 Hierarchical event passing

As the button example shows, mouse events normally go to the top window at the location of the mouse pointer. Keystrokes go to the window with the "keyboard focus," which is typically also the window under the mouse pointer. Events generated by sub-windows are sent to their owning windows. A window can also send events to any other window, identified by its name or "handle."

User events control output as well as input. Figure 11-7 shows an example. The user moves `Window 2` to a new position. In its old position, `Window 2` obscured part of `Window 1` (shown in gray). Most window managers assume that the information in the newly exposed part of `Window 1` may have changed since it was last drawn on the screen. To restore it, the window manager sends an *expose* or *paint* event to `Window 1`, passing it the area that must be repainted. Notice that `Window 1` has no control over this, and the user action may have been directed at `Window 2`, not `Window 1`.

Figure 11-8 shows the flow of event queuing and dispatching in a typical window management system. The primary sources of events are input devices used by the system. Device events generate synthetic events from visual controls, and the window system itself generates events to communicate with applications. Typical window systems define hundreds of different event types, and applications may define additional types.

The primary destination for events is the set of *widgets* that make up the interface. *Widget* is a term from X Windows, and it refers to a visual object such as a window, button, or menu, with the programming code that provides its behavior. In other systems, widgets are called *controls* or

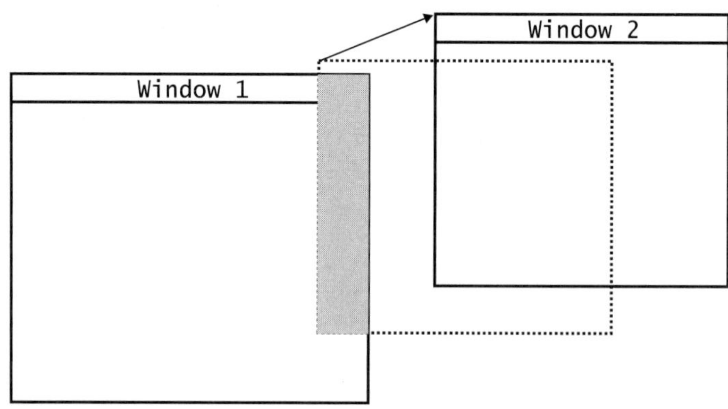

Figure 11-7 Window "expose" event

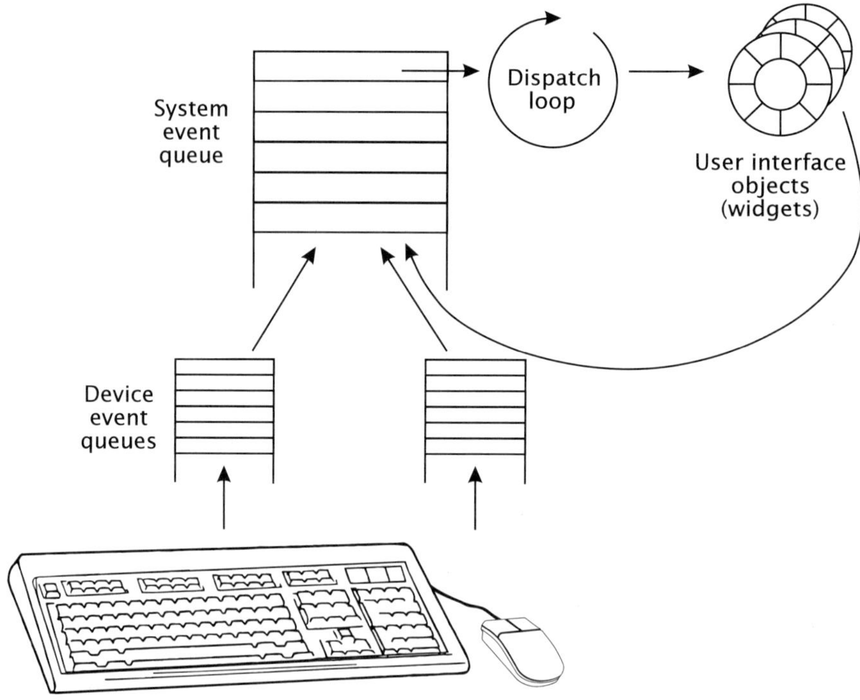

Figure 11-8 Events and event queues in a typical window system

windows. Widgets without visible behavior can also be created to handle events such as timer interrupts. OO class libraries for user interface development usually have a view class corresponding to each widget type, and a message corresponding to each event type.

The number of queues varies from system to system. Some window systems have queues that hold events for all the widgets belonging to a given application; some have a queue for each widget. Widgets may be able to register the event types they are interested in, discarding all others. The dispatching mechanism also varies. The important points to keep in mind are:

- Primitive events from input devices are queued and dispatched to the appropriate widget.
- Widgets can generate high-level events, based on combinations of primitives, that are queued for their owning widgets or windows.
- Output from widgets is controlled by events, such as *expose* and *resize*.
- Window system widgets are encapsulated by view and controller classes in OO class libraries used to develop applications.

Polling, Messages, and Callbacks

Event dispatching is handled in one of three ways, both in window systems and in OO classes that interface to window systems:

- Widgets or application programs may continually poll devices or queues for events.
- Events may be asynchronously sent as messages to widgets.
- A widget may register a *callback*, a pointer to a function or method that handles an event type. The window manager will call the function whenever the specified kind of event occurs.

The following example uses the Smalltalk-80 controller to illustrate these concepts. Smalltalk-80 uses a polling scheme, but this controller is enhanced to generate events as well. Comparing it to event dispatching in X Windows and Microsoft Windows will provide a representative sample of techniques found in commercial systems.

The Smalltalk `Controller` class has instance variables for its model, view, and sensor. A sensor is an instance of `InputSensor`, the interface to device queues for mouse and keyboard events. `Controller` also defines the flow of control for an event polling loop. In each controller, `controlLoop` calls `controlActivity` as long as it is active. Most controllers are active whenever the mouse pointer is inside their views (note the message to `sensor` in `isControlActive`).

```
Object subclass: #Controller
instanceVariableNames: 'model view sensor'
controlLoop
"Dispatch control events while the receiver is active."
       [self isControlActive] whileTrue: [
              self controlActivity].
```

```
isControlActive
"Answer true if the receiver is the active controller."
^view containsPoint: sensor cursorPoint.
```

When the controller answers `false` to `isControlActive`, control goes back to an instance of `ControlManager`, which polls all the controllers in the system until it finds one that wants to become active.

This subclass of Controller supports a direct manipulation dragging technique, useful for drawing "rubberband" lines in graphics programs, dragging icons, etc. Figure 11-9 shows its state transition diagram. It is implemented as a finite state machine with two states, and generates three mouse events. The instance variable `location` saves the mouse pointer location so it can detect movement.

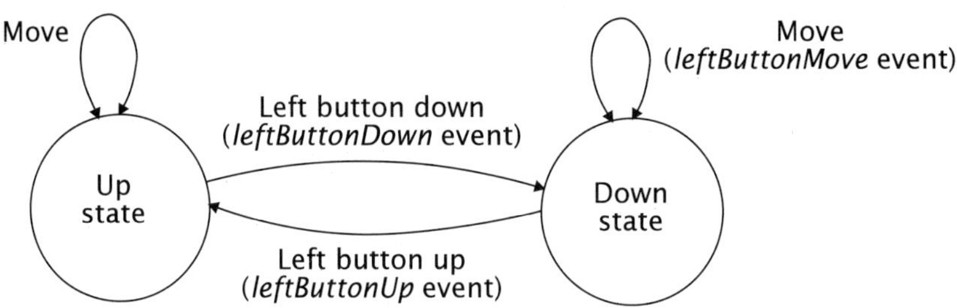

Figure 11-9 A mouse dragging controller

```
Controller subclass: #DrawingDMController
instanceVariableNames: 'state location'
controlActivity
"Sent while the receiver is the active controller."
   state = #down ifTrue: [self downState]
                 ifFalse: [self upState].
downState
"Control activity and mouse button is down."
   | newPoint |
   newPoint := sensor mousePoint.
   sensor leftButtonPressed ifFalse: [
      state := #up.
      location := newPoint.
      ^self leftButtonUp: location].1
   location = newPoint ifFalse: [
      location := newPoint.
      self leftButtonMove: location].
```

[1]The caret (^) in this line forces a return from the method.

```
upState
"Control activity and mouse button is up."
   sensor leftButtonPressed ifTrue: [
      location := sensor mousePoint.
      state := #down.
      self leftButtonDown: location].
```

The downState and upState methods poll sensor for mouse events. The results of the poll, however, are used to generate asynchronous events:[1]

```
leftButtonDown: aPoint
"User pressed the left mouse button at aPoint."
    self event: #leftButtonDown at: aPoint.
leftButtonMove: aPoint
 "User moved the mouse to aPoint with left button pressed."
     self event: #leftButtonMove at: aPoint.
leftButtonUp: aPoint
"User released the left mouse button."
    self event: #leftButtonUp at: aPoint.
```

All window systems allow polling when necessary. For example, suppose a widget receives an event indicating that the pointer has moved into its screen rectangle. If it needs to know whether a mouse button is down, it can query the window system to find out. The ongoing process of polling in the controlActivity method, however, is usually handled by the window system itself. Widgets see only the resulting events.

What happens to these events? They could be sent as messages directly to the controller's view. In Microsoft Windows there is a window procedure or *WndProc* associated with each widget. This procedure receives all events, and processes those it is interested in. It returns any unprocessed events to a default window procedure, which acts as a base class or superclass. For example, a procedure to handle our three mouse events would look like:

```
long FAR PASCAL WndProc (HWND hWnd, unsigned iMessage,
                         WORD wParam, LONG lParam)
   switch (imessage)
      case WM_LBUTTONDOWN: // Handle left button down event.
      . . . .
      case WM_MOUSEMOVE: // Handle mouse move event.
      . . . .
      case WM_LBUTTONUP: // Handle left button up event.
      . . . .
      default: // Default processing for other events.
```

[1] The event code is modeled after Digitalk Smalltalk/V, not Smalltalk-80.

```
            return DefWindowproc (hWnd, wParam, lParam);
    . . . .
```

Object-oriented systems handle this case statement under the covers, then send messages, usually named after the events, to views.

Some systems allow windows to register *callbacks* for events, particularly synthetic events from sub-windows or widgets they own. In Smalltalk/V, this is done with statements like:

```
myController when: #leftButtonDown perform: #startDrag:.
```

This causes the message `startDrag:` to be sent to the view whenever the `leftButtonDown` event occurs.

The use of callbacks in X Windows is similar to their use in Smalltalk/V, though the syntax is quite different. As an example, button widgets generate *activate* events when the user clicks the left mouse button inside them. The callback

```
XtAddCallback(myButton, XmNactivateCallback, fClicked, NULL);
```

tells X to call the function `fClicked` when `myButton` generates an *activate* event.

In Microsoft Windows, widgets send `WM_COMMAND` messages to their owning windows. Message parameters contain the widget's identifier and an event type, such as `BN_CLICKED` for a button press. Microsoft Windows supports callbacks as well as event messages for some events, such as timer interrupts.

Designing with Events

To provide the sense of "real objects," OOUIs need to respond quickly to low-level events. Time-sharing systems like JOSS demanded new, more interactive operating systems to respond to user events in seconds versus hours. OOUIs push the response criterion down to milliseconds for events such as mouse movements, and again require new architectures. These architectures are based on composition of fine-grained objects, which respond rapidly to low-level events and synthesize less frequent high-level events to trigger actions on application-domain objects.

Designers sometimes find it difficult to change from a "conventional" view to this event-based paradigm for program structure. I think the problem is an apparent loss of control. In systems architected like the one in Figure 11-4 (page 311), there is firm, centralized control. Everything flows according to plan. Event-based systems may seem chaotic in comparison.

This is an important issue, since well-designed OO systems share the characteristics of event-based systems. Control is distributed and cooperative, rather than centralized. "Conventional" systems are like hierarchical corporations, and have similar problems—they cannot respond fast enough to rapidly unfolding events. An event-based object system is more like an orchestra, and you, the designer, can think of yourself as the conductor.[1] You are still in control, but the need for fast response demands that you "empower" your objects.

Figure 11-10 relates object composition to event flow. There is indeed a hierarchy here, but its nodes are not just functional components, they are autonomous objects. Thinking of the design in terms of event flows maps to dynamic collaborations in the analysis model,[2] and helps provide good interactive performance. The composition of low-level events into high-level tasks is the reverse of the process of decomposing user tasks into basic interaction tasks, discussed in Chapter 10.

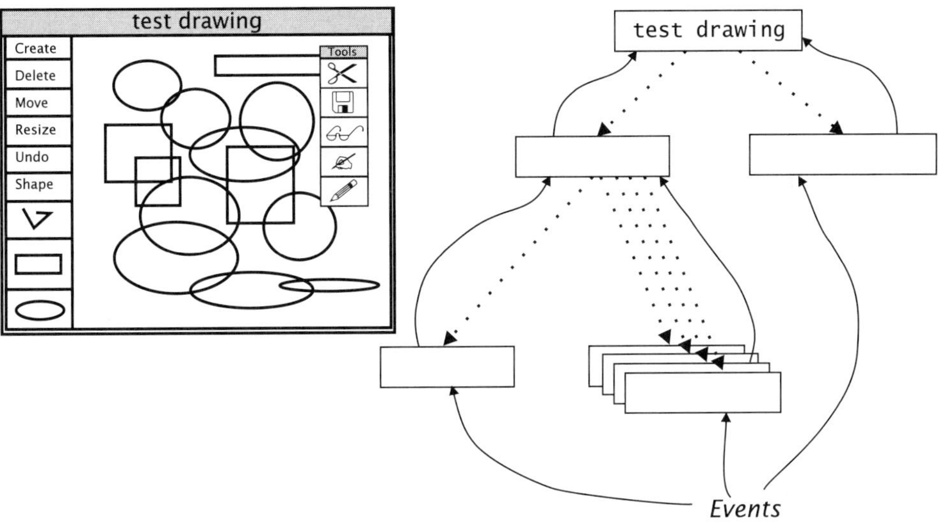

Figure 11-10 Composition hierarchy and event flow

11.4 Modular Separation of User Interface Code

This section is about general schemes for modularizing user interface code. The most obvious modular separation is between the code that implements the visible interface (the view and controller) and the information model. Separation of the information model from the technical infrastructure underneath it is also important because presenting a clear conceptual model is difficult if there is no clear software construct corresponding to it.

Object-oriented architectures are usually embodied in framework classes that are the basis for application development. These classes rep-

[1] Peter Drucker first used this analogy for corporations [Dru89].

[2] For a general treatment of event modeling in OO analysis, see [Rum91], Chapter 5.

resent abstractions ranging from arrays and collections to windows, icons, and menus. Most developers use (or start with) an existing class library, which strongly influences the possibilities for modularity. Understanding modularity issues will help to pick the right framework, or modify the one you choose.

The fundamental principle is separation of the view and information model. I hope that the solitaire game and other examples in this book are convincing, if you have not already learned this from experience. My experience, and that of other developers with whom I have discussed it, is that there are several good reasons for separating view and model:

- Views and models can be factored for high cohesion within each component and low coupling between them. Careful design can significantly reduce complexity.
- Once interfaces have been defined, user interface prototyping and development can proceed in parallel with development of the remainder of the application.
- Multiple views of the same information can be built without adding to the complexity of the system. This reduces the effort to support international products, provide for users with special needs, or build multiple prototypes for testing.
- The ability to change the user interface or the information model separately makes the system easier to maintain and extend.

Model-view separation for simple interfaces has been practiced for years. Object-orientation makes this possible in more complex interfaces. Composing interfaces from fine-grained objects provides a high total bandwidth without excessive coupling. Coupling is also reduced by isomorphism between the model and view, which substitutes implicit structural coupling for the explicit coupling of large interfaces between objects.

The MVC Architecture

Model-view-controller was described earlier as a reflection of the concept-presentation-action factoring of the external user interface. Here we look at it as a software engineering technique.

Early versions of Smalltalk [Ing78] had a two-way factoring of user interface classes. The idea of a model was implicit, and the explicit user interface objects were called *filters*, *browsers*, or *editors*. The addition of controllers in Smalltalk-80 was primarily motivated by a desire to achieve greater reusability of interface components [Kras88]. Many interface "views" differ only in the interaction mechanisms they provide to users. This suggested that factoring out the interaction mechanisms as separate components would increase the reusability of views. Experience has confirmed this intuition.

Many recent systems have classes corresponding to `View`, but not to `Controller`. Superficially, this seems like a step backward. Actually, controllers are still there in the form of *virtual devices* and *events*. Because virtual devices (such as menus and buttons) have acquired elaborate visual behavior, they are now placed in the `View` hierarchy.

MVC case study: a counter This small example concretely shows how MVC separates software into components. Although it uses Smalltalk-80, the concepts are language-independent, and they are found in many OO systems. The application is a simple counter, with the following requirements:

1. The counter must support the operations *increment* (add 1 to the counter value), *decrement* (subtract 1), *reset* (set the value to 0), and *value* (return the current counter value).
2. The current value of the counter must display as digits in a window.
3. Two versions are needed, with different interaction techniques:
   a. One in which a popup menu presents the operations for the user to click on with the mouse.
   b. One in which the user types +, -, and 0 on the keyboard to increment, decrement, and reset.

Figure 11-4 shows the user interface for the popup menu version, with the model, view, and controller objects.

Requirement (1) expresses the semantics of the counter, which will be implemented in a subclass of `Model`. Requirement (2) is for the presentation of the information supplied by the counter, and will be implemented in a subclass of `View`. Requirement (3) asks for two different

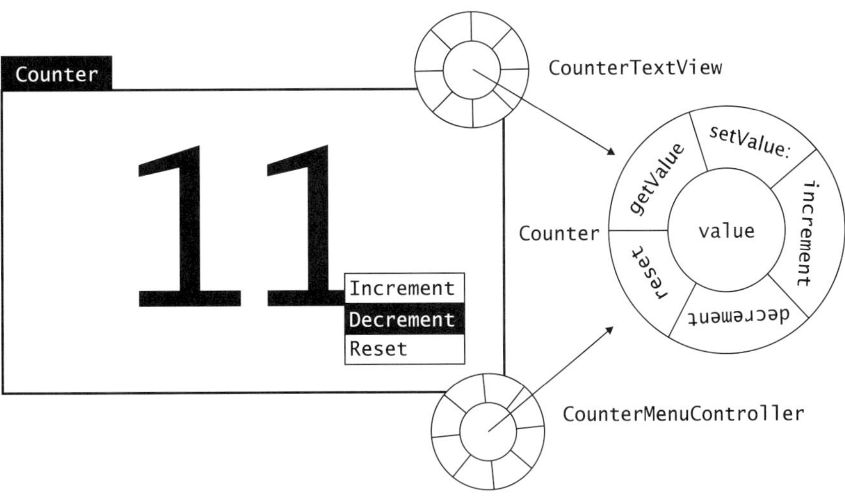

Figure 11-11 A simple MVC application

interaction techniques, which will correspond to two subclasses of Controller.

Requirement (3) shows the value of the component reusability of MVC. We could also easily imagine a requirement for multiple views.[1] We might even want to reuse the counter model in a situation where there is no user interface at all, for instance to count internal events in a program.

The following code answers requirement (1):[2]

```
Model subclass: #Counter
      instanceVariableNames: 'value'
decrement
"Decrement the value of the counter."
   self setValue: value - 1.
increment
"Increment the value of the counter."
   self setValue: value + 1.
reset
"Reset the value of the counter to 0."
   self setValue: 0.
getValue
"Answer the value of the counter."
   value isNil ifTrue: [self reset].
   ^value.
setValue: anInteger
"Private - set the value of the counter."
   value := anInteger.
   self changed.
```

This is straightforward, except the statement `self changed` in the method `setValue:`. Notice that no code in `Counter` refers to views or controllers. This feature of MVC helps separate application logic from user interface code. The abstract class `Model` supplies a protocol allowing views to register themselves as "dependents" of a model; the meaning of `self changed` is "broadcast a message to all my dependents, telling them I have changed." The dependents then update themselves appropriately (here, by getting the new counter value and displaying it).

Requirement (2) asks for just one type of view, and here is its code:

```
View subclass: #CounterTextView
      instanceVariableNames: 'controllerClass'
openOn: aCounter
"Open the receiver for viewing aCounter."
```

[1] As in the example shown in Chapter 10, Figure 10-12 (page 271).

[2] For brevity, in this and other examples I have removed some lines from the code that are not essential. All the classes and methods are shown.

```
| topView |
self model: aCounter;
      borderWidth: 2;
      insideColor: Form white.
topView := StandardSystemView new label: 'Counter.'.
topView addSubView: self.
topView controller open.
```

The gist of the `openOn:` method is that the `CounterTextView` instance is added as a subview to a `StandardSystemView` instance that provides the window frame. The message `self model: aCounter` saves the counter for later reference, and causes this view to be listed as a dependent of the counter.

```
controllerClass: aClass
"Set the controller class for this view."
   controllerClass := aClass.
defaultControllerClass
"Answer the controller class for this view."
   ^controllerClass.
```

The `controllerClass:` method is part of requirement (3). When the view is opened, `defaultControllerClass` is sent to find out what kind of controller to associate with it; `controllerClass:` allows the controller type to be specified as a parameter when the view is created.

```
update: aCounter
"The counter has been updated, update the view."
   ^self display.
```

The `update:` method is part of the dependency mechanism. The counter's sending `self changed` causes `update:` to be sent to all its dependents. The `display` method is implemented in the abstract class `View`, and calls `displayView`:

```
displayView
"Display the value of the counter."
   | box point |
   box := self insetDisplayBox.
   point := box origin + (box extent // 3).
   self model getValue printString
      displayAt: point.
```

This method contains the code to display the counter value as a text string. Notice that `self model getValue` is the only direct interface between the model and view.

Satisfaction of requirement (3) is completed by coding the two controllers. The first one, using a popup menu, is:

```
MouseMenuController subclass: #CounterMenuController
      instanceVariableNames: ''
initialize
"Initialize the popup menu for controlling the counter."
   super initialize.
   self yellowButtonMenu:
       (PopUpMenu labelList: #((Increment Decrement Reset)))
         yellowButtonMessages: #(increment decrement reset).
```

The Initialize method creates the popup menu for controlling the counter.[1] Selection of menu items invokes these methods:

```
decrement
"Decrement the counter."
   self model decrement.
increment
"Increment the counter."
   self model increment.
reset
"Reset the counter."
   self model reset.
```

Here is the second controller, which uses keystroke commands:

```
Controller subclass: #CounterKeyboardController
instanceVariableNames: ''
controlActivity
"If the user has pressed a key, process it."
   [sensor keyboardPressed]
            whileTrue:
         [self processCharacter: sensor keyboard].
processCharacter: aCharacter
"Check for input to control the Counter."
   aCharacter = $+ ifTrue:
      [^self model increment].
   aCharacter = $- ifTrue:
      [^self model decrement].
   aCharacter = $0 ifTrue:
      [^self model reset].
```

[1] "Yellow button" refers to the second mouse button; the term comes from the mouse on the Xerox Alto computer, which had color-coded buttons.

The method `processCharacter:` is straightforward. As discussed above, `controlActivity` is part of the Smalltalk event loop, and `sensor` provides the interface to the keyboard.

The following statements open views with the two controllers:

```
(CounterTextView new
      controllerClass: CounterMenuController)
      openOn: Counter new.
```

or

```
(CounterTextView new
      controllerClass: CounterKeyboardController)
      openOn: Counter new.
```

To illustrate the independence of models and views, two views can be opened on the same model:

```
| c |
c := Counter new.
(CounterTextView new
      controllerClass: CounterMenuController)
      openOn: c.
(CounterTextView new
      controllerClass: CounterKeyboardController)
      openOn: c.
```

Both counter displays will update when either one is changed.

Variants of MVC

Almost all OO user interface frameworks—for example, the many C++ user interface class libraries—can be understood as variants of MVC. Most of the differences are accounted for by three factors.

Early Smalltalks were standalone systems. They provided operating system facilities, window management, applications, and a software development environment in a single address space. Applications were tightly coupled with the base system and window manager. General purpose operating systems such as UNIX and Microsoft Windows, for reasons of security and reliability, separate applications and kernel processes. This means that making the application part of the basic event polling loop (as MVC does with `controlActivity` and other methods) is undesirable. Instead, the window manager maintains a separate event queue for each application.

The second factor is the increased graphics power of modern workstations. From the simple monochrome graphics of early systems, we have progressed to elaborate widgets using color and 3-D shading on platforms such as NeXT and OSF/Motif. Interaction techniques, meanwhile, have not changed much. As a result, the "view" portion of widgets has enlarged relative to the "control" portion.

The first factor reduces the work that a controller needs to do, and the second increases the work of views. The third factor is the increased use of direct manipulation. Because users act directly on displayed objects, direct manipulation controllers need to be coupled very closely to their views. The effect of these factors has been to merge view and controller into a single type.

Recent Smalltalk systems have joined this trend. Digitalk's Smalltalk/V [sDig92a,b], as well as ParcPlace Smalltalk-80 [Lei92], now interface with platform window managers. Smalltalk-80 retains the `Controller` class, while Smalltalk/V has given it up. Control behavior is a crucial conceptual element of the user interface, so separating display and control programming is still useful, even if they are in the same class.[1]

Model-view The prevailing paradigm in user interface software today is *model-view*, or MV. In MV structures, controller functions are distributed to widgets and mixed with view functions.

Apple's Lisa pioneered the architecture now used in most commercial window managers. The window manager fills an application event queue, and the application doles the events out to event handlers[2] (windows or widgets) it owns. The Lisa also pioneered the commercial use of OO class libraries for GUI development. The *Lisa Toolkit* was written in Object Pascal and had classes such as `TEvtHandler`, `TApplication`, `TView`, and `TWindow`.[3] It was the basis for an OO framework for the Macintosh, MacApp [Schm86].

Probably because it is a mature class library, built around a standard event architecture, MacApp has been widely imitated. Class libraries such as ET++ [Wein89], Intermedia [Yan88], and the Borland ObjectWindows library [sBor92] are at least partially based on it, as are commercial applications such as Aldus PageMaker [Fer89] and Adobe Photoshop [Olso94]. The next example illustrates parts of the MacApp MV structure.

A C++ counter Scores of different class libraries are available for C++, many with user interface classes that are similar to the MacApp classes. This example uses the Borland ObjectWindows Library on Microsoft Windows.[4]

The example is a counter, with requirements similar to those for the MVC example (page 326). With no controller, satisfying the third requirement (providing a version for each interaction technique) is more difficult, so this example supports only keyboard interaction. An alternative to controllers is writing code to support both interaction styles in the same view. A parameter and conditional test are added to turn off one or the other.

[1] Chapter 13 will show how controllers can be put back into systems such as Smalltalk/V and discuss why this is sometimes worthwhile.

[2] Event handlers are called *Responders* in the NeXT system.

[3] The "T" prefix is an Object Pascal convention; it stands for "Type."

[4] Some technical intricacies are omitted from the code (including some of the constructors), in order to simplify it. All functions are inlined to make it easier to read.

This is not an ideal solution, since it adds complexity and reduces component reusability. Discussion of other alternatives is deferred until Chapter 13.

MacApp has a class `TDocument` with some of the features of Smalltalk's `Model`, but it is not in ObjectWindows. I added the class `Model`, with a simple dependency mechanism—each model can have a single view:

```
class Model {
  private:
    View* pView;
  protected:
    void changed() { // Model has changed, update the view.
      pView->update(); }
  public:
    void setView(View* pv) {
      pView = pv;
      // Tell the view that this is its model.
      pView->setModel(this); }
};
```

`TWindow` is the ObjectWindows base class for windows. A `View` class is added with a member variable for the model, and the member function `update()`, required for views in the MV scheme.

```
class View: public TWindow {
  protected:
    Model* pModel;
  public:
    // Set the model for this view.
    void setModel(Model* pm) { pModel = pm; }
    virtual void update() { }
};
```

Here's the Counter class, which (aside from syntax) is almost the same as in the Smalltalk example:

```
class Counter: public Model {
  private:
    int value;
    void setValue(int val) {
      value = val;
      changed(); }
  public:
          Counter() : value(0) { } // Initialize to 0 value.
    void decrement() { setValue(--value); }
    void increment() { setValue(++value); }
```

```
    void reset() { setValue(0); }
    int getValue() { return value; }
};
```

The next class is the view. The main difference from the Smalltalk MVC example is the absence of a controller. The `WMChar()` function is essentially the same as `processCharacter:`, but it is now part of the view, not the controller. The `update()` function redisplays the counter value, as `update:` did in the MVC example.

Notice that `model()` casts `pModel` to type `Counter*` so the appropriate messages (`decrement`, etc.) can be sent to it; `pView` (in `Model`) did not need to be cast. This is because the only message sent by models to views is `update()`.[1] Since `update()` is defined in `View` as virtual, it can be sent to any class derived from `View`. In the opposite direction, we are not so lucky; views send all sorts of messages to their models (such as `decrement`, `increment`, `reset`, and `getValue`). We cannot define all possible messages to models as virtual functions in `Model`—we do not even know them *a priori*.

Smalltalk detects type mismatches only at run time, when the message is sent. C++ does type checking in the compiler, so the set of messages that can be sent must be known at compile time. We know that `pModel` will really point to a `Counter` object, so we must tell the compiler by casting `pModel` to `Counter*`.

```
class CounterTextView: public View {
  private:
    Counter* model() { // Answer the model, cast to Counter.
      return (Counter*) pModel; }
  public:
    CounterTextView(PTWindowsObject AParent, LPSTR ATitle)
             : View(AParent, ATitle) { } // Constructor.
    void WMChar(RTMessage Msg) {
      // Update the counter based on user keyboard input.
      if ( Msg.WP.Lo == '+') model()->increment();
      if ( Msg.WP.Lo == '-') model()->decrement();
      if ( Msg.WP.Lo == '0') model()->reset();
    }
    void update() {  // Update the display.
      HDC DC;
      DC = GetDC(HWindow);
      char val [10];
      sprintf(val, "%4d", model()->getValue());
      TextOut(DC, 50, 50, val, strlen(val));
```

[1] I use *message* synonymously with the technically accurate term, *member function call.*

```
        ReleaseDC(HWindow, DC)
    }
  };
```

ObjectWindows applications must have a class derived from TApplication. No equivalent class was present in the Smalltalk example.

```
class CounterApp: public TApplication {
  private:
    Counter appCounter;
    void InitMainWindow() {
      CounterTextView* myWindow;
      myWindow = new CounterTextView(NULL, Name);
      appCounter.setView(myWindow);
      MainWindow = myWindow;
    }
      . . . . .
};
```

This class is required because, as in MacApp, TApplication sets up a queue for the application and dispatches events from it to its windows. In more substantial applications than this, other processing might be done as well, such as coordinating the operation of multiple windows. The function of TApplication exists in Smalltalk too, since it is a requirement of the window manager, but it is provided "under the covers."

CounterApp might seem to be a good place to put the counter, avoiding the need for a Model class. This will work for small programs, but it violates the principle of MV separation. In a complex application, a TApplication derived class will probably include many functions related to window management and event handling. Mixing in the information model will result in a class that is hard to understand, error-prone, and difficult to maintain.

Finally, here is the main program that runs the counter.[1] Notice that this has the same structure as the skeletal object-oriented application on page 310. MyApp.Run() invokes the Run() function in TApplication, which calls InitMainWindow() in CounterApp, and kicks off the main event loop.

```
// Main program.
int PASCAL WinMain(HINSTANCE hInstance, HINSTANCE
              hPrevInstance, LPSTR lpCmdLine, int nCmdShow)
{
  CounterApp MyApp("Counter", hInstance, hPrevInstance,
                lpCmdLine, nCmdShow);
  MyApp.Run();
```

[1]WinMain is a special name for Microsoft Windows application main programs.

```
  return MyApp.Status;
}
```

The application ends when the user closes the CounterTextView window, which exits the Run() loop.

11.5 Summary

People typically understand a "conventional" system to be a structured collection of modules derived through top-down functional decomposition. Many systems, including operating systems, transaction-driven applications, and client-server systems, do not fit that model.

More and more systems and applications are best seen as object-based, regardless of whether they are implemented using object-oriented programming languages. In the object-based view, systems are composed of autonomous objects that communicate by message passing. In general, the objects may be distributed over a communications network.

Parts I and II of this book present a three-way factoring of the external user interface into conceptual model, presentation language, and action language. This factoring is mirrored in the model-view-controller (MVC) framework for implementing applications. Though developed in the Smalltalk-80 system, MVC concepts have been widely applied. Most other systems combine view and controller. Many systems use an Application class to represent the packaging of components comprising an application.

Interface designers should also understand the idea of a technical infrastructure layer underlying the information model. In real systems, information models rely on capabilities underneath them, such as databases and communications links. Synthesizing object behavior from non-OO components is an important task for designers in most current environments.

The best implementation model for graphical object-oriented user interfaces is called the event model. It is based on autonomous event handlers, or objects, that communicate by passing events. This model is essentially the same as the object-based view of systems, and it simplifies the construction of high-performance interactive applications. The event model is the basis for commercial window systems such as Microsoft Windows and the X Window System. Most commercial OO class libraries for building OOUIs provide classes matching the constructs in window systems.

Events, message passing, object classes, and composition are key tools for modularity in user interface implementation. As in object systems in general, control flow in OOUI implementations is distributed among autonomous objects. Understanding the principle of *model-view separation* is the basis for implementations that are well structured from a software engineering point of view.

The key messages for designers from this chapter are:

- Think of interactive systems and applications as networks of communicating objects that collaborate to provide visible interfaces to end users.
- The internals of the user interface design are organized using the same three-way factoring that describes the externals.
- Information models need to interface not only to user interface elements, but also to an infrastructure layer, which is often not OO.
- Window systems form an infrastructure layer for the view and controller components of the user interface. Window systems *do* have an object-based structure, based on events and event handlers.

11.6 To Explore Further

The view of applications in Section 11.1 has emerged from the convergence of two lines of research. One is the extension of message passing in object-oriented systems to objects separated by networks [McCu87]. The other is the quest for more robust, modular architectures for distributed services in heterogeneous networks. [Nic93] is a good summary of the role OO is playing in this arena. I learned a great deal about the role of OO in distributed systems from staff members at the IBM International Technical Support Organization. They developed the ITSO SAA Cooperative Processing Project [Nal91], which tested many of the ideas in Section 11.1.

The Seeheim model is explained in [Pfa85]. [Fol92] and [Shn92] discuss the language model in general terms. [Jaco83] describes the use of state transition diagrams and BNF grammars for specifying user interfaces. Harel has significantly extended state diagrams [Har88]; Harel statecharts have been used to specify the dynamics of OO models, for example in [Boo94] and [Rum91]. [Lar92], a textbook on user interface implementation, emphasizes high-level tools based on grammars and transition networks. [Gree86] compares transition networks, grammars, and event models. An understanding of the basics of language parsing can be found in compiler textbooks such as [Aho86], and is helpful in exploring the literature of grammars and transition networks applied to user interfaces.

The event model is more recent than the various flavors of the language model. [Gree86] is a good overview. [Jaco86] describes an implementation and covers the key ideas of events and event handling. [Jaco86], [Hud87], and [Sib86] explain why the event model is needed for graphical object-oriented interfaces.

I have not found a general treatment on the use of the event model in commercial window systems. Books on window system programming cover event processing, though it is often imbedded in complex code examples. [Berl91] and [You92], both for X Windows with OSF/Motif, provide quite readable overviews. Kurt Schmucker's book on MacApp [Schm86] also covers event handling in a general way, in the context of Macintosh programming. Comparing events and event handling between two or more platforms is the best way to develop a broad view. [Rosen83] discusses ideas that motivated the general shift to event-driven interfaces for graphical applications.

Model-view-controller is covered in more detail in Chapters 12 and 13. [Gol90] is a good overview, covering about the same ground as this chapter. Most of the literature on MVC, such as [Kras88], focuses on the technical aspects of programming MVC in Smalltalk-80, rather than on conceptual issues. [Schm86] is a good treatment of the MacApp structure. Many systems based on MV or MVC separation and fine-grained events are found in the research literature; see, for example, [Cou87a,b], [Hil86], and [Sib86].

11.7 Exercises

1. Consider a simplified version of the counter problem (page 325), in which only keyboard input is required.
   a. Design a solution using top-down functional decomposition—do not use MVC or any object-oriented technique.
   b. Can you map the lowest level modules in your decomposition to the methods in the MVC solution? (Disregard which object the methods are attached to.)
2. Do the same steps as in exercise 1, using the solitaire game of Chapter 5 as the problem.
   a. How would you compare the difficulty of this exercise and exercise 1? Does it seem to be a linear function of the problem size?
   b. Discuss your conclusion from (a) in terms of the "language" and "event" models of user interfaces presented in Section 11.2.
3. Draw a more complete state transition diagram for the `SimpleButton` on page 315. Instead of "left button clicked," explicitly consider the button up and button down events. Allow for situations such as that in which the user presses the mouse button, but moves out of `SimpleButton`'s rectangle before releasing it.
4. Describe synthetic events you think the following widgets should send to their owning windows:
   a. Popup menu.
   b. Prompt dialogue with text entry field and buttons (`OK`/`Cancel`) to accept or cancel the response.
   c. Same as (b), if you are using autocompletion (described in Chapter 10, Section 10.3) for the text entry field.

  d. A list box, in which the user can select one item from a list by clicking on it with the mouse.

5. Using documentation for a window system, compare your answer in (4) to what is actually provided.

6. Figure 7-5 (Chapter 7) shows an interaction diagram for the "transfer" task done through a bank ATM. Along the lines of Figure 11-10, draw a composition hierarchy and event flow diagram for a GUI version of this interface. You can assume an interface that has:

   - A list box showing accounts the customer can transfer *from.*
   - Another list box showing accounts the customer can transfer *to.*
   - `OK` and `Cancel` buttons to start the transfer (after selecting accounts) or cancel it.

   Notice that all the required logic cannot be expressed using only an event flow diagram. Try sketching a storyboard with annotation to show the entire sequence. (*For developers*: try this with a simple part of an application you are working on.)

12

Information Models

Chapter 5 quoted Trygve Reenskaug as saying "a bad system design can never be hidden from the user, even by a masterfully designed user interface" [Ree81]. Yet we must always conceal the deepest layers of the implementation, since they have nothing to do with the problem domain. This chapter is about general schemes for presenting a clear application model to users, while hiding details of the computer infrastructure.

Information models are the foundations for providing concrete views of the user's conceptual model.[1] That is, information models are software constructs that "realize" conceptual models and provide functional interfaces for external views. Though a model is seen by users only indirectly, through its views, its semantics are part of external design.

For user interface design, the critical part of the information model is its external protocol. All the rest is like wiring and plumbing in a building—not very interesting to the building's tenants. However, just as in the building metaphor, we occasionally need to think about the wiring and plumbing—for example, when it breaks down, or needs modification to accommodate an extension to the external edifice.

This chapter builds on Chapters 5 and 11 to provide more details on three aspects of information models:

- Protocols that support visible user interfaces.
- General structuring issues in designing information models.
- The "plumbing and wiring" infrastructure used to build information models from OO and non-OO components such as databases and communications links.

[1] For brevity and consistency with the well-established terminology of the model-view-controller architecture, information models will often be called simply "models."

Articles appear frequently suggesting that new "high level" tools will absolve designers of the responsibility for paying careful attention to structure. The following quotation, from an article on Microsoft's Visual Basic [Thé94], is typical:

> If you need computer-aided software engineering tools, code generators or Booch object-oriented analysis software, you won't find them for VB [Visual Basic]. But it may well be that component architectures make overall design so simple you don't need them.

Tools that make design simple are will-o'-the-wisps. Solving structure problems at one level enables larger systems to be attempted, and the problems reappear again at the next level. Designers always need to understand and model problem domain semantics in creative ways to build high-quality systems. This chapter merely scratches the surface of a large topic; I hope it will encourage further exploration.

12.1 Information Modeling

Information modeling in a general sense is the process of analyzing users' information needs and designing representations that will satisfy them. In this sense, information modeling far predates computers—librarians and accountants, among others, have practiced it for centuries. Computers have made the problems of modeling and organizing information more urgent. The amount of information held by institutions and individuals has multiplied exponentially, and the need to access it quickly has increased.

Information modeling can be approached from two directions. The bottom-up approach aims to conceal low-level implementation details from programmers and users. The top-down approach starts from a conceptual model of the domain and designs representations that are congruent with it. These approaches are found in OO and non-OO modeling methods, and designers use them iteratively.

Non-OO methods treat data and function separately, though I doubt they are ever fully separated in the designer's mind. OO modeling methods emphasize *behavior*, despite the data-centric connotation of "information model." This chapter focuses on information models in MVC and MV frameworks, but it does not exclude other aspects of modeling—as emphasized in Chapter 5, the information model we are discussing here is based on the analysis model for the system or application.

The Three-Schema Model for Data

There is an analogy between the structure of information models in OO systems and an idea from database theory, the *three-schema* model. Before discussing this model, however, I need to point out a conflict in terminology that the analogy brings out over the word *view*.

View, in computer graphics and human-computer interaction, refers to an area on a display, or a software object that presents information on a display. In the database literature, a view is a data structure that abstracts an application-specific "view" of physical data [Ull80].[1] For example, a customer database may have physical records containing thousands of bytes of data on each customer, including pointers to other records, indexing information, and device-dependent formatting. A program that prints envelopes for mailing to customers is only interested in the customer's name and address, and it may require a "view" of the customer data that looks like Figure 12-1:

Name	Street address	City	State	Postal code	Country

Figure 12-1 Logical view of a customer record

In a general sense, these two uses of "view" are similar—a view provides an appearance that abstracts part of a more complex lower-level object. What database people concretely call a view, however, has no direct connection with what is on the screen, and in fact the definition they use is close to what the object-oriented literature calls a model. In this book, I always mean *view* in the user interface sense. When referring to a database "view," I use the alternative term *external schema* [Elm89].

Figure 12-2 shows the three-schema model. At the top are people, who may be application programmers or end users of query languages. They deal with external schemas (also called external views in the database literature) like the one in Figure 12-1. These external schemas are models containing the data elements and structures that are of interest to a particular user or application.

External schemas are also called *subschemas*, because they are substructures of a *conceptual schema*, an overall model for data in a domain containing many applications. The conceptual schema is formulated using a data definition language such as SQL (structured query language), and is independent of the physical structure and storage of the data. Conceptual and external schemas use the same data definition language.

The *internal schema* describes the physical storage of the data and how it is accessed. In typical systems, a database management system (DBMS) uses the internal schema to access and update physical data corresponding to logical data specified by users in terms of the conceptual schema.

A Three-Schema Approach to OO Systems

Figure 11-2 in Chapter 11 implied a single information model tied to a single view, which is not a very realistic situation. More typically, an information model represents a large domain or enterprise, and many applications

[1] *View* is sometimes defined in the OO literature as it is in the database literature: "a class that renames or exports restricted properties of another" ([deCh93], p. 300).

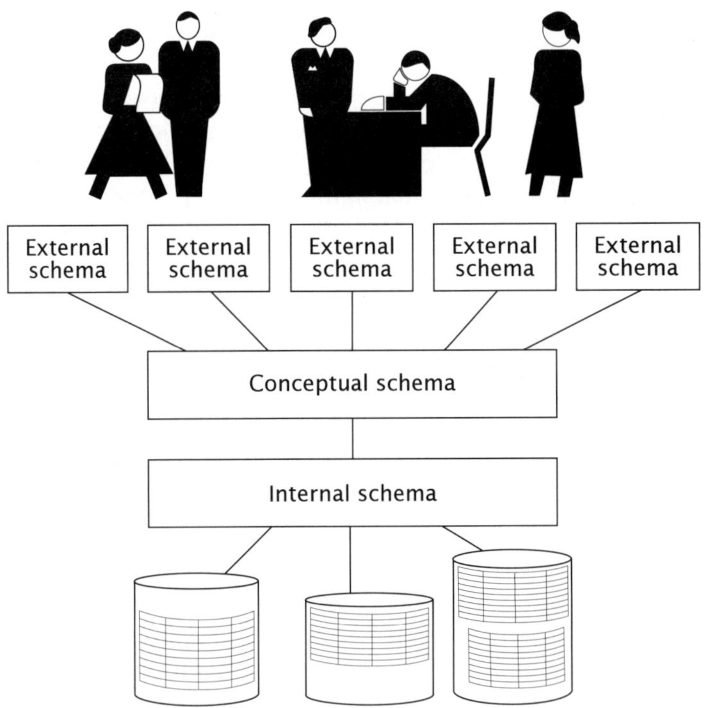

Figure 12-2 The three-schema model for databases

use parts of it. Each application has, at least implicitly, an external schema reflecting the part of the model it is interested in.

Figure 12-3 is a more complete picture, showing both external schemas and user interface views. This figure, unlike Figure 11-2, shows functional layers without asserting that they correspond to layers of objects. Deciding how to allocate these functions to objects is a key aspect of designing information models; the decision will be based on factors such as the size of the system, the number of applications, the type of database, and existing components that need to be reused.

To make the discussion of Figure 12-3 concrete, assume that applications are being developed for the TipTop Appliance Company, a retailer of household appliances such as refrigerators, stoves, and washing machines. The information model for the entire TipTop enterprise might include the following object classes:

- `Customer`, a person who purchases an item from TipTop.
- `Employee`, a TipTop person who sells to a customer.
- `Product`, an item TipTop sells.
- `Supplier`, a company supplying a product to TipTop.

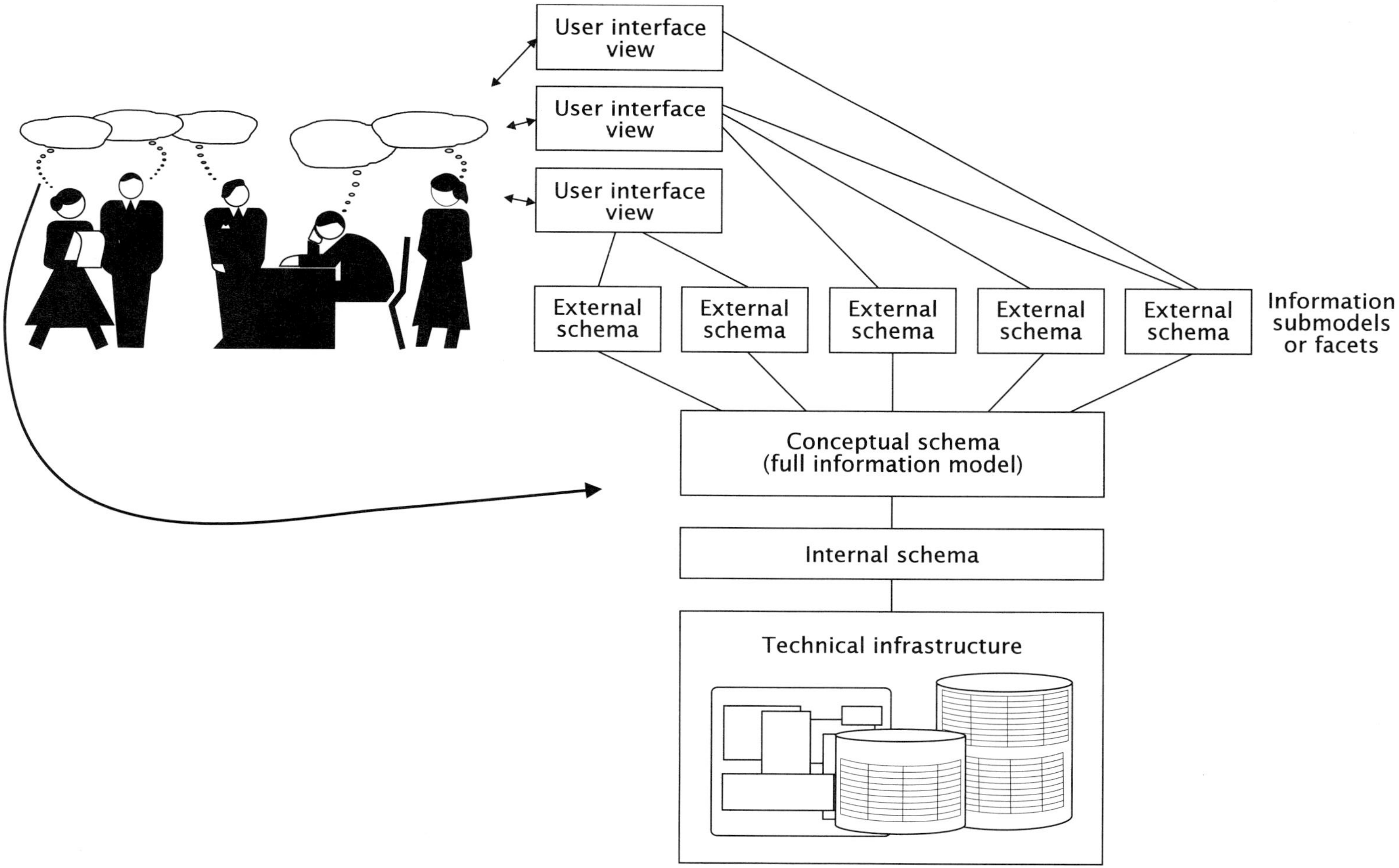

Figure 12-3 The three-schema model applied to an OO system

Besides these fundamental object types, the information model also contains objects that relate the fundamental types:

- `SupplierInvoice`, representing a purchase from a supplier.
- `SupplierOrder`, representing an order to a supplier.
- `CustomerInvoice`, representing a purchase by a customer.
- `CustomerOrder`, representing an order by a customer.
- `Account`, representing a history of transactions between TipTop and a given customer or supplier.
- `CreditHistory`, summarizing information on the credit-worthiness of a customer.
- `Inventory`, representing a collection of products on hand in the TipTop store or warehouse.

The users at the top left of Figure 12-3 can be thought of as different types of employee. The thought balloons indicate that each has a conceptual model of the objects that are important to TipTop. These conceptual models will be different, reflecting the job of each employee, though they should all be consistent with an overall enterprise conceptual model.

This "conceptual layer" is consistent with analysis methods in many disciplines. Peter Chen, for example, the developer of the *entity-relationship* (E-R) method for database analysis, recognized the need for another layer above the three schemas [Che76]. Chen wanted to capture more of the semantics of real-world entities—as did the developers of object-oriented programming languages such as Simula-67 [Nyg86].

Each user interface view in Figure 12-3 uses one or more external schemas, which represent subsets or aspects of the information model. External schemas may correspond to objects; for instance, the `CreditHistory` class is a schema for an aspect of the information model.

The internal schema describes how information in files and databases is mapped to objects in the information model; it may also involve communications links, non-OO programs, and so forth. As with external schemas, internal schemas may or may not correspond to object layers in the implementation.

We can classify methods or member functions in the information model into three categories:

1. Methods that return objects needed by applications, including what is needed to present views to end users.
2. Methods that implement the interface to the technical infrastructure.
3. Methods, other than those in (1) and (2), needed to keep the internal state of the information model consistent with the real-world entities it models.

The distribution of these methods helps to determine whether "schema" objects are necessary. If the number of methods in category (1) is large, factoring out external schema classes may be valuable. This is particularly true if (perhaps for security reasons) each application or view should be restricted to a subset of the interface provided by category (1) methods.

External schema classes are also useful if a subset of the methods in category (1) are used by only one application. In this case the external schema is simply the "model" (in the MVC sense) for that application. In many systems, the packaging class representing an application will automatically constitute an external schema for the application. This is true, for example, for `Model` subclasses in Smalltalk, and `TApplication` or `TDocument` subclasses in MacApp derivatives.

The existence of a large set of category (2) methods suggests factoring out internal schema classes. These can be particularly helpful if you anticipate changes in the infrastructure. Developers of commercial class libraries may provide internal schema classes, for instance, to help map relational database records to objects.

Where external and internal schemas are not factored into separate classes, they are subsets of methods in information model classes. As database people have discovered, a disadvantage of this is the lack of explicit, identifiable entities that document schemas. (Most database management systems provide libraries for storing schema specifications.) This can be partially addressed by protocol categories (as in Smalltalk-80), or in C++ by creating separate source files for storing schema function implementations.

Composite Information Models

Except in simple examples such as the counter of Chapter 11, information models are composite. In most real systems, models are sufficiently complex that packaging and structuring become serious concerns. Here I just summarize the issues that are important to user interface designers.[1]

"Part-of" hierarchies Hierarchical composition and decomposition are fundamental tools for managing complexity. The solitaire game provided a simple example of a composite model; its composition diagram is shown in Figure 5-5. Composition uses the part-subpart relation, implemented with instance variables (member data variables) containing or pointing to the parts.

Figure 12-4 shows a composite model for the `Customer` class. Like `KlondikeGame` in the solitaire game, the top object, the `Customer` instance, provides all the public protocols for applications and views dealing with customers. This can hide a great deal of complexity. Obtaining a list of customer orders might involve accessing a database and constructing `CustomerOrder` objects, but this is concealed from clients of the `Customer` object.

[1] For a more complete treatment, see Boo94], [deCh93], and [Jac92].

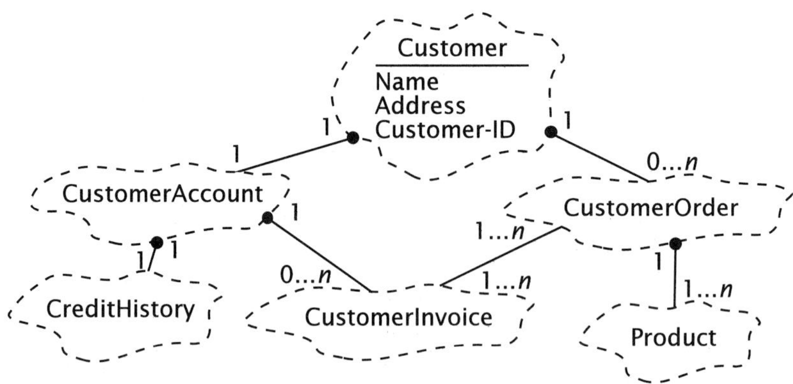

Figure 12-4 A composite information model for customers

The "top" in an information model may depend upon who the client is. For customer applications, `Customer` is on top, and `Product` instances are parts. On the other hand, consider a marketing application generating product promotion mailings that needs a list of customers who have purchased specified products. This application may see `Product` as the top object and `Customer` as a part.

Faceted models A model typically supports more than one view. Models often support several categories of views, where views in different categories use different aspects of the model. I call these models *faceted*; each facet provides behavior that is useful to a category of views, corresponding to a community of users.[1] This formalizes the situation just discussed, where customer information and marketing applications are interested in different facets of the same model. Figure 12-5 shows the facets of interest to various TipTop users.

Facets can be implementation constructs. Protocol categories, as in Smalltalk-80, can define sets of methods that correspond to facets. In Figure 12-4, for example, the Customer object might provide categories defining the interface to applications for sales, accounting, etc. Faceted models can also be implemented as true composites. Specific objects (corresponding to external schemas) can export only the interface needed by users of a particular facet. `Inventory` in the TipTop model is an example.

Layered models All the examples discussed so far assume a single information model layer, if we posit that the external schemas in Figure 12-3 are part of this layer. In most database systems, the three-schema model is really an *n*-schema model—external schemas can be built on top of other external schemas, as well as on the conceptual schema. The same principle applies in object-oriented systems—one layer of information models can be an "infrastructure" for higher layers.

[1] This is similar to the notion of facets in faceted classification [Prie91].

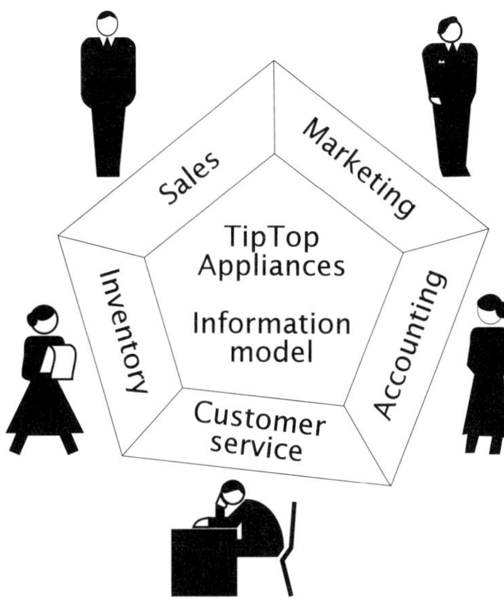

Figure 12-5 Facets in the TipTop Appliance information model

To illustrate layered models, suppose TipTop management wants to see certain reports and charts on the company's financial status in real time. If a customer has just purchased a refrigerator, for example, the transaction might immediately be reflected in an accounts receivable summary. (Even if "immediately" means at the end of the business day, the principle is the same.)

For this sort of reporting requirement, object types such as `AccountsReceivableSummary` and `AccountsPayableSummary` can be layered on top of `CustomerInvoice` and `SupplierInvoice` in the "basic" information model. These new types could simply be considered to be part of the enterprise information model—but in a real way, "second tier" objects like `AccountsReceivableSummary` are derivations or summaries of the more fundamental types.

To carry the layering another step, suppose various forms of displayed and printed reports are needed. An `AccountsReceivableSummaryReport` might be a combination of two things. First, the "data"—perhaps a time series for accounts receivable in various categories—along with behavior such as the ability to return the category data for a given date. There would also be a template for displaying the data, containing such things as chart format (line graph, histogram, etc.), legends for chart elements, and axis scaling.

Though this last layer might seem to be simply a view, in many "executive information systems" `Report` objects (composed of data objects and format templates) are persistent, and have stored instances for successive periods. Each report may have more than one view, specifying details such as colors, text fonts, and other rendering details.

Application domains for typical systems have models with tens or hundreds of object types. In these systems, intelligent composition of the information model is important to user interface designers, as well as to the developers of the model itself. Techniques such as layers, facets, and application-specific external schema objects are particularly helpful in managing the complexity of large user interfaces.

A quality often found in well-designed composite models is *coherence*. Easier to see than to analyze, coherence in an information model is a result of having a well-structured, coherent conceptual model, as described in Chapter 8. Coherence is often manifested in the use of polymorphic protocols to simplify composite models and reduce coupling between objects. That is, different object types can "plug and play" in an information model because its structure is defined by interfaces between generic types. Examples in the TipTop system could include an `Inventory` object that interfaces with any `Product` type, or an `Account` with many polymorphic transaction types.

12.2 Implementing Models

There are a host of issues, problems, and techniques connected with implementing information models. These mainly concern the developers of the information model; this section provides an overview for user interface designers and developers.

Middle-Out Implementation

I have seen three approaches to the development of interactive systems; they seem so deeply ingrained it is fair to call them paradigms. One is the *inside-out* or technology-based approach. This approach says we should base designs on the capabilities of existing technology, since technology dictates what can be delivered to end users. The second approach is *outside-in*, where the basis for design is the desired external appearance of the user interface. The rationale is that what users see "on the glass" is what ultimately decides the success or failure of a system.

The third approach is *middle-out* design, based on a conceptual model of the problem domain. Most published methodologies recommend something that is essentially middle-out, since the analysis model, and its corresponding design model, are the "middle" from which the technology infrastructure and the user interface are driven. In practice, many projects that claim to use these methods are actually using the outside-in or inside-out approaches.

My observation is that middle-out is usually abandoned because of the lack, in conventional systems, of implementation constructs corresponding to the middle. Clear-cut entities in the analysis model, such as customers, orders, and invoices, are fragmented across data structures and functional modules. As a result, developers focus on what is most real, namely the visible user interface and the technology infrastructure. I have also observed that developers pay more attention to the middle in object-oriented environments. I attribute this to the fact that the conceptual or analysis model now corresponds to a real piece of software, the information model.[1]

For the technology-driven, it may be useful to think of information models as *virtual machines.* In computer science, a virtual machine is a software or microcode layer that allows one machine architecture to simulate another, different architecture.[2] This may be done to build a high-level facility on top of a more primitive machine, or to present a standard machine appearance across different physical implementations.

In the user interface context, the information model is a virtual machine that makes the technology infrastructure look like an "application engine" designed for a specific problem domain. This allows applications and views to access domain-specific services instead of a more primitive technology infrastructure. It also fosters portability of applications and views by insulating them from changeable implementations.

In addition to the obvious case of moving from one platform to another, there are more subtle portability issues. Mission-critical applications often have lifetimes measured in decades, and migrate through several generations of infrastructure technology on the same platform. A well-structured information model can ease this process, as shown in Figure 12-6. It illustrates a situation faced by many organizations—the transition from "conventional" to object technology as the base for applications.

Step one in the migration is to build an object-oriented information model. An internal schema is added to use the existing application code as a technical infrastructure for the new model. Dietrich and colleagues describe a situation like this [Diet89], where the emphasis was on preserving a large investment in "legacy" application code within an OO system.

Step two is developing external schemas and views on the new model that are functionally similar or identical to existing user interfaces. User terminals or workstations can then be detached from direct interfaces to the old application (now the infrastructure for the new application), and attached to the new views. New schemas can be developed independently to provide new user interfaces. This is often done to migrate from character-based command or menu interfaces to graphical OOUIs. The new schemas may be distributed, for example if users are changing from directly attached terminals to networked workstations.

In step three, all or part of the old application can be "unplugged" and replaced with a new object-oriented infrastructure. The figure suggests replacing the entire infrastructure at once, but piecemeal replacement is also possible.

---

[1] Others have made similar observations; see, e.g., [Ross90].

[2] The Smalltalk virtual machine [Gol83] is an example of the standard usage of this term in computer science.

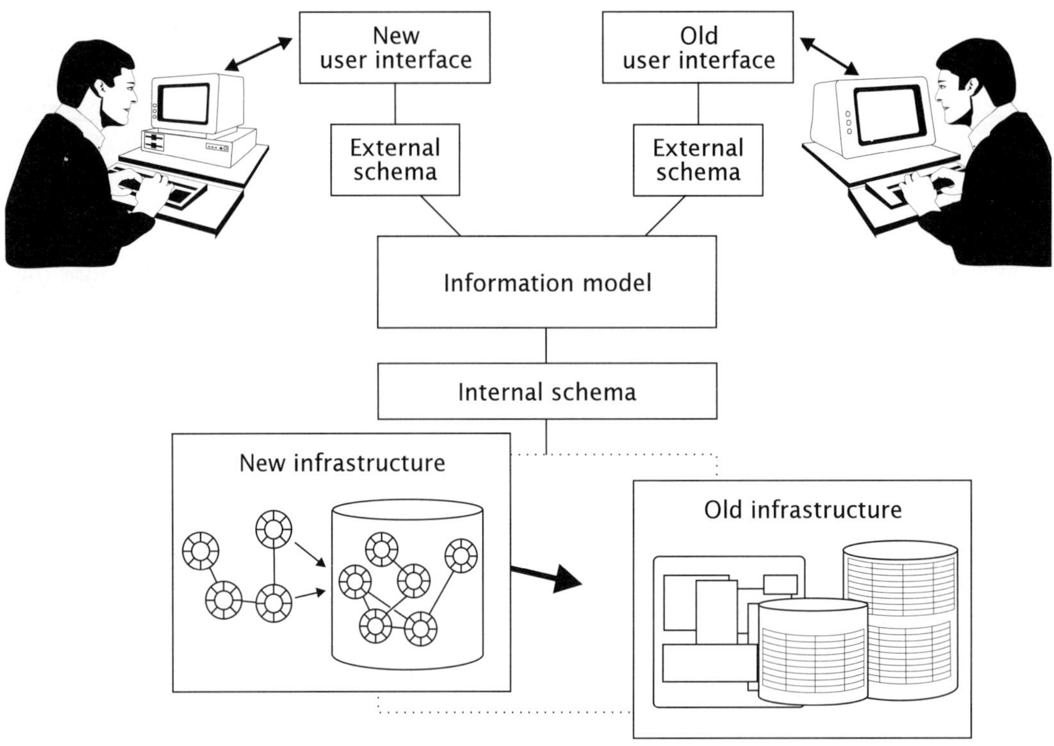

Figure 12-6 The ideal of an architecture with pluggable components

There are many variations on this scenario, and it must be executed with great care where mission-critical applications are involved. Some reverse engineering is typically required, since the information model may not correspond to any identifiable component in an existing system. Case studies such as [Diet89] and the Brooklyn Union Gas Company's CRIS-II system [Dav93] suggest significant benefits from using object technology in this way.

The technical infrastructure layer reflects the state of current technology, which changes rapidly over time. Specific applications and views represent business processes that are also subject to change. The information model is based upon the core entities of the business or organization, such as customers and products. These usually change more slowly than the processes that use them and more slowly than the implementation technology. This makes the information model a good anchor point for modularizing the remainder of the system.

Persistent Information Models

In all but the simplest systems, objects in the information model persist over time, independent of views and applications that access, create, or modify them. In these cases the persistence of objects is part of the user's conceptual model, so interface designers need to understand it.

Object persistence is a broad term. It may mean simply saving objects for later use by the same user, or it may mean making objects available for sharing between many users. Persistent objects may be under the control of an *object-oriented database manager* [KimW90]. This implies capabilities of database managers in general [Ull80]—reliable storage, sharing among multiple users, and the ability to find objects using a query facility. The discussion here uses simple examples to bring out key points that are relevant in any environment needing object persistence.

Object persistence in the solitaire game Figure 5-9 shows a simple user interface for the solitaire game example. Two of the menu commands in the figure are not mentioned in Chapter 5: `Save game` and `Restore game`. These commands allow a user to save the state of a game in progress, and resume the game later. This example shows the need for object persistence and shows that it can be visible at the user interface level.

Object-oriented databases can be built on simpler relational or file-based infrastructures. Saving and restoring solitaire games illustrates this. The information model for the solitaire game is an instance of `KlondikeGame`, which contains instances of `FoundationPile`, `TableauPile`, and so forth as sub-objects. The piles, in turn, are composed of `Card` objects. Each card must be saved, along with the structure of piles and the whole game.

The user is prompted for a file name after requesting that a game be saved. The following code is then executed:

```
saveGame: aFilename
   "Save the game in the file named aFilename."
   | stream |
   stream := (Filename named: aFilename) newReadWriteStream.
   self storeOn: stream.
   stream close.
```

The `storeOn:` method is defined for all objects in the game, and is recursively invoked to store the entire game. In `KlondikeGame`, the method is as follows:

```
storeOn: aStream
   "Append to aStream a sequence of characters that can be
        used to recreate the game."
   | name |
   aStream nextPutAll:
      (name := self class name asString); cr.
   aStream nextPutAll: 'Stock'; cr.
   self stock storeOn: aStream.
   aStream nextPutAll: 'End Stock'; cr.
   aStream nextPutAll: 'Talon'; cr.
```

```
    self talon storeOn: aStream.
    aStream nextPutAll: 'End Talon'; cr.
    self foundation do: [  : eachPile |
        eachPile storeOn: aStream.
        aStream cr].
    self tableau do: [  : eachPile |
        eachPile storeOn: aStream.
        aStream cr].
    aStream nextPutAll: 'End ', name.
```

Pile instances store themselves in a similar way:

```
storeOn: aStream
    "Append to aStream a sequence of characters that can be
         used to recreate the Pile."
    | name |
    aStream nextPutAll:
       (name := self class name asString); cr.
    self cards do: [  : eachCard |
        eachCard storeOn: aStream.
        aStream cr].
    aStream nextPutAll: 'End ', name; cr.
```

Finally, each Card instance stores itself:

```
storeOn: aStream
"Append to aStream a sequence of characters that can be
        used to recreate the Card."
aStream nextPutAll:
          self class name asString, ' ',
          self value asString, ' ',
          self suit asString.
```

A fragment of the resulting file looks like:

```
KlondikeGame
Stock
FaceDownPile
Card Ten spades
Card King spades
.....
End Stock
TableauPile
FaceUpPile
Card Ten diamonds
End FaceUpPile
```

```
FaceDownPile
End FaceDownPile
End TableauPile
....
End KlondikeGame
```

To reverse this process, the method `restoreFrom:` in `KlondikeGame` parses the file and recreates the stored game. It is essentially the reverse of the `storeOn:` process, though more complicated because of error checking.

The code maps to a similar design in C++, using the standard `ostream` and `istream` classes for file access. The equivalent to `restoreFrom:` can be placed in a constructor function for `KlondikeGame` that takes the filename as argument. This constructor creates an input stream on the file and recursively invokes the constructors for piles and individual cards:

```
class KlondikeGame {
      public:
              // Restore a game from filenameString.
              KlondikeGame(char* filenameString);
      .....
};
.....
class Card {
      public:
              // Restore a card from an input stream.
              Card(istream& is);
.....
};
KlondikeGame* pGame = new KlondikeGame("savegame.txt");
```

This simple example shows that objects can be transparently stored in standard file systems. "Transparently" means that the nature of the storage mechanism is known only to the methods that implement it.

Mapping objects to relational databases Suppose we have a class `CustomerMailingInfo`, used by programs that print envelopes and labels for customer mailings. Here is a fragment of the code for the class:

```
class CustomerMailingInfo {
      private:
              char* Name;
              char* StreetAddress;
              char* City;
              char* State;
              int PostalCode;
```

```
            char* Country;
        public:
            // Construct an object for customer "custName."
                CustomerMailingInfo(char* custName);
            // Return the mailing label format for printing.
            char* formatMailinglabel();
        . . . . .
    };
```

Notice that the member variables in this class correspond to the columns in the customer record shown in Figure 12-1 (page 341). This suggests that, just as a `KlondikeGame` instance was constructed from a file, a `CustomerMailingInfo` instance can be constructed from a row in a relational database table.

Many vendors of OO environments and class libraries provide classes that access relational databases. One of the functions typically provided is the ability to retrieve table rows based on SQL queries such as this:

```
SELECT Name, StreetAddress, City, State, PostalCode, Country
FROM CustomerMailingInfoTable
WHERE Name = custName
```

The `CustomerMailingInfo(char* custname)` constructor can use the result of this query to fill in its member variables—each variable corresponds to a column in the table.

When objects are stored in relational databases, no parsing or error checking is needed, and records can be retrieved using high-level query statements. Databases in general provide a higher level of sharing, security, and reliability than file systems.

Transparent Access to Persistent Objects

In the examples so far, both application programmers and end users are aware of the difference between "live" objects in the system and objects stored externally. There is value in hiding this distinction—imagine an avid solitaire player who wants to keep a "folder" of incomplete games. Ideally, the player would like to just pick a game and tell it to resume, dispensing with the extra conceptual baggage of live versus stored games.

For programmers, hiding the storage machinery makes programming less complex and avoids the need to learn a second language, such as SQL, for data access. Of course, someone has to program the data access functions, probably whoever creates a class such as `KlondikeGame`. But once it is written, other programmers can use the function without being aware of its existence.

There are several techniques for providing transparent access to stored persistent objects. They include lazy initialization, smart containers, smart pointers, and surrogate objects. As discussed below and in Chapter 13, these techniques can also provide transparent access to objects on remote servers.

Lazy initialization is a technique for delaying the fetching or materialization of stored parts of composite objects. As an example, take the Customer object shown in Figure 12-4 (page 346). A partial definition of the class might look like:

```
class CustomerAccount;
class Customer {
      private:
         char* Name, Address;
         int Customer-ID;
         CustomerAccount* account;
      . . . . .
};
```

Normally the constructor for Customer would instantiate the CustomerAccount for this customer at the time the Customer object was instantiated. It could be, though, that some applications only look at basic information such as name and address, and never reference account. To save the overhead of materializing it from the database, account can be initialized *only* when it is referenced:

```
CustomerAccount* Customer::getAccount() {
      if (account == NULL) initializeAccount();
      return account;
};
```

The private member function initializeAccount() does whatever is necessary to materialize the CustomerAccount object. This technique works in Smalltalk and C++, as does the next one, smart containers.

Smart containers Smalltalk and most C++ class libraries provide collection or container classes, such as Array, Set, Dictionary, etc. Enhanced with protocols for object creation and querying, they are good conceptual models for collections of objects stored on databases. Dictionary is a particularly good candidate, since it already supports storing objects with associated keys.

In Smalltalk, the protocol for retrieving an object—say, a customer—from a Dictionary instance looks like:

```
customerDictionary at: 'John Jones'
            ifAbsent: ["Error block"].
```

The error block contains code to be executed if the specified key does not exist. To create a dictionary of persistent objects, we need to supplement the code to fetch objects from a database:

```
Dictionary subclass: #PersistentDictionary
```

```
at: aKey ifAbsent: aBlock
    "Answer the object stored at aKey. Materialize from the
    database if necessary. Execute aBlock if not found."
    ^super at: aKey
        ifAbsent: [self databaseAt: aKey
            ifAbsent: aBlock].
```

The message to super returns the desired object if it is already in the dictionary. If not, databaseAt:ifAbsent: attempts to materialize it from the database, executing the application programmer's error block if it is not found.

Smart pointers C++ uses explicit pointers to objects, as in this example:

```
CustomerAccount* account;
. . . . .
if (account->balance() > 0) billCustomer(account);
```

CustomerAccount* is of type "pointer to CustomerAccount"; account-> *dereferences* the pointer to obtain the object. C++ pointers are simply storage addresses, but some object-oriented database systems[1] have introduced the idea of "smart pointers," which know whether an object is active or stored externally. When a smart pointer is dereferenced, it materializes (if necessary) the pointed-to object from external storage.

The O_2 system [Deux91] provides smart pointer classes o2_k, where k is the pointed-to class. Using this class, the example above would be coded:

```
o2_CustomerAccount account;
if (account->balance() > 0) billCustomer(account);[2]
```

Notice that except for the declaration of account, the change is transparent to the programmer. The need to have a specific pointer class for each pointed-to class is explained below.

Surrogate objects Smart pointers can be considered special cases of surrogate objects. These are directly accessible local objects that are proxies for objects stored on databases or residing on remote server machines. Ideally, users of surrogate objects can treat them as if they were fully materialized local objects. As in lazy initialization, the system will materialize them on demand when they receive a message.

In Smalltalk, no type checking is done until a message is actually sent to an object. If the object is of the wrong type, a protocol defined for all objects in class Object is invoked. It results in the object being sent the message:

[1] E.g., O_2 [Deux91] and GemStone [But91].

[2] This example also requires overloading the pointer dereferencing operator ->, a topic beyond the scope of this book.

```
doesNotUnderstand: badMessage.
```

The parameter badMessage is the message that was sent and not understood. The default behavior for doesNotUnderstand: is to simply raise a runtime error condition. This behavior can be overridden, allowing implementation of the following scheme:[1]

- A single class, ObjectID, is defined to act as a surrogate for other objects. Each instance of ObjectID contains a pointer (typically a database record ID) to its "real" object.
- ObjectID overrides doesNotUnderstand: in order to catch messages intended for its real (pointed-to) object.
- When an instance of ObjectID receives a message, it materializes its real object and resends the message to it.

Here is part of the implementation of ObjectID. DatabaseManager is a global variable referring to the system database manager:[2]

```
nil subclass: #ObjectID
    instanceVariableNames: 'oID realObject'
doesNotUnderstand: aMessage
    "Assume that aMessage is really for the receiver's
    real object."
    realObject isNil ifTrue: [
        realObject := DatabaseManager restore: oID].
    ^(aMessage receiver: realObject) perform.
```

In this scheme, surrogate objects can be almost completely transparent.

This will not work in C++, because a message (member function call) to the wrong object type is detected at compile time. We get around this by defining a specific surrogate type for each real type. The surrogate implements member functions whose signatures (names and argument types) are identical to those of the real objects. Each surrogate member function verifies that the real object is materialized, calls its corresponding member function, and returns the result. (The o2_k classes in O_2 are examples of this.) The definition of surrogate classes can be automated by preprocessing the C++ source code.

The "megadata" problem The solitaire game is an example of explicit visibility of persistence in a user interface. An important case where persistence accidentally (and undesirably) becomes visible has been christened "the megadata problem" by a colleague.[3] Systems like the TipTop example

---

[1] This roughly follows [Mal93].

[2] For the Smalltalk cognoscenti, this is more efficient if we add self become: realObject to the doesNotUnderstand: method. The nil superclass avoids "accidentally" understanding a message because it is inherited from class Object.

[3] Oliver Sims, of IBM UK.

in this chapter often contain very large numbers of objects. Large corporations, for example, may store thousands or even millions of `Customer` objects. In client-server and other distributed environments, most of the objects will be stored on machines remote from the user.

The combination of large object populations and remote storage makes transparency difficult to achieve. Even if remote objects are "functionally" transparent, the user may see variations in the responsiveness of objects. For example, opening a view on a `Customer` stored on the user's workstation might take one second, whereas the same view might take thirty seconds to open if the `Customer` were stored on a remote server.

Sometimes, we simply have to live with this problem. There are approaches, however, that can help to design around it. For example:

- There are algorithms in the database literature for preloading and caching objects based on the likelihood of their use.
- Surrogate objects and lazy initialization can provide basic information quickly without materializing large objects.

The second technique is particularly relevant to OOUIs because users often inspect object collections represented by lists or icons without opening detailed views. *Object handlers*, a specific technique for exploiting this, will be covered in Chapter 13. An example will be described in Chapter 15, where the objects are files containing digitized full-motion video.

These techniques are general and are used in object database management systems as well as the "roll your own" implementations shown here as examples. Besides persistence and transparency, databases have many other requirements that are beyond the scope of this book; they are addressed in commercial object database systems such as GemStone [But91] and ObjectStore [Lamb91].

Distributed Objects

So far the discussion of transparency has focused on live versus stored objects. The assumption was that once an object becomes live, all of its state and behavior exist on the same platform as any objects that communicated with it. In some situations, however, objects are never embodied on the local machine. Instead, a communications network passes method or function calls between objects.

Most platforms support some form of *remote procedure call* (RPC) [Laz93]. The idea is that a program calls what appears to be a local function or procedure, but is actually a *stub* that calls RPC routines to pass arguments to the real procedure. The real procedure, on a remote machine, uses the same process in reverse to return a result.

Figure 12-7 shows how RPC can be used to distribute the behavior of an object. Take as an example the image processing application mentioned in Chapter 11. Image display is done on a client machine, but we wish to use routines (such as a fast Fourier transform) that exist as ordinary programs or library routines on another machine. The client `Image` object

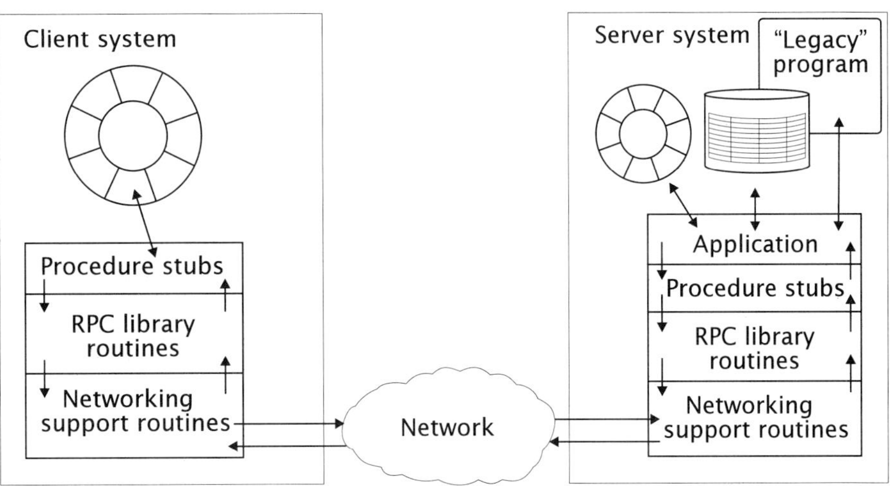

Figure 12-7 Distributed behavior via remote procedure calls

might have a member function FFT() that looks like:

```
Image* Image::FFT(); { // Return the Fourier transformed image.
        Image* newImage = new Image;
        char* bits = (char*) malloc(bitmapSize());
        copyBits(bits); // Copy the image bitmap.
        // Call the remote FFT function.
        newImage->setBits(remoteFFT(bits));
        return newImage;
}
```

The RPC library routines handle copying the bitmap across the network, invoking the remote procedure (which is unaware that its caller is remote), and returning the result.

This technique is applicable to Smalltalk also, with an extra level of indirection to call an external C function that calls the remote procedure. As shown in the figure, calls directed to a receiving program can invoke remote object services as well as programs.

Since every object method or member function looks like an ordinary function or procedure, a layer can be built on top of RPC to distribute complete objects, not just individual functions. This is shown in Figure 12-8. The client object, through an *object request broker* (ORB), instantiates what appears as a local object, but in fact is a surrogate for a remote object. Message passing is done through RPC.

The key to synthesizing the behavior of remote objects is an interface definition language (IDL) that defines the public interfaces of remote

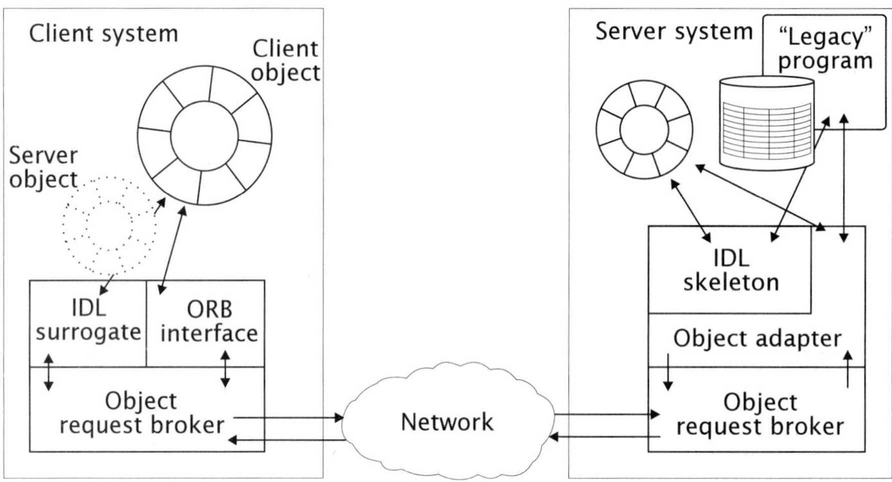

Figure 12-8 Distributed objects via object request broker (ORB)

object types. As an example, suppose we want to define a counter (like the example in Chapter 11) as a remote object. The IDL (on both local and remote machines) looks like:[1]

```
interface Counter { // counter.idl file
      void decrement();
      void increment();
      void reset();
      int getValue();       };
```

This looks very much like a C++ class definition, except that it only specifies the public interface for the class; no private functions or implementations are provided. On the server system, the IDL specifies method templates that describe how an ORB object adapter can access the interface. The interface can be implemented as a set of conventional programs, or by methods in objects.

Surrogate objects provided by an ORB can be created by the client using special ORB instantiation functions. Existing remote objects can be accessed using object references passed as strings. This example illustrates the client's use of an ORB to create a new counter and set it to the value of an existing counter:

```
#include "counter.idl"
copyCounter(char* counter_ref) {
      Counter *new, *old;
```

[1]The syntax is an approximation to the CORBA specification [Vino93].

```
        int count;
        old = ORB::string_to_objref(counter_ref);
        new = ORB::CounterNew();
        new->reset();
        for (count = old->getValue(); count < 0; count++)
              new->decrement(); // Decrement if old < 0
        for (count = old->getValue(); count > 0; count--)
              new->increment(); // Increment if old > 0
        return new;
}
```

The Object Management Group (OMG) has developed a standard for ORB services called the *common object request broker architecture* (CORBA) [Vino93]. As language bindings for CORBA in C++ and Smalltalk are developed and supported by class libraries, the complexity of dealing with ORBs will be hidden from application programmers. When this happens, well-structured information models will be more important than ever. Large models, written in several languages and distributed across heterogeneous networks, will be chaotic and unmaintainable otherwise.

12.3 Interfaces to Models

Information models communicate with other parts of the system through two major interface surfaces. One links the model to its views, the other links the model to its infrastructure. From a software engineering perspective, obvious benefits accrue from making these interfaces as clean as possible. From a user interface perspective, modular separation of the information model is essential if the implementation is to reflect a clear conceptual model.

Linking Models and Views

Information models are persistent, autonomous objects representing or simulating the state of problem domain entities. Views are transient relative to models. They are opened to display or manipulate models, and to change them in ways that become visible to other views.

Besides being changed directly by end users, a model's state may also be changed by events such as batch transactions, constraints imposed by business rules, or the expiration of time intervals. For example, the beginning of a new month may trigger TipTop's model to initiate the printing of reminder letters to customers who have not paid their bills. Ideally, if some facet of a model changes, views that are currently displaying that facet should be notified of the update.

Figure 12-9 shows how updates and changes might be communicated between a model and its views. The window labeled `Customer Information – John Jones` has three sub-windows. One shows basic information such as customer name, address, and telephone number. The second shows the customer's credit rating and related information. The third, on the right, shows detailed information on bills and payments; it also allows entry of data; for instance, the fact that a payment has been received from the customer.

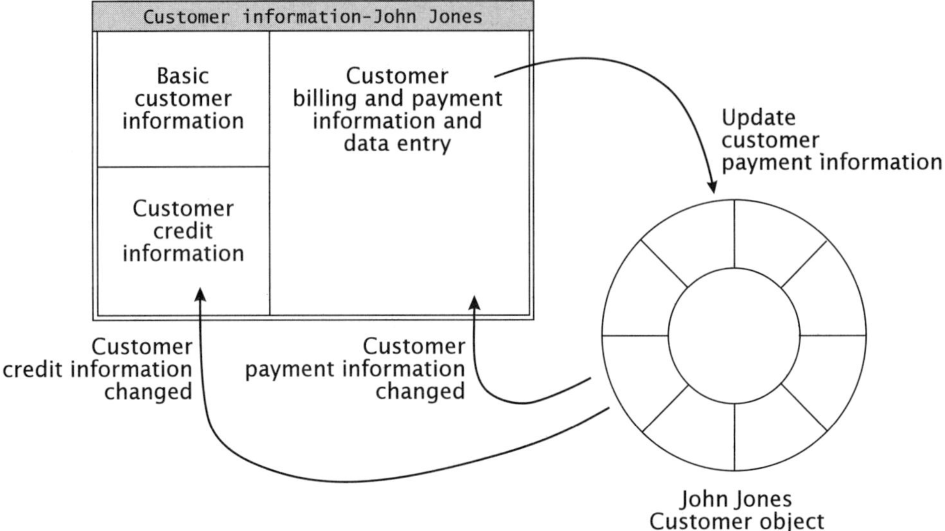

Figure 12-9 Dependency of a view on its model

Now suppose that a payment has been received, and it is entered. The view (or its controller) sends the payment information to the model, which changes its state as a result. The model then informs the view that changes have been made, which causes the view to obtain the updated information and display it. Two facets of the model that affect the view might change:

- Billing and payment information, such as payment history and the customer's current balance.
- Credit information; for instance, if the customer's credit rating is upgraded as a result of making a certain number of payments on time.

It might seem that the communication between the view and model could be simpler. Why, for example, can the view not go ahead and update its billing and payment information without waiting for the model to inform it that this facet has changed? After all, the view is the object that has initiated the change. This would be a mistake, for two reasons:

- Other events that the view is unaware of may be modifying the state of the model at the same time. For instance, the expiration of a time interval may trigger an interest charge that is added to the customer's balance.

- The view cannot, in general, know how its update will affect the state of the model. Perhaps, for example, the customer receives a 10% discount for a payment that is received more than 10 days before its due date.

Just as the view cannot anticipate the state changes of the model, the model cannot anticipate the presentation and interaction capabilities of its views. Its semantic content may be presented in many ways, for different users or for different purposes. The relative autonomy of models and views suggests a general purpose protocol for exchanging update requests and state changes between them. This results in better modularity, ease of maintenance, and models and views that are more reusable. It can also result in better performance, if views need to update only the portions of themselves that represent changed facets.

This picture of model-view interaction is very general, covering a many-to-many relationship between models and views in a distributed environment. In many cases, the situation is much simpler—a single view, designed to work with a specific model object that is never accessed by more than one view simultaneously. Smalltalk-80's MVC protocol exemplifies the general case. The MacApp framework illustrates a similar, but simpler, mechanism, designed for the more typical case.

MVC Dependency The counter example in Chapter 11 was a specific example of the Smalltalk-80 dependency protocol. Figure 12-10 shows the general flow of messages (somewhat simplified) in MVC. In MV architectures the classes `View` and `Controller` are combined, but the dependency portion of the protocol can be implemented in the same way.

The flow starts when a view is instantiated and the message `view openOn: model` is sent (typically by the object that represents the overall application). The view then registers itself as a dependent of the model, by sending `model addDependent: self`. The direction of this message reflects the fundamental point that the model is autonomous, and does not depend on the view. The view does depend on the model, since its mission in life is to provide a user interface for it.

The `addDependent:` method adds the view to a collection of dependent objects for the model. Any number of views may depend on a model and wish to be notified when the model's state changes.[1] Views might also want to send messages (not shown here) to indicate they are interested only in a certain facet of the model. This can improve performance in distributed systems, by eliminating messages to views that have not expressed interest in a facet that has changed.

[1] Actually, any object may depend on a model. This is useful in building layered models—higher layers can establish dependencies on lower layers.

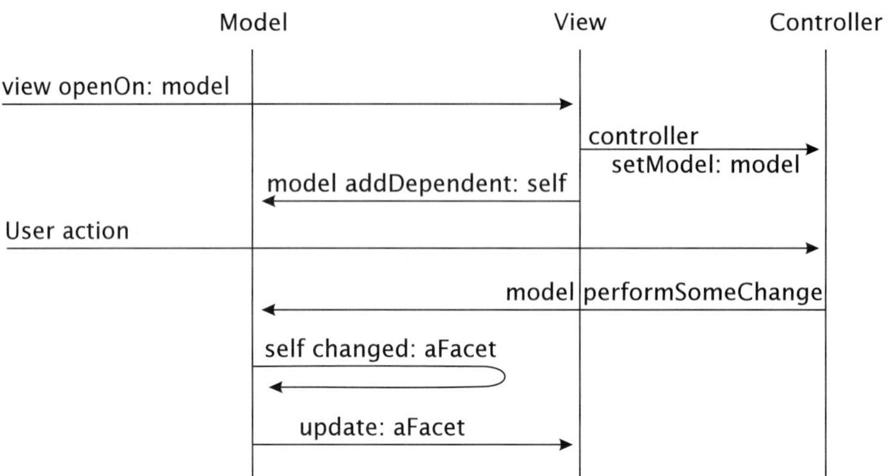

Figure 12-10 Interaction diagram for MVC dependency

Since there is a separate controller here, the view points it to the model. When the user performs an action that will change the model, the controller sends it the appropriate message. When the model changes its state, it sends `self changed: aFacet`. This invokes other processing (not shown in Figure 12-10) to send `update: aFacet` to all dependents of the model (or all dependents that have expressed interest in `aFacet`).

This is a case where the view needs to update itself to reflect a change it did not make. Here the change is made by its associated controller, but it could have been made by another view or by some external event. In any case, the view will send to the model whatever messages are required to update the portion of its presentation affected by `aFacet`.

Though this is a complex protocol, only a small part of it is implemented in specific model and view classes. The messages sent by the controller to update the model, and the messages sent by the view to update its presentation of the model, are application-specific. All the remaining messages are generic, and all are implemented in the abstract classes `Model`, `View`, `Controller`, and `Object`.

The MacApp approach Implementing the MVC dependency protocol in abstract classes reduces its complexity, but does not completely hide it. MacApp [Schm86] reduces the complexity, at the expense of generality, by focusing on a common application scenario. GUI applications such as word processing, spreadsheets, and graphical editors operate on information models that users think of as documents. Document processing is typically local to a single user, and views are specific to the document type.

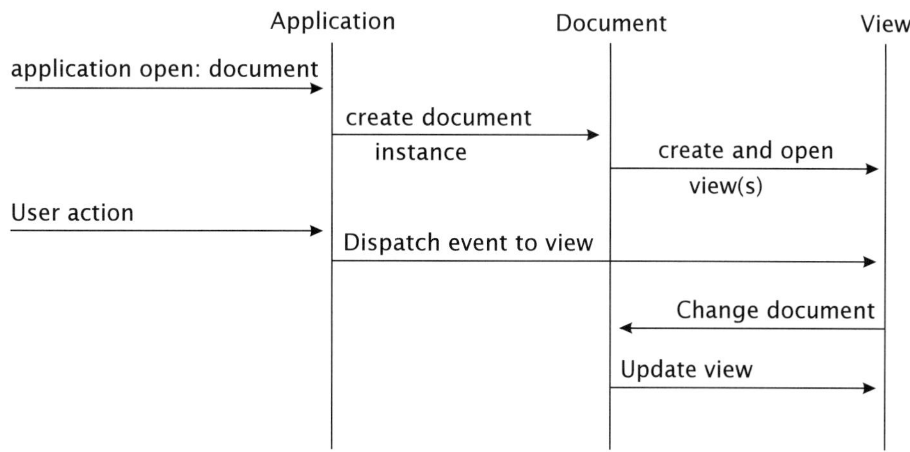

Figure 12-11 Interaction diagram for a MacApp application

In this kind of application, complex dependency protocols are not required, so MacApp and derivative frameworks do not use them. Figure 12-11 shows the general flow. The application is represented by an instance of `TApplication`, which has no analogue in MVC. The application contains the dispatch loop for user input events, which are sent to the appropriate view. Documents are instances of `TDocument`, which is similar to `Model` in MVC. Views are instances of `TView`.[1]

The key difference from MVC is that documents control their views. The user opens a document, which in turn opens its view or views. When the view closes, the document is also "closed," and reverts to its stored form. Since views are document-specific and controlled by their documents, the updating protocols are much simpler.

MVC-type dependency can be built on top of MacApp-style frameworks (the C++ counter in Chapter 11 is an example). MVC readily scales up to information models that have many autonomous views, to models that are active independent of their views, and to distributed objects; MacApp does not. On the other hand, many, perhaps the majority of, GUI applications are implemented in a style that is closer to MacApp than MVC. It is clearly a workable solution to many problems.

The lack of general dependency protocols in MacApp-style applications can be partially overcome by using object-linking capabilities provided by operating systems. Microsoft's *object linking and embedding* (OLE) is an example. Based on an underlying object system called the component object model (COM), OLE allows client documents to be composed from server objects that are either embedded in the document or accessed

[1]These MacApp classes are abstract; an actual application would define concrete subclasses of them. Changes to the document may be mediated by `TCommand` objects, not shown here (see [Schm86]).

through links. Links in several documents can refer to the same server object, thus establishing dependencies. OLE will, in the future, support distributed objects, as will the similar OpenDoc standard, being developed by a consortium of vendors [Way94a].

Language Pragmatics The generality of MVC requires that a model have a collection of all the objects (normally instances of `View` subclasses) that depend on it. Models and views send two kinds of messages to one another:

- Messages that are part of the general MVC protocol, which assume only that the receiver objects support the protocol.
- Messages that are specific to particular subclasses of `Model` and `View`.

In languages without compile-time type checking, such as Smalltalk, this is not problematic. Collections are untyped, so they can hold any type of object. The only requirement for views is that they understand the `update:` message at runtime.

In C++ and other languages with compile-time type checking, the situation is somewhat more complicated. Declared object types need to be generic, so they can be stored in common collections (for example, the collection of dependents of a model object). They also need to be specific, to call type-specific member functions. The `Counter` class in Chapter 11 was an example:

```
class Model {
      void changed() { . . .
. . .
class Counter : public Model { . . .
      void decrement() { . . .
```

The protocol to pass the counter to its view knows only that it is a `Model`; the view, however, must refer to it as a `Counter`, to call functions such as `reset()`. This requires some sort of typecast; in the example, the counter view class needed

```
CounterView :: Counter* model() { return (Counter*) pModel; }
```

whereas the same object was referred to as `Model*` in the abstract protocols. This sort of casting can be made safer using the runtime type identification extension to C++ [Str94]:

```
CounterView :: Counter* model() {
      if (Counter* c = dynamic_cast<Counter*>(pModel)) return c;
      else error("Error--model is not a Counter.");
}
```

The `if` statement returns true only if the real object type matches the cast.

Type systems should not discourage implementors from using generalized protocols. With care, classes can be designed to use dynamic binding and polymorphism without seriously compromising type safety. The effort will be rewarded with a more reliable and extensible system.

Linking Models and Infrastructure

The second major interface surface is between information models and the technical infrastructure of files, databases, communications software, etc. Though the details of these interfaces are beyond the scope of this book, user interface designers should be aware of some of the issues. Failure to cleanly separate model from infrastructure may result in infrastructure details becoming visible to end users—something that almost always detracts from the quality of the user interface.

As an example of an application where the separation between model and infrastructure is somewhat unclear, take the Klondike solitaire game. Only the `saveGame:` method (page 351) directly depends on the use of files to store solitaire games, though a search through all the `storeOn:` methods is needed to confirm this. There are also, however, indirect consequences of the decision to use files. The application will not allow arbitrary names for stored games, such as `MyLastSolitaireGame`—the system on which it is implemented (Microsoft Windows) requires file names to be eight characters or less, with a file extension of three characters or less. If the user specifies a nonexistent file for restoring a game, a runtime error window appears, providing diagnostic information that has no direct connection with the application.

Problems like this can be fixed, often at the expense of distributing infrastructure-dependent code throughout the application. This brings Reenskaug's point to mind again, about the difficulty of using the user interface to conceal design problems from the user. A better solution is to encapsulate infrastructure interfaces in schema objects that present a standard, infrastructure-independent interface to the information model.

A simple internal schema object for applications like the solitaire game might be an instance of a `DatabaseManager` class, satisfying the following requirements:

- The objects stored and retrieved by `DatabaseManager` instances are text streams.
- Stored objects are named with arbitrary character strings.
- `DatabaseManager` instances return a small set of standard codes indicating errors such as inability to retrieve an object. Applications are responsible for mapping these codes to messages that are meaningful in the application context.

`DatabaseManager` subclasses might support storage of objects on files, relational databases, network file servers, etc. This change would allow the solitaire application to deal with streams as before, but without the need to map text streams to and from the external file system.[1]

The interface to objects like `DatabaseManager` instances may be very direct. It can be less direct, as in the "smart containers" and "smart pointers" described above. An alternative to encapsulating interfaces in a separate class is to package them as methods in an abstract class to be inherited by classes that need them. This is particularly attractive in languages (such as C++) that support multiple inheritance; infrastructure interfaces can be inherited separately and privately.

Here is a sketch of inheritance of persistence for the solitaire game:

```
PersistentKlondikeGame :
        public KlondikeGame, private PersistentModel {
           public:
           // Recreate a stored game.
           PersistentKlondikeGame(char* nm) { . . . . . }
           private:
           // Return the game, flattened into a string.
           char* asString() { . . . . }
           // Set the name to identify this game.
           void setName(char* nm) { name = nm; }
           // Save the game.
           int saveGame() {
           // Invoke base class method to store game.
                 int errorCode = store(ClassName, name, asString())
                 if (!errorCode) return 0; // Stored OK.
                 else . . . // Handle error.
                 }
           static const char ClassName = "PersistentKlondikeGame";
                          char* name; // Game identifier.
                 . . . . .
```

The essential point is that methods such as `store()` are inherited from `PersistentModel`, which insulates the derived class from the details of the infrastructure interfaces.

Single-object applications An "architecture" that is common, particularly in small applications and prototypes, is to use only a single object, the view. The view goes directly to databases, files, etc. to get the data needed to present views of "objects" to the end user. A fragment from this sort of application, to display customer information, is shown here:

```
View subclass: #CustomerView
. . . . .
customerName
"Get name"
        ^self getNameFieldFromDatabase
```

[1]An alternative solution, using smart containers, is left to the reader—see Exercise 3.

```
getNameFieldFromDatabase
"Get the name field for the current customer."
      self getDatabaseRecordForKey: currentCustomer.
. . . . .
```

This approach may seem easy at first, particularly if the class library being used does not provide information model or schema classes. It suffers from major problems, though.

A good user interface requires a clean semantic model of the application domain. The lack of an information model in the implementation means the user interface code in the view must synthesize its appearance. For systems of any size, this is a difficult, if not impossible, task.

In addition, the software engineering benefits of modularity are lost with this approach. The view is dependent on low-level technical details that may change. There is no code reusability, since everything is application-specific. Over time, the view class gets larger, more complex, and more difficult to maintain or enhance.

12.4 Summary

From the user interface perspective, internal design of the information model has two main goals:

- To present a clear implementation of the objects and concepts in the user's conceptual model.
- To hide details of the "plumbing and wiring" from both users and application programmers.

Achieving these goals not only enhances the quality of the visible user interface, it makes the internal system components easier to understand and maintain, and more easily reusable.

Information models are usually composite, and have internal structure. They may have facets for specific applications, and layers that provide successively higher-level summary information. Analogous to the three-schema model for data, they have external schemas mapping from the model to end user views, and internal schemas mapping from the technical infrastructure to the model. Schemas in OO systems may be implemented as method (member function) categories, or as separate objects.

Objects in information models may have persistent forms on external storage (files or databases), and may be distributed over a network. User interface designers should understand enough about implementing these capabilities to appreciate the work required to hide the "plumbing and wiring" from end users.

Information models have two major interface surfaces to other parts of the system. One is to views and controllers that implement the visible user interface; the other is to the underlying technical infrastructure. Designing these interfaces well helps to insure:

- Reliability, maintainability, and extensibility of the system.
- Maximum reusability of the model, view, and controller objects.
- Portability, both across platforms and to new technology on the same platform.
- A user interface that performs well, reveals the information model structure, and hides details that users should not be aware of.

12.5 To Explore Further

Many of the concepts in this chapter germinated in my mind as a result of presentations by and conversations with Tom Morgan of the Brooklyn Union Gas Company. I am indebted to Tom for many insights into information modeling. The CRIS-II system, for which he was a principal designer, is described in [Dav93].

Information modeling, in the general sense, intersects a large part of the literature of knowledge-based systems, information science, and database systems, as well as that of OO analysis and design. [Coy90] discusses design based on knowledge. [Sow84] presents the philosophical and logical bases for many information modeling methods. [Ull80] and [Elm89] are two of many textbooks covering information modeling in non-OO database systems.

Information modeling (or *object modeling*) is central to OO analysis and design. [Rum91] especially emphasizes this. [Boo94] has an extensive bibliography of sources on OO analysis and design. Authors in the field vary in terms of the amount of attention they pay to data, function, and behavior.

Information modeling in the special sense in which it appears here and in [Gol90] is not treated explicitly in most of the literature. General object-modeling concepts and techniques are relevant and important, though not tied to MVC-type frameworks in texts such as [Boo94], [Rum91], and [Wir90]. [Jac92] does cover this aspect, and separates modeling of *interface* and *entity* objects.

[KimW90] is a good summary of issues in the field of object-oriented databases. *Communications of the ACM* 34, 10 (Oct. 1991) has a special section on "Next-Generation Database Systems." It is a good summary of current thinking on object persistence, and it describes several mature OODB systems. Some OODBMS, for example POET [Robi94], signal changes by generating events, thus facilitating remote MVC-type dependency protocols.

[Kun90] presents a general approach to mapping the state data for object classes to relational databases. [Prem90] describes an OODBMS system based on a relational sublayer. [Loo94] is a case study of the limitations of relational databases for storing complex object models.

Smalltalk-80 implements the most elaborate model-view dependency mechanism I am aware of, particularly in later releases [sPar92]. The mechanism can be implemented in other languages, and it is worth studying even if you do not implement all of it. [Gol90] is an overview; [Kras88] provides details, and [Lei92] is an update on recent enhancements. [Schm86] thoroughly explains the MacApp scheme, which has influenced most post-Smalltalk systems.

12.6 Exercises

1. How many examples can you find, from applications you use, where the user interface reveals unnecessary details of the technical infrastructure?
2. In OO systems, composite objects such as `KlondikeGame` instances use pointers to access their sub-objects. Relational databases do not support pointers. A case where, say, an `Employee` instance points to its `Department` instance is handled by the following relational table definitions:

EmpNumber	Name	Address	Salary	DeptNumber

DeptNumber	DeptName	Location	Manager

`DeptNumber` in the `Employee` table is a *foreign key* that maps to `DeptNumber` in the `Department` table. It is used to *join* the two tables, for instance in the following query that finds the location of John Jones's department:

```
SELECT Department.Location
FROM Employee, Department
WHERE Employee.Name = 'John Jones' AND
      Employee.DeptNumber = Department.DeptNumber
```

The `CustomerMailingInfo` example (page 353) did not need joins, because it had no component objects. What about the `KlondikeGame` example?

a. Based on Figure 5-5 in Chapter 5, list the relational tables needed to store solitaire games. Do you need a table for `Card`?

b. List pros and cons of storing solitaire games in relational tables versus flat files.

3. In the approach described on page 351 to make solitaire games persistent, all the information model objects were aware that they were storing on streams. Design a "smart container" class `KlondikeGameHolder` (along the lines of the one described on page 355) with the following properties:

   - `KlondikeGame` is the only class that is aware of `KlondikeGameHolder`.
   - `KlondikeGameHolder` does not duplicate information about the structure of a solitaire game that is already present in `KlondikeGame`.
   - Changing the infrastructure, for instance to use a database, requires changing only the `KlondikeGameHolder` class.

13

Presentation and Interaction Objects

Chapter 11 introduced architectural ideas for object-oriented systems, many motivated by the need to provide graphical object-oriented user interfaces in information-rich distributed systems. A key idea was *model-view-controlle*r (MVC), an implementation architecture corresponding to the three-way factoring of user interfaces into conceptual model, presentation language, and action language. Chapter 12 presented the model or *information model* of MVC, and discussed its interfaces with views and the implementation infrastructure.

This chapter expands on what was said about views and controllers in Chapter 11. *Presentation objects* are views or components of views that implement the presentation language. *Interaction objects* may be controllers, or they may be views (such as buttons, menus, or entry fields) that behave as virtual devices affording some user action. Interaction objects implement the action language. (Both kinds of components are often called *widgets.*)

In OOUIs, a great deal of the presentation language is directed at interactivity, at providing feedback that tells the user he or she is dealing with "real objects." This chapter emphasizes aspects of software structure that foster interactivity, since this is a topic that is not as well understood as static information presentation. The key points are:

- Trade-offs between closely coupling models and views, suggested by highly interactive interfaces, and the loose coupling that facilitates extensibility and software reuse.
- The pros and cons of MVC controllers and the components that substitute for them in MV frameworks.
- Software objects that extend controllers for encapsulating direct manipulation and other complex interaction techniques.

13.1 Components and Coupling

A goal of MVC is to reduce coupling between software objects, particularly the information model and its views and controllers. This makes presentation and interaction objects reusable across different applications, leading to high developer productivity, extensible applications, and consistent presentation and interaction techniques.

The counterargument to loose coupling is that tightly coupled components are easier to understand, faster, and highly optimized for particular applications. In recent years systems have become larger, users employ more applications, and there is a greater need for consistency and interoperability. These factors have swung the balance in favor of loose coupling, though the tension still remains.

User Interface Software Components

Chapter 14, *Tools for Prototyping and Implementation*, discusses specific component sets. Here we are mainly concerned with general characteristics of user interface widgets that affect the architecture of OOUI implementations.

Presentation and interaction objects in most systems are dependent on a window manager for receiving events and displaying themselves. Window managers also provide base or intrinsic widget classes, which are very much like OO classes, though typically written in the C language. Application programming interfaces (APIs) are provided for functions such as creating instances of widget classes and displaying them.

In principle, an OO application or system could rely on the window manager only to provide rectangular areas on the display and to signal events occurring within those areas. The OO system could then use the graphic services of the window manager to control the look and feel of its own widgets. In practice, almost all OO systems provide classes that "wrap" the platform's widgets. Advantages of this approach include:

- Automatic implementation of the appropriate platform style.
- Reuse of code, graphical elements, and design work from the base widget set.
- The ability to quickly support new platform widgets, or new versions of existing widgets.

Figure 13-1 shows the general scheme for using base widgets. A widget is defined in OO terms by events it generates and API calls corresponding to messages it can receive. The OO system includes a message dispatcher that handles the incoming events and an object that encapsulates the API for one or more widget classes.[1] The OO class that wraps the widget includes private code to interface with the window manager (di-

[1] The message dispatcher and API objects were shown in gray in Figure 11-2 (Chapter 11), and referred to as the *display manager* sublayer.

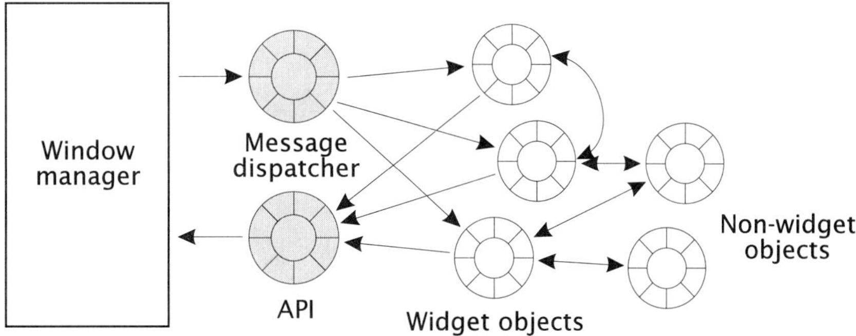

Figure 13-1 Interfaces between the window manager and OO widget objects

rectly or through an API object), and public methods for message passing between widgets and other objects.

For portability and ease of maintenance, it is good practice to localize code that interfaces with the window manager. This also facilitates providing high-level abstractions to programmers, rather than constructs based on a particular window manager. Window manager interfaces are usually based on C, and they can be called directly from any C++ member function. Consequently, discipline is needed in C++ class libraries to follow this localization practice.

Smalltalk systems need interlanguage communication modules to talk to the window manager, so of necessity they provide more code localization. Smalltalk/V for Windows [sDig92a], for example, supplies a `DynamicLinkLibrary` class, whose subclasses package various operating system and window manager APIs. An example API, for obtaining the position of the mouse cursor, is:

```
getCursorPos: aByteArray
    <api: GetCursorPos struct short>
```

Though localized, this is still platform-dependent; the parameter `aByteArray`, for example, supplies a window manager control block to receive the cursor location point. Normally, a programmer would use the platform-independent message `Cursor sense`. This in turn issues the platform-dependent message (`getCursorPos:` in the case of Microsoft Windows).

An example of an encapsulated platform widget is the following: Users often need to locate or specify files representing objects they need. GUI platforms all provide some sort of standard dialogue component for opening files. Figure 13-2 shows a sample file opening dialogue from OS/2.

This dialogue window is complex, containing a text entry field for the file name, drop-down lists for file type and drive, scrolling lists for file

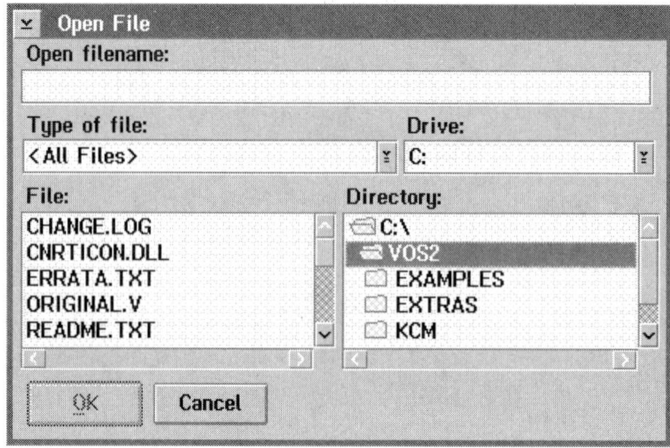

Figure 13-2 A file opening dialogue window

names and directories, and `OK` and `Cancel` buttons. The appearance of the window conforms to the CUA style, and OS/2 provides an API for instantiating this window. Whereas building this widget from primitive components could take hundreds of lines of code, the platform widget can be instantiated with one line:

```
filename := FileDialog new file.[1]
```

The `FileDialog` class is a wrapper for the platform widget. Sending `file` to the instance issues a synchronous call that returns when the user dismisses the dialogue by pushing one of the buttons. The variable `filename` is set to the file name string if `OK` is pushed, or to `nil` if the user pushes `Cancel`.

Generality and Coupling

File opening dialogues illustrates a tension between the close component coupling that facilitates highly interactive interfaces, and the loose coupling that facilitates extensibility and software reuse. The file dialogue in Figure 13-2 is highly reusable, because there is nothing application-specific about it. It is coupled to its using object only by the semantics of the `filename` variable.

Graphical editors and image processing applications often use file dialogues that are optimized for opening graphic or image files. Whereas the dialogue of Figure 13-2 can be used for any file, these have many features (such as sub-windows for visually previewing files) specialized for one particular type of file. Once learned, these dialogues are more useful to users of graphical or image editors; but they take longer for the user to learn and longer for the programmer to create.

[1] This example is from Digitalk Smalltalk/V.

Specificity at high levels may result from composition of general low-level components—the graphic file dialogues use many of the same components as the one in Figure 13-2 (drop-down lists, text entry fields, and so forth). If the composition is sensibly packaged as a reusable component, it offers a reasonable compromise—not quite as easy as the "one size fits all" approach, but more flexible.

Coupling between model and view Chapter 11 emphasized the importance of separating the semantics of an application from presentation and interaction. Experience with MVC shows that this decoupling leads to more component reusability. The protocols needed for decoupling, however, add complexity for small problems.

A simple graphical editor is one example of a class of problem in which it is tempting to bundle some aspects of presentation into the model objects. Imagine a "paint" program where simple elements such as lines, circles, and rectangles can be drawn on a bitmapped "canvas." An MV implementation might have the following classes:

- `Canvas` is the model class for drawings. A `Canvas` instance contains a collection of `PictureElements`.
- `PictureElement` is the model class for the elements of a drawing. It has subclasses for each element type, such as `Line`, `Circle`, and `Square`.
- `CanvasView` is the view class for drawings. It has a collection of subviews, one for each displayed `PictureElement`.
- `PictureElementView` instances draw individual elements on the canvas. It has subclasses corresponding to the subclasses of `PictureElement`.

Figure 13-3 shows a composition diagram for the application. The fine-grained MV separation introduces some complexity into a superficially simple problem. First, the `CanvasView` must interrogate each `PictureElement` to create the proper subview. Second, the dependency relationships are complicated. If the `CanvasView` simply depends on the `Canvas`, and redraws itself completely after any change, poor performance will result. Having each `PictureElementView` depend only on its corresponding `PictureElement` is efficient, but too simplistic. The `CanvasView` needs to be involved to redraw elements that overlay the changed element.[1]

Though logicians may disagree, for most people entities like squares and circles have visual properties that are intrinsic. `PictureElement` reinforces this by having properties such as `lineType` and `color`. A simpler design might place the behavior of drawing on a `CanvasView` in the

[1] Details are left as an exercise (see Exercise 4). The redrawing issues crop up regardless of the design that is chosen.

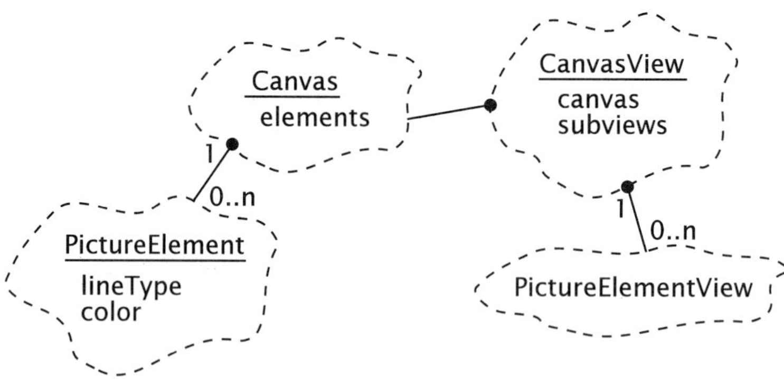

Figure 13-3 Composition diagram for a drawing editor

PictureElement itself. For the sort of shapes we are dealing with here, the drawing code is trivial, as this example for class Rectangle shows:

```
drawOn: aCanvasView
"Draw the receiver rectangle on aCanvasView."
      aCanvasView graphicTool goTo: self corner;
                              foreColor: self color;
                              setLineType: self lineType;
                              boxOfSize: self extent.
      aCanvasView invalidateRect: self boundingBox.
```

(The invalidateRect: message forces any overlapping picture elements to be redrawn.)

This design is plausible, and it is found as an example in the OO literature.[1] It is simple, but it may not scale up. The code in drawOn: is platform-dependent and therefore non-portable. Suppose the geometry of interest is not simple shapes, but complex machine parts generated in a CAD/CAM system? In such cases, portable models are often required, and managing complex model and view code in the same object is difficult. Nevertheless, there is no "right" solution for all cases. Where the shapes are simple and portability is not required, the simpler design may be preferable.

An objection sometimes raised against either one of these object-oriented solutions is the performance overhead of message passing (or member function calls) between many fine-grained objects. This overhead is small, and avoiding it requires conditional statements (branching on the object type to be drawn) that often introduce as much overhead as message passing. The work of Calder and Linton on *glyphs* (lightweight display

[1] See, e.g., [Mey88], Section 10.1; [Schm86], Chapter 8. Unidraw [Vlis90] is a good example of a framework that adheres to model-view separation, even for fine-grained components.

objects) [Cal90] is a good example of an OO system that couples large numbers of small objects without incurring a performance penalty.

Figure 13-4 summarizes aspects of the trade-off between generality and specificity. They apply to both externals and internals. The standard presentation and interaction styles are designed for reusability across multiple applications and users, in the same sense as OO code. Though conventional wisdom in software engineering falls on the side of generality, there are trade-offs. Working these out requires close cooperation between external designers, software architects, and programmers.

Generality	Specificity
Low coupling, good modularity	Models and views are coupled
Reusability of models and views	Harder to reuse models and views
Consistent cross-application presentation and interaction styles	Presentation and interaction styles optimized for application
Example: Smalltalk-80 MVC	Example: most "conventional" applications

Figure 13-4 The tension between generality and specificity in user interface components

Adapting Interfaces

A potent argument for loose coupling of user interface components is the need to support multiple interfaces for a single application. This may be required to accommodate users with differing abilities, to market an application internationally, or to allow tailoring for different work environments.

In most user interfaces presentation objects are visual, and interaction objects use standard techniques based on mouse and keyboard. These may not always be appropriate. Users with certain disabilities will never find them usable. Even "normal" users may not be able to use them in some contexts—for example, in "hands-off" or "eyes-off" applications.

Interfaces like the "audio GUIs" discussed in Chapter 9 (Section 9.6) have obvious implementation possibilities in an OO environment with separation of models and views. We simply create views and subviews that display to senses other than sight. For example, using a hypothetical speech output interface, the `drawOn:` method above could be recoded as:

```
drawOn: aView
"Present the receiver rectangle using speech."
      speechGenerator speechFromString:
       'rectangle at ' self corner asString,
```

```
    ' colored ' self color asString,
    ' line style' self lineType asString,
    ' diagonal extent ', self extent asString.
```

Conceptually, this is a simple extension to the design with a PictureElementView class—CanvasView can be parameterized with the name of a class whose instances will function polymorphically like PictureElementView instances. That is, they will respond to messages like drawOn: by presenting the appropriate display behavior. In practice, the situation is a little more complicated; for instance, when using speech output we may want the elements to display themselves only when pointed to, not whenever the window is exposed. In any case, this is easier than retrofitting speech output to an interface without modular view components.

Just as loosely coupled views are ideal for implementing multiple output modalities, loosely coupled controllers can accommodate special needs or preferences on the input side. This controller was given in Chapter 11 as an example of processing keyboard input:

```
controlActivity
"If the user has pressed a key, process it."
   [sensor keyboardPressed]
         whileTrue:
           [self processCharacter: sensor keyboard].
```

In a SpeechRecognitionController class this could be modified to process spoken input. Supposing the unit returned by the speech recognizer is a string representing an utterance, we might have:

```
controlActivity
"If the user has spoken, process the utterance."
       | string |
   (string := speechSensor inputString) notNil ifTrue: [
         string do: [ : eachChar |
                               self processCharacter: eachChar]].
```

This is similar to what is done "under the covers" by many commercial speech recognition products. Applications operate in a normal way; spoken input is translated by the recognizer into window manager events such as keystrokes and menu selections.

Internationalization also argues for modularity and loose coupling. Separation of translatable resources, such as text and icons, from the code that uses them is a first step. More difficult is the separation of object behavior that will change from culture to culture. Examples include time, date, and number formats, currency symbols, and the sorting order of characters.

Features of Digitalk's Smalltalk/V for Microsoft Windows [sDig92a] and OS/2 [sDig92b] illustrate how object-oriented systems can facilitate internationalization. Both systems provide classes and new behaviors that work with operating system facilities for national language support.

The class `NationalLanguageSupport` has a single instance, which is a repository of information and services. It provides an interface to the platform environment to obtain the language, keyboard type, date and time formats, and so forth, and it uses this information to provide services used by other classes. For example, the sorting order of characters may vary for different languages. Methods for class `Character`, such as < and <=, use `NationalLanguageSupport`, which maintains a collating table for all the characters in the current language.

Behavior is added to classes `Character`, `String`, and `FileStream` to transparently support the appropriate sorting order and format for different languages. This includes support for languages, such as Japanese, that use double-byte characters. The `Number`, `Date`, and `Time` classes are enhanced to support culture-dependent formatting. (For example, March 17, 1994 prints as `03/17/94` in the United States, and as `17/03/94` in Europe.)

The class `StringDictionaryReader` is provided to create dictionaries of translatable text strings from resource library modules. Dictionaries help avoid embedding language-dependent text in program source code. Suppose, for instance, the text label on a button is being set. Instead of writing

```
aButton label: 'Cancel'.
```

we can write

```
aButton label: (StringDictionary at: #buttonTextCancel)
```

If `StringDictionary` is loaded from a resource module, providing a new module at run time automatically changes the language for all messages and labels.

The power of object-oriented programming in this area is that supporting different languages and cultures no longer requires complex decision logic in programs. Polymorphic objects can simply implement the appropriate behavior for the given environment. Even complex objects such as right-to-left text editing windows are manageable with this philosophy.

Some people believe that the ultimate in usability is a user interface like the perfect butler—unobtrusive, but attentive to your every need. Achievement of interfaces that automatically adapt to user needs, however, will require breakthroughs in artificial intelligence technology that are probably years away. Meanwhile, simpler alternatives are quite feasible, and can make life easier for most users. *Adaptable* means "capable of adapting or being adapted." The first part of the definition is difficult to actualize, but the second part is achievable through careful attention to software structure. Software modularized on the basis of human capabilities can easily be changed to adapt to variations in these capabilities.

13.2 Interaction and Feedback

Though presentation and action are separable, their meaning comes from a context of ongoing interaction between the user and the computer. Some of the thorniest problems in "computer graphics" are those of interaction—how to respond appropriately to user actions.

As discussed in Chapter 10, the cycle of action and response occurs at several time scales, ranging from milliseconds to tens of seconds. Many operations in OOUIs require feedback at more than one scale. Immediate feedback is given while selecting operands and an action; after the action is complete, updates to the display reflect changes caused by the action. The objects that implement actions thus have certain aspects unique to OOUI environments, and certain aspects that are similar to operations in command languages.

Interaction and Commands in OOUIs

Most user actions in OOUIs involve some form of direct manipulation, involving continuous feedback. Once completed, however, they are semantically equivalent to command execution. Scrolling illustrates this. Figure 13-5 shows a text editing window with horizontal and vertical scroll bars. Scroll bars on different platforms have different "looks," but they all afford the same operations (described here for vertical scrolling):

- Clicking the mouse on the up or down arrows.
- Clicking the mouse in the area between the "thumb bar" (also called the scroll box or scroll knob) and the up or down arrows.
- Pressing the mouse button while over the thumb bar, moving the mouse, then releasing the button.

These actions are semantically equivalent to commands like these, communicated by events or callbacks to the window owning the scroll bar widget:

```
textWindow lineUp.
```

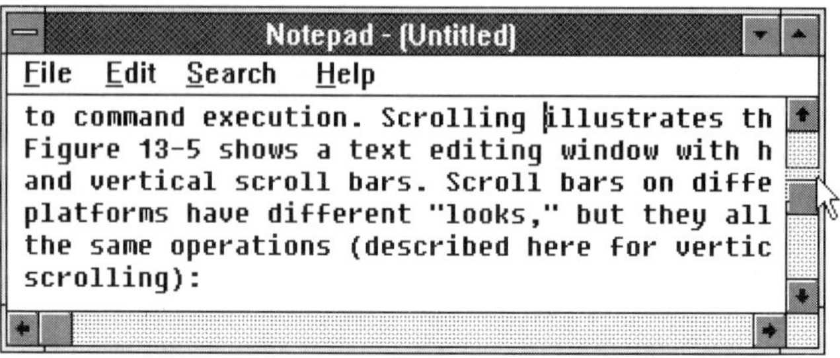

Figure 13-5 Scroll bar interaction

```
textWindow pageUp.
textWindow scrollTo: aPercentage.
```

The parameter aPercentage reflects the action of moving the thumb bar; The window is moved to a location in the text corresponding to the percentage of the scroll bar length above the thumb bar (or to the left if it is a horizontal scroll bar).

Once a scrolling operation is completed, the result is indistinguishable from a hypothetical case where a user actually typed the commands shown above. The syntax of entering a "command," however, is markedly different. Combining lexical parts into meaningful commands normally implies the possibility of invalid combinations. Most OOUIs have few, if any, syntactically invalid combinations. A series of motions may fail to accomplish its intent, for example if a user clicks on an inert part of the display; but the failure is known only to the user, who does not get the expected result.

The MacApp framework explicitly relies on semantic equivalence of user actions and commands directed at objects. The user action of picking a menu item causes DoMenuCommand to be sent to the document (an instance of TDocument).[1] The document does not directly change itself, but creates an instance of a subclass of TCommand. Each application-specific command has its own subclass. Sending the message doit to a TCommand effects the change in the document.

TCommand subclasses provide a uniform interface for changing the model, and may be reusable across different models. In one sense, they represent an alternative factoring of the user interface. Controllers in MVC understand physical interaction techniques as well as the semantics of actions on their models. MacApp places the physical interaction in TEvtHandler subclasses such as TView and TDocument, and the semantics of the action in TCommand. TCommand instances also differ from controllers in that they are transient—created to perform a specific action and then deleted.

Undoable commands One of the most useful aspects of TCommand, and a prime motivator for its creation, is its ability to support reversible commands. The effects of scrolling and other commands directed at views are easily undone by the user, simply by reversing the original actions. Commands that delete or permanently modify model objects are not. As anyone who has observed novice users knows, the fear of doing damage makes them reluctant to explore and discourages learning.[2] Providing a facility to undo the results of previous actions encourages novice learning; it also allows experts to work faster, since mistakes can be easily corrected.

[1] The target for menu events can be dynamically set to be the TDocument, TView, or TApplication subclass; TDocument is the normal default (see [Schm86]).

[2] Observation of users also shows that "command objects" are not artificial. Statements like "I did a *delete*, and now I want to undo *it*" (italics added) indicate that commands as objects are part of users' mental models.

To be most useful, such a facility should be able to undo an arbitrary number of previous actions.

Saving the state of affected model objects whenever they are changed is a "brute force" approach to undoing, usually impractical because of the storage required. A simpler and more efficient object-oriented approach is based on "objectification" of commands. Instances of classes modeling command types (such as `TCommand`) can save exactly the amount of information needed to undo (or redo) the given command. For example, suppose the user moves a graphic object in the "canvas" application described on page 377. The equivalent command (which we can call a `MoveCommand`) is:

```
aCanvas move: aPictureElement to: aPoint
```

An instance of `MoveCommand` needs to contain a pointer to the `PictureElement` instance affected, and two points giving the "from" and "to" locations for the move. This information suffices to undo the command (or redo it after an undo). Most commands have similarly simple inverses, and command instances can be placed on a stack to support *n*-level undo. Irreversible commands can warn the user before they execute, and implement an `undo` method that outputs a message indicating no undo is possible.

Commands and controllers Controllers can be defined as objects that translate event sequences into commands. They differ, however, from command language parsers. Since controllers are usually associated with visible objects, the main paradigm for command generation is *object selection.* There are two kinds of selection sequences. The first is:

1. Select the object(s).
2. Select the action.

This is often simplified by implicit object selection. In double-clicking on an icon to open it, for example, the action implicitly selects the object by virtue of the pointer position. Step (2) is simplified by that fact that once an object is selected, the user sees only the set of syntactically valid operations. Buttons such as the up and down arrows present the simplest possible case. Object selection is implicit, and the set of valid actions is a singleton; one "atomic" gesture thus executes the command.

The second selection sequence is:

1. Select the objects(s).
2. Select an object with an implied action (message) that takes the first selection as a parameter.

This sequence is often implemented by drag and drop—dragging the object(s) accomplishes the first step, dropping them on another object accomplishes the second. Examples are dragging documents to a printer icon, or to the trash. Drag-drop is complicated by the fact that the set of valid operations is determined not by one object, but by two.

Objects like scroll bars and menus are more or less permanent fixtures on the display. Controllers can also be transient, used to gather properties or parameters and then deleted. The standard file dialogue shown on page 376 is an example; it exists just long enough to obtain the user's input. Controllers for more complex interactions, such as drag-drop, can also be transient. The general idea is that controllers process in a thread that looks like:

```
BEGIN
  Set up and initiate command processing
  Form complete command
  Execute command
END
```

Where several command threads contain common processing, a controller class may be defined to embody it. `MouseMenuController` in Smalltalk-80, for example, contains logic common to all pop-up menu operations. `MouseMenuController` is an example of a controller that, once instantiated, is invoked many times, and thus it is permanently associated with its view. Infrequently used controllers, such as `FileDialog`, are instantiated only when necessary.

Controllers in Smalltalk-80 have two functions. One is to be part of the basic event polling loop, using methods such as `controlActivity`. In most other systems this is delegated to the operating system window manager. The second function is to generate commands from event sequences, and this remains in all OO frameworks used for OOUIs. Command generation has two phases. The first is to translate of a sequence of events, such as *mouseMove/leftButtonDown/leftButtonUp*, into a higher level event such as *upArrowPushed*. The second phase is to send a message associated with the event, such as `textWindow lineUp`, to effect a change in the controlled object.

Most controllers have visual properties. Except for keyboard shortcut commands or speech recognition, every user action directly involves a tangible object on the display—a menu, button, moving cursor, etc. Widgets such as buttons and menus include the first phase of command generation; they may also partially handle the second phase, by being parameterized with the message or callback function used to notify the controlled object. The main window owning the button or menu usually has some role in translating widget events into commands to itself or its model.

Combining Looks and Feels

There is a disadvantage to involving the window owning a control widget in translating events into commands. A variety of interaction techniques might be designed for the same information presentation—typing commands, function keys, pointing at objects and menus with a mouse, voice commands, etc. To adapt the interface to different users, or simply to test different techniques, it may be desirable to freely interchange them. Since the semantics of control can be expressed in commands that are independent of particular techniques, this ought to be feasible.

"Plugging in" different interaction techniques is simple in MVC. Models provide semantics-based interfaces that are independent of user interface details. `Controller` subclasses encapsulate interaction techniques by handling basic events such as keystrokes, instantiating control widgets, and handling their events. Controllers can be composite objects, built from subcontrollers to implement a full suite of interaction techniques for applications such as text and graphics editors.

Where control functions are integrated into views, pluggability is lost. The price paid for relegating event polling to window managers is that a single stream of events is generated, which includes control events such as keystrokes along with other events related only to the view. The single event stream encourages a programming style in which all events are funneled through a single handler—the view. In this situation, the only way to change interaction techniques is to selectively recode view functions that handle control events.

To illustrate this concretely, some aspects of interaction design are presented below in a more elaborate version of the counter example from Chapter 11. Recall that the information model (an instance of `Counter`), is controlled by the messages `decrement`, `increment`, and `reset`; it answers its value for display in response to `getValue`.

A Smalltalk/V Counter Suppose we want to provide keyboard and menu interaction as alternatives for the user interface, using Smalltalk/V (the structure of the example would be similar for typical C++ class libraries). There is no `Controller` class, so the code to support both interaction styles goes into the view. A parameter and conditional test are added to control which technique is used.

Here is the only class in the example, the view.[1] The `controlTechnique` instance variable selects the interaction technique to be used:

```
GraphPane subclass: #CounterTextView
  instanceVariableNames: 'controlTechnique'
controlTechnique: aSymbol
"Set the receiver's interaction style (#menu or #keyboard)."
   controlTechnique := aSymbol.
```

The next three methods are roughly the same as in the Smalltalk-80 example in Chapter 11.

```
openOn: aCounter
"Open the receiver for viewing aCounter."
```

[1] Smalltalk/V programmers may find the subclassing of `GraphPane` a little unorthodox; I did this to maintain the same structure as in the Smalltalk-80 example in Chapter 11.

```
   | topPane |
   self model: aCounter.
   topPane := TopPane new label: 'Counter'.
   topPane addSubpane: self.
   topPane openWindow.
   topPane activeTextPane: self. "Set keyboard focus."
update: aCounter
"The counter has been updated, update the view."
   ^self display.
displayWindow
"Display the value of the counter."
   | box point |
   box := self insetDisplayBox.
   point := box origin + (box extent // 3).
   self pen displayText: self model getValue printString
                          at: point.
```

Methods that were in the class CounterMenuController in the MVC example are now in the view. The ifFalse: [^self] in initialize exits the method if the popup menu interaction style is not being used:

```
initialize
"Initialize the popup menu for controlling the counter."
   super initialize.
   self controlTechnique = #menu ifFalse: [^self].
   self menu: (
       Menu new labels: #('Increment' 'Decrement' 'Reset')
                 lines: #()
             selectors: #(increment decrement reset)).
```

If the popup menu is created, selection of menu items invokes the same methods that were in CounterMenuController:

```
decrement
"Decrement the counter."
   self model decrement.
increment
"Increment the counter."
   self model increment.
reset
"Reset the counter."
   self model reset.
```

The characterInput: method implements the second interaction technique, keystroke commands. This corresponds to processCharacter: in the MVC example in Chapter 11. Event polling in the controlActivity

keyboard events for main windows. The most efficient place to handle events is in the system or application event dispatcher, but its source code may not be available for modification.

The event dispatcher sends a separate message to views for each event type, so an alternative is to override the methods or member functions that process these messages. In typical systems, this means overriding or modifying about two dozen methods. Two examples are given here, in C++ and in Smalltalk. They are again based on the counter.

A C++ example This first example uses Borland ObjectWindows for C++, as in Chapter 11. The class `Model` is the same. Class `View` is modified to maintain a pointer to a `Controller` instance, and to pass events to it. This example uses a keyboard controller to interact with a counter, and only shows the `WMChar` (keyboard character input) event. A complete implementation would forward all mouse and keyboard events.

```
class Model{
  . . . . // Same as Chapter 11 example. };
class View: public TWindow {
  protected:
    Model* pModel;
    Controller* pController;
    // Derived classes should override for appropriate
    // controller type.
    virtual Controller* controller() {
         return NULL; }
    void initController() {
      pController = controller();
      if (pController) {// If not NULL
             pController->setModel(pModel);
             pController->setView(this); }
  public:
   // Set the model for this view.
    void setModel(Model* pm) {
      pModel = pm;
      initController(); }
      virtual void update() { };
    virtual void WMChar(RTMessage Msg) {
         if (pController) // If not NULL
              pController->processCharacter(Msg.WP.Lo);
      // Overrides for other control events . . . . . }
};
```

The `Controller` class is added here:

```
class Controller {
```

```
  protected:
    Model* pModel;
    View* pView;
  public:
    // Set the model for this controller.
    void setModel(Model* pm) { pModel = pm; }
    // Set the view for this controller.
    void setView(View* pv) { pView = pv; }
    // Keyboard character input event.
    virtual void processCharacter(char c) { }
    // Other keyboard and mouse events . . .
       . . . . . . .
};
```

The class Counter, derived from Model, is unchanged from the Chapter 11 example. CounterTextView has two changes. The member function WM-Char() is missing, since the logic for processing characters and changing the Counter is now in the processCharacter() function of CounterKey-boardController. An instance of CounterKeyboardController is returned by the controller() function in CounterTextView.

```
class Counter: public Model {
  . . . . // Same as Chapter 11 example. };
class CounterTextView : public View {
  protected:
   Counter* model() { // Answer the model.
      return (Counter*) pModel; }
   Controller* controller() {
      return new CounterKeyboardController; }
  public:
       void update() {  // Update the display.
      . . . . // Same as Chapter 11 example. }
       void Paint(HDC PaintDC, PAINTSTRUCT _FAR & PaintInfo) {
      . . . . // Same as Chapter 11 example. }
       void display(HDC DC) {  // Display the counter value.
      . . . . // Same as Chapter 11 example. }
};
class CounterKeyboardController : public Controller {
  protected:
    Counter* model() {   // Answer the model.
      return (Counter*) pModel; }
  public:
    void processCharacter(char c) {
      if ( c == '+') model()->increment();
```

```
        if ( c == '-') model()->decrement();
        if ( c == '0') model()->reset();
    }
};
```

The overall logic is now just as in MVC. CounterTextView collaborates with Counter only to obtain its value for the display; CounterKeyboardController modifies the counter, letting the dependency mechanism take care of sending update() to the view.

A Smalltalk/V example A larger example is a reimplementation of the counters in Figure 13-6 with controllers. Typical non-controller solutions (like the one described starting on page 386) have a single class that contains all the view and control logic. A particular combination of display and interaction techniques is obtained by opening a CounterWindow instance with appropriate parameters.

The implementation with controllers has a view class CounterView with two subclasses, CounterTextView and CounterDialView. Corresponding to various interaction techniques are the classes CounterButtonController, CounterDMController, CounterKeyboardController, CounterMenuController, and CounterMouseController, all subclasses of Controller. As an example of their use, the following expression opens a counter view with dial display and menu interaction:

```
(CounterDialView new controllerClass: CounterMenuController)
        openOn: Counter new.
```

The code in this implementation follows the same general scheme as in the C++ example. The Smalltalk/V class Window (equivalent to TView in the C++ example) receives events from the system dispatcher. Here is an example showing how the event handling is modified for the wmRbuttonup event (right mouse button released):

```
wmRbuttonup: wordInteger with: longInteger
"Private - Process the right button up event."
        self sendInputEvent:
                (self controller notNil
                        ifTrue: [#button2UpMVC:]
                        ifFalse: [#button2Up:])
          with: ((WinPoint new:4) uLongAtOffset: 0
                    put: longInteger) asPoint.
        ^nil.
```

If a controller is present, button2UpMVC: is invoked to pass it the event:

```
button2UpMVC: aPoint
"Private - Right button released."
        ^self controller button2Up: aPoint.
```

A CounterMenuController handles this event by popping up a menu:

```
button2Up: aPoint
"Tell the view to do popup menu."
    self view doPopupMenuAt: aPoint.
```

As in the Smalltalk-80 example in Chapter 11, the controller creates the menu, but here it asks the view to pop the menu up. This is to allow for views without controllers, the normal case in Smalltalk/V. The code that accesses the menu in the view is modified to get it from the controller if there is one:

```
menu
"Private - Answer the popup menu for the pane."
self controller notNil ifTrue: [
      ^self controller menu].
"Normal processing if no controller. . ."
. . . . . . .
```

When these changes are made in class Window for all events of interest to controllers, and the Controller class itself is implemented, Smalltalk/V applications can be designed in a "pure" MVC style.

Once the base code was added to support the Controller class (about 500 lines), the two views and five controllers for the counter example totaled 395 lines of Smalltalk code. This is about the same as the code required for the original monolithic counter application (367 lines). The largest single instance of the MVC style counter is the dial display with direct manipulation interaction—this totals 295 lines.

In this example the use of composition to build an application, versus monolithic code with conditional logic, makes for a simpler structure. In addition, because they are smaller and more general, the components are reusable. The example was specifically chosen because it cries out for pluggable controllers, and many applications will not fit this model. Nevertheless, controllers are valuable additions to the developer's toolkit for situations that can benefit from pluggable interaction techniques.

13.3 Direct Manipulation

In direct manipulation (DM), displayed objects become the "input devices" that control the user interface. Well-designed direct manipulation interaction is a pleasure for end users, but often just the opposite for implementors.

The key characteristic of DM, continuous representation of object states, is the main difficulty in implementing it. Visible feedback is not only lexical (tracking the user's actions) but semantic. As the user moves an object, its state must visibly change in a way that is consistent with the user's intent. This involves deducing the intent, verifying that it does not violate constraints on action, and making appropriate changes to the display. All this must be done rapidly to provide the appearance of object continuity that is essential to the success of the technique.

Direct manipulation in OOUIs falls fairly neatly into two categories. In the first, simpler case, a single object is manipulated, such as the dial in the DM counter example. The second case involves interaction between multiple objects; iconic "drag and drop" is the standard example. Drag and drop may be supported by operating system protocols, in which case it becomes more than an end user interaction style. Direct manipulation can be the visible manifestation of a system-wide architecture for interaction between "plug-compatible" objects.

Semantic Feedback

The requirement for immediate and continuous semantic feedback is unique to direct manipulation. Other action language techniques provide lexical and syntactic feedback while a command is being formed; semantic feedback is provided only after it has been parsed and executed.

As an example, consider file deletion. This can be accomplished by typing a command:

```
delete myfile.doc
```

Echoing the typed characters on the display provides lexical feedback. Though seldom done, in principle syntactic feedback could be given as the command was typed. Supposing `delete` operates on a single file, if the user entered an additional token following `myfile.doc`, the system could signal the error immediately rather than after the entire line was typed.

Almost all GUIs support file deletion by selecting a visible object (an icon or text string representing the file), then selecting the `Delete` action from a popup or pulldown menu. Lexical feedback here includes highlighting the selected object and highlighting the menu items as they are selected. There may be a limited and discrete form of semantic feedback, the graying (disabling) of menu actions that are not valid for the selected object.

Figure 13-7 shows object deletion by direct manipulation in the OS/2 Workplace Shell; the icon for an object to be deleted is dragged to a `Shredder` icon and dropped. In the left half of the figure, the lack of any feedback other than the "target emphasis" box around the shredder shows that it is permissible to delete the document. In the right half, the international "do not enter" symbol means that the object `Calculator` cannot be deleted.

When dragging an icon in this way, there are three general possibilities for the user's intent. One is dropping it on the "desktop" (the surface of the icon's current containing window) at a location not occupied by another icon. A second is dropping it on another icon, and a third is dropping it on the surface of another open window. These correspond to

Figure 13-7 Semantic feedback based on object type—drop can/cannot occur

different commands. The user's intent cannot be known in advance; since the drop could occur anywhere, continuous feedback must be provided as to whether a drop is allowed or not. In OS/2, as in most other GUIs, feedback is binary—either "can't drop here," or "OK to drop."

Drag and drop is discussed in more detail below. A similar requirement for continuous semantic feedback exists when only a single object is manipulated. Use of the thumb bar for scrolling (described on page 382) is an example. As the bar is moved, the text is dynamically scrolled.[1]

Another example is shown in Figure 3-8. This is a simple graphic editor with only one function—drawing lines. The user presses the mouse button to anchor one end of a line, moves the mouse to the other end, and releases the button. Once the line is anchored, movement of the mouse is tracked by a "rubberband" line until the button is released to add the line to the drawing. The entire operation, once completed, is equivalent to the command

```
drawing add: (Line from: anchorPoint to: endpoint).
```

This points out that direct manipulation operations usually have two phases. In the first phase, a command is formed "by demonstration" and

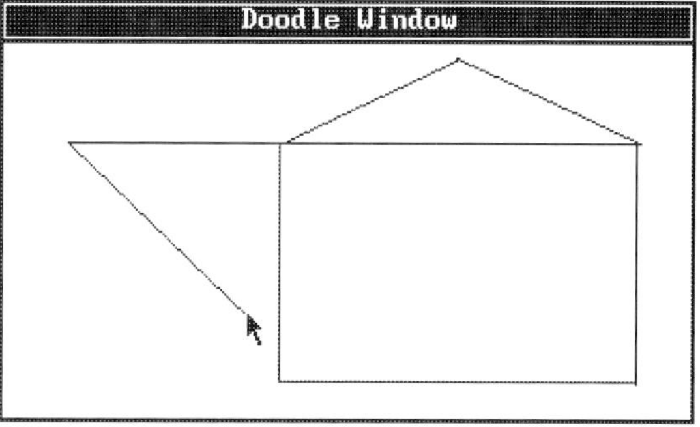

Figure 13-8 A simple direct manipulation application

[1] This is the behavior recommended in style guides; some text editors scroll the text only after the bar is released—a much less usable approach.

the user receives continuous feedback. In the second phase, the command is executed. The second phase can reuse command objects and services developed for non-DM operations. The DM text editor shown in Figure 10-11 (Chapter 10) is an example. Moving or copying text by direct manipulation is semantically equivalent to the menu commands `Cut` or `Copy`, followed by `Paste`. In the implementation of the example, these commands are reused "under the covers," and as a result the direct manipulation is implemented with very little additional code. It is also undoable, since the commands it reuses are undoable.

Operations are reversible in good DM interfaces. One aspect of this is providing ways of undoing the effects of completed operations—ideally, DM actions that invert the actions to be undone. An example is deletion by dragging an object to the trash; opening the trash and dragging the object back out undoes the operation. A global `Undo` action can also be provided.[1]

There is another aspect of reversibility, related to the principle of *feedback on button down, action on button up*. In the shredder example, at any point prior to releasing the mouse button, the user can reverse the intent of the operation by moving the dragged icon back to its original location or by canceling the drag with the `Esc` key. The operation has no effects before the user confirms his or her intent by releasing the button.

Undoing the effects of cancelled operations is not as simple as it might seem. In an MV or MVC application, the user's semantic actions change the model, which in turn changes the view. In general, more than one view may be open on a single model, creating a potential conflict—the requirement for reversibility suggests that only the view controlling the DM operation should see changes before they are "committed" by the user.

There are two ways to avoid changing the model object while DM is in progress. One is to have the view simulate the visible effect of changing the model, making the actual change when the operation is completed. The graphical editor shown in Figure 13-8 (whose implementation will be shown below) is an example of this. This technique is common in applications where precise visual feedback is essential.

Simulation reduces modularity by requiring the view to understand how the model will process a change. An alternative way of avoiding changes to the model is to provide minimal semantic feedback prior to completion of the operation. Iconic drag-drop is an example, where the feedback simply says "can drop" or "cannot drop." In many cases this is acceptable—the user needs detailed lexical feedback to coordinate the manipulation, but understands the operation well enough to not need exact semantic feedback.

Sometimes neither of these alternatives is possible. In the counter application shown in Figure 13-6, the whole point of modularizing model and view is that the model alone is responsible for what it does with mes-

[1] Some operations are irreversible; printing an object, or sending it out over a network connection, are examples. Irreversible deletion, as in OS/2, is common, but unnecessary.

sages such as `increment`—the view does not care whether the increment is by 1, 10, or any other value. So in the DM counter, the model is changed every time the mouse moves. In many applications, however, where information models are complex, distributed, or shared, this approach may not be feasible.

The scope of solutions to modifying shared models goes beyond the user interface. The logic of command processing described on page 385 may need to invoke system-wide locking protocols:

```
BEGIN
   Lock model
   Set up and initiate DM operation
   IF user canceled
      THEN back out model changes
   Unlock model
END
```

For reasons of complexity and performance, locking protocols are seldom feasible for direct manipulation operations.[1] They will become more feasible, though, as networks and workstations get faster and distributed object architectures such as CORBA are widely implemented. The case must also be considered where all users of a shared object *do* want to see immediate feedback from DM operations. Collaborative editing and computer conferencing are examples.

The situation today is that for single-user applications, well-designed DM techniques and rapid performance are the key requirements. With careful consideration of command semantics and good design, these can be accommodated without sacrificing modularity. For distributed applications, the key issue is providing the highest level of interactive performance consistent with remote objects. This will be discussed further in Section 13.4 under *Object Handlers.*

A DM Example

A typical example of direct manipulation feedback is the "rubberband line" in the application shown in Figure 13-8. The model for the application is an instance of `Drawing`, essentially just a collection of lines. `Line`, not shown here, contains a start and end point.

```
Model subclass: #Drawing
instanceVariableNames: 'lines '
addLine: aLine
"Add a line to the drawing. "
       lines add: aLine.
```

[1] MVC in Smalltalk-80 [sPar92] has protocols supporting a limited form of locking—models and views can synchronize their activities by exchanging `changeRequest` messages.

```
initialize
      lines := OrderedCollection new.
```

The application is launched on a blank drawing by

```
DrawingView new openOn: Drawing new.
```

The methods in the DrawingView class that are mainly of interest here are dragBegin:, dragMove:, and dragEnd. They handle the user actions of anchoring a line, moving its endpoint, and committing the line to the drawing by releasing the mouse button. The dragMove: method displays the rubberband line, by erasing the old line and drawing a new one each time the mouse is moved. Graphics code in DrawingView is platform-dependent, but conceptually similar to code on other platforms.[1]

```
View subclass: #DrawingView
instanceVariableNames: 'pen anchor endpoint'
defaultControllerClass
"Answer the controller class for this view."
      ^DrawingDMController.
dragBegin: aPoint
"Set the anchor point for a new line to aPoint."
   anchor := aPoint.
   endpoint := aPoint. "Initialize end to anchor."
dragEnd
"Save the line that was just constructed."
   pen up; black; "Redraw the line."
      combinationRule: Form over;
      goto: anchor;
      down; goto: endpoint.
   self model addLine:  "Add the line to the model."
      (Line from: anchor to: endpoint).
dragMove: aPoint
"Move the endpoint of the rubberband line to aPoint,
 erase the old line, and draw the new one. XOR the bits,
 to avoid erasing existing lines."
   pen combinationRule: Form reverse;
      white;
      up; goto: anchor;
      down; goto: endpoint; up; "Erase old line"
      goto: anchor;
      down; goto: aPoint.        "Draw new line."
      endpoint := aPoint.
```

[1] This example, and the one shown in Figure 13-10, was implemented on Smalltalk/V DOS [sDig86], modified for compatibility with Smalltalk-80.

```
initialize
"Initialize the receiver."
   super initialize.
   pen := Pen new defaultNib: 1; black.
openOn: aDrawing
"Open the receiver for creating/editing aDrawing."
   | topView |
   self model: aDrawing;
         borderWidth: 2;
         insideColor: Form white.
   topView := StandardSystemView new label: 'Doodle Window'.
   topView addSubView: self.
   topView controller open.
```

The controller, `DrawingDMController`,[1] generates drag messages to the view based on user actions with the mouse. Notice that, unlike previous examples, the controller does not send messages to the model; everything is done through the view, in order to provide the appropriate visual feedback.

```
MouseMenuController subclass: #DrawingDMController
instanceVariableNames: 'state location'
controlActivity
   "Sent while the receiver is the active controller."
   state = #down ifTrue: [self downState]
                ifFalse: [self upState].
downState
"Control activity and mouse button is down."
   | newPoint |
   newPoint := sensor mousePoint.
   sensor leftButtonPressed ifFalse: [
      state := #up.
      ^view dragEnd].
   location = newPoint ifFalse: [
      location := newPoint.
      view dragMove: location].
upState
"Control activity and mouse button is up."
   sensor leftButtonPressed ifTrue: [
      location := sensor mousePoint.
      state := #down.
      view dragBegin: location].
```

[1] A slightly different version of this controller was used to discuss event generation in Chapter 11 (Section 11.3).

Direct manipulation alters the relationship between the MVC components. The view does relatively more of the work, and the controller relatively less. Coupling between the view and the model is increased. This increase is explicit; the view now passes messages (to change the model) that the controller would normally handle. The increase is also implicit in situations like this one, where the view provides feedback by simulating the result of changing the model by adding a line. Correspondingly, coupling between the controller and the model is decreased.

The enhanced role of the view in this situation is one factor motivating the absence of controllers, as such, in most OO frameworks. Paradoxically, it also makes controllers more useful by increasing their reusability. The controllers in the counter example work only in counter applications, because they send model-specific messages such as `increment` and `decrement`.[1] `DrawingDMController`, on the other hand, is quite general—it can be used in any application that supports dragging.

A problem in reusing a class such as `DrawingDMController` is that real applications, unlike the examples shown so far, seldom use only one form of interaction. A full-function graphics editor, for example, will use direct manipulation for moving, rotating, and resizing objects, as well as for rubberband lines. An obvious way to scale up the application would be to add additional methods and conditional logic to handle the different cases. This could be done in the view, with code such as:

```
dragMove: aPoint
"Perform the appropriate drag operation."
      self drawingLine ifTrue: [^self moveEndpoint: aPoint].
      self resizing ifTrue: [^self sizeTo: aPoint].
      . . . . "And so forth for other modes."
```

Alternatively, code similar to this could be placed in the controller. In either case, the conditional logic increases code complexity and makes the components less reusable. Another solution to this problem involves dynamically selecting a controller based on the operation (moving, resizing, etc.) and the type of object being manipulated. This is discussed in Section 13.4, *Encapsulating Direct Manipulation.*

Drag and Drop

Drag and drop—the direct manipulation of iconic representations of objects—has been the signature interaction technique for graphical OOUIs since the Star, Lisa, and Macintosh. The "drop" in drag-drop is onto an icon or view representing some object, so the technique always involves the interaction of more than one object. Providing the appropriate feedback while the operation is in progress may require participation of the represented objects; this complicates the control flow and makes performance

[1] The impact on reusability can be lessened in some cases by parameterizing the messages sent by controllers to their models.

an issue. Providing good performance is especially challenging in a distributed environment.

Figure 13-7 illustrated feedback in a simple drag-drop operation. Semantic feedback there was dependent on the types of the objects represented by the icons. Figure 13-9 illustrates that semantic feedback cannot always be based just on object type, but may need to account for the state of individual objects. The example here is electronic mail; objects can be placed in envelopes, which are then addressed and sent over the network by being dropped on the `Outgoing mail` icon. On the left in the figure the mailbox does not accept the envelope because it has no address. On the right the drop is accepted, because the user had meanwhile dropped the object `Note to Dave` on the envelope and typed an e-mail address in response to a prompt.

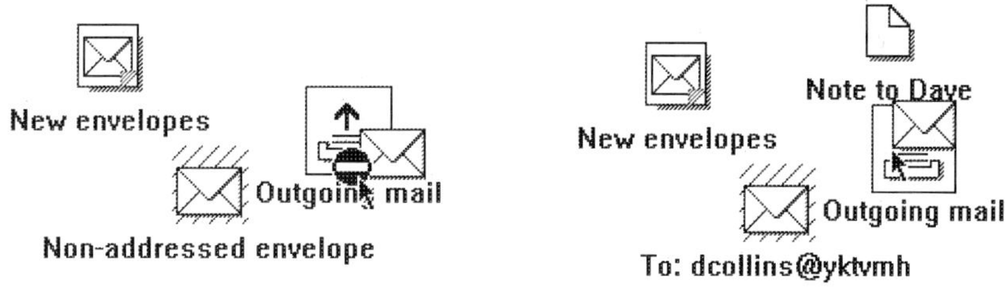

Figure 13-9 Semantic feedback based on object state—drop cannot/can occur

Drag and drop using MVC Direct manipulation involving multiple objects introduces significant complexity. To bring out some of the issues, consider how a drag and drop application might be implemented in an MVC framework. Figure 13-10 shows an example.[1] It has a `Desktop` folder containing two folders with open views. A drag-drop operation is in progress to move the document `January report` out of the folder `Pending items`.

There are any number of possibilities for the drop. The user might drop it on "whitespace" in `Desktop`, `Archive Folders`, or back in `Pending items`, in which case it would be added to those folders. The user could also drop it on a folder icon, for instance `1993`. Dropping it on an icon that has an open view will add the item to both the underlying model and to the view. For example, if `January report` is dropped on the `Archive folders` icon, it will appear in the open view of `Archive folders`.

Figure 13-11 shows some of the objects involved, and a yet-to-be-determined "drag and drop protocol" to handle their interaction (assuming the drop is onto `Archive folders`). The views are `FolderView` instances; their models are instances of `Folder`, which can contain text documents

[1] Implemented in Smalltalk/V DOS [sDig86], which has an MVC framework similar to that of Smalltalk-80.

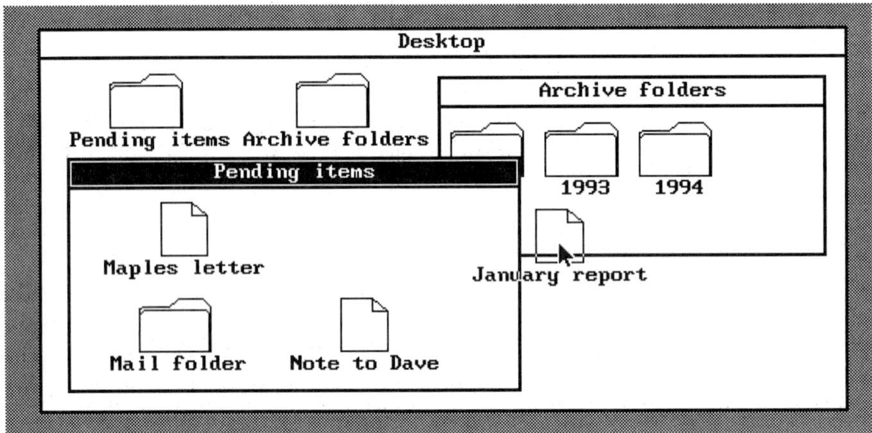

Figure 13-10 An MVC drag and drop application

(instances of `Note`) or other folders. `Folder` supports protocols such as `add:`, `remove:`, etc. `FolderController` is the controller class. The controller for the `FolderView` doesn't do much other than relay mouse events, so the problem is basically the same in MVC and MV frameworks.

A `Folder` has an instance variable `contents` pointing to a collection of the items it contains. The instance variable `icons` in `FolderView` is a dictionary of icons, indexed by the items contained in the `FolderView`'s model.

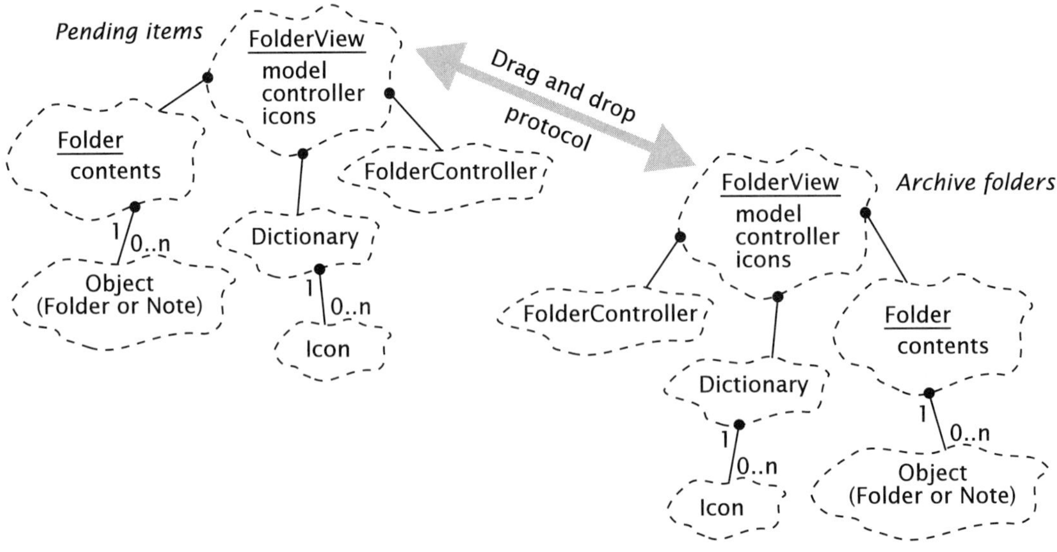

Figure 13-11 Composition diagram for MVC drag and drop

The icons are instances of the class Icon; besides the icon bitmap, they maintain their current location within the view and can draw themselves. The icon bitmap is determined by the type of object, and the Icon instances are created by the FolderView when it opens.

It is worth noting an alternative approach to maintaining the association between model objects and their icons. Recall the "canvas" application described on page 377—PictureElementView in that situation was like Icon in this one. The same design trade-off exists as well. Some implementors argue that it is simpler to fold the behavior of Icon into the class Model, so each model object knows how to locate and draw itself as an icon. This approach would avoid the need for the FolderView to initialize an icon dictionary. The other side of the argument is that doing this introduces platform dependency into model objects that may otherwise be portable.

To get a sense of the drag-drop protocol, consider the moment when the icon being dragged in Figure 13-10 is dropped. The FolderView from which the drag was done (Pending items) has tracked the mouse movement via its controller. When the user releases the mouse button, signaling a drop, the FolderController sends dropAt: to the FolderView. The drop point aPoint is expressed in coordinates relative to the display screen.

```
dropAt: aPoint
"The dragged icon has been dropped."
     | droppedOnView droppedOnIcon |
     "First find the view under the drop point."
     droppedOnView := self viewAt: aPoint.
     droppedOnView isNil ifTrue: [^self]. "Invalid drop."
     droppedOnView isFolder ifFalse: [^self]. "Invalid drop."
     droppedOnIcon := droppedOnView iconAt: aPoint.
     droppedOnIcon isNil ifTrue: [ "Dropped on whitespace."
       droppedOnObject := droppedOnView model]
                 ifFalse: [ "Dropped on an icon."
       droppedOnIcon isFolder ifFalse: [ "Icon not a folder."
           ^self]. "Invalid drop."
       droppedOnObject :=
                droppedOnView modelFor: droppedOnIcon].
     myDocument := self modelFor: self draggedIcon.
     self model remove: myDocument.
     droppedOnObject add: myDocument.
     droppedOnView icons at: myDocument
                   put: (self icons at: myDocument).
     self icons removeKey: myDocument.
```

Code in dropAt: handles verification and transfer of the model object and its icon after the drop. To provide dynamic feedback, portions of this logic are also in the `dragMove:` method, which tracks mouse movement while the drag is in progress. There is code in `dragBegin:` to initiate the drag, and in `initialize` to set everything up when the `FolderView` is opened. Because managing drag-drop operations is done by the view, the code would be substantially the same in MV frameworks.

The additional complexity here versus the single object case is partially because the operation itself is more complex. It also stems from the involvement of more than one instance of `FolderView` and the need for the source view to access icons and models in the target view. Superficially, it seems that the close coupling between control, visual feedback, and model semantics necessarily undermine modularity and encapsulation.

In the general (and most useful) case, a drag-drop protocol must handle communication between different applications, not just instances of the same application. This adds to the need for standard, reusable components that encapsulate as much as possible of the protocol. Suggestions for designing such components are the topic of the next section. Because this is a complex problem, many solutions are possible. The essential point is that there are solutions, like the one above, that are more complex, and others, like the ones described in the next section, that are less complex.

13.4 Encapsulating Direct Manipulation

We have seen some of the difficulties in implementing object-oriented direct manipulation interfaces, which stem from adding protocols to classes whose interfaces are already quite complex. This section examines ways of encapsulating DM protocols to make them simpler and more reusable.

Objects called *trackers* or *manipulators* have been developed to encapsulate direct manipulation interactions in graphical editors. These can be extended to *object handlers* for encapsulating drag-drop protocols. The general ideal is to provide fine-grained, special purpose controllers that can be instantiated to handle the first phase of DM, and emit commands based on the end result of the interaction.

Trackers and Manipulators

The MacApp framework's handling of menu commands, using `TCommand` instances, is described in Section 13.2. Menu and keyboard events in MacApp normally go to the document (`TDocument`); mouse events normally go to the view (`TView`). The typical mouse event is a single click used to select an object. The view informs its document of the selection, which becomes the target for the next menu command. When the document receives `DoMenuCommand`, indicating a menu selection, it creates an instance of the `TCommand` subclass corresponding to the menu item, passes it the selected object, and sends the message `doit` to apply the command.

What about direct manipulation operations, where the final form of the command is not known until the first phase of the DM operation is complete? By overriding three methods in `TCommand`, an application can use `TCommand` objects as *trackers* that retain control while a DM operation is in progress. The methods are:

- `TrackMouse` captures mouse events until the button is released, and forms the resultant command.
- `TrackFeedback` displays the appropriate visual feedback.
- `TrackConstrain` applies constraints to the mouse cursor, such as requiring that lines be straight, at right angles, etc.

To illustrate how this works, Figure 13-12 shows how the application shown in Figure 13-8 (page 395) could be recast using a tracker. Instead of being a permanent controller for `DrawingView`, `DrawingDMController` instances are now created on demand, as trackers, when the user presses the mouse button. When the button is released the tracker sends the message `add:` to update the drawing, and is saved for possible undo. The `undoit` method sends `remove:` to the drawing for the line that was added.

The example shown in Figure 13-8 has only a single function, drawing lines. For that situation, the only advantage to using `DMDrawingController` as a tracker (as opposed to a standard MVC controller) is that it simplifies undo processing. Real editors have many functions that use direct manipulation, and that is where trackers are most valuable. A single editor can have multiple tracker classes, for drawing lines, resizing, etc., and instantiate the appropriate one for each operation done by the user.

Some operations require more than a single direct manipulation ac-

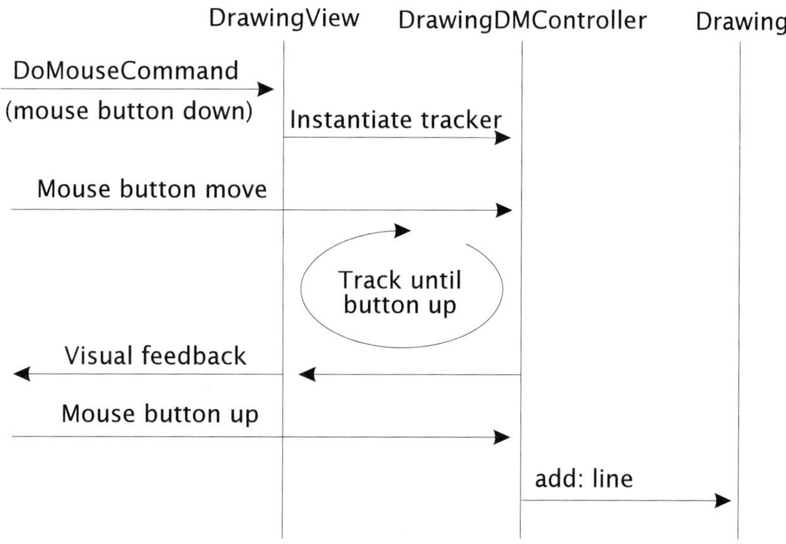

Figure 13-12 Using a tracker for the rubberband line example

tion. For example, to draw a polyline (sequence of connected line segments) a user may click to start a segment, drag and release to end it, click to start the next segment, and so forth—finally double clicking to signal the end of the polyline. In these cases a tracker may remain in a *pending* state, receiving control for each action, until a complete command can be formed.

Manipulators Unidraw [Vlis90], developed by John Vlissides at Stanford University, is an OO framework for building domain-specific graphical editors.[1] Domain-specific editors are things like circuit diagram applications, which use general graphical capabilities to lay out components with domain-specific semantics. The Unidraw architecture uses objects called *manipulators* to perform direct manipulation operations.

Figure 13-13 shows an example of a tool palette for a typical graphical editor. The horizontally arrayed buttons represent "tools" for writing text, drawing lines, creating rectangles, and so forth. In Unidraw, the user *grasps* a tool by selecting it from the palette, and *wields* the tool by moving the mouse cursor into the drawing area and pressing a mouse button. The *effect* of the tool is the complete command formed by the DM operation. When a tool is grasped it creates a manipulator, which functions like the MacApp tracker. After the wield phase is complete, the tool creates an undoable command object.

Figure 13-13 Tool palette for a graphics editor

Tools and manipulators are separated to allow for cases where tool operation may depend on the type of component object the user is operating on. For instance, in a circuit layout program the effect of resizing may be different for a transistor than for a connecting wire. The same tool can instantiate more than one manipulator to accommodate this sort of situation. Unidraw also allows composite manipulators for complex interactions. For example, imagine adjusting the size of a component with the mouse, while changing its color using the keyboard arrow keys.

The Unidraw scheme is more complex than either MacApp or MVC. The benefit is its ability to provide kits of standard tools and manipulators that can be quickly assembled into editors that use highly sophisticated interaction techniques.

[1]Unidraw runs on top of InterViews [Lin89], a C++ framework for building X Windows GUIs.

Object Handlers

Manipulators in Unidraw facilitate the implementation of complex direct manipulation techniques within a single view. A second dimension of complexity is the interchange of objects between more than one view through drag and drop. The idea of trackers can be extended to cover these interactions as well. By separating drag-drop protocols from application views, *object handlers* foster a "plug and play" environment that minimizes the effort required to move "standalone" applications into an iconic, direct manipulation environment.[1]

A metaphor for object handlers is the notion of "agents" with specialized expertise, who act on behalf of others; the use of lawyers at real estate closings is an example. These agents reduce the complexity of life for the principals they represent by carrying out their intentions in terms of some protocol that the principal does not care to understand in detail. Object handlers play an analogous role in OOUIs, and enhance the MVC paradigm by simplifying `Model` and `View` protocols. Object handlers are, in one sense, controllers for icons, but they also function as surrogate models.

There are three separable aspects to the problem of handling OOUI interactions involving iconic direct manipulation:

1. Performing icon manipulations and launching views from icons.
2. Performing semantic actions (executing commands) on model objects.
3. Managing views on objects once they are opened.

Items (2) and (3) are handled by "standard" MV and MVC frameworks. (1) is not—but for a given object, these activities are not concurrent. The user completes an icon manipulation and then either an action is performed such as adding an object to a folder, or a view is launched on an object, or both. This suggests factoring the responsibilities in (1) into a new class, `ObjectHandler`.

Figure 13-14 illustrates the use of object handlers in a reimplementation of the application shown in Figure 13-10. For simplicity, this uses an MV style, with no `FolderController`. For each item in the folder that needs to be displayed as an icon, an instance of `ObjectHandler` (actually a subclass of `ObjectHandler` appropriate for the object being handled) is created when the `FolderView` opens. The object handler takes responsibility for displaying the icon and interacting with other icons.

While a drag is in process, most of the messaging is between object handlers. Mouse events are passed by the `FolderView` to the handler for the object being dragged. The dragged handler asks the second view for the handler representing either the icon under the mouse pointer, or the

[1] The term *object handlers* comes from the KCM project at IBM Research ([Mac93], [Mal93]). It was originally suggested by Mark Wilkes.

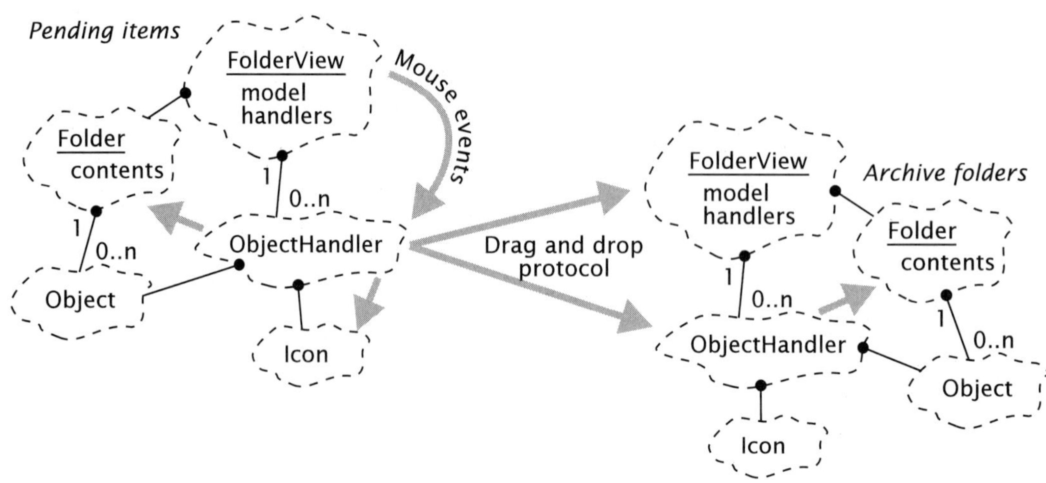

Figure 13-14 Drag and drop implemented with object handlers (compare Figure 13-11)

folder being viewed (if the pointer is over "whitespace" in the view). To find the handler at the mouse pointer position, the second FolderView interrogates its own collection of handlers:

```
handlerAt: aPoint
"Locate the handler at aPoint in the receiver view."
	self handlers do: [:each|
		(each isNear: aPoint) ifTrue: [^each]].
	^self handler. "Over whitespace, answer the view handler."
```

A two-way negotiation between object handlers determines whether a drop can occur. The handler for the dragged object sends `isDropOnable: self` to any handler it is dragged over. If a drop would be acceptable to the "dropped-on" handler, it sends `isDroppableOn: self` back to the dragged handler. If the dragged handler responds `true`, then the dropped-on handler also responds `true`. If either response is `false`, the user gets feedback indicating a drop would not be allowed. In some cases, responses are based on object type, as in Figure 13-7. In other cases, such as the envelope in Figure 13-9, the handler may send messages to its model object to make the determination.

Messages to model objects are sent only by the handlers representing them. Performing actions on model objects is mediated by object handlers so that the model objects are unaware of any protocol related to the interaction technique, and only receive semantically meaningful messages. For example, when an item is moved from one folder to another, the item's handler sends `remove: self` to the first `FolderHandler`, and `add: self` to the second. The `FolderHandler` instances then send the appropriate `add:` and `remove:` messages to their folders.

Managing a view on an object once it is opened is handled just as in MV or MVC. Figure 13-15 shows how a view is launched. When the user double-clicks the mouse, the `FolderView` sends `open` to the object handler under the mouse pointer. The handler is not aware of how `open` was generated; the mapping of a particular physical interaction to an `open` can be changed to suit the platform. The handler then sends

```
self defaultViewClass new openOn: self object.
```

The message labeled "Materialize object" implies that one of the functions of an object handler might be to materialize stored or remote objects; this is discussed below.

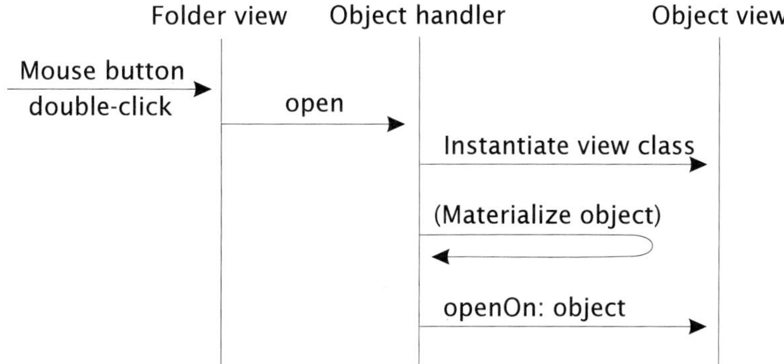

Figure 13-15 Launching a view using object handlers

In launching a view, as in direct manipulation operations involving multiple objects, neither models nor views are aware of the services of object handlers. As a result, existing "standalone" applications can be imported into OOUI environments with little modification of code.

Implementation of object handlers achieves substantial reuse, because most object handler behavior is "canonical" and can be fully or partially implemented in abstract classes. An overview of the main classes is shown in Figure 13-16. The hierarchy contains isomorphic subtrees under `Model`, `View`, and `ObjectHandler`; the subtree under `Controller` is present in an MVC framework.[1] Since object handlers are needed only to handle visual manipulation of icons, an object handler is created for each item whenever a view is opened on a folder or other container. The object handler class instantiated is based on the model object's type, which defaults to its class. There is a single `Icon` class, with no subclasses. Each `Icon` instance is parameterized with a bitmap and title string.

[1] Class `Object` and the `Controller` classes are shown in gray to indicate they are optional, depending on the framework.

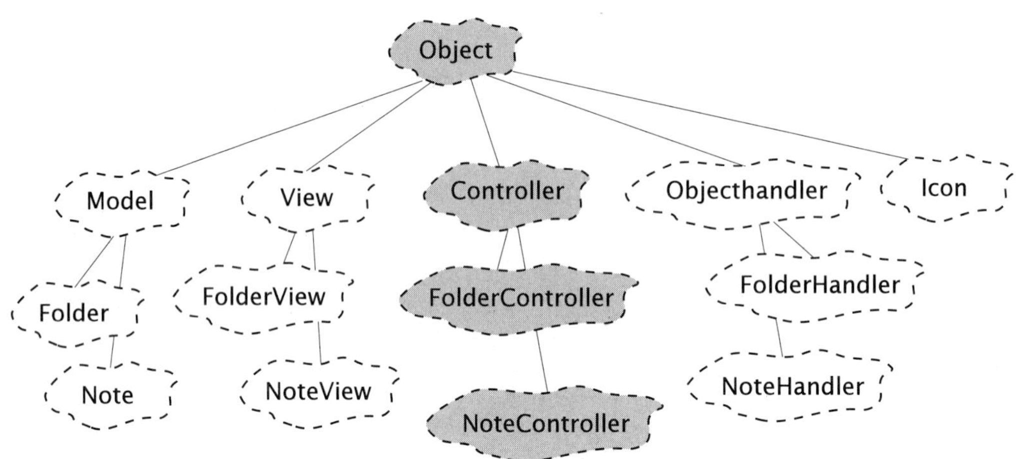

Figure 13-16 ObjectHandler in relation to other classes

Object handlers in client-server systems As mentioned above, object handlers can materialize their objects on demand, when the user launches a view. In the KCM system [Mal93], objects were stored on a database along with persistent, lightweight surrogates. These surrogates, instances of ContainerItemModel, were materialized when a folder was opened. A ContainerItemModel had an object type, title, and a pointer to the real object on the database. The object type and title were sufficient to create an object handler and display the object as an icon. When a view was launched, the database pointer was used to materialize the real object.

Experience with "megadata," large collections of remote objects presented to users, suggests that users typically view large collections of icons, but open only a few of them for detailed inspection. By substituting lightweight surrogates for the underlying model objects, collections such as folders can be opened and displayed rapidly. The performance penalty for materializing an object is paid only when the user has expressed interest by opening it.

Object handlers are also useful in client-server systems to conceal complex protocols from application developers. The application-specific behavior of an object handler is based on what kind of view it opens, and how it specifies drag-drop interactions between its model and other objects. Details of the drag-drop protocol and interfaces to infrastructure services are hidden, and of no concern to users, interface designers, or application programmers.

Encapsulating Platform Drag-Drop Protocols

Drag and drop is much more valuable if objects can be exchanged among multiple applications. Many applications available today allow users to freely interchange data between spreadsheets, text documents, graphical editors, etc., using drag-drop or the system clipboard. Whereas clipboard formats are standard, drag-drop protocols are often proprietary, and work only between applications from a single source.

This situation is changing, and platform-standard protocols are available for OSF/Motif on X Windows [Skl93], OS/2 [IBM92c], and Microsoft Windows [Broc93]. Though the different platform protocols are significantly different in detail, their "programmer's conceptual models" are all quite similar.[1] They are also similar to the ideas brought out in the discussion of trackers, manipulators, and object handlers. This reflects the fact that these schemes are all solutions to the same problem.

The protocols are based on the idea of "transferring" something from a drag source to a drag target. Microsoft's support is explicitly based on the cut/copy/paste model, and supports the same data types as the clipboard. Other models are semantically equivalent to clipboard transfer, though the data type names and formats may differ. This may seem limiting, but experience in systems ranging from the Xerox Star to KCM has shown that polymorphic `move` (cut/paste) and `copy` (copy/paste) operations cover the semantics of all currently used drag-drop functions. Operations in these protocols can be divided into four phases:[2]

1. During *initiation*, the end user selects a source icon and may also indicate an operation type (for example, by pressing the `Ctrl` key while dragging to indicate a `copy` operation). The source application program creates an object to represent the drag source; this object is normally not the source object itself, but a control block whose format is dictated by the drag-drop protocol. The source program then calls a platform API to start the *drag* phase. Either the source program or the API routine may build an object called a *drag controller* or *drag context* to maintain the overall state of the operation.

2. During the *drag* phase, the end user drags the icon, and the platform sends messages to potential targets (windows the icon passes over) in order to provide appropriate feedback to the user. Targets can examine the drag source object to decide whether it is droppable. Microsoft Windows and Motif provide the option of sending messages only to windows that have registered themselves with the window manager as drop targets. This improves performance in a distributed environment, where applications controlling windows on a display server may be scattered around a network. OS/2 always sends at least one message to a potential target, but the target response can indicate it will not accept the drop, and that no more messages are to be sent. (This response, `DOR_NEVERDROP`, is the default response for windows that do not support the drag-drop protocol.)

[1] Having struggled for several years with drag-drop protocols, I can attest that understanding the general conceptual model is a big step toward mastery of platform-specific details.

[2] The terminology here and in the remainder of this section is my own, since there is no standard across all the platforms.

3. When the user releases the mouse button or presses the Esc key to cancel the operation, the *drop* phase is entered. This ends the drag phase, and enters the *transfer* phase if the drop was accepted by the target.

4. During the *transfer* phase, objects or data are transferred from the source to the target. Depending on the platform and options, transfer can be handled by the window manager, the source, or the target. Drag source objects contain two types of information on the dragged object to guide the transfer. *Formats* are data types into which the source object can be transformed. For example, text can be formatted as a string, or placed in an ASCII file. *Mechanisms* are ways of transferring a given format from source to target. A string, for example, could be directly copied, copied through the system clipboard, or sent via a network connection. Platforms define standard formats and mechanisms that are passed in the drag source object. Provision is also made for "unknown" or private types, which must be transferred by proprietary messaging between the source and target.

Figure 13-17 shows the flow of interaction for a generic drag and drop.

There are two levels at which platform drag-drop protocols can be supported by OO class libraries. At the lowest level, libraries can simply

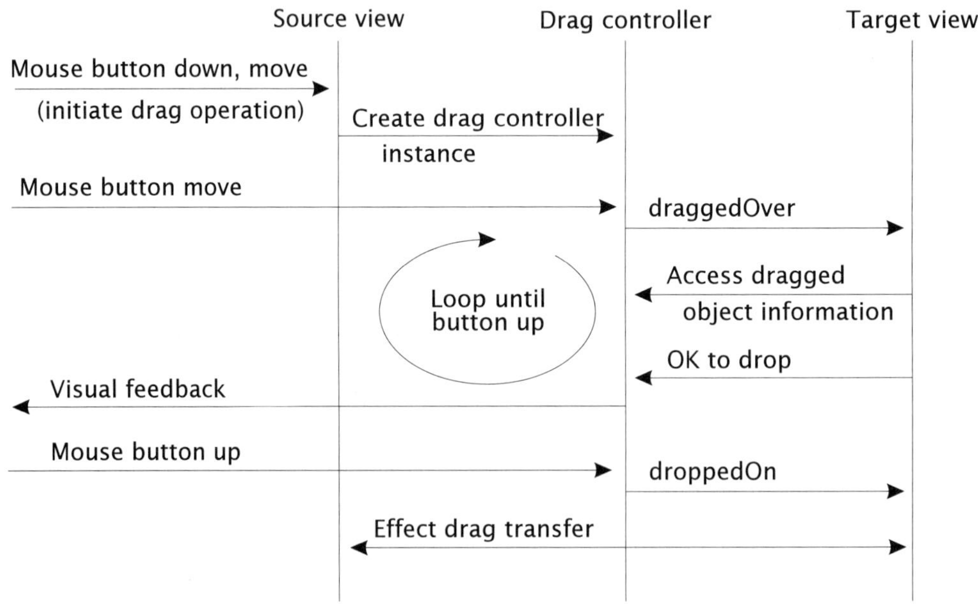

Figure 13-17 Generic platform drag/drop protocol

"wrap" the platform objects and APIs so they become accessible to other objects. The packaging of the OS/2 drag-drop protocol in Smalltalk/V [sDig92b] is an example:

- Messages are added to existing classes such as `Window` to handle initiation and termination of drag-drop operations, and forwarding messages such as `dragOver:` to the appropriate `DragDrop` instance.
- `DragDrop` instances represent drag protocols and control the overall flow. These are what the figure calls *drag controllers;* there is one `DragDrop` instance for each window that can be a drag source or target.
- `DragItem` represents an item being dragged. The drag source object mentioned above is a list of `DragItem` instances. The step *access dragged object information* in Figure 13-17 retrieves this list.
- `DragTransfer` controls the *transfer* phase. Subclasses of `DragTransfer` handle specific transfer mechanisms such as file copy.

At a higher level these classes can provide drag-drop capabilities to widgets and applications. In Smalltalk/V, `Container` is a subclass of `Window` that wraps the OS/2 container widget. `Container` instances hold icons representing objects, and have `DragDrop` instances to handle movement of icons between containers. `ContainerItem` instances represent individual icons in containers.

In KCM, Smalltalk/V `Container` instances were used to build `FolderViews`, and the `ObjectHandler` class insulated application programmers from the `ContainerItem` and `DragDrop` protocols. This technique works in Smalltalk or C++ and allows OO applications to "plug and play" with other applications in the system.

13.5 Summary

Implementors of presentation and interaction objects have several goals, which sometimes conflict. In the long run, developer productivity is maximized by components that are maintainable, extensible, and reusable. In the short run, it is often easier to build components that do not have these properties. Industry experience suggests that OO programming languages and architectures come closest to providing both productivity and reusability, but not without effort and discipline. The effort is rewarded by a stock of reusable components, and an architecture that is adaptable to international markets and special user needs.

Modular separation of information model and view code may appear difficult at first, but it is achievable, and usually without a performance penalty. Enforcing the separation makes code more portable across platforms, as well as more adaptable to changing needs and markets.

A key principle for modularizing interaction objects is the separation of command semantics, or the semantics of actions on objects, from the details of particular interaction techniques. An added benefit of defining objects representing commands is a relatively easy way to provide command undo and redo facilities to end users.

Direct manipulation, more than any other technique, contributes to the sense of "real objects" in an OOUI. The implementation requirements for direct manipulation are stringent, and achieving all of them together can be a significant technical challenge, particularly in the world of rich information models described in Chapter 12:

- Rapid interaction.
- Continuous visible feedback on the state of the object(s) involved in the direct manipulation operation.
- Easy reversibility of DM operations.

Techniques are described in this chapter for encapsulating direct manipulation in controller-like interaction objects within an MV or MVC framework. These objects can also support standard platform protocols for drag-drop interaction.

Acknowledgments In addition to cited sources, my understanding of drag-drop interactions was helped along by working with code developed by various people at IBM: Dave Dykstal at the Rochester lab, a team led by Tom Ruiz at the Westlake lab [Cav90], and John Richards at the Watson Research lab. Thanks also for comments by Bjorn Freeman-Benson and an anonymous reviewer of a paper submitted to OOPSLA, who sharpened my understanding of object handlers.

13.6 To Explore Further

Existing object-oriented systems and toolkits provide many examples of "wrapping" window system widgets as OO classes. At least for C++, a more promising approach may be to base the platform widgets on an OO language. *Fresco* [Bilo94] is a forthcoming C++ toolkit to be released with the X11R6 release of the X Window System.

Coupling between models and views is an ever-present issue in user interface implementation. The InterViews toolkit [Lin89] makes a distinction between *observers* (views) and *observables* (models). This idea is generalized to the *observer* design pattern in [Gam94]. Model-view separation for fine-grained graphical objects is found in Unidraw [Vlis90], based on InterViews, and in recent Smalltalk-80 systems from ParcPlace [sPar92]. [Edm92] provides a historical perspective on modularity in user interface software.

[Mart92], though directed at UNIX environments, is a good introduction to technical issues in internationalization. [Rei93b] discusses the problem of inputting ideographic languages such as Chinese from standard keyboards. [Brow92] and [Fil93] summarize adaptive technology for people with disabilities (an area that could be greatly benefitted by object-oriented architectures for GUIs).

In this chapter I have favored interaction over presentation, because I think interaction is less well understood. An extensive literature on the "pure presentation" aspect of GUIs exists; much of it is directed at specific platforms. [Fol92] is a good starting point for general knowledge, along with journals such as *ACM Transactions on Graphics, IEEE Computer Graphics and Applications*, and *Computer Graphics* (which publishes proceedings of the ACM SIGGRAPH conference as a special issue). The general trend is toward OO implementations; [Wiss90] is a good overview of issues in computer graphics from an OO perspective. [sPar92] is a commercial example of a full-function, platform-independent graphics model, in the context of Smalltalk-80 and MVC. An approach to standard imaging taken by many C++ libraries is to provide support for existing graphics standards such as PEX [Stew93]. (PEX is an emerging X Windows standard based on the industry-standard PHIGS [Fol92].)

Textbooks dealing with algorithms and software structure currently devote less attention to interaction than to graphical presentation. Papers on interaction software appear in the research literature of computer graphics and computer-human interaction, e.g., [Cou87a], [Cou87b], [Gree86], [Hil86], [Hud87], [Jaco86], [Sib86], and [Henr90]. [Hud92] describes a probabilistic approach to interaction where event occurrences are uncertain, for instance in speech, gesture, or handwriting recognition. The classic frameworks in MVC [Kras88] and MacApp [Schm86] have proven particularly enduring.

Undoable commands are supported in MacApp by the class `TCommand`, described in [Schm86]. Unidraw[Vlis90] has a similar scheme. [Mey88], Section 12.2, contains a thorough discussion of solving the undo/redo problem in object-oriented systems.

Drag-drop support in Motif is described in [Rei93a] and [Skl93]. [Mark91], published before the Motif support became available, is an excellent discussion of issues in supporting drag and drop for a distributed environment (the X Window System). [Broc93], Chapter 8, describes drag-drop in Microsoft Windows with OLE 2. [IBM92c], Volumes I and III, describe the programming interface to drag-drop in OS/2. [IBM93a], Chapter 10, describes the implementation of OS/2 drag-drop support in a C++ class library.

13.7 Exercises

1. Coupling between collaborating components has two aspects. *Essential* coupling is the sharing of information required for the collaboration. *Accidental* coupling is information sharing that is not, in principle, necessary. Give examples of how the following features of object-oriented programming languages reduce accidental coupling:

   a. Encapsulation

   b. Inheritance

   c. Polymorphism

2. Based on the ideas in Chapter 4, give examples of ways in which your answers to (1) are reflected in external aspects of OOUIs.

3. The file opening dialogue in Figure 13-2 is supplied as a single monolithic component. Design the syntax of a message to the `FileDialog` class to provide:

   a. Support for multiple languages.

   b. Support for a "talking" version of the dialogue for visually impaired users.

4. For the "Canvas" application (page 377), explain why a change in one `PictureElement` may require several elements to be redrawn. If both the model and view use the same coordinate system, what methods (member functions) are required in `PictureElement` to find the set of elements that need to be redrawn when a given element changes?

5. For the counter variations shown in Figure 13-6, briefly describe general requirements for which each of the two displays is optimal. Do likewise for the five interaction techniques. Assuming the MVC-like implementation described on page 392, suggest some ways of making the controller components more reusable in applications other than counters.

6. The control used as a "slider" in Figure 13-6 is really a scrollbar (the library used for implementing it did not have a slider control). Style guides such as [App92] and [IBM92b] specifically advise against this use of a scrolling control. Can you justify the style guide position, based on differences in the conceptual model for a scrollbar versus a slider (sliding switch)?

7. For the first implementation of the counters (with views, no controllers), design class hierarchies with a class for each of the ten counter variations. Use `View` as the root class for your hierarchies.

   a. Sketch two different single inheritance solutions.

   b. Sketch a multiple inheritance solution.

8. What additional object(s) need to be added to Figure 13-12 to support undoing multiple levels of command? Sketch the flow for drawing a line, resizing it, then undoing the resize operation.

14

Tools for Prototyping and Implementation

By the time this book is published, roughly one hundred million graphical user interface platforms will be in use on users' desks (and laps).[1] The market for applications to run on these platforms has grown dramatically over the last decade, while the cadre of experienced GUI programmers has grown more slowly. As a result, a substantial industry has sprung up to develop tools that help to reduce the gap between supply and demand.

The tools range from "power tools" for professional programmers, to "do it yourself" tools to help end users build their own applications. Tools may be intended for rapid prototypes or "one-off" applications that will be discarded after a few uses, or they may produce robust, industrial-strength code. They may support any or all phases of the software development process—analysis, design, coding, or testing.

The number of tools available, and the rate of change in the market, precludes detailed coverage in a book of this type. I can, however, offer some general principles, based on studying and using tools over several years:

- Ways of categorizing tools based on purpose, scope, and internal architecture.
- Factors in developing OOUIs on GUI platforms that make it hard to build an "ideal" tool for all purposes.

[1]Based on various market surveys—about half of them running Microsoft Windows, the remainder divided mostly between Apple Macintosh, IBM OS/2, and a variety of UNIX platforms running X Windows and OSF/Motif.

- Technical and organizational issues that should be considered when evaluating tools.

This chapter only covers tools that are in some sense "object-oriented," and focuses on tools that support prototyping and implementation of user interface code.

In surveying people for their experience, I have encountered a discomforting number of developers, consultants and managers who migrate from failure to failure, pursuing the "silver bullet"—a tool that will allow them to effortlessly develop robust, functional, usable object-oriented applications on GUI platforms. The silver bullet does not exist, but more modest tools can make a difference in productivity and quality. The aim of this chapter is to help you find them.

14.1 Tool Requirements

Many tools are available to help developers build or prototype user interfaces. Some are general-purpose CASE (computer aided software engineering) tools that only incidentally address user interfaces. Others specifically target the building of graphical user interfaces.

The ideal tool would provide seamless coverage for the entire development process, including user interface design and development. Real tools usually cover only part of the process. Assembling a suite of tools, and covering the seams where necessary, is left to the developer.

The Ideal Tool

Figure 14-1 is one view of what an ideal tool or suite of tools might cover. The central part of the figure shows an overview of the user interface design process. It connects to the larger development process at two important points. Much of the data from system analysis is also used for user interface design, so these processes must be coupled. Likewise the output from user interface design must feed into the process of detailed design and coding for the whole system.

The ideal tool suite would use the same notation, data formats, and content across the entire development process. Information model prototyping would be based on objects discovered in system analysis. Task analysis data would be exchanged between system analysis and the user interface design process. User interface prototyping would use an object-oriented class library compatible with the remainder of the development; it could be accessed, however, with high-level tools that allowed rapid prototyping by interface designers with minimal programming skills.

One might wish for a tool requiring *no* programming skills, and some tools claim to allow the creation of complex user interfaces or even entire systems "without programming." For example,

> Above is an interface for an airline reservation service. Typical of many systems now in use, it requires extensive programming and time to develop.
>
> Below that is the same interface developed without programming using TAE Plus. . .[1]

Although these claims may be technically valid (depending on the definition of "programming"), they are misleading. As Brooks points out [Broo87], the hard part of software is its intellectual content, not the form in which it is expressed. The content is expressed in this definition of *program*: "A procedure for solving a problem, including collection of data, processing, and presentation of results."[2] In this sense, development of a system always requires programming.

This is not to say that tools (including the one just cited) cannot ease the burden of prototyping and development. They do this by removing what Brooks calls "accidental complexity"—things like the syntactic details of a window manager API. But the "essential complexity" of the problem domain remains, and must be handled with programming. The programming may be done in a visual or non-procedural language as opposed to C++ or Smalltalk, but it is still programming.

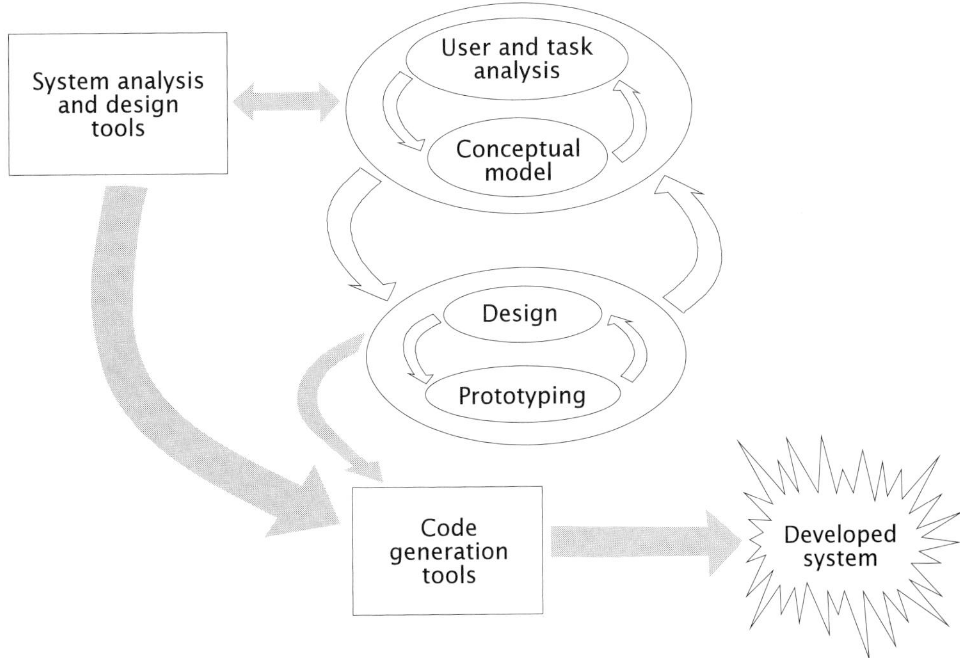

Figure 14-1 The "ideal" tool suite for user interface designers and implementors

[1]From an advertisement for *TAE Plus* [sCen93].

[2]From *The American Heritage Dictionary of the English Language* (Houghton Mifflin).

Real Tools

More typical tools, covering design-prototyping iterations in the user interface design process, resemble Figure 14-2. Because they cover only part of the development process, making the splices to other tools used in the overall process is left to the tool user.

The flow through the tool starts with the creation of a set of resources and a specification for the user interface. Resources include text files, graphics, icons, and other objects stored separately from programs that implement the interface. A tool with good coverage will provide editors and other tools for creating and managing these resources.[1] The user interface specification may take a variety of forms, for example:

- A programming language source code file.
- A high-level textual specification of appearance and dialogue flow, independent of any particular programming language.

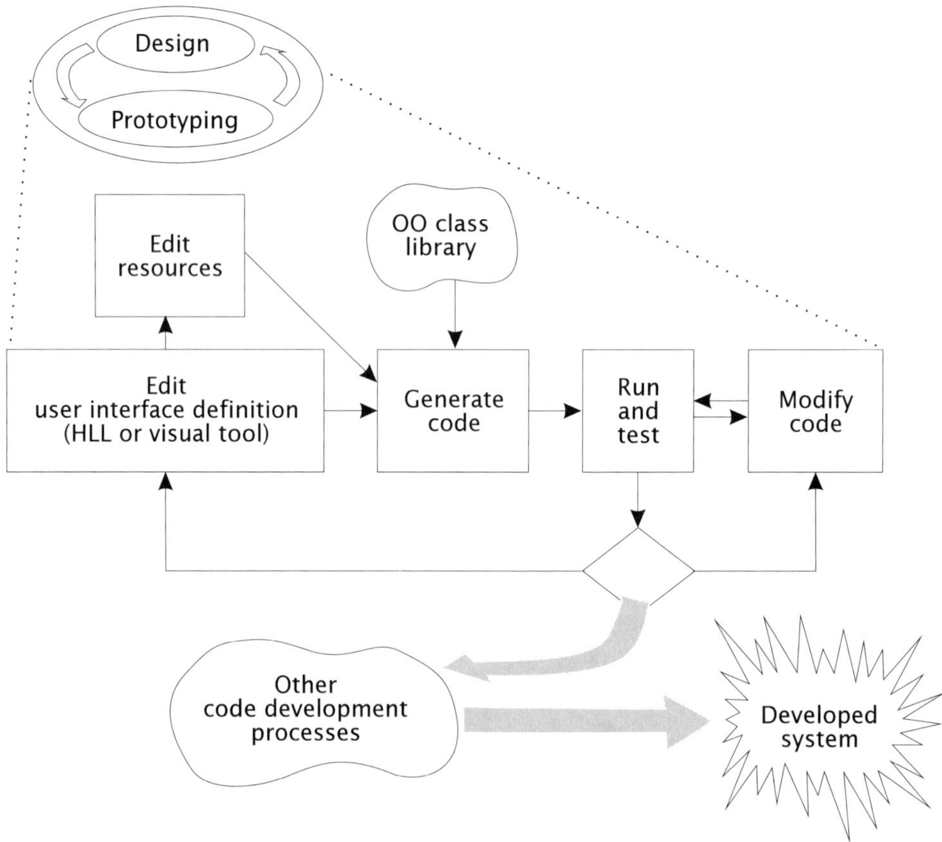

Figure 14-2 A typical "real" tool for user interface designers and implementors

[1]Note that *tool* is used to describe both the overall package, and "subtools" within it.

- A visual layout of the components of the user interface, often accompanied by textual specifications of the behavior of individual components.

Some tools use a mixture of these, or allow different views of the same specification. The type of specification is usually coupled to the intended users, and uses, of the tool. Designers who are not programmers favor very high-level visual or textual specifications. Programming language specifications are harder to use, but more likely to produce code that can become part of the delivered product.

Since we are discussing OO tools, there will probably be a class library of reusable code representing user interface objects. Sometimes the whole tool is simply a class library for use with a standard development environment.[1] From the library and the specification, code is generated to build a prototype of the user interface, which is then run and tested. Typically, many iterations of build-test-modify occur.

With some tools, there are two options for the *modify* part of the cycle. Either the original specification is changed, or changes are made to the generated code. This could be true, for example, if the tool used a high-level specification to generate C++ code. Changing the generated code might be done because it is quicker, or there might be low-level changes that can only be done to the generated source code. This complicates the process—if several iterations have changed generated code, the code must be reverse-engineered to update the original specification.

When the iterative design process is complete, the results go into the larger development process. Depending on the tool, the results might include only the external design, both external and internal design, or source code that will become part of the delivered system.

Object-oriented testing A discussion of the full range of development activities that might be facilitated by user interface tools is beyond the scope of this book. Testing is a representative example, and important because of the complexity of graphical OOUIs.

Two sorts of testing are applicable to user interfaces. The first is external usability testing, monitoring end users to discover problems or verify that the interface is efficient and easy to use. The second type is reliability or regression testing, in which test scripts are executed to verify that the software is free of errors and operates within performance specifications. An ideal tool would integrate testing into the total design and development process:

- During task analysis and synthesis, a library of usage scenarios would be created.

[1]For example, the View.h++ [sRog93] Motif class library can be used in many C++ development environments, and can be integrated with modular visual interface builders such as UIM/X [sVis93].

- The scenarios would be expanded into detailed scripts during the design of the presentation and action languages.
- During usability testing, actual end user behavior would be logged and compared against the scripts.
- During regression testing, scripts would be run by an automated driver to verify compliance with performance, reliability, and functional specifications.

For OOUIs, scripts specify object behavior, and test drivers operate by sending sequences of messages to objects.

Various approximations to the ideal can be found in real tools. In a Smalltalk environment, HOMSuite [sHat94] collects usage scripts with cross-references to the classes involved, and descriptions of the "contracts" between collaborating classes. In principle, a tool like this could be extended to provide enough information for a test driver. This is a top-down approach to testing.

Bottom-up testing tools are more common. The typical approach allows manual specification of a sequence of user actions, or recording of actions as they are done. Action sequences are used to build scripts to feed a test driver. SQA TeamTest [sSQA92] is a good example; it is object-oriented, in the sense that scripts are based on objects such as windows and icons, rather than screen positions. SQA runs on Microsoft Windows, and generates test scripts in Visual Basic [sMic93d]. Whereas SQA is strictly a testing tool, TAE Plus [sCen93], for X Windows and UNIX, is a GUI building tool with integrated script recording and playback facilities. The recording facility can log user actions during a usability test, as well as generate test scripts.

MVC architectures allow a two-level testing scheme. Chapter 5 discusses building test scripts for objects in the information model, before the user interface is built. This idea can be elaborated based on the discussion in Chapter 13 of separating command semantics from specific interaction techniques. Just as it is valuable to be able to develop the look and feel of the interface separately from the information model, testing them separately can be valuable also.

14.2 Components and Portability

Many technical issues in tools relate to the components a tool provides for interface construction, and how components can be ported for use in different contexts. This section just skims the surface, with minor excursions into the depths. It should encourage you to investigate issues of this sort when developing your own tool strategy. Early exploration can save much wasted time later.

Portability

The general idea of portability explains much of what developers are looking for in tools. Portability of *concepts* means that a developer who understands the paradigm of OOUI development in the context of one tool, can apply the same concepts to a different tool or platform. Portability of *look and feel* means end users will perceive that an application has the same look and feel on different platforms, though surface details change to reflect each platform's style. Portability of *design and code* means that low-level design and/or code can be ported to different platforms, or moved from one tool or language to another.

Many commercial developers are faced with an explicit portability requirement—they need to market a product for several platforms. Projects with no requirement for explicit portability can still have implicit (and easily overlooked) requirements. Multiple tools may be used on a project for prototyping and product development. Portability between tools, of concepts, design, or code, enhances productivity. Portability to new generations of technology is another implicit requirement, which requires separating technology-dependent and technology-independent layers.

"Hello, world" A traditional benchmark for portability, and undoubtedly the best known short program in the world, is Kernighan and Ritchies's "hello, world," which appears in their text on the C language [Ker78]. It simply prints "hello, world" on the console:

```
#include <stdio.h>
main ()
{
printf("hello, world\n");
}
```

Programs like this defined portability for a generation of programmers. If a program was moved to another system—say from BSD 4.0 to AT&T System V UNIX—and it still typed out "hello, world," it was portable.

Part of the portability of this program comes from the C language itself, which is standard. Part lies outside the language, in `stdio.h`. This is the standard I/O library for C; it is different for every platform, but guarantees that its platform-specific implementation of `printf` will correctly print the argument. Does this idea of portability scale up to GUIs? In principle, yes; in practice, the current answer is no. The problem is the complexity of graphical user interfaces compared to the simple line-oriented I/O of programs like "hello, world."

The closest approach to `stdio.h` in the realm of GUIs is the X Window System, a standard across most UNIX platforms. Here is a C language "hello, world" program for X Windows.[1]

[1]Based on one published in a paper by David Rosenthal, provocatively subtitled "How hard can it really be to write 'Hello, World'?" [Rosen88]. This is written to X11R3.

```
#include <X11/Xlib.h>
#include <X11/Xutil.h>
#define HELLO "hello, world"
main(int argc, char** argv) //***Main Program***
{
Display *display;  // X server connection
Window *win;        // Window ID
GC gc;  // Graphics context for text display in window
int bw = 2; // Border width
int bc = BlackPixel; // Border color
int bgc = WhitePixel; // Window background color
XSizeHints hints;  // Window sizing hints
XEvent event;       // Event data structure
// Open the display
display = XOpenDisplay(NULL);
// Set hints for initial window size and position
hints.x = 200; hints.y = 200;
hints.width = 300; hints.height = 200;
hints.flags = PPosition | PSize;
// Create the window
win = XCreateSimpleWindow(display,
      DefaultRootWindow(display), hints.x, hints.y,
      hints.width, hints.height, bw, bc, bgc);
XSetStandardProperties(display, win, HELLO, HELLO,
       argv, argc, &hints);
// Create a graphics context for writing the text
gc = XCreateGC(display, win, NULL, NULL);
// Specify events of interest (only exposure)
XSelectInput(display, win, ExposureMask);
XMapWindow(display, win);  // Show the window
// Event loop
while (TRUE)  {
  XNextEvent(display, &event);
  // Discard all but the most recent expose event
  if (event type == Expose && event.xexpose.count == 0) {
  int x, y;
    while (XCheckTypedEvent(display, Expose, &event));
  XClearWindow(display, win);
    //***Print "hello world"!!***
    XDrawImageString(display, win, gc, 50, 50,
            HELLO, strlen(HELLO));
  }
}
```

```
exit(0);
}
```

The most obvious change from the original "hello, world" is increased complexity, making it more likely that two vendors' implementations will have subtle differences. This suggests that even if X were standard across all platforms, portability would not be guaranteed, though life would certainly be easier.

Programs written for other GUI environments, such as Microsoft Windows or the Apple Macintosh toolkit, exhibit similar complexity. Most of it comes from generating visual and interaction behavior that is standard on any given platform, and similar across all GUI platforms. Comparing programs from different platforms will show that very different syntaxes cover up the same semantics.

Here is a "hello, world" program in C++, using the Borland ObjectWindows class library [sBor92] on Microsoft Windows. This example is 27 lines (excluding comment lines), versus the 37 lines of the C/X Windows version.[1] A good deal of this code still has the flavor of a magical incantation, because it directly reflects the Windows API.

```
#include <owl.h>
const char* HELLO = "hello, world";
class HelloWindow: public TWindow {
public:
    HelloWindow(PTWindowsObject AParent, LPSTR ATitle)
       : TWindow(AParent, ATitle) { }
    void Paint(HDC PaintDC, PAINTSTRUCT _FAR &PaintInfo) {
      //***Print "hello world"!!***
      TextOut(PaintDC, 50, 50, HELLO, strlen(HELLO));
    }
  };
class HelloApp: public TApplication {
    void InitMainWindow() {
      MainWindow = new HelloWindow(NULL, Name);
    }
 public:
    HelloApp(LPSTR AName, HINSTANCE hInstance, HINSTANCE
      hPrevInstance, LPSTR lpCmdLine, int nCmdShow)
      : TApplication(AName, hInstance, hPrevInstance,
            lpCmdLine, nCmdShow) { }
};
```

[1]These examples are atypical because they are small; larger OO programs reuse more code. Typically, C++ and Smalltalk reduce code bulk in GUI programs by factors of 3-5, compared to C.

```
//***Main program***
int PASCAL WinMain(HINSTANCE hInstance, HINSTANCE
hPrevInstance, LPSTR lpCmdLine, int nCmdShow) {
    HelloApp MyApp(HELLO, hInstance, hPrevInstance,
                lpCmdLine, nCmdShow);
    MyApp.Run();
    exit(0);
}
```

The examples so far suggest one approach to portability—pick an API and declare it to be the standard. X Windows is standard on most UNIX platforms. Some tools, such as XVT [Roch92], have developed "synthetic" standard APIs that they provide on multiple platforms.[1] The Microsoft Windows API is a *de facto* standard because it is so widely used, and tools exist that implement it on other platforms. Wind/U [Win94], for example, provides the Windows API on UNIX platforms by mapping it to X and OSF/Motif. Standard APIs solve part of the problem by providing platform portability, but they do not attack the complexity problem.

To better illustrate the ability of OO programming to reduce complexity, here is another C++ "hello, world," using the CommonView class library [sGlo89].

```
#include <commonvu.hxx>
const char* HELLO = "hello, world";
class HelloWindow : public AppWindow {
public:
    HelloWindow() : AppWindow() {
      Caption(HELLO);
      Commit(); }
    long Expose(ExposeEvt) {
      //***Print "hello world"!!***
      TextPrint(HELLO, Point(50, 50));
    }
  };
void App::Start()  {
  HelloWindow helloWin;
  Exec();
}
int main(int argc, char** argv)  //***Main Program***
{
HelloApp App;
HellpApp.Start();
```

[1] XVT has been proposed as a POSIX standard for a uniform window system API.

```
exit(0);
}
```

CommonView programs are portable across MS Windows, OS/2 Presentation Manager, and several UNIX platforms using X Windows. Portability is achieved through *abstraction*—raising the level of the code above the details of particular APIs. Compare the ObjectWindows `Paint` function call with CommonView's `Expose`. `Paint` explicitly uses the MS Windows structures `HDC` (handle of a device graphics context) and `PAINTSTRUCT` (which provides information on the window rectangle that needs to be displayed). CommonView's `Expose` is more generic, and relies on platform-specific private member functions (called by `TextPrint`) to take care of the details.

Here is yet another "hello, world," in Smalltalk/V; this example is portable across the Windows, OS/2, and Macintosh versions, again because the level of abstraction is high enough. It is not, however, portable to other Smalltalk systems, such as ParcPlace Smalltalk-80. With Smalltalk, as with C++, the language is standard but user interface class libraries are not.

```
ApplicationWindow subclass: #HelloWindow
open
  self addSubpane: (
  TextPane new
       owner: self;
       when: #getContents perform: #paint:).
  self openWindow.
paint: aTextPane
  "***Print 'hello world'!!***"
  aTextPane contents: 'hello, world'.
Object subclass: #HelloApp
  instanceVariableNames: 'mainWindow'
initMainWindow
  mainWindow := HelloWindow new.
  mainWindow label: 'Hello window'.
run
  mainWindow open.
```

The application is started up by the statement

```
| myApp |
myApp := HelloApp new.
myApp initMainWindow; run.
```

Component Sets

Interface-building tools provide libraries of classes or functions representing presentation and interaction components. There are many existing component sets, including commercial offerings and research toolkits.

These can be divided into two categories:

- "Base widgets" supplied by platform vendors (or consortiums of vendors, such as OSF and the X Consortium). These usually implement the content of a particular style guide, and are accessed by programmers through library routines.
- User interface class libraries written in a language such as C++ or Smalltalk. Typically, many of the classes supplied are OO "wrappers" for a base widget set.

These will probably merge as vendors start providing OO class libraries for base widgets. An example is Fresco [Bilo94], a forthcoming version of the X Toolkit based on C++. Widget sets based on the X Toolkit [McC88], such as the Motif widgets, already have a strong OO flavor. Though implemented in C, the X Toolkit provides explicit facilities for encapsulation, classes, and inheritance.

Widgets have "interaction semantics," independent of their look and feel. Scroll bars, for example, provide the same semantics on all platforms, sending messages to their owning windows to scroll up or down by some number of lines or pages. Their appearance and the exact details of their interaction behavior, however, differ from platform to platform. Similar considerations apply to buttons, text entry fields, etc.[1]

Abstracting interaction semantics is key to providing class libraries that work on multiple platforms. User interface classes represent visible objects with similar or identical semantics across platforms; as a result, the libraries have many similarities. The following subsections briefly summarize generic components provided in typical class libraries. Sources consulted include Smalltalk systems ([sDig92a], [sDig92b], [sPar92]); MacApp and several derivative frameworks ([Schm86], [Fer89], [Wein89], [sBor92]); X Windows and OSF/Motif ([Sch86], [McC88], [Berl91], [You92]); the C++ frameworks CommonView [sGlo89], C++/Views [sLia93], the Microsoft C++ Foundation Classes [sMic93c], and the IBM C++ User Interface Class Library [IBM93a]; and the NeXTSTEP Objective-C class library [Garf93]. Most of these are general-purpose programming environments, but only their user interface components are shown here.

Indentation of class names indicates hierarchical order. The hierarchies are "typical"; specific libraries differ in where classes are placed, how they are named, and the division of responsibilities between them. Some differences only affect abstract classes, so programmers may not need to be aware of them. For example, some libraries provide an abstract `EventHandler` class to hold behavior inherited by all objects that receive events (called `TEvtHandler` in MacApp, and `Responder` in NeXTSTEP). Other differences are more significant, such as classes (not shown in the lists

[1]The issue of interaction semantics is discussed in more detail in Chapter 13, Section 13.2. [vSIGGRAPH90] provides excruciatingly detailed examples of widget appearance and semantics for all the major platforms.

below) provided by Motif and ParcPlace Smalltalk for managing the geometry of composite display objects.[1]

Note that in discussing differences between libraries, two portability issues arise. A library can support code that ports to many platforms, while differing from other portable libraries. Differences between libraries affect the portability of code between them (on the same or different platforms), for example if one is used for prototyping and another for implementation.

Graphical objects and functions provide abstract interfaces to platform graphic services, functions such as drawing lines and filling areas, and drawn objects such as rectangles and circles:

- `GraphicsMedium` (or `Drawable`, a medium for drawing)
  - `Bitmap` (or `PixMap`, an off-screen drawing medium)
  - `Metafile` (a context for external file storage of graphic orders)
  - `Printer` (a context for printed graphics)
  - `Screen` (a context for graphics display on the screen)
- `GraphicsTool` (an object type representing drawing functions)
  - `Brush` (for filling areas with colors or patterns)
  - `Pen` (for drawing lines and closed shapes)
- `Color` (an object type representing a color)
- `Font` (an object type representing a text font)
- `Palette` (or `ColorMap`, representing a particular set of colors)
- `GraphicElement` (`Rectangle`, `Circle`, `Ellipse`, etc.)

Graphics classes vary considerably, both in terminology and semantics. Many libraries do not provide `GraphicElement` classes such as `Rectangle`; instead, they supply methods such as `drawRectangle` in `GraphicsMedium` or `GraphicsTool` subclasses. Most libraries support standard 2-D graphics primitives [Fol92] and *BitBlt* (bitmapped) primitives originally developed for Smalltalk [Gol83]. The syntax for invoking these primitives, however, varies widely. Sun NeWS [Ster87] and NeXT [Garf93] use imaging models based on the PostScript page description language [Ado86], which is quite different from typical graphics models. Even where two platforms use imaging models that are conceptually the same, interface details differ (Microsoft Windows and OS/2 are examples), and tools often do not do a good job of hiding the differences. This can significantly affect portability.

Two classes under *Widget classes* below are related to graphics classes—`Icon` and `MouseCursor` are similar to `Bitmap`, but also have interactive properties. `Widget` or `Window` instances in most libraries have an associated instance of some `GraphicsMedium` subclass, so they can display on the screen. In some libraries, visible windows may inherit from `GraphicsMedium`.

[1]ParcPlace reduces the impact by transparently instantiating reasonable defaults; many tools based on Motif also insulate developers from `Shell`, `Manager`, and `Constraint` protocols.

Widget classes Widgets (also called windows or views) are the most numerous classes. These classes map directly to visible objects, and are often "wrappers" for objects accessed through the platform API or low-level toolkit. Because platforms differ, these are not standard, but there are more similarities than differences across class libraries.

- `Icon` (represents "desktop" icons)
- `Menu` (collections of `MenuItem` instances; associated with `MenuWindow` instances)
  - `PopupMenu`
- `MenuItem` (corresponds roughly to `TCommand` in MacApp)
- `MouseCursor` (represents the behavior of the mouse-tracking icon)
- `Widget` (or `Window`, an abstract class supplying common behavior)
  - `ApplicationMainWindow` (the top-level window for an application)
  - `DialogWindow` (a special kind of widget optimized for quick display of transient information or prompts; called `Panel` in NeXTSTEP)
    - `FileSelectDialog` (for selecting a file from the file system)
    - `FontSelectDialog` (for selecting a text font)
    - `MessageBox` (displays transient information or action messages)
    - `PrinterSelectDialog` (for selecting a printer to print a document)
    - `Prompter` (requests a single item of information from the user)
  - `MenuWindow` (displays popup or pulldown menus)
  - `SubPane` (represents part of an application main window)
    - `Control` (widgets used as components in a `DialogWindow` or `SubPane`)
      - `Button` (abstract base class for buttons)
        - `DrawnButton` (client program draws the button label)
        - `PushButton` (standard push button)
        - `CheckBox` (used for inclusive choices)
        - `RadioButton` (used for mutually exclusive choices)
      - `TextControl` (abstract base class for text entry/edit controls)
        - `EntryField` (text entry for dialogs and prompters)
        - `StaticText` (non-editable text label)
        - `TextEdit` (editable text field, supports cut/copy/paste)
          - `MultiLineEdit` (multiple line text editor)
          - `SingleLineEdit` (single line editable entry field)
      - `GroupBox` (Coordinated or aligned group of controls)
        - `ButtonGroup`
          - `InclusiveGroup` (groups check boxes, for example)
          - `ExclusiveGroup` (groups radio buttons, for example)
      - `ListBox` (represents a list of selectable objects)
        - `ComboBox` (text entry with drop-down list of choices)
            - `MultipleSelectListBox` (`ListBox` permitting multiple selections)
        - `ScrollBar` (vertical or horizontal scroll bar)
    - `GraphPane` (`SubPane` specialized for drawing graphics)
    - `GroupPane` (`SubPane` for grouping other subpanes)

Event classes Most class libraries represent events from the window system as messages or member functions in a `Window` or `EventHandler` class. The arguments to these functions are often platform-dependent data structures. Some libraries, such as CommonView, provide an `Event` class to represent events at a more abstract level.[1]

`Event` (abstract class of events)
- `ControlEvent` (a child widget has generated an event for its parent; for example, a button has been pushed)
- `ExposeEvent` (the receiving widget has been exposed and needs to be redrawn)
- `FocusChangeEvent` (keyboard focus moved to a new widget)
- `InitEvent` (the receiving widget has just been opened)
- `KeyEvent` (a keyboard key was pressed or released)
- `MenuCommandEvent` (a menu command was picked)
- `MenuSelectEvent` (a menu item was selected, but the mouse button was not released to pick the menu command)
- `MouseEvent` (mouse button pressed or released, or mouse moved)
- `MoveEvent` (the receiving widget was moved on the display)
- `ResizeEvent` (the receiving widget was resized)
- `ScrollEvent` (vertical or horizontal scrolling)

Miscellaneous classes These are classes provided in some libraries that do not fit into any of the above categories.

`Application` (represents applications; like MacApp `TApplication`)
`HelpManager` (represents interfaces to the system help manager)
`NationalLanguageSupport` (represents interfaces to platform support for internationalization)
`Notifier` (system or application event dispatcher; may be subsumed by `EventHandler`, `Application`, or `Window` class)
`Point` (used generally for point location)
`Rectangle` (used generally for rectangles; for example, bounding rectangles of windows)
`Resource` (represents an externally stored resource such as an icon, dialog window specification, or text string)

Non-visual widgets Missing from all the leading user interface class libraries are components to handle non-visual presentation. (Support for audio output in NeXTSTEP is a notable exception.) Most libraries cover only the common-denominator forms of visual presentation and interaction that are found in platform style guides. Finding libraries supporting "advanced" media and techniques ranging from sound and video to handwriting recognition is possible, but no standard components exist in these areas.

[1]See Exercise 3 for other possible uses for event classes.

Platform-specific widgets There are many similarities between platforms, but there are significant differences too. Drag-drop support is missing from many tools, because not all platforms support it. Some platforms support unique interface objects; an example is the OS/2 *Notebook*, shown in Figure 1-2 in Chapter 1, and Figure 9-4 (c) in Chapter 9. Another example, shown in Figure 14-3, is the MDI (multiple document interface) window, used in MS Windows and early versions of OS/2.

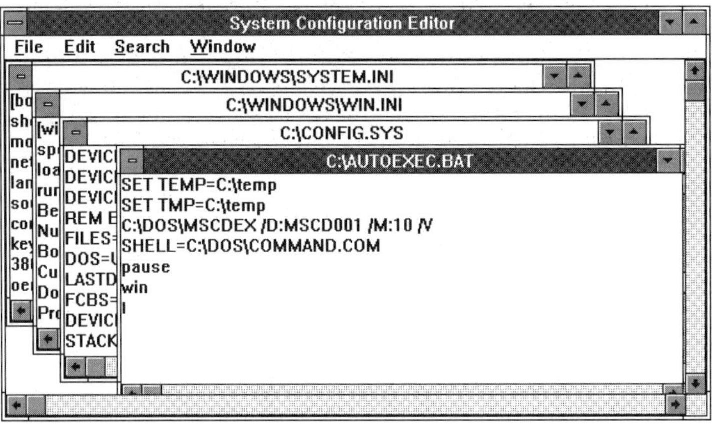

Figure 14-3 A multiple document interface (MDI) window

The MDI is easy to emulate on other platforms, since it is simply a collection of standard windows clipped by a parent window that contains them. The notebook is more difficult, since it is a custom graphic control, and it illustrates a common problem faced by developers and users of portable libraries. Supposing a library is to be portable between OS/2 and Motif, here are the possibilities for handling the notebook control:

- Do not use it, because it is not supported on both platforms; this is the *least common denominator* approach.
- Use the native control on OS/2, and emulate it on Motif; this and the next solution are variants of the *superset* approach.
- Develop a class that emulates the notebook, and use it on both platforms.

None of these solutions is entirely satisfactory. The first is easy for the library developer. The second provides the native "look and feel" on OS/2. The third sacrifices native look and feel, but provides more cross-platform compatibility. Recent standards, such as OSF/Motif 2.0 [Jol94] and the Common Open Software Environment (COSE) [Star94], will result in more commonality between widget sets, but compromises are still necessary today.

Domain-specific widgets Some toolkits and class libraries supply complex, high-level widgets designed for a particular application domain. LabVIEW [sNat89], shown in Figure 8-6 (Chapter 8), is an example—it comes with a kit of dials, buttons, indicators, etc. for building laboratory instrument control panels. Pinball Construction Set [sEle87], shown in Figure 10-2, is another domain-specific toolkit, for building pinball games. "Business widgets," such as graphical chart objects and spreadsheets, are included in some libraries.

The value of domain-specific widgets sometimes dominates other considerations in determining the value of a class library. One of the objectives of "plug and play" architectures such as OLE [Broc93] and CORBA [Vino93] is to allow reuse of domain-specific objects across different libraries and languages.

Architecting for Portability

Figure 14-4 shows an architecture that has evolved in many class libraries. Its primary aim is to foster portability by minimizing the interface between user interface classes and particular window manager APIs. In moving from one platform to another, only the layer labeled "platform-dependent objects" needs to change. Platform-independent user interface objects and applications (clients of library classes) are unaffected.

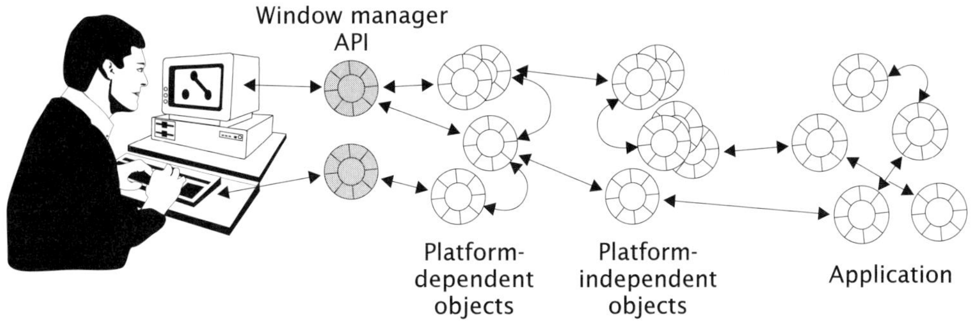

Figure 14-4 Layered abstractions in a user interface class library

The platform-dependent objects fall into two categories:

- Abstract classes with private methods or member functions that communicate with the platform-specific API.
- Concrete classes to which platform-dependent behavior is delegated by platform-independent classes.

An example of the first category is the `Window` class in Smalltalk/V. It receives platform-dependent messages such as `wmLbuttondown:with:`, and resends them as platform-independent messages such as `button1Down:`.

An example of the second category, also from Smalltalk/V, is the `CommonDialogDLL`. This class encapsulates the interface to standard platform dialogue windows, and has different versions for MS Windows and OS/2 Presentation Manager.

14.3 Categorizing OO Tools

Developing object-oriented user interface software requires components and tools for assembling and integrating them. The assembly tools may include generic blueprints that guide construction by showing how typical systems are put together. "Assembly" may include analysis, design, and testing, though most tools support only the building process.

One dimension for categorizing tools is whether the emphasis is on "raw" components and assembly tools, or on blueprints for entire applications. This differentiates toolkits from application frameworks, though both are usually packaged as object-oriented class libraries. A second dimension is the paradigm for assembly. Some tools emphasize visual methods, where developers lay out and "wire together" components to build a user interface. Others rely on textual specification. Many tools are hybrid, providing both visual and non-visual methods.

Toolkits and Class Libraries

Section 14.2 summarizes the kinds of objects provided by typical OO class libraries for user interface building, and shows a few samples of their use. Chapters 11-13 provide other samples, such as the various versions of the counter application. These examples fit the common metaphor of *toolkits*—organized collections of objects that a skilled craftsperson can use to build things.

Event-driven GUIs are inherently object-based, no matter how they are implemented. Early toolkits such as the Macintosh Toolbox [App88] and Xlib [Nye90] provided the developer with a set of function or procedure calls. Here is a simplified pseudocode example:[1]

```
windowProcedure(event) {
  switch(event.type) {
     case EXPOSE: callHandleExposeEvent(event);
. . . . . .
main() {
  window = callWindowCreateFunction(windowProcedure);
  callSetWindowProperties(window, properties);
  callOpenWindow(window);
  exit(0); // Exit when window closes
}
```

[1]The X Windows "hello, world" (page 425) is a real example.

In spite of the programming style, the semantic content here is an object of type `Window`, which receives events as messages and responds to them. It is a short step to an object-oriented toolkit that provides facilities for object creation and message dispatching:

```
class Window {
  public:
      ExposeEvent(event);
. . . . . . . };
main() {
  window = new Window();
  window.setProperties(properties);
  window.open();
  exit(0); // Exit when window closes
}
```

Procedural toolkits are generally considered esoteric, difficult to learn, and hard to use, except by the minority of programmers who have become experts. Object-oriented toolkits are easier, for several reasons:

- They provide a better fit to the semantics of the problem domain.
- Encapsulation conceals implementation details.
- Encapsulation and inheritance allow new objects to be created based on composition of existing objects, or differences from existing objects.

OO toolkits, except some visual toolkits, require a knowledge of programming. Like toolkits in other crafts, they also require a knowledge of the plans for building things. Frameworks, discussed below, reduce the requirement for detailed knowledge of plans. All toolkits, even procedural ones, provide substantial code reuse. Since most of them implement GUI style guides, they also reuse graphic and human factors design work.

An advantage of low-level toolkits is that they can produce production-quality code. This means that code from a user interface prototype can be reused in the delivered product. Higher skill requirements and longer development time for the prototype may be a corresponding disadvantage, but this is not always true. In some cases, high-level tools cannot provide the function or performance needed to accurately prototype an OOUI, so toolkit-level programming is required.

Application Frameworks

Application frameworks address the issue of reusing software components larger than functions or classes. This requires modeling assemblies as well as objects. Frameworks can be generic or domain-specific; they can cover facets, such as the user interface, or encompass the entire structure of an application.

Object-oriented frameworks are class libraries of software components with preestablished connections embodying the function, structures, and design patterns needed for applications. Like toolkits, they include classes representing the kinds of objects used in a domain, but they also capture interconnections and relations between objects. They may include abstract classes intended to be subclassed, concrete classes that can be instantiated to provide services to applications, and sample applications illustrating the use of the framework.

The boundary between toolkits and frameworks is fuzzy.[1] Almost all toolkits incorporate some knowledge of component assembly. Like toolkits, frameworks reuse code, graphics design, and human factors work. Frameworks also embody a (perhaps very general) conceptual model of what an entire application looks like. The Smalltalk MVC scheme is an example—it represents the structure of an abstract application.

As in many other frameworks, the `View` and `Controller` subtrees in the MVC hierarchy contain concrete classes that most applications will use, whereas the `Model` branch does not. This reflects the fact that it is intended for a particular domain of user interfaces, not a particular domain of applications. Because GUIs are difficult for developers, many frameworks (and toolkits) emphasize user interface components. They must be extended with information model classes, or combined with domain-specific frameworks, to build complete applications.[2]

MacApp has been mentioned several times as a mature and widely imitated framework. The number of MacApp "clones" validates a statement by Peter Deutsch, echoing Brooks's thought on what is hard about software: "Interface design and functional factoring constitutes the key intellectual content of software and is far more difficult to recreate than code" [Deut91]. MacApp itself is available in both Object Pascal and C++; its essence is the structure of an event driven application, not some particular set of code sources.

"If you choose MacApp to develop Macintosh application, it will probably save you months of effort as compared with the traditional approach." This statement, by Kurt Schmucker [Schm86], once seemed radical; it has since been confirmed by experience with MacApp and other frameworks. The following table, from [Schm88], indicates the kind of effort that frameworks capture for reuse. This shows statistics for MacApp and its predecessor, the Lisa Toolkit.

	Classes	**Methods**	**LOC**	**Person-Years**
Lisa Toolkit	96	1163	44,391	18
MacApp	39	562	23,849	9

[1] Most of the examples in this chapter and Chapters 11-13 are on the border between toolkits and frameworks.

[2] Exercises 4 and 5 explore the idea of domain and industry-specific frameworks, an important concept that is beyond the scope of this book.

The effort reflected here (in person-years of development time) is effort avoided by users of MacApp.

Visual Interface Builders

At least since Ivan Sutherland's Sketchpad system, tools that exploit human visual processing have generated excitement. Given that graphical OOUIs themselves are examples of this, it seems natural that visual tools should be applied to specifying them.

Visual versus textual specification is not an either-or proposition. Certain aspects of an interface, such as the general layout and appearance of objects, lend themselves to direct manipulation with visual feedback. Other aspects do not. Most people would agree that computational logic is easier to express textually than visually, though completely visual tools do exist.[1]

Figure 14-5 shows Digitalk's PARTS Workbench [sDig92c], a representative visual interface builder.[2] The `PARTS.CAT` window on the left is a notebook with tabs showing various categories of parts, such as windows, buttons, menus, etc. Moving the mouse pointer over a visual part causes a textual description to appear in an information area at the bottom of the `PARTS Workbench` window. An application titled `My Application` is being constructed by dragging parts from the notebook to the workbench and linking them.

Six parts have been placed: a main window, a menu bar, two menu labels (`File` and `Edit`), and the standard `File` and `Edit` pulldown menus. Dragging from the `Edit` label to the `Edit` menu links them (shown by the dotted line) and pops up a prompt with the suggested action—to send the message `popup` to the menu when its label generates the `clicked` event. The already completed link on the `File` menu has been labeled with these names. At any point, the interface can be dynamically tested. In Figure 14-6, the interface constructed in Figure 14-5 is being tested to verify the behavior of the `Edit` menu.

PARTS permits textual and visual specification. Developers can create visual parts from Smalltalk objects and add them to the catalog. The behavior of visual parts can also be supplemented by writing scripts in PARTSTalk, a Smalltalk-like language. In this regard, PARTS resembles Apple's HyperCard [Goo87] and Microsoft's Visual Basic [sMic93d]. The construction paradigm is that the interface is a container for event-driven visual parts. Behavior of parts is either intrinsic to the part, or defined by a script. The script languages used are PARTSTalk, HyperTalk, and Basic, respectively.

An interesting feature of HyperCard is its rich set of graphics tools, and complete lack of constraints on the look and feel of the interface. As a

[1]For example LabVIEW [sNat89] and Prograph [sTGS90]. See [Shu88] for a general discussion of visual programming.

[2]PARTS, like the NeXT Interface Builder [Garf93], allows the construction of complete applications, not just user interfaces.

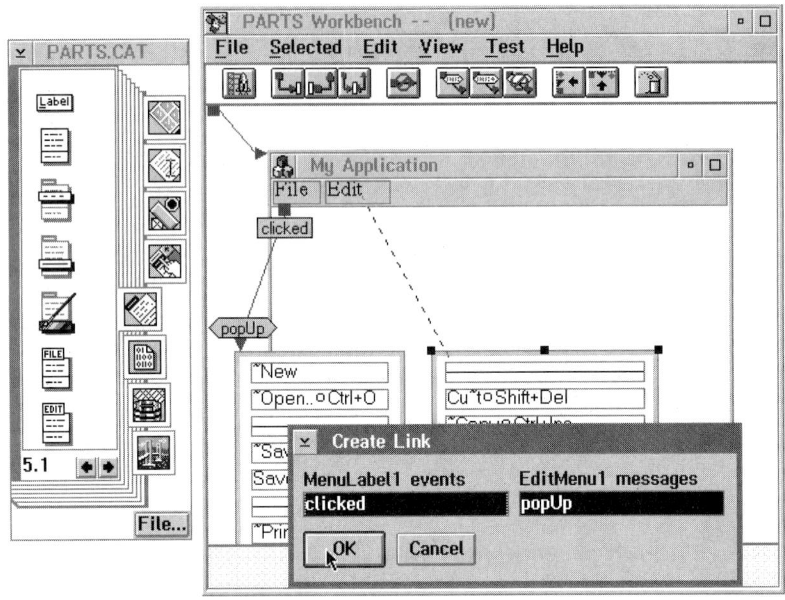

Figure 14-5 Linking objects in a visual interface builder (PARTS)

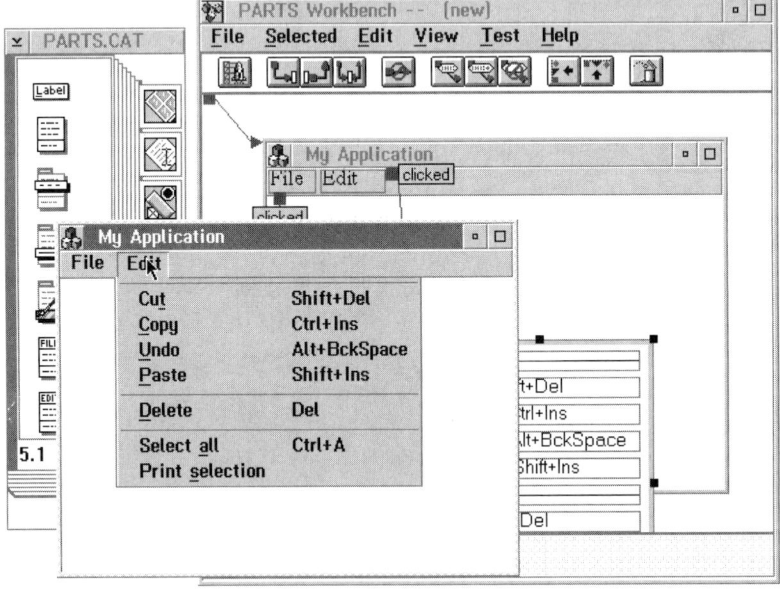

Figure 14-6 Testing the interface construction (PARTS)

result, though it runs only on the Macintosh, it can be used to prototype interfaces for other platforms. PARTS and Visual Basic use native platform widgets, so they are restricted to building interfaces with the look and feel of the platforms they run on (OS/2 and Microsoft Windows).

In PARTS, the only way of building an interface (or an application) is by parts assembly. A more common paradigm is to generate an executable specification for the interface (typically programming language code), which is then supplemented with "logic" code to complete the application or prototype. This is the scheme used by VisualWorks [sPar92], an interface builder packaged with ParcPlace Smalltalk. The Smalltalk code generated by VisualWorks includes a `windowSpec` method, used to create an instance of `UISpecification`. This in turn is used by a `UIPainter` to instantiate the widgets making up the user interface.

VisualWorks, like HyperCard, is independent of the look and feel of the platform it runs on. Unlike HyperCard, it is not freeform, but provides a fixed set of platform styles. This is more easily seen than explained, and it is illustrated in Figure 14-7.

In the figure, VisualWorks (running under Microsoft Windows) is being used to test interfaces for Macintosh and OSF/Motif. The two windows being tested (`My Application - Motif` and `My Application - Macintosh`) have the same interaction semantics. The `Canvas Control` window associated with each one sets the desired style. By emulating widgets instead of using the native widgets, VisualWorks achieves remarkable portability. The price paid is an interface that does not exploit all the details of each platform's style.

Visual builders can dramatically increase productivity for parts of

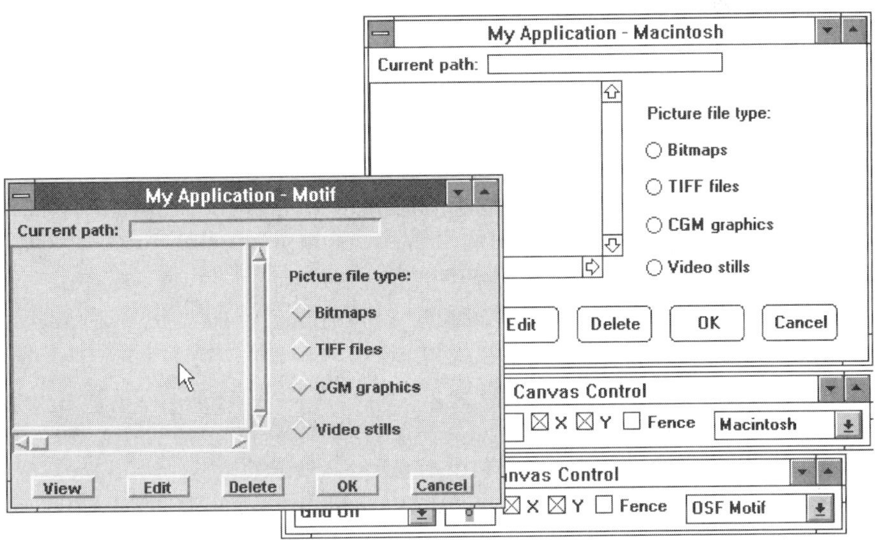

Figure 14-7 Testing multiple platform versions of an interface (VisualWorks)

the interface building task that are inherently visual, such as window layout. For logic functions or interactions between multiple objects, a text specification is often superior. Even in layout tasks, a textual specification of the interface may be valuable. For example, we might want to specify the approximate location of two widgets visually, but also specify that their top edges should be aligned exactly—something difficult to accomplish by visual alignment. A good tool will support both modes.

14.4 Evaluating Tools

I spend hours every day keeping up with developments in this field, but I cannot list, let alone knowledgeably discuss, all the available tools. Any detailed discussion would soon be obsolete, since vendors continually release new versions. Because of the scalability problem (described below), even those who work full time on tool evaluation, such as product reviewers for trade journals, cannot provide all the necessary information. So it is essential to understand your tool needs and develop a methodology for evaluating tools in your own environment.

Scalability

Figure 14-8 shows how two hypothetical tools, "A" and "B," scale up with problem size. (Size may be measured in lines of code, number of developers, function points, etc.) Based on small sample problems used to demonstrate or evaluate the tools, tool "A" appears superior; this remains true with medium-sized problems used for in-depth evaluation. But tool "A" scales up non-linearly. Truly large problems (which may be the reason for purchasing the tool) are *more* difficult than with tool "B," perhaps even impossible.

There are many reasons for scaling problems, for example:

- Features required for the large problem, such as drag-drop or client-server communications, are not supported by the tool.
- The tool lacks management and coordination features, which causes breakdowns when the code volume or number of people on the project becomes large.
- The tool has technical problems, such as poor runtime performance or very long compile times, that only surface in large projects.

Ideally, you can avoid using a tool that has never been used on a project whose scope and size are similar to yours. If that is not possible, a measure of the tool vendor's credibility is willingness to help analyze requirements and point out possible pitfalls. Evolutionary or incremental development is another defense against the scalability problem—delivery of a system in increments reduces the size of the deliverables, and provides earlier warning of problems.

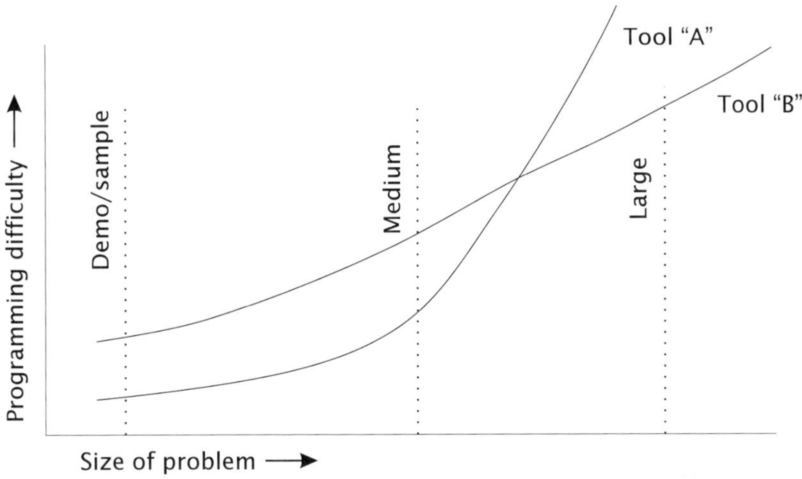

Figure 14-8 Comparing scalability of two tools

Issues Checklist

The following may seem like a "laundry list," when what you really want is a flowchart that guides you to a decision. Unfortunately, there are too many contextual variables, so there is no generally valid decision procedure. Fortunately, an understanding of your environment and object-oriented tool technology will usually lead to a good decision.

Note that "tool" here can be a single tool, an add-on such as a class library, or an entire suite of tools intended to work together.

Contextual factors The following are some significant variables that will affect how you look at the issues.

- *How risky is the project?* If it has been done before, "tried and true" tools may be available. Sometimes the only way to reduce the risk is to pursue several tools in parallel until one emerges as clearly superior.
- *What are the critical success factors?* If high-quality detailing of the interface is key, or if you need specialized components, custom programming in a language like C or C++ may be the answer. If end users are willing to make sacrifices in return for rapid delivery, low cost, or portability, then higher-level tools may be appropriate. Keep in mind that progress in tools is rapid, so there may be a high-level tool that generates low-level code that can be "tweaked" to fit your needs.
- *How large is the project?* The larger it is, the more important are things like source code management, quality control, and tool integration across the development life cycle.

- *Are the system requirements well understood?* If not, the ability to do rapid prototyping and exploratory programming is important. If requirements are well-understood, there is a better chance of finding domain-specific tools such as frameworks that package the needed functionality.
- *What skills exist?* Other things being equal, the tool with the shortest learning curve is best. When existing skills do not match the selected tool, training and support are important issues.
- *What components exist?* Availability of required components with a particular tool will bias your decision in its favor.

In dealing with these contextual variables, I frequently find a dichotomy between two types of tool. On one side are tools specialized for particular development contexts or problem domains. These are easier to use within the intended domain, but harder to extend or scale up. On the other side are general-purpose "power tools"—typically, integrated development environments for languages such as C++ and Smalltalk. These are harder to learn and use initially, but easier to extend and scale up.

Issues Here is a summarized list of issues that will affect your choice of tools. They are framed as questions to ask of yourself or the tool vendor. They should be weighted based on the importance of each one in the context of a particular project or range of projects.

- What phases of the development life cycle does the tool cover? Most tools embody assumptions about the development process and methodology. Are they consistent with practices and existing tools within your organization? Can data be shared between this tool and others used on the project? For user interface tools, an important special case is how the tool supports external design, human factors, usability testing, etc.
- Is the tool fully object-oriented, supporting encapsulation, classes, and inheritance? Does it provide OO development facilities for the entire application, or just the user interface?
- Can the facilities and objects provided by the tool be extended? Can you add your own domain-specific classes? Can it be integrated with other class libraries?
- Who will use the tool? Have you tested its ease of use and learning for the intended users? (Note that "users" here are the developers using the tool.)
- If you move to a different tool, can work done with this one be salvaged? The extremes are tools that produce source code in industry-standard languages, versus "black box" tools using closed, proprietary formats.

- Is the tool expected to generate code for use in the delivered product? If so, can it be integrated with other tools such as source code library managers? If the tool supplies a class hierarchy, does it conflict with the naming or structure of other libraries in your organization? Is time and space performance of the generated code adequate for its intended uses? (Scale-up problems are common in the area of performance.) If the tool does not use a standard programming language, does it provide interfaces to operating system services that you need?
- If output from the tool will be part of the delivered product, what are the runtime requirements? Is there a per-user licensing charge?
- If the tool is for prototyping, do its capabilities match those of the implementation language? This can work both ways—the tool may allow features that cannot be delivered, or it may be unable to prototype required features. Does the tool support a fast change-test cycle, or must large amounts of code be recompiled and relinked for each change?
- Does the tool address requirements that go beyond the standard GUI, such as audio and video? Does it support internationalization?
- Is platform portability required for user interfaces built with the tool? What, if anything, are you willing to sacrifice in return for portability? (For example, do you need full native look and feel for each platform?) Will the tool keep up with new releases of platform software?
- Does the tool have a sound architecture, with layered abstractions appropriate for its intended uses? Can it be extended to new abstractions?

14.5 Summary

It is unlikely that a single tool or suite of tools will be ideal for all your requirements. Because of the large number of tools on the market, and their complexity, keeping up can be a daunting task. The best intellectual tools for this task are a thorough knowledge of your requirements and of enabling technologies such as class libraries and frameworks.

Besides the checklists above, here are a few points to keep in mind:

- Tools for rapid prototyping and code generation enhance the design process; they do not substitute for task analysis, conceptual model design, etc.
- Problems with scalability have caused many disasters. Do not judge tools based on how they solve small problems.
- Studies and experience show that the dominant productivity factor is

good people. If you hire good people and train them well, they will find or build good tools.

14.6 To Explore Further

The world of commercial and research interface-building tools is a chaotic one, resulting from the collision of several technology waves. Starting in the early 1980s, the availability of powerful desktop computers lent credibility to the emerging idea of CASE, computer-aided engineering for software professionals. In the middle to late '80s, CASE vendors with tools based on older "structured" methods scrambled to maintain a foothold as the market began to swing to object-orientation, client-server, and GUIs. Meanwhile there is a long history of research tools for building user interfaces from high-level specifications [Löw88].

Today, the tools market has hundreds of players. These include old-line CASE vendors with updated offerings, language vendors supporting GUIs with offerings ranging from "fourth-generation" database languages to COBOL, platform vendors trying to ease the burden of coding to their APIs, vendors of object-oriented class libraries supporting GUI development, and many more. New players and new tools enter the market monthly. Since development on GUI platforms is relatively new, relatively difficult, and very important, most development tools at least advertise some GUI development capability.

While this technology churn exists, there will not be any systematic, up-to-date "literature" in the field. To keep up, know the contexts that interest you. That includes technical knowledge of platforms and application domains, development methods, and organizational factors. The literature, such as it is, is primarily found in the more serious trade journals such as *BYTE*, *Dr. Dobb's Journal*, and *Software Development*. *DATAMATION* primarily covers tools of interest in distributed systems that include mainframe and midrange computers. *UNIX Review* and *The X Journal* cover the UNIX, X Windows, and Motif market. *Object* and the *Journal of Object-oriented Programming* focus on "pure" object-oriented tools.

Vendors of specific tools can provide references to the research literature that relate to their tools. Vendors may also provide seminars, and demonstration or evaluation versions of their tools. The consensus among developers I have consulted is that it takes at least a week of solid work with a tool to properly understand and evaluate it. This means that you will usually learn more from an in-depth study of a few tools than a more cursory study of many. The journals cited above can help in selecting representative samples of tools.

One good way to learn about a tool is to discuss experiences with a developer who has completed a substantial project using the tool—if possible, one with characteristics similar to your applications.

[Löw88] and [Mye89] are useful surveys of tools, capabilities, issues and definitions. These two papers, and [Pfa85], provide discussions of user interface management systems (UIMS).[1] [Dea90] and [Nic91], descriptions of tool development efforts, are useful because they abstract general principles. [Hix91] describes a detailed methodology for formally evaluating user interface development tools. [DeS93], though produced by a tool vendor [sLia93], is a comprehensive summary of issues in evaluating multi-platform GUI builders (with emphasis on C++ tools).

[Johns88] discusses the general idea of frameworks. MacApp, the best known commercial framework, is described in [Schm86]. [Fer89] describes a MacApp derivative used by developers at Aldus. [Yan88] describes the use of a framework derived and extended from MacApp in the InterMedia project at Brown University. InterMedia and Unidraw [Vlis90] are examples of domain-specific frameworks.

14.7 Exercises

1. In the "hello, world" examples starting on page 425, suppose you want to show the text in one of several languages; the choice of language is to be made at runtime. Propose a method for doing this in the C/X Windows example. Could your method be simplified if you were using C++ or Smalltalk?
2. Suppose you want to provide the capability of having "hello, world" spoken by a synthesizer instead of being displayed. Compare the difficulty of doing this in C/X Windows, and the C++/CommonView and Smalltalk examples.
3. Describe new classes representing events (like the ones on page 433) that would help in the following problems:
   a. Hierarchical event passing as shown in Chapter 11, Figure 11-6.
   b. Linking models and views (described in Chapter 12, Section 12.3) in a distributed client-server environment.
4. Figure 8-6, in Chapter 8, showed a screen created with LabVIEW, a user interface building tool for laboratory instrumentation. Based on "reverse engineering" the interface, diagram a hierarchy of visual object classes that could be used in LabView.
5. Design a framework for office applications such as word processing and spreadsheets. Your design can take the form of sketched class and composition hierarchies. Think about information model objects, presentation and interaction objects, and how you might package and document the framework.

[1] I do not use the term UIMS in referring to user interface tools, because it means too many things in too many contexts.

6. Extend the framework in (5) with industry-specific objects for one of the following applications:
    - Insurance claims processing
    - Processing loan applications in a bank
    - Invoices, bills of lading, etc. in a warehouse.

15

Design Examples

This chapter describes four applications with object-oriented user interfaces, developed using object-oriented design and programming. One is a successful commercial product, two are research projects, and the fourth is a prototype for a potential product. They illustrate aspects of OOUI design methodology in the context of substantial development efforts.

Journalist, the first example, shows the power of a new conceptual model—not only to make the interface better, but to provide a cleaner internal structure for the system. KCM, the second, had a vision that exceeded the available development resources. By focusing on concepts and architecture, however, it produced a robust platform for future efforts. The developers of VR-DECK, the third case, also focused on architecture. They capitalized on their substantial experience building virtual reality applications to provide a toolkit for other developers. The last case is a prototype of the fax application described in Appendix 1.

I hope these examples encourage you to make "case studies" from projects you are involved in or projects done by people you know. Most of the lessons anyone needs on object-oriented development have already been learned from the successes and failures of the last couple of decades. They only wait to be documented and disseminated.

15.1 Journalist: Seamless Online News[1]

Journalist [sPED93] was discussed in Chapter 8 as an example of the use of metaphor. It provides facilities for laying out a "personal newspaper," which is then filled in by downloading text and images from online news services.[2] The use of the newspaper metaphor not only affects the user

[1] I am indebted to Gail De Lano, of De Lano Communications, and Gregory Hassett, of PED Software, for providing me with information on the development of Journalist.

[2] Currently, services accessed through CompuServe or Prodigy.

interface, but changes the internal design of the application as well.

The problem that Journalist aims to solve is the proliferation of on-line sources for local, national, and international news. These sources provide up-to-the-minute news, and in principle a user can access just the information of interest—but in practice, the task of finding the desired information may be like finding a needle in a haystack. Looking just at one service, CompuServe, there are many sources of news articles, photographs, maps, and so forth. Here is the main menu for the `News and Weather` category:

```
BASIC NEWS SERVICES
 1 Associated Press Online
 2 Weather
 3 U.S. News & World Report Magazine
 4 UK News/Sports
 5 Deutsche Presse-Agentur Kurznachrichtendienst
 6 Deutsche Wahlen '94
 7 Online Today Daily Edition
 8 Syndicated Columns
EXTENDED NEWS SERVICES
 9 Executive News Service ($)
10 U.S. News Online
11 NewsGrid US/World News  +
12 Sports
13 News Source USA
14 Detroit Free Press
15 Reuter News Pictures Forum  +
16 Florida Today Forum  +
17 Global Crises Forum  +
18 The Business Wire  +
19 Citibank's Global Report
20 Soviet Politics
21 Entertainment News/Info
22 New York Newslink Forum +
```

Each of these may unfold to another list of sources; for example, under `Weather` we find:[1]

```
1 Short-Term Weather Forecasts
2 U.S. National Weather Service Reports
3 Other Regions of the World
4 Radar (for 12:45 EST 27-Apr-94)
5 Depiction (for 12:41 EST 27-Apr-94)
```

[1] This session occurred on April 27, 1994.

```
 6 CompuServe Temperatures (for 12:41 EST 27-Apr-94)
 7 Satellite (for 12:00 EST 27-Apr-94)
 8 Satellite - Pacific (for 22:00 EST 26-Apr-94)
 9 Current Weather (for 12:00 EST 27-Apr-94)
10 Tomorrow's Weather (for 12:00 EST 28-Apr-94)
11 48-Hour Weather (for 07:00 EST 29-Apr-94)
12 Current Temperatures (for 12:00 EST 27-Apr-94)
13 Tonight's Lows (for 28-Apr-94)
14 Tomorrow's Highs (for 28-Apr-94)
15 Northeast NA (for 27-Apr-94)
16 Southeast NA (for 27-Apr-94)
17 North Central NA (for 27-Apr-94)
18 South Central NA (for 27-Apr-94)
19 Northwest NA (for 27-Apr-94)
20 Southwest NA (for 27-Apr-94)
```

When the desired source is reached, there may still be a list of items to browse. Depending on the service and the type of terminal, users can view the items online, or download the files and display them on local computers. To take one task as an example, suppose I want to see a weather map for the northeast US. The steps involved are:

1. Invoke a terminal emulator program, dial in, and log on to CompuServe.
2. Either access the weather maps through the series of menus shown above, or type `go maps` to get there directly.
3. Select `Northeast NA`.
4. Depending on the terminal emulator, a viewer may open on the map, or I may need additional steps:
   a. Download the file to my computer.
   b. Exit the terminal emulator.
   c. Invoke an image viewer application and open the weather map file.

I always need to download the file if I want to print the map. If I want to print the map with text (for example, the weather forecast) I must import it into a word processing or desktop publishing application.

What users often want is something like a daily newspaper, but one that is available on demand and contains only items that interest the individual reader. The newspaper, with its standard layout, is a good metaphor, but existing CompuServe facilities implicitly define the system and task models in terms of files, applications, and download procedures. Journalist supplies the missing layer. Users can lay out pages with frames for specific kinds of stories and pictures. Frames fill themselves by downloading the appropriate data from CompuServe.

The newspaper metaphor adds a new layer to the implementation, with objects like pages, frames, and news categories. The "old" model, of links, files, and downloads, becomes the technical infrastructure for the new layer and is hidden from the user. This is a good example of the importance—and pervasiveness—of a conceptual model. Here it leads to a different object model in analysis, changes the design model, and affects implementation of the whole system, not just the user interface.

Figure 15-1 shows the process of creating and filling a layout with Journalist. On the left, frames have been placed on a page, using icons to select categories such as sports, weather, etc. Frames can be further configured through property dialogues that allow a user to specify, for example, the geographic area to show in a weather map. Text properties, such as size and font, can be adjusted using typical word processing controls. Some frames are static, for example, the banner saying ****Dave's Daily News****. Others must be filled, which is done through scripts that execute processes to download files from CompuServe and display them in the desired format.

Any number of pages can be laid out in a "newspaper," which is saved in a file. When the file is loaded and the `Fill all` menu command is picked, all the necessary downloads are done, and the page appears as on

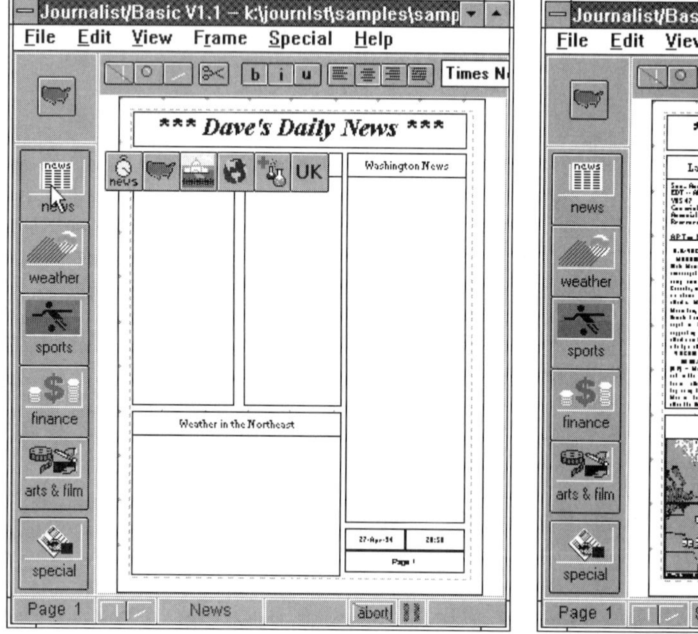

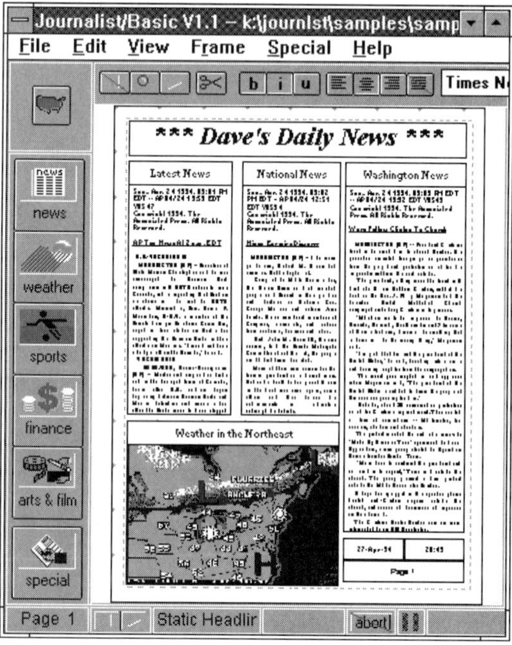

Figure 15-1 Page layout and filling in Journalist

World News

Sat., Feb. 05 1994, 11:26 PM EST

Big News At 11 p.m.

BOMBING IN SARAJEVO

SARAJEVO, Bosnia-Herzegovina -- Bombs landed in two shopping malls Friday, killing more than 50 people and wounding 100. Serb leader Radoxan Varadzic asserted that Bosnian government soldiers "bombed their own people" to be persuading the UN to go ahead with threatened attacks on Serb positions. In Washington, President Clinton vilified the slaughter and called on the United Nations to "please, please investigate" and blame the guilty parties. The French arranged for a Foreign Legion medical team to arrive in Sarajevo early Sunday to take out victims of the attack.

BOSNIA-FRENCH HELP

SARAJEVO, Bosnia-Herzegovina -- A French plane began taking out the wounded on Saturday. Fifty people were killed and 100

U.S. News

Sun., Feb. 06 1994, 11:08 AM EST.

Discovery Shuttle Will Release Device

NASA, Houston -- Astronaut James Smilov will release an experimental device from the Shuttle Discovery on Saturday.

The Shield Facility causes radio interference and uses solar energy to retransmit radio signals beamed to it and elsewhere.

Tilting the satellite will improve transmissions and allow the Shuttle crew to deploy it one day later than scheduled. NASA officials reported that yesterday's difficulties were "minor" and had been corrected. "Everybody's ready to go today."

The 60-foot shield satellite weighs 4,500 pounds and looks like a flying saucer. Astronauts will hoist it high over the shuttle and dangle it overboard so a rush of atomic oxygen will clean its sensitive

Weather in the United States

Washington News

Sun., Feb. 06 1994, 11:09 AM EST.

Latest from Somalia

WASHINGTON -- The Clinton administration plans to get Americans out of Somalia after April 1. A battalion of Marines will guard civilians during the evacuation and leave later.

Military commanders are concerned with whether the security provided will be adequate. They are transporting troops and civilians out of the country on a luxury cruise ship so as not to risk having air transport planes bombed or sabotaged.

Maj. Bovanic Tarski, operations officer for the Marines, wrote in a Jan. 2 letter to Ambassador Bogosian Richards in Mogadishu that his battalion's "firepower is insufficient for protecting diplomats and their families."

Other Washington News

WASHINGTON -- The Clinton administration plans to leave Washington after April 1. A battalion of Marines will provide security during the evacuation. Military commanders are concerned with whether the security provided will be adequate. They are transporting troops and civilians out of the country in a stretch limo so as not to risk having air transport planes bombed or sabotaged.

International Politics

WASHINGTON -- Administration plans to sponsor an international monetary conference in Washington starting April 14 are "going forward" according to a top-ranked official who chose to remain anonymous. Leading bankers and politicians will discuss interest rates, the fall of the dollar versus other currencies, and unemplotment rates. Representatives from both Europe and Japan have reportedly been invited.

TOKYO -- Japanese officials who declined to be directly quoted "are bothered by the U.S. position on trade deficits." The Japanese claim that U.S.

Figure 15-2 Front page of a "personal newspaper" created with Journalist

the right in Figure 15-1. Frames can then be viewed in Journalist, or the newspaper can be printed, producing the result shown in Figure 15-2. Besides filling on command, frames can fill on a preset schedule. For example, a user might want to fill financial data frames every day after the New York Stock Exchange closes.

What are the pros and cons of Journalist? It might seem that users wanting to see only a few items could retrieve them faster by going straight to CompuServe, but that turns out not to be true. Once the layout is done, the use of automated scripts allows Journalist to fill many pages faster than a user could log on and download a single file. Layout is a nontrivial task, but needs to be done only once; sample files provided as templates make it easier. Journalist's page layout capabilities are not up to those of high-end publishing packages, but adequate for most uses.

Journalist only works with a fixed set of news sources (primarily from the Associated Press); though these are fairly comprehensive, it would be desirable to be able to work with any source for which a download script could be written. One could imagine a "plug and play" architecture allowing any number of information sources to be tapped in constructing a personal newspaper.

Journalist runs on Microsoft Windows, and was developed using Microsoft Visual C++ and the Microsoft Foundation Class Library [sMic93c]. The internal structure of the software reflects the visible interface and the user's conceptual model. For example, *frames*, which contain text, images, etc., are prominent components in the interface. Internally, frames are modeled as subclasses of the abstract class `TPlaceable`, which specifies general behavior such as printing the frame, painting it on the screen, and spilling to continuation pages. Subclasses of `TPlaceable` include `TPIText` and `TPIImage`, for text and image frames, and `TPIChart` for things like stock price graphs.

Gregory Hassett, President of PED Software and one of the lead developers of Journalist, offers this advice to other developers: "Try to make objects mirror the real world—it's always a challenge, but a clean interface to your objects will pay off in spades." He also emphasizes the importance of understanding the services that objects provide to users: "Can you completely describe the purpose and function of your object in terms of the real-world metaphor to which it maps? . . . not being able to do so is an indication that more design work is called for." These services should be clearly exposed, while as much as possible of the implementation is private. This philosophy proved itself when a new version of Journalist was developed to run on Prodigy, an information service whose infrastructure is different from CompuServe's. Changes mainly affected the "back end,"[1] not the functional interface to end users.

The metaphor (and implementation model) of a document and its sub-objects as a unifying layer for disparate information sources is quite general. It is found in schemes ranging from Microsoft's Object Linking and Embedding (OLE) [Broc93], to the World-Wide Web [Mark93], a hypermedia architecture for linking document components across the Internet. We revisit it below in KCM.

15.2 KCM: Distributed Multimedia[2]

The Knowledge and Collaboration Machine (KCM) was a project done at IBM's T. J. Watson Research center during 1992 and 1993 [Mac93]. Its purpose was to prototype an environment in which an object-oriented user interface supports tasks involving the storage, retrieval, and management of multimedia information located on remote servers. The end user interface was written in Smalltalk [sDig92b] to run on OS/2, and it used a database server, written in C and Perl,[3] running under AIX.

[1] This is what Chapter 11 calls the *internal schema*, and Aldus's developers call *edge code* [Fer89].

[2] I am indebted to Bob Mack, manager of the KCM project, for assistance in preparing this section. Participants in the project included Bob, Peter Malkin, Mak Utpat, Mark Laff, Linn Marks, John Richards, and myself.

[3] Perl is an interpreted language found on many UNIX systems.

The problem domain for KCM is one that is becoming increasingly important—integrating a variety of applications and tools to help users navigate productively through very large information spaces. This section will discuss the system as a whole, and then present one of its tools, a video browser, in more detail.

General Goals

KCM began as an attempt to apply several existing lines of technical work to an emerging problem domain, online access to large multimedia databases. The project, originally called Interact, brought together research in high-speed networks, multimedia authoring and presentation, linguistic-based information retrieval, and object-oriented user interfaces. Figure 15-3 shows the target environment for Interact/KCM, with end users reflecting a typical usage scenario:

- Teachers and students in a school or university would have access to databases containing multimedia objects ranging from illustrated encyclopedias to video clips of news stories. The databases might be provided by libraries, book publishers, television networks, etc.
- Teachers would develop curricula that used the database content both for classroom presentation and as a research resource for students.
- Assignments given to students would include the preparation of multimedia "essays" or "scrapbooks" presenting the results of their research.

In this environment, users are interested in understanding the content of the databases, finding objects of interest, and using them in creative and productive ways. They do not need or want to understand the

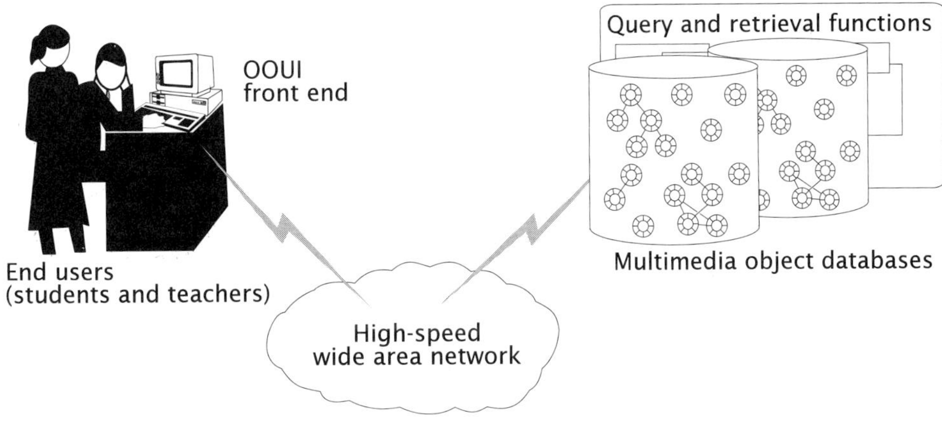

Figure 15-3 Target environment for KCM/Interact

underlying storage and accessing mechanisms. Interact thus had goals similar to those of Journalist—to let users work with objects consistent with their conceptual models of tasks, and hide the machinery of retrieving files stored on remote servers.

The project was rechristened KCM to reflect longer-term goals—developing interfaces and tools enabling knowledge workers to work collaboratively in information-rich environments. In these environments users would do research by searching multimedia databases, and could retrieve and store subsets of the databases to use in composing and sharing multimedia documents. After exploring scenarios with various types of users and content, we concluded that the KCM interface and tools were appropriate for a broad range of application domains.

Figure 15-4 shows the KCM prototype configuration that was built over about a one-year period, through several iterations. The end user's workstation was an IBM PS/2, running OS/2, with a framework and applications written in Smalltalk. The user interface was based on the CUA concept of *workplaces* [IBM92b], containers that group documents and tools related to particular projects. Besides project-specific workplaces, a general workplace provided tools for searching databases, composing multimedia documents, and collaborating with other users through electronic mail and shared folders. Though not all the envisioned tools were fully implemented, the architecture provided slots for them, and visual objects appeared in the prototype to represent both implemented and future functionality.

Limitations of the original prototype, including the video technology that was chosen, precluded realtime video transmission on the network (a token-ring LAN). To simulate remote video, video clip objects stored on

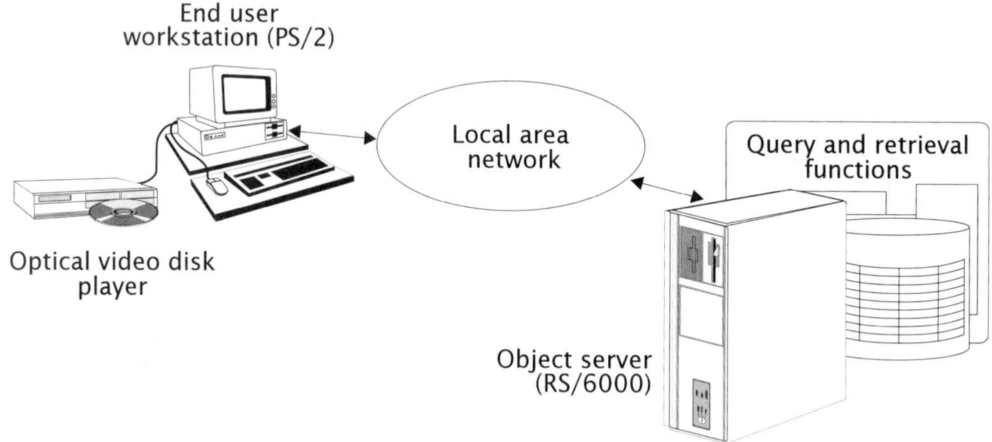

Figure 15-4 KCM prototype environment

the database contained only starting and stopping frame addresses. The video frames themselves were stored on an optical video disk attached to the user's workstation. Subsequent work (including the browser described below) has been based on standard digital video formats that would permit true distribution.

Figure 15-5 shows the KCM user interface for a representative end user. A student is using KCM to prepare an essay on the 1945 Yalta conference for a Political Science course.[1] The `Author works` folder on the left contains video copies of film clips and other media with information on the conference, along with editing tools. Documents and pages in notebooks (such as `Poli Sci notes`) are composite, and can contain text, graphics, still images, and video. The `Tools` workplace on the right contains general tools such as templates for queries on content or "card catalog" information for the electronic libraries the user is searching. The buttons on the lower right, which are always visible, help users navigate within the interface itself. `Tools` surfaces the `Tools` workplace, `Folders` and `Windows` pop up lists of folders and open windows, and the + and - buttons cycle sequentially through all the open windows.

The internal architecture of KCM embodied many of the ideas

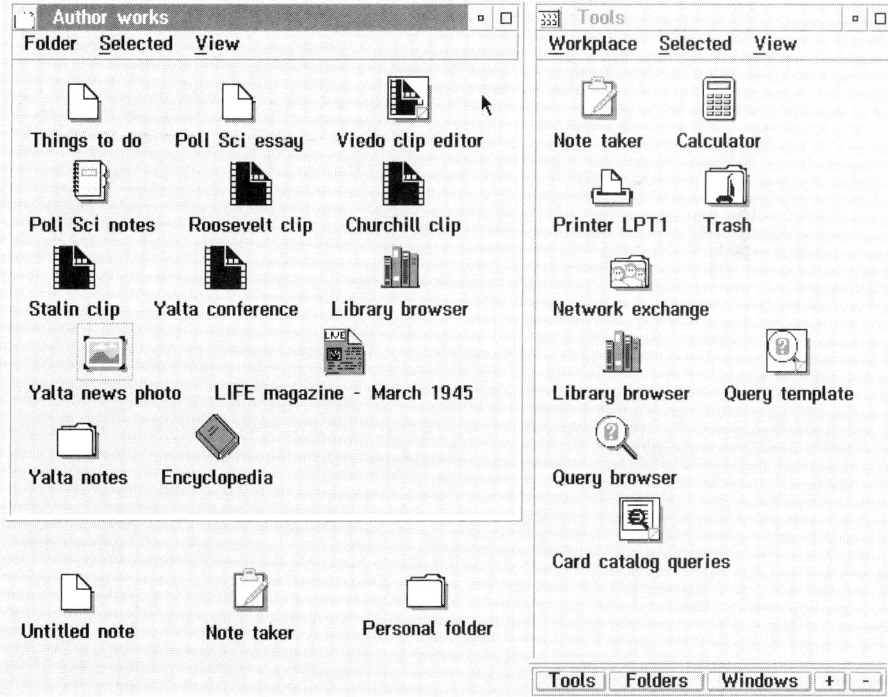

Figure 15-5 Typical KCM end user workplace

[1] I constructed this particular scenario specifically for this book, but it is similar to the university scenarios that originally motivated KCM/Interact.

discussed in Chapters 11-14. Figure 15-6 shows the class hierarchy. It contains isomorphic subtrees for models, views, and object handlers, as discussed in Chapter 13. Abstract classes and "service" classes, such as object handlers and containers, make up the KCM framework—an application framework as defined in Chapter 14. A key component of KCM's database subsystem is the `KCMOID`, a surrogate object as described in Chapters 12 and 13. The use of object handlers and surrogate objects greatly simplifies building applications. Components in the applications subsystem of KCM enjoy the benefits of persistent storage and drag-drop interaction with little added complexity.

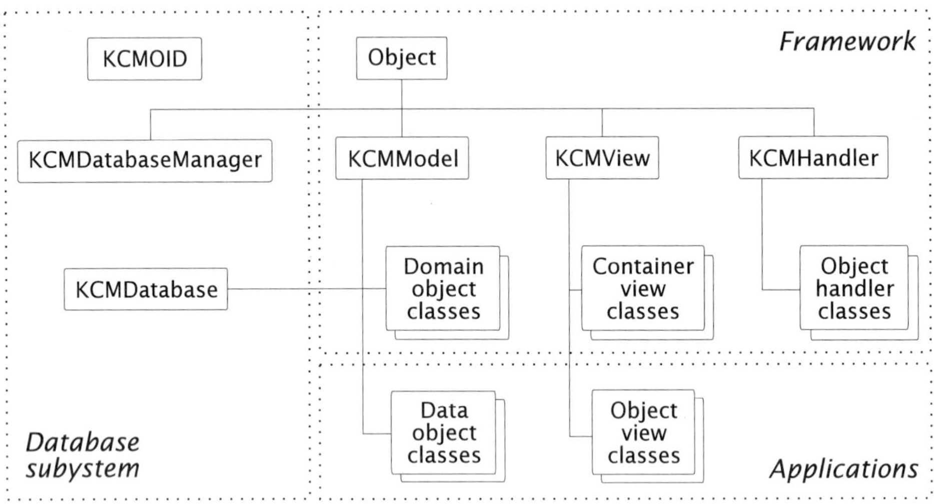

Figure 15-6 Outline of the KCM class hierarchy and subsystems

"Domain object classes" represent persistent objects that are part of the administrative framework of KCM, such as users, collaborating groups, folders, mailboxes, etc. "Data object classes" represent information models for applications. These include composite multimedia documents and information retrieval tools. Much of the information retrieval function is built into `Query` objects, which encapsulate query and search operations, and serve as containers for objects returned. Queries themselves are persistent objects, so users can store them for later use.

The Smalltalk portion of KCM was about 50,000 lines of source code, of which nearly half were reused from earlier projects. Most of the reused code provided text formatting, video display, and multimedia editing capabilities. The high level of reuse was made possible by several factors, particularly the use of object-oriented programming and a modular architecture. The robustness of the framework architecture has been validated by its subsequent use on projects as diverse as an information retrieval system [Byrd94], a visual interface builder, and a learning environment for OO programming.

Visual Browsing[1]

High-speed networking turns the computer display into a window on a very large information space. As the space increases in size and complexity, providing users with easy and intuitive ways of getting to information is increasingly important. This problem provided a focus for much of the KCM work.

Imagine walking through a crowded stadium and suddenly picking out a friend's familiar face. The ability to immediately recognize complex visual patterns is so commonplace that we often forget how extraordinary it is. Steven Pinker, summarizing studies of visual cognition in people and machines [Pin85], wrote in the mid-1980s that "Recognizing and reasoning about the visual environment is something that people do extraordinarily well; it is often said that in these abilities an average three-year old makes the most sophisticated computer vision system look embarrassingly inept."

Much computer science research on accessing visual information is directed toward replacing, rather than exploiting, the power of the human visual system. Many developers of large image databases focus on feature recognition algorithms that use textual queries for searching libraries of images [Gro89]. Commercial image database systems that allow visual searches are beginning to appear [Pars94], but the use of visual processing in database systems is typically limited to simple iconic representation of functions, rather than the much richer visual representation of content.

KCM included purely text-based tools for searching text components of documents, and tools such as "idea browsers" for exploring semantic content. In light of the power of the human visual system to recognize and reason about the visual environment, we also developed visual interfaces. By providing a direct representation of content in multimedia databases, they give users simple ways of searching for visual information. They also provide an overview of the information space, to help users decide whether to search it in the first place.

The experience of leafing through a photo album or "channel surfing" with television inclines us to take visual browsing for granted, but it is a non-trivial problem. The time taken to transmit complex images and video over a network and display them on a local workstation makes browsing expensive. KCM aimed to reduce both the network and human costs of browsing.

Instances of `KCMOID` (described above), along with `ContainerItemModel` instances, comprise lightweight surrogates for multimedia objects in the database. Users can browse through surrogate object collections, requesting the real (usually very large) object only if the surrogate appears interesting. Much of the KCM architecture is aimed at making the existence of surrogate objects and the network transparent—users perceive that objects, once found, are local to the workstation.

[1] General aspects of visual browsing in this section are summarized from [Dav94].

Picons (picture icons) are one class of surrogate object in KCM. Picons are small bitmaps (usually images of single frames) associated with video clips. They also carry publication data and brief descriptions of the clips in text form. Picon browsers allow users to view the picons and related text in successive "pages." Collections of picons are generated in response to user queries, and pre-selected collections may also appear as folders on the user's desktop. An example is shown in Figure 15-7.[1]

Figure 15-7 A vicon browser, based on the KCM picon browser

Picons are displayed in rows and columns (12 to a page in Figure 15-7, 36 to a page in the original KCM version). The user can navigate from page to page using buttons on the screen or the PgUp and PgDn keys on the keyboard. Movement and selection within a page use the mouse or the keyboard arrow keys. The browser also has a scrollable list of titles; selecting a title pages the browser and positions the cursor on the corresponding picon. When the user selects a particular picon, the title of its associated clip is highlighted in the list, and a short description appears in a text pane in the lower part of the window. The clip can be played in place, overlaying the picon; or, as in the example shown, the user can open a separate viewer with VCR controls.

[1] The application in the figure is a recent reimplementation of the picon browser, now called the *vicon* (video icon) browser, on Microsoft Windows. It uses the standard Microsoft/Intel AVI file format for digitized video.

A clip is retrieved from the database only if the user expresses interest by double-clicking on its picon or opening a viewer. A picon uses at least two orders of magnitude less storage than a video clip, so it can be retrieved and displayed in tenths of a second, versus tens of seconds. The user can view and compare many picons at a time, adding an additional order of magnitude improvement in performance. Our experience is that "many are called, but few are chosen"—that is, users will inspect, and quickly reject, many objects before finding one they wish to view in detail. Even if networks could transmit video in zero time, at zero cost, the human efficiency of this sort of browsing would still hold and would be an important consideration in the design of a visual browser.

15.3 VR-DECK: A Virtual Reality Toolkit[1]

The ultimate object-oriented interface would completely immerse the user in a world of objects with arbitrarily complex behavior. This sort of virtual world is achievable today only for small numbers of objects with simple behaviors, but is being pursued by many researchers. A limitation on the "reality" of such worlds is the availability of enough computational power to simulate complex objects in real time.

Alan Kay has pointed out [Kay93] that conceptually, objects in an OO system are like autonomous computers. Some researchers have applied this principle literally, building "computer per object" simulations. Examples include a system for accurate simulation of sound sources relative to a moving observer, needing hundreds of MIPS per simulated source [Wen93]. Another example is a system providing kinesthetic feedback such as the "feel" of a wrench contacting a bolt [Stan93]. This system requires real-time collision detection and calculation of dynamics in a many-object simulation. It is implemented on an Inmos Transputer, which connects a large number of processor chips in a network. Each processor models a single object, and the processors are dynamically linked as objects contact one another.

Figure 15-8 shows an idealized view of this sort of "computer per object" architecture. It suggests that OO design can be done without concern for the location of objects; later, in a separate step, object implementations are distributed across several computers. As is typical, such an architecture is easy to envision, but difficult to implement. VR-DECK (Virtual Reality Distributed Environment and Construction Kit),[2] part of an ongoing project at IBM Research, is a successful attempt to separate object design and implementation from object location and distribution.

VR-DECK is a toolkit for building distributed "virtual worlds." Appli-

[1] I am indebted to Christopher Codella, manager of the Virtual Worlds project at IBM Research, and Reza Jalili, a staff member on the project, for assistance in preparing this section.

[2] The name also alludes to the consoles or "decks" used by computer jockeys to navigate cyberspace in the science fiction novels of William Gibson, e.g. [Gib84].

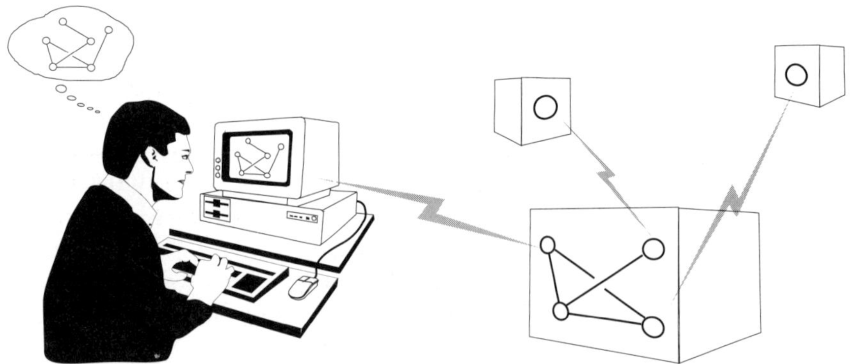

Figure 15-8 Event-driven "computer per object" architecture

cations range from multi-person interactive games to "surrogate travel" through virtual buildings. The implementor of a virtual world codes rule-based modules corresponding to objects. In a separate step, modules are connected and assigned to nodes in a heterogeneous local area network. Communication between modules is by event passing, which is done transparently across the network.

VR-DECK has two language levels. At the higher level, *modules* contain *rulesets*, which contain *rules* specifying how events are produced and handled. A ruleset looks like this (words in **boldface** are supplied by the programmer):

```
ruleSet ruleset_name {
      rule rule_name
            when(event_handling_specification)
            produce(event_specification) {
                  // Rule body code
      }
      rule another_rule_name
      . . . . .
      }
} // End ruleset
```

An **event_specification** looks very much like a C or C++ variable definition, consisting of a type for the data carried by the event (if any), and the event name. An **event_handling_specification** consists of event specifications and logical qualifiers, for example:

```
when (void initialize and int startingValue)
```

The lower level, the rule body, is C or C++ code, with two extensions. It can examine incoming events, and produce new events (the events produced must be declared with `produce()` in the rule header). The flow of a rule is that it "fires" when the specified combination of events occurs, its body code executes, and it may produce new events that fire other rules. So rulesets are like objects, and rules are like methods or member functions. The point of the module layer is to supply a transparent event-passing mechanism, allowing modules to be distributed in arbitrary ways.

As an example, here is an implementation of a simple counter, like the ones in Chapters 11 and 13. The `Counter` ruleset is the model (in the MVC sense); its rules are fired by `increment` and `decrement` events, and it produces the `counterValue` event whenever it is changed; `counterValue` in turn fires `CounterValue`, which broadcasts the new value of the counter. The view is not shown, but it would have a rule that consumed the `counter` event and displayed its value to the end user. The MVC controller is the ruleset `handleXEvents`. It uses standard X Windows code to receive events when the user presses mouse button 1 or 2, and produces `increment` and `decrement` events.

```
#include <X11/Xlib.h>
int count;  // Value of the counter
ruleset Counter {
  rule Initialize when(void start)
                    produce(void counterValue) {
    count = 0;
    produce(counterValue);
  }
  rule Increment when(void increment)
                    produce(void counterValue) {
    count++;
    produce(counterValue);
  }
  rule Decrement when(void decrement)
                    produce(void counterValue) {
    count--;
    produce(counterValue)
  }
  rule CounterValue when(void counterValue)
                    produce(int counter) {
    counter = count;
    produce(counter); // New value for interested parties
  }
}
ruleset handleXEvents {
  rule handleEvent when(XEvent anEvent)
          produce(void increment, void decrement) {
    if (anEvent.type == ButtonPress) {
```

```
        switch (((XButtonEvent)anEvent).button) {
          case 1: produce(increment);
                  break;
          case 2: produce(decrement);
        }
      }
    }
  }
```

Compiling rules involves translating statements such as `rule`, `when`, and `produce` into standard C++ code, then compiling the C++. Output from compiling the programmer's rules is linked with predefined standard rules, communications routines, and event dispatching routines to form a module. Physically, modules are executable programs. Properties such as startup parameters, the location of the machine on which they will run, and their connections to other modules are specified using *vbuild*, described below.

Figure 15-9 shows the configuration for a non-trivial application built with VR-DECK. The machine on the lower right has modules handling events from a dataglove and head-mounted tracker. The upper machines are running modules that simulate objects. Modules on the remaining machine are consuming events giving the state of the simulated objects, and the position and orientation of the user's hand and head. These events are used to generate a stereoscopic display that provides the user with a sense of immersion in the virtual world. The dataglove allows the user to manipulate objects in the world.

Figure 15-10 shows *vbuild*, the interface used to connect VR-DECK modules into an application. Modules are selected from the list on the left side of the window, placed into the center part of the window, and connected. Connection implies event visibility; if two modules are connected, rules in one may be fired by events produced in the other. Connectivity is transparent to the rule programmer—a produced event has no explicit destination, but is available to any connected module.

Figure 15-11 shows a virtual world built with VR-DECK. This is a simulation of the interior of a church in Dresden that was destroyed by bombing during World War II.[1] The church is in process of reconstruction, and the application provides a virtual "walking tour" of what it will look like when completed. In actual use, the user wears a head-mounted display or views a stereoscopic display through polarized glasses. This provides a three-dimensional immersive view of the church in which the user can move around.

Data for constructing the virtual church was not generated specifically for this application. It was already available in a CAD (computer-

[1] The church in the figure is actually a simplified demonstration version of the fully detailed church used in Germany for the on-site application.

aided design) system being used to prepare plans for the reconstruction. Reuse of preexisting objects is an important factor in this kind of application. The design of objects ranging from airplanes to office buildings is increasingly being done with CAD systems. With a tool like VR-DECK, these CAD object models are potential components of virtual worlds in which one or more users can interact with the objects.

VR-DECK supports object-oriented design principles, particularly the separation of models and views. It also separates high-level object models from the technical infrastructure, including details of connectivity to other objects. Its high-level rule specifications and event architecture can be used to wrap objects from disparate sources for use in "plug and play" worlds. As the objects in interactive applications become more complex, amortizing their development cost by enhancing reusability will make such a capability highly desirable.

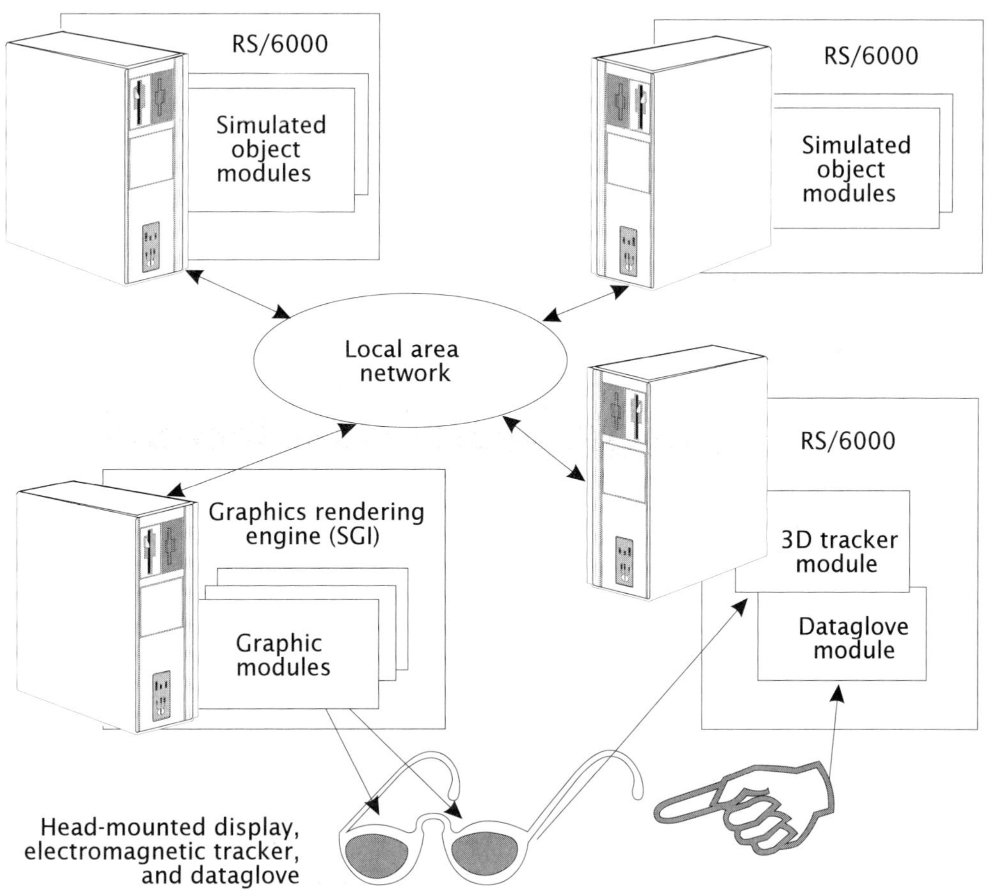

Figure 15-9 A sample configuration for VRDECK

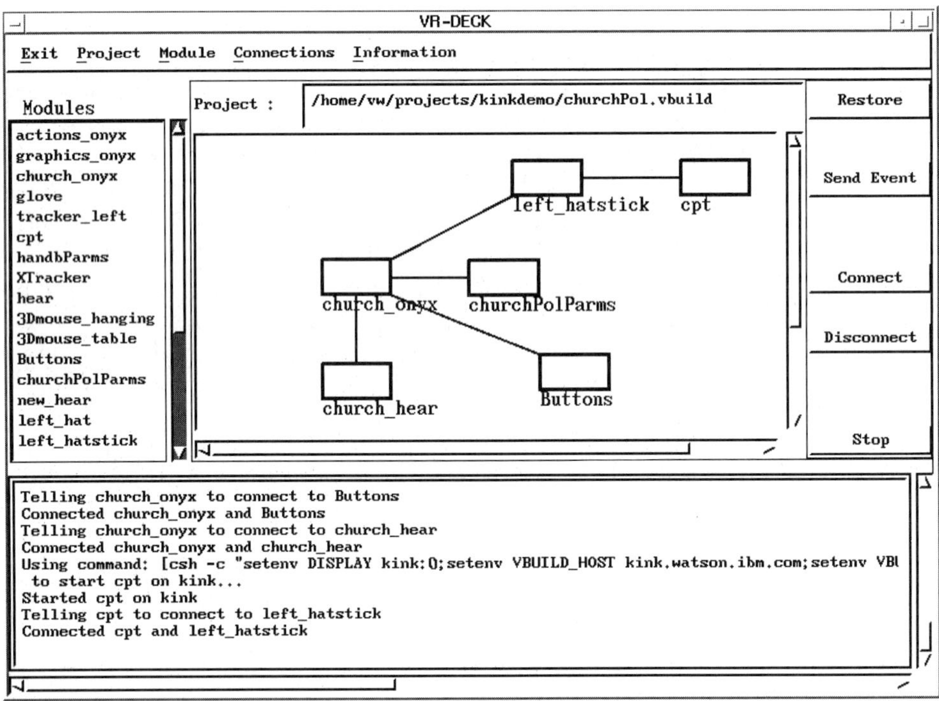

Figure 15-10 The vbuild programmer's interface for VR-DECK

15.4 Adding Fax to an Office System

This section discusses ideas and prototypes for adding facsimile transmission functions to an existing "desktop" office environment. The problem is described in Appendix 1, *Fax Case Study*, and used as a basis for exercises in Chapters 7-10.

When I developed this as an exercise for classes in user interface design, in the late 1980s, I assumed we would shortly see a real commercial implementation. It was widely predicted that object-oriented "shells" such as Hewlett-Packard's NewWave [sHew92] would dominate users' desktops in the '90s. In fact, widespread adoption of fully object-oriented workplaces, along the lines of KCM, still sits on the horizon. The realization of the vision probably awaits closer integration of OO capabilities with base operating systems; systems such as OS/2 and Macintosh System/7 are the beginnings of this, with Microsoft's "Cairo" and Taligent's "Pink" (perhaps) coming closer.[1]

Meanwhile, laptop computers with built-in fax-capable modems became widely available, and "standalone" fax applications have prolifer-

[1] "Cairo" and "Pink" are code names for operating systems forthcoming from the respective vendors in the 1996 time frame.

Figure 15-11 A virtual world constructed with VR-DECK

ated, running under shells such as Microsoft Windows. These provide a rich set of functions, though they are application-oriented, not object-oriented.

Step-by-Step Approach

Case studies for several courses in user interface design have used the fax application. Here are the steps from a typical series of design sessions:

- Required capabilities are discussed in the context of scenarios for using existing fax systems, and possible extensions based on new technology. Representative scenarios are written down, along with rough sketches illustrating them. Figure 15-12 is a typical sketch, showing three main scenarios. Fax machines may be private, used only by one person; they may be shared, for instance a fax machine in a company mailroom; or they may be integral parts of a personal computer. All these machine types must interact.
- The scenarios are used to determine objects that people use. Conceptual models are discussed; these include ways of thinking about the

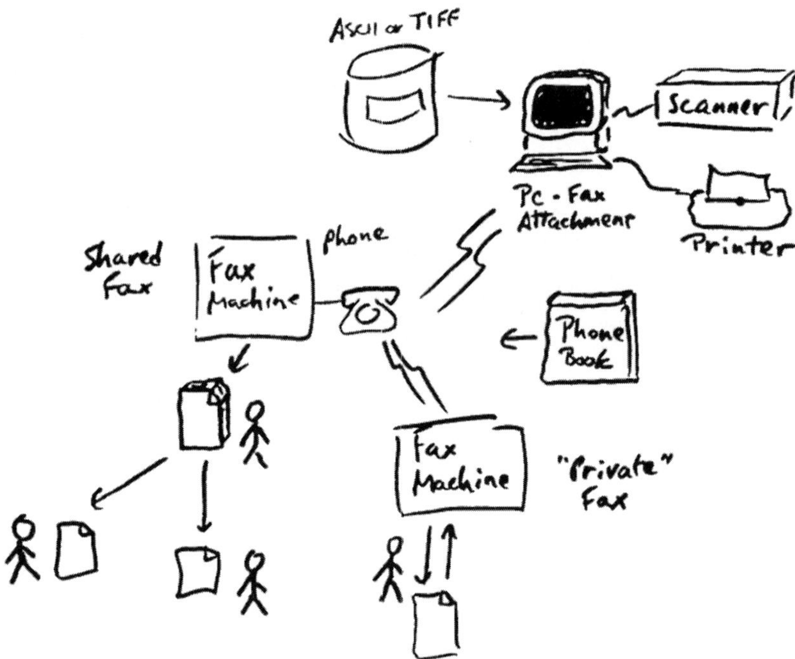

Figure 15-12 A rough sketch for understanding the fax application

objects, how they interact, and how conceptual models for fax objects fit into larger contexts, such as the entire scope of office work. The discussion includes classification issues, for example whether fax documents in a computer are like paper notes. Objects may come out of this discussion that are not at first obvious, such as the phone book in Figure 15-12.

- The objects are formalized, and their behaviors are documented using a method such as CRC cards. In this discussion, decisions are made about which objects are new (for example fax documents), and where extensions can be made to objects that already exist in an office system (for instance the phone book). Subclassing and collaboration relations between new and existing objects are also established.
- Icons and content representations for the new objects are designed.
- Control mechanisms are designed; both presentation and interaction designs are evaluated for consistency with the existing desktop user interface.
- The design is sketched on screen dumps from the existing system, to illustrate the usage scenarios.

A Prototype, and Some Issues

There are issues and trade-offs in the fax problem at many levels, from conceptual model to implementation. A few of them are discussed here in the context of a simple prototype. The prototype cannot transmit or receive real faxes, but has enough simulated function to do basic testing. It was built using the KCM framework described in Section 15.2.

A key issue in this problem is how to represent the basic functionality, transmitting and receiving facsimile documents. All solutions I have seen use an object representing the document, but there are two lines of thought on how the functions should be shown to users. One possibility, shown on the right in Figure 15-13, is to provide a "fax machine" icon encapsulating both functions. The argument is that this maps closely to experience with real fax machines. In this solution, documents dropped on the fax icon are transmitted; the icon "opens" to a container view showing documents that have been received.[1]

The argument against this solution is that it unnecessarily introduces a new object, and one that is complex because it incorporates two functions. An alternative is to reuse the incoming and outgoing mail trays that have become standard for representing electronic mail. This is shown on the left in Figure 15-13. The real-world metaphor here is that people would rather just put their fax transmissions in an out box for pickup, and have someone deliver incoming faxes along with other incoming mail.

Figure 15-13 Alternative visible models of fax functionality

Assuming the use of mail trays, what does a user drop into them? Figure 15-12 does not show the fax cover sheet, which usually precedes the pages in a transmission. It contains information such as the sender's name and phone number, a company logo, and comments on the content of the transmission. The KCM framework uses an envelope metaphor for sending electronic mail; an example is shown in Chapter 13, Figure 13-9. Documents to be mailed are dropped into an envelope, which is then addressed and dropped on the outgoing mail tray. In fax transmission, the role of the envelope—to be a container for documents sent to a single recipient—is subsumed by the cover sheet. So in the prototype, `FaxCoverSheet` was modeled as a subclass of `Envelope`.

KCM, following the CUA style, supports templates for creating new

[1] In commercial fax programs such as WinFax [sDel94], the "fax machine" icon is common; however, it represents the send and receive functions on a tool bar, and is not a true object. WinFax uses mail tray icons to access logs of incoming and outgoing faxes.

instances. Figure 15-14 shows the user dragging from a template to create a new fax cover sheet. In Figure 15-15, `Godwin Letter` is being dropped on the cover sheet. Just as dropping a document on an envelope brings up a dialogue asking for the e-mail address, dropping on a fax cover sheet brings up an appropriate dialogue, shown in Figure 15-16.

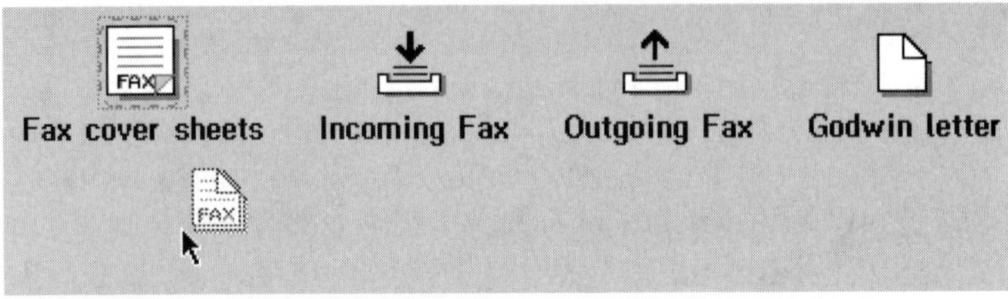

Figure 15-14 Creating a fax cover sheet from a template

Figure 15-15 Dropping a document on the cover sheet

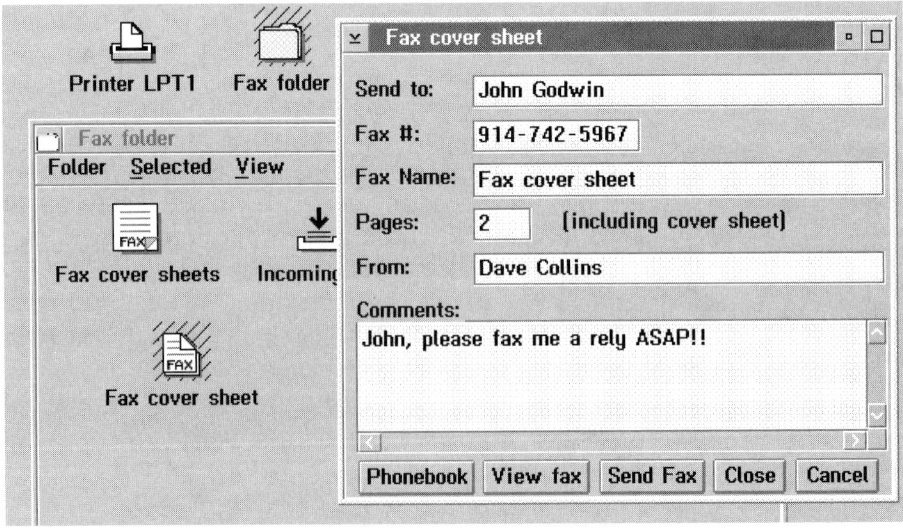

Figure 15-16 Filling in the fax cover sheet

It could be argued that the distinction between fax and e-mail is unnecessary—that a single envelope and addressing dialogue would serve for both. On the other hand, users really do have different models of fax and e-mail, which argues for a visible distinction. A significant difference is that received faxes are image documents (an example is shown in Figure 15-17), and e-mail is formatted text. This means, for example, that the sender of an e-mailed document can be determined automatically, but the sender of a fax cannot.

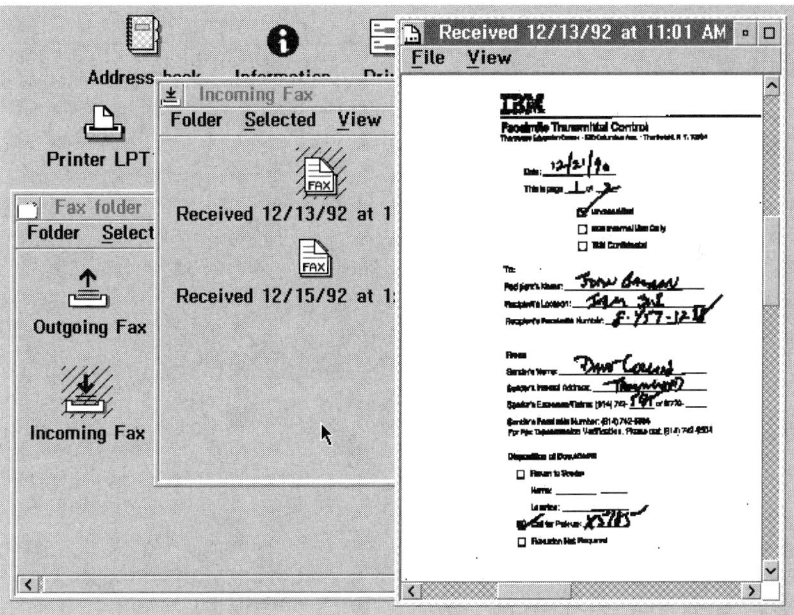

Figure 15-17 Viewing an incoming fax

A fully functional fax application in an OOUI would address many other issues beyond the basic functionality. We would expect at least the capabilities of available application-oriented fax programs, described in Appendix 1. Given the maturity of these applications, they provide a good benchmark for any object-oriented design. The challenge is to provide all the functions users have come to expect, with a level of integration and ease-of-use that would make the OOUI version superior.

15.5 Summary

Four examples have been presented, illustrating development of systems with object-oriented user interfaces. Key principles exemplified by these cases include:

- The value of a user-centered conceptual model in guiding the design of both the user interface and system internals.

- Isomorphism between visible objects and internal software structures.
- Separation of views and information models from the technical infrastructure.
- The use of application frameworks and modular components to foster reuse and high developer productivity.

15.6 To Explore Further

Journalist [sPED93], like most commercial products, is developed by people who do not take time out to write papers about what they have done. That does not make them less worthy of study, so by all means become a user of leading edge applications. Even a brief conversation with the developer of a good application is worthwhile. Greg Hassett's remarks on Journalist (sent by fax) were invaluable, because his product exemplifies the principles he talks about.

The World-Wide Web (WWW) is a mechanism for accessing composite and linked documents on the Internet; it addresses issues similar to those in Journalist and KCM. Additional information on WWW, Mosaic (a viewing program for web documents), and HTML (HyperText Markup Language, used for constructing web documents), can be obtained from various FTP sites. NCSA (National Center for Supercomputer Applications), the developer of Mosaic, maintains a site at `ftp.ncsa.uiuc.edu`. CERN, where WWW was "invented," has a site at `info.cern.ch`.

KCM is described in detail in [Mac93]. [Mal93] describes the distributed database used in KCM. [Dav94] presents a general perspective on the need for visual browsers in networked multimedia environments.

[Jal93] is a tutorial on VR-DECK; [Codel93] summarizes the toolkit and its philosophy. [Codel92] describes an earlier VR toolkit. [Kov93] describes GROOP, an object-oriented graphics toolkit used for constructing objects used in VR-DECK applications. The bombed church in Dresden is described in an article in the *New York Times*: "From the ruins shall rise a church, and a symbol" (April 7, 1994, p. A4).

Appendix 1, *Fax Case Study*, has further references for the fax problem.

16

Summary and Directions

This book has introduced object-oriented user interfaces and presented methods for designing their conceptual models, external appearance, interactivity, and internal software architectures. The methodology was supplemented with background on the history and psychology of OOUIs, and illustrated with examples. Throughout, I have tried to maintain a focus on OOUIs as components of object-oriented systems and applications.

This chapter first summarizes the most important points in the book—the critical success factors for OOUI designers. The overarching principle is isomorphism, introduced in Chapter 5—that structural correspondences between different aspects of an object-oriented system (including the user's and designer's conceptual models) can be exploited to build better systems, faster.

The next section presents a view of the current state of OOUIs—the interfaces themselves, and development tools for building them. Within the prevailing GUI paradigm, today's leading applications set a high standard. It is based on mature styles and metaphors, such as desktops and spreadsheets. The best tools make this standard accessible to developers, at least in terms of its visible parts, the look and feel. Conceptual models for applications continue to be based on knowledge and creativity, not tools.

This chapter also talks about the future, about where OOUIs are headed as we move toward the 21st century. Improvements in technology will provide huge gains in performance parameters—what will we use them for? A key message here is that platform architects can give us sixteen million colors, or the power to execute many tasks concurrently—but we must decide how to use those colors, and what tasks users can actually do. Advances in platform technology will never eliminate the need for good design.

Many aspects of future user interfaces are predictable—pervasive object-orientation, three-dimensional displays, handwriting, speech, and gesture recognition, integrated multimedia. These are evolutionary extensions of today's GUI paradigm, enabled by cheaper, more powerful technology. Many aspects of tools and methods are also predictable—OO toolkits, application frameworks, "plug and play" distributed objects.

Not so easily predictable, except by the creative geniuses who invent them, are the new paradigms, the metaphors that will take interactive computing far beyond the desktop and spreadsheet. They probably already exist, just as OOUIs, windows, and desktops existed before the Macintosh. You may find them in research laboratories, or in video game arcades. That is the last message in this book: though the principles here are necessary for designing object-oriented user interfaces, they do not define the limits of the interfaces you can design.

16.1 Success Factors

In general terms, any object-oriented system can be described along the lines of the definition of an OOUI in Chapter 1:

- There are objects.
- Objects can be classified based on their behavior.
- Objects fit together into a coherent whole.

This describes internals and externals, design and implementation. It is based on how people think about the world, which is one reason why object-orientation works as a paradigm for system development.

Because object-orientation is based in human cognition, "user interface" issues pervade the design of a system or application. The obvious human interface is between end users and the system. The less obvious, but just as important, human interface is between and among end users and developers. Both are simplified by a uniform, object-oriented view of what the system is and does.

This perspective integrates the "three domains" described in Chapter 5—conceptual, user interface, and implementation models. They are all critical to a good user interface.

Conceptual Models

The most important point in this book is the value of a common conceptual model for what the system is and does. This model cuts across the system in two directions, shown in Figure 16-1. In the system dimension, it unifies the three domains. In the "people" dimension, it unites the

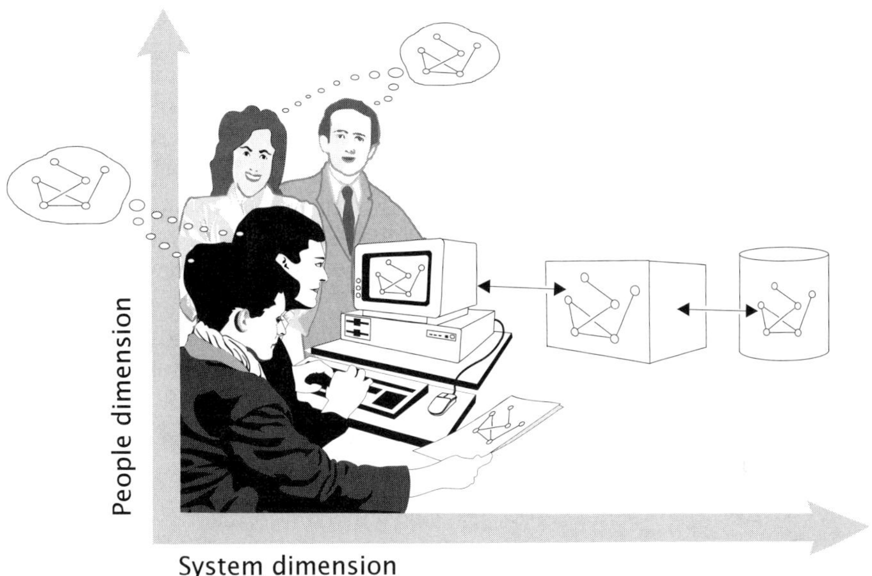

Figure 16-1 Dimensions of the common conceptual model

development team around a model of the system they share with its users.[1]

The conceptual model is a map of the system that provides an overview of objects and capabilities. Starting with data from system and task analysis, it drives the design of the "look and feel" of the user interface, and contributes to internal design. It thus cuts across a third dimension as well, not shown in the figure—time, and the development life cycle.

Software engineering methodologies advocate basing system design (and implicitly user interface design) on an analysis model that defines object semantics and relationships. In many projects, clear-cut entities in the analysis model are fragmented in design. This can happen in OO as well as "conventional" systems. Developers then focus on the fragments—pieces of the visible user interface and the technology infrastructure.

In successful OO designs, the conceptual or analysis model is real, and implemented in software—the information model. Information models "realize" conceptual models, providing functional interfaces for views of the information that users interact with. Though users access the model only indirectly, through views, its semantics are part of external design.

Representation and Interactivity

Computers are media that can simulate other media. A computer display can be a book, a painting, or a television. Computers surpass all other

[1] The important idea of mappings between the designer's and user's conceptual models was introduced by Don Norman [Nor88].

media in interactivity, the dimension in which objects (including people) act and react. They can thus simulate not only media—information about objects—but the objects themselves.

"Reality" and "real objects," as perceived by people, are broad concepts. To mathematicians, the expression $\Sigma f(x)\Delta x$ represents a perfectly good object; in general, any constellation of properties we frequently encounter and use can become an object. As designers, we do not want to deny the abstract nature of objects such as these, but to provide useful, concrete ways of seeing and interacting with them.[1]

Whatever the objects, OOUIs provide views on the display that make them tangible.[2] The root meaning of tangible comes from *touch*—people identify objects by actively exploring ("touching"), so presentation and interaction are intertwined. In designing the behavior of objects, it is often useful to analyze presentation and user action separately; nevertheless, appearance and other behaviors play out within cycles of interaction:

- Based on a task and the current state of objects, a user plans a sequence of actions to produce a result.
- An action taken on objects begins a process in the implementation model; when it finishes, an output presentation acknowledges that the action is complete, shows changes in object states, and indicates the range of possible new actions.
- The user modifies the state of his or her mental model based on the presentation, and the cycle repeats.

The time scales of these cycles ranges from milliseconds to hours, and each cycle may include smaller cycles. Users may engage in several cycles concurrently, starting a new one while waiting for a previous action to finish.

Object and action representations (affordances) in a good interface minimize the effort of translating conceptual intentions into the action language, and translating from the presentation language back into the conceptual model. Direct manipulation is the signature interaction technique of OOUIs because it represents the conceptual model as directly as possible. This avoids encumbering the display (and the user's mind) with a complicated visible infrastructure of buttons, scroll bars and popup menus. Like the internal infrastructure, these are not part of the user's model; unlike the internal infrastructure, they cannot be hidden, so they should be used sparingly.

Combining directness, efficiency, and consistency has top-down and bottom-up aspects. Top-down issues include things like matching visible controls to metaphors in the user's conceptual model. Bottom-up issues relate to basic interactions such as pointing or entering text, from which

[1] Concrete views of abstract objects are not contradictory—no matter what it represents, anything we put on the screen is concrete.
[2] "Views" covers any representation of objects, including visual, audio, tactile etc.

larger interactions are synthesized. Interactions should be consistent across similar objects, and operations should be polymorphic—applicable to different object types. This reduces the number of interaction behaviors and simplifies the interface. Visible controls should be congruent with one another and with the user's conceptual model.

Objects and their interactions on the display correspond to real objects in the implementation—views and controllers, in the Smalltalk model-view-controller terminology. Views separate the semantics of what is being presented from the specifics of presentation. Controllers separate the semantics of actions from the details of particular interaction techniques.

Architecture and Performance

Graphical OOUIs, though easy on users, can be hard on developers. Simply getting the job done is often not enough. Quality, time to market, portability, and ease of enhancement are all important. Poor interactive performance can make an otherwise good design awkward and frustrating.

Architecture is key to attaining these goals. Object layers that separate major functions such as application logic, user interface, and communications infrastructure modularize the large-scale structure of systems and applications. Explicit coupling between layers is reduced through the implicit coupling of isomorphism, shown along the system dimension in Figure 16-1. In the small, OO systems are built from communicating objects driven by events from the end user, processes external to the system, or other objects.

MVC Model-view-controller or its derivative, model-view, is the basis for many layered OO architectures. MVC is a scalable architecture for implementing interactive applications. Its three components are software objects corresponding to the external components of the user interface—conceptual model, presentation, and interaction. Underneath the MVC objects is a technical infrastructure—objects that provide general services, such as database and communications access.

Objects like files and communications sockets have no place in the user's model and thus do not fit the isomorphism principle, but they are essential parts of systems. The infrastructure is the rug under which we sweep these objects. This is legitimate as long as the interfaces between them and the MVC objects are clear and modular. The objective is to hide as much as possible of the infrastructure from higher layers.[1]

Infrastructure reflects current technology, which changes over time. Applications and views represent business processes that are also subject to change. The information model is based on core entities of the business or organization, such as customers and products, that seldom change, and is the best anchor for modularizing the remainder of the system. Think of

[1] This is an ideal that is difficult to attain in many environments. Getting as close as you can, however, is worth the effort.

information models as virtual machines that make the technology infrastructure look like "application engines" designed for specific problem domains. This allows applications and views to access domain-specific services instead of more primitive technology, and fosters portability by insulating applications from changeable implementations.

Particularly in distributed systems, views cannot anticipate the state changes of their models and models cannot anticipate the presentation and interaction capabilities of their views. Autonomy of models and views is fostered by a general-purpose protocol for exchanging update requests and state changes between them. MVC provides this, resulting in better modularity, ease of maintenance, and more reusable models and views. It can also lead to better performance, if views only need to update portions of themselves representing changed facets of a model.

The classical MVC controller encapsulates interactions such as keyboard entry or menu selection. Controller-like interaction objects can also encapsulate direct manipulation, hiding details such as platform protocols for drag-drop interactions. The key principle for modularizing interaction objects is the separation of command or action semantics from the details of particular interaction techniques. Defining objects representing commands and actions is also the easiest way to provide undo and redo facilities.

Event-driven architecture Object responses to actions should be consistent with the conceptual models users have of them. Expectations about the general behavior of physical objects dictate that many responses must be "instantaneous."[1] These include visual feedback in response to selecting text, dragging icons, and pushing buttons. Responses involving collaboration between multiple objects can be slower, if feedback is given on the progress of operations.

Individual objects in the world respond rapidly to simple stimuli because they are autonomous, and the same principle applies to computer systems. Non-OO systems are often monolithic "fortress" objects; input and output flow through constrained, centrally controlled channels. Like bureaucratic organizations, they are slow and unresponsive. In OO systems, control is distributed to "empowered" objects, and operations are accomplished through collaboration, not centralized control.

These ideas lead to event-driven architectures for input and output. They make systems more robust and extensible, and provide better performance. Objects at the periphery of a system receive low-level events and provide immediate responses. Combinations of low-level events generate higher-level events, which are handled by higher-layer objects. The idea is to handle an event as close to its origin as possible, requesting services from more distant objects when necessary.

Event-driven architectures are characteristic of OO systems; their prevalence in modern window systems reflects the heritage of interactive

[1] In a sense that can be determined by testing users; always less than 100 milliseconds.

object systems such as Smalltalk. There appears to be a long-term trend away from monolithic, centrally controlled architectures, toward those based on loosely coupled objects and events. Client-server systems are examples. An extension of this trend, discussed below, is detached "agents" that travel through networks, performing services for their owning systems.

16.2 The State of the OOUI

Object-oriented user interfaces date from Ivan Sutherland's Sketchpad system, now more than thirty years old. Major commercial offerings go back about half as far, to the Xerox Star and Apple Lisa. Object-oriented frameworks for building applications on these platforms, such as Smalltalk MVC, the Lisa Toolkit, and MacApp, have been around for well over a decade. How far have we come in these years?

Interfaces

Hardware is enormously faster and cheaper—the personal computer on my desk has more power than the world's largest mainframe circa 1963. Software has not made commensurate progress, and this is nowhere more evident than in user interfaces. Early interfaces such as Sketchpad and GRAIL still excite admiration for functionality, conceptual clarity, and even snappy performance. I occasionally use a 128K Macintosh computer; it is about ten years old, and its plastic case is beginning to yellow with age. But its interface is still crisp and fast, even compared to modern interfaces running on much more powerful systems.

On the other hand, this simplistic judgement masks the difficulty of the problem we have set in software. Hardware progress is measured—in MIPS, megabytes, etc.—by its ability to do the same thing, only faster, or more of it. We measure software progress by how fast we can customize hardware to solve an array of problems whose scope is limited only by imagination.

Tens of millions of people now use interfaces that were once seen only by the privileged few, and do things that were impossible until recently. Old film clips of Sketchpad show that 2-D drawings with only a few tens of lines degraded its display to the point of limited usefulness. High-end workstations today easily show 3-D drawings with thousands of lines and fully rendered surfaces, and permit movement and rotation in real time.

Today's graphical user interfaces are successful, by the criterion of making powerful functions accessible to a large population. Where could they improve? Chapter 2 describes how GUI platforms are converging on a "canonical" style, and one area of potential improvement lies within the confines of that style. A second area is in the use of new technologies and interaction paradigms that are only dimly visible at present. This area will be deferred to the next section, *21st Century OOUIs.*

Graphical elements in GUIs set a high standard today, and tools are available to implement them rapidly. Tools to incorporate custom, content-specific graphics also exist, though they are not as easy to use. The design of static information displays is a mature discipline, since it draws on centuries of experience in print media. Designing multimedia information presentations is also well established, based on experience in the motion picture and television industries.

Graphic and multimedia design are specialized skills, not traditionally found in software development teams. The skills do exist, along with the tools and platforms, so there is little excuse today for a user interface whose "look" is inelegant or clumsy. Increasing awareness of this has raised the standard of graphical excellence in user interfaces, and will continue to do so.

Leading-edge graphic and multimedia applications push the limits of human visual performance. The same is not true for motor performance, or for senses other than vision. This is not entirely a problem, since it is a successful response to the market. The rapid increase in popularity of GUIs resulted from their relative ease of use. Ease of use is not inconsistent with graphical sophistication—our visual systems have already been trained by exposure to print media, films, and television.

The only complex input device used on most computers is the keyboard, and this is enabled by prior experience with typewriters and calculators. The mouse is extremely simple, but remarkably good at one highly versatile task that we are all experts at—pointing. These devices have brought millions of users into the fold, but they do not push the upper bound of what is possible for experts. They also do not reach those who, due to age or injury, lack motor coordination in the hands. Watching the skilled performances of people ranging from carpenters to musicians, it seems clear that greater exploitation of motor skills could significantly improve OOUIs. Both human factors knowledge and the hardware to do this already exist.

Though the graphical OOUI, as we know it today, is not the ultimate user interface, its best examples provide users with remarkable power in a form that is easy to use. The two main challenges within the current GUI paradigm are to bring the average application closer to the best, and to fully develop the action side of the interface.

Methods and Tools

Looking back over three decades, certain characteristics of OOUIs stand out. Those that succeed are difficult to design and implement. Good people with many skills are needed—successful products involve hardware and software people, human factors experts, graphic designers, and writers. The hardest, and least obvious, part of design is developing the right conceptual model for the domain. New interface metaphors, such as the spreadsheet and the desktop, come along rarely; once developed, they dominate their field of application, and are used repeatedly.

Raising the average standard closer to the best requires methods, training, and tools that answer these questions:

- How can we increase the pool of skilled designers, or reduce the amount of skill required?
- What organizational structures are required to foster the interdisciplinary teams needed for OOUI design?
- How can we increase the productivity of OOUI implementors?
- Where will we find new user interface metaphors to expand computing in the 1990s and beyond as the spreadsheet and the desktop did in the 1980s?

The industry has made significant progress toward answering these questions, as I hope this book helps to illustrate.

Design is hard, and highly skilled designers will remain few and far between—but we can do a better job of capturing their designs in a reusable and extensible form. This effectively reduces the amount of skill required to do interface design, since most designs are based on existing concepts. Application frameworks, toolkits, and uniform notations are the primary means of doing this.

New organizational structures are possible, based on the isomorphism principle and tools to support it. Current object-oriented methods are adequate to produce common representations for collaboration among interdisciplinary teams. Many tools are available to support the translation of common design languages into working implementations. These range from data repositories supporting the development life cycle, to OO programming toolkits.

New user interface metaphors will emerge slowly and painfully, and belong mainly to the "futures" discussion below. This is an area that will continue to rely on individual creativity, not new technology. The good news about metaphors is that we need only a few, and those few can be packaged for reuse with object-oriented toolkits and frameworks. An area where significant progress is possible with existing tools is the development of frameworks tailored to specific industries such as banking and insurance.

The knowledge base for user interface design contains much more than technology. In psychology and human factors, many experiments remain to be done to explore the way users perceive, think about, and act upon objects displayed at the interface. An interface must capture the work of these experts, as well as that of software engineers. Current tools do this implicitly, through the knowledge embodied in artifacts. Existing research tools suggest that commercial tools could do a better job of facilitating human factors iteration and experimentation. This will probably happen as part of an increased focus on the action language side of the interface.

Many tools are available to help developers build or prototype user interfaces. The right tool can make a big difference, but the "silver bullet"—a tool that allows effortless development of robust, functional, usable object-oriented applications on GUI platforms—does not exist. Tools do not substitute for design expertise, or replace creative people. Application frameworks, however, do reduce the need for expertise in well-understood domains.

Will Objects Go Away?

I am sure at least one reader is wondering when "all this object stuff" will go away, so we can get on to more appropriate paradigms for user interface design. I have met people who think that command lines and text display are the be-all and end-all of user interfaces, that icons are childish "pretty pictures," or that some as-yet-undiscovered technology, such as brain-wave reading, will be the basis for interfaces of the future.

Objects will not go away, because the issue of objects is not about user interfaces, or OO programming, or anything to do with computers. It is about how people perceive and act upon the world. We—end users, everyone—have evolved to deal with objects since the dawn of time. What *can* go away are the naive or confused portrayals of physical objects that are often seen today. The best antidote to these is paying careful attention to developing conceptual models that reflect the thinking of experts in the application domains.

The trend toward object-orientation in business applications is obvious to any reader of the computer trade press. Scientific and engineering applications as well are moving to graphical representations of abstract objects [Far91]. Scientists are not abandoning more traditional symbolic representations, but they are recognizing that these representations are often inadequate to deal with large quantities of data. Human perceptual systems, particularly vision, have fantastic abilities to summarize and recognize patterns ([Held74], [Kos83], [Pin85]). It is natural that these systems should be exploited, now that computers have the power to represent the data graphically.

To help confirm this trend, I looked at all the advertisements for software packages in a recent issue of *IEEE Spectrum*, a magazine catering to electrical and electronic engineers. Of nineteen products, five had user interfaces that were fully object-oriented—graphical representations of domain objects were used both as input and output. Eleven more had interfaces with at least graphical displays of domain objects.[1] Application areas covered by the products include communications network analysis, mathematics and statistics, electromagnetic analysis, antenna design, dynamical systems analysis, digital oscilloscope data management, circuit design, power engineering, neural networks, and realtime temperature sensing.

[1] The remaining three provided no information about their user interfaces.

This example is typical. In engineering as in many other areas, "real world" conceptual models and graphical representations have taken a radical transformation in computing and made it accessible to everyone in the field.

16.3 21st Century OOUIs

Predicting the uses of future technology becomes more difficult as the rate of change increases. But the future is "in your face," as the kids say—something you cannot ignore. This section is frankly speculative, but grounded in clearly visible social, economic, and technological trends.

There are two practical messages here. First, there are fixed points in human-computer interaction that will help to chart a course through the future. Second, whatever is not fixed will change rapidly, even chaotically. This will put a premium on methods, tools, and organizational structures that support exploratory prototyping, rapid development, and incremental delivery.

Channeled Technology Growth

The fact that technology does not evolve in a vacuum is discussed in Chapter 2. Figure 16-2 shows some factors that condition its evolution.[1] Hardware and software can grow and change in many directions, but their growth is channeled by the needs, capabilities, and tasks of individuals and groups.

The channeling of growth is subtle and complex. As an example,

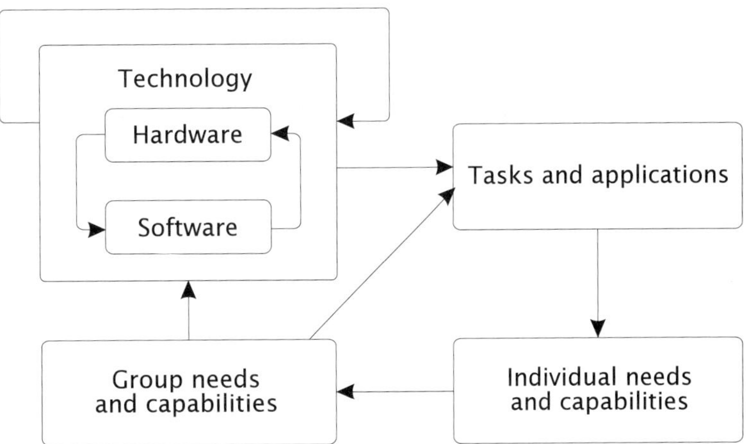

Figure 16-2 The cycle of technological change

[1] This figure is based on Figure 2-12.

consider video recording media. Optical video "laserdisc" technology was promising in the 1970s, and companies invested large sums in its development. It never really succeeded, and it is now approaching obsolescence, while the use of videotape has grown explosively. Paradoxically, sometime in the next couple of decades, CD-ROM optical disks will probably obsolete tape for many video storage applications. This is only partly due to anticipated technical advances that will allow high-quality video to be stored on the more conveniently sized CD-ROM format. A second factor in the success of tape was its recordability, which allowed consumers to see TV shows "on demand" rather than at the time of broadcast. This need will be satisfied by improvements in high-speed networking, leading to "video on demand" services from centralized databases.

Factors underlying these relationships operate at different time scales, which helps us to understand how they operate:

- Hardware technology changes quickly, on a scale of months. Exact predictions, such as which chip design will dominate, are difficult. General predictions, such as how many MIPS or gigabytes of storage will be available in a given year, are easier—or rather, have been easier to date. Over the last thirty years, aggregate progress has been quite predictable; where predictions have been wrong, it is usually because they were too conservative.

- Software technology seems to change quickly, but this is a superficial phenomenon, mainly due to marketing. Significant developments take place on a scale of years. Using object-orientation as an example, commercial products exploit principles and algorithms that have been documented in the research literature for at least several years.

  The difference between hardware and software time scales is partly because the raw materials we work with are manufactured goods in the case of hardware, but mostly designs and specifications in software. This may change if we come to rely more on packaged software components purchased on the open market.[1]

- Major changes in group needs and applications occur on a scale ranging from years to decades and longer. At any point in time, significant discontinuity may exist between the needs and capabilities of different groups. These changes are dominated by social and cultural factors that are not well understood, so they are hard to predict. Many seemingly rapid changes in needs related to technology are only apparent, caused by the application of new technology to preexisting needs.

- Significant changes in individuals, other than those mediated by society and culture, occur over millennia and are not factors in technological change. Human capabilities as they exist *are* significant

[1] [Ude94] has an interesting perspective on "componentware." [Cox91] explicitly links hardware and software component concepts in the notion of "software-ICs."

factors, particularly for technology affecting user interfaces. Chapters 4 and 8-10 presented fundamental cognitive, sensory, and motor capabilities as a basis for interface design; they are also a basis for the development of new interface technology.

Staying afloat in the sea of change within the computer industry requires a knowledge of where the safe harbors and anchor points lie. These are the deep structures of human needs and capabilities, which anchor aspects of computer technology and applications that use technology.

Most computer usage is accounted for by a few application categories—spreadsheets, text processing, graphics, publishing, communication of notes and documents, filing and retrieval, and filling in forms. The tasks these applications automate have existed for centuries. Even *avant garde* applications, such as digital video editing [MacN92], satisfy needs that have been understood for years. "Advanced" features such as hypertext are often simply new ways of supplying old capabilities.[1]

The relative stability of applications means that technology directions can often be predicted by the following questions, asked iteratively:[2]

- Where are the breakdowns in existing ways of doing an application—points of inefficiency, inaccuracy, or frustration?
- Could these breakdowns be fixed by exploiting human capabilities better, or eliminating the need for human intervention in some process step?
- Does (or will) technology exist that can be applied to removing the breakdowns?
- What other applications or processes will be affected (perhaps eliminated, or improved, or caused to reveal other breakdowns) by the hypothesized application of new technology?

Development methods also have stable points based on human needs and capabilities. Most major truths about managing large projects were probably known to the builders of the Egyptian pyramids—certainly they were known before there was such a thing as "software."

Though some members of the OO community might disagree, object-orientation is more a consequence of knowledge about good software structure than its cause. There is a general level of "software object principles" that cuts across *all* good systems.[3] Software techniques are based only partially on pure computer science considerations; equally important is to have structures that reflect what human programmers can reliably generate and comprehend.

[1] The semantics of hypertext have been used for centuries in encyclopedias, Bible concordances, bibliographies, etc.

[2] Notice the resemblance here to the process of task analysis and synthesis described in Chapter 7.

[3] Even the dreaded "functional decomposition" is a useful technique in the small, for structuring methods in a single class.

These stable points, though helpful, define only the broad outlines of the channels in which technology will evolve. There is an old saying, "God is in the details"—and another old saying, "the devil is in the details." Predicting the details is hard, so here we must rely on flexible methods and architectures that can react to changes in technology, user needs, and perhaps taste and styles.

Object ecosystems An insight that seems to be emerging from many disciplines—economics and management, politics and government, urban studies, computer science—is that large, centralized systems do not work very well. These systems are characterized by functional hierarchies, central control, and slow responses to events.

Many successful object systems illustrate an opposing set of principles, described above under *Event-driven architecture*—control is distributed, operations are collaborative, and most events are handled close to their origins. The largest examples are not "pure OO" systems, but heterogeneous networks of computers that communicate by message passing.[1] The Internet, for instance, has tens of thousands of connected domains, over two million computer nodes, and twenty-five million end-user terminals, with no central control.[2] Yet it is more robust, reliable, and functional than many centrally designed and controlled networks that are orders of magnitude smaller.

It is tempting to compare these large object systems with examples of successful systems in nature, such as stable societies and ecosystems. Though most obvious in ecosystems, they all are self-regulating, self-organizing and decentralized. Global order comes primarily from local interactions. They are very complex, and causal chains stemming from single events are difficult to follow. This complexity, however, seems to contribute to their ability to adapt (maintain global stability, or homeostasis) within a broad range ([May74], [Lovel87]).[3]

This comparison is speculative, but relevant to readers of this book. Many future OOUIs will be parts of, and provide access to, huge networks of connected objects. These interfaces and their underlying systems will no longer be in the realm of designed objects that can be well understood and completely determined. That does not mean they cannot be designed—but we may need to think of ourselves more as landscape architects than workers in steel and stone.

Researchers in Japan are taking these ideas seriously. Mario Tokoro, of the Sony Computer Science Laboratory, talks about "the society of objects" [Tok93], a vast network of fixed and mobile computers, servers, and "volitional agents" operating on behalf of users. He views the sum of all this activity as a globe-spanning "computational field." Tokoro and other

[1] Networked computers see each other as finite state machines—which are formally equivalent to objects without classes or inheritance.

[2] The statistics are as of mid-1994 [Lewis94]. It is growing at over 10% per month.

[3] I leave it as an exercise to verify that these systems satisfy Booch's "five attributes of well-formed complex systems," described in Chapter 5, Section 5.1.

researchers are working on concrete problems associated with this vision, ranging from new operating system architectures and concurrent object computing, to user interface paradigms. As an example of the latter, work is in progress on software to generate facial expressions for the volitional agents in interfaces to future computers [Tak93].

These distributed, heterogeneous networks of agents and servers contrast with the Japanese "Fifth Generation" project [Hendl94] of the early 1980s, which projected the development of centralized intelligent computers. In Tokoro's "society of objects," intelligence emerges from an evolving social web of computer agents. This idea is strikingly similar to Marvin Minsky's "society of mind" [Minsk86], which attempts to explain the human mind based on similar societies of neural agents: "Each mental agent by itself can only do some simple thing that needs no mind or thought at all. Yet when we join these agents in societies—in certain very special ways—this leads to true intelligence."[1]

In the 21st century, for the first time, the society of mind may meet a society of objects of similar complexity. The consequences for interface designers are hard to predict, but they will surely be enormous.

New Technologies

All new computer technologies affect user interfaces—either directly, or by providing new functions and power that interfaces must access. Figure 16-3 shows one of many possible ways to classify changes that will determine the nature of future OOUIs. The dimensions of change in the figure map roughly to the three domains of Chapter 5—conceptual model (intellectual content and connectivity), user interface model (sensory/motor engagement), and implementation model (platform and network capability). The last one will be treated first, since it is the substrate for the others.

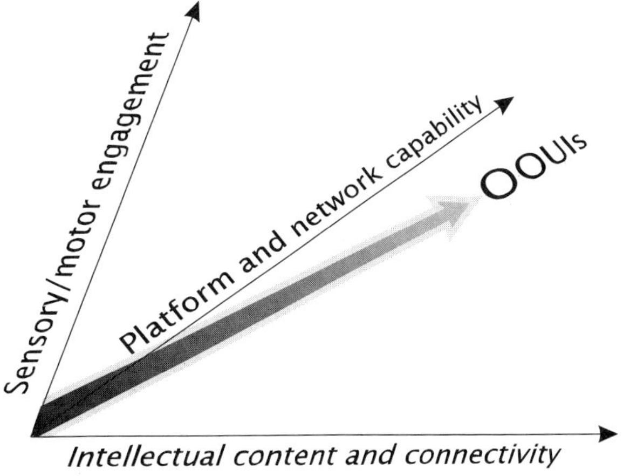

Figure 16-3 Dimensions of the future for object-oriented user interfaces

[1] [Minsk86], p. 17.

Platform and network capability determines the power of the implementation models underlying user interfaces. Application domains determine the content of implementation models, but more powerful platforms move new domains onto computers and allow problems of larger scale to be attacked. This creates new challenges for interface designers—making new capabilities easily accessible, and scaling current interfaces up to larger object spaces.

Figure 16-4 illustrates what some people call "straight-ahead" technology growth or improvement, because it is measured as a straight line on a logarithmic graph. This means that as time proceeds linearly, the technology improves exponentially. Take a characteristic such as the number of transistors on a microprocessor chip, or the data capacity of the fastest telecommunications links. If the number increases tenfold within some period, say three years, in six years it will increase one hundredfold, in nine years one thousandfold, and so forth. This straight-ahead growth has held in many areas of hardware capability, from storage capacity to processor speed.

How does this affect user interface designers? For one thing, it brings new realms of content to interfaces. Multimedia, for example, including full-motion video, needs both powerful microprocessors and large-capacity storage. Technology improvement also permits new looks and feels, such as head-mounted displays and other computationally expensive virtual reality techniques. Designers of user interface and application internals need to pay close attention to isolating infrastructure layers, as described in Chapter 12; these layers will change rapidly as growth in raw technology leads to new operating system architectures to support it.

Quantitative increases in platform capabilities may force qualitative

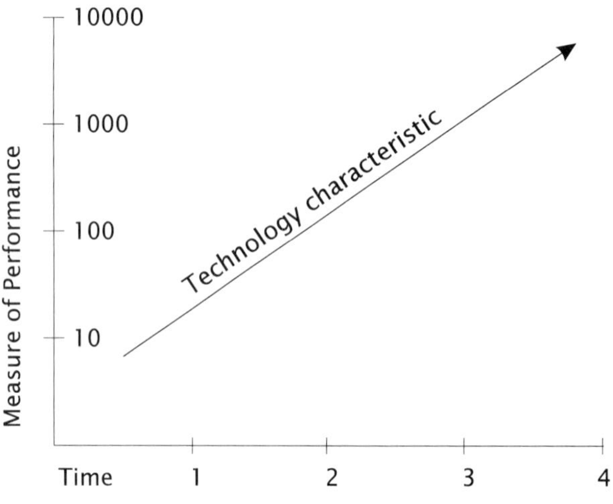

Figure 16-4 "Straight-ahead" technology improvement

changes in user interfaces. As an example, consider information storage. Hard disk storage units in typical personal computers today hold 100-300 megabytes of data, about equal to what might be found in the filing cabinets and bookshelves of an individual office.[1] Interface metaphors such as file cabinets, folders, and bookshelves are adequate to manage this amount of information.

Gigabyte (10^9 byte) drives are already common in desktop machines, and will be shortly be common in notebook computers. Within ten years, desktop machines may have storage in the terabyte (10^{12} byte) range, equaling the amount of information in a large library.[2] Through high-speed networks, users will have nearly instant access to thousands of terabytes of information. Existing metaphors for organizing things are inadequate to deal with information on this scale, so new ones must be developed.

Not only will there be more powerful computers, but there will simply be *more* computers. A typical automobile, for example, already has several computers controlling fuel injection, brakes, etc. In the future it will have additional ones, for purposes ranging from route-finding to collision avoidance. Some of these "ubiquitous computers" [Weis91] will be invisible, but many will need some sort of user interface, possibly quite different from standard GUIs.

Sensory/motor engagement is the extent to which the look and feel of an interface matches the sensory and motor capabilities of users. Engagement implies that users take pleasure in using the interface, besides using it effectively. This area is driven both by technology and by basic research in human factors.

As a technology category, it covers input and output devices. Though the human need for technology in general is unlimited, in certain areas, such as visual perception, there are finite limits based on sensory capabilities. As a result the growth curve often looks like Figure 16-5. The capability of the technology (display resolution, say) rises asymptotically to the limits of the human sense (vision in this case).

There are several reasons why the curve is typically asymptotic, rather than a straight line. The figure looks like a classic "learning curve," and the slow accumulation of knowledge about how our senses work is indeed one issue. Others relate to how much raw technology is needed to provide a given increment in perceived quality. In vision, for example, because of how computer graphics problems scale up, exponential improvements in raw technology provide only linear improvements in quality as seen by users.

A useful set of subcategories for this technology area is based on the

[1] By a rough calculation, the *Encyclopedia Britannica* could be stored in 125 megabytes. Word count in the complete *Britannica* equals about 160 average books.

[2] One to two million (10^6) books. This only considers text; as a comparison, the amount of storage consumed by the text of the *Britannica* would only hold about ten minutes of compressed video, or thirty seconds of uncompressed video.

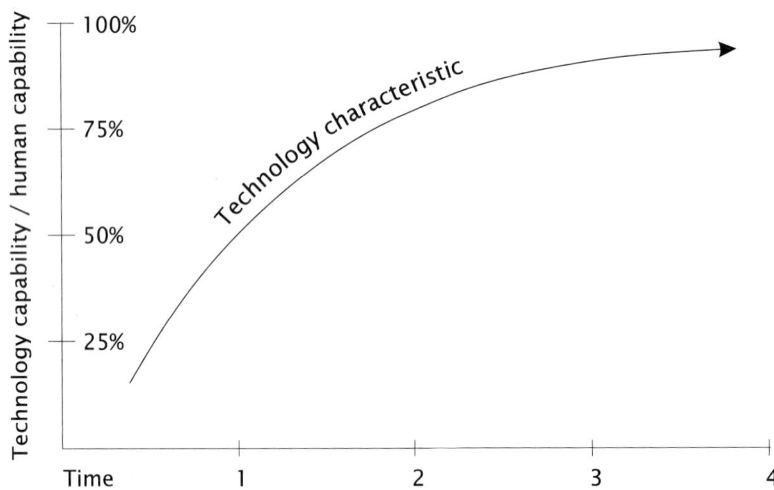

Figure 16-5 Asymptotic approach of technology to human capabilities

size of displays, which in turn influences input devices, systems, tasks and environments in which they will be used:

- *Tiny.* This includes user interfaces for appliances such as microwave ovens, credit-card computers used for banking, and wristwatch computers. Though too small for conventional GUIs, they can support OOUIs. As an example, Nintendo's *StarFox* Game Watch provides a highly interactive video game, with sound and graphics, on a wristwatch with about a one inch square (6-7 cm^2) display and four buttons. Buttons, touch panels, and voice recognition will be the typical input devices associated with these displays.
- *Small.* Mobile "personal digital assistants" (PDAs) [Hal93] such as the one shown in Figure 16-6 will become widespread within the next few years. They resemble Alan Kay's *Dynabook* [Kay77a]—a computer, about the size of a book, that responds to handwriting as a notebook would. The size of PDAs will be determined by the need to carry them in pockets, briefcases, and purses. Cellular networks will connect them wherever they go. To reduce their size and weight, most will not have keyboards or mice. Preferred input modes will be handwriting and gesture recognition (using a stylus), and speech recognition. Neural networks and other artificial intelligence technologies will prove useful in developing input recognizers. Because of their use in business, PDAs will probably have interfaces that look like simplified versions of popular GUIs.
- *Large.* Desktop computers will be extensions of those we have today, though extensively networked with other machines (including their users' PDAs). Displays will be larger, have better resolution, and

Figure 16-6 A mobile, wireless, "personal digital assistant"

support video. This is probably the only area where CRT displays will persist, at least for a few years; for most other uses, LCD displays will dominate. Variations on keyboards, mice, joysticks, styluses, and touch screens will likely continue to be the dominant input devices. Polarizing glasses[1] or lightweight head-mounted displays will be used for applications requiring stereoscopic 3-D display.

- *Very large.* Displays up to several meters on a side will function as "whiteboard" displays for use by groups. Prototypes are already in use [Elr92]. These displays may also support videoconferencing, high-definition TV, video games, etc. Input will include chalk-like styluses, remote control button pads, laser pointers, direct touch, and speech. Large displays can, through wireless connections, mirror information displayed on PDAs used by meeting participants.
- *Immersive.* Many future computers will provide users with the sense of being immersed in a virtual space rather than of "using a computer." Current virtual reality systems do this with head-mounted displays (HMDs) or rooms with wall-sized displays.[2] The latter are particularly appropriate for shared spaces, such as virtual conference rooms. Wall displays will use the same technology as the *very large* category.

  Probably within the next ten years, HMDs will be reduced in size and weight to not much more than a pair of glasses, making them practical for a range of applications. For input, tracking the user's head position is required, and other inputs, such as grasping and pointing, are optional. Multimodal input, particularly mixing speech and pointing, will be important. Expect to see rapid change in these technologies over the next decade.

[1] This is the same technology used for 3-D movies, where two images with different polarization are shown simultaneously; the glasses route one image to each eye.
[2] For true 3-D, these rooms require users to wear passive polarizing glasses.

Lightweight HMDs will enable "augmented reality" applications, where computer-generated 3-D objects are superimposed on real objects in the world. For example, a surgeon might see a patient's internal organs, synthesized from scan data, dynamically superimposed on the patient.

Three-dimensional display and visualization will be an important component of the presentation language for many interfaces. Figure 16-6, based on [Macki91], is an instructive example. A user of the system can control his or her position along a large wall showing information. Information around the selected point appears on the center wall, the focus of the user's attention, and peripheral information is placed on the two receding walls. Perspective reduces the amount of space required to display background information—each of the outer walls takes about half the display space of the central wall. The result is that a large amount of peripheral information is shown in a small space, surrounding the information at the center of the user's point of view. As the user moves, the display changes smoothly to keep the central information on the center wall.

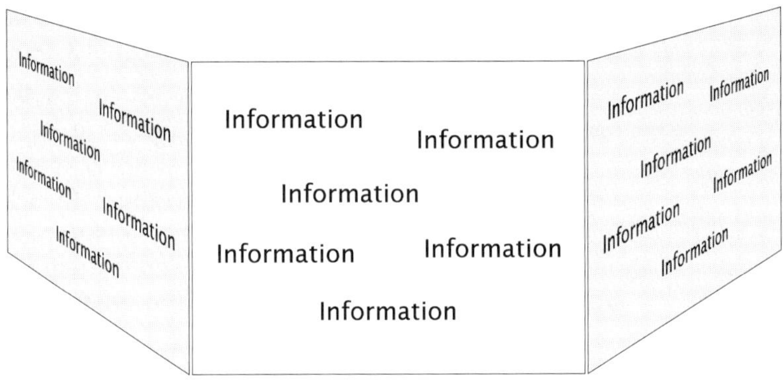

Figure 16-7 A "perspective wall" [Macki91]

The perspective wall does not just give a 3-D "look" to the interface. It, and other 3-D representations described in [Macki91], provide a context for users as they navigate in large information spaces. Context and continuity reduce the cognitive effort required to use the interface. A dynamic example of the value of continuous navigation in a 3-D space appears toward the end of the Steven Spielberg film *Jurassic Park*, when Lex "flies" through the computer file system while she is attempting to reactivate the park's security system. The interface shown in the film is a real product, *Info Navigator* from Silicon Graphics.

Notice that in the examples just cited, the sense of immersive space does not come from true 3-D display, but from the user's ability to move around in it. Using products such as Sense8's *WorldToolKit* [sSen93], 3-D spaces in which users can move can be built even on low-end desktop computers; such toolkits may be standard parts of future user interface builders. Current 2-D metaphors have been pushed nearly to their limits, and 3-D is an obvious next step.

Intellectual content and connectivity include the content of conceptual models for application domains and the way the objects comprising the content are linked. The obvious effects of technology will be to bring larger quantities of information, new media types, and more users into existing applications. Our ability to design representations that make new content and connectivity accessible and comprehensible to users will gate the application of technology.

The application categories mentioned on page 485 (spreadsheets, text processing, etc.) have well-established models, but new media types and networking capabilities may induce significant changes in their interfaces. The example on page 488, of quantitative increases in content creating a need for new interface models, is one example. Another is the incorporation of motion video, graphical animation, and sound into composite documents, which will result in new interaction paradigms for editing such documents.

Coordinating work between individuals will become a required feature of many applications, and will cause significant changes in some interfaces. There are many potential metaphors for collaborative work—whiteboards, conference rooms, routing slips, marginal annotations, etc. Interfaces that exploit these metaphors are in their infancy, and they may change radically as they become more pervasive.

Really new conceptual models are rare, but have large effects. The introduction of spreadsheets and desktops can be compared to the switch from the Ptolemaic (earth-centered) to the Copernican (sun-centered) model of the solar system. Organizing information content in new ways can lead to progress that would have been difficult to predict beforehand. At this point, we can only speculate about what new models might drive the "killer apps" of the 21st century.

Top Ten Trends in OOUIs

If I were asked to pick the most important trends for developers to pay attention to, my list would include the following. They are consistent with the general idea of putting users in touch with "real objects," and proof-of-concept examples for most of them exist today.[1]

1. *Direct manipulation* will continue to be the signature interaction technique for OOUIs. Drag-drop will become pervasive for the sorts of objects found on computer desktops today—icons, text, graphics, video, etc. Manipulation will become more tactile as input devices with force feedback become available. Spaces of manipulable objects will enlarge, as networks make object location increasingly

[1] Many examples were pointed out in Chapters 8, 9, and 10.

transparent to users. New direct manipulation metaphors will evolve, based on 3-D presentation and a richer set of input devices. Direct manipulation will be combined synergistically with other modalities, such as speech.

2. *3-D spatial navigation metaphors* based on "haptic" spaces. (A haptic space is one in which a user actively moves around and explores, as opposed to "pure visual" spaces such as the one shown in Figure 8-9.) Simplifying navigation in huge, ever-changing cyberspaces will certainly be an important problem for 21st century interface designers. Space seems to be the best metaphor available, but there are infinitely many variants. Enabling technologies include displays (flat and head-mounted), and navigation controls such as joysticks and "flying mice" with six degrees of freedom.

3. *Integrated, concurrent multimodal input.* Technology exists today, and will improve, for speech, handwriting, and gesture recognition. Most commercial uses of the technology are fragmented, offering users a choice of several discrete input modes. It is obvious from observing people (and validated by more formal studies[1]) that we can integrate several modes, say pointing, gesturing, and speaking simultaneously. Concurrent and coordinated use of input modalities will characterize the best future OOUIs.

4. *Integrated multimedia output.* By the 21st century, the majority of computers will be capable of high-quality sound and full-motion video output. Not integrating multimedia into applications will amount to throwing away important capabilities. Uses abound, from voice annotation and online video help, to things like the "sonic finder" described in Chapter 10.

   An ancillary trend is the blending of graphics and video, leading to video-quality photorealistic graphic objects, and video in which individual objects can be selected and manipulated by users [Tan92].

5. *Diverse, heterogeneous user populations.* As technology becomes cheaper and more widespread, almost everyone on the planet will become a computer user. This, and the divergence of display types and sizes, may end the trend toward "standard interfaces" across platforms and users. Future successful interfaces will be rapidly customizable to suit different nationalities, abilities, and preferences.

6. *Focus on groups, not individual users.* People mostly work and play in groups. Two trends are driving computers toward supporting groups, not individuals. One is the availability of fast networks and powerful desktop machines to support cooperative work and play. The second is widespread perception of negative aspects of the current transportation infrastructure (noise, pollution, lost time,

[1] [Hau89] and [Bol80], for example.

etc.). These combine to suggest that many collaborations can effectively take place electronically.[1]

7. *Decentralized services.* Banking has moved from the teller's cage to the ATM, and will move to home computers. The same will occur with shopping centers, movie theaters, and many other services. Service companies have set the stage for this by moving toward "assembly line" service delivery; if the service can be delivered (or at least ordered) by computer there is thus little loss, and the benefit of avoiding travel. Technology exists, or will soon exist, to bring shops, theaters, concert halls, museums, etc. into homes.

8. *Task-based agents.* Over time, natural language understanding and other "artificial intelligence" techniques will dramatically enhance agent capabilities.[2] However, agents with any degree of general intelligence (like "Phil" in Apples's *Knowledge Navigator* [vApp87]) are unlikely to appear anytime soon. The key to making agents useful is to confine them to specific tasks that are difficult for users because they require rote knowledge, are repetitive, or involve "brute force" computation or information searching.

   For tasks such as searching databases, dispatching autonomous agents to remote nodes in a network may improve both performance and ease of use, as opposed to downloading large quantities of information [Way94b]. Autonomous remote agents will eventually lead to the "societies of objects" discussed above.

   Agents, properly used, are not inconsistent with direct manipulation. As Brenda Laurel points out [Lau90], "It doesn't feel like indirection when an agent does something for me that I can't or don't want to do myself." Well-designed agents do not force users to give up control, or seem so "human" that they raise expectations that can't be fulfilled. Nor are they just "pasted on" to cover up an overly complicated system—they perform tasks that are fundamentally difficult for human users.

9. *Network-aware collaborating component objects.* Many complete interfaces and applications will be built from components by system integrators, end user organizations, or end users themselves. Components will make minimal assumptions about the location of collaborating objects, allowing distribution across networks. Distribution may include dynamic migration of objects within a network based on failures or load conditions. It will include mobile users, who can move around a network while remaining continuously connected.

[1] See [For94] and [Weis91] for a discussion of some of the subtleties of supporting cooperative work, such as tracking and locating individuals users, and moving work from one place to another. [Rhei93] presents issues in networking communities of people for purposes ranging from play to politics.

[2] Note that agents are just software objects, and not fundamentally different from other objects. The name *agent* simply reflects their purpose, to act as surrogates for users in the performance of specific tasks.

Interface components will be customizable, so they can "plug and play" in multiple environments.

An extension, enabled by cheap microprocessors and wireless networks, is to "animate" real objects (automobiles and coffee makers, for example) with computers so they can collaborate with simulated objects inside other computers [Wel93].

10. *Application frameworks.* Frameworks, described in Chapter 14, will be the dominant method of providing platform services such as network access and window management. There will also be a large market for frameworks specific to application domains, such as graphics, or industries, such as insurance. Component objects sold separately will be designed to interoperate with popular frameworks.

We are at a watershed between the past and the future. An intellectual base painstakingly constructed over the last three decades by Ivan Sutherland, Doug Engelbart, Alan Kay, Charles Irby, Larry Tesler, and thousands of other researchers and developers is now available to everyone. A generation of designers and programmers has grown up in a world of graphical, event-driven systems. Powerful hardware and a rich set of object-oriented development tools will soon be taken for granted. As new technology becomes available, OOUIs more powerful than anything we see today will be possible.

User interface designers, collectively, design experiences that fill significant parts of the lives of computer users. Over time, more and more people will use computers. What kinds of experiences will we create for them? There is ample evidence that computers can engage people and make them happy, augment their intelligence and productivity, and foster a sense of community with other users. Computers can also create anxiety, frustration, and stress. The difference between happiness and frustration is in the experiences our interfaces provide. My hope is that what you have learned from this book will help you to make a difference.

16.4 To Explore Further

My perspective on the state of the OOUI is based on sources cited in earlier chapters, particularly observation and use of today's leading-edge applications and tools. Staying in touch with the future requires inputs from sources too diverse to cite in detail. Future systems are driven by available technology, by the wants and needs of end users, and by the economics of work and play. Keeping up with all this involves reading a variety of journals, and "hanging out" in places where the future is being created—from the Internet to video game arcades.

I have found *IEEE Spectrum* particularly useful for the hardware side of technology trends (not just in computers), and *Fortune* for their social and economic impact. *Spectrum* runs an annual issue entirely devoted to analyzing and forecasting technology trends [Bell94]. *Communications of the ACM* and *Computer (IEEE)* are good sources for computer hardware and software trends, particularly periodic special issues like [Man93], [Wel93], [Pal94], and [Rie94]. *BYTE* and *DATAMATION* are good sources of fast-breaking news. *Mondo 2000* and *Wired* report on fringe issues that may become mainstream.

To go beyond this book, I suggest three things.

In learning design, there is no substitute for doing it. As in other arts and crafts, good design requires new ways of seeing as well as new ways of building. Acquiring these new ways through lectures or books is almost impossible. The cycle of ideas, implementation, and improvement based on feedback is indispensable for improving your skills.

Isaac Newton said that if he seemed to see farther than others, it was because he stood on the shoulders of giants. This is good advice to anyone in any field. There are giants even in the young field of human-computer interface design—and superb examples of information design in other media stretch back for centuries. You probably will not go beyond the work of the past until you thoroughly understand it. Analyze examples of user interfaces that are judged very good—or very bad—by their users. What are the factors that led to the judgement? Find out why the developers did what they did, and what they would do differently if given the chance.

Talk—and listen—to end users. Without exception, great user interfaces are great because they provide innovative and efficient solutions to existing problems. Experts in the application domain are the richest source of information about the problems, information that often leads to new solutions. "Listen" also means observe, because people are not always able to articulate their sources of frustration. If you are skilled in the solution technologies, watching people work with existing tools, questioning when necessary, may reveal solvable problems users themselves are not aware of. The Xerox Star's desktop metaphor and Dan Bricklin's spreadsheet are just two examples of enduring ideas that developed in the context of analyzing how people worked.

The proof of your mastery of these concepts is in designing user interfaces that work—and the users of your product are the final judges of that.

Appendix 1

Fax Case Study

This appendix describes facsimile transmission (usually called *fax*), discusses typical applications, and positions fax in the market relative to other forms of electronic communication. Information here is used for exercises in Chapters 7-10 that ask you to understand the requirements, analyze users' tasks, and design a user interface for a fax application.

The design problem that is posed in Chapters 7-10 is typical of real-life development—a substantial new application (to support facsimile transmission) must be designed, and it must be integrated into a "desktop" shell. Besides fax, this appendix also describes the shell and presents a brief style guide for it.

A1.1 Background

Digital facsimile transmission, a technology for electronically transmitting document images, has been commercially available for more than a century. Its use grew explosively during the 1980s, rapidly outstripping text-based electronic mail (e-mail). By 1990, applications for sending and receiving faxes on personal computers had become popular. Fax continues to grow rapidly, on standalone machines and computers.

History and Usage of Fax

Fax is a fairly old technology, having been in commercial use since the late 19th century [Coo93]. Until the 1980s, however, it was confined to niches such as transmission of "wirephotos" to newspapers.

Two factors were significant in moving fax into the mainstream. One was that written characters in Japan (kana and kanji) were not supported by telex, telegraph, or other forms of electronic mail; this led to a major

Japanese investment in improving fax technology. The second factor was the development of facsimile transmission standards by the CCITT, allowing any two fax machines anywhere to connect using the public telephone network.

Today robust fax machines, which are nearly as easy to use as telephones, cost around $500 US. There are tens of millions of them worldwide, many shared by multiple users. By dialing a standard telephone number, a user can send a fax anywhere in the world where there is another machine. In 1991, 17 billion pages were transmitted in the US alone, and sales of machines were doubling annually [Coo93].

Technically, facsimile transmission involves scanning and digitizing a page, compressing the image, and transmitting it through a modem over the telephone line. The receiving machine decompresses and prints the image. Images can be scanned at resolutions up to 200 dots per inch (dpi) with 64 gray levels. (A future CCITT standard will support transmission in color.) A transmission typically consists of several pages following a cover page (also called a cover sheet) that gives information on the sender, receiver, and subject. For shared machines, the receiver's identity is critical; unlike e-mail, faxes have no electronic addressing other than the phone number of the machine to which they are transmitted.

Here is an informal scenario for using a fax machine (exercises in Chapter 7 ask for a more formal analysis):

1. The person sending the fax gathers the pages to be sent and prepares a cover page. Cover pages are usually preprinted with fixed information, such as the sender's company; other information is handwritten in spaces provided. For verification, the sender writes on the cover page the number of pages in the transmission.

2. The user loads pages to be transmitted into the feeder tray of the fax machine and keys in the receiving machine's phone number. The transmitting machine establishes a connection and then feeds and transmits the pages. Most machines provide features such as the ability to store frequently called numbers and to continuously redial a number if it is busy. Some machines are also able to scan the pages once, store the images, and transmit them to each person on a list of recipients.

3. As each page is received, the receiving machine prints it. Most transmission errors are corrected automatically. Some errors, such as paper jams, require manual intervention either at the sending or the receiving machine. When the transmission is completed successfully, the sending machine prints an acknowledgment showing the number of pages and the time they were sent.

This scenario assumes a single user at each end. Fax machines are often shared by many users and located next to a secretary or in a company mailroom. Step (1) is then broken into two parts. The sender prepares the pages to be transmitted (including the cover page) and delivers them to the fax operator, who executes step (1) as described above. When a fax is received at a shared machine, the operator uses the information on the cover page to hand-deliver it to the recipient. Operators of shared fax machines usually maintain a log of transmissions sent and received.

Public fax machines, where users pay to transmit, are available at locations ranging from office-supply stores to airports. Some businesses provide incoming fax service as well, charging users per page received. Telephone companies, for example AT&T, supply incoming numbers that receive faxes and store them on a database. Users can then dial in and download their faxes or have them forwarded. This service is useful for those who want to receive faxes while traveling.

In the US at least, shops and restaurants often accept orders by fax. There are many innovative uses of fax. For example, one application allows users to query a database by telephone and fax. Queries are entered through the buttons on a touchtone phone, and abstracts of results are read back through a speech synthesizer. If the user wants to see the full text, pressing a button sends it to his or her fax machine.

Computer Fax Applications

Facsimile transmission hardware and software have been available for computers since around 1985. As with real fax machines, a user can have a personal fax computer, or a server on a network may receive faxes and redistribute them to individual users.

Initially, personal fax required adding an attachment card to a personal computer. Today most modems will support fax, and processors are fast enough to receive and transmit without any additional hardware. As a result, almost all laptop and notebook computers are now sold with built-in modems and bundled fax software. Software packages are also widely sold for desktop machines.

The scenario for using a PC as a fax machine satisfies the same goals as the scenario on the previous page, but differs in its details:

1. The person sending the fax generates pages to be sent and prepares a cover page. Cover page images are usually stored with fixed information, and variable information (such as the receiver of the fax) is typed by the user. The fax program will count the pages in the transmission and put the number on the cover page. Transmitted pages can come from a variety of sources:

   a. Fax programs supply print drivers that present a standard interface to applications but format documents for fax transmission instead of printing them. Thus anything that can be printed from any application can be transmitted as a fax.

   b. Any bitmapped image can be reformatted for fax.

   c. A scanner can generate image files from paper documents, just as in a real fax machine.

2. The user keys in the receiving machine's phone number or selects it from an online phone directory. The transmitting machine establishes a connection and transmits the pages. Fax programs, like fax machines, support features such as distribution lists and automatic redialing.
3. When a fax is received by a computer, the pages are stored in a file that can be viewed online or printed. Received fax images can also be retransmitted by fax, or sent to other people using file transfer protocols. Some fax programs provide optical character recognition (OCR), so printed pages received as faxes can be converted to ASCII (machine readable) files.

Delrina's *WinFax* [sDel94], a popular program for personal computers, illustrates the functions provided by fax applications. Besides the basic capabilities just described, it provides:

- Phone books for storing telephone numbers of fax recipients; phone books also support distribution lists for multiple recipients.
- Scheduling of fax transmissions to account for time zone differences, or to take advantage of lower rates at certain times of day.
- A library of cover page designs that users can customize.
- The ability to combine outputs from multiple applications into a single fax.
- The ability to view and annotate a fax before it is sent.
- Capabilities for monitoring the status of transmissions and logging sent and received faxes.
- Encryption and electronic signatures to verify the identity of fax senders.
- Bitmapped "rubber stamps" for marking fax pages as *draft*, *confidential*, etc.

Fax and E-Mail

Through the 1980s and early 90s, fax usage grew much faster than e-mail [Bor91]. The reason for this in Japan has already been discussed. In the US and Europe, the situation is more complex.

Observation suggests that ease of use must be a factor—most fax users seem more comfortable with fax machines than with computers and computer e-mail systems. On the other hand, e-mail usage on the Internet has recently increased dramatically [Lewis94] without any significant change in the accessing technology. As discussed in Chapter 2, social factors probably play a role in this shift—the fact that some people accept e-mail (or fax) will encourage others to do so, independent of any "rational" factors.

There is also an "avalanche effect" that can occur with any two-way communications technology. Whether it be telephone, fax, or e-mail, the value of the technology to an individual is proportional to the number of people he or she can contact. This suggests that if n people are connected in a network, the aggregate value of connectivity grows proportionally to n^2. At the same time, economies of scale will tend to reduce the cost per individual as more people join the network. These factors can combine to produce rapid growth.

Translation and interconnection are possible between fax and e-mail. Fax transmissions received by computer can be resent as e-mail—either directly as image data, or after translation to text using OCR. In the other direction, Lewis [Lewis94] describes a business that caters to people who do not use e-mail, but need to receive mail from the Internet. They are given an Internet e-mail address that is actually a port on a computer. When the system receives mail, it "prints" the note to an image file, uses a directory to map the e-mail address to a phone number, and sends the note to the recipient as a fax.

The exercises will ask you to integrate fax into a shell that already supports e-mail. This is why e-mail is relevant to the problem—the design will need to account for several different types of users:

- Users who are comfortable with computer e-mail, but not computer fax.
- Those who have used both "standalone" computer fax applications and e-mail.
- Users of real fax machines, who may or may not be comfortable with either computer fax or e-mail.

This does not exhaust the permutations, but it suggests the range of experience in the user community. The basic tension is between making the fax function consistent with the e-mail function, and making it consistent with the operation of a real fax machine.

A1.2 Case Study Application Requirements

Existing fax programs are quite mature and leave little to be desired for users operating in a "fax-centric" environment. General users, who use fax documents as one of many object types in their work, might want more. In particular, the need to launch an application and enter a new context may be disruptive. In an object-oriented environment it is possible to have fax documents that "plug and play" seamlessly with other objects. This section describes a general framework for office work, and suggests requirements for integrating fax into it.

codesigned with the "Office" base. This appearance should work at all levels—conceptual as well as "look and feel."

A1.3 The "Office" Style Guide

The "Office" prototype was developed with Smalltalk/V [sDig92b] on OS/2, and follows the CUA (Common User Access) style [IBM92b]. The style elements it uses, however, are typical of GUI platforms such as the Apple Macintosh, Microsoft Windows, OSF/Motif, OpenLook, etc.[1]

This section provides a brief "style guide" with enough look and feel elements to do the exercises in Chapters 9 and 10. Figures A1-1 and A1-2 illustrate style elements, and Figure A1-3 provides a template that can be copied and used to sketch trial designs.

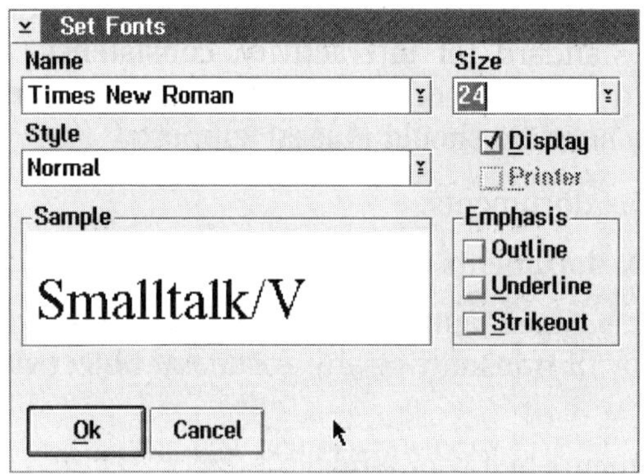

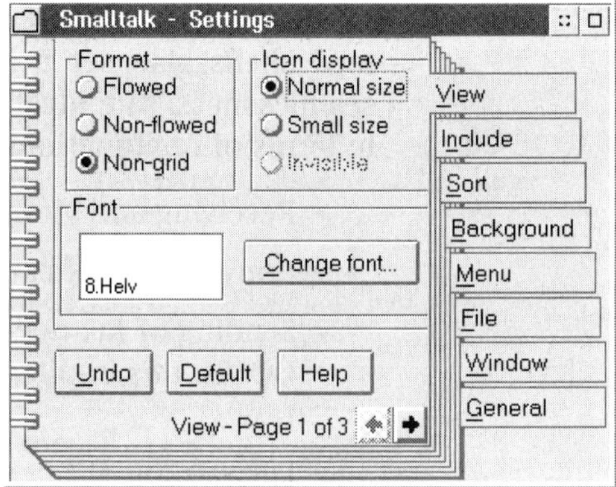

Figure A1-2 Dialogue controls

The most important elements are:

- Content views of objects, also called "application main windows" in application-oriented environments such as Microsoft Windows. In Figure A2-1, `Electronic mail` and `Word processing` are content views of folders; `Pentawidget announcement` is a content view of a text document.
- Dialogue windows (also called "popup windows") are transient windows used to display or modify the properties of objects. As an example, the lefthand window in Figure A1-2 allows a user to change the font for text display in a content window.
- Icons for information objects, containers, and templates. Icons are

[1] Published guides for these styles are cited in the general discussion of style guides in Chapter 11.

straightforward, except perhaps for templates. Figure 4-8 (Chapter 4) shows an example of template usage, for the `New envelopes` template in Figure A1-1. Icons can have various forms of emphasis to indicate their state; for instance, highlighting with reverse video to indicate selection. In OS/2, cross-hatching shows that the icon is "in use" because a content view is opened on it (in Figure A1-1, the `Word processing` and `Electronic mail` icons are examples of this).

- Drag and drop, expressing object interactions by dropping icons on one another, is discussed in Chapter 10.
- Menus. As illustrated by the `View` menu in Figure A1-1, menus may cascade—selecting a menu entry, `Icon` in this case, displays a submenu showing different types of icon views. Menu operations that change the state of objects can be checked to show the current state (in this example, `Normal icons` and `Show icon names` are properties of the folder's content view). Though not shown in the figure, menu items can be "grayed out" or disabled to show that they do not apply to the currently selected object.
- Context menus can be "popped up" directly over an icon by clicking the right mouse button. This feature of OS/2 is not present in all GUIs, though it has been around for a long time—a Smalltalk-80 example is shown in Figure 11-11. A context menu shows only the actions that apply to the object over which it is popped up.
- Push buttons, such as `OK` and `Cancel` in Figure A1-2, invoke actions.
- Radio buttons are used in groups to select one and only one of a set of options. Pressing any button in a group turns it on, and all the others off. In the righthand window in Figure A1-2, there are radio button groups under `Format` and `Icon display`. This window also illustrates use of a notebook control; different sets of properties are controlled by different "pages" in the notebook. (Notebooks are OS/2 features, not supported by all GUIs.)
- Check boxes are also grouped, but show sets of options from which any number can be selected. The group under `Emphasis` in the `Set Fonts` dialogue (Figure A1-2) is an example; any combination of `Outline`, `Underline`, and `Strikeout` can be set.
- List boxes are vertical lists of textual elements or icons, of which one or more can be selected. Drop-down lists are space-saving list boxes. `Name` in the `Set Fonts` dialogue is an example; clicking on the arrow to the right of `Times New Roman` causes a list to drop down showing other type faces. The appearance is similar to the way a menu drops down from the menu bar when it is selected.

Acknowledgments Thanks to John Bennett and Bob Mack for helpful discussions of fax, and to the many students in my classes who presented sample solutions.

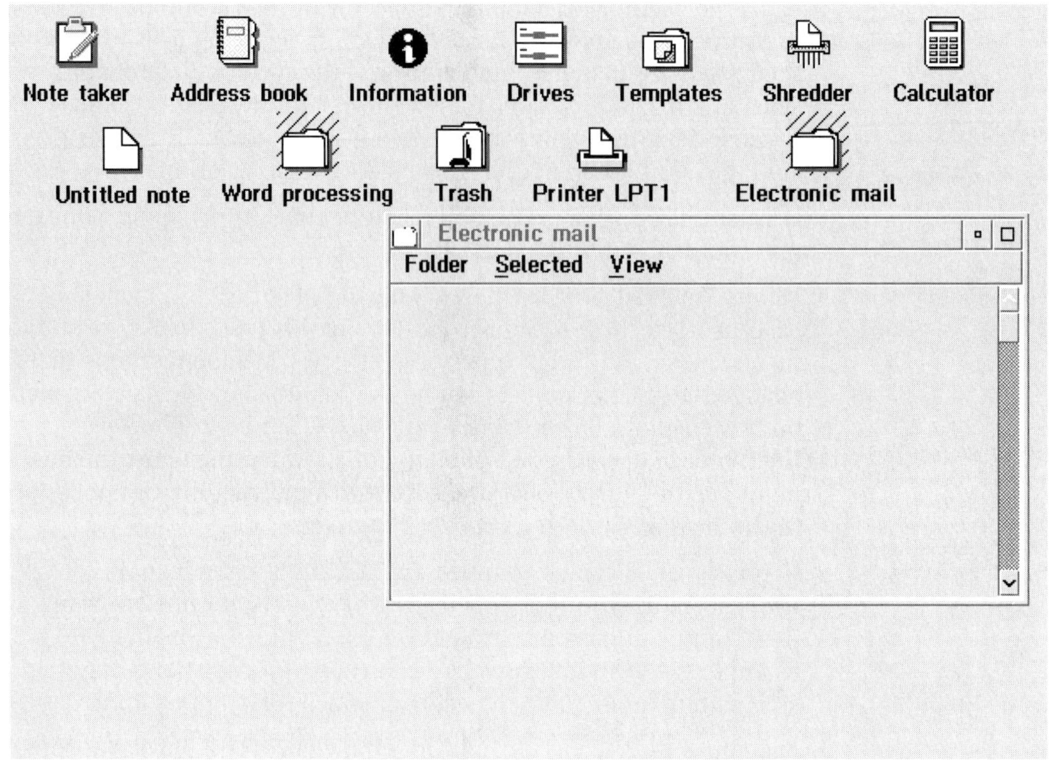

Figure A1-3 A template for sketching solutions to the exercises

Appendix 2

Introduction to Object-Orientation

You should read all of this appendix if you have no prior experience or training in any object-oriented discipline. "Prior experience or training" typically means experience or training in object-oriented programming, but might come from fields as varied as cognitive psychology, artificial intelligence, or the theory of distributed computer systems. This list indicates the number of fields that have been influenced by, or have contributed to, the set of ideas called "object-orientation."

This book contains programming examples to reinforce implementation concepts, mostly in Chapters 5 and 11–15. The examples use the object-oriented programming languages Smalltalk and C++, which are the most important OO languages used in developing OOUIs. If you are already familiar with OO concepts, but not with these languages, you can skip immediately to page 517, *The Smalltalk Language*, or page 519, *The C++ Language*.

If you have not previously studied the fundamental ideas of object-orientation, expect to have to struggle a bit to grasp them. Your reward will be an understanding of one of the half dozen or so big, crucially important ideas to come out of the last several decades of computer and information technology. After reading this appendix, you will begin to understand the basic principles behind all object-oriented disciplines, and to appreciate the broad range of applicability of those ideas.

Besides providing the positive benefits of understanding, learning the basic principles of objects has a defensive value as well. Object-orientation is a "hot topic," and peddling object-oriented products, methods, literature, and expertise has become a major industry. As in any fast-growing industry, many of the goods are of dubious quality. A good general understanding of terms and concepts, and their applications, will provide intellectual ammunition for dealing with the barrage of "object-oriented" products that assault you.

A2.1 What Is All This "Object-Oriented" Stuff?

In the 1970s and 80s, the field of information technology was dominated by "structured" things—structured programming, structured analysis, structured design, structured database, etc. "Structured" was the answer to the universal desire for a free lunch, the panacea that would solve all the hard problems of software development. "Object-oriented" (OO) has replaced "structured" as the hot buzzword and cure-all for the 1990s. OO appeared first in the context of object-oriented programming (OOP), and was presented as the answer to the demand for higher levels of productivity in building functionally rich, extensible, and easy-to-use applications. Subsequently, "object-oriented," just like "structured," was tacked onto just about every important discipline and technique in information technology, and every kind of product.

A novice setting out to understand the concept of "object-orientation" may get the impression that the whole thing is a hoax, or a marketing ploy to sell dubious products. A newcomer's first impression, from articles in the popular press and the academic literature, is typically something like this:

- It seems to have started with Smalltalk, though real programmers nowadays use C++.
- Programming people talk about encapsulation, classes, and inheritance, or (sometimes) prototyping and delegation.
- Some say that the programming language Ada is object-oriented, others say that Ada is not object-oriented. Ada 9X is definitely OO.
- User interface people talk about icons, windows, and bitmapped displays as "object-oriented."
- Databases can be object-oriented.
- In the trade press, and in product literature from vendors, just about anything at all that someone is trying to sell can be "object-oriented."

Confusing? What do all these things—user interfaces, programs, databases—have in common? First, understand that some of what people say and write about object-orientation is genuinely wrong, or just does not make sense. This is usually because the author of the misinformation is misinformed or confused. Occasionally it is deliberate, where someone is trying to sell something as "good" because it is "object-oriented."

There are some legitimate differences of opinion about what makes up object-orientation in a particular area such as databases, user interfaces, etc. Many of these differences are, in my opinion, too subtle to be of great concern to nonspecialists. (This book, of course, does address the specialist issues in OOUIs.)

The key point is that there are a small number of ideas, with a few variants, that represent the core of what it means to be object-oriented. Mastery of these will allow you to deal with most of what you read and hear, and to recognize confusion (or sleaze) when you see it. The next section is about these core ideas of object-orientation.

A2.2 Core Concepts of Object-Orientation

The most basic and important idea in any discussion of object-orientation is the notion of an *object*. This is a familiar word, and I would ask you to take a few moments and think about what it means in ordinary language.

The common notion of objects can be helpful in understanding the technical sense of *object*, but it can be deceptive as well. Some aspects of objects in the technical sense may at first appear strange or contradictory. Carefully analyzing how people perceive and think about objects will help to resolve the apparent problems. Although the object-oriented paradigm[1] is most mature in the field of programming languages, it was not primarily motivated by considerations of computer science. Its roots lie in efforts to make computers more comprehensible to people (this thesis is presented in Chapter 4, *Applying Object-Orientation to User Interfaces*).

Let us look at the characteristics of an object in the world as we might perceive it:

- It is closed or *encapsulated*; that is, it is a "thing in itself," separate from other things, revealing itself by its external behavior (which includes tangible properties such as color, size, texture, as well as motion, sound, etc.). The internal structure of the object is accessible only if it is "cut open" in some way.
- An object may be *composed* of other objects, which determine how it behaves. For example, a car is composed of body, engine, suspension, etc.; and these in turn are also composed of simpler objects.
- Although the object is unique, it is usually so similar to certain other objects that we can put them into the same category or *class*. The quarter (25 cent coin) I have in my pocket is unique, but I can think of it as differing from other quarters only by a few parameters such as date, location, etc. The particular quarter can be considered an *instance* of its class. Another way of looking at it is to say that we could clone one instance from another, with minor differences.
- Different classes of objects often have enough in common that we

[1] I use the term *paradigm* to mean roughly "a way of looking at the world."

would like to lump them together. Quarters and pennies[1] are significantly different, but they are both *coins*. Technically, we can say that the class of pennies and the class of quarters are both *subclasses* of the class of coins, or that the class of coins is a *superclass* of the classes of pennies and quarters. This idea, though somewhat abstract, has existed at least since Aristotle. Think of the biological classification scheme—horses are mammals, mammals are animals, animals are living things, etc.[2] It economizes resources in perceiving and thinking—as soon as we fit a horse into the category (or class) *mammal*, we know that it is warm-blooded, because horses derive or "inherit" that characteristic from *mammal*.

Two other aspects of objects turn out to be important. They stem from the relation between an object and its name:

- Proper names of objects do not usually specify what kind of object they refer to. For instance, I might have a son named "Johnny," or a father, a pet dog, a truck, etc.
- If I take some action on "Johnny," for example saying "Johnny, go to bed," the results will depend very much on what sort of object Johnny is. (My son might go to bed, my father would probably object, my dog might give me a puzzled look, my truck would do nothing.)

The history of science shows that fundamental principles often become simpler as a discipline matures. The appearance of complexity follows from the far-reaching consequences of fundamental principles. This is by way of explaining that you now understand, in a basic way, *all* the fundamental principles of object-orientation. Investigating the ramifications of these principles can be the work of an entire career, and I will explore only a few of them in this appendix. This entire book, of course, is about applying the principles to the design and development of user interfaces.

To make this discussion more concrete, consider some examples of what "objects" might be in the technical sense of object-oriented programming, object-oriented database, etc.

Software modules, "things" that a programmer builds to provide some externally visible behavior or function, can be objects. In OOP, these modules encapsulate both programs and the data that makes an individual object unique. (Examples are given in the next section.) Things stored in OO databases are also objects. Without going into the technical details, these "things" are not just passive data. They are more like the objects of OOP, except that they are *persistent*; they do not go away when the program ends. Most relevant to the topic of this book, things that users interact with in an interface to a computer system can be objects.

[1] For those outside the US, think of any two coins of different denominations.

[2] Our modern system of biological classification was developed by Carl von Linné (Linnaeus) in the 18th century, but its roots go back to Aristotle.

Let me summarize the principles of object-orientation as follows:

- *Encapsulation*, the idea that objects reveal their "outside" through tangible behavior, but keep their "inside" hidden. Another way of saying this is that we do not need to know how an object works to know how it behaves.
- *Composition*, the notion that the behavior of an object may result from the collective behavior of objects from which it is composed or constructed. Many authors do not include composition as a characteristic of OO systems, since it is not unique to them, but occurs in all complex systems. My justification for including it is that building up behavior by composition is a salient feature of object-oriented systems in general, and OOUIs in particular.
- *Classes*, groups of objects that share common characteristics or that can be cloned from a common prototype. Objects are said to be *instances* of their classes.
- *Inheritance*, the notion that the general behavior of a superclass can be "handed down" to (or *inherited by*) its subclasses.

A2.3 Object-Oriented Programming

You will probably see the term "object-oriented" most frequently in "object-oriented programming," commonly called "OOP." This is also where researchers have formulated the OO principles most clearly. If you have never done any programming, this will be hard going, so do not feel that you must master all the details. Even if you are a graphic designer or human factors specialist, and never intend to program, you will find this knowledge valuable. The language of OOP is a cultural bond uniting diverse people in the field, and it will help you communicate with other team members involved with design and development.

If you have programmed in languages like COBOL, FORTRAN, LISP, Pascal, PL/I, or C, you will find that OOP is a radically different way of looking at programming. Do not worry if it looks strange at first.

Applying the OO Principles

Here is a quick tour of how the general principles of object-orientation apply to programming. In the following sections, we will look at two specific examples of OO programming languages: Smalltalk and C++.

Encapsulation The behavior of a program depends on both algorithms and data structures. In many programming languages, algorithms are coded into program modules (usually called procedures or functions), and data structures are represented separately. When a function is called, the programmer must pass the data structure it will operate on.

An object-oriented program module—usually called simply "an object"—encapsulates both algorithms (code) and data.[1] Other objects communicate with it by calling it or sending messages, and never see its internal structure. There is a function, or method, that gets executed for every message. Each object has instance variables that hold its unique, private data.

Typically, these "objects" represent things in the real world. As an example, consider the object "my savings account" (in a bank). In real life I might want to deposit money into it, query the balance, withdraw, etc. So a programming object, `mySavingsAccount`, in a banking application might respond to the calls `deposit(amount)`, `queryBalance`, `withdraw(amount)`, etc. `mySavingsAccount` probably has an instance variable called `balance`, and others for account number, customer name, and so forth.

Proponents of OOP believe that this kind of design for an application is easier to understand, and thus easier to implement and maintain. Software engineers will recognize this sort of thing as "information hiding," "separation of concerns," etc. The difference from classical software engineering or "structured" approaches, however, is that the problem has been decomposed into *objects* rather than *functions*.

Composition Expanding on the banking example, imagine an application for a full-service institution. It might provide `FinancialPortfolio` objects that contain, or are composed from, `BankAccount`, `Stock`, `Bond`, `InsurancePolicy`, etc., objects. (In a fully object-oriented system, an application is itself an object composed of other objects.)

Classes In the bank example, do we want to code each `SavingsAccount` object individually? After all, they differ only by a few parameters (account holder name, balance, etc.). Classes in an OOP system are templates or prototypes from which programs can create new objects. `mySavingsAccount`, for example, is an instance of the class `SavingsAccount`. Typically it would be created by sending a message to the class telling it to create a new object. The message would include arguments or parameters to initialize the object's instance variables, in this case the customer name and balance:

```
mySavingsAccount :=
    SavingsAccount new('Dave Collins', 1500.00)
```

The ability to support classes is one of the differences between OOP languages, such as Smalltalk and C++, and "conventional" languages such as Pascal, PL/I, and C. Technically, the class holds the programming code for the object's methods. The object itself holds its data (which is unique)

[1] Technically, as mentioned below in the discussion of classes, the algorithms or methods are shared between all objects (instances) of a given class. It is conceptually easier, though, to think of each object as encapsulating all its methods, along with its data. The term *module* is not very precise, and is used in various senses to refer to some collection of program code.

but points to the class for methods (which all instances of the class share).

Inheritance Think about implementing a class called `CheckingAccount`. Clearly it has a lot in common with `SavingsAccount`; why not factor out the common behavior into a superclass `BankAccount`? There is a cognitive economy in thinking of savings accounts and checking accounts as special kinds of bank accounts; OOP systems mirror this by providing mechanisms to code the `SavingsAccount` and `CheckingAccount` classes not from scratch, but by specifying how they *differ* from a `BankAccount` superclass. The code in `BankAccount` defines all the common characteristics of savings and checking accounts. This results in code reuse and conceptual clarity. The example just given might be coded as

```
BankAccount subclass: SavingsAccount.
```

Figure A2-1 is a "doughnut diagram" showing an object of class `SavingsAccount` receiving the message `withdraw(50.00)`. The message will be processed by the `withdraw()` method (or member function). The center of the doughnut holds instance variables. Methods are around the outside, surrounding the instance data; this shows graphically that instance data is private, and can be accessed only by the object's methods.

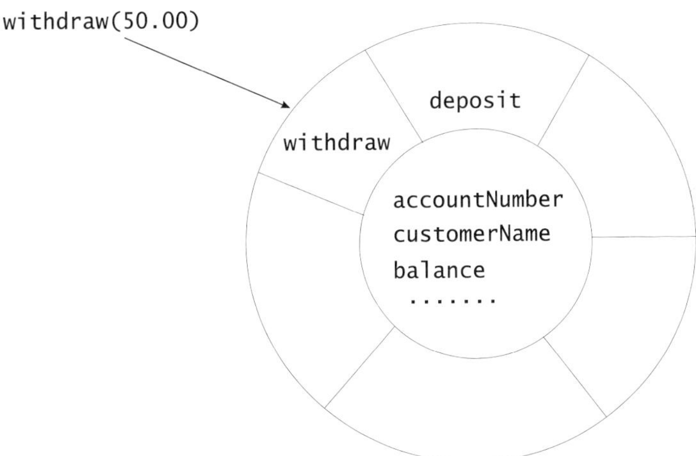

Figure A2-1 Sending a message to an object

Figure A2-2 is a common way of representing the inheritance relationship between different kinds of bank accounts. Suppose, in this situation, we wanted a class representing "negotiable order of withdrawal" (NOW) accounts. NOW accounts are similar in some ways to both savings and checking accounts. Could we inherit from `SavingsAccount` *and* `CheckingAccount` to form the `NOWAccount` class? Some languages (such as C++) allow *multiple inheritance*, and for them the answer is yes. Others (such as

Smalltalk) allow only single inheritance, and the answer is no.[1]

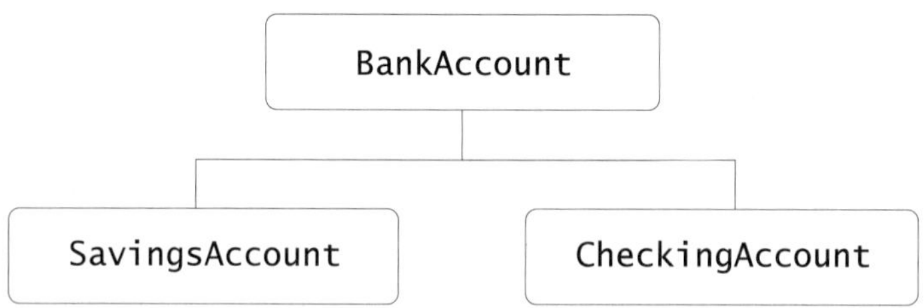

Figure A2-2 Inheritance between classes

Dynamic binding I mentioned two other significant aspects of objects, related to naming them. When we declare the name of a variable in a conventional programming language, we usually specify what type of object it refers to (for example, a real number, an integer, a character string, etc.). This can be a problem in object-oriented languages. Suppose I want to process all the accounts for a given bank in some way that does not depend on whether an account is savings or checking. It seems natural to declare a variable to be simply a `BankAccount`, and let it actually (when the program is running) be either a `SavingsAccount` or a `CheckingAccount`. In the terminology of programming languages, functions to be invoked by messages to the object referenced by the variable are *dynamically bound* at the time the program is run. (As opposed to being *statically bound* at the time the program is compiled.)[2]

If we do not know the type of an object, how can we (or the language compiler) figure out which method to execute when the object receives a message? In object-oriented languages, the answer is simple. Since operations are "packaged" into the object itself, it just does whatever is appropriate. Though this may sound strange, notice that it is exactly how objects in the real world behave.

Since object behavior in response to an action may take many forms, depending on the object, this is called *polymorphism*, from a Greek word meaning "many forms." Polymorphism makes OOPLs very flexible. New kinds of objects can be added without changing existing code, as long as they respond to the same messages. For example, imagine adding a `MoneyMarketAccount` class in the banking example. If `MoneyMarketAccount` objects respond to `deposit`, `withdraw`, etc., they can easily be added to existing applications.

[1]Reasons for this are beyond the scope of this appendix. Multiple inheritance adds significant complexity to OO programming, which is why some languages disallow it.
[2]Dynamic binding is also found in some non-OO languages, for example LISP and APL.

Language

eveloped in the early 1970s at the Xerox Palo Alto Research and has since become an important commercial OO lan- Simula-67 [Nyg81] was the first OO programming language, en more influential. One of the ways its influence is felt is -most people in the OO community understand Smalltalk *message*, though other languages may have different terms ncepts.

alk language is very simple and is based on sending mes- Every statement has one of three forms:

```
aMessage.

firstMessage;
secondMessage;
astMessage.

me := anObject aMessage.
```

colons separate a series of messages to the same object. erminated with periods. (3) is the same as (1) or (2), except eturned from sending the message is assigned to a variable so it can be used later. Here are examples of these three forms:

1. `aSavingsAccount balance.`
2. ```
   aSavingsAccount deposit: 200;
                   withDraw: 100;
                   balance.
   ```
3. `mySavingsAccount := SavingsAccount new.`

In (3), notice that the object receiving the message is a class. The message `new` is *unary*; that is, it has no arguments. `deposit:` is a *keyword* message, taking the number `200` as its argument. Keyword messages can have any number of arguments:

```
mySavingsAccount initializeBalance: 100
                              name: 'Dave Collins'.
```

The message name in this example is `initializeBalance:name:`, and its arguments are `100` and `'Dave Collins'`. Though the syntax is different, semantically this is the same as a function call with multiple arguments in other languages.

There is an important difference between

```
SavingsAccount new initializeBalance: 100
                              name: 'Dave Collins'.
```

and the message series in (2) above, even though in both cases multiple messages are sent (in this example two messages are sent, `new` and `initializeBalance:name:`). Here the two messages are *not* going to the same
```

object. initializeBalance:name: is sent to the object that is returned by the expression SavingsAccount new, which is a new instance of SavingsAccount.

Smalltalk has one other type of message, the *binary*. Binary messages are named with special characters and take a single argument. Their purpose is mainly to provide syntactic compatibility with other languages for common operations such as +, *, <, and so forth. An example is

```
X := 1 + 5
```

where the object 1 is sent the message +, with the argument 5.

One of the reasons for the simplicity of the Smalltalk language is that control structures, such as conditional execution, are defined as messages to objects. In

```
(anInteger > 10)
        ifTrue: [ "code for true case" . . . ]
        ifFalse: [ "code for false case" . . . ].
```

the expression (anInteger > 10) evaluates to a Boolean object, which receives the message ifTrue:ifFalse:. There are two booleans in Smalltalk, true and false; true responds to ifTrue:ifFalse: with the result of executing the "true" block; false responds with the result from the "false" block.

Classes in Smalltalk are defined as in the following example:

```
BankAccount subclass: #SavingsAccount
        instanceVariableNames: 'balance name'
```

This says that SavingsAccount is a subclass of BankAccount, with instance variables (data) named balance and name. The # indicates that #SavingsAccount is just a symbol at this point, since it is being defined in this statement. Notice that this is just like any other Smalltalk expression—it is a message to the object BankAccount.

The behavior of objects is defined by *methods* associated with their classes. Each message has a corresponding method, for example:[1]

```
initializeBalance: anInteger name: aString
  "Set the balance and account name."
  balance := aninteger.
  name := aString.
  ^self
```

[1] In the text of this book, subclass names in definitions and method names are in **boldface**.

```
balance
   "Answer the account balance."
   ^balance
```

The caret (^) exits the method and returns a result to the message sender. The keyword `self` means "this object," the receiver of the message. The default object returned is `self`, so it is not really necessary to specify it. The explicit return *is* required in the `balance` method.

The convention for indicating which class a method belongs to is >>, as in `BankAccount>>balance`.[1] (>> is actually a Smalltalk message that can be sent to a class, which returns the code for the named method.) In typical Smalltalk systems, the entry and compilation of code for methods is done through an interactive code browser.

You have probably noticed that there are no type declarations in Smalltalk, such as integer, character, etc. Argument names, such as `anInteger`, are suggestive but not enforced. Type errors are manifested at run time when an object of the wrong type does not understand a message that is sent to it.

Something else that Smalltalk does not have is storage allocation. Storage is dynamically allocated when an object is created and deallocated by a *garbage collector* when all references to the object have been deleted.

The C++ Language

C++ is an object-oriented language based on C and Simula-67. It has been characterized by its principal designer, Bjarne Stroustrup of AT&T Bell Laboratories, as "a better C" [Str86]. It extends the C language with objects, classes, and inheritance. Unlike Smalltalk, it supports strong typing and multiple inheritance. It does not use garbage collection; as in C, programmers explicitly allocate and free object storage. Because of these factors, C++ is more complicated than either C or Smalltalk. This tutorial covers only a very small fragment of the language, mainly through examples. It should be adequate, however, for understanding the examples in this book.

To understand C++, it is first necessary to know a little C. Keep in mind that any C program is automatically a C++ program, since C is a subset of C++. The following, from [Ker78], is a simple C program:

```
#include <stdio.h>
main () // A very simple program
{
      printf("hello, world\n");
}
```

The `#include` embeds definitions from the standard I/O library

[1] Note that the same >> is used in C++ as the input stream operator; this is unrelated to Smalltalk's usage.

needed for the printf statement. Every C and C++ program has a main() function, which is called when the program is executed. Braces ({ }) delineate blocks of statements, in this case the single statement making up the body of main(). This statement prints "hello, world" when the program is executed. The semicolon terminates a statement (notice the difference from Smalltalk). The double quote is the character string delimiter in C; the comment delimiter is a double slash (//).

In addition to main(), a program can have any number of other functions.

```
#include <stdio.h>
int cube(int x) {
        return x * x * x;
}
main () {
        int i;
        for(i = 1; i++; i < 10)
                printf(i, " cubed is ", cube(i));
}
```

This example adds the function cube(int x), which returns x^3 and is called from main(), plus a few other complications. The expression i++ is common in C and C++; it means "use the value of i, then increment i by one." The entire for expression means "start with i set to 1; use i in the statement (or block of statements) after the for; increment i by 1; keep doing this until i gets to 10; then continue the program after the for."

The C if and while control structures resemble the for. Here is an example of if:

```
int i, j;
if (i == 0) {
        j = 10;
        i++;
        printf(i);
        }
```

Notice that the equality test in C is ==, and = is used for assignment. Most other operators are like those in other languages; != means "not equal."

C and C++, unlike Smalltalk, explicitly differentiate accessing an object directly (by value) from accessing it through a pointer (by reference). This is illustrated in the following example:

```
int sum1(int x, int y) {
        return x + y;
}
int sum2(int *x, int *y) {
        return *x + *y;
```

```
}
int result1, result2;
int i, j; int *pi, *pj;
i = j = 10;
pi = &i; pj = &j;
result1 = sum1(i, j);
result2 = sum2(pi, pj);
```

The variables `i` and `j` are declared as integers and set to 10. The variables `pi` and `pj` are declared as *pointers* to integers, and set to the *addresses* of `i` and `j` (`int *i` means "the object pointed to by `i` is an integer"; `&i` means "the address of `i`"). Pointer references are useful when objects are large, because passing a pointer is faster than copying the object. They are needed when objects are dynamically allocated, since their locations are not known at the time the program is compiled.

C++ adds objects, classes, and inheritance to C.[1] The equivalent of a method in C++ is a *member function*; this is just like an ordinary C function, except it is defined as part of a class, and has an implicit argument that is the object receiving the "message." The equivalent of a message in C++ is a *member function call.*

Because objects in C++ can be referenced directly or through a pointer, there are two somewhat different equivalents for Smalltalk's message sending:

```
SavingsAccount account;
SavingsAccount *pAccount;
int a, b;
pAccount = new SavingsAccount;
a = account.balance();
b = pAccount->balance();
```

The object `account` is allocated when the program is compiled. The `pAccount` declaration only allocates a pointer, and the assignment to `new SavingsAccount` dynamically allocates the object it points to. Direct references to object member functions use the "dot" (.), and references by pointer use the -> notation.[2]

A fragment of the C++ class and member function definitions for bank accounts look like this:

```
class BankAccount {
        private:
         int balance;
```

[1] C++ also adds other features, but a full discussion is not necessary here.

[2] The notation is inherited from C data structure referencing. In general, C and C++ have the feel of being lower level, "closer to the metal," than Smalltalk. This can be good or bad, depending on what you are trying to do.

```
        char* name;
       public:
        // Set the balance and account name
        void initialize(int b char* n) {
              balance = b;
              name = n;
        }
        int balance() {
              return balance;
        }
       . . . . .
};

class SavingsAccount public: BankAccount {
       private:
        float interestRate;
       public:
        virtual void postInterest() {
              balance = balance + balance*interestRate; }
       . . . . .
};
```

BankAccount is called a *base class*, and SavingsAccount is a *derived class*. Unlike Smalltalk, C++ differentiates between public and private members. Data members (equivalent to instance variables) and member functions can be *public*, accessible to any other object, or *private*, accessible only to member functions in the class in which they are defined. Members can also be *protected*, accessible to the class and its derived classes. One other thing to notice in this example is the void keyword, indicating that a function does not return anything.

The C++ analogue to BankAccount>>balance in Smalltalk is BankAccount::balance(). In C++ :: is an important part of the language (the *scoping operator*), and is used frequently when the code for a member function is placed outside the class definition.

The initialize() function in the example is not typical. C++ classes use *constructor* functions that are invoked when an object of the class is created. Constructors can take arguments, and are the usual ways of initializing objects. In this case, we might define the constructor as:

```
SavingsAccount::SavingsAccount(int b char* n)
                                   : balance(b) name(n) { }
```

Though C++ objects are strongly typed, it uses a limited form of dynamic binding. We can have

```
BankAccount *pAccount; int b1, b2;
pAccount = new SavingsAccount(1000, "Dave Collins");
```

```
b1 = pAccount->balance();
delete pAccount; // Delete old object
pAccount = new CheckingAccount(2000, "Dave Collins");
b2 = pAccount->balance();
```

The compiler can guarantee that `balance()` is a valid function call, since it is implemented in `BankAccount` and `pAccount` points to an object of some class derived from `BankAccount`. The delete call here is necessary to free the storage for the first account before it is disconnected from its pointer.

To help with terminology differences between Smalltalk and C++, the following table shows corresponding terms.

Smalltalk	**C++**
Object	Object
Class	Class
Method	Member function
Instance variable	Member data variable
Message	Member function call
Superclass	Base class
Subclass	Derived class
`anObject doIt` (message send)	`anObject.doIt()` (direct) `anObject->doIt()` (pointer)
`self` (the object executing a method)	`this` (usually not written)
^ (caret)	`return`
`methodName: argument`	`memberFunctionName (argu-ment)`
:= (assignment)	=
= (equality test)	==
>> (indicates a method's class)	`::` (scoping operator)
`"Comment"`	`// Comment`
`'string constant'`	`"string constant"`
`$c` (character constant)	`'c'` (character constant)

A2.4 Other Object-Oriented Disciplines

From the OO principles presented in Section A2.2, the general notion of an object-oriented database (OODB) follows naturally—how do we store `SavingsAccount` and `CheckingAccount` objects permanently, so that multiple users can access them concurrently, update them, etc.? The details of this are beyond the scope of this appendix, but there are a number of commercially available OODB products.

You may be familiar with data modeling techniques such as Entity-Relationship (ER) modeling. ER models things in the world of an application as entities and relationships between entities. In the bank example, `FinancialPortfolio` entities are aggregated, or composed from, `BankAccount`, `Stock`, `Bond`, `InsurancePolicy`, etc., entities.

If you think entities sound somewhat like objects, you are right. But whereas ER focuses on just the data, object-oriented modeling also includes the processes or methods. Since objects resemble real-world entities, there is a discipline of object-oriented analysis (OOA), that models the business requirements for applications. Since we already have OOP and OODB, it makes sense to use OO design methods as well. Thus we have OOD. Proponents of OO claim a couple of things based on all this:

- Since all the disciplines are OO and talk roughly the same language, developers in all areas of a software project can communicate better.
- Since objects model their real-world counterparts, developers stay focused on the problem the application is intended to solve.

The user interface issue also arises very naturally: How do we present all these objects to users in a way that is meaningful, given the tasks that they have to accomplish? That is the subject of the main body of this book, to which you can now return.

A2.5 To Explore Further

The job of this entire book is to explore the application of object-oriented ideas, methods, and technology to user interfaces. To explore other areas of OO, here are a few suggestions. David Taylor's book, *Object-Oriented Technology: A Manager's Guide* [Tay90], is a clear and simple overview of OO as applied to programming and databases. Brad Cox's *Object-Oriented Programming: An Evolutionary Approach* [Cox91] is a good second book. It discusses OOP in general, with examples in several programming languages, but features Cox's Objective-C (a hybrid of C and Smalltalk). Grady Booch's *Object Oriented Analysis and Design with Applications* [Boo94] is a comprehensive and more advanced book. [Cox91] and [Boo94] assume a knowledge of programming.

Training vendors and universities offer courses at all levels. The industry trade press, particularly publications that specialize in OO, are a good source of course advertisements, as well as keeping you up to date on the field.

My experience in learning and teaching OO is that reading and lecture courses will not give you more than a superficial understanding of OO technology. You need hands-on work to really learn it. For most people, the most practical approach is to learn an OO programming language and complete a few small applications. I recommend Smalltalk as a first language because it is a pure OO language. If you already know a language like C or Pascal, you can learn from their OO variants (C++, Objective-C, and Object Pascal). Since these are hybrid languages, though, there is a strong temptation to continue programming in a procedural style. Smalltalk avoids this problem.

Glossary

abstract class A **class** that has no **instances**, but has **concrete classes** as subclasses.[1] *Mammal* is an abstract class, and *horse* is a concrete class (there are no actual entities that are mammals without also being horses, cows, dogs, etc.). In the real world, this is a little fuzzy—we might consider *horse* abstract, whereas, for example, *Clydesdale* would be concrete. **OOPLs** can make the concept precise by preventing the **instantiation** of classes defined as abstract.

affordance A tangible aspect of an object that suggests and permits some sort of action. You can think of affordances as "handles," and in fact handles are affordances—they afford opening and closing doors, picking up luggage, etc. Buttons, knobs, and switches are also common affordances in everyday life. In computer interfaces, scroll bars, buttons, entry fields, etc., are affordances.

analysis The application of some rational technique for decomposing a complex whole into its elements. In the development of computer **applications** or **systems**, analysis usually means analysis of the users' wants and needs into a set of precise "requirements" for what the system is supposed to do. These requirements do not specify *how* the system is to do these things; that is the job of **design**. In practice, it is difficult to attain the precision implied here, so analysis and design share a large gray area.

ANSI American National Standards Institute, an agency of the US government that develops and promulgates standards for, among other things, programming languages. ANSI works closely with ISO, the International Organization for Standardization.

API Application programming interface. The term is usually applied to a formal description of the syntax and semantics of function calls or messages implementing an **operating system** service interface.

application A specific use; in the context of computer technology, usually a software package supporting a specific set of tasks for a **domain** of work such as word processing, accounting, etc. Applications normally use general services provided by a **system** or **platform**.

[1] Words in **boldface** have their own entries in this glossary.

ASCII American Standard Code for Information Interchange, a widely used standard for encoding text characters in computer files. ASCII uses one byte per character, so it is not adequate for encoding languages such as Chinese, which require two bytes per character.

architecture A general plan or set of concepts or principles governing the construction of some type of **system**. Architectures in the computer field vary greatly in the amount of detail they specify, ranging from precise specifications to loosely applied general concepts.

bandwidth The capacity of a channel or medium to carry information, usually measured in bits per second. A bit is one "unit" of information—on a monochrome display, for example, one bit is needed for each pixel (the bit can be coded 0 for black, 1 for white). A monochrome display with 1 million pixels, refreshed 30 times a second, thus has an output bandwidth of 30 million bits (megabits) per second.

base class see **superclass**.

bitmap An internal stored representation of a screen image in which each **pixel** displayed on the screen is represented by a stored bit (for monochrome images) or group of bits (for color images). Images with more than one bit per pixel are also called *pixmaps*.

C++ An **object-oriented programming language** developed by Bjarne Stroustrup at AT&T Bell Labs in the early 1980s; he wanted to combine the object-oriented features of the programming language **Simula-67** with the good performance of C.

CAD Computer aided (or assisted) design, the use of computer graphics and simulation to aid designers of buildings, mechanical parts, etc.

CASE Computer aided software engineering, the use of computers to support software engineering processes. CASE tools are often tied to specific software engineering methodologies and notations.

CCITT *Comité Consultatif Internationale Télégraphique et Téléphonique* (International Telegraph and Telephone Consultative Committee), an international body that develops communications standards.

CD-ROM Compact disk-read only memory, a computer disk that is physically identical to an audio CD. Holds 600 megabytes of data using optical recording and playback. Standard CDs are read-only. CDs using magneto-optical technology are writable as well.

CHI Computer-human interaction; see **HCI**. Sometimes used as a short form of **SIGCHI**.

class One of the fundamental **object-oriented principles**. A class **models** the general characteristics of a set of objects that are important in a particular **domain**. Classes may be specialized through **inheritance**. Compare **prototype**.

CLOS Common Lisp Object System, an **ANSI** standard **object-oriented programming language** developed during the 1980s, which combines and standardizes many features of various **OOPLs** based on the programming language Lisp.

cognition The set of faculties by which people process information and acquire knowledge, involving both perception and thought. C*ognitive psychology* and *cognitive science* attempt to explain cognition, based on experimental evidence and formal **models**.

COM Component object model, an **architecture** developed by Microsoft for sharing distributed objects. Similar to in purpose to **CORBA**, though it does not conform to the CORBA standard.

concrete class A **class** that can have **instances**, as opposed to an **abstract class**.

CORBA Common Object Request Broker Architecture, developed by the **OMG** as a standard for distributed objects.

CRC Class, responsibilities, collaborators. An OO design method in which these items are written on small cards for each class in the design [Bec89].

CRT Cathode ray tube, a common computer display technology; essentially the same as the traditional television display. Compare **LCD**.

CUA Common User Access, a user interface style developed by IBM [IBM92b], and used in OS/2 and Microsoft Windows.

derived class see **subclass**.

design The process of creating of a plan or "blueprint" for building something, or the plan created by this process. In the development of computer **applications** or **systems**, design takes the output of **analysis** and specifies a concrete system that will satisfy the users' requirements.

domain An area of concern or function. Usually qualified to indicate the area, as in **application** domain, indicating the tasks or functions addressed by an application.

effector A limb, muscle, or appendage (for example, an arm or finger) used for **motor** action.

ergonomics Derived from Greek roots meaning roughly "laws of work," reflecting its origin in the study of the physical environment of workers and their interface to machines. Ergonomics is related to industrial psychology, which addresses the design of efficient work environments from a broader perspective (including training, management styles, organizational form, etc.). The application of ergonomic principles to software interfaces is sometimes qualified as "software ergonomics." Compare **human factors** (which overlaps ergonomics to a great extent), **industrial design**.

function points A measure of the size of a software development project, based on the external functions provided to end users; unlike the typical "lines of code" metric, it is intended to be independent of the implementation language.

gestalt German for "shape" or "form." The Gestalt theory in psychology asserts that people perceive forms "all at once" based on all their characteristics in relationship, rather then by summing up individual features. From this usage, gestalt has come to mean holistic as opposed to reductionist.

GUI Graphical user interface, a user interface based on bitmapped graphics (see **bitmap**), as opposed to character display. Typically, GUIs feature **widgets** such as moveable, overlapping windows for information display, **icons** representing objects, popup dialog boxes, menus that pull down like window shades, and graphical buttons that can be "pushed" to invoke actions.

haptic Literally means "touch." In psychology, haptic touch is the use of movement in conjunction with touch to discover the spatial or textural qualities of an object. This book uses the term "haptic perception" more generally to refer to any use of active exploration to discover object characteristics.

HCI Human computer interaction. Refers to a variety of topics and disciplines involved in understanding and designing user interfaces. Typically used in a more inclusive sense than **human factors**, since it may include graphic design, etc.

HLL High level language (applied to programming languages). "Level" is relative—C is high level relative to assembler, low level relative to Smalltalk.

human factors The discipline that concerns itself with the scientific and engineering aspects of the human side of interfaces between humans and machines. It uses basic knowledge from psychology, physiology, etc. In Europe, human factors is roughly synonymous with **ergonomics**; in the US, ergonomics is sometimes reserved for the physical, as opposed to psychological, aspects of human-machine interaction.

hypermedia The use of **hypertext**-style links to refer to media other than text. For instance, following a link from a text document might cause a video clip to be shown.

hypertext The capability of linking arbitrary regions of text in a document to text in other documents, or in other parts of the same document. The links are used for referring the reader to related ideas, definitions, etc.

icon A likeness or symbolic representation of an object, usually visual. In GUIs, icons are small **bitmaps** displayed on the screen, which also have interaction behavior.

IEEE Institute of Electrical and Electronic Engineers, a professional society for engineers which includes committees that set standards for various electrical and communications interfaces.

industrial design Design of the form (as opposed to the function) of utilitarian artifacts such as furniture, appliances, etc. In the computer industry, industrial designers are responsible for the physical form of the computer "box," the keyboard, etc. Since this involves design and placement of knobs, switches, etc., there is some overlap with **human factors**. Industrial design differs from **ergonomics** in being motivated by engineering simplicity and aesthetics, rather than human physiology and biomechanics.

inheritance One of the fundamental **object-oriented principles**. A class may be specialized through **inheritance** (for example, "horse" is a specialization of "mammal"). Inheritance allows reuse of characteristics of the **superclass** when creating the **subclass**. In **object-oriented programming**, this is called "programming by difference." Inheritance hierarchies, or taxonomies, for classifying knowledge have been in use for thousands of years.

instance A particular **object**, as opposed to a **class**. For example, my dog Rover is an instance of the class *dog*. Instance is generally synonymous with **object**, but is used where the emphasis is on the object's connection to its class. An instance can also be viewed as a copy or clone of a **prototype**.

instantiation The process of creating a new **instance** of a **class**.

isomorphism In mathematics, a one-to-one mapping between objects and object relationships in two **domains**. In general, a similarity in form or structure that approximates the mathematical ideal.

KLOC Kilo-lines of code, thousands of source code lines in a program.

LAN Local area network, a high-speed communications network for linking computers, usually located within a single building. Various types exist, such as Ethernet and token-ring.

LCD Liquid crystal display, a display in which light shining through from the back is modulated by an array of liquid crystal cells that are turned on and off electronically. LCDs are thinner and use less power than **CRTs**.

LOC Lines of code, the number of source code lines in a program.

MIPS Millions of instructions executed per second, a measure of the performance of computers.

model A structure in one **domain** used to represent an object in some other domain, for the purpose of understanding or controlling it. For example, model airplanes help to understand real ones. As a verb, "model" refers to the process of creating a model or the state of being a model.

monospaced In a monospaced font for text, each character occupies a fixed space: `this is monospaced`. Also called non-proportional, in contrast to a proportional font, where characters take varying amounts of space. Monospaced fonts are easier to render, but less readable.

motor refers to human "output," such as motion or speech, as opposed to sensory "input."

MVC Model-view-controller, an **architecture** for user interface software, developed as part of Smalltalk-80.

object One of the fundamental **object-oriented principles**. An object encapsulates all the attributes and behavior of a "thing" that is important in a particular **domain**. An object is usually considered to be an **instance** of a **class** or **prototype**. "Object" is also used as an adjective roughly synonymous with "object-oriented," for example, in the context of "object technology" or "the object paradigm."

Object Management Group (OMG) A consortium of companies in the computer industry that have banded together to develop standard definitions of terms and common formats and protocols related to object technology, particularly the sharing of objects and object definitions in heterogeneous networks.

object-oriented analysis An **analysis** in which the problem decomposition results in a set of **objects** and **classes**, the relationships between them, and the services they provide; or the process of doing such an analysis. Proponents of object-oriented analysis claim that it feeds naturally into **object-oriented design**.

object-oriented database A database that stores objects, as opposed to records, relations, etc.

object-oriented design The application of **object-oriented principles** to the **design** of a **system**. Many methods for object-oriented design exist;

they all agree on including **objects** and **classes**, relationships between them, and the services they provide.

object-oriented principles A set of principles, generally including objects, classes, and inheritance, on which are based **object-oriented programming**, **object-oriented design**, etc.

object-oriented programming Programming done with a language that supports **object-oriented principles**. Object-oriented languages such as **Simula-67**, **Smalltalk**, **C++**, **CLOS**, etc., provide language constructs for defining **classes**, creating **objects** (**instances** of classes), and allowing objects to communicate with one another.

object-oriented programming language A computer language for doing **object-oriented programming**.

object-oriented user interface A user interface that **models** the task **domain** with **objects**, **classes**, and relationships such as **inheritance**. It presents objects from the task domain to the user, along with capabilities for viewing and manipulating them.

OLE Object linking and embedding, an **architecture** developed by Microsoft for linking objects in Microsoft Windows applications.

OMG **Object Management Group**.

OO A frequently used abbreviation for **object-oriented** or **object-orientation**. May be seen in the context of **OOUI**, **OOD**, **OOA**, or **OODB**.

OOA **Object-oriented analysis.**

OOD **Object-oriented design**.

OODB **Object-oriented database**.

OODBMS **Object-oriented database manager**.

OOPL **Object-oriented programming language**.

OOP **Object-oriented programming**.

OOUI **Object-oriented user interface**.

operating system A software package that controls a computer and translates primitive capabilities of the hardware into higher level services (such as storage management and input/output) to applications. MS-DOS, MVS, OS/2, UNIX, and VMS are all examples.

OSF/Motif A user interface style for UNIX systems with GUIs, developed by the Open Systems Foundation. Similar to **CUA** in look and feel.

paradigm A pattern or **model**, usually a model for thinking about some area. Often found in the context of "paradigm shift," meaning a period when the way people think about some area changes—not only in terms of what they think about it, but *how* they think about it. I like Ted Nelson's definition: "A paradigm is an idea that's too big to get in the door." (Or, one might add, to get *out* the door when its usefulness is over.)

PARC Xerox Corporation's Palo Alto Research Center, an important center for user interface research since the 1970s.

PERT/CPM Project evaluation and review technique/critical path method, a project management technique featuring network diagrams showing the duration and ordering of activities.

pixel Picture element, one of the small dots on a display screen or printed output that physically form the image. Also called *pel*.

platform A base for providing services to computer applications. It may be applied to the computer system hardware, the **operating system**, the **window manager**, or a combination of all three.

polymorphism The ability of objects of different types to respond to a common message or function call. For instance, letters, pictures, and fax documents might all respond to `print`. Some authors consider polymorphism an essential characteristic of object-orientation. The word come from Greek roots meaning "many forms."

POSIX A set of standards for a subset of typical UNIX **operating system** service **APIs**, developed by the **IEEE** Technical Committee on Operating Systems.

prototype 1. In software development, a mock-up of a proposed system that allows inspection and testing to begin before the final product has been built. "Rapid prototyping" is the technique of building a prototype as quickly as possible, to guide the early stages of **analysis** or **design**.
2. In psychology, a "typical" example of a species or type of thing, which is used as a general mental **model** of the type.
3. In some **object-oriented programming languages**, such as **Self**, an **instance** used to create other instances by copying (as opposed to instantiating a **class**).

Self An object-oriented programming language developed by David Ungar at MIT, which is based on **prototypes** instead of **classes**. Used primarily for research.

self In **Smalltalk**, a keyword referring to the receiver of a message.

semantics In linguistics, the meaning of a sentence as opposed to its syntax (grammatical form). For example, "I saw John" and "It was John I saw" have different syntax but the same semantics. More generally, semantics refers to the meaning or content of something as opposed to the form in which it is presented. (Though plural in form, *semantics* is a singular noun; *semantic* is the adjective.)

SIGCHI Special Interest Group on Computer-Human Interaction, part of the Association for Computing Machinery (ACM).

Simula-67 Generally considered the first **object-oriented programming language**. Simula-67 is based on the programming language ALGOL, but adds the notions of **objects**, **classes**, and **inheritance**. It was motivated by, among other things, the desire for a simulation language that non-programmers could understand.

Sketchpad An electronic drafting system developed at MIT by Ivan Sutherland in 1962. Sketchpad implemented many ideas now associated with **object-oriented programming** and **object-oriented user interfaces**.

Smalltalk A programming language developed at Xerox **PARC** in 1972, by Alan Kay and others in the Learning Research Group. Influenced by the languages Lisp, Logo, and **Simula-67**, and by the **Sketchpad** system, Smalltalk was designed to be powerful, yet easy enough for children to use.

Smalltalk-80 The last of a series of **Smalltalk** implementations done at Xerox **PARC**. Named after its year of development (1980), it became the base for subsequent commercial implementations. (Smalltalk-80 is a trademark of Xerox Corporation.)

SOM System object model, an **architecture** developed by IBM for sharing distributed objects. Similar to **CORBA**.

SQL Structured query language, an industry-standard language for accessing relational databases from programs.

subclass In an **inheritance** hierarchy, a specialized version of a more general **superclass**. Called a *derived class* in **C++**.

superclass In an **inheritance** hierarchy, a generic **class** from which a **subclass** can inherit, or be derived from. Called a *base class* in **C++**.

system In general, a group of interacting parts viewed as a whole. In the computer context, "system" usually refers to a complete, standalone environment, which defines all the basic services available to end users (often used synonymously with **platform**). A system may be a base for one or more **applications**.

task A meaningful unit of work, composed of a series of steps that lead to some well-defined goal.

timbre A dimension of sound perception; the quality or "color" of a sound. A piano and a flute sound different when playing the same note because their timbres are different. Technically, timbre reflects wave shape, as opposed to pitch.

UIMS **user interface management system**.

user interface management system A software component that implements the style (presentation and interaction components) of a user interface. The essence of a UIMS is that it separates application functionality from the user interface. "Management system" implies that it provides a general, centralized function to many applications.

VCR Videocassette recorder.

VGA Video graphics array, a standard for displays on IBM-compatible personal computers. VGA displays have 640 horizontal, and 480 vertical **pixels**. Each pixel is represented by 4 bits, so it can have one of 16 colors. SVGA (super VGA) has 8 bits per pixel, thus 256 colors.

widget A visual object presented as part of a **GUI**, such as a window, dialog box, button, scroll bar, etc. In some contexts, a widget is taken to include the programming code that implements it.

WIMP Windows, icons, pointers, and menus—typical paraphernalia of the modern GUI. Probably coined as a pejorative reference to those who used them.

window manager In the narrow sense, the functional module that allocates and manages display space for application windows in a **GUI** environment. More broadly, the term is often used to cover all platform services related to graphic output and event handling for a **GUI**.

Bibliography

This is a guide to resources for further study. It has three sections, with information on software, videotapes, and a complete list of the sources that were consulted in preparing this book.

Software

Software is an indispensable source of information and ideas for interface designers. Commercial software applications referenced in this book are listed below. Bibliographical entries for software are prefixed with **s** to distinguish them when they are referenced in the text.

The fact that a product is mentioned here does not constitute an endorsement, and other products may be available for the same application. My knowledge of the products may be based on firsthand experience, product reviews, or demonstration versions. The product versions cited here may not be current when this book is published.

The following list gives addresses for vendors of cited software packages that are not generally available in retail stores. Unless indicated otherwise, addresses are in the USA.

Ark Interface, Inc.
1201 Third Avenue
Suite 2380
Seattle, WA 98101

Digitalk Incorporated
5 Hutton Centre Drive
Santa Ana, CA 92707

Frame Technology Corporation
1010 Rincon Circle
San Jose, CA 95131

Golden Technologies, Inc.
14251 Camden Lane
Lake Oswego, OR 97035

Century Computing, Inc.
1014 West Street
Laurel, MD 20707

The ForeFront Group
1360 Post Oak Blvd., Suite 1660
Houston, TX 77056

Glockenspiel Ltd.
19 Belvedere Place
Dublin, Ireland

Hatteras Software, Inc.
208 Lochside Drive
Cary, NC 27511

Liant Software Corporation
959 Concord St.
Framingham, MA 01701

National Instruments
6504 Bridge Point Pky.
Austin, TX 78730

ParcPlace Systems
999 E. Arques Ave.
Sunnyvale, CA 94086

PED Software Corporation
1340 Saratoga-Sunnyvale Road
San Jose, CA 95129

Rogue Wave Software
P.O. Box 2328
Corvallis, OR 97339

Sense8
4000 Bridgeway, Suite 101
Sausalito, CA 94965

SQA, Inc.
10 State St.
Woburn, MA 01801

TGSSystems
447 Battery St.
San Francisco, CA 94111

Ulead Systems, Inc.
970 West 190th St.
Torrance, CA 90502

Visual Edge Software, Ltd.
3870 Cote Vertu
St-Laurent, Quebec H4R 1V4
Canada

Xsoft
3400 Hillview Ave.
Palo Alto, CA 94304

[sAri92] Aristosoft, Inc. *Talking Icons.* Adds various sound capabilities to Microsoft Windows.

[sArk92] Ark Interface, Inc. *Ark Workspace.* A "shell" that provides a 3-D room in which objects are stored. Versions are available for Apple Macintosh and Microsoft Windows.

[sBor92] Borland International, Inc. *Turbo C++.* A C++ compiler and environment for Microsoft Windows; includes the ObjectWindows class library. Versions are also available for MS-DOS and OS/2.

[sCen93] Century Computing, Inc. *TAE Plus.* A visual programming tool for GUI building on various UNIX platforms.

[sCor92] Corel, Inc. *CorelDRAW! 3.0.* A popular graphics package for Microsoft Windows.

[sDel94] Delrina Technology, Inc. *WinFax Pro 4.0.* A fax program for Microsoft Windows.

[sDig86] Digitalk Inc. *Smalltalk/V.* The original $99 Smalltalk (now somewhat more expensive). Runs on IBM-compatible PCs under MS-DOS.

[sDig92a] Digitalk Inc. *Smalltalk/V for Windows.*

[sDig92b] Digitalk Inc. *Smalltalk/V for OS/2.*

[sDig92c] Digitalk, Inc. *PARTS Workbench 2.0.* A visual interface builder and visual programming environment for OS/2 and Microsoft Windows.

[sEle87] Electronic Arts. *Pinball Construction Set.* Users can play pinball on the screen and construct custom pinball games. Versions were published for Macintosh, IBM, and Commodore machines; unfortunately this package is now "out of print."

[sFor93] The ForeFront Group. *The Virtual Notebook System.* A system supporting collaboration, based on a notebook metaphor. Versions available for Macintosh, Microsoft Windows, and UNIX platforms.

[sFra92] Frame Technology Corporation. *FrameMaker.* A desktop publishing application available for Macintosh, Microsoft Windows, and UNIX platforms.

[sFuj93] Fujitsu Networks Industry, Inc. *Fujitsu DeskTop Conferencing.* Allows sharing of Microsoft Windows applications between conference participants over a network.

[sGlo89] Glockenspiel Ltd. *CommonView.* A portable C++ class library for OS/2, Microsoft Windows, and X Windows. See also [Dea90].

[sGol92] Golden Technologies, Inc. *Sliders & Dials.* Allows users to attach slider and dial controls to cells in Microsoft Excel spreadsheets.

[sHat94] Hatteras Software, Inc. *HOMSuite* (Hatteras Object Modeling Tool Suite). A software engineering tool supporting responsibility-driven design [Wir90].

[sHew92] Hewlett Packard, Inc. *NewWave 4.0.* An object-oriented shell for Microsoft Windows, first released in 1987.

[sLia93] Liant Software Corporation. *C++/Views 2.0.* A portable C++ class library for OS/2, Microsoft Windows, X Windows/Motif, and Apple Macintosh.

[sLot93] Lotus Development Corp. *Lotus Organizer.* Provides an address book, calendar, etc. via a user interface that looks like "organizer" notebooks such as the Daytimer. Runs on Microsoft Windows.

[sMic92] Microsoft Corporation. *Microsoft Word 2.0.* A popular word processing application for Microsoft Windows.

[sMic93a] Microsoft Corporation. *Microsoft Flight Simulator.* One of many flight simulator "games" that provide a level or realism found, until recently, only in systems used for pilot training.

[sMic93b] Microsoft Corporation. *Microsoft Office for Windows.* Integrates other Microsoft products, such as Word and Excel.

[sMic93c] Microsoft Corporation. *Microsoft Visual C++.* C++ compiler, development environment, and user interface builder; includes the Microsoft Foundation Class Library.

[sMic93d] Microsoft Corporation. *Microsoft Visual Basic.* A popular Basic compiler and user interface builder. While not an OO language, VB has an object-based visual construction paradigm for GUIs.

[sNat89] National Instruments. *LabVIEW.* A graphical interface builder used to create virtual control panels for data acquisition hardware. Versions are available for Microsoft Windows, Macintosh, and Sun.

[sPar89] ParcPlace Systems. *Objectworks\Smalltalk.* This is "classic" Smalltalk-80. Objectworks\Smalltalk versions run on MS-DOS, Microsoft Windows, OS/2, and UNIX platforms. See also [sPar92].

[sPar92] ParcPlace Systems. *ParcPlace Smalltalk Release 4.* A major upgrade to earlier releases [sPar89], incorporating architectural changes to MVC and *VisualWorks*, a visual user interface builder.

[sPED93] PED Software Corporation. *Journalist.* A Microsoft Windows application that allows users to "compose" newspaper page layouts and fill them with material downloaded from online sources.

[sRog93] Rogue Wave Software. *View.h++.* A C++ class library for OSF/Motif interfaces.

[sSen93] Sense8. *WorldToolKit for Windows.* A software tool for building realtime 3-D graphic and virtual reality simulations on Microsoft Windows. Versions are also available for MS-DOS and UNIX.

[sSQA92] SQA, Inc. *TeamTest.* An automated test tool for GUI applications on Microsoft Windows.

[sTGS90] TGSSystems. *Prograph.* A visual object-oriented program development environment for the Macintosh.

[sUle93] Ulead Systems, Inc. *ImagePals 2.0.* An image processing application for publishing, etc. Runs under Microsoft Windows.

[sVis93] Visual Edge Software, Ltd. *UIM/X.* A GUI builder for OSF Motif and Sun OpenLook.

[sXer92] Xsoft (a division of Xerox). *Rooms for Windows.* An implementation of the research described in [Hen86] for Microsoft Windows.

[sXer93] Xsoft (a division of Xerox). *InConcert.* Workflow management software available for Microsoft Windows and UNIX.

Videotapes

Seeing an interface on videotape is the next best thing to using it. Many systems that are no longer commercially available, such as the Xerox Star, are still worth studying. Tapes narrated by the designers are particularly valuable.

Many research systems are videotaped for conferences, chiefly ACM SIGGRAPH (special interest group on graphics) and SIGCHI (Special Interest Group on Computer-Human Interaction). Marketing videotapes may also be valuable, to provide a look at innovative commercial systems.

Bibliographical entries for videotapes are prefixed with **v** to distinguish them when they are referenced in the text.

The following list gives sources for cited videotapes. Unless otherwise indicated, addresses are in the USA. The default format for videotapes sent from the US is ½ inch VHS, NTSC. Check before ordering if you need another format, such as PAL or SECAM.

Apple Computer, Inc.
20525 Mariani Avenue
Cupertino, CA 95014

First Priority
Box 576
Itasca, IL 60143-0576

University Video Communications
P.O. Box 2666
Stanford, CA 94309

[vApp87] Apple Computer. *Knowledge Navigator.* A short tape containing Apple's vision of the future of personal computing, which includes global networking and intelligent software agents.

[vIBM90] IBM Research Division. "In-Keyboard Analog Pointing Device." [vSIGGRAPH] 55, 1 (1990). Describes the use of a small joystick-like device embedded in a standard keyboard.

[vIBM92] IBM Corp. *Introducing Screen Reader/2.* Atlanta, GA: IBM Corp., 1992 (IBM form number GV21-9052). Demonstrates the Screen Reader/2 product, which makes OS/2 Presentation Manager applications accessible to blind people by providing audible speech feedback as the user moves a pointer around the screen.

[vKay87] Kay, Alan. *Doing with Images Makes Symbols: Communicating with Computers.* Stanford, CA: University Video Communications, 1987. Discusses the origin of many of the ideas in modern GUIs, and shows film clips of early interfaces. See also [Kay93].

[vSIGGRAPH] *SIGGRAPH Video Review.* Association for Computing Machinery, Special Interest Group on Graphics. Several issues of this review are published yearly, containing compilations of videotapes submitted to SIGGRAPH and SIGCHI (ACM Special Interest Group on Computer-Human Interaction). It is an invaluable source of material on user interfaces. References are by issue number and segment; for instance, "[vSIGGRAPH] 13, 6 (1984)" is Segment 6 of Issue 13, released in 1984. Tapes can be obtained from First Priority (address above). Some tapes have more than one issue.

[vSIGGRAPH90] "All the Widgets." [vSIGGRAPH] 57 (1990). This really does show *all* the widgets used in commercial and research GUIs—16 minutes of scroll bars, 30 minutes of menus, etc.

[vWang89] Wang Laboratories. *Freestyle.* [vSIGGRAPH] 45, 3 (1989). Despite the strong marketing flavor of this video, the Freestyle interface, with miniature images of documents as icons, is worth a look.

Books, Papers, and Articles

Here is a complete list of sources used for this book. Text in square brackets, such as [Bak89], corresponds to citations within the body of the book. Entries marked with an asterisk (*) are items I consider particularly valuable to developers. Entries marked with a dagger (†) are good starting points for delving into the research literature.

The following abbreviations are used for frequently referenced publications: *CACM* stands for *Communications of the ACM.*
JOOP stands for *Journal of Object-Oriented Programming.*

[Ada86] Adams, James L. *Conceptual Blockbusting: A Guide to Better Ideas.* Reading, MA: Addison-Wesley, 1986 (3rd edition). A handbook of techniques for creative thinking.

[Ado86] Adobe Systems, Inc. *PostScript® Language: Tutorial and Cookbook.* Reading, MA: Addison-Wesley, 1986.

[Agh87] Agha, Gul, and Carl Hewitt. "Actors: a Conceptual Foundation for Concurrent Object-Oriented Programming." in [Shr87], pp.49-74.

[Agr86] Agresti, William W. *New Paradigms for Software Development.* Washington, DC: IEEE Computer Society Press, 1986. A collection of articles on software development "beyond the waterfall." It contains an extensive section on prototyping.

[Ahl92] Ahlberg, Christopher, Christopher Williamson, and Ben Shneiderman. "Dynamic Queries for Information Exploration: An Implementation and Evaluation." [CHI92], pp. 667-668. Describes query interfaces with dynamic parameter specification by direct manipulation. A videotape appears in [vSIGGRAPH] 76 (1992).

[Aho86] Aho, Alfred V., Ravi Sethi, and Jeffrey D. Ullman. *Compilers: Principles, Techniques, and Tools.* Reading, MA: Addison-Wesley, 1986.

[Ala84] Alavi, Maryam. "An Assessment of the Prototyping Approach to Information Systems Development." *CACM* 27, 6 (June 1984), pp. 556-563. Reprinted in [Agr86].

[Alex79] Alexander, Christopher. *The Timeless Way of Building.* New York: Oxford University Press, 1979. A theory of how large entities such as buildings and towns are built from smaller architectural patterns. See also [Gam94].

[All92] Allen, Phillip. *The Atlas of Atlases: The Map Maker's Vision of the World.* New York: Harry N. Abrams, Inc., 1992. Maps are good examples of information design on a flat surface. This book has many historical examples of useful and aesthetically pleasing maps.

[Ans84] American National Standards Institute. *Graphical Kernel System* (draft proposed standard). Reprinted in *Computer Graphics* 18, 2 (February 1984).

[Aoy93] Aoyama, Mikio. "Concurrent-Development Process Model." *IEEE Software* 10, 4 (July 1993), pp. 46-55. Describes a highly concurrent software development process used for developing large systems.

[Apo61] Apostel, Leo. "Towards the Formal Study of Models in the Non-Formal Sciences." In Hans Freudenthal, ed. *The Concept and the Role of the Model in Mathematics and Natural and Social Sciences.* Dordrecht, The Netherlands: D. Reidel Publishing Co., 1961. Introduces the notion of "approximate isomorphism."

[App88] Apple Computer, Inc. *Programmer's Introduction to the Macintosh Family.* Reading, MA: Addison-Wesley, 1988.

[App92] Apple Computer, Inc. *Macintosh Human Interface Guidelines.* Reading, MA: Addison-Wesley, 1992. An illustrated style guide for the Macintosh user interface. Because the Macintosh has influenced many other GUIs, this is worthwhile for non-Macintosh developers as well. A companion videotape is available from Apple.

[Bad76] Baddeley, Alan D. *The Psychology of Memory.* New York: Basic Books, Inc., 1976.

[Bae91] Baecker, Ronald, Ian Small, and Richard Mander. "Bringing Icons to Life." [CHI91], pp. 1-6. Describes the use of animated GUI icons.

[Bas86] Bashe, Charles J., *et al. IBM's Early Computers.* Cambridge, MA: MIT Press, 1986. A history of IBM computers up to the mid-1960s.

[Bak89] Baker, Walter E. "Human Factors, Ergonomics, and Usability: Principles and Practice." In Edmund T. Klemmer, ed. *Ergonomics: Harness the Power of Human Factors in Your Business.* Norwood, NJ: Ablex Publishing Corp., 1989. A summary of basic ergonomics principles and experience in applying them.

[Bay84] Bayman, Piraye, and Richard E. Mayer. "Instructional manipulation of users' mental models for electronic calculators." *International Journal of Man-machine Studies* 20 (1984), pp. 189-199.

[Bec89] Beck, Kent, and Ward Cunningham. "A Laboratory for Teaching Object-Oriented Thinking." [OOPSLA89], pp. 1-6. A description of the CRC card method for OO design.

[Bel80] Bell, Daniel. "The Social Framework of the Information Society." [Der80], pp. 164-211. A discussion of the information sector of the economy, an analysis of demographic trends, and some predictions.

[Bell94] Bell, Trudy E. "Technology 1994." *IEEE Spectrum* 31, 1 (Jan. 1994), pp. 20-21. Introduces *Spectrum*'s yearly technology analysis and forecast issue.

[Ben77] Bennett, John. "User-Oriented Graphics Systems for Decision Support in Unstructured Tasks." *User-Oriented Design of Interactive Graphics Systems.* ACM/SIGGRAPH, 1977. (Based on the ACM/SIGGRAPH workshop, Pittsburgh, PA, October 14-15, 1976.)

[Ben83] Bennett, John. "Analysis and Design of the User interface for Decision Support Systems." In John Bennett, ed. *Building Decision Support Systems.* Reading, MA: Addison-Wesley, 1983. An expanded version of [Ben77]. Contains an important perspective on OOUIs (though Bennett does not use this term), based on the idea of visual presentation providing a context for user actions.

[Ben84a] Bennett, John, *et al.*, eds. *Visual Display Terminals: Usability Issues and Health Concerns.* Engelwood Cliffs, NJ: Prentice-Hall, Inc., 1984.

[Ben84b] Bennett, John. "Managing to Meet Usability Requirements," in [Ben84a]. Defines usability and presents an approach to managing usability objectives in the development process. See also [Whi88].

[Ber67] Berger, Peter L., and Thomas Luckmann. *The Social Construction of Reality: A Treatise in the Sociology of Knowledge.* Garden City, NY: Doubleday Anchor Books, 1967. The authors argue that what we perceive as "reality" is partly determined by the societies in which we live and work.

[Berl91] Berlage, Thomas. *OSF/Motif: Concepts and Programming.* Wokingham, England: Addison-Wesley, 1991. A good balance between general principles, the architecture of X Windows and Motif, and programming details.

[Bew83] Bewley, William L., *et al.* "Human Factors Testing in the Design of Xerox's 8010 'Star' Office Workstation." *Human Factors in Computing Systems* (CHI'83 Conference proceedings). New York: Association for Computing Machinery, 1983. See also [Joh89].

[Bie94] Biederman, Hans. *Dictionary of Symbolism: Cultural Icons and the Meaning Behind Them.* New York: Meridian/Penguin, 1994. Symbols and their meanings, indexed by names and visual images.

[Bil88] Billingsley, Patricia A. "Taking Panes: Issues in the Design of Windowing Systems." Chapter 19 in [Hel88]. Issues and studies on systems with multiple windows.

[Bilo94] Bilow, Steven C. "Object-oriented X: Adopting Fresco as Your X Toolkit." *The X Journal* 3, 3 (Jan.-Feb. 1994), pp. 76-77.

[Bla89] Blattner, Meera M., Denise A. Sumikawa, and Robert M. Greenberg. "Earcons and Icons: Their Structure and Common Design Principles." *Human-Computer Interaction* 4 (1989), pp. 11-44. Presents analogues between auditory and visual icons.

[Ble88] Bleser, Teresa W., John L. Sibert, and J. Patrick McGee. "Charcoal Sketching: Returning Control to the Artist." *ACM Transactions on Graphics* 7, 1 (January 1988), pp. 76-81. Describes a paint program using a stylus with four degrees of freedom that control line width and darkness in addition to stroke location.

[Boe76] Boehm, Barry. "Software Engineering." *IEEE Transactions on Computers* 25, 12 (December 1976), pp. 1226-1241. Reprinted as Chapter 21 in

[Your79]. Boehm pioneered an approach based on analysis of empirical data from software development projects.

[Boe81] Boehm, Barry W. *Software Engineering Economics.* Engelwood Cliffs, NJ: Prentice-Hall, 1981. This book collects empirical data, cost models, etc. on the software development process.

[Boe88] Boehm, Barry W. "A Spiral Model of Software Development and Enhancement." *Computer (IEEE)* 21, 5 (May 1988).

[Bog85] Bogue, Donald J. *The Population of the United States: Historical Trends and Future Projections.* New York: The Free Press, 1985. Statistics on long-term demographic trends for major world countries.

[Bol80] Bolt, Richard A. " 'Put-That-There': Voice and Gesture at the Graphics Interface." *Computer Graphics* 14, 3 (August 1980), pp.262-270. A video clip of 'Put-That-There' appears as [vSIGGRAPH] 13, 4 (1984).

[Bol81] Bolt, Richard A. "Gaze-Orchestrated Dynamic Windows." *Computer Graphics* 15, 3 (August 1981), pp.109-119. Describes a system that tracks the direction and timing of the user's eye gaze and uses it to control a user interface. See [Sta90] for more recent work.

*__[Boo94]__ Booch, Grady. *Object-Oriented Analysis and Design with Applications.* Redwood City, CA: Benjamin/Cummings, 1994 (2nd edition). A comprehensive treatise on all aspects of object-oriented design. It includes a widely used design notation, worked-out examples in C++, and an extensive bibliography.

[Bor91] Borenstein, Nathaniel S. "Why Do People Prefer FAX to E-mail?" In P. Schicker and E. Steferud, eds. *Message Handling Systems and Application Layer Communication Protocols.* Amsterdam: Elsevier Science Publishers, 1991. Discusses factors that have slowed the acceptance of electronic mail relative to facsimile transmission.

[Boro94] Boroughs, Don L. "Profits on a Platter: The CD-ROM Business Rounds the Corner and Heads for Giant Growth." *US News & World Report* 116, 16 (April 25th, 1994), pp. 69-72.

[Bow93] Bower, Bruce. "A Child's Theory of Mind." *Science News* 144, 3 (July 17, 1993), pp. 39-41. A summary of recent views on the staged development of intelligence in children. See also [Pia74].

[Bra74] Brand, Stewart. *II Cybernetic Frontiers.* New York: Random House, 1974. Reprints articles by Brand; one describes Spacewar, the earliest graphical computer game, developed by the legendary early-60s hackers at MIT; another is about Xerox PARC.

[Broc93] Brockschmidt, Kraig. *Inside OLE 2.* Redmond, WA: Microsoft press, 1993. Technical details on Microsoft's Object Linking and Embedding, Version 2.

[Broo87] Brooks, Frederick P. Jr. "No Silver Bullet: Essence and Accidents of Software Engineering." *Computer (IEEE)* 20, 4 (April 1987), pp. 10-19. Explains why Brooks thinks there is no "silver bullet" for improving software development processes. Contains valuable insights into the nature of complexity in software development.

[Broo90] Brooks, Frederick P. Jr., *et al.* "Project GROPE—Haptic Displays for Scientific Visualization." *Computer Graphics* 24, 4 (August 1990), pp. 177-185. Describes a series of systems utilizing force feedback for solving molecular docking problems in chemistry.

[Bro58] Brown, Roger. "How Shall a Thing Be Called?" *Psychological Review*

65 (1958), pp. 14-21. A pioneering study of how people classify objects.

[Brow92] Brown, Carl. "Assistive Technology, Computers, and Persons with Disabilities." *CACM* 35, 5 (May 1992), pp. 36-44. Summarizes computer technology for people with various disabilities. Includes sources of additional information and products. Part of a special issue on "Computers and People with Disabilities." See also [Fil93].

[Bru66] Bruner, Jerome S. *Toward a Theory of Instruction.* Cambridge, MA: Harvard University Press, 1966. Bruner's theory of three parallel systems for human information processing influenced the group at Xerox PARC that developed Smalltalk (see [Kay93]).

[Bry93] Brynjolfsson, Erik. "The Productivity Paradox of Information Technology." *CACM* 36, 12 (December 1993), pp. 67-77. Reviews studies of the relationship between information technology investment and productivity. See also [Lov91].

[Bur46] Burks, Arthur W., Herman H. Goldstine, and John von Neumann. *Preliminary Discussion of the Logical Design of an Electronic Computing Instrument.* Report to the US Army Ordinance Department, 1946. Reprinted in *DATAMATION*, Sept. 1962, pp. 24-31, and Oct. 1962, pp. 36-41.

[But91] Butterworth, Paul, Allen Otis, and Jacob Stein. "The GemStone Object Database Management System." *CACM* 34, 10 (Oct. 1991), pp. 64-77.

[Bux85] Buxton, William, Ralph Hill, and Peter Rowley. "Issues and Techniques in Touch-Sensitive Tablet Input." *Computer Graphics* 19, 3 (July 1985, Proceedings of SIGGRAPH'85), pp. 215-224.

[Bux86] Buxton, William, and Brad Myers. "A Study in Two-Handed Input." *Human Factors in Computing Systems* (CHI'86 Conference proceedings). New York: ACM/Addison-Wesley, 1986. Describes experiments showing that users can easily and effectively use two hands simultaneously for pointing and selection tasks.

†[Bux89] Buxton, William. "Introduction to This Special Issue on Nonspeech Audio." *Human-Computer Interaction* 4 (1989), pp. 1-9. Overview of a prime source of information on the use of audio in user interfaces. See also [Bla89], [Edw89], and [Gav89].

[Bux90a] "A Three State Model of Graphical Input." In D. Diaper *et al.* (eds), *Human-Computer Interaction—INTERACT '90.* Amsterdam: Elsevier Science Publishers, 1991, pp. 449-456.

[Bux90b] "The 'Natural' Language of Interaction: A Perspective on Nonverbal Dialogues." In [Lau90], pp. 405-416. Discusses the concept of "natural" as applied to computer systems interaction.

[Bux91] Buxton, William. *The Pragmatics of Haptic Input.* Tutorial notes, 1991. Cambridge, England: Cambridge University Press (in press). This is the most complete treatment I have seen of the input side of the user interface. It is currently available only as tutorial notes from various ACM SIGGRAPH and SIGCHI conferences. See also [Bux85], [Bux90a], [Bux90b], [Car90], [Fol92] (Chapter 8), [Green88], [MacK91], and [Shn92] (Chapter 6).

[Byl93] Bylinsky, Gene. "The Payoff from 3-D Computing." *Fortune* 128, 7 (Autumn 1993 special issue on information technology), pp. 32-40. Describes 3-D "visualization" interfaces such as SGI's *Info Navigator*, and their potential value in business applications.

[Byrd94] Byrd, R., Y. Ravin, and J. Prager. "Lexical Assistance at the Information-Retrieval User Interface." IBM Research Division technical report RC 19484, 1994.

[Byrn93] Byrne, Michael D. *Using Icons to Find Documents: Simplicity Is Critical.* [CHI93], pp. 446-453. Concludes that simple icons can be recognized faster, so fine discrimination is best done with text labels.

[Cal90] Calder, Paul R., and Mark A. Linton. "Glyphs: Flyweight Objects for User Interfaces." *UIST* (Proceedings of the 1990 ACM Symposium on user Interface Software and Technology). New York: Association for Computing Machinery, 1990, pp. 92-101.

[Can58] Canaday, John. *Metropolitan Seminars in Art: Portfolio 5—Composition as Pattern.* New York: Metropolitan Museum of Art, 1958.

[Car78] Card, Stuart K, William K. English, and Betty J. Burr. "Evaluation of Mouse, Rate-Controlled Isometric Joystick, Step Keys, and Text Keys for Text Selection on a CRT." *Ergonomics* 21 (1978). Reprinted as Chapter 23 in [Ven90]. A study showing the superiority of the mouse for selection tasks in text editing.

†[Car83] Card, Stuart K., Thomas P. Moran, and Allen Newell. *The Psychology of Human-Computer Interaction.* Hillsdale, NJ: Lawrence Erlbaum Associates, 1983. Applies theory and experimental results from psychology to the prediction of human performance in using computers. A valuable source of data and ideas.

[Car88] Card, Stuart K., and Thomas P. Moran. "User Technology: From Pointing to Pondering." In [Gol88], pp. 493-526. A history of how scientists from various disciplines developed our current understanding of user interaction with computer workstations.

[Car90] Card, Stuart K., Jock D. Mackinlay, and George G. Robertson. "The Design Space of Input Devices." [CHI90], pp. 117-124. Presents a taxonomy of input devices based on physical and logical capabilities.

[Car91] Card, Stuart K., George G. Robertson, and Jock D. Mackinlay. "The Information Visualizer: An Information Workspace."[CHI91], pp. 181-188. A technique for 3-D visualization of data. See also [Macki91], [Rob91].

[Carr82] Carroll, John, and John Thomas. "Metaphor and the Cognitive Representation of Computing Systems." *IEEE Transactions on Systems, Man, and Cybernetics* 12, 2 (March/April 1982), pp. 107-116.

[Carr84] Carroll, John M., and Robert L. Mack. "Learning to Use a Word Processor: By Doing, by Thinking, and by Knowing." In J. C. Thomas and M. Schneider, eds., *Human Factors in Computers.* Norwood, NJ: Ablex, 1984. Discusses "active learning." See also [Carr85].

[Carr85] Carroll, John M., and Robert L. Mack. "Metaphor, Computer Systems, and Active Learning." *International Journal of Man-Machine Studies* 22, 39-57. See also [Carr84].

[Carr87] Carroll, John M., ed. *Interfacing Thought: Cognitive Aspects of Human-Computer Interaction.* Cambridge, MA: MIT Press, 1987.

[Carr88a] Carroll, John M., and Judith Reitman Olson. "Mental Models in Human-Computer Interaction." Chapter 2 in [Hel88].

[Carr88b] Carroll, John M., Robert L. Mack, and Wendy A. Kellogg. "Interface Metaphors and User Interface Design." Chapter 3 in [Hel88]. Advice for designers on the use of metaphor in user interfaces.

[Cav90] Cavendish, Cathy, Stacey Ramos, and R. J. Torres. "Practically O-O." Roanoke, Texas: IBM ASD Software Development Lab, 1990.

[Cha82] Chapman, J. A., *et al. Computing for the Information Age: The Report of the Interactive Systems Task Force (INTERSYS).* Chicago, IL: SHARE, Inc., 1982. Spells out pervasive problems the authors saw inhibiting the growth of interactive computing.

[Che76] Chen, Peter. "The Entity-Relationship Model—Toward a Unified View of Data." *ACM Transactions on Database Systems* 1, 1 (March 1976), pp. 9-36.

[CHI88] Soloway, Elliot, *et al.*, eds. *Human Factors in Computing Systems* (CHI'88 conference proceedings). New York: ACM/Addison-Wesley, 1988.

[CHI89] Bice, Ken, and Clayton Lewis, eds. *Human Factors in Computing Systems* (CHI'89 conference proceedings). New York: ACM/Addison-Wesley, 1989.

[CHI90] Chew, Jane Carrasco, and John Whiteside, eds. *Human Factors in Computing Systems* (CHI'90 conference proceedings). New York: ACM/Addison-Wesley, 1990.

[CHI91] Robertson, Scott P., *et al.* (eds.). *Human Factors in Computing Systems* (CHI'91 conference proceedings). New York: ACM/Addison-Wesley, 1991.

[CHI92] Bauersfeld, Penny, *et al.*, eds. *Human Factors in Computing Systems* (CHI'92 conference proceedings). New York: ACM/Addison-Wesley, 1992.

[CHI93] Ashlund, Stacey, *et al.*, eds. *Human Factors in Computing Systems* (INTERCHI'93—INTERACT'93 and CHI'93 conference proceedings). New York: ACM/Addison-Wesley, 1993.

[Cho72] Chomsky, Noam. *Language and Mind.* New York: Harcourt Brace Jovanovich, 1972.

[Coc93] Cockburn, A. A. R. "The Impact of Object-Orientation on Application Development." *IBM Systems Journal* 32, 3 (1993), pp. 420-444. A good survey of key issues in "conventional" and object-oriented approaches to development.

[Cod79] Codd, E. F. "Extending the Database Relational Model to Capture More Meaning." *ACM Transactions on Database Systems* 4, 4 (Dec. 1979), pp. 397-434.

[Codel92] Codella, Christopher, *et al.* "Interactive Simulation in a Multi-Person World." [CHI92], pp. 329-334. Describes "rubber rocks," a two-person virtual reality application.

[Codel93] Codella, Christopher, *et al.* "A Toolkit for Developing Multi-User, Distributed Virtual Environments." *IEEE Virtual Reality Annual International Symposium.* IEEE, 1993, pp. 401-407. Describes VR-DECK.

[Col90] Collins, Dave. "What Is an Object-Oriented User Interface?" *Proceedings of the Symposium on Object-Oriented Programming Emphasizing Practical Applications.* Poughkeepsie, NY: ACM/Marist College, 1990, pp. 269-306.

[Con92] Conger, James L. *The Waite Group's Windows API Bible: The Definitive Programmer's Reference.* Mill Valley, CA: The Waite Group, 1992. A programming reference for Microsoft Windows 3.1.

[Coo93] Coopersmith, Jonathan. "Facsimile's False Starts." *IEEE Spectrum* 30, 2 (Feb. 1993), pp. 46-49. A brief history of fax technology.

[Cot93] Cotton, Bob, and Richard Oliver. *Understanding Hypermedia: From Multimedia to Virtual Reality.* London: Phaidon Press, 1993. A lavishly illustrated tour of user interfaces ranging from Dynabook and Sensorama to modern multimedia and virtual reality systems.

[Cou87a] Coutaz, Joelle. "PAC, an Object Oriented Model for Dialog Design." [INTER87], pp. 431-436.

[Cou87b] Coutaz, Joelle. "The Construction of User interfaces and the Object Paradigm." *Proceedings of ECOOP'87* (European Conference on Object-Oriented Programming). Berlin: Springer-Verlag, 1987.

[Coy90] Coyne, R. D., *et al. Knowledge-Based Design Systems.* Reading, MA: Addison-Wesley, 1990.

[Cox91] Cox, Brad J., and Andrew J. Novobilski. *Object-Oriented Programming: An Evolutionary Approach.* Reading, MA: Addison-Wesley, 1991. A general introduction to OOP and exposition of the Objective-C language. (The first edition, by Cox, appeared in 1986.)

[Cur85] Curtois, P.-J. "On Time and Space Decomposition of Complex Structures." *CACM* 28, 6 (June 1985), p. 590-603.

[Curt88] Curtis, Bill, Herb Krasner, and Neil Iscoe. "A Field Study of the Software Design Process for Large Systems." *CACM* 31, 11 (November 1988), pp. 1268-1287. An analysis of the software development process based on interviews with personnel from 17 large projects.

[Dav93] Davis, John, and Tom Morgan. "Object-Oriented Development at Brooklyn Union Gas." *IEEE Software* 10, 1 (January 1993). Development of a large commercial mainframe application using OO.

[Dav94] Davis, Ben, Linn Marks, Dave Collins, et al. "The Human Interface to Large Multimedia Databases." *Symposium on Electronic Imaging Science and Technology: High-Speed Networking and Multimedia Applications.* San Jose, CA: IS&T/SPIE, 1994.

[Dea90] Dearle, Fergal. "Designing Portable Application Frameworks for C++." *The C++ Journal*, Summer 1990, pp. 55-59. Discusses the CommonView framework [sGlo89].

[deCh93] de Champeaux, Dennis, Douglas Lea, and Penelope Faure. *Object-Oriented System Development.* Reading, MA: Addison-Wesley, 1993. A good discussion of both high- and low-level design issues.

[Der80] Dertouzos, Michael L., and Joel Moses, eds. *The Computer Age: A Twenty-Year View.* Cambridge, MA: MIT Press, 1980. An assessment and forecast of the influence of computers in many different areas. This collection of essays is still worthwhile today.

[DeS93] DeSantis, Joseph. "How to Evaluate Multi-Platform Development Tools." Liant Software Corporation, 1993. (Available from Liant; address above under *Software.*)

[Des93] Desmond, Michael. "Finding the Perfect Touch." *PC World* 11, 9 (September 1993), pp. 213-225. Lists vendors of keyboards, mice, and trackballs.

[Deut91] Deutsch, L. Peter. "Objects: Just Another Technology?" *Symposium on Object-Oriented Computing.* Thornwood, NY: IBM Corp., 1991.

[Deux91] Deux, O., *et al.* "The O_2 System." *CACM* 34, 10 (Oct. 1991), pp. 34-48. Describes an object-oriented database management system.

[Dich93] Dichter, Carl. "One for All . . ." *UNIX Review* 11, 10 (October 1993). A review and comparison of five portable GUI builders.

[Dic84] Dickerson, O. Bruce, and Walter E. Baker. "Health Considerations at the Information Workplace." In [Ben84a], pp. 271-286.

[Diet89] Dietrich, Walter C., et al. "Saving a Legacy with Objects." [OOPSLA89], pp. 77-83.

[Dit87] Ditchburn, Robert William. "Visual Information Rate." In [Greg87], pp. 795-796. Discusses estimates of information bandwidth for human sensory channels.

[Doh86] Doherty, Walter J., and William G. Pope. "Computing as a Tool for Human Augmentation." *IBM Systems Journal* 25, 3/4 (1986), pp. 306-320. Reports experiences in increasing the productivity of scientists through the use of computers and high-speed networks.

[Doh91] Doherty, Walter J. "The Computer as a Tool for Human Augmentation." Presentation at the IBM User Interface Symposium, Thornwood, NY, Feb. 1991. A theme begun by Engelbart [Eng68].

[Don78] Donnelly, James H., James L. Gibson, and John M. Ivancevich. *Fundamentals of Management.* Dallas, TX: Business Publications, Inc., 1978 (3rd edition). A textbook of management theory.

[Dre72] Dreyfuss, Henry. *Symbol Sourcebook: An Authoritative Guide to International Graphic Symbols.* New York: McGraw-Hill Book Co., 1972. 200+ pages of iconic symbols, indexed by where the symbols are used, their meaning, and their graphic form. It has sections on graphic elements that recur in symbols, and on uses and symbolism of colors, including cross-cultural differences. See also [Mod76].

[Dru68] Drucker, Peter. *The Age of Discontinuity.* New York: Harper & Row, 1968. Drucker saw early on that shifts such as that from production to knowledge work would have a profound effect on society. [Dru89] is a more recent perspective.

[Dru74] Drucker, Peter. *Management: Tasks, Responsibilities, Practices.* New York: Harper & Row, 1974.

[Dru89] Drucker, Peter. *The New Realities.* New York: Harper & Row, 1989. Describes changes in the social, political, and economic world order, many of which have to do with information technology.

[Edm92] Edmonds, Ernest A. *The Separable User Interface.* London: Academic Press, 1992. A collection of papers written over the past several decades on modular separation of user interface code.

[Edw89] Edwards, Alistair D. N. "Soundtrack: An Auditory Interface for Blind Users." *Human-Computer Interaction* 4 (1989), pp. 45-66. Describes an audio interface to a word processing application.

[Ega88] Egan, Dennis E. "Individual Differences in Human-Computer Interaction." Chapter 24 in [Hel88]. Summarizes studies of individual differences in areas ranging from text editing to programming, with suggestions for interfaces that compensate for differences.

[Ell91] Ellis, C. A., S. J. Gibbs, and G. L. Rein. "Groupware: Some Issues and Experiences." *CACM* 34, 1 (January 1991), pp. 39-58. An overview of issues in systems that support collaboration between users.

[Elm89] Elmasri, Ramez, and Shamkant B. Navathe. *Fundamentals of Database Systems.* Redwood City, CA: Benjamin/Cummings, 1989.

[Elr92] Elrod, Scott, et al. "Liveboard: A Large Interactive Display Supporting Group Meetings, Presentations and Remote Collaboration." [CHI92], pp. 599-607.

[Eng68] Engelbart, Douglas C., and William K. English. "A Research Center for Augmenting Human Intellect." *AFIPS Proceedings* 33 (Fall Joint Computer Conference, 1968), pp. 395-410. Engelbart and colleagues invented the mouse and the idea of multiple windows, and developed a working system supporting hypertext and collaborative work. A brief film clip of this work is included in [vKay87].

[Eng73] Engelbart, Douglas C., Richard W. Watson, and James C. Norton. "The Augmented Knowledge Workshop." *AFIPS Proceedings* 42 (National Computer Conference, 1973), pp. 9-21. An update on [Eng68].

[Far91] Farrell, Edward J., ed. "Visual Interpretation of Complex Data." *IBM Journal of Research and Development* 35, 1/2 (Jan./March 1991). A special edition on visualization of numeric data.

[Fei93] Fein, Robert M., Gary M. Olson, and Judith S. Olson. "A Mental Model Can Help with Learning to Operate a Complex Device." *INTERCHI'93 Adjunct Proceedings.* New York: Association for Computing Machinery, 1993, pp. 157-158. Experiments on the use of conceptual models versus rote procedure learning, with references to other studies.

[Fer89] Ferrel, Patrick J., and Robert F. Meyer. "Vamp: The Aldus Application Framework." [OOPSLA89], pp. 185-189. Describes a framework, based on MacApp [Schm86], used to develop Aldus products.

[Fil93] Filipczak, Bob. "Adaptive Technology for the Disabled." *Training,* March 1993, pp. 23-29. Summarizes technology (primarily computer-related) to help workers with various disabilities. Includes sources of additional information and products. See also [Brow92].

[Fin84] Finzer, William, and Laura Gould."Programming by Rehearsal." *BYTE* 9, 6 (June 1984), pp. 187-210. Presents a visual programming system based on a theater metaphor. Also described in [Shu88], Chapter 5.

[Fit47] Fitts, Paul M., and R. E. Jones. *Analysis of Factors Contributing to 460 "Pilot-Error" Experiences in Operating Aircraft Controls.* Memorandum Report TSEAA-694-12, Aero Medical Laboratory, Wright-Patterson Air Force Base. Dayton, OH: July 1, 1947.

[Fit53] Fitts, Paul M., and Charles M. Seeger. "Compatibility: Spatial Characteristics of Stimulus and Response Codes." *Journal of Experimental Psychology,* 46 (1953). Reprinted as Chapter 13 in [Ven90]. Presents the notion of stimulus-response compatibility.

[Fit54] Fitts, Paul M. "The Information Capacity of the Human Motor System in Controlling the Amplitude of Movement." *Journal of Experimental Psychology,* 47 (June 1954). Exposition of Fitts's law, widely used in studying performance of mice and other pointing devices.

[Fol74] Foley, James D., and Victor L. Wallace. "The Art of Natural Man-Machine Conversation." *Proceedings of the IEEE* 62, 4 (April 1974). Early work on the "language model" of interaction.

*__[Fol92]__ Foley, James D., *et al. Computer Graphics: Principles and Practice.* Reading, MA: Addison-Wesley, 1992. A comprehensive textbook on graphics and interaction; Chapters 8-10 deal with user interface design.

[For94] Forman, George H., and John Zahorjan. "The Challenges of Mobile Computing." *Computer (IEEE)* 27, 4 (April 1994), pp. 38-47. Technical issues in networking portable, highly mobile computers.

[Fur93] Furger, Roberta. "Danger at Your Fingertips." *PC World* 11, 5 (May 1993), pp. 118-124. A warning to PC users about repetitive strain injury (RSI) due to typing.

[Gam94] Gamma, Erich, Richard Helm, Ralph Johnson, and John Vlissides. *Design Patterns: Elements of Object-Oriented Software Architecture.* Reading MA: Addison-Wesley, 1994. Applies Alexander's theory of pattern languages [Alex79] to OO design.

[Garb92] Garber, Sharon R., and Mitch B. Grunes. "The Art of Search: A Study of Art Directors."[CHI92], pp. 157-164. Describes a "light table" interface prototype.

[Gard82] Gardner, Howard. *Art, Mind, and Brain: A Cognitive Approach to Creativity.* New York: Basic Books, Inc., 1982.

†**[Gard85]** Gardner, Howard. *The Mind's New Science: A History of the Cognitive Revolution.* New York: Basic Books, Inc., 1985. A comprehensive treatise on theories of cognition.

[Garf93] Garfinkel, Simson L., and Michael K. Mahoney. *NeXTSTEP Programming: Step One, Object-Oriented Applications.* Santa Clara, CA: Telos/Springer-Verlag, 1993. A tutorial for developers using the Objective-C language and the NeXT Interface Builder.

[Gat83] Gates, William. "The Future of Software Design." BYTE 8, 8 (August 1983), pp. 401-403.

[Gav89] Gaver, William W. "The SonicFinder: An Interface that Uses Auditory Icons." *Human-Computer Interaction* 4 (1989), pp. 67-94. Describes an extension to the Apple Macintosh Finder application to support audio behavior for objects.

[Gib79] Gibson, J. J. *The Ecological Approach to Visual Perception.* Boston: Houghton-Mifflin, 1979.

[Gib84] Gibson, William. *Neuromancer.* New York: Ace Books, 1984. The book in which Gibson coined the term "cyberspace," the "consensual hallucination" of an enormous space holding all the world's data. Interfaces are already starting to look like his ideas [Byl93].

*__[Gil88]__ Gilb, Tom. *Principles of Software Engineering Management.* Wokingham, England: Addison-Wesley, 1988. Gilb's ideas about attributes versus functions, measurable objectives, and evolutionary development are invaluable, even when applied at the level of the individual developer. [Whi88] applies them to usability engineering.

[Gle93] Gleckman, Howard, *et al.* "The Technology Payoff: A Sweeping Reorganization of Work Itself Is Boosting Productivity." *Business Week* 3323 (June 14, 1993), pp. 56-68. Interviews and case studies supporting the assertion that information technology requires reengineering of work processes to pay off. See also [Stewa93].

[Gold58] Goldman, Robert N. "Simplicity and The Computer." *DATAMATION*, May/June 1958, pp. 40-42. A prophetic article describing the plight of the "computer illiterate" user.

[Gol83] Goldberg, Adele, and David Robson. *Smalltalk-80: The Language and Its Implementation.* Reading, MA: Addison-Wesley, 1983.

[Gol88] Goldberg, Adele, ed. *A History of Personal Workstations.* Reading, MA: Addison-Wesley, 1988. Based on the proceedings of an ACM conference on personal workstations, which involved many of the industry's pioneers.

[Gol90] Goldberg, Adele. "Information Models, Views, and Controllers." *Dr. Dobb's Journal* (July 1990), pp. 54-60. An overview of the model-view-controller paradigm in Smalltalk. See [Kras88] for the gory details, and [Lei92] for recent changes in MVC.

[Goo87] Goodman, Danny. *The Complete HyperCard Handbook.* Toronto: Bantam Books, 1987. A comprehensive tutorial on using and developing applications for Apple's HyperCard.

[Gou85] Gould, John D., and Clayton Lewis. "Designing for Usability: Key Principles and What Designers Think." *CACM* 28, 3 (March 1985), pp. 300-311. Summarizes a set of principles for designing usable systems (presented in more detail in [Gou88]), and discusses why these principles often are not practiced by designers.

[Gou87] Gould, John D., *et al.* "The 1984 Olympic Messaging System: A Test of Behavioral Principles of Design." *CACM* 30, 9 (Sept. 1987), pp. 758-769. Describes the development of an audio messaging system for athletes at the 1984 Summer Olympics.

***[Gou88]** Gould, John D. "How to Design Usable Systems." Chapter 35 in [Hel88]. Offers a wealth of practical techniques for using user input to design better systems. See also [Whi88], which complements this, focusing more on formal objectives for the design process.

[Gou91] Gould, John D., Stephen J. Boies, and Clayton Lewis. "Making Usable, Useful, Productivity-Enhancing Computer Applications." *CACM* 34, 1 (January 1991), pp. 74-85. Summarizes principles of usability design [Gou88], and presents an approach to applying them based on organizational structure and tool support. [Wie90] presents more details on the tool they discuss.

[Gree85] Green, Mark. "Report on Dialogue Specification Tools." In [Pfa85], pp. 9-20.

†[Gree86] Green, Mark. "A Survey of Three Dialogue Models." *ACM Transactions on Graphics* 5, 3 (July 1986), pp. 244-275. Compares transition network, grammar-based, and event (object-oriented) models for user interfaces.

[Green88] Greenstein, Joel S., and Lynn Y. Arnaut. "Input Devices." Chapter 22 in [Hel88].

[Greg79] Gregory, Richard L. *Eye and Brain: The Psychology of Seeing.* New York: McGraw-Hill, 1979 (third edition). A readable and informative treatise on all aspects of human vision.

[Greg86] Gregory, Richard L. *Odd Perceptions.* New York: Routledge, Chapman & Hall, Inc., 1986. Essays on mind and perception.

[Greg86a] Gregory, Richard L. "Whatever Happened to Information Theory?" In [Greg86], pp. 187-194. Information theory and psychology; an important application not mentioned here is Fitts's law [Fit54].

†[Greg87] Gregory, Richard L. (editor). *The Oxford Companion to the Mind.* Oxford: Oxford University Press, 1987. A short encyclopedia of the human mind, dealing primarily with topics from psychology and physiology. The articles are informative summaries, and contain citations of the research literature.

[Greg87a] Gregory, Richard L. "Recovery from Blindness." In [Greg87], pp. 94-96. Summarizes cases of people who have recovered their sight after lifelong (or nearly lifelong) blindness. See also [Sac93].

[Gro89] Grosky, W. I., and R. Mehrotra, eds. *Computer (IEEE)* 22, 12 (Dec. 1989). Special issue on "Image Database Management."

[Gut84] Guterl, Fred. "Design Case History: Apple's Macintosh." *IEEE Spectrum* 21, 12 (Dec. 1984), pp. 34-43. The Macintosh is particularly important because it was the first commercially successful computer based on an OOUI.

[Guy88] Guynes, Jan L. "Impact of System Response Time on State Anxiety." *CACM* 31, 3 (March 1988), pp. 342-347. A study finding that anxiety correlated with longer response time.

[Had54] Hadamard, Jacques. *An Essay on the Psychology of Invention in the Mathematical Field.* New York: Dover Books, 1954. Hadamard, a mathematician, based this on descriptions of the creative process from scientific colleagues.

[Hak91] Hakiel, S. R. *Evaluating Icons for Human-Computer Interfaces.* IBM UK Laboratories technical report, 1991. A summary of research and testing methods for computer icons.

[Hal93] Halfhill, Tom R. "PDAs Arrive But Aren't Quite Here Yet." *BYTE* 18, 11 (October 1993), pp. 66-86. Reviews architectures and applications for the first generation of "personal digital assistants."

[Har88] Harel, David. "On Visual Formalisms." *CACM* 31, 5 (May 1988), pp. 514-530. Describes higraphs and statecharts for representing complex systems.

[Hau89] Hauptmann, Alexander G. "Speech and Gestures for Graphic Image Manipulation." [CHI89], pp. 241-245. A study showing that people prefer gestures and speech to either alone.

***†[Hel88]** Helander, Martin, ed. *Handbook of Human-Computer Interaction.* Amsterdam: North-Holland, 1988. A massive (nearly 1200 pages) compendium on all aspects of user interface design and the human factors of HCI. Has 52 chapters written by psychologists, human factors engineers, and designers. Though many of these papers are not for the average developer, some of them, such as [Gou88] and [Whi88], offer practical techniques not readily available elsewhere.

[Held74] Held, Richard (ed.). *Image, Object, and Illusion.* San Francisco: W. H. Freeman, 1974. Reprints of articles from *Scientific American* on visual perception.

[Hen86] Henderson, D. Austin Jr., and Stuart K. Card. "Rooms: The Use of Multiple Virtual Workspaces to Reduce Space Contention in a Window-Based Graphical User Interface." *ACM Transactions on Graphics* 5, 3 (July 1986), pp. 211-243. See also [sXer92].

[Hendl94] Hendler, J. "Beyond the Fifth Generation: Parallel AI Research in Japan." *IEEE Expert* 9, 1 (Feb. 1994) pp. 2-7

[Henr90] Henry, Tyson R., Scott E. Hudson, and Gary L. Newell. "Integrating Gesture and Snapping into a User Interface Toolkit." *UIST* (Proceedings of the 1990 ACM Symposium on User Interface Software and Technology). New York: Association for Computing Machinery, 1990, pp. 112-122.

[Hil86] Hill, Ralph D. "Supporting Concurrency, Communication, and Synchronization in Human-Computer Interaction—The Sassafras UIMS." *ACM Transactions on Graphics* 5, 3 (July 1986), pp. 179-210.

[Hil88] Hill, Ralph, *et al.* "UIMSs: Threat or Menace?" [CHI88], pp. 197-200. Panel discussion on the pros and cons of user interface management systems [Löw88].

[Hix91] Hix, Deborah, and Robert S. Schulman. "Human-Computer Interface Development Tools: A Methodology for Their Evaluation." *CACM* 34, 3 (March 1991), pp. 75-87.

[Hoa78] Hoare, C. A. R. "Communicating Sequential Processes." *CACM* 21, 8 (August 1978), pp. 666-677.

[Hol93] Holtzblatt, Karen, and Hugh Beyer. "Making Customer-Centered Design Work for Teams." *CACM* 36, 10 (October 1993), pp. 93-103. More details on contextual design methods described in [Wix90].

[How87] Howard, Ian P. "Spatial Co-ordination of the Senses." In [Greg87], pp. 727-733. Describes how human senses and motor activities coordinate to locate objects in space.

[HudI90] Hudson Institute and Towers Perrin. *Workforce 2000.* Hudson Institute/Towers Perrin report, 1990. Follows up a 1987 study by the Hudson Institute, *Workforce 2000: Work and Workers in the 21st Century.* Examines whether US corporations are prepared for forecasted demographic changes in the workforce.

[Hud86] Hudson, Scott E., and Roger King. "A Generator of Direct Manipulation Office Systems." *ACM Transactions on Office Information Systems* 4, 2, (April 1986).

[Hud87] Hudson, Scott. "UIMS Support for Direct Manipulation Interfaces." *Computer Graphics* 21, 2 (April 1987), pp. 120-124. Argues that the Seeheim model [Pfa85] is inadequate for implementing direct manipulation user interfaces.

[Hud92] Hudson, Scott, and Gary L. Newell. "Probabilistic State Machines: Dialog Management for Inputs with Uncertainty." *UIST* (Proceedings of the 1992 ACM Symposium on User Interface Software and Technology). New York: Association for Computing Machinery, 1992, pp. 199-208.

[Hur93] Hurst, E. Gerald Jr. "PERT/CPM." [Ral93], pp. 1061-1062.

†[Hut85] Hutchins, Edwin L., James D. Hollan, and Donald A. Norman. "Direct manipulation Interfaces." *Human-Computer Interaction* 1, 1985. Direct manipulation from the point of view of cognitive psychology. Another version of this paper appears in [Nor86].

[IBM89] IBM Corporation. *IBM Data Interpretation System: General Information Manual.* IBM Form number GH21-0437, 1989.

[IBM91] IBM Corporation. *Icon Reference Book.* IBM Form number SC34-4348, 1991. Presents guidelines for designing and producing icons, and catalogs icon designs for IBM products running on OS/2.

[IBM92a] IBM Corporation. *OS/2 2.0 Technical Library: Application Design Guide.* IBM form number S10G-6260-0, 1992.

[IBM92b] IBM Corporation. *Object-Oriented Interface Design: IBM Common User Access Guidelines.* Carmel, IN: Que, 1992. Briefly discusses OOUIs in a general way, then presents the specifics of IBM's CUA interface style.

[IBM92c] IBM Corporation. *OS/2 2.0 Technical Library: Presentation Manager Programming Reference* (3 vols.). IBM form numbers S10G-6264, 6265, 6272, 1992.

[IBM93a] IBM Corporation. *C/C++ Tools Version 2.01: User Interface Class Library User's Guide.* IBM form number S82G-3743.

[Ing78] Ingalls, Daniel H. "The Smalltalk-76 Programming System: Design and Implementation." *Conference Record of the Fifth Annual Symposium on Principles of Programming Languages.* Tucson, AZ: Association for Computing Machinery, 1978, pp. 9-15.

[Ing81] Ingalls, Daniel H. "Design Principles Behind Smalltalk." *BYTE* 6, 8 (August 1981), pp. 286-298.

[Ing86] Ingalls, Daniel H. "A Simple Technique for Handling Multiple Polymorphism." [OOPSLA86], pp. 347-349.

[INTER87] Bullinger, H.-J., B. Shackel, and K. Kornwachs, eds. *Human-Computer Interaction—Interact '87* (Proceedings of the Second IFIP Conference on Human-Computer Interaction). Amsterdam: North Holland, 1987.

[Irb77] Irby, Charles, Linda Bergsteinsson, Thomas Moran, William Newman, and Larry Tesler. *A Methodology for User Interface Design.* Palo Alto, CA: Xerox Palo Alto Research Center, Jan. 1977. An attempt to capture available knowledge at Xerox about interface design methods. Though it was never published except as a Xerox technical report, the ideas have influenced (directly or indirectly) most OOUI design methods. A more accessible source for some of this material is [Smi82]. See also [Joh89].

[Irb89] Irby, Charles. *User Interface Design.* Presentation given at the IBM Technical Education Center, Thornwood, NY, April 7, 1989.

[Ish92] Ishii, Hiroshi, and Minoru Kobayashi. "ClearBoard: A Seamless Medium for Shared Drawing and Conversation with Eye Contact." [CHI92], pp. 525-532. Describes a clear "blackboard" for collaborative design work. Video is used to show a remote collaborator as if on the other side of the board.

[ISO92] International Organization for Standardization. *Information Technology - Text and Office Systems - Graphic Symbols Used on Screens: Interactive Icons.* Reference number JTC 1/SC 18 N 3737. Committee Draft of a proposed ISO standard on screen icons.

*__[Jac92]__ Jacobson, Ivar. *Object-Oriented Software Engineering: A Use Case Driven Approach.* Reading, MA: Addison-Wesley, 1992. Use cases should be understood by every OO designer. Includes a chapter comparing Jacobson's approach with other methods.

[Jaco83] Jacob, Robert. "Using Formal Specifications in the Design of a Human-Computer Interface." *CACM* 26, 4 (April 1983), pp. 259-264. Shows the use of transition diagrams and BNF in specifying a UI.

[Jaco86] Jacob, Robert. "A Specification Language for Direct-Manipulation User Interfaces." *ACM Transactions on Graphics* 5, 4 (October 1986), pp. 283-317.

[Jal93] Jalili, Reza. *Architecture for Distributed Multi-User Environments.* IEEE Virtual Reality Applications International Symposium, 1993, Tutorial 9. Describes VR-DECK, a tool for building virtual reality applications. See also [Codel93].

†**[Lak87]** Lakoff, George. *Women, Fire, and Dangerous Things: What Categories Reveal about the Mind.* Chicago: University of Chicago Press, 1987. A summary and synthesis of the modern view of categories and classes, drawing on the work of linguists, psychologists, and philosophers.

[Lamb91] Lamb, Charles, *et al.* "The ObjectStore Database System." *CACM* 34, 10 (Oct. 1991), pp. 64-77. Describes an OODBMS.

*__[Lam86]__ Lammers, Susan. *Programmers at Work: Interviews with 19 Programmers Who Shaped the Computer Industry.* Redmond, WA: Microsoft Press, 1986. Interviews with people like Dan Bricklin (who conceived VisiCalc) and Andy Hertzfield (principal developer of the Macintosh operating system) about how they turn ideas into systems.

[Lan93] Lang, Laura. "Getting There with Software Maps." *PC World* 11, 3 (March 1993), pp. 182-189. Examples of atlases and other mapping software for personal computers.

[Lar92] Larson, James A. *Interactive Software: Tools for Building Interactive User Interfaces.* Engelwood Cliffs, NJ: Yourdon press, 1992. Emphasizes high-level tools for building user interfaces.

*__[Lau90]__ Laurel, Brenda, ed. *The Art of Human-Computer Interface Design.* Reading, MA: Addison-Wesley, 1990. A collection of short chapters written by experts in the field. A terrific source of ideas, and a fun book to browse in.

[Lau90a] Laurel, Brenda. "Interface Agents: Metaphors with Character." [Lau90], pp. 355-365.

[Lau92] Laurel, Brenda, *et al.* "Anthropomorphism: From ELIZA to *Terminator 2.*" [CHI92], pp. 67-70. Summarizes a panel discussion on the benefits and hazards of making computers seem human.

[Laz93] Lazowska, Edward D. "Operating Systems." [Ral93], pp. 966-989.

[Lea92] Lea, Doug. "Run Time Type Information and Class Design." *Usenix C++ Technical Conference Proceedings.* Usenix Association, 1992, pp. 341-347.

[Lei92] Leibs, David J., and Kenneth S. Rubin. "Reimplementing Model-View-Controller." *The Smalltalk Report* 1, 6, March/April 1992. Describes recent changes to MVC in ParcPlace Smalltalk-80 [sPar92].

[Lem90] LeMaster, Ron, and Ulla Merz. "Design of a Loading Plan Format for an Expert Cargo Loading System." [CHI90], pp. 369-378. A case study of task analysis done in the workplace.

[Lew90] Lewis, Clayton, *et al.* "Testing a Walkthrough Methodology for Theory-Based Design of Walk-Up-and-Use Interfaces." [CHI90], pp. 235-242. Presents the "cognitive walkthrough" technique for evaluating user interfaces.

[Lewi91] Lewis, Michael. "Situated Visualization: Building Interfaces from the Mind Up." *Multimedia Review* (Winter 1991/Spring 1992), pp. 23-39. An account of metaphor and visualization based on an ecological approach [Gib79] to cognition.

[Lewis94] Lewis, Peter H. "Getting Down to Business on the Net." The *New York Times*, Sunday, June 19, 1994; section 3, pp. 1, 6. Discusses the growth of the Internet and its use for business purposes.

[Lib89] Libes, Don, and Sandy Ressler. *Life with UNIX: A Guide for Everyone.* Engelwood Cliffs, NJ: Prentice Hall, 1989. UNIX is the mother of all command line interfaces (though it was based on earlier mainframe user interfaces), a paradigmatic example of everything that is bad—and good—about command lines.

[Lic89] Licklider, Tracy Robnett. "Ten Years of Rows and Columns." *BYTE* 14, 12 (Dec. 1989), pp. 324-331. A brief history of computer spreadsheets. See also the interview with Dan Bricklin in [Lam86].

[Lim92] Lim, K. Y., and Long, J. B. "A Method for (Recruiting) Methods: Facilitating Human Factors Input to System Design."[CHI92], pp. 549-556. A method for integrating human factors techniques into a structured development process.

[Lin89] Linton, Mark, *et al.* "Composing User Interfaces with InterViews." *Computer (IEEE)* 22, 2 (Feb. 1989). Describes the InterViews C++ user interface framework and class library.

[Lip82] Lipkie, Daniel, *et al.* "Star Graphics: An Object-Oriented Implementation." *Computer Graphics* 16, 3 (July 1982), pp. 115-124. Discusses aspects of the implementation of the Xerox Star.

[Lis74] Liskov, Barbara, and Stephen Zilles. "Programming with Abstract Data Types." *SIGPLAN Notices* 9, 4 (April 1974).

[Loo94] Loomis, Mary E. S. "Hitting the relational wall." *JOOP* 6, 8 (Jan. 1994), pp. 56-59. Hazards of using relational DBMS in OO systems.

[Lov91] Loveman, Gary. "Cash Drain, No Gain." *Computerworld* 25, 47 (Nov. 25, 1991), pp. 69-72. Loveman's influential study, "An Assessment of the Productivity Impact of Information Technologies" (at the MIT Sloan School of Management) found no productivity gains in US companies that had invested heavily in information technology. Similar results have been reported by others [Pow92], though there is some debate [Bry93]. Here he argues that gains can be realized only by improving management and organizational structure (similar to the conclusion in [Gle93]).

[Love93] Love, Tom. *Object Lessons: Lessons Learned in Object-Oriented Development Projects.* New York: SIGS Books, 1993. Advice for developers and managers, based on Love's consulting experience.

[Lovel87] Lovelock, J. E. *Gaia: A New Look at Life on Earth.* Oxford: Oxford University Press, 1987. A theory of stability and homeostasis in very large ecosystems.

[Löw88] Löwgren, Jonas. "History, State, and Future of User Interface Management Systems." *SIGCHI Bulletin* 20, 1 (July 1988), pp. 32-44. A useful overview of UIMS issues.

[Mac87] Mack, Robert L., and Jakob Nielsen. "Software Integration in the Professional Work Environment: Observations on Requirements, Usage, and Interface Issues." IBM Research Division technical report RC 12677, 1987.

[Mac93] Mack, Robert L., Peter Malkin, Dave Collins, *et al.* "Smalltalk prototyping of CUA 1991 workplace and multimedia information management concepts." IBM Research Division technical report, 1993.

[MacK91] MacKenzie, I. Scott, Abigail Sellen, and William Buxton. "A Comparison of Input Devices in Elemental Pointing and Dragging Tasks." [CHI91], pp. 161-166. Experiments comparing mouse, tablet, and trackball for GUI tasks.

[MacK93a] MacKenzie, I. Scott, and William Buxton. "A Tool for the Rapid Evaluation of Input Devices Using Fitts' Law Models." *SIGCHI Bulletin* 25, 3 (July 1993), pp. 58-63. Describes a Macintosh program for input device research. It is available by anonymous FTP from `snowhite.cis.uoguelph.ca`, in `pub/fitts-law`.

[MacK93b] MacKenzie, I. Scott, and Colin Ware. "Lag as a Determinant of Human Performance in Interactive Systems." [CHI93], pp. 488-493. Discusses tracking lag and experiments quantifying performance degradation resulting from lag.

[Macki91] Mackinlay, Jock D., George G. Robertson, and Stuart K. Card. "The Perspective Wall: Detail and Context Smoothly Integrated. [CHI91], pp. 173-179. A technique for 3-D visualization of data. See also [Car91], [Rob91].

[MacL89] Maclean, Allan, Richard M. Young, and Thomas P. Moran. "Design Rationale: The Argument Behind the Artifact." [CHI89], pp. 247-252. Argues that one of the products of user interface design ought to be a rationale for the chosen design.

[MacN92] MacNicol, Gregory. "Video Editing Hits the Desktop." *Computer Graphics World* 15, 4 (April 1992), pp. 32-40. Reports on video editing applications for PCs and workstations.

[Mal93] Malkin, Peter. "The KCM Distributed Database Management System." IBM Research Division technical report RC 18608, 1993.

[Man93] Mandelkern, Dave. "Graphical User Interfaces: The Next Generation." *CACM* 36, 4 (April 1993), pp. 37-39. Introduces a special issue on the topic.

[Mand92] Mander, Richard, Gitta Salomon, and Yin Yin Wong. "A 'Pile' metaphor for Casual Organization of Information." [CHI92], pp. 627-634.

[Mar92] Marcus, Aaron. *Graphic Design for Electronic Documents and User Interfaces.* Reading, MA: ACM/Addison-Wesley, 1992. Covers information design, use of color and typography, icon design, user interface style manuals, and an analysis of commercial GUIs.

[Mark93] Markoff, John. "A Free and Simple Computer Link." The *New York Times*, Dec. 8, 1993, pp. D1, D5. Describes Mosaic and the World-Wide Web on the Internet.

[Mark82] Marks, Shirley. "JOSS—Conversational Computing for the Nonprogrammer." *Annals of the History of Computing* 4, 1 (Jan. 1982), pp. 35-52. Describes an early interactive timesharing system at the Rand Corporation. [Thi90], pp. 209-211 also discusses JOSS.

[Mark91] Marks, Stuart W. "Implementing Drag and Drop in X11." *Proceeding of NCGA '91.* Chicago: National Computer Graphics Association, 1991, pp. 450-457. Issues in implementing drag and drop for X Windows. See also [Rei93a], [Skl93]

[Marks95] Marks, Linn, and Ben Davis. *Integrative Multimedia Design.* Cambridge, MA: MIT Press, 1995 (in press). A design process for multimedia applications that integrates "form" and "content."

[Mart92] Martin, Sandra. *Internationalization Explored.* Santa Clara, CA: UniForum, 1992. Available from UniForum, 2901 Tasman Dr., Santa Clara, CA 95054. A detailed presentation of translation issues, primarily for C/UNIX environments.

[May74] Maynard Smith, J. *Models in Ecology.* London: Cambridge University Press, 1974.

[McC60] McCarthy, John. "Recursive Functions of Symbolic Expressions." *CACM* 3, 4 (April 1960), pp. 184-195. The basis for LISP.

[McC88] McCormack, Joel, and Paul Asente. "Using the X Toolkit or How to Write a Widget." *Proceedings of the USENIX Summer Conference.* San Francisco, CA: USENIX Association, 1988.

[McCu87] McCullough, Paul. "Transparent Forwarding: First Steps." [OOPSLA87], pp. 331-341. A scheme for remote Smalltalk objects.

[McE93] McEnery, Paul. "Last Exit to VRcadia." *Mondo 2000* 11 (1993), pp. 111-116. Describes high-end arcade virtual reality experiences.

[McLu65] McLuhan, Marshall. *Understanding Media: The Extensions of Man.* New York: McGraw-Hill Book Company, 1965.

[Mey88] Meyer, Bertrand. *Object-Oriented Software Construction.* New York: Prentice Hall, 1988. Though it emphasizes the author's Eiffel language, this has a wealth of good general advice on OO design.

[Mez93] Mezick, Dan. "Pen Computing Catches On." *BYTE* 18, 11 (October 1993), p. 112. An overview of "pen-based" computing. See also [Hal93].

[Mic92] Microsoft Corporation. *The Windows Interface: An Application Design Guide.* Redmond, WA: Microsoft Press, 1992. A style and design guide for Microsoft Windows applications; includes diskettes containing visual examples and sample code and bitmaps.

[Mil94] Miller, Arthur. "From here to ATM." *IEEE Spectrum* 31, 6 (June 1994). Describes ATM (asynchronous transfer mode) communications networks.

[Min89] Minsky, Margaret, *et al.* "Recent Progress Creating Environments With the Sense of Feel: Giving 'Look and Feel' Its Missing Meaning." [CHI89], pp. 189-190. Summarizes a panel discussion on systems with tactile and force feedback.

[Min90] Minsky, Margaret, Ming Ouh-young, *et al.* "Feeling and Seeing: Issues in Force Display." *Computer Graphics* 24, 2 (March 1990). Discusses research on user interfaces that allow users to feel textures (such as sandpaper) using a joystick with force feedback.

[Minsk86] Minsky, Marvin. *The Society of Mind.* New York: Simon & Schuster, 1986.

[Mod76] Modley, Rudolf. *Handbook of Pictorial Symbols: 3,250 Examples from International Sources.* New York: Dover Publications, 1976. A sourcebook for iconic symbols. See also [Dre72], [Bie94].

[Moo87] Moore, Brian C. J. "Hearing." In [Greg87], pp. 303-308.

[Mor83] Morgan, Chris. "An Interview with Wayne Rosing, Bruce Daniels, and Larry Tesler: A Behind-the-Scenes Look at the Development of Apple's Lisa." *BYTE* 8, 2 (February 1983), pp. 90-114. See also [Wil83].

[Mor91] Morgan, K., R. L. Morris, and S. Gibbs. "When Does a Mouse Become a Rat? or . . . Comparing Performance and Preferences in Direct Manipulation and Command Line Environment." *The Computer Journal* (UK) 34, 3 (1991).

[Moran81] Moran, Thomas P. "The Command Language Grammar: A Representation for the User Interface of Interactive Computer Systems." *International Journal of Man-Machine Studies* 15 (1981), pp. 3-50.

Though perhaps too detailed to be used in development, CLG can help designers understand how users understand interfaces.

[Mye88] Myers, Brad. "A Taxonomy of Window Manager User Interfaces." *Computer Graphics and Applications (IEEE)* 8, 5 (Sept. 1988). Compares the look and feel of interfaces on 21 window management systems. See also [Ster87].

[Mye89] Myers, Brad. "User Interface Tools: Introduction and Survey." *IEEE Software* 6, 1 (Jan. 1989).

[Mye92] Myers, Brad, and Mary Beth Rosson. "Survey on User Interface Programming." [CHI92], pp. 195-202. Results of a survey of 74 applications. On average, about 50% of both code and development effort was devoted to the user interface.

[Nal91] Nally, Martin, Anna Ottobelli, Chris Dekkers, and Andreas Rudolf. *Cooperative Processing in an Object-Oriented Environment.* Raleigh, NC: IBM International Technical Support Organization, 1991 (IBM form number GG24-3801).

[Nel87] Nelson, Ted. *Computer Lib/Dream Machines.* Redmond, WA: Microsoft Press, 1987. Opinions on user interface design that are provocative, sometimes outrageous, but always thought-provoking. This double book is an updated reprint of work originally published in the '60s and '70s. Many of Nelson's critical comments on user interfaces are still valid today.

[Nic91] Nicholson, Robert T. "Designing a Portable GUI Toolkit." *Dr. Dobb's Journal*, Jan. 1991, pp. 68-75. Describes the author's experience in designing a toolkit, and prescribes general principles.

[Nic93] Nicol, John R., Thomas Wilkes, and Frank A. Manola. "Object Orientation in Heterogeneous Distributed Computer Systems." *Computer (IEEE)* 26, 6 (June 1993), pp. 57-67. Discusses the role of OO in providing flexible integrated services in heterogeneous networks.

[Nid93] Nidumolu, S. R., and S. E. Goodman. "Computing in India: An Asian Elephant Learning to Dance." *CACM* 36, 4 (June 1993), pp. 15-22. See also [Pres93].

[Nie90a] Nielsen, Jakob, and Rolf Molich. "Heuristic Evaluation of User Interfaces." [CHI90], pp. 249-256. A relatively fast, cheap technique for evaluating user interfaces. See [Nie94] for a more thorough treatment of this subject.

[Nie90b] Nielsen, Jakob, *et al.* "Designing for International Use." [CHI90], pp. 291-294. Summarizes a panel discussion on designing user interfaces for international use.

[Nie90c] Nielsen, Jakob, ed. *Designing User Interfaces for International Use.* Amsterdam: Elsevier Science Publishers, 1990. A collection of papers on aspects of designing internationalized user interfaces.

[Nie92a] Nielsen, Jakob. "Teaching Experienced Developers to Design Graphical user Interfaces." [CHI92], pp. 557-564.

***[Nie92b]** Nielsen, Jakob. "The Usability Engineering Life Cycle." *Computer (IEEE)* 25, 3 (March 1992), pp. 12-22. Presents activities for incorporating usability engineering into the development process.

***[Nie94]** Nielsen, Jakob, and Robert L. Mack, eds. *Usability Inspection Methods.* New York: John Wiley & Sons, 1994. A compendium of methods for evaluating and improving usability. Focuses on "discount" techniques with high return for the effort, and on using inspection results within the development process.

[Nor64] Norman, Donald. "Categorization of Action Slips." Psychological Review 88 (1964). Reprinted as Chapter 7 in [Ven90]. Classifies, by cause, human errors in performing actions. See also [Nor83b].

[Nor83a] Norman, Donald. "Some Observations on Mental Models." In Stevens and Gentner, eds., *Mental Models.* Hillsdale, NJ: Lawrence Erlbaum Associates, 1983.

[Nor83b] Norman, Donald. "Design Rules Based on Analyses of Human Error." *CACM* 26, 4 (April 1983), pp. 254-258.

[Nor86] Norman, Donald A., and S. W. Draper, eds. *User Centered Design: New Perspectives on Human-Computer Interaction.* Hillsdale, NJ: Lawrence Erlbaum Associates, 1986.

***[Nor88]** Norman, Donald A. *The Psychology of Everyday Things.* New York: Basic Books, 1988. (A second edition has been published, with the title changed to *The Design of Everyday Things.*) Challenges us to take a fresh look at things like doors, kitchen appliances, automobiles, etc. They often do not work very well, and Norman derives general design principles from exploring why.

[Nye90] Nye, Adrian. *Xlib Programming Manual.* Sebastopol, CA: O'Reilly & Associates, 1990.

[Nye93] Nye, Adrian, and Tim O'Reilly. *X Toolkit Intrinsics Programming Manual.* Sebastopol, CA: O'Reilly & Associates, 1993.

[Nyg81] Nygaard, Kristen, and Ole-Johan Dahl. "The Development of the Simula Language." In *History of Programming Languages.* New York: ACM/Academic Press, 1981. Nygaard and Dahl were the designers of Simula-67, the first OO programming language.

[Nyg86] Nygaard, Kristen. "Basic Concepts in Object Oriented Programming." *SIGPLAN Notices* 21, 10 (Oct. 1986). pp. 128-132.

[Nygr92] Nygren, E., *et al.* "The Art of the Obvious." [CHI92], pp. 235-239. Presents research on how people utilize visual patterns and other low-level information in text documents.

[Olm92] Olmert, Michael. *The Smithsonian Book of Books.* Washington, DC: Smithsonian Books, 1992. Good books are marvels of information design; this book provides examples, techniques, and the history of book-crafting. See also [All92].

[Ols92] Olson, Andrew W. "Object-Oriented Analysis of Visual Computer-Human Interfaces." *Journal of Visual Languages and Computing* 3 (1992), pp. 399-414. A formal method of describing and analyzing visual, object-oriented interfaces.

[Olso94] Olson, Douglas K. "Developing for Multiple Platforms." *BYTE* 19, 2 (February 1994), pp. 91-96. A discussion of code portability for GUI applications; uses Adobe Photoshop as an example.

[OOPSLA86] Meyrowitz, Norman, ed. *Object-Oriented Programming Systems, Languages and Applications.* Special edition, *SIGPLAN Notices* 21, 11 (Nov. 1986). Proceedings of the 1986 OOPSLA conference.

[OOPSLA87] Meyrowitz, Norman, ed. *Object-Oriented Programming Systems, Languages and Applications.* Special edition, *SIGPLAN Notices* 22, 12 (Dec. 1987). Proceedings of the 1987 OOPSLA conference.

[OOPSLA88] Meyrowitz, Norman, ed. *Object-Oriented Programming Systems, Languages and Applications.* Special edition, *SIGPLAN Notices* 23, 11 (Nov. 1988). Proceedings of the 1988 OOPSLA conference.

[OOPSLA89] Meyrowitz, Norman, ed. *Object-Oriented Programming Systems, Languages and Applications.* Special edition, *SIGPLAN Notices* 24, 10 (Oct. 1989). Proceedings of the 1989 OOPSLA conference.

[OOPSLA90] Meyrowitz, Norman, ed. *Conference on Object-Oriented Programming Systems, Languages and Applications/European Conference on Object-Oriented Programming.* Special edition, *SIGPLAN Notices* 25, 10 (Oct. 1990). Proceedings of the 1990 OOPSLA/ECOOP conference.

[OOPSLA91] Paepcke, Andreas, ed. *Object-Oriented Programming Systems, Languages and Applications.* Special edition, *SIGPLAN Notices* 26, 11 (Nov. 1991). Proceedings of the 1991 OOPSLA conference.

[OOPSLA92] Paepcke, Andreas, ed. *Object-Oriented Programming Systems, Languages and Applications.* Special edition, *SIGPLAN Notices* 27, 10 (Oct. 1992). Proceedings of the 1992 OOPSLA conference.

[OOPSLA93] Paepcke, Andreas, ed. *Object-Oriented Programming Systems, Languages and Applications.* Special edition, *SIGPLAN Notices* 28, 10 (Oct. 1993). Proceedings of the 1993 OOPSLA conference.

[OSF90] Open Software Foundation. *Motif Style Guide.* Engelwood Cliffs, NJ: Prentice-Hall, Inc., 1990. The official style guide for Motif, a "look and feel" standard for GUIs on UNIX platforms. An update, to version 1.1, was released in 1991. Motif 2.0 [Jol94] will be released in 1994, so this will be revised.

[Pak85] Pake, George E. "Research at Xerox PARC: A Founder's Assessment." *IEEE Spectrum* 22, 10 (Oct. 1985), pp. 54-61. See also [Per85].

[Pal94] Palmer, James D., and N. Ann Fields. "Computer-Supported Cooperative Work." *Computer (IEEE)* 27, 5 (May 1994), pp. 15-17. Introduces a special issue on the topic.

[Pap70] Papert, Seymour, and Cynthia Solomon. "NIM: A Game-Playing Program." Artificial Intelligence Memo Number 254, MIT Artificial Intelligence Laboratory, January 1970. This contains the first reference I can find to the anthropomorphic metaphor for computing, widely used by object-oriented programmers and designers.

[Pap80] Papert, Seymour. "Computers and Learning." In [Der80], pp. 74-86. Describes the use of the LOGO language for teaching children, and presents Papert's philosophy of computer use for learning.

[Par69] Parnas, David L. "On the Use of Transition Diagrams in the Design of a User Interface for an Interactive Computer System." *CACM,* 1969, reprinted in [Edm92]. An early paper on this subject. See [Gree86] for recent views.

[Pars94] Parisi, Paula. "The Picture Exchange." *Wired* 2, 1 (Jan. 1994), p. 32. Describes an online image database with visual browsing.

[Pau92] Pausch, Randy, Laura Vogtle, and Matthew Conway. One Dimensional Motion Tailoring for the Disabled: A User Study." [CHI92], pp. 405-411. Reports on a novel input device to allow children with cerebral palsy to play Pong on a computer.

[Pay91] Payne, Stephen J. "A descriptive study of mental models." *Behavior & Information Technology* 10, 1 (1991), pp. 3-21. A study of the mental models of users of bank teller machines, with a summary of previous research on mental models.

[Pen93] Penz, Franz, and Manfred Tscheligi. "The Feelmouse: An Interaction Device with Force Feedback." *INTERCHI'93 Adjunct Proceedings.* New York: Association for Computing Machinery, 1993, pp. 121-122. Describes an enhanced mouse that conveys a different level of friction or "stickiness" for each point it passes over.

[Per82] Perry, Tekla, *et al.* "Video Games: The Electronic Big Bang." *IEEE Spectrum* 19, 12 (Dec. 1982). Discusses technical and marketing factors related to the explosive growth of video games in the US in the late 1970s.

[Per85] Perry, Tekla S., and Paul Wallich. "Inside the PARC: The 'Information Architects.' " *IEEE Spectrum* 22, 10 (Oct. 1985), pp. 62-75. A history of the first ten years at Xerox PARC. See also [Pak85].

[Per89] Perry, Tekla S., and John Voelcker. "Of Mice and Menus: Designing the User-Friendly Interface." *IEEE Spectrum* 26, 9 (Sept. 1989), pp. 46-51. A historical summary of the people, places, and machines that led to what we now call the GUI.

[Pfa85] Pfaff, Gunther E. *User Interface Management Systems.* Berlin: Springer-Verlag, 1985. Proceedings of the Seeheim conference on user interface management systems (UIMS), which defined basic concepts and requirements for UIMS.

†[Phi81] Phillips, John L. Jr. *Piaget's Theory: A Primer.* An introduction to the work of Jean Piaget.

[Phil88] Phillips, Mark D., *et al.* "A Task Analytic Approach to Dialogue Design." Chapter 38 in [Hel88]. Presents a rationale and methodology for task analysis.

[Pia67] Piaget, Jean, and Barbel Inhelder. *The Child's Conception of Space.* New York: W. W. Norton & Co., 1967. Describes how children's sensory and motor activities lead to increasingly sophisticated conceptions of physical space.

[Pia74] Piaget, Jean. *The Child and Reality.* New York: The Viking Press, 1974. Piaget showed that capabilities of object recognition, classification, etc. develop over time in stages. For an overview of Piaget's work, see [Phi81].

[Pin85] Pinker, Stephen. *Visual Cognition.* Cambridge, MA: MIT Press, 1985. How people process visual information.

[Pla92] Plaisant, Catherine, and Daniel Wallace. "Touchscreen Toggle Design." [CHI92], pp. 667-668. Describes the design of toggle switches for touchscreen display and activation. A videotape appears in [vSIGGRAPH] 76 (1992).

[Por92] Poretta, James. "Omegamon II for MVS: An Object-Oriented User Interface for the Nonprogrammable Terminal." *Proceedings of the SHARE Conference* Winter '92 (February 1992).

[Pot89] Potosnak, Kathleen. "Keys and Keyboards." Chapter 21 in [Hel88].

[Pot89] Potosnak, Kathleen. "Human Factors: When a Usability Test Is *Not* the Answer." *IEEE Software* 6, 7 (July 1989), pp. 105-106. A brief summary of task analysis.

[Pow92] Powell, Doug. "The Productivity Paradox." *Computing Canada* 18, 24 (Nov. 23, 1992), pp. 1, 8. A summary of studies on the relation between investment in information technology and resultant productivity changes. See also [Bry93], [Lov91].

[Prem90] Premeriani, William J., *et al.* "An Object-Oriented Relational Database." *CACM* 33, 7 (July 1990), pp. 117-125.

[Pres93] Press, Larry. "Software Export from Developing Nations." *Computer (IEEE)* 26, 12 (December 1993), pp. 63-67. Market aspects of internationalization. See also [Nid93], [Russ93].

[Pri71] Pribram, Karl H. *Languages of the Brain: Experimental Paradoxes and Principles in Neuropsychology.* Engelwood Cliffs, NJ: Prentice-Hall, 1971.

[Prie91] Prieto-Díaz, Rubén. "Implementing Faceted Classification for Software Reuse." *CACM* 34, 5 (May 1991), pp. 89-97.

[Ral93] Ralston, Anthony, and Edwin D. Reilly, eds. *Encyclopedia of Computer Science.* New York: IEEE Press, 1993 (third edition).

[Ran85] Rand, Paul. *A Designer's Art.* New Haven, CT: Yale University Press, 1985. This book by a well-known graphic designer is not about computers, but has a wealth of ideas for visual design.

[Rap93] Rappaport, Ari, and Maarten van Emmerik. "User-Interface Devices for Rapid and Exact Number Specification." *ACM Transactions on Graphics* 12, 4 (October 1993), pp. 348-354. Describes virtual controls for specifying high-precision numbers rapidly using only a mouse.

[Ree81] Reenskaug, Trygve. "User-Oriented Descriptions of Smalltalk Systems." *BYTE* 6, 8 (August 1981), pp. 148-166.

[Rei93a] Reichard, Kevin, and Eric F. Johnson. "Life Is a Drag." *UNIX Review* 11, 4 (April 1993), pp. 97-106. Examples of drag and drop implementation for Motif. See also [Mark91], [Skl93].

[Rei93b] Reichard, Kevin, and Eric F. Johnson. "Internationalizing Motif." *UNIX Review* 11, 12 (Dec. 1993), pp. 91-98. Discusses keyboard input of ideographic characters.

[Rhei91] Rheingold, Howard. *Virtual Reality.* New York: Simon & Schuster, 1991. Rheingold traveled worldwide to interview researchers, who are extensively quoted. The best summary I have seen of technical and human interface issues in virtual reality.

[Rhei93] Rheingold, Howard. *The Virtual Community.* Reading, MA: Addison-Wesley, 1993. An introduction to new forms of collaboration and community emerging in large networks.

[Rhy87] Rhyne, Jim. "Dialogue Management for Gestural Interfaces." *Computer Graphics* 21, 2 (April 1987), pp. 137-142. A good example of a gestural interface, developed by Rhyne and colleagues at IBM research, is the "Paper-Like Interface," in [vSIGGRAPH] 47, 1 (1989).

[Rie94] Riecken, Doug. "Intelligent Agents." *CACM* 37, 7 (July 1994), pp. 18-21. Introduces a special issue on the topic.

[Rob91] Robertson, George G., Jock D. Mackinlay, and Stuart K. Card. "Cone Trees: Animated 3D Visualizations of Hierarchical Information." [CHI91], pp. 189-194. A technique for 3-D visualization of data. See also [Car91], [Macki91].

[Robi94] Robie, Jonathan. "Event Handling in Object-Oriented Databases." *C++ Report* 6, 6 (July-Aug. 1994), pp. 24-27. Describes an OODBMS that supports event triggers based on database changes.

[Roch92] Rochkind, Marc J. "An Extensible Virtual Toolkit (XVT) for Portable

GUI Applications." *COMPCON Spring 1992.* San Francisco: IEEE, 1992, pp. 485-489.

[Rock74] Rock, Irwin. "The Perception of Disoriented Figures." In [Held74], pp. 71-78. Discusses perceptual issues in things like the upside-down faces in Figure 4-7.

[Roo93] Root, Robert W., and Kathy M. Uyeda. "A Headsup on GUI Styleguides: Report on the CHI'92 Styleguide SIG." *SIGCHI Bulletin* 25, 3 (July 1993), pp. 32-35. Summarizes pragmatic issues in developing and using style guides, based on a survey of designers.

[Rosch78] Rosch, Eleanor, and Barbara B. Lloyd, eds. *Cognition and Categorization.* Hillsdale, NJ: Lawrence Erlbaum Associates, 1978. Presents psychological theories of categorization and classification.

[Rosen83] Rosenthal, David. "Managing Graphical Resources" *Computer Graphics* 17, 1 (Jan. 1983), pp. 38-45. Motivates the event model for graphical user interfaces.

[Rosen88] Rosenthal, David. "A Simple X11 Client Program -or- How Hard Can it Really Be to Write 'Hello, World'?" *Proceedings of the USENIX Winter Conference.* Dallas, TX: USENIX Association, 1988.

[Ross90] Rosson, Mary Beth, and Sherman Alpert. "The Cognitive Consequences of Object-Oriented Design." *Human-Computer Interaction* 5, 4 (1990). A cognitive psychology perspective on differences between object-oriented and other design paradigms.

[Rost88] Rost, Randi J. "Adding a Dimension to X." *UNIX Review* 6, 10 (Oct. 1988), pp. 51-59. Describes PEX, a proposed 3-D graphics standard for X Windows.

***[Rub92]** Rubin, Kenneth S., and Adele Goldberg. "Object Behavior Analysis." *CACM* 35, 9 (September 1992), pp. 48-62. OBA and the "use cases" of [Jac92], are examples of "user-driven" or "use-driven" design.

***[Rubin84]** Rubinstein, Richard, and Harry Hersh. *The Human Factor: Designing Computer Systems for People.* Bedford, MA: Digital Press, 1984. Human factors guidelines for designing computer systems, with examples. This is a good first aid manual for ailing interfaces, but most effective if used preventively (during design).

***[Rum91]** Rumbaugh, James, *et al. Object-Oriented Modeling and Design.* Engelwood Cliffs, NJ: Prentice-Hall, 1991. Presents OMT (object modeling technique), a widely used method and notation for OO analysis and design.

[Rush86] Rushinek, Avi, and Sara F. Rushinek. "What Makes Users Happy?" *CACM* 29, 7 (July 1986), pp. 594-598. Results of a survey finding response time the prime determinant of user satisfaction.

[Russ93] Russo, Patricia, and Stephen Boor. "How Fluent Is Your Interface? Designing for International Users." [CHI93], pp. 342-347. Guidelines for designing user interfaces that "translate well." See also [Mart92], [Nie90b], [Nie90c].

[Sac93] Sacks, Oliver. "To See and Not to See." The *New Yorker* LXIX, 12 (May 10, 1993), pp. 59-73. Describes the case of a man, blind for 40 years, who recovers his sight. See also [Greg87a].

[Saf90] Saffo, Paul. "Racing Change on a Merry-Go-Round." *Personal Computing,* May 25, 1990, pp. 67-70. Relates Loveman's report on productivity

[Lov91] to Engelbart's recent work on augmenting human capabilities ([Eng68] and [Eng73] describe his early work).

[San85] Sanford, Anthony J. *Cognition and Cognitive Psychology.* New York: Basic Books, 1985.

[Sch86] Scheifler, Robert W., and Jim Gettys. "The X Window System." *ACM Transactions on Graphics* 5, 2 (April 1986), pp. 79-109. A history and architectural review of the X Window System.

[Schm86] Schmucker, Kurt. *Object-Oriented Programming for the Macintosh.* Hasbrouck Heights, NJ: Hayden Book Co., 1986. Describes MacApp, an object-oriented framework for Macintosh applications.

[Schm88] Schmucker, Kurt. "Using Objects to Package User Interface Functionality." *JOOP* April/May 1988.

[Sea92] Sears, Andrew, Catherine Plaisant, and Ben Shneiderman. "A New Era for Touchscreen Applications: High Precision, Dragging Icons, and Refined Feedback." In R. H. Hartson and D. Hix, eds. *Advances in Human-Computer Interaction,* Vol. 3. Norwood, NJ: Ablex, 1992.

[See90] Seetharaman, K., C. F. Rei, and B. R. Montague. "A C++ Binding for OSF/Motif." Computer Science Technical report R-90-009. Lowell, MA: University of Lowell, 1990.

[Sen91] Sengupta, Kishore, and Dov Te'eni. "Direct Manipulation and Command Language Interfaces: A Comparison of Users' Mental Models," in H. J. Bullinger, ed., *Human Aspects in Computing: Design and Use of Interactive Systems and Work with Terminals* (Proceedings of the Fourth International Conference on Human-Computer Interaction). Amsterdam: Elsevier, 1991. Proposes that superiority of direct manipulation interfaces is due to a simpler mental model of tasks. See also [Kar87].

[Shi93] Shimoga, Karun B. "A Survey of Perceptual Feedback Issues in Dextrous Telemanipulation" (Part I, "Finger Force Feedback," and Part II, "Finger Touch Feedback"). *IEEE Virtual Reality Applications International Symposium.* Piscataway, NJ: IEEE, 1993, pp. 263-279. Summarizes research on force and tactile feedback to the hands and its value in remote manipulation tasks.

[Shn83] Shneiderman, Ben. "Direct Manipulation: A Step Beyond Programming Languages." *Computer (IEEE)* 16, 8 (Aug. 1983). A classic paper. Chapter 5 in [Shn92] is an updated version.

***†[Shn92]** Shneiderman, Ben. *Designing the User Interface: Strategies for Effective Human-Computer Interaction.* Reading, MA: Addison-Wesley, 1992 (2nd edition). A comprehensive treatment of the theories, processes, and technologies involved in designing user interfaces. Provides essential background knowledge for user interface designers, as well as lots of examples and ideas for interfaces. Includes references to the research literature in each chapter.

[Shr87] Shriver, Bruce, and Peter Wegner, eds. *Research Directions in Object-Oriented Programming.* Cambridge, MA: MIT press, 1987.

[Shu88] Shu, Nan C. *Visual Programming.* New York: Van Nostrand Reinhold, 1988. Though the primary topic of this book is visual *programming,* it is relevant to developers of any visual interface.

[Sib86] Sibert, John L., William D. Hurley, and Teresa W. Bleser. "An Object-Oriented User Interface Management System." *Computer Graphics* 20, 4, Aug. 1986, pp. 259-268.

[Skl93] Sklar, David F. "A Gentle Introduction to Implementing Drag-and-Drop." *The X Journal* 3, 2 (Nov.-Dec. 1993), pp. 24-35. Drag and drop with Motif. See also [Mark93], [Rei93a].

[Smi75] Smith, David C. *Pygmalion: A Creative Programming Environment* (Ph.D. thesis). Palo Alto, CA: Stanford University, 1975. This introduced the use of icons to represent objects. Still worth reading, though the interface now looks dated.

***[Smi82]** Smith, David C., Charles Irby, Ralph Kimball, Bill Verplank, and Eric Harslem. "Designing the Star User Interface." *BYTE* 7, 4 (April 1982), pp. 242-282. Describes the design and design process for the Xerox Star. See also [Joh89].

[Smit93] Smith, Ben, and Howard Eglowstein. "In Good Electronic Form." *BYTE* 18, 12 (November 1993), pp. 67-76. Case studies, issues, and advice on shifting from paper to electronic forms processing.

[Smith87] Smith, Randall B. "Experiences with the Alternate Reality Kit: An Example of the Tension Between Literalism and Magic." *Human Factors in Computing Systems* (CHI + GI 1987 Conference proceedings). New York: ACM/Addison-Wesley, 1987, pp. 61-67.

[Sny93] Snyder, Alan. "The Essence of Objects: Terms and Concepts." *IEEE Software* 10, 1 (January 1993), pp. 31-42. An attempt to develop standard definitions across disciplines for the concepts of object-orientation.

[Snyd88] Snyder, Harry L. "Image Quality." Chapter 20 in [Hel88]. Discusses human vision in relation to computer displays.

†[Sow84] Sowa, John F. *Conceptual Structures: Information Processing in Mind and Machine.* Reading, MA: Addison-Wesley, 1984. How knowledge is acquired and represented, in people and computers.

[Sta90] Starker, India, and Richard A. Bolt. "A Gaze-Responsive Self-Disclosing Display." [CHI90], pp. 3-9. Describes a system that uses the user's gaze as a pointing and selection device. See also [Bol81].

[Stan93] Stanley, Michael C., and James E. Colgate. "Real Time Simulation of Stiff Dynamic Systems via Distributed Memory Parallel Processors." *IEEE Virtual Reality Annual International Symposium.* IEEE, 1993, pp. 456-462. A "computer per object" architecture.

[Star94] Starks, Cindy. "A Developer's Look at the COSE Desktop." *UNIX Review* 12, 3 (March 1994), pp. 41-45. Summarizes the Common Open Software Environment common desktop standard for UNIX.

[Stea89] Stearns, Glenn. "Agents and the HP NewWave Application Program interface." *Hewlett-Packard Journal* Aug. 1989, pp. 32-37.

[Ste89] Stein, Lynn Andrea, Henry Lieberman, and David Ungar. "A Shared View of Sharing: *The Treaty of Orlando."* In Won Kim and Frederick H. Lochovsky, eds. *Object-Oriented Concepts, Databases, and Applications,* pp. 31-48. New York: ACM Press, 1989. Resolves a debate about mechanisms for sharing behavior in OO systems.

[Ster87] Stern, Hal L. "Comparison of Window Systems." *BYTE* 12, 11 (Nov. 1987), pp. 265-272. Compares the internal architectures of Microsoft Windows, X Windows, Apple Macintosh, and Sun NeWS. See also [Mye88].

[Stew93] Stewart, Joseph, and Robert J. Weidemen. "Graphics and Imaging in

X." *The X Journal* 3, 2 (Nov./Dec. 1993), 18-22. Describes the PEX graphics standard for X Windows. See also [Rost88].

[Stewa93] Stewart, Thomas A. "Reengineering: The Hot New Management Tool." *Fortune* 128, 4 (Aug. 23, 1993), pp. 40-48. Pros and cons of business process reengineering. See also [Gle93].

[Str86] Stroustrup, Bjarne. *The C++ Programming Language.* Reading, MA: Addison-Wesley, 1986 (second edition, 1992).

[Str94] Stroustrup, Bjarne. *The Design and Evolution of C++.* Reading, MA: Addison-Wesley, 1994.

[Stri92] Strijland, Paulien. *Icon Design.* Tutorial number 34. ACM Conference on Human Factors in Computing Systems (CHI'92), 1992.

[Sun90] Sun Microsystems, Inc. *Open Look Graphical User Interface Application Style Guide.* Reading, MA: Addison-Wesley, 1990. A style guide for applications on Sun workstations using the Open Look standard. Sun also supports the Motif standard [OSF90].

[Sut63a] Sutherland, Ivan. *Sketchpad, a Man-Machine Graphical Communication System* (Ph.D. thesis). Cambridge MA: MIT, 1963.

[Sut63b] Sutherland, Ivan. "Sketchpad, a Man-Machine Graphical Communication System." *AFIPS Proceedings* (Spring Joint Computer Conference, 1963), pp. 329-346. A more accessible summary of [Sut63a]. [vKay87]and [vSIGGRAPH] 13, 6 (1984) contain film clips of Sketchpad.

[Sut66] Sutherland, Ivan. "Computer Graphics: Ten Unsolved Problems." *DATAMATION* May 1966, pp. 22-27.

[Swi85] Switchenko, Debra M. "In Defense of the Traditional (Non-Icon) Interface: A Position Based on a Selective Review of the Literature." *Trends in Ergonomics/Human Factors II.* Amsterdam: North-Holland, 1985, pp. 373-379. Reviews studies of iconic interfaces; finds no unequivocal evidence of the superiority of icons over text.

[Tak93] Takeuchi, Akikazu, and Katashi Nagao. "Communicative Facial Displays as a New Conversational Modality." [CHI93], pp. 187-193. Describes a system that adds synthesized facial expressions to a speech generator.

[Tan92] Tani, Masayuki, *et al.* "Object-Oriented Video: Interaction with Real-World Objects through Live Video." [CHI92], pp. 593-598.

[Tay90] Taylor, David A. *Object-Oriented Technology: A Manager's Guide.* Reading, MA: Addison-Wesley, 1990. A brief overview of many aspects of OO, intended for those with no prior background.

[TBS90] Temple, Barker, & Sloane, Inc. *The Benefits of the Graphical User Interface: A Report on New Primary Research.* 1990. Based on research done by TBS for Microsoft and Zenith Data Systems. Compares graphical with character-based user interfaces for the same set of tasks, using both novice and expert computer users as subjects. The results reported are favorable to the GUI, in terms of user performance and satisfaction.

[Tei86] Teitleman, Warren. "Ten Years of Window Systems—A Retrospective View." In F.R.A. Hopgood, *et al.*, eds., *Methodology of Window Management.* Berlin: Springer-Verlag, 1986. Discusses systems such as Smalltalk and DLisp, whose user interface concepts led to the structure of modern window management systems.

[Tel90] Telles, Marcy. "Updating an Older interface." [CHI90], pp. 243-247. Describes problems in changing the user interface of a product (WordStar) with millions of users.

[Tes81] Tesler, Larry. "The Smalltalk Environment." *BYTE* 6, 8 (Aug. 1981), pp. 90-149. This article presents Tesler's views on user interface "modes," and compares modal interfaces to those he designed for editing text in the Smalltalk environment.

[Tes83] Tesler, Larry. "Object Oriented User Interfaces and Object Oriented Languages." *ACM Conference on Personal and Small Computers*, pp. 3-5. New York: ACM, 1983. Here Tesler coins the phrase "object-oriented user interface." He focuses on the analogy between OOP languages and OOUIs, using Object Pascal (used in the Apple Lisa Toolkit) as an example.

[Tetz93] Tetzeli, Rick. "Videogames: Serious Fun." *Fortune* 128, 16 (December 27, 1993). An overview of technical and marketing issues in the multibillion dollar video game industry.

[Tetzl91] Tetzlaff, Linda and David R. Schwartz. "The Use of Guidelines in Interface Design." [CHI91], pp. 329-333. Results of a study of how interface designers use style guidelines. See also [Thov91].

[Tha81] Thadani, A. J. "Interactive User Productivity." *IBM Systems Journal* 20, 4 (1981), pp. 407-423. Reports on measurements relating productivity and system response time.

[The94] Thé, Lee. "Get It Together with Visual Basic." *DATAMATION* 40, 2 (Jan. 21, 1994), pp. 45-52.

[Thi90] Thimbleby, Harold. *User Interface Design.* Wokingham, England: Addison-Wesley/ACM Press, 1990.

[Tho80] Thomas, John C., and Wendy A. Kellogg. "Minimizing Ecological Gaps in Interface Design." *IEEE Software* 6, 1 (January 1989), pp. 78-86. The "ecological" approach looks at individual users in the context of relations between them and other people, the environment, etc.

[Thom89] Thomas, Dave. "In Search of an Object-Oriented Development Process." *JOOP* May/June 1989, pp. 60-63. A summary of experience in OO development.

[Thov91] Thovtrup, Henrik, and Jakob Nielsen. "Assessing the Usability of a User Interface Standard." [CHI91], pp. 335-341. Results of experiments done to see whether designers could produce user interfaces that complied to a standard. See also [Tet91].

[Tof85] Toffler, Alvin. *The Adaptive Corporation.* New York: Bantam Books, 1985. Originally written as a report to AT&T, this is Toffler's view of how modern companies need to change in order to survive in a more information-intensive world.

*__[Tog92]__ Tognazzini, Bruce. *Tog on Interface.* Reading, MA: Addison-Wesley, 1992. Based on Tog's column in *Apple Direct*, a magazine for Macintosh developers—but most of it is relevant and important for any GUI platform. Also one of the most entertaining books you will find on the topic. I disagree with his position on OOP, but otherwise this is a wonderful book.

[Tog93] Tognazzini, Bruce. "Principles, Techniques, and Ethics of Stage Magic and Their Application to User Interface Design." [CHI93], pp. 355-362. Points out interesting parallels between magic and design.

[Tok93] Tokoro, Mario. "The Society of Objects." Invited talk given at OOPSLA'93 (Sept. 30, 1993), Washington DC.

[Tuf83] Tufte, Edward R. *The Visual Display of Quantitative Information.* Cheshire, CT: Graphics Press, 1983. This and [Tuf90] are landmarks in graphic design. Besides their merits as expositions of the subject matter, they are superb examples of the printer's art.

***[Tuf90]** Tufte, Edward R. *Envisioning Information.* Cheshire, CT: Graphics Press, 1990. More directly relevant than [Tuf83] to interface designers. Most of the examples come from print media, but the principles are applicable to presentation on computer displays.

[Tul88] Tullis, Thomas S. "Screen Design." Chapter 18 in [Hel88]. Focuses mainly on alphanumeric displays.

[Tur84] Turkle, Sherry. *The Second Self: Computers and the Human Spirit.* New York: Simon & Schuster, 1984. Studies the effects of computers on individuals and culture in the US. See also [Zub88].

[Tve64] Tversky, Barbara, and Kathleen Hemenway. "Objects, Parts, and Categories." *Journal of Experimental Psychology: General* 113, 2 (June 1984), pp. 169-191. Explains Rosch's "basic level categories" [Rosch78] in terms of the subject's ability to discriminate parts of prototypical objects in the category.

[Ude94] Udell, Jon. "Componentware." *BYTE* 19, 5 (May 1994), pp. 46-56. Argues that OO has failed as a reuse technology because it hasn't paid enough attention to distribution and assembly of components.

[Ull80] Ullman, Jeffrey D. *Principles of Database Systems.* Potomac, MD: Computer Science Press, 1980.

†[Ven90] Venturino, Michael (editor). *Selected Readings in Human Factors.* Santa Monica, CA: The Human Factors Society, 1990.

[Ver88] Verplank, William. "Graphic Challenges in Designing Object-Oriented User Interfaces." [Hel88], pp. 365-376.

[Vin93] Vines, Don, and Zen Kishimoto. "Smalltalk's Runtime Type Support for C++." *C++ Report* 5, 1 (Jan. 1993), pp. 44-52. Argues that supporting the CORBA specification [Vino93] in C++ requires a Smalltalk-like runtime (dynamic) type system.

[Ving87] Vinge, Vernor. *True Names . . . and Other Dangers.* New York: Baen Books, 1987. This collection contains Vinge's novella *True Names*, a thought-provoking look at what virtual reality might be like in the future.

[Vino93] Vinoski, Steve. "Distributed Object Computing with CORBA." *C++ Report* 5, 6 (July-August 1993), pp. 33-38. Describes the OMG's CORBA specification for client-server networks.

[Vlis90] Vlissides, John M., and Mark A. Linton. "Domain-Specific Graphical Editors." *ACM Transactions on Information Systems* 8, 3 (July 1990), pp. 237-268. Describes the Unidraw framework.

[Wal93] Walker, Neff, David E. Meyer, and John B. Smelcer. "Spatial and Temporal Characteristics of Rapid Cursor-Positioning Movements with Electromechanical Mice in Human-Computer Interaction." *Human Factors* 35, 3 (Sept. 1993), pp. 431-458.

[Way94a] Wayner, Peter. "Objects on the March." *BYTE* 19, 1 (Jan. 1994), pp. 139-150. Describes distributed object technologies.

[Way94b] Wayner, Peter. "Agents Away." *BYTE* 19, 5 (May 1994), pp. 113-118. Describes General Magic's concept of *telescript*, a language for implementing distributed agents.

[Web93] Weber, Gerhard. "Adapting Direct Manipulation for Blind Users." *INTERCHI'93 Adjunct Proceedings.* New York: Association for Computing Machinery, 1993, pp. 21-22. Describes a touch display allowing pointing and Braille reading.

[Weg76] Wegner, Peter. "Programming Languages—The First 25 Years." *IEEE Transactions on Computers* Dec. 1976, pp. 1207-1225. Reprinted in Ellis Horowitz, ed., *Programming Languages: A Grand Tour.* Rockville, MD: Computer Science Press, 1987 (third edition).

[Weg87a] Wegner, Peter. "Dimensions of Object-Based Language Design." In [OOPSLA87]. Defines an OO language as one that supports encapsulated objects, classes, and inheritance.

[Weg87b] Wegner, Peter. "The Object-Oriented Classification Paradigm." [Shr87], pp. 479-560. An exhaustive treatment of classes and types in object-oriented programming languages.

[Wein89] Weinand, André, Erich Gamma, and Rudolf Marty. "Design and Implementation of ET++, a Seamless Object-Oriented Framework." *Structured Programming* 10, 2 (1989), pp. 63-87.

[Weis91] Weiser, Mark. "The Computer for the 21st Century." *Scientific American* 265, 3 (Sept. 1991), pp. 94-104.

[Wel93] Wellner, Pierre, Wendy Mackay, and Rich Gold. "Computer-Augmented Environments: Back to the Real World." *CACM* 36, 7 (July 1993), pp. 24-26. Introduces a special issue on the topic of augmenting "real objects" with computers.

[Wen93] Wenzel, Elizabeth M., and Scott H. Foster. *Tutorial on the Psychophysics and Technology of Virtual Acoustic Displays.* IEEE Virtual Reality Applications International Symposium, 1993, Tutorial 3. Discusses creation of sound sources in virtual 3-D spaces.

[Wer93] Werner, Kenneth I. "The Flat Panel's Future." *IEEE Spectrum* 30, 11 (November 1993), pp. 18-26. Describes LCD and other current and future flat panel display technologies.

***[Whi88]** Whiteside, John, John Bennett, and Karen Holtzblatt. "Usability Engineering: Our Experience and Development." Chapter 36 of [Hel88]. This, [Gou88], and [Nie92b] are excellent treatments of usability engineering in the development process.

[Who56] Whorf, Benjamin L. *Language, Thought, and Reality: Selected Writings of Benjamin Lee Whorf* (edited by John B. Carroll). Cambridge, MA: MIT Press, 1956. Whorf is best known for the "Whorfian hypothesis" that a speaker's native language conditions not only what can be *said*, but what can be *thought*.

[Wie90] Wiecha, Charles, et al. "ITS: A Tool for Rapidly Developing Interactive Applications." *ACM Transactions on Information Systems* 8, 3 (July 1990), pp. 204-236. ITS enforces a strong separation between the "style" and "content" of an application. See also [Gou91].

[Wil83] Williams, Gregg. "The Lisa Computer System." *BYTE* 8, 2 (Feb. 1983), pp. 33-50. A review of the Apple Lisa workstation. An Apple videotape showing the Lisa appears as [vSIGGRAPH] 8, 2 (1983).

[Win94] Wingo, Scot. "Implementing the Windows API on UNIX/Motif." *The X Journal* 3, 6 (July-Aug. 1994), pp. 62-66.

***[Wir90]** Wirfs-Brock, Rebecca, Brian Wilkerson, and Lauren Wiener. *Designing Object-Oriented Software.* Engelwood Cliffs, NJ: Prentice Hall, 1990. A good general treatment of design and related issues. I like their idea of "responsibility driven" design, which helps to keep the focus on requirements rather than technology.

[Wiss90] Wisskirchen, Peter. *Object-Oriented Graphics.* Berlin: Springer-Verlag, 1990. An OO perspective on computer graphics.

[Wix90] Wixon, Dennis, Karen Holtzblatt, and Stephen Knox. "Contextual Design: An Emergent View of System Design." [CHI90], pp. 329-336. Describes how designers can work with end users in the workplace. See also [Hol93]. See [Lem90] for a case study.

[Wol83] Wolf, Catherine, and James Rhyne. "A Taxonomic Approach to Understanding Direct Manipulation." *Proceedings of the Human Factors Society 31st Annual Meeting.* Santa Monica, CA: Human Factors Society, 1987.

[Woo93] Woods, Wilton. "The Jobs Americans Hold." *Fortune* 128, 1 (July 12, 1993), pp. 54-55. Summarizes information and forecasts on employment by category from the US Bureau of Labor Statistics.

[Wur84] Wurman, Richard Saul. *Tokyo Access.* Los Angeles: ACCESSPRESS, 1984. The *Access* guidebooks are dense with information, yet easy to use and aesthetically pleasing. As such, they are sources of visual ideas for computer interface designers.

[Wur89] Wurman, Richard Saul. *Information Anxiety.* New York: Doubleday, 1989. Offers antidotes to the malaise described in the title, and advice on graphic and information design.

[Yan88] Yankelovich, Nicole, *et al.* "Intermedia: The Concept and Construction for a Seamless Information Environment." *Computer (IEEE)* 21, 1 (Jan. 1988), pp. 81-96. Describes Brown University's Intermedia hypermedia system.

[You81] Young, Richard M. "The Machine Inside the Machine: Users' Models of Pocket Calculators." *International Journal of Man-Machine Studies* 15 (1981), pp. 51-85.

[You92] Young, Douglas A. *Object-Oriented Programming with C++ and OSF/Motif.* Englewood Cliffs, NJ: Prentice Hall, 1992.

[Your79] Yourdon, Edward Nash. *Classics in Software Engineering.* New York: Yourdon Press, 1979. Reprints of significant papers.

[Zub88] Zuboff, Shoshana. *In the Age of the Smart Machine.* New York: Basic Books, 1988. Studies the effects of information technology on work and workers. Mostly anecdotal, this is valuable for its historical perspective, and a wealth of interviews. See also [Tur84].

Index

B

C

D

E

N

- Professional development is crucial to maintain staff commitment to the high school and to sustain the solution focused approach.
- Sustaining a solution focused high school over time requires that leadership and staff share a clear vision and identity as a solution focused school.
- Leadership changes require identifying candidates who understand and buy in to the mission and of the solution focused high school and its solution focused approach.
- Solution focused high schools are data driven and maintain ongoing efforts to evaluate and monitor the school's effectiveness. This data is used for reflection and to sustain its growth and practices.

Summary

This chapter addresses ways to sustain an effective solution focused alternative high school across time, explaining elements of a school organization that makes this possible. The importance of embracing a mission and set of values and the commitment to professional development and the growth of everyone within the system is also described. It further summarizes how to change leadership in a way that won't derail the school's solution focused practices. Finally, the importance of continued evaluation and data collection are explained as necessary for self-reflection and the continued success within the alternative high school. Five studies are described as examples of how the solution focused alternative high school, Gonzalo Garza Independence High School, used research to improve the school's practices.

Note

1 Cases presented in this chapter are taken from research interviews of students that attend an alternative high school and staff experiences working with these students. Names and some information have been changed to protect the confidentiality of the students involved. Some of these interviews were made possible by the generous support of the Hogg Foundation for Mental Health at The University of Texas at Austin.

References

Franklin, C., Montgomery, K., Baldwin, V., & Webb, L. (2012). Research and development of a solution-focused high school. In C. Franklin, T. Trepper, W. Gingerich, & E. McCollum (Eds.) *Solution-focused brief therapy: A handbook of evidence-based practice* (pp. 371–389). New York, NY: Oxford University Press.

Franklin, C., Streeter, C. L., Belcuig, C., Webb, L., & Szlyk, H. (2017). An evaluation of on-time graduation rates and college enrollment in a solution-focused alternative school for at-risk students. Manuscript submitted for publication.

Franklin, C, Streeter, C. L., Kim, J. S., & Tripodi, S. J. (2007). The effectiveness of a solution-focused, public alternative school for dropout prevention and retrieval. *Children and Schools, 29,* 133–144. doi:10.1093/cs/29.3.133

Glisson, C., & James, L. R. (2002). The cross-level effects of culture and climate in human services teams. *Journal of Organizational Behavior, 23,* 767–794. doi:10.1002/job.162

Jaskyte, K., & Dressler, W. W. (2005). Organizational culture and innovation in nonprofit human service organizations. *Administration in Social Work, 29,* 23–41. doi:10.1300/J147v29n02_03

Kelly, M. S., Kim. J. S., & Franklin, C. (2008). *Solution-focused brief therapy in schools: A 360-degree view of research and practice.* New York, NY: Oxford University Press.

Lagana-Riordan, C., Aguilar, J. P., Franklin, C., Streeter, C. L., Kim, J. S., Tripodi, S. J., & Hopson, L. M. (2011). At-risk students' perceptions of traditional schools and a solution-focused public alternative school. *Preventing School Failure, 55*(3), 105–114. doi:10.1080/10459880903472843

Streeter, C. L., Franklin, C., Kim, J. S., & Tripodi, S. J. (2011). Concept mapping: An approach for evaluating a public alternative school program. *Children & Schools, 33*(4), 197–214. doi:10.1093/cs/33.4.197

Szlyk, H. (2017). Fostering independence through an academic culture of social responsibility: A grounded theory for engaging at-risk students. *Learning Environments Research,* (4), 1–15. doi: 10.1007/s10984-017-9245-x

Index

NOTE: pages with a *t* can be found in tables

Made in the USA
Lexington, KY
07 August 2019